BUSINESS LAW AND PRACTICE:
LEGISLATION HANDBOOK

BUSINESS LAW AND PRACTICE: LEGISLATION HANDBOOK

Co-ordinating Editor

Trevor Adams BSc, PhD, Solicitor

JORDANS

2003

Published by
Jordan Publishing Limited
21 St Thomas Street
Bristol BS1 6JS

British Library Cataloguing-in-Publication Data
A catalogue record for this book is available from the British Library.

ISSN 1360–4503
ISBN 0 85308 884 5

Printed in Great Britain by Hobbs the Printers Ltd of Southampton

PREFACE TO THE FIRST EDITION

We would like to express our appreciation and gratitude to everyone who helped in the preparation of this book. Janet Hughes, Pat Humphries, Ann Goulding and Sarah Smith from The College of Law Wordprocessing Department in Chester and Moira Smith, Paula Peterson and the late Jean Buchan of the Wordprocessing Department in Guildford spent many hours expertly typing the materials for this book. Special thanks go to our fellow tutor at Chester, Raymond Henley for his invaluable technical knowledge of computers and wordprocessing.

Thanks are also due to the tutors in Chester, who devoted many mind-numbing hours to proof-reading the material, namely Sarah Hutchinson, Sara Maccallum, Jane Mackenzie, Tracy Savage and Melanie Shoesmith.

We would also like to thank the staff at Jordans who transformed what was originally a publication purely for students at The College of Law into one of more general application.

ANDREW HARVEY
ALISON HARVEY
ALEXIS LONGSHAW
TIM SEWELL

PREFACE TO THIS EDITION

This edition builds on the work of previous years. Material has been updated where amendments have been made to the legislation, as usual. Some material no longer of relevance to business law has been omitted. Chris Morris remains responsible for the section on taxation.

TREVOR ADAMS
Chester
April 2003

CONTENTS

HOW TO USE THIS BOOK

FORMAT

This book is intended for use in conjunction with the Legal Practice Course Resource Book *Business Law and Practice* (Jordans) and is divided into seven parts: Partnership, Company, Taxation, Insolvency, Commercial, EU and Company Forms. Within each Part, the legislation is arranged chronologically.

To aid speed of reference, a detailed arrangement of sections has been included at the beginning of this book. This lists every section of every statute included in this book with its page reference.

AMENDMENTS

The statutory materials included in this book are presented with all the subsequent amendments incorporated and are up to date to 1 May 2003, with the exception of Part III: Taxation, which is up to date to 31 March 2003.

At the time of going to press, the Finance Bill 2003 has yet to complete its passage through Parliament. Those sections of the legislation that appear in Part III: Taxation should therefore be checked with reference to the Finance Act 2003 once it has received Royal Assent.

Full details of all amending legislation will be found in the Table of Amendments and Repeals.

Every effort has been made to present the text in a clear and easily digestible form. To this end, the use of textual notes and annotations has been kept to a minimum.

Where prospective changes have been made to the material but have not yet been brought into force, the text of the original section is retained with the prospective change noted in italic type. In this case, brief textual notes have been added to explain the nature of the change.

TABLE OF LEGISLATION

References in the right-hand column are to page numbers.

TABLE OF AMENDMENTS AND REPEALS

ABBREVIATIONS

Am	Amended by	Ins	Inserted by
CA 1989	Companies Act 1989	IA 1985	Insolvency Act 1985
FA 1986	Finance Act 1986	IA 1986	Insolvency Act 1986
FA 1987	Finance Act 1987	IA 1994	Insolvency Act 1994
FA 1988	Finance Act 1988	IA 2000	Insolvency Act 2000
FA 1989	Finance Act 1989	ICTA 1988	Income and Corporation
FA 1990	Finance Act 1990		Taxes Act 1988
FA 1991	Finance Act 1991	Ital	Italics
FA (No 2) 1992	Finance (No 2) Act 1992	Para	Paragraph
FA 1993	Finance Act 1993	Prosp am	Prospective amendment
FA 1994	Finance Act 1994	Prosp ins	Prospective insertion
FA 1997	Finance Act 1997	Prosp rep	Prospective repeal
FA (No 2) 1997	Finance (No 2) Act 1997	Prosp sub	Prospective substitution
FA 1998	Finance Act 1998	Rep	Repealed by
FA 1999	Finance Act 1999	Sch	Schedule
FA 2000	Finance Act 2000	SLR 1908	Statute Law Revision Act 1908
FLA 1996	Family Law Act 1996	SL(R)A 1998	Statute Law (Repeals) Act 1998
FSA 1986	Financial Services Act 1986	Sub	Substituted by

PARTNERSHIP

Partnership Act 1890

s 1	*Sub-s (2)*: Am SL(R)A 1998, s 1(1), Sch 1, Pt X
s 23	*Sub-s (1)*: Am SLR Act 1908
	Sub-s (2): Am Courts Act 1971, s 56(4), Sch 11, Pt II
	Sub-s (4): Rep SL(R)A 1998, s 1(1), Sch 1, Pt X
s 35(a)	Rep Mental Health Act 1959, s 149(2), Sch 8

Limited Liability Partnerships Act 2000

s 2	*Sub-ss (2A), (2B)*: Ins Limited Liability Partnerships (Particulars of Usual Residential Address) (Confidentiality Orders) Regulations 2002, SI 2002/915
s 9	*Sub-ss (3A), (3B)*: Ins Limited Liability Partnerships (Particulars of Usual Residential Address) (Confidentiality Orders) Regulations 2002, SI 2002/915

COMPANY

Company and Business Names Regulations 1981, SI 1981/1685

reg 3	Am Company and Business Names (Amendment) Regulations 1992, SI 1992/1196, reg 2(1), (2)
reg 4	Am Company and Business Names (Amendment) Regulations 1992, SI 1992/1196, reg 2(1), (3)

Company and Business Names Regulations 1981, SI 1981/1685 *cont*

Sch	Company and Business Names (Amendment) Regulations 1982, Am SI 1982/1653, reg 2, Company and Business Names (Amendment) Regulations 1992, SI 1992/1196, reg 2(1), (4), (5), Company and Business Names (Amendment) Regulations 1995, SI 1995/3022, reg 3, SI 2001/259, reg 3, Transfer of Functions (Miscellaneous) Order 2001, SI 2001/3500, art 8, Sch 2, Pt II, para 14, Secretaries of State for Education and Skills and for Work and Pensions Order 2002, SI 2002/1397, art 12, Sch, Pt II, para 17

Business Names Act 1985

s 1	Am Limited Liability Partnerships Regulations 2001, SI 2001/1090, reg 9(1), Sch 5, para 10
s 2	*Sub-s (1)*: Am Scotland Act 1999 (Consequential Modifications) (No 2) Order 1999, SI 1999/1820, art 4, Sch 2, Pt I, para 79
s 4	Am Limited Liability Partnerships Regulations 2001, SI 2001/1090, reg 9(1), Sch 5, para 11

Companies Act 1985

s 1	*Sub-s (3A)*: Ins Companies (Single Member Private Limited Companies) Regulations 1992, SI 1992/1699, reg 2, Sch, para 1
s 2	*Sub-s (6)*: Am Companies Act 1985 (Electronic Communications) Order 2000, SI 2000/3373
	Sub-s (6A): Ins Companies Act 1985 (Electronic Communications) Order 2000, SI 2000/3373
s 3A	Ins CA 1989, s 110(1)
s 4	Sub CA 1989, s 110(2)
s 7	*Sub-s (3)(c)*: Am Requirements of Writing (Scotland) Act 1995, s 14(2), Sch 5; Am Companies Act 1985 (Electronic Communications) Order 2000, SI 2000/3373
	Sub-s (3A): Ins Companies Act 1985 (Electronic Communications) Order 2000, SI 2000/3373
s 10	*Sub-s (2A)*: Ins Companies (Particulars of Usual Residential Address) (Confidentiality Orders) Regulations 2002, SI 2002/912, reg 16, Sch 2, para 1(1), (2)
	Sub-s (3): Am Companies (Particulars of Usual Residential Address) (Confidentiality Orders) Regulations 2002, SI 2002/912, reg 16, Sch 2, para 1(1), (3)
s 12	*Sub-s (3)*: Am Companies Act 1985 (Electronic Communications) Order 2000, SI 2000/3373
	Sub-ss (3A), (3B): Ins Companies Act 1985 (Electronic Communications) Order 2000, SI 2000/3373
s 13	*Sub-s (4)*: Am IA 1986, s 439(1), Sch 13, Pt I
s 26	*Sub-s (1)(bb)*: Ins Open-Ended Investment Companies (Investment Companies with Variable Capital) Regulations 1996, SI 1996/2827, reg 75, Sch 8, Pt I, para 4(a); Sub Open-Ended Investment Companies Regulations 2001, SI 2001/1228, reg 84, Sch 7, para 3
	Sub-s (1)(bbb): Ins Limited Liability Partnerships Regulations 2001, SI 2001/1090, reg 9, Sch 5, para 9

Companies Act 1985 *cont*

s 26 *cont*	*Sub-s (3)(b)*: Am Open-Ended Investment Companies (Investment Companies with Variable Capital) Regulations 1996, SI 1996/2827, reg 75, Sch 8, 1 Pt I, para 4(b), Open-Ended Investment Companies Regulations 2001, SI 2001/1228, reg 84, Sch 7, para 3
s 29	*Sub-ss (2), (3)*: Am Companies Act 1985 (Electronic Communications) Order 2000, SI 2000/3373
s 35	Sub CA 1989, s 108(1); Am Charities Act 1993, s 98(1), para 20(1), (2)
s 35A	Ins CA 1989, s 108(1)
	Sub-s (6): Am Charities Act 1993, s 98(1), para 20(1), (2)
s 35B	Ins CA 1989, s 108(1)
s 36	Sub CA 1989, s 130(1)
s 36A	Ins CA 1989, s 130(2)
s 36C	Ins CA 1989, s 130(4)
s 40	Am Companies Act 1989, s 130(7), Sch 17, para 3; Am Requirements of Writing (Scotland) Act 1995, s 14(2), Sch 4, para 54
s 43	*Sub-s (3)*: Am Companies Act 1985 (Electronic Communications) Order 2000, SI 2000/3373
	Sub-ss (3A), (3B): Ins Companies Act 1985 (Electronic Communications) Order 2000, SI 2000/3373
s 44	*Sub-s (7)(a)*: Am Insolvency Act 1986, ss 437, 439(1), Sch 11, Pt I, Sch 13, 1 Pt I, Vol 4
s 46	*Sub-ss (2)–(4)*: Sub CA 1989, s 23, Sch 10, para 1
s 47	*Sub-s (2)*: Am Companies Act 1985 (Electronic Communications) Order 2000, SI 2000/3373
s 80	*Sub-s (1)*: Am CA 1989, s 115(1)
s 80A	Ins CA 1989, s 115(1)
s 81	Rep for certain purposes FSA 1986, s 212(3), Sch 17, Pt I
s 85	Am FSA 1986, s 212(3), Sch 17, Pt I
s 117	*Sub-s (2)*: Am Companies Act 1985 (Electronic Communications) Order 2000, SI 2000/3373
	Sub-s (3A): Ins Companies Act 1985 (Electronic Communications) Order 2000, SI 2000/3373
	Sub-s (5): Am Companies Act 1985 (Electronic Communications) Order 2000, SI 2000/3373
	Sub-s (7A): Ins Companies Act 1985 (Electronic Communications) Order 2000, SI 2000/3373
s 153	*Sub-s (3)*: Am IA 1985, s 109, Sch 6, para 8; Am IA 1986, ss 437, 439(1), Sch 11, Pt I, Sch 13, Pt I
	Sub-s (4): Am FSA 1986, s 196(2); Am CA 1989, ss 132, 144(4), Sch 18, para 33
	Sub-s (5): Ins FSA 1986, s 196(3); Am CA 1989, ss 132, 144(4), Sch 18, para 33
s 155	*Sub-s (6)*: Am Companies Act 1985 (Electronic Communications) Order 2000, SI 2000/3373
	Sub-s (6A): Ins Companies Act 1985 (Electronic Communications) Order 2000, SI 2000/3373
s 156	*Sub-s (1A)*: Ins Companies Act 1985 (Electronic Communications) Order 2000, SI 2000/3373
	Sub-ss (2), (4), (5), (7): Am Companies Act 1985 (Electronic Communications) Order 2000, SI 2000/3373
	Sub-s (3): Am IA 1986, ss 437, 439(1), Sch 11, Pt I, Sch 13, Pt I
s 157	Am Companies Act 1985 (Electronic Communications) Order 2000, SI 2000/3373

Companies Act 1985 *cont*

s 158	*Sub-s (4)*: Am Companies Act 1985 (Electronic Communications) Order 2000, SI 2000/3373
s 159A	Prosp ins CA 1989, s 133(1), (2)
s 160	*Sub-s (3)*: Prosp rep CA 1989, ss 133(1), (3), 212, Sch 24
	Sub-s (4): Prosp am CA 1989, ss 133(1), (3), 212, Sch 24
s 162	*Sub-s (2)*: Prosp am CA 1989, ss 133(1), (4), 212, Sch 24
s 163	*Sub-ss (1)–(4)*: Am FSA 1986, s 212(2), Sch 16, para 17
	Sub-s (2)(a): Am Financial Services and Markets Act 2000 (Consequential Amendments and Repeals) Order 2001, SI 2001/3649, art 6
	Sub-ss (4), (5): Sub for sub-s (4) Financial Services and Markets Act 2000 (Consequential Amendments and Repeals) Order 2001, SI 2001/3649, art 6
s 169	Sub-s (5): Am CA 1989, ss 143(2), 212, Sch 24
s 171	*Sub-s (5)(b)*: Am CA 1985 (Accounts of Small and Medium-sized Companies and Minor Accounting Amendments) Regulations 1997, SI 1997/220, reg 7(1)
s 173	*Sub-s (4)*: Am IA 1986, ss 437, 439(1), Sch 11, Pt I, Sch 13, Pt I
s 175	*Sub-s (6)*: Am CA 1989, ss 143(3), 212, Sch 24
s 178	*Sub-s (7)*: Rep IA 1985, s 235(3), Sch 10, Pt II
s 185	*Sub-s (4)*: Am FSA 1986, s 194 (5)
	Sub-s (4): Sub Financial Services and Markets Act 2000 (Consequential Amendments and Repeals) Order 2001, SI 2001/3649, art 7
	Sub-ss (4A)—(4D): Ins Financial Services and Markets Act 2000 (Consequential Amendments and Repeals) Order 2001, SI 2001/3649, art 7
s 186	Sub CA 1989, s 130 (7), Sch 17, para 5
	Sub-s (1): Am Law Reform (Miscellaneous Provisions) (Scotland) Act 1990, s 74, Sch 8, para 33(4), Sch 9
s 196	Sub IA 1986, ss 437, 439(1), Sch 11, Pt I, Sch 13, Pt I
s 221	Ins CA 1989, s 2
s 222	Ins CA 1989, s 2
s 223	Ins CA 1989, s 3
s 224	Ins CA 1989, s 3
	Sub-s (2): Am CA 1985 (Miscellaneous Accounting Amendments) Regulations 1996, SI 1996/189, reg 2(2)
	Sub-s (3): Am CA 1989 (Commencement No 4 and Transitional Savings Provisions) Order 1990, SI 1990/355, art 15; Am CA 1985 (Miscellaneous Accounting Amendments) Regulations 1996, SI 1996/189, reg 2(3)
	Sub-s (3A): Ins CA 1985 (Miscellaneous Accounting Amendments) Regulations 1996, SI 1996/189, reg 2(4)
s 225	Ins CA 1989, s 3
	Sub-s (1): Am CA 1985 (Miscellaneous Accounting Amendments) Regulations 1996, SI 1996/189, reg 3(2)
	Sub-s (2): Rep CA 1985 (Miscellaneous Accounting Amendments) Regulations 1996, SI 1996/189, reg 3(3)
	Sub-s (4): Am CA 1985 (Miscellaneous Accounting Amendments) Regulations 1996, SI 1996/189, reg 3(4); Prosp am Enterprise Act 2002, s 248(3), Sch 17, paras 3, 4(a)
	Sub-s (5): Am CA 1985 (Miscellaneous Accounting Amendments) Regulations 1996, SI 1996/189, reg 3(5)
	Sub-s (6): Prosp am Enterprise Act 2002, s 248(3), Sch 17, paras 3, 4(b)
	Sub-s (7): Ins CA 1985 (Miscellaneous Accounting Amendments) Regulations 1996, SI 1996/189, reg 3(6)

Companies Act 1985 *cont*

s 226	Ins CA 1989, s 4(1)
s 233	Ins CA 1989, s 7
s 234	Ins CA 1989, s 8(1)
	Sub-s (1): Am CA 1985 (Miscellaneous Accounting Amendments) Regulations 1996, SI 1996/189, reg 5(2)
	Sub-s (4): Am CA 1985 (Miscellaneous Accounting Amendments) Regulations 1996, SI 1996/189, reg 5(3); Am Companies Act 1985 (Directors' Report) (Statement of Payment Practice) Regulations 1997, SI 1997/571, reg 2(1)
s 234A	Ins CA 1989, s 8(1)
ss 234B, 234C	Ins Directors' Remuneration Report Regulations 2002, SI 2002/1986, reg 3
s 235	Ins CA 1989, s 9; Am Directors' Remuneration Report Regulations 2002, SI 2002/1986, reg 4
s 238	Ins CA 1989, s 10; Am Companies Act 1985 (Electronic Communications) Order 2000, SI 2000/3373, Directors' Remuneration Report Regulations 2002, SI 2002/1986, reg 10
s 240	Ins CA 1989, s 10; Am CA 1985 (Audit Exemption) Regulations 1994, SI 1994/1935
s 241	Ins CA 1989, s 11; Am Directors' Remuneration Report Regulations 2002, SI 2002/1986, reg 10
s 241A	Ins Directors' Remuneration Report Regulations 2002, SI 2002/1986, reg 7
s 242	Ins CA 1989, s 11; Am Directors' Remuneration Report Regulations 2002, SI 2002/1986, reg 10
	Sub-s (1): Am Welsh Language Act 1993, s 30
s 244	Ins CA 1989, s 11
s 246	Ins CA 1989, s 13(1)
	Sub CA 1985 (Accounts of Small and Medium-sized Companies and Minor Accounting Amendments) Regulations 1997, SI 1997/220, reg 2(1)
	Sub-s (3): Sub Company Accounts (Disclosure of Directors' Emoluments) Regulations 1997, SI 1997/570, reg 6(1)
	Sub-s (9): Am Companies Act 1985 (Audit Exemption) (Amendment) Regulations 2000, SI 2000/1430, reg 8(1)
s 246A	Ins CA 1985 (Accounts of Small and Medium-sized Companies and Minor Accounting Amendments) Regulations 1997, SI 1997/220, reg 3
s 247	Ins CA 1989, s 13(1)
	Sub-ss (2)–(3): Am CA 1985 (Accounts of Small and Medium-sized Enterprises and Publications of Accounts in ECUs) Regulations 1992, SI 1992/2452, reg 5
	Sub-s (5): Am CA 1985 (Accounts of Small and Medium-sized Companies and Minor Accounting Amendments) Regulations 1997, SI 1997/220, reg 7(2)
s 247A	Ins CA 1985 (Accounts of Small and Medium-sized Companies and Minor Accounting Amendments) Regulations 1997, SI 1997/220, reg 4
	Sub-ss (1)(a), (2)(b), (c): Sub Financial Services and Markets Act 2000 (Consequential Amendments and Repeals) Order 2001, SI 2001/3649, art 11
	Sub-s (2)(d): Rep Financial Services and Markets Act 2000 (Consequential Amendments and Repeals) Order 2001, SI 2001/3649, art 11
s 247B	Ins CA 1985 (Accounts of Small and Medium-sized Companies and Minor Accounting Amendments) Regulations 1997, SI 1997/220, reg 5
	Sub-s (1): Am Companies Act 1985 (Audit Exemption) (Amendment) Regulations 2000, SI 2000/1430, reg 8(2)

Companies Act 1985 *cont*

Companies Act 1985 *cont*

s 366A *cont*	*Sub-s (5A)*: Ins Companies Act 1985 (Electronic Communications) Order 2000, SI 2000/3373
s 368	*Sub-s (8)*: Ins CA 1989, s 145, Sch 19, para 9
s 369	*Sub-s (4)*: Am CA 1989, s 115(3)
	Sub-ss (4A)–(4G): Ins Companies Act 1985 (Electronic Communications) Order 2000, SI 2000/3373
s 370A	Ins Companies (Single Member Private Limited Companies) Regulations 1992, SI 1992/1699
s 372	*Sub-ss (2A), (2B)*: Ins Companies Act 1985 (Electronic Communications) Order 2000, SI 2000/3373
	Sub-ss (5), (6): Am Companies Act 1985 (Electronic Communications) Order 2000, SI 2000/3373
	Sub-s (6A): Ins Companies Act 1985 (Electronic Communications) Order 2000, SI 2000/3373
s 373	*Sub-s (2)*: Am Companies Act 1985 (Electronic Communications) Order 2000, SI 2000/3373
s 378	*Sub-s (3)*: Am CA 1989, s 115(3)
s 379A	Ins CA 1989, s 116(1), (2)
	Sub-s (2A): Ins Deregulation (Resolutions of Private Companies) Order 1996, SI 1996/1471, reg 2
	Sub-ss (2B)–(2F): Ins Companies Act 1985 (Electronic Communications) Order 2000, SI 2000/3373
	Sub-s (5): Am Companies Act 1985 (Electronic Communications) Order 2000, SI 2000/3373
	Sub-s (5A): Ins Companies Act 1985 (Electronic Communications) Order 2000, SI 2000/3373
s 380	Am CA 1989, s 116(1), (3); Am IA 1986, ss 437, 439(1), Sch 11, Pt I, Sch 13, Pt I; Am Uncertified Securities Regulations 1995, SI 1995/3272, reg 40(3), Uncertificated Securities Regulations 2001, SI 2001/3755, reg 51, Sch 7, para 10
s 381A	Ins CA 1989, s 113(1), (2)
	Sub-s (5): Am Deregulation (Resolutions of Private Companies) Order 1996, SI 1996/1471, reg 3(2)
s 381B	Ins CA 1989, s 113(1), (2)
	Am Deregulation (Resolutions of Private Companies) Order 1996, SI 1996/1471, reg 3(1)
s 381C	Ins CA 1989, s 113(1), (2)
	Sub-s (1): Am Deregulation (Resolutions of Private Companies) Order 1996, SI 1996/1471, reg 4
s 382A	Ins CA 1989, s 113(1), (2)
s 382B	Ins Companies (Single Member Private Limited Companies) Regulations 1992, SI 1992/1699
s 383	Am CA 1989, ss 143(9), 212, Sch 24
s 384	Ins CA 1989, s 119(1); Am SI 1994/1935
s 385	Ins CA 1989, s 119(1)
s 385A	Ins CA 1989, s 119(1)
s 386	Ins CA 1989, s 119(1)
	Sub-s (2)(a): Sub Companies Act 1985 (Audit Exemption) (Amendment) Regulations 2000, SI 2000/1430, reg 8(8)
s 389A	Ins CA 1989, s 120(1)
s 390	Ins CA 1989, s 120(1)

Companies Act 1985 *cont*

s 390 *cont*	*Sub-s (1A):* Ins Companies Act 1985 (Electronic Communications) Order 2000, SI 2000/3373
	Sub-s (2): Rep Deregulation (Resolutions of Private Companies) Order 1996, SI 1996/1471, reg 3(2)
s 390A	Ins CA 1989, s 121
s 390B	Ins CA 1989, s 121
s 391	Ins CA 1989, s 122(1)
s 392	Ins CA 1989, s 122(1)
s 392A	Ins CA 1989, s 122(1)
s 394	Ins Companies Act 1989, ss 118, 123(1)
s 395	*Sub-s (1):* Am IA 1985, s 109(1), Sch 6, para 10
s 403	*Sub-s (1):* Am Companies Act 1985 (Electronic Communications) Order 2000, SI 2000/3373
s 459	*Sub-s (1):* Am CA 1989, s 145, Sch 19, para 11(a)
	Sub-s (3): Ins Water Act 1989, s 190(1), Sch 25, para 71(3); Am Water Consolidation (Consequential Provisions) Act 1991, s 2(1), Sch 1, para 40(2)
s 461	Am Insolvency Act 1985, s 109(1), Sch 6, para 24; Am Insolvency Act 1986, s 439(1), Sch 13, Pt I
s 653	Am Deregulation and Contracting Out Act 1994, s 13 (1), Sch 5
	Sub-s (1): Prosp am Financial Services and Markets Act 2000, s 263
s 716	Rep Regulatory Reform (Removal of 20 Member Limit in Partnerships etc) Order 2002, SI 2002/3203
s 736	Sub CA 1989, s 144(1)
s 736A	Ins CA 1989, s 144(1)
s 741	*Sub-s (3):* Am Companies (Single Member Private Limited Companies) Regulations 1992, SI 1992/1699, reg 2, Sch, para 3(2)
Sch 1	Paras 1–3: Am CA 1989, ss 23, 145, Sch 10, para 17, Sch 19, para 7
	Para 2(2)(a): Am Companies Act 1985 (Audit Exemption) (Amendment) Regulations 2000, SI 2000/1430, reg 8(10)
	Para 4: Sub CA 1989, ss 23, 145, Sch 10, para 17, Sch 19, para 7
Sch 7A	Ins Directors' Remuneration Report Regulations 2002, SI 2002/1986, reg 9, Sch
Sch 8	Sub CA 1985 (Accounts of Small and Medium-sized Companies and Minor Accounting Amendments) Regulations 1997, SI 1997/220, reg 2(2), Sch 1
	Para 51A ins Companies Act 1985 (Audit Exemption) (Amendment) Regulations 2000, SI 2000/1430, reg 6
	Para 54 sub Financial Services and Markets Act 2000 (Consequential Amendments and Repeals) Order 2001, SI 2001/3649, art 34
Sch 8A	Ins Companies Act 1985 (Accounts of Small and Medium-sized Companies and Minor Accounting Amendments) Regulations 1997, SI 1997/220, reg 2(3), Sch 2
	Para 9A ins Companies Act 1985 (Audit Exemption) (Amendment) Regulations 2000, SI 2000/1430, reg 7
Sch 13	Para 11: Sub FSA 1986, s 212(2), Sch 16, para 25; Am Charities Act 1992, s 78(1), Sch 6, para 11(b); Am Charities Act 1993, s 98(1), Sch 6, para 20(1), (3); Am Financial Services and Markets Act 2000 (Consequential Amendments and Repeals) Order 2001, SI 2001/3649, art 37
	Para 25: Am CA 1989, ss 143(10), 212, Sch 24
	Para 26: Am CA 1989, ss 143(10), 212, Sch 24
Sch 15A	Ins CA 1989, s 114(1)

Table A as prescribed by Companies (Tables A to F) Regulations 1985, SI 1985/805

reg 1	Am Companies Act 1985 (Electronic Communications) Order 2000, SI 2000/3373, art 32(1), Sch 1, para 1
reg 4	Am Companies (Tables A to F) (Amendment) Regulations 1985, SI 1985/1052, reg 2
reg 41	Am Companies (Tables A to F) (Amendment) Regulations 1985, SI 1985/1052, reg 2
reg 60	Am Companies Act 1985 (Electronic Communications) Order 2000, SI 2000/3373, art 32(1), Sch 1, para 2
reg 61	Am Companies Act 1985 (Electronic Communications) Order 2000, SI 2000/3373, art 32(1), Sch 1, para 3
reg 62	Am Companies Act 1985 (Electronic Communications) Order 2000, SI 2000/3373, art 32(1), Sch 1, para 4
reg 63	Am Companies Act 1985 (Electronic Communications) Order 2000, SI 2000/3373, art 32(1), Sch 1, para 5
reg 111	Sub Companies Act 1985 (Electronic Communications) Order 2000, SI 2000/3373, art 32(1), Sch 1, para 6
reg 112	Am Companies Act 1985 (Electronic Communications) Order 2000, SI 2000/3373, art 32(1), Sch 1, para 7
reg 115	Am Companies (Tables A to F) (Amendment) Regulations 1985, SI 1985/1052, reg 2; Companies Act 1985 (Electronic Communications) Order 2000, SI 2000/3373, art 32(1), Sch 1, para 8

Company Directors Disqualification Act 1986

s 1	*Sub-s (1)*: Am Insolvency Act 2000, s 5(1); Prosp am Enterprise Act 2002, s 204(1), (3)
	Sub-s (2): Am Insolvency Act 2000, s 5(2)
	Sub-s (3): Am Insolvency Act 2000, s 8, Sch 4, Pt I, paras 1, 2
s 1A	Ins Insolvency Act 2000, s 6(1), (2)
s 2	*Sub-s (1)*: Am Deregulation and Contracting Out Act 1994, s 39, Sch 11, para 6; Am Insolvency Act 2000, s 8, Sch 4, Pt I, paras 1, 3
s 3	*Sub-s (3)*: Am CA 1989, s 23, Sch 10, para 35(1), (2)(a)
s 4	*Sub-s (1)(b)*: Am Insolvency Act 2000, s 8, Sch 4, Pt I, paras 1, 4
s 6	Prosp am Enterprise Act 2002, s 248(3), Sch 17, paras 40, 41
	Sub-ss (3), (3A)–(3C): Sub for sub-s (3) Insolvency Act 2000, s 8, Sch 4, Pt I, paras 1, 5
s 7	Prosp am Enterprise Act 2002, s 248(3), Sch 17, paras 40, 42
	Sidenote: Sub Insolvency Act 2000, s 8, Sch 4, Pt I, paras 1, 6(b)
	Sub-s (1)(b): Am Insolvency Act 2000, s 8, Sch 4, Pt I, paras 1, 6(a)
	Sub-s (2A): Ins Insolvency Act 2000, s 6(1), (3)
s 8	*Sub-s (2A)*: Ins Insolvency Act 2000, s 6(1), (4)
s 8A	Ins Insolvency Act 2000, s 6(1), (5)
s 9	*Sub-s (1)*: Am Insolvency Act 2000, ss 8, 15(1), Sch 4, Pt I, paras 1, 7(a), Sch 5
	Sub-s (1A): Ins Insolvency Act 2000, s 6(1), (6)
	Sub-s (2): Am Insolvency Act 2000, s 8, Sch 4, Pt I, paras 1, 7(b)
ss 9A–9E	Prosp ins Enterprise Act 2002, s 204(1), (2)
s 11	Sub-s (1): Prosp sub Enterprise Act 2002, s 257(3), Sch 21, para 5
s 12A	Ins Insolvency Act 2000, s 7(1)
s 13	Am Insolvency Act 2000, s 8, Sch 4, Pt I, paras 1, 8
s 14	*Sub-s (1)*: Am Insolvency Act 2000, s 8, Sch 4, Pt I, paras 1, 9

Company Directors Disqualification Act 1986 *cont*

s 15   *Sub-s (1)*: Am Insolvency Act 2000, s 8, Sch 4, Pt I, paras 1, 10(1), (2)
                        Sub-s (5): Am Insolvency Act 2000, s 8, Sch 4, Pt I, paras 1, 10(1), (3)

s 16   Prosp am Enterprise Act 2002, s 204(1), (6), (7)
                        Sub-s (2): Am Insolvency Act 2000, s 8, Sch 4, Pt I, paras 1, 11

s 17   Sub Insolvency Act 2000, s 8, Sch 4, Pt I, paras 1, 12; Prosp am Enterprise Act
                        2002, s 204(1), (8)–(10)

s 18   *Sidenote*: Sub Insolvency Act 2000, s 8, Sch 4, Pt I, paras 1, 13(1), (6)
                        Sub-s (1)(b)–(d): Am Insolvency Act 2000, s 8, Sch 4, Pt I, paras 1, 13(1), (2)
                        Sub-s (2A): Ins Insolvency Act 2000, s 8, Sch 4, Pt I, paras 1, 13(1), (3); Prosp sub
                        Enterprise Act 2002, s 204(1), (11)
                        Sub-s (3): Am Insolvency Act 2000, s 8, Sch 4, Pt I, paras 1, 13(1), (4)
                        Sub-s (4A): Ins Insolvency Act 2000, s 8, Sch 4, Pt I, paras 1, 13(1), (5)

s 20   Prosp re-numbered as sub-s (1) Youth Justice and Criminal Evidence Act 1999,
                        s 59, Sch 3, para 8
                        Sub-ss (2)–(4): Prosp ins Youth Justice and Criminal Evidence Act 1999, s 59,
                        Sch 3, para 8

s 21   *Sub-s (2)*: Am Insolvency Act 2000, s 8, Sch 4, Pt I, paras 1, 14(1), (2)
                        Sub-s (3): Am Insolvency Act 2000, s 8, Sch 4, Pt I, paras 1, 14(1), (3)

s 22   *Sub-s (3)*: Am Insolvency Act 2000, s 8, Sch 4, Pt I, paras 1, 15(1), (2)
                        Sub-s (4): Am Insolvency Act 2000, s 8, Sch 4, Pt I, paras 1, 15(1), (3)
                        Sub-s (10): Ins Insolvency Act 2000, s 5(3)

Sch 1   Para 4: Am CA 1989, ss 23, 139(4), Sch 10, para 35(1), (3); Prosp am CA 1989,
                        s 107, Sch 16, para 4
                        Para 5: Sub CA 1989, ss 23, 139(4), Sch 10, para 35(1), (3)
                        Para 5A: Ins Open-Ended Investment Companies (Investment Companies with
                        Variable Capital) Regulations 1996, SI 1996/2827, reg 75, Sch 8, Pt I, para 10;
                        Am Open-Ended Investment Companies Regulations 2001, SI 2001/1228, reg 84,
                        Sch 7, para 9

TAXATION

Inheritance Tax Act 1984

s 3A   Ins FA 1986, s 101, Sch 19, para 1; Am FA (No 2) 1987, ss 96, 104, Sch 9, Pt III

s 19   *Sub-s (3A)*: Ins FA 1986, s 101, Sch 19, para 5

s 21   *Sub-s (3)*: Am ICTA 1988, s 844, Sch 29, para 32

s 23   *Sub-s (5)*: Am FA 1998, ss 143(2), 171(2)

s 94   *Sub-ss (2), (3)*: Am ICTA 1988, s 844(1), Sch 29, para 32, Sch 30

s 103   *Sub-s (2)*: Am CA 1989, s 144(2), Sch 18, para 30(1), (3); Am Companies
                        (Consequential Provisions) Act 1985, s 30, Sch 2

s 104   *Sub-s (1)*: Am FA 1987, s 58, Sch 8, para 4; Am FA (No 2) 1992, s 73, Sch 14,
                        para 1

s 105   *Sub-s (1)*: Am FA 1987, s 58, Sch 8, para 5; Am FA (No 2) 1992, s 73, Sch 14,
                        para 2; Am FA 1996, s 184(2)
                        Sub-ss (1A), (1B), (2A): Ins FA 1987, s 58, Sch 8, para 5; Rep FA 1996, ss 184(1),
                        (2), (6), 205, Sch 41
                        Sub-s (1ZA): Ins FA (No 2) 1992, s 73, Sch 14, para 2; Am FA 1996, Sch 38,
                        para 2(1)
                        Sub-s (4): Am FA 1986, s 106(1)–(3)

Inheritance Tax Act 1984 *cont*

s 105 *cont*	*Sub-s (7)*: Ins FA 1986, s 106(1)–(3)
s 107	*Sub-s (4)*: Am FA 1987, s 58, Sch 8, para 6; Am FA 1996, s 184(1), (3), (6), 205, Sch 41
s 113A	Ins FA 1986, s 101, Sch 19, Part I, para 21
	Sub-s (3): am FA 1987, s 58, Sch 8, para 8
	Sub-s (3A): Ins FA 1987, s 58, Sch 8, para 8(2); Am FA 1996, s 184(4), (6)
	Sub-s (3B): Ins Finance (No 2) Act 1992, s 73, Sch 14, paras 3, 8; Am FA 1996, s 199, Sch 38, para 2
	Sub-s (6): Am Taxation of Chargeable Gains Act 1992, s 290(1), Sch 10, para 8(5)
	Sub-s (7A): Ins FA 1996, s 184(5), (6)(a)
s 113B	Ins FA 1986, s 101, Sch 19, Part I, para 21
	Sub-s (2): Am FA 1994, s 247(1)(a), (3)
	Sub-s (5): Am FA 1994, s 247(1)(a), (3)
	Sub-s (8): Am FA 1994, s 247(1)(b), (3)
s 116	*Sub-s (2)*: Am FA (No 2) 1992, s 73, Sch 14, paras 4, 8; Am FA 1995, ss 155, 162, Sch 29
	Sub-s (2A): Rep FA 1996, ss 185(3), (6), 205, Sch 41
	Sub-s (4): Am FA (No 2) 1992, s 73, Sch 14, paras 4, 8
	Sub-ss (5A)–(5E): Ins FA 1996, s 185(2), (5)
s 227	*Sub-s (1A)*: Ins FA 1986, s 101(1), (3), Sch 19, Pt I, para 31; Sub FA 1987, s 58, Sch 8, para 15
	Sub-s (1AA): Ins FA (No 2) 1992, s 73, Sch 14, para 5; Am FA 1996, Sch 38, para 5(1)
	Sub-s (1B): Ins FA 1986, s 101(1), (3), Sch 19, Pt I, para 31; Am FA 1987, s 58, Sch 8, para 15
	Sub-s (1C): Ins FA 1987, s 58, Sch 8, para 15
s 228	*Sub-s (1)*: Am FA 1987, s 58, Sch 8, para 15
	Sub-s (3A): Ins FA 1987, s 58, Sch 8, para 16
	Sub-s (5): FA (No 2) 1992, s 73, Sch 14, para 6; Am FA 1996, Sch 38, para 5(1)
s 270	Am Taxation of Chargeable Gains Act 1992, s 290(1), Sch 10, para 8(1), (12)

Income and Corporation Taxes Act 1988

s 1	*Sub-s (1):* Am FA 1996, s 79(2), Sch 7, paras 1, 2, 32
	Sub-s (2): Am FA 1988, ss 24(2), 148, Sch 14, Pts IV, V; Am FA 1996, s 72(2); Am FA 1999, ss 22(1)–(6), (12); Am Income Tax (Indexation Order) 2000, SI 2000/806; Am FA 2001, s 51(1); Am Income Tax (Indexation) Order 2002, SI 2002/707; Am Income Tax (Earnings and Pensions) Act 2003, s 722, Sch 6, Pt 1, paras 1, 2; Am Income Tax (Indexation) Order 2003, SI 2003/840
	Sub-s (2A): Ins FA 1992, s 9; Sub FA 1999, ss 22(1)–(6), (12)
	Sub-s (3): Am FA 1988, ss 24(2), 148, Sch 14, Pts IV, V; Am FA 1992, s 9; Am FA 1999, ss 22(1)–(6), (12)
	Sub-s (4): Am FA 1992, s 9; Am FA 1993, ss 107, 213, Sch 23, Pt III(10); Am FA 1999, ss 22(1)–(6), (12). Does not apply for year 2001–2002 so far as relates to amount specified in sub-s (2)(aa)
	Sub-s (5): Rep FA 1993, ss 107, 213, Sch 23, Pt III(10)
	Sub-s (5A): Ins FA 1999, ss 22(1)–(6), (12); Am Finance Act 2002, s 27(a); Am Income Tax (Earnings and Pensions) Act 2003, s 722, Sch 6, Pt 1, paras 1, 2
	Sub-s (6): Am FA 1992, s 9
	Sub-s (6A): Ins FA 1992, s 9; Am FA 1999, ss 22(1)–(6), (12)

Income and Corporation Taxes Act 1988 *cont*

s 1A   Ins FA 1996, s 73(1), (3)

Sub-s (1): Am FA (No 2) 1997, s 31(1)–(4); Am FA 1998, s 100; Am FA 2000, s 32(1), (2)

Sub-s (1AA): Ins FA 2000, s 32(1), (3)

Sub-s (1A): Ins FA (No 2) 1997, s 31(1)–(4)

Sub-s (1B): Ins FA 1999, s 22(7), (12)

Sub-s (2): Am FA 1997, s 113, Sch 18, Pt VI(2)

Sub-s (5): Sub FA (No 2) 1997, s 31(1)–(4)

Sub-s (6A): Ins FA 1999, s 22(7), (12)

s 1B   Ins FA (No 2) 1997, s 31(5)

s 8   *Sub-ss (4)–(6)*: Rep FA 1993, ss 206(1), 213, Sch 23, Pt VII

s 9   *Sub-s(3)*: Am Income Tax (Earnings and Pensions) Act 2003, s 722, Sch 6, Pt 1, paras 1, 4

s 15   *Sub-s (1)*: Am FA 1995, s 39(1), (3), (4), Sch 6, para 1; Am FA 1998, ss 38, 165, Sch 5, Pt I, paras 1, 2, Sch 27, Pt III(4), FA 2002, ss 83(1)(b), 141, Sch 27, paras 1, 2, Sch 40, Pt 3(10)

Sub-s (1A): Ins FA 1998, ss 38, 165, Sch 5, Pt I, paras 1, 2, Sch 27, Pt III(4)

Sub-s (2): Rep FA 1998, ss 38, 165, Sch 5, Pt I, paras 1, 2, Sch 27, Pt III(4)

Sub-s (3): Rep FA 1988, s 148, Sch 14, Pt V

s 18   Am FA 1988, s 148, Sch 14, Pt V; Am FA 1995, s 39, Sch 6, para 2

Sub-ss (1), (3): Am Income Tax (Earnings and Pensions) Act 2003, s 722, Sch 6, Pt 1, paras 1, 5

Sub-ss (1), (3), (5): Am FA 1996, Sch 7, para 4

Sub-s (3): Am FA 1996, Sch 41, Pt V(2)

Sub-s (3A): Ins FA 1996, Sch 14, para 5

Sub-ss (3B)–(3E): Ins FA 1996, Sch 7, para 4(3)

s 19   *Sub-s (1)*: Am FA 1989, s 36; Am FA 1996, Sch 7, para 5; Am FA 1998, ss 63(3), 165, Sch 27, Pt III(11)

s 20   *Sub-s (1)*: Am FA 1993, s 181(1), 184(3); Am FA 1997, s 69, Sch 7, para 8(2)(a); Am FA (No 2) 1997, ss 22(5), 24(10)

Sub-s (2): Am FA 1988, s 61(1), (5); Am FA 1994, s 217(5)

s 60   Sub FA 1994, s 200; Am FA 1998, s 46(3), Sch 7

s 61   Sub FA 1994, s 201

Sub-s (1): Am FA 1998, s 46(3), Sch 7

Sub-s (4): Am FA 1988, s 146, Sch 13, Pt I, paras 1, 2

s 62   Sub FA 1994, s 200

s 62A   Ins FA 1994, s 201

Sub-s (3): Am FA 1996, Sch 21, para 1

s 63   Sub FA 1994, s 204

Sub-ss (1)–(2): Am FA 1988, s 35, Sch 3, paras 1, 3

s 63A   Ins FA 1994, s 205

Sub-ss (1), (3), (5): Am FA 1998, s 46(3), Sch 7

s 74   Am FA 1994, s 81, Sch 9, para 1

Sub-s (1): Ins FA 1994, s 144(1); Am FA 1996, Sch 20, para 4; Sch 41, Pt V(10); Am FA 1998, s 46(3), Sch 7

Sub-s (1)(q): Rep FA 1997, Sch 18, Pt VI (2)

Sub-s (2): Ins FA 1994, s 144(2)

s 113   *Sub-s (1)*: Sub for certain purposes FA 1994, s 215(4); Am FA 1998, s 46(3), Sch 7

Sub-s (2): Sub for certain purposes FA 1994, s 215(4)

Income and Corporation Taxes Act 1988 *cont*

s 384 *cont*	*Sub-s (10)*: Am Capital Allowances Act 1990, s 164, Sch 1, para 8(1), (14); Am Capital Allowances Act 2001, ss 578, 580, Sch 2, para 29(2), Sch 4
	Sub-s (11): Ins Capital Allowances Act 2001, s 578, Sch 2, para 29(2)
s 384A	Ins Capital Allowances Act 2001, s 578, Sch 2, para 30
s 385	*Sub-s (1)*: Sub FA 1994, s 209(4)
	Sub-s (2): Rep for certain purposes FA 1994, s 216(3)
	Sub-s (3): Rep for certain purposes FA 1994, s 209(5)
	Sub-s (4): Am FA 1998, s 46(3), Sch 7, para 1
	Sub-s (5): Rep for certain purposes FA 1994, s 216(4)
	Sub-s (6): Rep FA 1988, s 148, Sch 14, Pt V
	Sub-s (8): Rep for certain purposes FA 1994, s 209(5)
s 386	*Sub-s (1)*: Am FA 1998, s 46(3), Sch 7, para 1
	Sub-s (4): Rep for certain purposes FA 1994, s 215(4)
s 388	Am FA 1994, ss 209(6), 211(2); Am FA 1998, s 46(3), Sch 7, para 1
s 393	*Sub-s (1)*: Am FA 1990, s 99(1), (2), (4),132, Sch 19, Pt V; Am FA 1991, ss 73(2–5),123, Sch 15, para 8, Sch 19, Pt V
	Sub-ss (2)–(6): Ins FA 1990, s 61; Rep FA 1991, s 73(2)-(5), 123, Sch 15, para 8, Sch 19, Pt V
	Sub-s (11): Rep FA 1991, s 73(2), (5),123, Sch 15, para 8, Sch 19, Pt V
s 393A	Ins FA 1991, s 73(1), (4), (5)
	Sub-s (2): Am FA (No 2) 1997, s 39(1), (2)
	Sub-ss (2A)–(2C): Ins FA (No 2) 1997, s 39(1), (3)
	Sub-s (2C): Am Capital Allowances Act 2001, s 578, Sch 2, para 32(1)
	Sub-ss (3), (4): Am FA 1996, Sch 20, para 26
	Sub-ss (5), (6): Rep Capital Allowances Act 2001, s 578, 580, Sch 2, para 32(2), Sch 4
	Sub-s (7): Am FA (No 2) 1997, s 39(1), (4)
	Sub-ss (7A), (12): Ins FA (No 2) 1997, s 39(1), (5), (6)
	Sub-ss (11), (12): Am Capital Allowances Act 2001, s 578, Sch 2, para 32(3)(a), (4)
s 414	*Sub-ss (2)–(2D)*: Sub FA 1989, ss 104, 187(1), Sch 17, Pt V
	Sub-s (3): Rep FA 1989, ss 104, 187(1), Sch 17, Pt V
	Sub-s (5): Am FA 1989, ss 104, 187(1), Sch 17, Pt V
s 416	*Sub-s (1)*: Am FA 1989, s 187(1), Sch 17, Pt V
s 417	*Sub-s (3)*: Am FA 1995, s 74, Sch 17, para 6
s 419	Am FA 1996, s 173; Am FA 1998, ss 31(5), 117(3)–(5), 165, Schs 3, 19, 27
s 420	*Sub-s (2)*: Am FA 1988, s 35, 148, Sch 3, Pt I
s 421	*Sub-s (1)*: Am FA (No 2) 1992, s 19(6), (7); Am FA 1993, s 77(4), (5); Am FA 1996, Sch 6, para 9; Am FA(No 2) 1997, s 34, Sch 4, para 11
s 839	*Sub-ss (3), (3A)*: Sub FA 1995, s 74, Sch 17, para 20
	Sub-s (8): Am ICTA 1988 (Appointed Day) Order, SI 1988/745
Sch 7	Am FA 1994, s 88, 258, Sch 26; Am FA 1995, s 45(4); Am FA 1996, s 107(2), (3); Sch 41, Pt V(10); Am FA 2000, s 57, Sch 10, paras 1, 6

Finance Act 1991

s 72	*Sub-s (4)*: Am Taxation of Chargeable Gains Act 1992, s 290(1), Sch 10, para 23; Am FA 2002, s 48(1)
	Sub-s (8): Am FA 1994, s 258, Sch 26, Pt V(24)

Taxation of Chargeable Gains Act 1992

s 2	Am FA 1998, s 121(3), Sch 21, para 2
s 2A	Ins FA 1998, s 121(1), (4)
	Sub-s (5): Am FA 2000, s 66(1), (2); Am FA 2002, s 46(1)
	Sub-s (8): Am FA 1999, s 72(3)(a) ; Sub FA 2000, s 66(1), (3); Am FA 2002, s 47, Sch 10, para 2, Sch 40, Pt 3(3)
	Sub-s (9): Sub FA 2000, s 66(1), (3)
s 3	Am FA 1998, s 121(3), Sch 21, para 3
	Sub-s (2): Am Capital Gains Tax (Annual Exempt Amount) Order 2002, SI 2002/702, art 2
s 152	*Sub-s (4)*: Am FA 1996, ss 121(8), 141(1)
s 153A	Ins FA 1996, s 141(2)
s 155	Am FA 1993, s 86(1), (4), (Fish Quota) Order 1999, SI 1999/564; FA 1999, s 84
s 156	Am FA 1998, s 41(2)–(7)
s 156A	Ins Limited Liability Partnerships Act 2000, s 10(4)
s 157	Am FA 1993, s 87, Sch 7, Pt I, para 1(1); Am FA 1998, s 140(1), (3), (6)
s 163	*Sub-ss (1), (4), (6)*: Am FA 1996, s 176(1)
	Sub-ss (3), (5): Am FA 1993, s 87, Sch 7, Pt I, para 2(1), 1(1)
	Sub-s (7): Am FA 1993, s 87, Sch 7, Pt I, para 2(1), 1(1); Am FA 1993, s 87, Sch 7, Pt I, para 2(2)
s 164	*Sub-ss (1), (2), (4), (5)*: Am FA 1996, s 176(1)
	Sub-ss (2): Am FA 1993, s 87, Sch 7, Pt I, para 2(3)
	Sub-s (4): Am FA 1993, s 87, Sch 7, Pt I, para 2(1)
s 165	*Sub-ss (1)–(3)*: Am FA 2000, s 90(1), (3), (4)
	Sub-ss (2), (8): Am FA 1993, s 87, Sch 7, Pt 1, para 1(1)
	Sub-s (2): Am FA 1996, Sch 38, para 10(2)
	Sub-s (2)(a), (b): Rep FA 1998, s 165, Sch 27, Pt III(31)
	Sub-s (6): Am FA 1998, s 165, Sch 27, Pt III(31)
	Sub-s (8): Am FA 1998, s 140(4)
s 170	*Sub-s (2)(a)*: Rep FA 2000, ss 102, 156, Sch 29, para 1(1)(a), Sch 40, Pt II(12)
	Sub-s (3): Am FA 1996, Sch 38, para 10(2)
	Sub-s (5): Am FA 1996, Sch 18, para 15(2)
	Sub-s (6): Am FA 1996, Sch 18, para 15(3)
	Sub-s (7): Am FA 1996, Sch 18, para 15(4)
	Sub-s (8): Am FA (No 2) 1992, s 24, Sch 6, paras 5, 10
	Sub-s (8): Am FA 2000, s 156, Sch 40, Pt II(11)
	Sub-s (9): Am FA 1998, s 136(1), (4); Am FA 2000, ss 102, 156, Sch 29, para 1(1)(b), Sch 40, Pt II(12); Am FA 2001, s 75(4), (6)
s 281	*Sub-s (3)(c)*: Am FA 1996, s 199, Sch 38, para 10
	Sub-ss (5)(a), (6), (7): Am FA 1996, s 132, Sch 18, paras 15, 17(3)
s 286	Am FA 1995, s 74, Sch 17, para 31
Sch A1	Ins FA 1998, s 121(2), (4), Sch 20; Am FA 1999, s 72(3)(b); Am FA 2000, ss 67, 156, Sch 40, Pt II(6); Am FA 2001, s 78, Sch 26; Am Financial Services and Markets Act 2000 (Consequential Amendments) (Taxes) Order 2001, SI 2001/3629; Am FA 2002, ss 45(1), 47, 141, Sch 9, Pt 2, para 5(1), (13), Sch 10, paras 1–12, Sch 40, Pt 3(3)
Sch 6	Rep FA 1998, ss 140(2)(c), 165, Sch 27, Pt III(3)
Sch 7	*Para 2*: Am FA 2000, s 90(3)
	Para 7: Am FA 1993, s 87, Sch 7, para 1(1)
	Para 8: Rep FA 1998, s 165, Sch 27, Pt III(31)

Capital Allowances Act 2001

ss 45A–45C	Ins FA 2001, Sch 17, s 65, para 2
s 45D	Ins FA 2002, s 59, Sch 19, paras 1, 3, 4
s 46	Am FA 2001, ss 65, 110, Sch 17, para 3, Sch 33, Pt 2(4); Am FA 2002, ss 59, 61, 62(1), 63(3), 141, Sch 19, paras 1, 4(1)-(3), Sch 20, paras 1, 4, Sch 21, Pt 1, paras 1, 5, Sch 40, Pt 3(7)
s 52	*Sub-s (3)*: Am FA 2001, s 65, Sch 17
s 57	*Sub-s (2)*: Am FA 2001, s 68, Sch 20

INSOLVENCY

Insolvency Act 1986

s 1	*Sub-s (2)*: Am Insolvency Act 2000, s 2, Sch 2, paras 1, 2
	Sub-s (4): Ins Insolvency Act 1986 (Amendment) (No 2) Regulations 2002, SI 2002/1240, regs 3, 4
s 1A	Ins Insolvency Act 2000, s 1, Sch 1, paras 1, 2
s 2	*Sub-s (1)*: Am Insolvency Act 2000, s 2, Sch 2, paras 1, 3
	Sub-s (2)(a), (aa): Am Insolvency Act 2000, s 2, Sch 2, paras 1, 3(a)
	Sub-s (4): Sub Insolvency Act 2000, s 2, Sch 2, paras 1, 3(b)
s 4	*Sub-s (2)*: Am Insolvency Act 2000, s 2, Sch 2, paras 1, 4
s 4A	Ins Insolvency Act 2000, s 2, Sch 2, paras 1, 5
s 5	*Sub-s (1)*: Sub Insolvency Act 2000, s 2, Sch 2, paras 1, 6(a)
	Sub-s (2): Am Insolvency Act 2000, s 2, Sch 2, paras 1, 6(b)
	Sub-s (2)(b): Sub Insolvency Act 2000, s 2, Sch 2, paras 1, 6(c)
	Sub-s (2A): Ins Insolvency Act 2000, s 2, Sch 2, paras 1, 6(c)
	Sub-s (3): Am Insolvency Act 2000, s 2, Sch 2, paras 1, 6(b)
s 6	*Sub-s 1(a)*: Am Insolvency Act 2000, s 2, Sch 2, paras 1, 7(1), (2)
	Sub-s 2(aa): Ins Insolvency Act 2000, s 2, Sch 2, paras 1, 7(1), (3)
	Sub-s (3): Am Insolvency Act 2000, s 2, Sch 2, paras 1, 7(1), (4)
	Sub-s (4)(a): Am Insolvency Act 2000, s 2, Sch 2, paras 1, 7(1), (5)
	Sub-s (5): Am Insolvency Act 2000, s 2, Sch 2, paras 1, 7(1), (6)
	Sub-s (6): Am Insolvency Act 2000, s 2, Sch 2, paras 1, 7(1), (7)
	Sub-s (7): Am Insolvency Act 2000, s 2, Sch 2, paras 1, 7(1), (8)
s 6A	Ins Insolvency Act 2000, s 2, Sch 2, paras 1, 8
s 7	*Sub-s (1)*: Am Insolvency Act 2000, s 2, Sch 2, paras 1, 9(a)
	Sub-s (2)(a): Sub Insolvency Act 2000, s 2, Sch 2, paras 1, 9(b)
	Sub-s (5): Sub Insolvency Act 2000, s 2, Sch 2, paras 1, 9(c)
s 7A	Ins Insolvency Act 2000, s 2, Sch 2, paras 1, 10
s 7B	Ins Insolvency Act 2000, s 2, Sch 2, paras 1, 10
s 8	*Sub-ss (1A), (1B)*: Ins Financial Services and Markets Act 2000 (Consequential Amendments and Repeals) Order 2001, SI 2001/3649, art 303
	Sub-s (4): Am Banking Act 1987, s 108(1), Sch 6, para 25(1)
	Sub-ss (4)–(6): Sub for sub-s (4)
	Sub-s (5)(a): Sub Financial Services and Markets Act 2000 (Consequential Amendments) Order 2002, SI 2002/1555, Art 14(1), (2)
	Sub-s (5)(b): Am Financial Services and Markets Act 2000 (Consequential Amendments) Order 2002, SI 2002/1555, Art 14(1), (3)

Insolvency Act 1986 *cont*

s 8 *cont*	*Sub-s (7)*: Ins Insolvency Act 1986 (Amendment) (No 2) Regulations 2002, SI 2002/1240, regs 3, 5
s 9	*Sub-s (1)*: Am Criminal Justice Act 1988, s 62(2)(a); Am Access to Justice Act 1999, s 90, Sch 13, para 133
	Sub-s (3): Am CA 1989, s 107, Sch 16, para 3
s 10	*Sub-s (1)(aa)*: Ins Insolvency Act 2000, s 9(1), (2)
s 11	*Sub-s (3)(ba)*: Ins Insolvency Act 2000, s 9(1), (3)
s 27	*Sub-s (3)(a)*: Prosp am IA 2000, ss 1, 15(1), Sch 1, paras 1, 5, Sch 5
s 31	Prosp sub Enterprise Act 2002, s 257, Sch 21, para 1
s 44	*Sub-s (1)*: Am IA 1994, s 2(2)
	Sub-ss (2A)–(2D): Ins IA 1994, s 2(3)
ss 72A–72H	Ins Enterprise Act 2002, s 250(1) (s 72H(2)–(5) only; remainder prosp ins)
s 84	*Sub-s (4)*: Prosp ins Commonhold and Leasehold Reform Act 2002, s 68, Sch 5, para 6
s 122	*Sub-s (1)*: Companies (Single Member Private Limited Companies) Regulations 1992, SI 1992/1699, reg 2, Sch, para 8
	Sub-s (1)(fa): Ins Insolvency Act 2000, s 1, Sch 1, paras 1, 6
s 124	*Sub-s (1)*: Am Criminal Justice Act 1988, s 62(2)(b); Am Access to Justice Act 1999, s 90, Sch 13, para 133; Am Insolvency Act 1986 (Amendment) (No 2) Regulations 2002, SI 2002/1240, regs 3, 8
	Sub-s (3A): Ins Insolvency Act 2000, s 1, Sch 1, paras 1, 7
	Sub-s (4): Am CA 1989, s 60(2)
s 124A	Ins Companies Act 1989, s 60(3)
	Sub-s (1): Am Financial Services and Markets Act 2000 (Consequential Amendments and Repeals) Order 2001, SI 2001/3649, art 305
s 218	*Sub-s (1)*: Am Insolvency Act 2000, s 10(1), (2)
	Sub-s (2): Rep Insolvency Act 2000, ss 10(1), (3), 15(1), Sch 5
	Sub-s (4): Am Insolvency Act 2000, s 10(1), (4)
	Sub-s (5): Sub Insolvency Act 2000, s 10(1), (5)
	Sub-s (6)(b): Am Insolvency Act 2000, ss 10(1), (6), 15(1), Sch 5
s 219	*Sub-s (1)*: Am Insolvency Act 2000, s 10(1), (7)(a)
	Sub-ss (2A), (2B): Ins Insolvency Act 2000, s 11
	Sub-s (3): Am Insolvency Act 2000, s 10(1), (7)(b)
	Sub-s (4): Am Insolvency Act 2000, s 10(1), (7)(c)
s 240	*Sub-s (3)*: Para (aa) ins Insolvency Act 1986 (Amendment) (No 2) Regulations 2002, SI 2002/1240, regs 3, 11
s 241	Am Insolvency (No 2) Act 1994, s 1
s 247	*Sub-s (3)*: Ins Insolvency Act 1986 (Amendment) (No 2) Regulations 2002, SI 2002/1240, regs 3, 12
s 252	*Sub-s (2)(aa)*: Ins Insolvency Act 2000, s 3, Sch 3, paras 1, 2(a)
	Sub-s (2)(b): Am Insolvency Act 2000, s 3, Sch 3, paras 1, 2(b)
s 253	*Sub-s (1)*: Am Insolvency Act 2000, s 3, Sch 3, paras 1, 3(a)
	Sub-s (2): Am Insolvency Act 2000, s 3, Sch 3, paras 1, 3(b)
	Sub-s (4): Am Insolvency Act 2000, s 3, Sch 3, paras 1, 3(c)
s 254	*Sub-s (1)*: Am Insolvency Act 2000, s 3, Sch 3, paras 1, 4
s 255	*Sub-s (1)(a)*: Am Insolvency Act 2000, s 3, Sch 3, paras 1, 5(a)
	Sub-s (1)(d): Am Insolvency Act 2000, ss 3, 15(1), Sch 3, paras 1, 5(b), Sch 5
s 256	*Sub-s (1)(a), (aa)*: Am Insolvency Act 2000, s 3, Sch 3, paras 1, 6(a)

Insolvency Act 1986 *cont*

s 256 *cont*	*Sub-s (3)*: Am Insolvency Act 2000, s 3, Sch 3, paras 1, 6(b)
	Sub-s (3A): Ins Insolvency Act 2000, s 3, Sch 3, paras 1, 6(b)
s 256A	Ins Insolvency Act 2000, s 3, Sch 3, para 1
s 257	*Sub-s (1)*: Am Insolvency Act 2000, s 3, Sch 3, paras 1, 8
s 258	*Sub-s (3)*: Am Insolvency Act 2000, s 3, Sch 3, paras 1, 9
s 260	*Sub-s (2)(b)*: Sub Insolvency Act 2000, s 3, Sch 3, paras 1, 10
	Sub-s (2A): Ins Insolvency Act 2000, s 3, Sch 3, paras 1, 10
s 262	*Sub-s (2)(b), (c)*: Am Insolvency Act 2000, s 3, Sch 3, paras 1, 11(1)
	Sub-s (3)(a), (b): Am Insolvency Act 2000, s 3, Sch 3, paras 1, 11(2)
s 262A	Ins Insolvency Act 2000, s 3, Sch 3, paras 1, 12
s 262B	Ins Insolvency Act 2000, s 3, Sch 3, paras 1, 12
s 262C	Ins Insolvency Act 2000, s 3, Sch 3, paras 1, 12
s 263	*Sub-s (2)*: Am Insolvency Act 2000, s 3, Sch 3, paras 1, 13(a)
	Sub-s (5): Prosp am Insolvency Act 2000, s 3, Sch 3, paras 1, 13(b)
ss 263A–263G	Prosp ins Enterprise Act 2002, s 264(1), Sch 22, para 2
s 264	*Sub-s (1)*: Prosp am Criminal Justice Act 1988, s 170(2), Sch 16; Am Insolvency Act 1986 (Amendment) (No 2) Regulations 2002, SI 2002/1240, regs 3, 13
s 265	Sub-s (3): Ins Insolvency Act 1986 (Amendment) (No 2) Regulations 2002, SI 2002/1240, regs 3, 14
s 266	*Sub-s (4)*: Prosp rep Criminal Justice Act 1988, s 170(2), Sch 16
s 267	*Sub-s (3)*: Prosp rep Criminal Justice Act 1988, s 170(2), Sch 16
s 279	Prosp sub Enterprise Act 2002, s 256(1)
s 281	*Sub-s (4A)*: Ins Proceeds of Crime Act 2002, s 456, Sch 11, paras 1, 16(1), (2)
	Sub-s (5): Am Consumer Protection Act 1987, s 48, Sch 4, para 12; Am Children Act 1989, ss 92(11), 108(7), Sch 11, Pt II, para 11(1), Sch 15; Am Child Support Act 1991, s 58(13), Sch 5, para 7; Prosp am Child Support, Pensions and Social Security Act 2000, s 26, Sch 3, para 6
	Sub-s (8): Am Children Act 1989, ss 92(11), 108(7), Sch 11, Pt II, para 11(1), Sch 15
s 281A	Prosp ins Enterprise Act 2002, s 257(1)
s 282	*Sub-s (2)*: Prosp rep Criminal Justice Act 1988, s 170(2), Sch 16
s 283	*Sub-s (3A)*: Ins Housing Act 1988, s 117(1)
s 283A	Prosp ins Enterprise Act 2002, s 261(1)
s 289	Prosp sub Enterprise Act 2002, s 258
ss 306A–306C	Ins Proceeds of Crime Act 2002, s 456, Sch 11, paras 1, 16(1), (3)
s 308	*Sub-s (1)*: Am Housing Act 1988, s 140(1), Sch 17
s 308A	Ins Housing Act 1988, s 117(2)
s 309	*Sub-s (1)(b)*: Am Housing Act 1988, s 117(3)
s 310	*Sub-s (2)*: Am Pensions Act 1995, s 122, Sch 3, para 15
	Sub-s (7): Am Pensions Act 1995, s 122, Sch 3, para 15; Am Welfare Reform and Pensions Act 1999, s 18, Sch 2, para 2
	Sub-ss (8), (9): Ins Pensions Act 1995, s 122, Sch 3, para 15
s 310A	Prosp ins Enterprise Act 2002, s 260
s 313A	Prosp ins Enterprise Act 2002, s 261(3)
s 335A	Ins Trusts of Land and Appointment of Trustees Act 1996, s 25(1), Sch 3, para 23
s 336	*Sub-ss (1), (2), (4)*: Am FLA 1996, s 66(1), Sch 8, Pt III, para 57
	Sub-s (3): Rep Trusts of Land and Appointment of Trustees Act 1996, s 25(2), Sch 4
	Sub-s (4): Am Trusts of Land and Appointment of Trustees Act 1996, s 25(2), Sch 4

Insolvency Act 1986 *cont*

s 337	*Sub-ss (2), (4), (5)*: Am FLA 1996, s 66(1), Sch 8, Pt III, para 57
	Sub-s (3): Sub FLA 1996, s 66(1), Sch 8, Pt III, para 57
s 341	*Sub-ss (4)–(5)*: Prosp rep Criminal Justice Act 1988, s 170(2), Sch 16
s 342	Am Insolvency (No 2) Act 1994, s 2
s 342A	Ins (for purposes only of making regs) Pensions Act 1995, s 95(1); Sub (for purposes only of making subordinate legislation) Welfare Reform and Pensions Act 1999, s 15
s 342B	Ins (for purposes only of making regs) Pensions Act 1995, s 95(1); Sub (for purposes only of making subordinate legislation) Welfare Reform and Pensions Act 1999, s 15
s 342C	Ins (for purposes only of making regs) Pensions Act 1995, s 95(1); Sub (for purposes only of making subordinate legislation) Welfare Reform and Pensions Act 1999, s 15
s 342D	Prosp ins Welfare Reform and Pensions Act 1999, s 84(1), Sch 12, paras 70, 71
s 342E	Prosp ins Welfare Reform and Pensions Act 1999, s 84(1), Sch 12, paras 70, 71
s 342F	Prosp ins Welfare Reform and Pensions Act 1999, s 84(1), Sch 12, paras 70, 71
s 360	*Sub-ss (5), (6)*: Prosp ins Enterprise Act 2002, s 257(3), Sch 21, para 3
s 389A	Ins Insolvency Act 2000, s 4(1), (4)
s 389B	Prosp ins Enterprise Act 2002, s 264(1), Sch 22, para 3
s 390	*Sub-s (4)*: Am Insolvency Act 2000, s 8, Sch 4, Pt II, para 16(1), (2); Am Adults with Incapacity (Scotland) Act 2000, s 88(2), Sch 5, para 18
	Sub-s (5): Prop ins Enterprise Act 2002, s 257(3), Sch 21, para 4
s 436	Am Insolvency Act 1986 (Amendment) Regulations 2002, SI 2002/1037, regs 2, 4
s 436A	Ins Insolvency Act 1986 (Amendment) (No 2) Regulations 2002, SI 2002/1240, regs 3, 18
Sch A1	Ins Insolvency Act 2000, s 1, Sch 1, paras 1, 4
Sch B1	Prosp ins Enterprise Act 2002, s 248, Sch 16
Sch 4	Prosp am Enterprise Act 2002, s 253
Sch 4A	Prosp ins Enterprise Act 2002, s 257, Sch 20
Sch 6	*Paras 1–2*: Am ICTA 1988, s 844, Sch 29
	Para 3: Am VAT Act 1994, s 100, Sch 14
	Para 3A: Ins FA 1994, s 65, Sch 7, para 7
	Para 3B: Ins FA 1996, s 60, Sch 5, Pt III, para 12(1)
	Para 3C: Ins FA 2000, s 30(2), Sch 7, para 3(1)(b), (2)
	Para 3D: Ins FA 2001, s 27, Sch 5, para 17(1)(b), (2)
	Para 5: Am FA 1997, ss 13(2), 113, Sch 2, Pt II, para 6, Sch 18, Pt II
	Para 5A: Ins FA 1991, s 7(4), (5), Sch 2, para 22
	Para 5B: Ins FA 1993, a 36(2)
	Para 5C: Ins FA 1994, s 40, Sch 6, para 13(1)
	Para 6: Am Social Security (Consequential Provisions) Act 1992, s 4, Sch 2, para 73
	Para 8: Am Pension Schemes Act 1993, s 190, Sch 8, para 18
	Para 13: Am Trade Union and Labour Relations (Consolidation) Act 1992, s 300(2), Sch 2, para 33; Am Trade Union Reform and Employment Rights Act 1993, s 49, Sch 8; Am Employment Rights Act 1996, s 240, Sch 1, para 29
	Para 15A: Ins Insolvency (ECSC Levy Debts) Regulations 1987, SI 1987/2093, reg 2(1), (3)

COMMERCIAL

Misrepresentation Act 1967

s 3   Sub UCTA 1977, s 8(1)

Unfair Contract Terms Act 1977

s 1   *Sub-s (3)*: Am Occupiers Liability Act 1984, s 2
s 6   *Sub-ss (1)–(2)*: Am Sale of Goods Act 1979, s 63, Sch 2, para 19
s 7   *Sub-s (3A)*: Ins Supply of Goods and Services Act 1982, s 17(2), (3)
                             Sub-s (4): Ins Supply of Goods and Services Act 1982, s 17(2), (3)
                             Prosp am Enterprise Act 2002, s 251
s 12   *Sub-s (1A)*: Ins Sale and Supply of Goods to Consumers Regulations 2002,
                             SI 2002/3045, reg 14(1), (2)
                             Sub-s (2): Sub Sale and Supply of Goods to Consumers Regulations 2002,
                             SI 2002/3045, reg 14(1), (3)
s 14   Am Sale of Goods Act 1979, s 63, Sch 2, para 20
s 27   *Sub-s (1)*: Am Contracts (Applicable Law) Act 1990, s 5, Sch 4, para 4
Sch 1   *Para 1:* Am Copyright, Designs and Patents Act 1988, s 303(1), Sch 7, para 24

Sale of Goods Act 1979

s 11   Am Sale and Supply of Goods Act 1994
s 12   Am Sale and Supply of Goods Act 1994
s 13   Am Sale and Supply of Goods Act 1994
s 14   Am Sale and Supply of Goods Act 1994
                             Sub-ss (2D)–(2F): Ins Sale and Supply of Goods to Consumers Regulations 2002,
                             SI 2002/3045, reg 3(1), (2)
s 15   Am Sale and Supply of Goods Act 1994
s 15A   Ins Sale and Supply of Goods Act 1994
s 16   Am Sale of Goods (Amendment) Act 1995, s 1(1)
s 18   Am Sale of Goods (Amendment) Act 1995, s 1(2)
s 20   Am Sale and Supply of Goods to Consumers Regulations 2002, SI 2002/3045,
                             reg 4(1), (2)
ss 20A, 20B   Ins Sale of Goods (Amendment) Act 1995, s 1(3)
s 30   Am Sale and Supply of Goods Act 1994
s 32   *Sub-s (4)*: Ins Sale and Supply of Goods to Consumers Regulations 2002,
                             SI 2002/3045, reg 4(3)
s 34   Am Sale and Supply of Goods Act 1994
s 35   Am Sale and Supply of Goods Act 1994
s 35A   Ins Sale and Supply of Goods Act 1994
ss 48A–48F   Ins Sale and Supply of Goods to Consumers Regulations 2002, SI 2002/3045,
                             reg 5
s 53   Am Sale and Supply of Goods Act 1994
s 55   Am Sale and Supply of Goods Act 1994
s 61   Am Insolvency Act 1985, s 235(3), Sch 10, Pt III; Am Bankruptcy (Scotland) Act
                             1985, s 75(2), Sch 8; Am Sale and Supply of Goods Act 1994; Am Sale of Goods
                             (Amendment) Act 1995, s 2; Am Sale and Supply of Goods to Consumers
                             Regulations 2002, SI 2002/3045, reg 6

Commercial Agents (Council Directive) Regulations 1993, SI 1993/3053

reg 1	Am SI 1998/2868, reg 2(a)
reg 2	Am SI 1998/2868, reg 2(b)
reg 17	Am SI 1998/2868, reg 2(c)
reg 18	Am SI 1993/3173, reg 2

EU

Treaty of Rome 1957 (EC Treaty)

Table of Derivatives (Articles of the EC Treaty as re-numbered by the Treaty of Amsterdam)

Treaty of Amsterdam	Treaty of Rome
Article 1	Article 1
Article 2	Article 2
Article 3	Article 3
Article 4	Article 3a
Article 5	Article 3b
Article 6	Article 3c
Article 7	Article 4
Article 8	Article 4a
Article 9	Article 4b
Article 10	Article 5
Article 11	Article 5a
Article 12	Article 6
Article 13	Article 6a
Article 14	Article 7a
Article 15	Article 7c
Article 16	Article 7d
Article 17	Article 8
Article 18	Article 8a
Article 19	Article 8b
Article 20	Article 8c
Article 21	Article 8d
Article 22	Article 8c
Article 23	Article 9
Article 24	Article 10
Article 25	Article 12
Article 26	Article 28
Article 27	Article 29
Article 28	Article 30
Article 29	Article 34
Article 30	Article 36
Article 31	Article 37
Article 32	Article 38
Article 33	Article 39
Article 34	Article 40
Article 35	Article 41
Article 36	Article 42
Article 37	Article 43

Treaty of Amsterdam *cont*	**Treaty of Rome** *cont*
Article 38	Article 46
Article 39	Article 48
Article 40	Article 49
Article 41	Article 50
Article 42	Article 51
Article 43	Article 52
Article 44	Article 54
Article 45	Article 55
Article 46	Article 56
Article 47	Article 57
Article 48	Article 58
Article 49	Article 59
Article 50	Article 60
Article 51	Article 61
Article 52	Article 63
Article 53	Article 64
Article 54	Article 65
Article 55	Article 66
Article 56	Article 73b
Article 57	Article 73c
Article 58	Article 73d
Article 59	Article 73f
Article 60	Article 73g
Article 61	Article 63i
Article 62	Article 73j
Article 63	Article 73k
Article 64	Article 6731
Article 65	Article 73m
Article 66	Article 73n
Article 67	Article 73o
Article 68	Article 73p
Article 69	Article 73q
Article 70	Article 74
Article 71	Article 75
Article 72	Article 76
Article 73	Article 77
Article 74	Article 78
Article 75	Article 79
Article 76	Article 80
Article 77	Article 81
Article 78	Article 82
Article 79	Article 83
Article 80	Article 84
Article 81	Article 85
Article 82	Article 86
Article 83	Article 87
Article 84	Article 88
Article 85	Article 89
Article 86	Article 90
Article 87	Article 92

Treaty of Amsterdam *cont*	**Treaty of Rome** *cont*
Article 88	Article 93
Article 89	Article 94
Article 90	Article 95
Article 91	Article 96
Article 92	Article 98
Article 93	Article 99
Article 94	Article 100
Article 95	Article 100a
Article 96	Article 101
Article 97	Article 102
Article 98	Article 102a
Article 99	Article 103
Article 100	Article 103a
Article 101	Article 104
Article 102	Article 1044
Article 103	Article 104b
Article 104	Article 104c
Article 105	Article 105
Article 106	Article 105a
Article 107	Article 106
Article 108	Article 107
Article 109	Article 108
Article 110	Article 108a
Article 111	Article 109
Article 112	Article 109a
Article 113	Article 109b
Article 114	Article 109c
Article 115	Article 109d
Article 116	Article 109e
Article 117	Article 109f
Article 118	Article 109g
Article 119	Article 109h
Article 120	Article 109i
Article 121	Article 109j
Article 122	Article 109k
Article 123	Article 109l
Article 124	Article 109m
Article 125	Article 109n
Article 126	Article 109o
Article 127	Article 109p
Article 128	Article 109q
Article 129	Article 109r
Article 130	Article 109s
Article 131	Article 110
Article 132	Article 112
Article 133	Article 113
Article 134	Article 115
Article 135	Article 116
Article 136	Article 117
Article 137	Article 118

Treaty of Amsterdam *cont*	**Treaty of Rome** *cont*
Article 138	Article 118a
Article 139	Article 118b
Article 140	Article 118c
Article 141	Article 119
Article 142	Article 119a
Article 143	Article 120
Article 144	Article 121
Article 145	Article 122
Article 146	Article 123
Article 147	Article 124
Article 148	Article 125
Article 149	Article 126
Article 150	Article 127
Article 151	Article 128
Article 152	Article 129
Article 153	Article 129a
Article 154	Article 129b
Article 155	Article 129c
Article 156	Article 129c
Article 157	Article 130
Article 158	Article 130a
Article 159	Article 130b
Article 160	Article 130c
Article 161	Article 130d
Article 162	Article 130c
Article 163	Article 130f
Article 164	Article 130g
Article 165	Article 130h
Article 166	Article 130i
Article 167	Article 130j
Article 168	Article 130k
Article 169	Article 130l
Article 170	Article 130m
Article 171	Article 120n
Article 172	Article 130o
Article 173	Article 130p
Article 174	Article 130r
Article 175	Article 130s
Article 176	Article 130t
Article 177	Article 130u
Article 178	Article 130v
Article 179	Article 130w
Article 180	Article 130x
Article 181	Article 130y
Article 182	Article 131
Article 183	Article 132
Article 184	Article 133
Article 185	Article 134
Article 186	Article 135
Article 187	Article 136

Treaty of Amsterdam *cont*	**Treaty of Rome** *cont*
Article 188	Article 136a
Article 189	Article 137
Article 190	Article 138
Article 191	Article 138a
Article 192	Article 138b
Article 193	Article 138c
Article 194	Article 138d
Article 195	Article 138e
Article 196	Article 139
Article 197	Article 140
Article 198	Article 141
Article 199	Article 142
Article 200	Article 143
Article 201	Article 144
Article 202	Article 145
Article 203	Article 146
Article 204	Article 147
Article 205	Article 148
Article 206	Article 150
Article 207	Article 151
Article 208	Article 152
Article 209	Article 153
Article 210	Article 154
Article 211	Article 155
Article 212	Article 156
Article 213	Article 157
Article 214	Article 158
Article 215	Article 159
Article 216	Article 160
Article 217	Article 161
Article 218	Article 162
Article 219	Article 163
Article 220	Article 164
Article 221	Article 165
Article 222	Article 166
Article 223	Article 167
Article 224	Article 168
Article 225	Article 168a
Article 226	Article 169
Article 227	Article 170
Article 228	Article 222
Article 230	Article 173
Article 231	Article 174
Article 232	Article 175
Article 233	Article 176
Article 234	Article 177
Article 235	Article 178
Article 236	Article 179
Article 237	Article 180
Article 238	Article 181

Treaty of Amsterdam *cont*	**Treaty of Rome** *cont*
Article 239	Article 182
Article 240	Article 183
Article 241	Article 184
Article 242	Article 185
Article 243	Article 186
Article 244	Article 187
Article 245	Article 188
Article 246	Article 188a
Article 247	Article 188b
Article 248	Article 188c
Article 249	Article 189
Article 250	Article 189a
Article 251	Article 189b
Article 252	Article 189c
Article 253	Article 190
Article 254	Article 191
Article 255	Article 191a
Article 256	Article 192
Article 257	Article 193
Article 258	Article 194
Article 259	Article 195
Article 260	Article 196
Article 261	Article 197
Article 262	Article 198
Article 263	Article 198a
Article 264	Article 198b
Article 265	Article 198c
Article 266	Article 198d
Article 267	Article 198e
Article 268	Article 199
Article 269	Article 201
Article 270	Article 201a
Article 271	Article 202
Article 272	Article 203
Article 273	Article 204
Article 274	Article 205
Article 275	Article 205a
Article 276	Article 206
Article 277	Article 207
Article 278	Article 208
Article 279	Article 209
Article 280	Article 209a
Article 281	Article 210
Article 282	Article 211
Article 283	Article 212
Article 284	Article 213
Article 285	Article 213a
Article 286	Article 213b
Article 287	Article 214
Article 288	Article 215

Treaty of Amsterdam *cont*	**Treaty of Rome** *cont*
Article 289	Article 216
Article 290	Article 217
Article 291	Article 218
Article 292	Article 219
Article 293	Article 220
Article 294	Article 221
Article 295	Article 222
Article 296	Article 223
Article 297	Article 224
Article 298	Article 225
Article 299	Article 227
Article 300	Article 228
Article 301	Article 228a
Article 302	Article 229
Article 303	Article 230
Article 304	Article 231
Article 305	Article 232
Article 306	Article 233
Article 307	Article 234
Article 308	Article 235
Article 309	Article 236
Article 310	Article 238
Article 311	Article 239
Article 312	Article 240
Article 313	Article 247
Article 314	Article 248

PART I

PARTNERSHIP

Partnership Act 1890

1. Definition of partnership

(1) Partnership is the relation which subsists between persons carrying on a business in common with a view of profit.

(2) But the relation between members of any company or association which is—

(a) Registered as a Company under the Companies Act 1862 or any other Act of Parliament for the time being in force and relating to the registration of joint stock companies; or

(b) Formed or incorporated by or in pursuance of any other Act of Parliament or letters patent, or Royal Charter;

is not a partnership within the meaning of this Act.

2. Rules for determining existence of partnership

In determining whether a partnership does or does not exist, regard shall be had to the following rules:

(1) Joint tenancy, tenancy in common, joint property, common property, or part ownership does not of itself create a partnership as to anything so held or owned, whether the tenants or owners do or do not share any profits made by the use thereof.

(2) The sharing of gross returns does not of itself create a partnership, whether the persons sharing such returns have or have not a joint or common right or interest in any property from which or from the use of which the returns are derived.

(3) The receipt by a person of a share of the profits of a business is prima facie evidence that he is a partner in the business, but the receipt of such a share, or of a payment contingent on or varying with the profits of a business, does not of itself make him a partner in the business; and in particular—

(a) The receipt by a person of a debt or other liquidated amount by instalments or otherwise out of the accruing profits of a business does not of itself make him a partner in the business or liable as such:

(b) A contract for the remuneration of a servant or agent of a person engaged in a business by a share of the profits of the business does not of itself make the servant or agent a partner in the business or liable as such:

(c) A person being the widow or child of a deceased partner, and receiving by way of annuity a portion of the profits made in the business in which the deceased person was a partner, is not by reason only of such receipt a partner in the business or liable as such:

(d) The advance of money by way of loan to a person engaged or about to engage in any business on a contract with that person that the lender shall receive a rate of interest varying with the profits, or shall receive a share of the profits arising from carrying on the business, does not of itself make the lender a partner with the person or persons carrying on the business or liable as such. Provided that the contract is in writing, and signed by or on behalf of all the parties thereto:

(e) A person receiving by way of annuity or otherwise a portion of the profits of a business in consideration of the sale by him of the goodwill of the business is not by reason only of such receipt a partner in the business or liable as such.

5. Power of partner to bind the firm

Every partner is an agent of the firm and his other partners for the purpose of the business of the partnership; and the acts of every partner who does any act for carrying on in the usual way business of the kind carried on by the firm of which he is a member bind the firm and his partners, unless the partner so acting has in fact no authority to act for the firm in the particular matter, and the person with whom he is dealing either knows that he has no authority, or does not know or believe him to be a partner.

6. Partners bound by acts on behalf of firm

An act or instrument relating to the business of the firm and done or executed in the firm-name, or in any other manner showing an intention to bind the firm, by any person thereto authorised whether a partner or not, is binding on the firm and all the partners.

Provided that this section shall not affect any general rule of law relating to the execution of deeds or negotiable instruments.

7. Partner using credit of firm for private purposes

Where one partner pledges the credit of the firm for a purpose apparently not connected with the firm's ordinary course of business, the firm is not bound, unless he is in fact specially authorised by the other partners: but this section does not affect any personal liability incurred by an individual partner.

8. Effect of notice that firm will not be bound by acts of partner

If it has been agreed between the partners that any restriction shall be placed on the power of any one or more of them to bind the firm, no act done in contravention of the agreement is binding on the firm with respect to persons having notice of the agreement.

9. Liability of partners

Every partner in a firm is liable jointly with the other partners, and in Scotland severally also, for all debts and obligations of the firm incurred while he is a partner; and after his death his estate is also severally liable in a due course of administration for such debts and obligations, so far as they remain unsatisfied, but subject in England or Ireland to the prior payment of his separate debts.

10. Liability of the firm for wrongs

Where, by any wrongful act or omission of any partner acting in the ordinary course of the business of the firm, or with the authority of his co-partners, loss or injury is caused to any person not being a partner in the firm, or any penalty is incurred, the firm is liable therefor to the same extent as the partner so acting or omitting to act.

14. Persons liable by 'holding out'

(1)   Every one who by words spoken or written or by conduct represents himself, or who knowingly suffers himself to be represented, as a partner in a particular firm, is liable as a partner to any one who has on the faith of any such representation given credit to the firm, whether the representation has or has not been made or communicated to the person so giving credit by or with the knowledge of the apparent partner making the representation or suffering it to be made.

(2)   Provided that where after a partner's death the partnership business is continued in the old firm-name, the continued use of that name, or of the deceased partner's name as part thereof shall not of itself make his executors or administrators estate or effects liable for any partnership debts contracted after his death.

17. Liabilities of incoming and outgoing partners

(1)   A person who is admitted as a partner into an existing firm does not thereby become liable to the creditors of the firm for anything done before he became a partner.

(2)   A partner who retires from a firm does not thereby cease to be liable for partnership debts or obligations incurred before his retirement.

(3)   A retiring partner may be discharged from any existing liabilities, by an agreement to that effect between himself and the members of the firm as newly constituted and the creditors, and this agreement may be either express or inferred as a fact from the course of dealing between the creditors and the firm as newly constituted.

19. Variation by consent of terms of partnership

The mutual rights and duties of partners, whether ascertained by agreement or defined by this Act, may be varied by the consent of all the partners, and such consent may be either express or inferred from a course of dealing.

23. Procedure against partnership property for a partner's separate judgment debt

(1)   A writ of execution shall not issue against any partnership property except on a judgment against the firm.

(2)   The High Court, or a judge thereof, or a county court may, on the application by summons of any judgment creditor of a partner, make an order charging that partner's interest in the partnership property and profits with payment of the amount of the judgment debt and interest thereon, and may by the same or a subsequent order appoint a receiver of that partner's share of profits (whether already declared or accruing), and of any other money which may be coming to him in respect of the partnership, and direct all accounts and inquiries, and give all other

orders and directions which might have been directed or given if the charge had been made in favour of the judgment creditor by the partner, or which the circumstances of the case may require.

(3)   The other partner or partners shall be at liberty at any time to redeem the interest charged, or, in case of a sale being directed, to purchase the same.

(5)   [Applies to Scotland only.]

24.   Rules as to interests and duties of partners subject to special agreement

The interests of partners in the partnership property and their rights and duties in relation to the partnership shall be determined, subject to any agreement express or implied between the partners, by the following rules:

(1)   All the partners are entitled to share equally in the capital and profits of the business, and must contribute equally towards the losses whether of capital or otherwise sustained by the firm.

(2)   The firm must indemnify every partner in respect of payments made and personal liabilities incurred by him—

      (a)   In the ordinary and proper conduct of the business of the firm; or
      (b)   In or about anything necessarily done for the preservation of the business or property of the firm.

(3)   A partner making, for the purpose of the partnership, any actual payment or advance beyond the amount of capital which he has agreed to subscribe, is entitled to interest at the rate of five per cent per annum from the date of the payment or advance.

(4)   A partner is not entitled, before the ascertainment of profits, to interest on the capital subscribed by him.

(5)   Every partner may take part in the management of the partnership business.

(6)   No partner shall be entitled to remuneration for acting in the partnership business.

(7)   No person may be introduced as a partner without the consent of all existing partners.

(8)   Any difference arising as to ordinary matters connected with the partnership business may be decided by a majority of the partners, but no change may be made in the nature of the partnership business without the consent of all existing partners.

(9)   The partnership books are to be kept at the place of business of the partnership (or the principal place, if there is more than one), and every partner may, when he thinks fit, have access to and inspect and copy any of them.

25.   Expulsion of partner

No majority of the partners can expel any partner unless a power to do so has been conferred by express agreement between the partners.

26.   Retirement from partnership at will

(1)   Where no fixed term has been agreed upon for the duration of the partnership, any partner may determine the partnership at any time on giving notice of his intention so to do to all the other partners.

(2)   Where the partnership has originally been constituted by deed, a notice in writing, signed by the partner giving it, shall be sufficient for this purpose.

27.   Where partnership for term is continued over, continuance on old terms presumed

(1)   Where a partnership entered into for a fixed term is continued after the term has expired, and without any express new agreement, the rights and duties of the partners remain the same as they were at the expiration of the term, so far as is consistent with the incidents of a partnership at will.

(2)   A continuance of the business by the partners or such of them as habitually acted therein during the term, without any settlement or liquidation of the partnership affairs, is presumed to be a continuance of the partnership.

28.   Duty of partners to render accounts, etc

Partners are bound to render true accounts and full information of all things affecting the partnership to any partner or his legal representatives.

29.   Accountability of partners for private profits

(1)   Every partner must account to the firm for any benefit derived by him without the consent of the other partners from any transaction concerning the partnership, or from any use by him of the partnership property, name or business connection.

(2)   This section applies also to transactions undertaken after a partnership has been dissolved by the death of a partner, and before the affairs thereof have been completely wound up, either by any surviving partner or by the representatives of the deceased partner.

30.   Duty of partner not to compete with firm

If a partner, without the consent of the other partners, carries on any business of the same nature as and competing with that of the firm, he must account for and pay over to the firm all profits made by him in that business.

32.   Dissolution by expiration or notice

Subject to any agreement between the partners, a partnership is dissolved—

(a)   If entered into for a fixed term, by the expiration of that term:

(b)   If entered into for a single adventure or undertaking, by the termination of that adventure or undertaking:

(c)   If entered into for an undefined time, by any partner giving notice to the other or others of his intention to dissolve the partnership.

In the last-mentioned case the partnership is dissolved as from the date mentioned in the notice as the date of dissolution, or, if no date is so mentioned, as from the date of the communication of the notice.

33.   Dissolution by bankruptcy, death or charge

(1)   Subject to any agreement between the partners, every partnership is dissolved as regards all the partners by the death or bankruptcy of any partner.

(2)   A partnership may, at the option of the other partners, be dissolved if any partner suffers his share of the partnership property to be charged under this Act for his separate debt.

34.   Dissolution by illegality of partnership

A partnership is in every case dissolved by the happening of any event which makes it unlawful for the business of the firm to be carried on or for the members of the firm to carry it on in partnership.

35.   Dissolution by the Court

On application by a partner the Court may decree a dissolution of the partnership in any of the following cases:

(b)   When a partner, other than the partner suing, becomes in any other way permanently incapable of performing his part of the partnership contract:

(c)   When a partner, other than the partner suing, has been guilty of such conduct as, in the opinion of the Court, regard being had to the nature of the business, is calculated to prejudicially affect the carrying on of the business:

(d)   When a partner, other than the partner suing, wilfully or persistently commits a breach of the partnership agreement, or otherwise so conducts himself in matters relating to the partnership business that it is not reasonably practicable for the other partner or partners to carry on the business in partnership with him:

(e)   When the business of the partnership can only be carried on at a loss:

(f)   Whenever in any case circumstances have arisen, which, in the opinion of the Court, render it just and equitable that the partnership be dissolved.

36.   Rights of persons dealing with firm against apparent members of firm

(1)   Where a person deals with a firm after a change in its constitution he is entitled to treat all apparent members of the old firm as still being members of the firm until he has notice of the change.

(2)   An advertisement in the *London Gazette* as to a firm whose principal place of business is in England or Wales, in the *Edinburgh Gazette* as to a firm whose principal place of business is in Scotland, and in the *Dublin Gazette* as

to a firm whose principal place of business is in Ireland, shall be notice as to persons who had not dealings with the firm before the date of the dissolution or change so advertised.

(3)   The estate of a partner who dies, or who becomes bankrupt, or of a partner who, not having been known to the person dealing with the firm to be a partner, retires from the firm, is not liable for partnership debts contracted after the date of the death, bankruptcy, or retirement respectively.

38.   Continuing authority of partners for purposes of winding up

After the dissolution of a partnership the authority of each partner to bind the firm, and the other rights and obligations of the partners, continue notwithstanding the dissolution so far as may be necessary to wind up the affairs of the partnership, and to complete transactions begun but unfinished at the time of the dissolution, but not otherwise.

Provided that the firm is in no case bound by the acts of a partner who has become bankrupt; but this proviso does not affect the liability of any person who has after the bankruptcy represented himself or knowingly suffered himself to be represented as a partner of the bankrupt.

39.   Rights of partners as to application of partnership property

On the dissolution of a partnership every partner is entitled, as against the other partners in the firm, and all persons claiming through them in respect of their interests as partners, to have the property of the partnership applied in payment of the debts and liabilities of the firm, and to have the surplus assets after such payment applied in payment of what may be due to the partners respectively after deducting what may be due from them as partners to the firm; and for that purpose any partner or his representatives may on the termination of the partnership apply to the court to wind up the business and affairs of the firm.

42.   Rights of outgoing partner in certain cases to share profits made after dissolution

(1)   Where any member of a firm has died or otherwise ceased to be a partner, and the surviving or continuing partners carry on the business of the firm with its capital or assets without any final settlement of accounts as between the firm and the outgoing partner or his estate, then, in the absence of any agreement to the contrary, the outgoing partner or his estate is entitled at the option of himself or his representatives to such share of the profits made since the dissolution as the court may find to be attributable to the use of his share of the partnership assets, or to interest at the rate of five per cent per annum on the amount of his share of the partnership assets.

(2)   Provided that where by the partnership contract an option is given to surviving or continuing partners to purchase the interest of a deceased or outgoing partner, and that option is duly exercised, the estate of the deceased partner, or the outgoing partner or his estate, as the case may be, is not entitled to any further or other share of profits; but if any partner assuming to act in exercise of the option does not in all material respects comply with the terms thereof, he is liable to account under the foregoing provisions of this section.

44.   Rule for distribution of assets on final settlement of accounts

In settling accounts between the partners after a dissolution of partnership, the following rules shall, subject to any agreement, be observed—

(a)   Losses, including losses and deficiencies of capital, shall be paid first out of profits, next out of capital, and lastly, if necessary, by the partners individually in the proportion in which they were entitled to share profits.

(b)   The assets of the firm, including the sums, if any, contributed by the partners to make up losses or deficiencies of capital, shall be applied in the following manner and order:

1.   In paying the debts and liabilities of the firm to persons who are not partners therein:
2.   In paying to each partner rateably what is due from the firm to him for advances as distinguished from capital:
3.   In paying to each partner rateably what is due from the firm to him in respect of capital:
4.   The ultimate residue, if any shall be divided among the partners in the proportion in which profits are divisible.

45. Definitions of 'court' and 'business'

In this Act, unless the contrary intention appears,—

The expression 'court' includes every court and judge having jurisdiction in the case:

The expression 'business' includes every trade, occupation, or profession.

Limited Liability Partnerships Act 2000

1.　Limited liability partnerships

(1)　There shall be a new form of legal entity to be known as a limited liability partnership.

(2)　A limited liability partnership is a body corporate (with legal personality separate from that of its members) which is formed by being incorporated under this Act; and—

(a)　in the following provisions of this Act (except in the phrase 'oversea limited liability partnership'), and

(b)　in any other enactment (except where provision is made to the contrary or the context otherwise requires),

references to a limited liability partnership are to such a body corporate.

(3)　A limited liability partnership has unlimited capacity.

(4)　The members of a limited liability partnership have such liability to contribute to its assets in the event of its being wound up as is provided for by virtue of this Act.

(5)　Accordingly, except as far as otherwise provided by this Act or any other enactment, the law relating to partnerships does not apply to a limited liability partnership.

(6)　The Schedule (which makes provision about the names and registered offices of limited liability partnerships) has effect.

Incorporation

2.　Incorporation document etc

(1)　For a limited liability partnership to be incorporated—

(a)　two or more persons associated for carrying on a lawful business with a view to profit must have subscribed their names to an incorporation document,

(b)　there must have been delivered to the registrar either the incorporation document or a copy authenticated in a manner approved by him, and

(c)　there must have been so delivered a statement in a form approved by the registrar, made by either a solicitor engaged in the formation of the limited liability partnership or anyone who subscribed his name to the incorporation document, that the requirement imposed by paragraph (a) has been complied with.

(2)　The incorporation document must—

(a)　be in a form approved by the registrar (or as near to such a form as circumstances allow),

(b)　state the name of the limited liability partnership,

(c)　state whether the registered office of the limited liability partnership is to be situated in England and Wales, in Wales or in Scotland,

(d)　state the address of that registered office,

(e)　state the name and address of each of the persons who are to be members of the limited liability partnership on incorporation, and

(f)　either specify which of those persons are to be designated members or state that every person who from time to time is a member of the limited liability partnership is a designated member.

(2A)　Where a confidentiality order, made under section 723B of the Companies Act 1985 as applied to a limited liability partnership, is in force in respect of any individual named as a member of a limited liability partnership under subsection (2) that subsection shall have effect as if the reference to the address of the individual were a reference to the address for the time being notified by him under the Limited Liability Partnerships (Particulars of Usual Residential Address) (Confidentiality Orders) Regulations 2002 to any limited liability partnership of which he is a member or if he is not such a member either the address specified in his application for a confidentiality order or the address last notified by him under such a confidentiality order as the case may be.

(2B)　Where the incorporation document or a copy of such delivered under this section includes an address specified in reliance on subsection (2A) there shall be delivered with it or the copy of it a statement in a form approved by the registrar containing particulars of the usual residential address of the member whose address is so specified.

(3)　If a person makes a false statement under subsection (1)(c) which he—

(a)   knows to be false, or

(b)   does not believe to be true,

he commits an offence.

(4)   A person guilty of an offence under subsection (3) is liable—

(a)   on summary conviction, to imprisonment for a period not exceeding six months or a fine not exceeding the statutory maximum, or to both, or

(b)   on conviction on indictment, to imprisonment for a period not exceeding two years or a fine, or to both.

3.   Incorporation by registration

(1)   When the requirements imposed by paragraphs (b) and (c) of subsection (1) of section 2 have been complied with, the registrar shall retain the incorporation document or copy delivered to him and, unless the requirement imposed by paragraph (a) of that subsection has not been complied with, he shall—

(a)   register the incorporation document or copy, and

(b)   give a certificate that the limited liability partnership is incorporated by the name specified in the incorporation document.

(2)   The registrar may accept the statement delivered under paragraph (c) of subsection (1) of section 2 as sufficient evidence that the requirement imposed by paragraph (a) of that subsection has been complied with.

(3)   The certificate shall either be signed by the registrar or be authenticated by his official seal.

(4)   The certificate is conclusive evidence that the requirements of section 2 are complied with and that the limited liability partnership is incorporated by the name specified in the incorporation document.

Membership

4.   Members

(1)   On the incorporation of a limited liability partnership its members are the persons who subscribed their names to the incorporation document (other than any who have died or been dissolved).

(2)   Any other person may become a member of a limited liability partnership by and in accordance with an agreement with the existing members.

(3)   A person may cease to be a member of a limited liability partnership (as well as by death or dissolution) in accordance with an agreement with the other members or, in the absence of agreement with the other members as to cessation of membership, by giving reasonable notice to the other members.

(4)   A member of a limited liability partnership shall not be regarded for any purpose as employed by the limited liability partnership unless, if he and the other members were partners in a partnership, he would be regarded for that purpose as employed by the partnership.

5.   Relationship of members etc

(1)   Except as far as otherwise provided by this Act or any other enactment, the mutual rights and duties of the members of a limited liability partnership, and the mutual rights and duties of a limited liability partnership and its members, shall be governed—

(a)   by agreement between the members, or between the limited liability partnership and its members, or

(b)   in the absence of agreement as to any matter, by any provision made in relation to that matter by regulations under section 15(c).

(2)   An agreement made before the incorporation of a limited liability partnership between the persons who subscribe their names to the incorporation document may impose obligations on the limited liability partnership (to take effect at any time after its incorporation).

6.   Members as agents

(1)   Every member of a limited liability partnership is the agent of the limited liability partnership.

(2)   But a limited liability partnership is not bound by anything done by a member in dealing with a person if—

(a) the member in fact has no authority to act for the limited liability partnership by doing that thing, and

(b) the person knows that he has no authority or does not know or believe him to be a member of the limited liability partnership.

(3) Where a person has ceased to be a member of a limited liability partnership, the former member is to be regarded (in relation to any person dealing with the limited liability partnership) as still being a member of the limited liability partnership unless—

(a) the person has notice that the former member has ceased to be a member of the limited liability partnership, or

(b) notice that the former member has ceased to be a member of the limited liability partnership has been delivered to the registrar.

(4) Where a member of a limited liability partnership is liable to any person (other than another member of the limited liability partnership) as a result of a wrongful act or omission of his in the course of the business of the limited liability partnership or with its authority, the limited liability partnership is liable to the same extent as the member.

7.   Ex-members

(1) This section applies where a member of a limited liability partnership has either ceased to be a member or—

(a) has died,

(b) has become bankrupt or had his estate sequestrated or has been wound up,

(c) has granted a trust deed for the benefit of his creditors, or

(d) has assigned the whole or any part of his share in the limited liability partnership (absolutely or by way of charge or security).

(2) In such an event the former member or—

(a) his personal representative,

(b) his trustee in bankruptcy or permanent or interim trustee (within the meaning of the Bankruptcy (Scotland) Act 1985) or liquidator,

(c) his trustee under the trust deed for the benefit of his creditors, or

(d) his assignee,

may not interfere in the management or administration of any business or affairs of the limited liability partnership.

(3) But subsection (2) does not affect any right to receive an amount from the limited liability partnership in that event.

8.   Designated members

(1) If the incorporation document specifies who are to be designated members—

(a) they are designated members on incorporation, and

(b) any member may become a designated member by and in accordance with an agreement with the other members,

and a member may cease to be a designated member in accordance with an agreement with the other members.

(2) But if there would otherwise be no designated members, or only one, every member is a designated member.

(3) If the incorporation document states that every person who from time to time is a member of the limited liability partnership is a designated member, every member is a designated member.

(4) A limited liability partnership may at any time deliver to the registrar—

(a) notice that specified members are to be designated members, or

(b) notice that every person who from time to time is a member of the limited liability partnership is a designated member,

and, once it is delivered, subsection (1) (apart from paragraph (a)) and subsection (2), or subsection (3), shall have effect as if that were stated in the incorporation document.

(5) A notice delivered under subsection (4)—

(a) shall be in a form approved by the registrar, and

(b) shall be signed by a designated member of the limited liability partnership or authenticated in a manner approved by the registrar.

(6) A person ceases to be a designated member if he ceases to be a member.

9. Registration of membership changes

(1) A limited liability partnership must ensure that—

(a) where a person becomes or ceases to be a member or designated member, notice is delivered to the registrar within fourteen days, and

(b) where there is any change in the name or address of a member, notice is delivered to the registrar within 28 days.

(2) Where all the members from time to time of a limited liability partnership are designated members, subsection (1)(a) does not require notice that a person has become or ceased to be a designated member as well as a member.

(3) A notice delivered under subsection (1)—

(a) shall be in a form approved by the registrar, and

(b) shall be signed by a designated member of the limited liability partnership or authenticated in a manner approved by the registrar,

and, if it relates to a person becoming a member or designated member, shall contain a statement that he consents to becoming a member or designated member signed by him or authenticated in a manner approved by the registrar.

(3A) Where a confidentiality order under section 723B of the Companies Act 1985 as applied to limited liability partnerships is made in respect of an existing member, the limited liability partnership must ensure that there is delivered within 28 days to the registrar notice in a form approved by the registrar containing the address for the time being notified to it by the member under the Limited Liability Partnerships (Particulars of Usual Residential Address) (Confidentiality Orders) Regulations 2002.

(3B) Where such a confidentiality order is in force in respect of a member the requirement in subsection (1)(b) to notify a change in the address of a member shall be read in relation to that member as a requirement to deliver to the registrar, within 28 days, notice of—

(a) any change in the usual residential address of that member; and

(b) any change in the address for the time being notified to the limited liability partnership by the member under the Limited Liability Partnerships (Particulars of Usual Residential Address) (Confidentiality Orders) Regulations 2002,

and the registrar may approve different forms for the notification of each kind of address.

(4) If a limited liability partnership fails to comply with subsection (1), the partnership and every designated member commits an offence.

(5) But it is a defence for a designated member charged with an offence under subsection (4) to prove that he took all reasonable steps for securing that subsection (1) was complied with.

(6) A person guilty of an offence under subsection (4) is liable on summary conviction to a fine not exceeding level 5 on the standard scale.

Taxation

10. Income tax and chargeable gains

(1) In the Income and Corporation Taxes Act 1988, after section 118 insert—

'Limited liability partnerships

118ZA.   Treatment of limited liability partnerships
For the purposes of the Tax Acts, a trade, profession or business carried on by a limited liability partnership with a view to profit shall be treated as carried on in partnership by its members (and not by the limited liability partnership as such); and, accordingly, the property of the limited liability partnership shall be treated for those purposes as partnership property.

118ZB.   Restriction on relief

Sections 117 and 118 have effect in relation to a member of a limited liability partnership as in relation to a limited partner, but subject to sections 118ZC and 118ZD.

118ZC.   Member's contribution to trade

(1) Subsection (3) of section 117 does not have effect in relation to a member of a limited liability partnership.

(2) But, for the purposes of that section and section 118, such a member's contribution to a trade at any time ("the relevant time") is the greater of—

> (a)   the amount subscribed by him, and
>
> (b)   the amount of his liability on a winding up.

(3) The amount subscribed by a member of a limited liability partnership is the amount which he has contributed to the limited liability partnership as capital, less so much of that amount (if any) as—

> (a)   he has previously, directly or indirectly, drawn out or received back,
>
> (b)   he so draws out or receives back during the period of five years beginning with the relevant time,
>
> (c)   he is or may be entitled so to draw out or receive back at any time when he is a member of the limited liability partnership, or
>
> (d)   he is or may be entitled to require another person to reimburse to him.

(4) The amount of the liability of a member of a limited liability partnership on a winding up is the amount which—

> (a)   he is liable to contribute to the assets of the limited liability partnership in the event of its being wound up, and
>
> (b)   he remains liable so to contribute for the period of at least five years beginning with the relevant time (or until it is wound up, if that happens before the end of that period).

118ZD.   Carry forward of unrelieved losses

(1) Where amounts relating to a trade carried on by a member of a limited liability partnership are, in any one or more chargeable periods, prevented from being given or allowed by section 117 or 118 as it applies otherwise than by virtue of this section (his "total unrelieved loss"), subsection (2) applies in each subsequent chargeable period in which—

> (a)   he carries on the trade as a member of the limited liability partnership, and
>
> (b)   any of his total unrelieved loss remains outstanding.

(2) Sections 380, 381, 393A(1) and 403 (and sections 117 and 118 as they apply in relation to those sections) shall have effect in the subsequent chargeable period as if—

> (a)   any loss sustained or incurred by the member in the trade in that chargeable period were increased by an amount equal to so much of his total unrelieved loss as remains outstanding in that period, or
>
> (b)   (if no loss is so sustained or incurred) a loss of that amount were so sustained or incurred.

(3) To ascertain whether any (and, if so, how much) of a member's total unrelieved loss remains outstanding in the subsequent chargeable period, deduct from the amount of his total unrelieved loss the aggregate of—

> (a)   any relief given under any provision of the Tax Acts (otherwise than as a result of subsection (2)) in respect of his total unrelieved loss in that or any previous chargeable period, and
>
> (b)   any amount given or allowed in respect of his total unrelieved loss as a result of subsection (2) in any previous chargeable period (or which would have been so given or allowed had a claim been made).'

(2)   In section 362(2)(a) of that Act (loan to buy into partnership), after 'partner' insert 'in a limited partnership registered under the Limited Partnerships Act 1907'.

(3)   In the Taxation of Chargeable Gains Act 1992, after section 59 insert—

'59A.   Limited liability partnerships

(1) Where a limited liability partnership carries on a trade or business with a view to profit—

> (a)   assets held by the limited liability partnership shall be treated for the purposes of tax in respect of chargeable gains as held by its members as partners, and

(b)　any dealings by the limited liability partnership shall be treated for those purposes as dealings by its members in partnership (and not by the limited liability partnership as such),

and tax in respect of chargeable gains accruing to the members of the limited liability partnership on the disposal of any of its assets shall be assessed and charged on them separately.

(2) Where subsection (1) ceases to apply in relation to a limited liability partnership with the effect that tax is assessed and charged—

(a)　on the limited liability partnership (as a company) in respect of chargeable gains accruing on the disposal of any of its assets, and

(b)　on the members in respect of chargeable gains accruing on the disposal of any of their capital interests in the limited liability partnership,

it shall be assessed and charged on the limited liability partnership as if subsection (1) had never applied in relation to it.

(3) Neither the commencement of the application of subsection (1) nor the cessation of its application in relation to a limited liability partnership is to be taken as giving rise to the disposal of any assets by it or any of its members.'

(4)　After section 156 of that Act insert—

'156A.　Cessation of trade by limited liability partnership

(1) Where, immediately before the time of cessation of trade, a member of a limited liability partnership holds an asset, or an interest in an asset, acquired by him for a consideration treated as reduced under section 152 or 153, he shall be treated as if a chargeable gain equal to the amount of the reduction accrued to him immediately before that time.

(2) Where, as a result of section 154(2), a chargeable gain on the disposal of an asset, or an interest in an asset, by a member of a limited liability partnership has not accrued before the time of cessation of trade, the member shall be treated as if the chargeable gain accrued immediately before that time.

(3) In this section "the time of cessation of trade", in relation to a limited liability partnership, means the time when section 59A(1) ceases to apply in relation to the limited liability partnership.'

11.　Inheritance tax

In the Inheritance Tax Act 1984, after section 267 insert—

'267A.　Limited liability partnerships

For the purposes of this Act and any other enactments relating to inheritance tax—

(a)　property to which a limited liability partnership is entitled, or which it occupies or uses, shall be treated as property to which its members are entitled, or which they occupy or use, as partners,

(b)　any business carried on by a limited liability partnership shall be treated as carried on in partnership by its members,

(c)　incorporation, change in membership or dissolution of a limited liability partnership shall be treated as formation, alteration or dissolution of a partnership, and

(d)　any transfer of value made by or to a limited liability partnership shall be treated as made by or to its members in partnership (and not by or to the limited liability partnership as such).'

12.　Stamp duty

(1)　Stamp duty shall not be chargeable on an instrument by which property is conveyed or transferred by a person to a limited liability partnership in connection with its incorporation within the period of one year beginning with the date of incorporation if the following two conditions are satisfied.

(2)　The first condition is that at the relevant time the person—

(a)　is a partner in a partnership comprised of all the persons who are or are to be members of the limited liability partnership (and no one else), or

(b)　holds the property conveyed or transferred as nominee or bare trustee for one or more of the partners in such a partnership.

(3)　The second condition is that—

(a)   the proportions of the property conveyed or transferred to which the persons mentioned in subsection (2)(a) are entitled immediately after the conveyance or transfer are the same as those to which they were entitled at the relevant time, or

(b)   none of the differences in those proportions has arisen as part of a scheme or arrangement of which the main purpose, or one of the main purposes, is avoidance of liability to any duty or tax.

(4)   For the purposes of subsection (2) a person holds property as bare trustee for a partner if the partner has the exclusive right (subject only to satisfying any outstanding charge, lien or other right of the trustee to resort to the property for payment of duty, taxes, costs or other outgoings) to direct how the property shall be dealt with.

(5)   In this section 'the relevant time' means—

(a)   if the person who conveyed or transferred the property to the limited liability partnership acquired the property after its incorporation, immediately after he acquired the property, and

(b)   in any other case, immediately before its incorporation.

(6)   An instrument in respect of which stamp duty is not chargeable by virtue of subsection (1) shall not be taken to be duly stamped unless—

(a)   it has, in accordance with section 12 of the Stamp Act 1891, been stamped with a particular stamp denoting that it is not chargeable with any duty or that it is duly stamped, or

(b)   it is stamped with the duty to which it would be liable apart from that subsection.

13.   Class 4 national insurance contributions

In section 15 of the Social Security Contributions and Benefits Act 1992 and section 15 of the Social Security Contributions and Benefits (Northern Ireland) Act 1992 (Class 4 contributions), after subsection (3) insert—

'(3A) Where income tax is (or would be) charged on a member of a limited liability partnership in respect of profits or gains arising from the carrying on of a trade or profession by the limited liability partnership, Class 4 contributions shall be payable by him if they would be payable were the trade or profession carried on in partnership by the members.'

14.   Regulations Insolvency and winding up

(1)   Regulations shall make provision about the insolvency and winding up of limited liability partnerships by applying or incorporating, with such modifications as appear appropriate, Parts I to IV, VI and VII of the Insolvency Act 1986.

(2)   Regulations may make other provision about the insolvency and winding up of limited liability partnerships, and provision about the insolvency and winding up of oversea limited liability partnerships, by—

(a)   applying or incorporating, with such modifications as appear appropriate, any law relating to the insolvency or winding up of companies or other corporations which would not otherwise have effect in relation to them, or

(b)   providing for any law relating to the insolvency or winding up of companies or other corporations which would otherwise have effect in relation to them not to apply to them or to apply to them with such modifications as appear appropriate.

(3)   In this Act 'oversea limited liability partnership' means a body incorporated or otherwise established outside Great Britain and having such connection with Great Britain, and such other features, as regulations may prescribe.

15.   Application of company law etc

Regulations may make provision about limited liability partnerships and oversea limited liability partnerships (not being provision about insolvency or winding up) by—

(a)   applying or incorporating, with such modifications as appear appropriate, any law relating to companies or other corporations which would not otherwise have effect in relation to them,

(b)   providing for any law relating to companies or other corporations which would otherwise have effect in relation to them not to apply to them or to apply to them with such modifications as appear appropriate, or

(c)   applying or incorporating, with such modifications as appear appropriate, any law relating to partnerships.

Part I   Partnership

16.   Consequential amendments

(1)   Regulations may make in any enactment such amendments or repeals as appear appropriate in consequence of this Act or regulations made under it.

(2)   The regulations may, in particular, make amendments and repeals affecting companies or other corporations or partnerships.

17.   General

(1)   In this Act 'regulations' means regulations made by the Secretary of State by statutory instrument.

(2)   Regulations under this Act may in particular—

(a)   make provision for dealing with non-compliance with any of the regulations (including the creation of criminal offences),

(b)   impose fees (which shall be paid into the Consolidated Fund), and

(c)   provide for the exercise of functions by persons prescribed by the regulations.

(3)   Regulations under this Act may—

(a)   contain any appropriate consequential, incidental, supplementary or transitional provisions or savings, and

(b)   make different provision for different purposes.

(4)   No regulations to which this subsection applies shall be made unless a draft of the statutory instrument containing the regulations (whether or not together with other provisions) has been laid before, and approved by a resolution of, each House of Parliament.

(5)   Subsection (4) applies to—

(a)   regulations under section 14(2) not consisting entirely of the application or incorporation (with or without modifications) of provisions contained in or made under the Insolvency Act 1986,

(b)   regulations under section 15 not consisting entirely of the application or incorporation (with or without modifications) of provisions contained in or made under Part I, Chapter VIII of Part V, Part VII, Parts XI to XIII, Parts XVI to XVIII, Part XX or Parts XXIV to XXVI of the Companies Act 1985,

(c)   regulations under section 14 or 15 making provision about oversea limited liability partnerships, and

(d)   regulations under section 16.

(6)   A statutory instrument containing regulations under this Act shall (unless a draft of it has been approved by a resolution of each House of Parliament) be subject to annulment in pursuance of a resolution of either House of Parliament.

18.   Supplementary Interpretation

In this Act—

'address', in relation to a member of a limited liability partnership, means—

(a)   if an individual, his usual residential address, and

(b)   if a corporation or Scottish firm, its registered or principal office,

'business' includes every trade, profession and occupation,
'designated member' shall be construed in accordance with section 8,
'enactment' includes subordinate legislation (within the meaning of the Interpretation Act 1978),
'incorporation document' shall be construed in accordance with section 2,
'limited liability partnership' has the meaning given by section 1(2),
'member' shall be construed in accordance with section 4,
'modifications' includes additions and omissions,
'name', in relation to a member of a limited liability partnership, means—

(a)   if an individual, his forename and surname (or, in the case of a peer or other person usually known by a title, his title instead of or in addition to either or both his forename and surname), and

(b)   if a corporation or Scottish firm, its corporate or firm name,

'oversea limited liability partnership' has the meaning given by section 14(3),
'the registrar' means—

(a)   if the registered office of the limited liability partnership is, or is to be, situated in England and Wales or in Wales, the registrar or other officer performing under the Companies Act 1985 the duty of registration of companies in England and Wales, and

(b)   if its registered office is, or is to be, situated in Scotland, the registrar or other officer performing under that Act the duty of registration of companies in Scotland, and

'regulations' has the meaning given by section 17(1).

19.   Commencement, extent and short title

(1)   The preceding provisions of this Act shall come into force on such day as the Secretary of State may by order made by statutory instrument appoint; and different days may be appointed for different purposes.

(2)   The Secretary of State may by order made by statutory instrument make any transitional provisions and savings which appear appropriate in connection with the coming into force of any provision of this Act.

(3)   For the purposes of the Scotland Act 1998 this Act shall be taken to be a pre-commencement enactment within the meaning of that Act.

(4)   Apart from sections 10 to 13 (and this section), this Act does not extend to Northern Ireland.

(5)   This Act may be cited as the Limited Liability Partnerships Act 2000.

PART II

COMPANY

Company and Business Names Regulations 1981, SI 1981/1685

1.   These Regulations may be cited as the Company and Business Names Regulations 1981 and shall come into operation on 26th February 1982.

2.   In these Regulations, unless the context otherwise requires, 'the Act' means the Companies Act 1981.

3.   The words and expressions stated in column (1) of the Schedule hereto together with the plural and the possessive forms of these words and expressions are hereby specified as words and expressions for the registration of which as or as part of a company's corporate name of the approval of the Secretary of State is required by section 22(2)(b) of the Act or for the use of which as or as part of a business name his approval is required by section 28(2)(b) of the Act.

4.   Subject to Regulation 5, each Government department or other body stated in column (2) of the Schedule hereto is hereby specified as the relevant body for the purposes of section 31(2) and (3) of the Act in relation to the word or expression and the plural and the possessive forms of that word or expression opposite to it in column (1).

5.   Where two Government departments or other bodies are specified in the alternative in Column (2) of the Schedule hereto the second alternative is to be treated as specified,

    (a)   in the case of the corporate names of a company,

        (i)   if the company has not yet been registered and its principal or only place of business in Great Britain is to be in Scotland or, if it will have no place of business in Great Britain, its proposed registered office is in Scotland, and

        (ii)   if the company is already registered and its principal or only place of business in Great Britain is in Scotland or, if it has no place of business in Great Britain, its registered office is in Scotland, and

    (b)   in the case of a business name, if the principal or only place of the business carried on or to be carried on in Great Britain is or is to be in Scotland,

and the first alternative is to be treated as specified in any other case.

SCHEDULE

Regulations 3–5

SPECIFICATION OF WORDS, EXPRESSIONS AND RELEVANT BODIES

Column (1)	Column (2)
Word or expression	Relevant body
Abortion	Department of Health (formerly of Health and Social Security)
Apothecary	Worshipful Society of Apothecaries of London or Pharmaceutical Society of Great Britain
Association	
Assurance	
Assurer	
Authority	
Benevolent	
Board	
British	
Building Society	
Chamber (or Chambers) of Business (or their Welsh equivalents, Siambr Fusnes; Siambrau Busnes)	

Column (1)	Column (2)
Word or expression	Relevant body
Chamber (or Chambers) of Commerce (or their Welsh equivalents, Siambr Fasnach; Siambrau Masnach)	
Chamber (or Chambers) of Commerce and Industry (or their Welsh equivalents, Siambr Masnach a Diwydiant; Siambrau Masnach a Diwydiant)	
Chamber (or Chambers) of Commerce, Training and Enterprise (or their Welsh equivalents, Siambr Masnach, Hyfforddiant a Menter; Siambrau Masnach, Hyfforddiant a Menter)	
Chamber (or Chambers) of Enterprise (or their Welsh equivalents, Siambr Fenter; Siambrau Menter)	
Chamber (or Chambers) of Industry (or their Welsh equivalents, Siambr Diwydiant; Siambrau Diwydiant)	
Chamber (or Chambers) of Trade (or their Welsh equivalents, Siambr Fasnach; Siambrau Masnach)	
Chamber (or Chambers) of Trade and Industry (or their Welsh equivalents, Siambr Masnach a Diwydiant; Siambrau Masnach a Diwydiant)	
Chamber (or Chambers) of Training (or their Welsh equivalents, Siambr Hyfforddiant; Siambrau Hyfforddiant)	
Chamber (or Chambers) of Training and Enterprise (or their Welsh equivalents, Siambr Hyfforddiant a Menter; Siambrau Hyfforddiant a Menter)	
Charitable	} Charity Commission or the Scottish Ministers
Charity	
Chartered	
Chemist	
Chemistry	
Contact Lens	General Optical Council

Column (1)	Column (2)
Word or expression	Relevant body
Co-operative	
Council	
Dental Dentistry	} General Dental Council
District Nurse	Panel of Assessors in District Nurse Training
Duke	Home Office or the Scottish Ministers
England	
English	
European	
Federation	
Friendly Society	
Foundation	
Fund	
Giro	
Great Britain	
Group	
Health Centre Health Service	} Department of Health (formerly of Health and Social Security)
Health Visitor	Council for the Education and Training of Health Visitors
Her Majesty His Majesty	} Home Office or the Scottish Ministers
Holding	
Industrial and Provident Society	
Institute	
Institution	
Insurance	
Insurer	
International	
Ireland	
Irish	
King	Home Office or the Scottish Ministers
Midwife Midwifery	} Central Midwives Board or Central Midwives Board for Scotland
National	
Nurse Nursing	} General Nursing Council for England or General Nursing Council for Scotland
Patent	
Patentee	

Column (1)	Column (2)
Word or expression	Relevant body
Police	Home Office or Scottish Home and Health Department
Polytechnic	Department for Education and Skills
Post Office	
Pregnancy Termination	Department of Health (formerly of Health and Social Security)
Prince Princess	} Home Office or the Scottish Ministers
Queen	
Reassurance	
Reassurer	
Register	
Registered	
Reinsurance	
Reinsurer	
Royal Royale Royalty	} Home Office or the Scottish Ministers
Scotland	
Scottish	
Sheffield	
Society	
Special School	
Stock Exchange	Department for Education and Skills
Trade Union	
Trust	
United Kingdom	
University	The Privy Council
Wales	
Welsh	
	Home Office or the Scottish Ministers

Note: The reference in Column (2) to the Home Office shall be treated as a reference to the Lord Chancellor's Department in relation to the following entries in Column (1)—

    (a)   Duke,
    (b)   Her Majesty,
    (c)   His Majesty,
    (d)   King,
    (e)   Prince,
    (f)   Princess,
    (g)   Queen,
    (h)   Royal,
    (i)   Royale,
    (j)   Royalty, and
    (k)   Windsor.

Business Names Act 1985

1. Persons subject to this Act

(1) This Act applies to any person who has a place of business in Great Britain and who carries on business in Great Britain under a name which—

    (a) in the case of a partnership, does not consist of the surnames of all partners who are individuals and the corporate names of all partners who are bodies corporate without any addition other than an addition permitted by this Act;

    (b) in the case of an individual, does not consist of his surname without any addition other than one so permitted;

    (c) in the case of a company, being a company which is capable of being wound up under the Companies Act 1985, does not consist of its corporate name without any addition other than one so permitted;

    (d) in the case of a limited liability partnership, does not consist of its corporate name without any addition other than one so permitted.

(2) The following are permitted additions for the purposes of subsection (1)—

    (a) in the case of a partnership, the forenames of individual partners or the initials of those forenames or, where two or more individual partners have the same surname, the addition of 's' at the end of that surname; or

    (b) in the case of an individual, his forename or its initial;

    (c) in any case, any addition merely indicating that the business is carried on in succession to a former owner of the business.

2. Prohibition of use of certain business names

(1) Subject to the following subsections, a person to whom this Act applies shall not, without the written approval of the Secretary of State, carry on business in Great Britain under a name which—

    (a) would be likely to give the impression that the business is connected with Her Majesty's Government, with any part of the Scottish Administration, or with any local authority; or

    (b) includes any word or expression for the time being specified in regulations made under this Act.

(2) Subsection (1) does not apply to the carrying on of a business by a person—

    (a) to whom the business has been transferred on or after 26th February 1982; and

    (b) who carries on the business under the name which was its lawful business name immediately before that transfer,

during the period of 12 months beginning with the date of that transfer.

(3) Subsection (1) does not apply to the carrying on of a business by a person who—

    (a) carried on that business immediately before 26th February 1982; and

    (b) continues to carry it on under the name which immediately before that date was its lawful business name.

(4) A person who contravenes subsection (1) is guilty of an offence.

3. Words and expressions requiring Secretary of State's approval

(1) The Secretary of State may by regulations—

    (a) specify words or expressions for the use of which as or as part of a business name his approval is required by section 2(1)(b); and

    (b) in relation to any such word or expression, specify a Government department or other body as the relevant body for purposes of the following subsection.

(2) Where person to whom this Act applies proposes to carry on a business under a name which is or includes any such word or expression, and a Government department or other body is specified under subsection (1)(b) in relation to that word or expression, that person shall—

    (a) request (in writing) the relevant body to indicate whether (and if so why) it has any objections to the proposal; and

(b)   submit to the Secretary of State a statement that such a request has been made and a copy of any response received from the relevant body.

4.   Disclosure required of persons using business names

(1)   A person to whom this Act applies shall—

(a)   subject to subsections (3) and (3A), state in legible characters on all business letters, written orders for goods or services to be supplied to the business, invoices and receipts issued in the course of the business and written demands for payment of debts arising in the course of the business—

(i)   in the case of a partnership, the name of each partner,

(ii)   in the case of an individual, his name,

(iii)   in the case of a company, its corporate name,

(iiia) in the case of a limited liability partnership, its corporate name and the name of each member, and

(iv)   in relation to each person so named, an address in Great Britain at which service of any document relating in any way to the business will be effective; and

(b)   in any premises where the business is carried on and to which the customers of the business or suppliers of any goods or services to the business have access, display in a prominent position so that it may easily be read by such customers or suppliers a notice containing such names and addresses.

(2)   A person to whom this Act applies shall secure that the names and addresses required by subsection (1)(a) to be stated on his business letters, or which would have been so required but for subsection (3) or (3A), are immediately given, by written notice to any person with whom anything is done or discussed in the course of the business and who asks for such names and addresses.

(3)   Subsection (1)(a) does not apply in relation to any document issued by a partnership of more than 20 persons which maintains at its principal place of business a list of the names of all the partners if—

(a)   none of the names of the partners appears in the document otherwise than in the text or as a signatory; and

(b)   the document states in legible characters the address of the partnership's principal place of business and that the list of the partners' names is open to inspection at that place.

(3A) Subsection (1)(a) does not apply in relation to any document issued by a limited liability partnership with more than 20 members which maintains at its principal place of business a list of the names of all the members if—

(a)   none of the names of the members appears in the document otherwise than in the text or as a signatory; and

(b)   the document states in legible characters the address of the principal place of business of the limited liability partnership and that the list of the members' names is open to inspection at that place.

(4)   Where a partnership maintains a list of the partners' names for purposes of subsection (3), any person may inspect the list during office hours.

(4A) Where a limited liability partnership maintains a list of the members' names for the purposes of subsection (3A), any person may inspect the list during office hours.

(5)   The Secretary of State may by regulations require notices under subsection (1)(b) or (2) to be displayed or given in a specified form.

(6)   A person who without reasonable excuse contravenes subsection (1) or (2), or any regulations made under subsection (5), is guilty of an offence.

(7)   Where an inspection required by a person in accordance with subsection (4) or (4A) is refused, any partner of the partnership concerned, or any member of the limited liability partnership concerned, who without reasonable excuse refused that inspection, or permitted it to be refused, is guilty of an offence.

5.   Civil remedies for breach of s 4

(1)   Any legal proceedings brought by a person to whom this Act applies to enforce a right arising out of a contract made in the course of a business in respect of which he was, at the time the contract was made, in breach of subsection (1) or (2) of section 4 shall be dismissed if the defendant (or, in Scotland, the defender) to the proceedings shows—

(a) that he has a claim against the plaintiff (pursuer) arising out of that contract which he has been unable to pursue by reason of the latter's breach of section 4(1) or (2), or

(b) that he has suffered some financial loss in connection with the contract by reason of the plaintiff's (pursuer's) breach of section 4(1) or (2),

unless the court before which the proceedings are brought is satisfied that it is just and equitable to permit the proceedings to continue.

(2) This section is without prejudice to the right of any person to enforce such rights as he may have against another person in any proceedings brought by that person.

Companies Act 1985

PART I

FORMATION AND REGISTRATION OF COMPANIES, JURIDICAL STATUS AND MEMBERSHIP

1. Mode of forming incorporated company

(1) Any two or more persons associated for a lawful purpose may, by subscribing their names to a memorandum of association and otherwise complying with the requirements of this Act in respect of registration, form an incorporated company, with or without limited liability.

(2) A company so formed may be either—

(a) a company having the liability of its members limited by the memorandum to the amount, if any, unpaid on the shares respectively held by them ('a company limited by shares');

(b) a company having the liability of its members limited by the memorandum to such amount as the members may respectively thereby undertake to contribute to the assets of the company in the event of its being wound up ('a company limited by guarantee'); or

(c) a company not having any limit on the liability of its members ('an unlimited company').

(3) A 'public company' is a company limited by shares or limited by guarantee and having a share capital, being a company—

(a) the memorandum of which states that it is to be a public company, and

(b) in relation to which the provisions of this Act or the former Companies Acts as to the registration or re-registration of a company as a public company have been complied with on or after 22nd December 1980;

and a 'private company' is a company that is not a public company.

(3A) Notwithstanding subsection (1), one person may, for a lawful purpose, by subscribing his name to a memorandum of association and otherwise complying with the requirements of this Act in respect of registration, form an incorporated company being a private company limited by shares or by guarantee.

(4) With effect from 22nd December 1980, a company cannot be formed as, or become, a company limited by guarantee with a share capital.

2. Requirements with respect to memorandum

(1) The memorandum of every company must state—

(a) the name of the company;

(b) whether the registered office of the company is to be situated in England and Wales, or in Scotland;

(c) the objects of the company.

(2) Alternatively to subsection (1)(b), the memorandum may contain a statement that the company's registered office is to be situated in Wales; and a company whose registered office is situated in Wales may by special resolution alter its memorandum so as to provide that its registered office is to be so situated.

(3) The memorandum of a company limited by shares or by guarantee must also state that the liability of its members is limited.

(4) The memorandum of a company limited by guarantee must also state that each member undertakes to contribute to the assets of the company if it should be wound up while he is a member, or within one year after he ceases to be a member, for payment of the debts and liabilities of the company contracted before he ceases to be a member, and of the costs, charges and expenses of winding up, and for adjustment of the rights of the contributories among themselves, such amount as may be required, not exceeding a specified amount.

(5) In the case of a company having a share capital—

(a) the memorandum must also (unless it is an unlimited company) state the amount of the share capital with which the company proposes to be registered and the division of the share capital into shares of a fixed amount;

(b) no subscriber of the memorandum may take less than one share; and

(c)   there must be shown in the memorandum against the name of each subscriber the number of shares he takes.

(6)   Subject to subsection (6A), the memorandum must be signed by each subscriber in the presence of at least one witness, who must attest the signature; and that attestation is sufficient in Scotland as well as in England and Wales.

(6A)   Where the memorandum is delivered to the registrar otherwise than in legible form and is authenticated by each subscriber in such manner as is directed by the registrar, the requirements in subsection (6) for signature in the presence of at least one witness and for attestation of the signature do not apply.

(7)   A company may not alter the conditions contained in its memorandum except in the cases, in the mode and to the extent, for which express provision is made by this Act.

3.   Forms of memorandum

(1)   Subject to the provisions of sections 1 and 2, the form of the memorandum of association of—

(a)   a public company, being a company limited by shares,
(b)   a public company, being a company limited by guarantee and having a share capital,
(c)   a private company limited by shares,
(d)   a private company limited by guarantee and not having a share capital,
(e)   a private company limited by guarantee and having a share capital, and
(f)   an unlimited company having a share capital,

shall be as specified respectively for such companies by regulations made by the Secretary of State, or as near to that form as circumstances admit.

(2)   Regulations under this section shall be made by statutory instrument subject to annulment in pursuance of a resolution of either House of Parliament.

3A.   Statement of company's objects: general commercial company

Where the company's memorandum states that the object of the company is to carry on business as a general commercial company—

(a)   the object of the company is to carry on any trade or business whatsoever, and
(b)   the company has power to do all such things as are incidental or conducive to the carrying on of any trade or business by it.

4.   Resolution to alter objects

(1)   A company may by special resolution alter its memorandum with respect to the statement of the company's objects.

(2)   If an application is made under the following section, an alteration does not have effect except in so far as it is confirmed by the court.

5.   Procedure for objecting to alteration

(1)   Where a company's memorandum has been altered by special resolution under section 4, application may be made to the court for the alteration to be cancelled.

(2)   Such an application may be made—

(a)   by the holders of not less in the aggregate than 15 per cent in nominal value of the company's issued share capital or any class of it or, if the company is not limited by shares, not less than 15 per cent of the company's members; or
(b)   by the holders of not less than 15 per cent of the company's debentures entitling the holders to object to an alteration of its objects;

but an application shall not be made by any person who has consented to or voted in favour of the alteration.

(3)   The application must be made within 21 days after the date on which the resolution altering the company's objects was passed, and may be made on behalf of the persons entitled to make the application by such one or more of their number as they may appoint in writing for the purpose.

(4)   The court may on such an application make an order confirming the alteration either wholly or in part and on such terms and conditions as it thinks fit, and may—

(a)   if it thinks fit, adjourn the proceedings in order that an arrangement may be made to its satisfaction for the purchase of the interests of dissentient members, and

(b)   give such directions and make such orders as it thinks expedient for facilitating or carrying into effect any such arrangement.

(5)   The court's order may (if the court thinks fit) provide for the purchase by the company of the shares of any members of the company, and for the reduction accordingly of its capital, and may make such alterations in the company's memorandum, and articles as may be required in consequence of that provision.

(6)   If the court's order requires the company not to make any, or any specified, alteration in its memorandum or articles, the company does not then have power without the leave of the court to make any such alteration in breach of that requirement.

(7)   An alteration in the memorandum or articles of a company made by virtue of an order under this section, other than one made by resolution of the company, is of the same effect as if duly made by resolution; and this Act applies accordingly to the memorandum or articles as so altered.

(8)   The debentures entitling the holders to object to an alteration of a company's objects are any debentures secured by a floating charge which were issued or first issued before 1st December 1947 or form part of the same series as any debentures so issued; and a special resolution altering a company's objects requires the same notice to the holders of any such debentures as to members of the company.

In the absence of provisions regulating the giving of notice to any such debenture holders, the provisions of the company's articles regulating the giving of notice to members apply.

6.   Provisions supplementing ss 4, 5

(1)   Where a company passes a resolution altering its objects, then—

(a)   if with respect to the resolution no application is made under section 5, the company shall within 15 days from the end of the period for making such an application deliver to the registrar of companies a printed copy of its memorandum as altered; and

(b)   if such an application is made, the company shall—

(i)   forthwith give notice (in the prescribed form) of that fact to the registrar, and

(ii)   within 15 days from the date of any order cancelling or confirming the alteration, deliver to the registrar an office copy of the order and, in the case of an order confirming the alteration, a printed copy of the memorandum as altered.

(2)   The court may by order at any time extend the time for the delivery of documents to the registrar under subsection (1)(b) for such period as the court may think proper.

(3)   If a company makes default in giving notice or delivering any document to the registrar of companies as required by subsection (1), the company and every officer of it who is in default is liable to a fine and, for continued contravention, to a daily default fine.

(4)   The validity of an alteration of a company's memorandum with respect to the objects of the company shall not be questioned on the ground that it was not authorised by section 4, except in proceedings taken for the purpose (whether under section 5 or otherwise) before the expiration of 21 days after the date of the resolution in that behalf.

(5)   Where such proceedings are taken otherwise than under section 5, subsections (1) to (3) above apply in relation to the proceedings as if they had been taken under than section, and as if an order declaring the alteration invalid were an order cancelling it, and as if an order dismissing the proceedings were an order confirming the alteration.

7.   Articles prescribing regulations for companies

(1)   There may in the case of a company limited by shares, and there shall in the case of a company limited by guarantee or unlimited, be registered with the memorandum articles of association signed by the subscribers to the memorandum and prescribing regulations for the company.

(2)   In the case of an unlimited company having a share capital, the articles must state the amount of share capital with which the company proposes to be registered.

(3)   Articles must—

    (a)   be printed,

    (b)   be divided into paragraphs numbered consecutively, and

    (c)   subject to subsection (3A) be signed by each subscriber of the memorandum in the presence of at least one witness who must attest the signature.

(3A)   Where the articles are delivered to the registrar otherwise than in legible form and are authenticated by each subscriber to the memorandum in such manner as is directed by the registrar, the requirements in subsection (3)(c) for signature in the presence of at least one witness and for attestation of the signature do not apply.

8.   Tables A, C, D and E

(1)   Table A is as prescribed by regulations made by the Secretary of State; and a company may for its articles adopt the whole or any part of that Table.

(2)   In the case of a company limited by shares, if articles are not registered or, if articles are registered, in so far as they do not exclude or modify Table A, that Table (so far as applicable, and as in force at the date of the company's registration) constitutes the company's articles, in the same manner and to the same extent as if articles in the form of that Table had been duly registered.

(3)   If in consequence of regulations under this section Table A is altered, the alteration does not affect a company registered before the alteration takes effect, or repeal as respects that company any portion of the Table.

(4)   The form of the articles of association of—

    (a)   a company limited by guarantee and not having a share capital,

    (b)   a company limited by guarantee and having a share capital, and

    (c)   an unlimited company having a share capital,

shall be respectively in accordance with Table C, D or E prescribed by regulations made by the Secretary of State, or as near to that form as circumstances admit.

(5)   Regulations under this section shall be made by statutory instrument subject to annulment in pursuance of a resolution of either House of Parliament.

9.   Alteration of articles by special resolution

(1)   Subject to the provisions of this Act and to the conditions contained in its memorandum, a company may by special resolution alter its articles.

(2)   Alterations so made in the articles are (subject to this Act) as valid as if originally contained in them, and are subject in like manner to alteration by special resolution.

10.   Documents to be sent to registrar

(1)   The company's memorandum and articles (if any) shall be delivered—

    (a)   to the registrar of companies for England and Wales, if the memorandum states that the registered office of the company is to be situated in England and Wales, or that it is to be situated in Wales; and

    (b)   to the registrar of companies for Scotland, if the memorandum states that the registered office of the company is to be situated in Scotland.

(2)   With the memorandum there shall be delivered a statement in the prescribed form containing the names and requisite particulars of—

    (a)   the person who is, or the persons who are, to be the first director or directors of the company; and

    (b)   the person who is, or the persons who are, to be the first secretary or joint secretaries of the company;

and the requisite particulars in each case are those set out in Schedule 1.

(2A)   Where any statement delivered under subsection (2) includes an address specified in reliance on paragraph 5 of Schedule 1 there shall be delivered with the statement, a statement in the prescribed form containing particulars of the usual residential address of the director or secretary whose address is so specified.

(3)   The statement under subsection (2) shall be signed by or on behalf of the subscribers of the memorandum and shall contain a consent signed by each of the persons named in it as a director, as secretary or as one of joint secretaries, to act in the relevant capacity.

(4)   Where a memorandum is delivered by a person as agent for the subscribers, the statement shall specify that fact and the person's name and address.

(5)   An appointment by any articles delivered with the memorandum of a person as director or secretary of the company is void unless he is named as a director or secretary in the statement.

(6)   There shall in the statement be specified the intended situation of the company's registered office on incorporation.

12.   Duty of registrar

(1)   The registrar of companies shall not register a company's memorandum delivered under section 10 unless he is satisfied that all the requirements of this Act in respect of registration and of matters precedent and incidental to it have been complied with.

(2)   Subject to this, the registrar shall retain and register the memorandum and articles (if any) delivered to him under that section.

(3)   Subject to subsection (3A), a statutory declaration in the prescribed form by—

   (a)   a solicitor engaged in the formation of a company, or
   (b)   a person named as a director or secretary of the company in the statement delivered under section 10(2),

that those requirements have been complied with shall be delivered to the registrar of companies, and the registrar may accept such a declaration as sufficient evidence of compliance.

(3A)   In place of the statutory declaration referred to in subsection (3), there may be delivered to the registrar of companies using electronic communications a statement made by a person mentioned in paragraph (a) or (b) of subsection (3) that the requirements mentioned in subsection (1) have been complied with; and the registrar may accept such a statement as sufficient evidence of compliance.

(3B)   Any person who makes a false statement under subsection (3A) which he knows to be false or does not believe to be true is liable to imprisonment or a fine, or both.

13.   Effect of registration

(1)   On the registration of a company's memorandum, the registrar of companies shall give a certificate that the company is incorporated and, in the case of a limited company, that it is limited.

(2)   The certificate may be signed by the registrar, or authenticated by his official seal.

(3)   From the date of incorporation mentioned in the certificate, the subscribers of the memorandum, together with such other persons as may from time to time become members of the company, shall be a body corporate by the name contained in the memorandum.

(4)   That body corporate is then capable forthwith of exercising all the functions of an incorporated company, but with such liability on the part of its members to contribute to its assets in the event of its being wound up as is provided by this Act and the Insolvency Act.

This is subject, in the case of a public company, to section 117 (additional certificate as to amount of allotted share capital).

(5)   The persons named in the statement under section 10 as directors, secretary or joint secretaries are, on the company's incorporation, deemed to have been respectively appointed as its first directors, secretary or joint secretaries.

(6)   Where the registrar registers an association's memorandum which states that the association is to be a public company, the certificate of incorporation shall contain a statement that the company is a public company.

(7)   A certificate of incorporation given in respect of an association is conclusive evidence—

   (a)   that the requirements of this Act in respect of registration and of matters precedent and incidental to it have been complied with, and that the association is a company authorised to be registered, and is duly registered, under this Act, and
   (b)   if the certificate contains a statement that the company is a public company, that the company is such a company.

14.   Effect of memorandum and articles

(1)   Subject to the provisions of this Act, the memorandum and articles, when registered, bind the company and its members to the same extent as if they respectively had been signed and sealed by each member, and contained covenants on the part of each member to observe all the provisions of the memorandum and of the articles.

(2)   Money payable by a member to the company under the memorandum or articles is a debt due from him to the company, and in England and Wales is of the nature of a specialty debt.

22.   Definition of 'member'

(1)   The subscribers of a company's memorandum are deemed to have agreed to become members of the company, and on its registration shall be entered as such in its register of members.

(2)   Every other person who agrees to become a member of a company, and whose name is entered in its register of members, is a member of the company.

25.   Name as stated in memorandum

(1)   The name of a public company must end with the words 'public limited company' or, if the memorandum states that the company's registered office is to be situated in Wales, those words or their equivalent in Welsh ('cwmncyfyngedig cyhoeddus'); and those words or that equivalent may not be preceded by the word 'limited' or its equivalent in Welsh ('cyfyngedig').

(2)   In the case of a company limited by shares or by guarantee (not being a public company), the name must have 'limited' as its last word, except that—

(a)   this is subject to section 30 (exempting, in certain circumstances, a company from the requirement to have 'limited' as part of the name); and

(b)   if the company is to be registered with a memorandum stating that its registered office is to be situated in Wales, the name may have 'cyfyngedig' as its last word.

26.   Prohibition on registration of certain names

(1)   A company shall not be registered under this Act by a name—

(a)   which includes, otherwise than at the end of the name, any of the following words or expressions, that is to say, 'limited, 'unlimited' or 'public limited company' or their Welsh equivalents ('cyfyngedig', 'anghyfyngedig' and 'cwmni cyfyngedig cyhoeddus' respectively);

(b)   which includes, otherwise than at the end of the name, an abbreviation of any of those words or expressions;

(bb)   which includes, at any place in the name, the expressions 'investment company with variable capital' or 'open-ended investment company' or their Welsh equivalents ('cwmni buddsoddi â chyfalaf newidiol' and 'cwmni buddsoddiant penagored' respectively);

(bbb)   which includes, at any place in the name, the expression 'limited liability partnership' or its Welsh equivalent ('partneriaeth atebolrwydd cyfyngedig');

(c)   which is the same as a name appearing in the registrar's index of company names;

(d)   the use of which by the company would in the opinion of the Secretary of State constitute a criminal offence; or

(e)   which is the opinion of the Secretary of State is offensive.

(2)   Except with the approval of the Secretary of State, a company shall not be registered under this Act by a name which—

(a)   in the opinion of the Secretary of State would be likely to give the impression that the company is connected in any way with Her Majesty's Government or with any local authority; or

(b)   includes any word or expression for the time being specified in regulations under section 29.

'Local authority' means any local authority within the meaning of the Local Government Act 1972 or the Local Government (Scotland) Act 1973, the Common Council of the City of London or the Council of the Isles of Scilly.

(3)   In determining for purposes of subsection (1)(c) whether one name is the same as another, there are to be disregarded—

(a)   the definite article, where it is the first word of the name;

(b)   the following words and expressions where they appear at the end of the name, that is to say—

'company' or its Welsh equivalent ('cwmni'),

'and company' or its Welsh equivalent ('a'r cwmni'),

'company limited' or its Welsh equivalent ('cwmni cyfyngedig'),

'and company limited' or its Welsh equivalent ('a'r cwmni cyfyngedig'),

'limited' or its Welsh equivalent ('cyfyngedig'),

'unlimited' or its Welsh equivalent ('anghyfyngedig'),

'public limited company' or its Welsh equivalent ('cwmni cyfyngedig cyhoeddus');

'investment company with variable capital' or its Welsh equivalent ('cwmni buddsoddi â chyfalaf newidiol'); and

'open-ended investment company' or its Welsh equivalent ('cwmni buddsoddiant penagored');

(c) abbreviations of any of those words or expressions where they appear at the end of the name; and

(d) type and case of letters, accents, spaces between letters and punctuation marks;

and 'and' and '&' are to be taken as the same.

27. Alternatives of statutory designations

(1)   A company which by any provision of this Act is either required or entitled to include in its name, as its last part, any of the words specified in subsection (4) below may, instead of those words, include as the last part of the name the abbreviations there specified as alternatives in relation to those words.

(2)   A reference in this Act to the name of a company or to the inclusion of any of those words in a company's name includes a reference to the name including (in place of any of the words so specified) the appropriate alternative, or to the inclusion of the appropriate alternative, as the case may be.

(3)   A provision of this Act requiring a company not to include any of those words in its name also requires it not to include the abbreviated alternative specified in subsection (4).

(4)   For the purposes of this section—

(a) the alternative of 'limited' is 'ltd';

(b) the alternative of 'public limited company' is 'p.l.c.';

(c) the alternative of 'cyfyngedig' is 'cyf'; and

(d) the alternative of 'cwmni cyfyngedig cyhoeddus' is 'c.c.c.'.

28. Change of name

(1)   A company may by special resolution change its name (but subject to section 31 in the case of a company which has received a direction under subsection (2) of that section from the Secretary of State).

(2)   Where a company has been registered by a name which—

(a) is the same as or, in the opinion of the Secretary of State, too like a name appearing at the time of the registration in the registrar's index of company names, or

(b) is the same as or, in the opinion of the Secretary of State, too like a name which should have appeared in that index at that time,

the Secretary of State may within 12 months of that time, in writing, direct the company to change its name within such period as he may specify.

Section 26(3) applies in determining under this subsection whether a name is the same as or too like another.

(3)   If it appears to the Secretary of State that misleading information has been given for the purpose of a company's registration with a particular name, or that undertakings or assurances, have been given for that purpose and have not been fulfilled, he may within 5 years of the date of its registration with that name in writing direct the company to change its name within such period as he may specify.

(4)   Where a direction has been given under subsection (2) or (3), the Secretary of State may by a further direction in writing extend the period within which the company is to change its name, at any time before the end of that period.

(5)   A company which fails to comply with a direction under this section, and any officer of it who is in default, is liable to a fine and, for continued contravention, to a daily default fine.

(6)   Where a company changes its name under this section, the registrar of companies shall (subject to section 26) enter the new name on the register in place of the former name and shall issue a certificate of incorporation altered

Part II   Company

to meet the circumstances of the case; and the change of name has effect from the date on which the altered certificate is issued.

(7)   A change of name by a company under this section does not affect any rights or obligations of the company or render defective any legal proceedings by or against it; and any legal proceedings that might have been continued or commenced against it by its former name may be continued or commenced against it by its new name.

29.   Regulations about names

(1)   The Secretary of State may by regulations—

   (a)   specify words or expressions for the registration of which as or as part of a company's corporate name his approval is required under section 26(2)(b), and

   (b)   in relation to any such word or expression, specify a Government department or other body as the relevant body for purposes of the following subsection.

(2)   Where a company proposes to have as, or as part of, its corporate name any such word or expression and a Government department or other body is specified under subsection (1)(b) in relation to that word or expression, a request shall be made (in writing) to the relevant body to indicate whether (and if so why) it has any objections to the proposal; and the person to make the request is—

   (a)   in the case of a company seeking to be registered under this Part, the person making the statutory declaration under section 12(3) or statement under section 12(3A) (as the case may be),

   (b)   in the case of a company seeking to be registered under section 680, the persons making the statutory declaration under section 686(2) or statement under section 686(2A) (as the case may be), and

   (c)   in any other case, a director or secretary of the company concerned.

(3)   The person who has made that request to the relevant body shall submit to the registrar of companies a statement that it has been made and a copy of any response received from that body, together with—

   (a)   the requisite statutory declaration or statement, or

   (b)   a copy of the special resolution changing the company's name,

according as the case is one or other of those mentioned in subsection (2).

(4)   Sections 709 and 710 (public rights of inspection of documents kept by registrar of companies) do not apply to documents sent under subsection (3) of this section.

(5)   Regulations under this section may contain such transitional provisions and savings as the Secretary of State thinks appropriate and may make different provision for different cases or classes of case.

(6)   The regulations shall be made by statutory instrument, to be laid before Parliament after it is made; and the regulations shall cease to have effect at the end of 28 days beginning with the day on which the regulations were made (but without prejudice to anything previously done by virtue of them or to the making of new regulations), unless during that period they are approved by resolution of each House. In reckoning that period, no account is to be taken of any time during which Parliament is dissolved or prorogued or during which both Houses are adjourned for more than 4 days.

34.   Penalty for improper use of 'limited' or 'cyfyngedig'

If any person trades or carries on business under a name or title of which 'limited' or 'cyfyngedig', or any contraction or imitation of either of those words, is the last word, that person, unless duly incorporated with limited liability, is liable to a fine and, for continued contravention, to a daily default fine.

35.   A company's capacity not limited by its memorandum

(1)   The validity of an act done by a company shall not be called into question on the ground of lack of capacity by reason of anything in the company's memorandum.

(2)   A member of a company may bring proceedings to restrain the doing of an act which but for subsection (1) would be beyond the company's capacity; but no such proceedings shall lie in respect of an act to be done in fulfilment of a legal obligation arising from a previous act of the company.

(3)   It remains the duty of the directors to observe any limitations on their powers flowing from the company's memorandum; and action by the directors which but for subsection (1) would be beyond the company's capacity may only be ratified by the company by special resolution.

A resolution ratifying such action shall not affect any liability incurred by the directors or any other person; relief from any such liability must be agreed to separately by special resolution.

(4)   The operation of this section is restricted by section 65(1) of the Charities Act 1993 and section 112(3) of the Companies Act 1989 in relation to companies which are charities; and section 322A below (invalidity of certain transactions to which directors or their associates are parties) has effect notwithstanding this section.

35A.   Power of directors to bind the company

(1)   In favour of a person dealing with a company in good faith, the power of the board of directors to bind the company, or authorise others to do so, shall be deemed to be free of any limitation under the company's constitution.

(2)   For this purpose—

    (a)   a person 'deals with' a company if he is a party to any transaction or other act to which the company is a party;

    (b)   a person shall not be regarded as acting in bad faith by reason only of his knowing that an act is beyond the powers of the directors under the company's constitution; and

    (c)   a person shall be presumed to have acted in good faith unless the contrary is proved.

(3)   The references above to limitations on the directors' powers under the company's constitution include limitations deriving—

    (a)   from a resolution of the company in general meeting or a meeting of any class of shareholders, or

    (b)   from any agreement between the members of the company or of any class of shareholders.

(4)   Subsection (1) does not affect any right of a member of the company to bring proceedings to restrain the doing of an act which is beyond the powers of the directors; but no such proceedings shall lie in respect of an act to be done in fulfilment of a legal obligation arising from a previous act of the company.

(5)   Nor does that subsection affect any liability incurred by the directors, or any other person, by reason of the directors' exceeding their powers.

(6)   The operation of this section is restricted by section 65(1) of the Charities Act 1993 and section 112(3) of the Companies Act 1989 in relation to companies which are charities; and section 322A below (invalidity of certain transactions to which directors or their associates are parties) has effect notwithstanding this section.

35B.   No duty to enquire as to capacity of company or authority of directors

A party to a transaction with a company is not bound to enquire as to whether it is permitted by the company's memorandum or as to any limitation on the powers of the board of directors to bind the company or authorise others to do so.

36.   Company contracts: England and Wales

Under the law of England and Wales a contract may be made—

    (a)   by a company, by writing under its common seal, or

    (b)   on behalf of a company, by any person acting under its authority, express or implied;

and any formalities required by law in the case of a contract made by an individual also apply, unless a contrary intention appears, to a contract made by or on behalf of a company.

36A.   Execution of documents: England and Wales

(1)   Under the law of England and Wales the following provisions have effect with respect to the execution of documents by a company.

(2)   A document is executed by a company by the affixing of its common seal.

(3)   A company need not have a common seal, however, and the following subsections apply whether it does or not.

(4)   A document signed by a director and the secretary of a company, or by two directors of a company, and expressed (in whatever form of words) to be executed by the company has the same effect as if executed under the common seal of the company.

(5)   A document executed by a company which makes it clear on its face that it is intended by the person or persons making it to be a deed has effect, upon delivery, as a deed; and it shall be presumed, unless a contrary intention is proved, to be delivered upon its being so executed.

(6)   In favour of a purchaser a document shall be deemed to have been duly executed by a company if it purports to be signed by a director and the secretary of the company, or by two directors of the company, and, where it makes it clear on its face that it is intended by the person or persons making it to be a deed, to have been delivered upon its being executed.

A 'purchaser' means a purchaser in good faith for valuable consideration and includes a lessee, mortgagee or other person who for valuable consideration acquires an interest in property.

36C.   Pre-incorporation contracts, deeds and obligations

(1)   A contract which purports to be made by or on behalf of a company at a time when the company has not been formed has effect, subject to any agreement to the contrary, as one made with the person purporting to act for the company or as agent for it, and he is personally liable on the contract accordingly.

(2)   Subsection (1) applies—

     (a)   to the making of a deed under the law of England and Wales, and

     (b)   [Applies to Scotland only],

as it applies to the making of a contract.

40.   Official seal for share certificates etc

(1)   A company which has a common seal may have, for use for sealing securities issued by the company and for sealing documents creating or evidencing securities so issued, an official seal which is a facsimile of its common seal with the addition on its face of the word 'Securities'.

The official seal when duly affixed to a document has the same effect as the company's common seal.

(2)   Nothing in this section shall affect the right of a company registered in Scotland to subscribe such securities and documents in accordance with the Requirements of Writing (Scotland) Act 1995.

42.   Events affecting a company's status

(1)   A company is not entitled to rely against other persons on the happening of any of the following events—

     (a)   the making of a winding-up order in respect of the company, or the appointment of a liquidator in a voluntary winding up of the company, or

     (b)   any alteration of the company's memorandum or articles, or

     (c)   any change among the company's directors, or

     (d)   (as regards service of any document on the company) any change in the situation of the company's registered office,

if the event had not been officially notified at the material time and is not shown by the company to have been known at that time to the person concerned, or if the material time fell on or before the 15th day after the date of official notification (or, where the 15th day was a non-business day, on or before the next day that was not) and it is shown that the person concerned was unavoidably prevented from knowing of the event at that time.

(2)   In subsection (1)—

     (a)   'official notification' and 'officially notified' have the meanings given by section 711(2) (registrar of companies to give public notice of the issue or receipt by him of certain documents), and

     (b)   'non-business day' means a Saturday or Sunday, Christmas Day, Good Friday and any other day which is a bank holiday in the part of Great Britain where the company is registered.

PART II

RE-REGISTRATION AS A MEANS OF ALTERING A COMPANY'S STATUS

43. Re-registration of private company as public

(1)   Subject to this and the following five sections, a private company (other than a company not having a share capital) may be re-registered as a public company if—

(a)   a special resolution that it should be so re-registered is passed; and

(b)   an application for re-registration is delivered to the registrar of companies, together with the necessary documents.

A company cannot be re-registered under this section if it has previously been re-registered as unlimited.

(2)   The special resolution must—

(a)   alter the company's memorandum so that it states that the company is to be a public company; and

(b)   make such other alterations in the memorandum as are necessary to bring it (in substance and in form) into conformity with the requirements of this Act with respect to the memorandum of a public company (the alterations to include compliance with section 25(1) as regards the company's name); and

(c)   make such alterations in the company's articles as are requisite in the circumstances.

(3)   The application must be in the prescribed form and be signed by a director or secretary of the company; and the documents to be delivered with it are the following—

(a)   a printed copy of the memorandum and articles as altered in pursuance of the resolution;

(b)   a copy of a written statement by the company's auditors that in their opinion the relevant balance sheet shows that at the balance sheet date the amount of the company's net assets (within the meaning given to that expression by section 264(2)) was not less than the aggregate of its called-up share capital and undistributable reserves;

(c)   a copy of the relevant balance sheet, together with a copy of an unqualified report (defined in section 46) by the company's auditors in relation to that balance sheet;

(d)   if section 44 applies, a copy of the valuation report under subsection (2)(b) of that section; and

(e)   subject to subsection (3A), a statutory declaration in the prescribed form by director or secretary of the company—

(i)   that the special resolution required by this section has been passed and that the conditions of the following two sections (so far as applicable) have been satisfied, and

(ii)   that, between the balance sheet date and the application for re-registration, there has been no change in the company's financial position that has resulted in the amount of its net assets becoming less than the aggregate of its called-up share capital and undistributable reserves.

(3A)   In place of the statutory declaration referred to in paragraph (e) of subsection (3), there may be delivered to the registrar of companies using electronic communications a statement made by a director or secretary of the company as to the matters set out in sub-paragraphs (i) and (ii) of that paragraph.

(3B)   Any person who makes a false statement under subsection (3A) which he knows to be false or does not believe to be true is liable to imprisonment or a fine, or both.

(4)   'Relevant balance sheet' means a balance sheet prepared as at a date not more than 7 months before the company's application under this section.

(5)   A resolution that a company be re-registered as a public company may change the company name by deleting the word 'company' or the words 'and company', or its or their equivalent in Welsh ('cwmni', 'a'r cwmni'), including any abbreviation of them.

44. Consideration for shares recently allotted to be valued

(1)   The following applies if shares have been allotted by the company between the dates as at which the relevant balance sheet was prepared and the passing of the special resolution under section 43, and those shares were allotted as fully or partly paid up as to their nominal value or any premium on them otherwise than in cash.

(2)   Subject to the following provisions, the registrar of companies shall not entertain an application by the company under section 43 unless beforehand—

(a)   the consideration for the allotment has been valued in accordance with section 108, and

(b)   a report with respect to the value of the consideration has been made to the company (in accordance with that section) during the 6 months immediately preceding the allotment of the shares.

(3)   Where an amount standing to the credit of any of the company's reserve accounts, or of its profit and loss account, has been applied in paying up (to any extent) any of the shares allotted or any premium on those shares, the amount applied does not count as consideration for the allotment, and accordingly subsection (2) does not apply to it.

(4)   Subsection (2) does not apply if the allotment is in connection with an arrangement providing for it to be on terms that the whole or part of the consideration for the shares allotted is to be provided by the transfer to the company or the cancellation of all or some of the shares, or of all or some of the shares of a particular class, in another company (with or without the issue to the company applying under section 43 of shares, or of shares of any particular class, in that other company).

(5)   But subsection (4) does not exclude the application of subsection (2), unless under the arrangement it is open to all the holders of the shares of the other company in question (or, where the arrangement applies only to shares of a particular class, all the holders of the other company's shares of that class) to take part in the arrangement.

In determining whether that is the case, shares held by or by a nominee of the company allotting shares in connection with the arrangement, or by or by a nominee of a company which is that company's holding company or subsidiary or a company which is a subsidiary of its holding company, are to be disregarded.

(6)   Subsection (2) does not apply to preclude an application under section 43, if the allotment of the company's shares is in connection with its proposed merger with another company; that is, where one of the companies concerned proposes to acquire all the assets and liabilities of the other in exchange for the issue of shares or other securities of that one to shareholders of the other, with or without any cash payment to shareholders.

(7)   In this section—

(a)   'arrangement' means any agreement, scheme or arrangement, including an arrangement sanctioned in accordance with section 425 (company compromise with creditors and members) or section 110 of the Insolvency Act (liquidator in winding up accepting shares as consideration for sale of company's property), and

(b)   'another company' includes any body corporate and any body to which letters patent have been issued under the Chartered Companies Act 1837.

45.   Additional requirements relating to share capital

(1)   For a private company to be re-registered under section 43 as a public company, the following conditions with respect to its share capital must be satisfied at the time the special resolution under that section is passed.

(2)   Subject to subsections (5) to (7) below—

(a)   the nominal value of the company's allotted share capital must be not less than the authorised minimum, and

(b)   each of the company's allotted shares must be paid up at least as to one-quarter of the nominal value of that share and the whole of any premium on it.

(3)   Subject to subsection (5), if any shares in the company or any premium on them have been fully or partly paid up by an undertaking given by any person that he or another should do work or perform services (whether for the company or any other person), the undertaking must have been performed or otherwise discharged.

(4)   Subject to subsection (5), if shares have been allotted as fully or partly paid up as to their nominal value or any premium on them otherwise than in cash, and the consideration for the allotment consists of or includes an undertaking to the company (other than one to which subsection (3) applies), then either—

(a)   the undertaking must have been performed or otherwise discharged, or

(b)   there must be a contract between the company and some person pursuant to which the undertaking is to be performed within 5 years from the time the resolution under section 43 is passed.

(5)   For the purpose of determining whether subsection (2)(b), (3) and (4) are complied with, certain shares in the company may be disregarded; and these are—

(a)   subject to the next subsection, any share which was allotted before 22nd June 1982, and

(b)   any share which was allotted in pursuance of an employees' share scheme and by reason of which the company would, but for this subsection, be precluded under subsection (2)(b) (but not otherwise) from being re-registered as a public company.

(6)   A share is not to be disregarded under subsection (5)(a) if the aggregate in nominal value of that share and other shares proposed to be so disregarded is more than one-tenth of the nominal value of the company's allotted share capital; but for this purpose the allotted share capital is treated as not including any shares disregarded under subsection (5)(b).

(7)   Any shares disregarded under subsection (5) are treated as not forming part of the allotted share capital for the purposes of subsection (2)(a).

46.   Meaning of 'unqualified report' in s 43(3)

(1)   The following subsections explain the reference in section 43(3)(c) to an unqualified report of the company's auditors on the relevant balance sheet.

(2)   If the balance sheet was prepared for a financial year of the company, the reference is to an auditors' report stating without material qualifications the auditors' opinion that the balance sheet has been properly prepared in accordance with this Act.

(3)   If the balance sheet was not prepared for a financial year of the company, the reference is to an auditors' report stating without material qualification the auditors' opinion that the balance sheet has been properly prepared in accordance with the provisions of this Act which would have applied if it had been so prepared.

For the purposes of an auditors' report under this subsection the provisions of this Act shall be deemed to apply with such modifications as are necessary by reason of the fact that the balance sheet is not prepared for a financial year of the company.

(4)   A qualification shall be regarded as material unless the auditors state in their report that the matter giving rise to the qualification is not material for the purpose of determining (by reference to the company's balance sheet) whether at the balance sheet date the amount of the company's net assets was not less than the aggregate of its called up share capital and undistributable reserves.

In this subsection 'net assets' and 'undistributable reserves' have the meaning given by section 264(2) and (3).

47.   Certificate of re-registration under s 43

(1)   If the registrar of companies is satisfied, on an application under section 43, that a company may be re-registered under that section as a public company, he shall—

(a)   retain the application and other documents delivered to him under the section; and
(b)   issue the company with a certificate of incorporation stating that the company is a public company.

(2)   The registrar may accept a declaration under section 43(3)(e) or a statement under section 43(3A) as sufficient evidence that the special resolution required by that section has been passed and the other conditions of re-registration satisfied.

(3)   The registrar shall not issue the certificate if is appears to him that the court has made an order confirming a reduction of the company's capital which has the effect of bringing the nominal value of the company's allotted share capital below the authorised minimum.

(4)   Upon the issue to a company of a certificate of incorporation under this section—

(a)   the company by virtue of the issue of that certificate becomes a public company; and
(b)   any alterations in the memorandum and articles set out in the resolution take effect accordingly.

(5)   The certificate is conclusive evidence—

(a)   that the requirements of this Act in respect of re-registration and of matters precedent and incidental thereto have been complied with; and
(b)   that the company is a public company.

PART IV

ALLOTMENT OF SHARES AND DEBENTURES

80. Authority of company required for certain allotments

(1)   The directors of a company shall not exercise any power of the company to allot relevant securities, unless they are, in accordance with this section or section 80A, authorised to do so by—

(a)   the company in general meeting; or

(b)   the company's articles.

(2)   In this section 'relevant securities' means—

(a)   shares in the company other than shares shown in the memorandum to have been taken by the subscribers to it or shares allotted in pursuance of an employees' share scheme; and

(b)   any right to subscribe for, or to convert any security into, shares in the company (other than shares so allotted);

and a reference to the allotment of relevant securities includes the grant of such a right but (subject to subsection (6) below), not the allotment of shares pursuant to such a right.

(3)   Authority under this section may be given for a particular exercise of the power or for its exercise generally, and may be unconditional or subject to conditions.

(4)   The authority must state the maximum amount of relevant securities that may be allotted under it and the date on which it will expire, which must be not more than 5 years from whichever is relevant of the following dates—

(a)   in the case of an authority contained in the company's articles at the time of its original incorporation, the date of that incorporation; and

(b)   in any other case, the date on which the resolution is passed by virtue of which the authority is given;

but such an authority (including an authority contained in the articles) may be previously revoked or varied by the company in general meeting.

(5)   The authority may be renewed or further renewed by the company in general meeting for a further period not exceeding 5 years; but the resolution must state (or restate) the amount of relevant securities which may be allotted under the authority or, as the case may be, the amount remaining to be allotted under it, and must specify the date on which the renewed authority will expire.

(6)   In relation to authority under this section for the grant of such rights as are mentioned in subsection (2)(b), the reference in subsection (4) (as also the corresponding reference in subsection (5)) to the maximum amount of relevant securities that may be allotted under the authority is to the maximum amount of shares which may be allotted pursuant to the rights.

(7)   The directors may allot relevant securities, notwithstanding that authority under this section has expired, if they are allotted in pursuance of an offer or agreement made by the company before the authority expired and the authority allowed it to make an offer or agreement which would or might require relevant securities to be allotted after the authority expired.

(8)   A resolution of a company to give, vary, revoke or renew such an authority may, notwithstanding that it alters the company's articles, be an ordinary resolution; but it is in any case subject to section 380 of this Act (copy to be forwarded to registrar within 15 days).

(9)   A director who knowingly and wilfully contravenes, or permits or authorises a contravention of, this section is liable to a fine.

(10)   Nothing in this section affects the validity of any allotment.

(11)   This section does not apply to any allotment of relevant securities by a company, other than a public company registered as such on its original incorporation, if it is made in pursuance of an offer or agreement made before the earlier of the following two dates—

(a)   the date of the holding of the first general meeting of the company after its registration or re-registration as a public company, and

(b)   22nd June 1982,

but any resolution to give, vary or revoke an authority for the purposes of section 14 of the Companies Act 1980 or this section has effect for those purposes if passed at any time after the end of April 1980.

80A. Election by private company as to duration of authority

(1)   A private company may elect (by elective resolution in accordance with section 379(A) that the provisions of this section shall apply, instead of the provisions of section 80(4) and (5), in relation to the giving or renewal, after the election, of an authority under that section.

(2)   The authority must state the maximum amount of relevant securities that may be allotted under it and may be given—

(a)   for an indefinite period, or
(b)   for a fixed period, in which case it must state the date on which it will expire.

(3)   In either case an authority (including an authority contained in the articles) may be revoked or varied by the company in general meeting.

(4)   An authority given for a fixed period may be renewed or further renewed by the company in general meeting.

(5)   A resolution renewing an authority—

(a)   must state, or re-state, the amount of relevant securities which may be allotted under the authority or, as the case may be, the amount remaining to be allotted under it, and
(b)   must state whether the authority is renewed for an indefinite period or for a fixed period, in which case it must state the date on which the renewed authority will expire.

(6)   The references in this section to the maximum amount of relevant securities that may be allotted shall be construed in accordance with section 80(6).

(7)   If an election under this section ceases to have effect, an authority then in force which was given for an indefinite period or for a fixed period of more than five years—

(a)   if given five years or more before the election ceases to have effect, shall expire forthwith, and
(b)   otherwise, shall have effect as if it had been given for a fixed period of five years.

81.   Restriction on public offers by private company

(1)   A private limited company (other than a company limited by guarantee and not having a share capital) commits an offence if it—

(a)   offers to the public (whether for cash or otherwise) any shares in or debentures of the company; or
(b)   allots or agrees to allot (whether for cash or otherwise) any shares in or debentures of the company with a view to all or any of those shares or debentures being offered for sale to the public (within the meaning given to that expression by sections 58 to 60).

(2)   A company guilty of an offence under this section, and any officer of it who is in default, is liable to a fine.

(3)   Nothing in this section affects the validity of any allotment or sale of shares or debentures, or of any agreement to allot or sell shares or debenture. [Section rep for certain purposes]

85.   Effect of irregular allotment

(1)   An allotment made by a company to an applicant in contravention of section *83 or* 84 is voidable at the instance of the applicant within one month after the date of the allotment, and not later, and is so voidable notwithstanding that the company is in the course of being wound up. [Words in italics rep for certain purposes]

(2)   If a director of a company knowingly contravenes, or permits or authorises the contravention of, any provision of either of those sections with respect to allotment, he is liable to compensate the company and the allottee respectively for any loss, damages or costs which the company or the allottee may have sustained or incurred by the contravention.

(3)   But proceedings to recover any such loss, damages or costs shall not be commenced after the expiration of 2 years from the date of the allotment.

Part II Company

89.   Offers to shareholders to be on pre-emptive basis

(1)   Subject to the provisions of this section and the seven sections next following, a company proposing to allot equity securities (defined in section 94)—

(a)   shall not allot any of them on any terms to a person unless it has made an offer to each person who holds relevant shares or relevant employee shares to allot to him on the same or more favourable terms a proportion of those securities which is as nearly as practicable equal to the proportion in nominal value held by him of the aggregate of relevant shares and relevant employee shares, and

(b)   shall not allot any of those securities to a person unless the period during which any such offer may be accepted has expired or the company has received notice of the acceptance or refusal of every offer so made.

(2)   Subsection (3) below applies to any provisions of a company's memorandum or articles which requires the company, when proposing to allot equity securities consisting of relevant shares of any particular class, not to allot those securities on any terms unless it has complied with the condition that it makes such an offer as is described in subsection (1) to each person who holds relevant shares or relevant employee shares of that class.

(3)   If in accordance with a provisions to which this subsection applies—

(a)   a company makes an offer to allot securities to such a holder, and

(b)   he or anyone in whose favour he has renounced his right to their allotment accepts the offer,

subsection (1) does not apply to the allotment of those securities, and the company may allot them accordingly; but this is without prejudice to the application of subsection (1) in any other case.

(4)   Subsection (1) does not apply to a particular allotment of equity securities if these are, or are to be, wholly or partly paid up otherwise than in cash; and securities which a company has offered to allot to a holder of relevant shares or relevant employee shares may be allotted to him, or anyone in whose favour he has renounced his right to their allotment, without contravening subsection (1)(b).

(5)   Subsection (1) does not apply to the allotment of securities which would, apart from a renunciation or assignment of the right to their allotment, be held under an employees' share scheme.

90.   Communication of pre-emption offers to shareholders

(1)   This section has effect as to the manner in which offers required by section 89(1), or by a provision to which section 89(3) applies, are to be made to holders of a company's shares.

(2)   Subject to the following subsections, an offer shall be in writing and shall be made to a holder of shares either personally or by sending it by post (that is to say, prepaying and posting a letter containing the offer) to him or to his registered address or, if he has no registered address in the United Kingdom, to the address in the United Kingdom supplied by him to the company for the giving of notice to him.

If sent by post, the offer is deemed to be made at the time at which the letter would be delivered in the ordinary course of post.

(3)   Where shares are held by two or more persons jointly, the offer may be made to the joint holder first named in the register of members in respect of the shares.

(4)   In the case of a holder's death or bankruptcy, the offer may be made—

(a)   by sending it by post in a prepaid letter addressed to the persons claiming to be entitled to the shares in consequence of the death or bankruptcy by name, or by the title of representatives of the deceased, or trustee of the bankrupt, or by any like description, at the address in the United Kingdom supplied for the purpose by those so claiming, or

(b)   (until such an address has been so supplied) by giving the notice in any manner in which it might have been given if the death or bankruptcy had not occurred.

(5)   If the holder—

(a)   has no registered address in the United Kingdom and has not given to the company an address in the United Kingdom for the service of notices on him, or

(b)   is the holder of a share warrant,

the offer may be made by causing it, or a notice specifying where a copy of it can be obtained or inspected, to be published in the *Gazette*.

(6)   The offer must state a period of not less than 21 days during which it may be accepted; and the offer shall not be withdrawn before the end of that period.

(7)   This section does not invalidate a provision to which section 89(3) applies by reason that that provision requires or authorises an offer under it to be made in contravention of any of subsections (1) to (6) above; but, to the extent that the provision requires or authorises such an offer to be so made, it is of no effect.

91.   Exclusion of ss 89, 90 by private company

(1)   Section 89(1), section 90(1) to (5) or section 90(6) may, as applying to allotments by a private company of equity securities or to such allotments of a particular description, be excluded by a provision contained in the memorandum or articles of that company.

(2)   A requirement or authority contained in the memorandum or articles of a private company, if it is inconsistent with any of those subsections, has effect as a provision excluding that subsection; but a provision to which section 89(3) applies is not to be treated as inconsistent with section 89(1).

92.   Consequences of contravening ss 89, 90

(1)   If there is a contravention of section 89(1), or of section 90(1) to (5) or section 90(6), or of a provision to which section 89(3) applies, the company, and every officer of it who knowingly authorised or permitted the contravention, are jointly and severally liable to compensate any person to whom an offer should have been made under the subsection or provision contravened for any loss, damage, costs or expenses which the person has sustained or incurred by reason of the contravention.

(2)   However, no proceedings to recover any such loss, damage, costs or expenses shall be commenced after the expiration of 2 years from the delivery to the registrar of companies of the return of allotments in question or, where equity securities other than shares are granted, from the date of the grant.

93.   Saving for other restrictions as to offers

(1)   Sections 89 to 92 are without prejudice to any enactment by virtue of which a company is prohibited (whether generally or in specified circumstances) from offering or allotting equity securities to any person.

(2)   Where a company cannot by virtue of such an enactment offer or allot equity securities to a holder of relevant shares or relevant employee shares, those sections have effect as if the shares held by that holder were not relevant shares or relevant employee shares.

94.   Definitions for ss 89–96

(1)   The following subsections apply for the interpretation of sections 89 to 96.

(2)   'Equity security', in relation to a company, means a relevant share in the company (other than a share shown in the memorandum to have been taken by a subscriber to the memorandum or a bonus share), or a right to subscribe for, or to convert securities into, relevant shares in the company.

(3)   A reference to the allotment of equity securities or of equity securities consisting of relevant shares of a particular class includes the grant of a right to subscribe for, or to convert any securities into, relevant shares in the company or (as the case may be) relevant shares of a particular class; but such a reference does not include the allotment of any relevant shares pursuant to such a right.

(4)   'Relevant employee shares', in relation to a company, means shares of the company which would be relevant in it but for the fact that they are held by a person who acquired them in pursuance of an employees' share scheme.

(5)   'Relevant shares', in relation to a company, means shares in the company other than—

    (a)   shares which as respects dividends and capital carry a right to participate only up to a specified amount in a distribution, and

    (b)   shares which are held by a person who acquired them in pursuance of an employees' share scheme or, in the case of shares which have not been allotted, are to be allotted in pursuance of such a scheme.

(6)   A reference to a class of shares is to shares to which the same rights are attached as to voting and as to participation, both as respects dividends and as respects capital, in a distribution.

(7)   In relation to an offer to allot securities required by section 89(1) or by any provision to which section 89(3) applies, a reference in sections 89 to 94 (however expressed) to the holder of shares of any description is to whoever

was at the close of business on a date, to be specified in the offer and to fall in the period of 28 days immediately before the date of the offer, the holder of shares of that description.

95. Disapplication of pre-emption rights

(1) Where the directors of a company are generally authorised for purposes of section 80, they may be given power by the articles, or by a special resolution of the company, to allot equity securities pursuant to that authority as if—

(a) section 89(1) did not apply to the allotment, or

(b) that subsection applied to the allotment with such modifications as the directors may determine;

and where the directors make an allotment under this subsection, sections 89 to 94 have effect accordingly.

(2) Where the directors of a company are authorised for purposes of section 80 (whether generally or otherwise), the company may by special resolution resolve either—

(a) that section 89(1) shall not apply to a specified allotment of equity securities to be made pursuant to that authority, or

(b) that that subsection shall apply to the allotment with such modifications as may be specified in the resolution;

and where such a resolution is passed, sections 89 to 94 have effect accordingly.

(3) The power conferred by subsection (1) or a special resolution under subsection (2) ceases to have effect when the authority to which it relates is revoked or would (if not renewed) expire; but if the authority is renewed, the power or (as the case may be) the resolution may also be renewed, for a period not longer than that for which the authority is renewed, by a special resolution of the company.

(4) Notwithstanding that any such power or resolution has expired, the directors may allot equity securities in pursuance of an offer or agreement previously made by the company, if the power or resolution enabled the company to make an offer or agreement which would or might require equity securities to be allotted after it expired.

(5) A special resolution under subsection (2), or a special resolution to renew such a resolution, shall not be proposed unless it is recommended by the directors and there has been circulated, with the notice of the meeting at which the resolution is proposed, to the members entitled to have that notice a written statement by the directors setting out—

(a) their reasons for making the recommendation,

(b) the amount to be paid to the company in respect of the equity securities to be allotted, and

(c) the directors' justification of that amount.

(6) A person who knowingly or recklessly authorises or permits the inclusion in a statement circulated under subsection (5) of any matter which is misleading, false or deceptive in a material particular is liable to imprisonment or a fine, or both.

100. Prohibition on allotment of shares at a discount

(1) A company's shares shall not be allotted at a discount.

(2) If shares are allotted in contravention of this section, the allottee is liable to pay the company an amount equal to the amount of the discount, with interest at the appropriate rate.

PART V

SHARE CAPITAL, ITS INCREASE, MAINTENANCE AND REDUCTION

117. Public company share capital requirements

(1) A company share registered as a public company on its original incorporation shall not do business or exercise any borrowing powers unless the registrar of companies has issued it with a certificate under this section or the company is re-registered as a private company.

(2) The registrar shall issue a company with such a certificate if, on an application made to him by the company in the prescribed form, he is satisfied that the nominal value of the company's allotted share capital is not less than

the authorised minimum, and there is delivered to him a statutory declaration complying with the following subsection. This subsection is subject to subsection (3A).

(3)   The statutory declaration must be in the prescribed form and be signed by a director or secretary of the company; and it must—

    (a)   state that the nominal value of the company's allotted share capital is not less than the authorised minimum;

    (b)   specify the amount paid up, at the time of the application, on the allotted share capital of the company;

    (c)   specify the amount, or estimated amount, of the company's preliminary expenses and the persons by whom any of those expenses have been paid or are payable; and

    (d)   specify any amount or benefit paid or given, or intended to be paid or given, to any promoter of the company, and the consideration for the payment or benefit.

(3A)   In place of the statutory declaration referred to in subsection (2), there may be delivered to the registrar of companies using electronic communications a statement made by a director or secretary of the company complying with the requirements of subsection (3)(a) to (d).

(4)   For the purposes of subsection (2), a share allotted in pursuance of an employees' share scheme may not be taken into account in determining the nominal value of the company's allotted share capital unless it is paid up at least as to one-quarter of the nominal value of the share and the whole of any premium on the share.

(5)   The registrar may accept a statutory declaration or statement delivered to him under this section as sufficient evidence of the matters stated in it.

(6)   A certificate under this section in respect of a company is conclusive evidence that the company is entitled to do business and exercise any borrowing powers.

(7)   If a company does business or exercises borrowing powers in contravention of this section, the company and any officer of it who is in default is liable to a fine.

(7A)   Any person who makes a false statement under subsection (3A) which he knows to be false or does not believe to be true is liable to imprisonment or a fine, or both.

(8)   Nothing in this section affects the validity of any transaction entered into by a company; but, if a company enters into a transaction in contravention of this section and fails to comply with its obligations in that connection within 21 days from being called upon to do so; the directors of the company are jointly and severally liable to indemnify the other party to the transaction in respect of any loss or damage suffered by him by reason of the company's failure to comply with those obligations.

118. The authorised minimum

(1)   In this Act, 'the authorised minimum' means £50,000, or such other sum as the Secretary of State may by order made by statutory instrument specify instead.

(2)   An order under this section which increases the authorised minimum may—

    (a)   require any public company having an allotted share capital of which the nominal value is less than the amount specified in the order as the authorised minimum to increase that value to not less than that amount or make application to be re-registered as a private company;

    (b)   make, in connection with any such requirement, provisions for any of the matters from which provision is made by this Act relating to a company's registration, re-registration or change of name, to payment for any share comprised in a company's capital and to offers of shares in or debentures of a company to the public, including provision as to the consequences (whether in criminal law or otherwise) of a failure to comply with any requirement of the order; and

    (c)   contain such supplemental and transitional provisions as the Secretary of State thinks appropriate, make different provision for different cases and, in particular, provide for any provision of the order to come into operation on different days for different purposes.

(3)   An order shall not be made under this section unless a draft of it has been laid before Parliament and approved by resolution of each House.

121. Alteration of share capital (limited companies)

(1)   A company limited by shares or a company limited by guarantee and having a share capital, if so authorised by its articles, may alter the conditions of its memorandum in any of the following ways.

(2)   The company may—

    (a)   increase its share capital by new shares of such amount as it thinks expedient;

    (b)   consolidate and divide all or any of its share capital into shares of larger amount than its existing shares;

    (c)   convert all or any of its paid-up shares into stock, and re-convert that stock into paid-up shares of any denomination;

    (d)   sub-divide its shares, or any of them, into shares of smaller amount than is fixed by the memorandum (but subject to the following subsection);

    (e)   cancel shares which, at the date of the passing of the resolution to cancel them, have not been taken or agreed to be taken by any person, and diminish the amount of the company's share capital by the amount of the shares so cancelled.

(3)   In any sub-division under subsection (2)(d) the proportion between the amount paid and the amount, if any, unpaid on each reduced share must be the same as it was in the case of the share from which the reduced share is derived.

(4)   The powers conferred by this section must be exercised by the company in general meeting.

(5)   A cancellation of shares under this section does not for purposes of this Act constitute a reduction of share capital.

123. Notice to registrar of increased share capital

(1)   If a company having a share capital (whether or not its shares have been converted into stock) increases its share capital beyond the registered capital, it shall within 15 days after the passing of the resolution authorising the increase, give to the registrar of companies notice of the increase, and the registrar shall record the increase.

(2)   The notice must include such particulars as may be prescribed with respect to the classes of shares affected and the conditions subject to which the new shares have been or are to be issued.

(3)   There shall be forwarded to the registrar together with the notice a printed copy of the resolution authorising the increase, or a copy of the resolution in some other form approved by the registrar.

(4)   If default is made in complying with this section, the company and every officer of it who is in default is liable to a fine and, for continued contravention, to a daily default fine.

130. Application of share premiums

(1)   If a company issues shares at a premium, whether for cash or otherwise, a sum equal to the aggregate amount or value of the premiums on those shares shall be transferred to an account called 'the share premium account'.

(2)   The share premium account may be applied by the company in paying up unissued shares to be allotted to members as fully paid bonus shares, or in writing off—

    (a)   the company's preliminary expenses; or

    (b)   the expenses of, or the commission paid or discount allowed on, any issue of shares or debentures of the company, or in providing for the premium payable on redemption of debentures of the company.

(3)   Subject to this, the provisions of this Act relating to the reduction of a company's share capital apply as if the share premium account were part of its paid up share capital.

(4)   Sections 131 and 132 below give relief from the requirements of this section, and in those sections references to the issuing company are to the company issuing shares as above mentioned.

135. Special resolution for reduction of share capital

(1)   Subject to confirmation by the court, a company limited by shares or a company limited by guarantee and having a share capital may, if so authorised by its articles, by special resolution reduce its share capital in any way.

(2)   In particular, and without prejudice to subsection (1), the company may—

    (a)   extinguish or reduce the liability on any of its shares in respect of share capital not paid up; or

    (b)   either with or without extinguishing or reducing liability on any of its shares, cancel any paid-up share capital which is lost or unrepresented by available assets; or

    (c)   either with or without extinguishing or reducing liability on any of its shares, pay off any paid-up share capital which is in excess of the company's wants;

and the company may, if and so far as is necessary, alter its memorandum by reducing the amount of its share capital and of its shares accordingly.

(3)   A special resolution under this section is in this Act referred to as 'a resolution for reducing share capital'.

136.   Application to court for order of confirmation

(1)   Where a company has passed a resolution for reducing share capital, it may apply to the court for an order confirming the reduction.

(2)   If the proposed reduction of share capital involves either—

(a)   diminution of liability in respect of unpaid share capital; or
(b)   the payment to a shareholder of any paid-up share capital,

and in any other case if the court so directs, the next three subsections have effect, but subject throughout to subsection (6).

(3)   Every creditor of the company who at the date fixed by the court is entitled to any debt or claim which if that date were the commencement of the winding up of the company, would be admissible in proof against the company is entitled to object to the reduction of capital.

(4)   The court shall settle a list of creditors entitled to object, and for that purpose—

(a)   shall ascertain, as far as possible without requiring an application from any creditor, the names of those creditors and the nature and amount of their debts or claim; and
(b)   may publish notices fixing a day or days within which creditors not entered on the list are to claim to be so entered or are to be excluded from the right of objecting to the reduction of capital.

(5)   If a creditor entered on the list whose debt or claim is not discharged or has not determined does not consent to the reduction, the court may, if it thinks fit, dispense with the consent of that creditor, on the company securing payment of his debt or claim by appropriating (as the court may direct) the following amount—

(a)   if the company admits the full amount of the debt or claim or, though not admitting it, is willing to provide for it, then the full amount of the debt or claim;
(b)   if the company does not admit, and is not willing to provide for, the full amount of the debt or claim, or if the amount is contingent or not ascertained, then an amount fixed by the court after the like enquiry and adjudication as if the company were being wound up by the court.

(6)   If a proposed reduction of share capital involves either the diminution of any liability in respect of unpaid share capital or the payment to any shareholder of any paid-up share capital, the court may, if having regard to any special circumstances of the case it thinks proper to do so, direct that subsections (3) to (5) of this section shall not apply as regards any class or any classes of creditors.

137.   Court order confirming reduction

(1)   The court, if satisfied with respect to every creditor of the company who under section 136 is entitled to object to the reduction of capital that either—

(a)   his consent to the reduction has been obtained; or
(b)   his debt or claim has been discharged or has determined, or has been secured,

may make an order confirming the reduction on such terms and conditions as it thinks fit.

(2)   Where the court so orders, it may also—

(a)   if for any special reason it thinks proper to do so, make an order directing that the company shall, during such period (commencing on or at any time after the date of the order) as is specified in the order, add to its name as its last words the words 'and reduced'; and
(b)   make an order requiring the company to publish (as the court directs) the reasons for reduction of capital or such other information in regard to it as the court thinks expedient with a view to giving proper information to the public and (if the court thinks fit) the causes which led to the reduction.

(3)   Where a company is ordered to add to its name the words 'and reduced', those words are, until the expiration of the period specified in the order, deemed to be part of the company's name.

143. General rule against company acquiring own shares

(1)   Subject to the following provisions, a company limited by shares or limited by guarantee and having a share capital shall not acquire its own shares, whether by purchase, subscription or otherwise.

(2)   If a company purports to act in contravention of this section, the company is liable to a fine, and every officer of the company who is in default is liable to imprisonment or a fine, or both; and the purported acquisition is void.

(3)   A company limited by shares may acquire any of its own fully paid shares otherwise than for valuable consideration; and subsection (1) does not apply in relation to—

    (a)   the redemption or purchase of shares in accordance with Chapter VII of this Part,
    (b)   the acquisition of shares in a reduction of capital duly made,
    (c)   the purchase of shares in pursuance of an order of the court under section 5 (alteration of objects), section 54 (litigated objection to resolution for company to be re-registered as private) or Part XVII (relief to members unfairly prejudiced), or
    (d)   the forfeiture of shares, or the acceptance of shares surrendered in lieu, in pursuance of the articles, for failure to pay any sum payable in respect of the shares.

144. Acquisition of shares by company's nominee

(1)   Subject to section 145, where shares are issued to a nominee of a company mentioned in section 143(1), or are acquired by a nominee of such a company from a third person as partly paid up, then, for all purposes—

    (a)   the shares are to be treated as held by the nominee on his own account; and
    (b)   the company is to be regarded as having no beneficial interest in them.

(2)   Subject to that section, if a person is called on to pay any amount for the purpose of paying up, or paying any premium on, any shares in such a company which were issued to him, or which he otherwise acquired, as the company's nominee and he fails to pay that amount within 21 days from being called on to do so, then—

    (a)   if the shares were issued to or acquired by him as subscriber to the memorandum by virtue of an undertaking of his in the memorandum, the other subscribers to the memorandum, or
    (b)   if the shares were otherwise issued to or acquired by him, the directors of the company at the time of the issue or acquisition,

are jointly and severally liable with him to pay that amount.

(3)   If in proceedings for the recovery of any such amount from any such subscriber or director under this section it appears to the court—

    (a)   that he is or may be liable to pay that amount, but
    (b)   that he has acted honestly and reasonably and, having regard to all the circumstances of the case, he ought fairly to be excused from liability,

the court may relieve him, either wholly or partly, from his liability on such terms as the court thinks fit.

(4)   Where any such subscriber or director has reason to apprehend that a claim will or might be made for the recovery of any such amount from him, he may apply to the court for relief; and the court has the same power to relieve him as it would have had in proceedings for the recovery of that amount.

151. Financial assistance generally prohibited

(1)   Subject to the following provisions of this Chapter, where a person is acquiring or is proposing to acquire shares in a company, it is not lawful for the company or any of its subsidiaries to give financial assistance directly or indirectly for the purpose of that acquisition before or at the same time as the acquisition takes place.

(2)   Subject to those provisions, where a person has acquired shares in a company and any liability has been incurred (by that or any other person), for the purpose of that acquisition, it is not lawful for the company or any of its subsidiaries to give financial assistance directly or indirectly for the purpose of reducing or discharging the liability so incurred.

(3)   If a company acts in contravention of this section, it is liable to a fine, and every officer of it who is in default is liable to imprisonment or a fine, or both.

152. Definitions for this Chapter

(1) In this Chapter—

    (a) 'financial assistance' means—

        (i) financial assistance given by way of gift,

        (ii) financial assistance given by way of guarantee, security or indemnity, other than an indemnity in respect of the indemnifier's own neglect or default, or by way of release or waiver,

        (iii) financial assistance given by way of a loan or any other agreement under which any of the obligations of the person giving the assistance are to be fulfilled at a time when in accordance with the agreement any obligation of another party to the agreement remains unfulfilled, or by way of the novation of, or the assignment of rights arising under, a loan or such other agreement, or

        (iv) any other financial assistance given by a company the net assets of which are thereby reduced to a material extent or which has no net assets;

    (b) 'distributable profits', in relation to the giving of any financial assistance—

        (i) means those profits out of which the company could lawfully make a distribution equal in value to that assistance, and

        (ii) includes, in a case where the financial assistance is or includes a non-cash asset, any profit which, if the company were to make a distribution of that asset, would under section 276 (distributions in kind) be available for that purpose, and

    (c) 'distribution' has the meaning given by section 263(2).

(2) In subsection (1)(a)(iv), 'net assets' means the aggregate of the company's assets, less the aggregate of its liabilities ('liabilities' to include any provision for liabilities or charges within paragraph 89 of Schedule 4).

(3) In this Chapter—

    (a) a reference to a person incurring a liability includes his changing his financial position by making an agreement or arrangement (whether enforceable or unenforceable, and whether made on his own account or with any other person) or by any other means, and

    (b) a reference to a company giving financial assistance for the purpose of reducing or discharging a liability incurred by a person for the purpose of the acquisition of shares includes its giving such assistance for the purpose of wholly or partly restoring his financial position to what it was before the acquisition took place.

153. Transactions not prohibited by s 151

(1) Section 151(1) does not prohibit a company from giving financial assistance for the purpose of an acquisition of shares in it or its holding company if—

    (a) the company's principal purpose in giving that assistance is not to give it for the purpose of any such acquisition, or the giving of the assistance for that purpose is but an incidental part of some larger purpose of the company, and

    (b) the assistance is given in good faith in the interests of the company.

(2) Section 151(2) does not prohibit a company from giving financial assistance if—

    (a) the company's principal purpose in giving the assistance is not to reduce or discharge any liability incurred by a person for the purpose of the acquisition of shares in the company or its holding company, or the reduction or discharge of any such liability is but an incidental part of some larger purpose of the company, and

    (b) the assistance is given in good faith in the interests of the company.

(3) Section 151 does not prohibit—

    (a) a distribution of a company's assets by way of dividend lawfully made or a distribution made in the course of the company's winding up,

    (b) the allotment of bonus shares,

    (c) a reduction of capital confirmed by order of the court under section 137,

    (d) a redemption or purchase of shares made in accordance with Chapter VII of this Part,

    (e) anything done in pursuance of an order of the court under section 425 (compromises and arrangements with creditors and members),

(f) anything done under an arrangement made in pursuance of section 110 of the Insolvency Act (acceptance of shares by liquidator in winding up as consideration for sale of property), or

(g) anything done under an arrangement made between a company and its creditors which is binding on the creditors by virtue of Part I of the Insolvency Act.

(4) Section 151 does not prohibit—

(a) where the lending of money is part of the ordinary business of the company, the lending of money by the company in the ordinary course of its business,

(b) the provision by a company, in good faith in the interests of the company, of financial assistance for the purposes of an employees' share scheme,

(bb) without prejudice to paragraph (b), the provision of financial assistance by a company or any of its subsidiaries for the purposes of or in connection with anything done by the company (or a company in the same group) for the purpose of enabling or facilitating transactions in shares in the first-mentioned company between, and involving the acquisition of beneficial ownership of those shares by, any of the following persons—

(i) the bona fide employees or former employees of that company or of another company in the same group; or

(ii) the wives, husbands, widows, widowers, children or stepchildren under the age of eighteen of any such employees or former employees,

(c) the making by a company of loans to persons (other than directors) employed in good faith by the company with a view to enabling those persons to acquire fully paid shares in the company or its holding company to be held by them by way of beneficial ownership.

(5) For the purposes of subsection (4)(bb) a company is in the same group as another company if it is a holding company or subsidiary of that company, or a subsidiary of a holding company of that company.

154. Special restriction for public companies

(1) In the case of a public company, section 153(4) authorises the giving of financial assistance only if the company has net assets which are not thereby reduced or, to the extent that those assets are thereby reduced, if the assistance is provided out of distributable profits.

(2) For this purpose the following definitions apply—

(a) 'net assets' means the amount by which the aggregate of the company's assets exceeds the aggregate of its liabilities (taking the amount of both assets and liabilities to be as stated in the company's accounting records immediately before the financial assistance is given);

(b) 'liabilities' includes any amount retained as reasonably necessary for the purpose of providing for any liability or loss which is either likely to be incurred, or certain to be incurred but uncertain as to amount or as to the date on which it will arise.

155. Relaxation of s 151 for private companies

(1) Section 151 does not prohibit a private company from giving financial assistance in a case where the acquisition of shares in question is or was an acquisition of shares in the company or, if it is a subsidiary of another private company, in that other company if the following provisions of this section, and section 156 to 158, are complied with as respects the giving of that assistance.

(2) The financial assistance may only be given if the company has net assets which are not thereby reduced or, to the extent that they are reduced, if the assistance is provided out of distributable profits.

Section 154(2) applies for the interpretation of this subsection.

(3) This section does not permit financial assistance to be given by a subsidiary, in a case where the acquisition of shares in question is or was an acquisition of shares in its holding company, if it is also a subsidiary of a public company which is itself a subsidiary of that holding company.

(4) Unless the company proposing to give the financial assistance is a wholly-owned subsidiary, the giving of assistance under this section must be approved by special resolution of the company in general meeting.

(5) Where the financial assistance is to be given by the company in a case where the acquisition of shares in question is or was an acquisition of shares in its holding company, that holding company and any other company which is both the company's holding company and a subsidiary of that other holding company (except, in any case,

a company which is a wholly-owned subsidiary) shall also approve by special resolution in general meeting the giving of the financial assistance.

(6)   Subject to subsection (6A), the directors of the company proposing to give the financial assistance and, where the shares acquired or to be acquired are shares in its holding company, the directors of that company and of any other company which is both the company's holding company and a subsidiary of that other holding company shall before the financial assistance is given make a statutory declaration in the prescribed form complying with the section next following.

(6A) In place of the statutory declaration referred to in subsection (6), there may be delivered to the registrar of companies under section 156(5) a statement made by the persons mentioned in subsection (6) above complying with the section next following.

156. Statutory declaration under s 155

(1)   A statutory declaration made by a company's directors under section 155(6) shall contain such particulars of the financial assistance to be given, and of the business of the company of which they are directors, as may be prescribed, and shall identify the person to whom the assistance is to be given.

(1A) A statement made by a company's directors under section 155(6A) shall state—

    (a)   the names and addresses of all the directors of the company,

    (b)   whether the business of the company is that of a banking company or insurance company or some other business,

    (c)   that the company or (as the case may be) a company (naming such company) of which it is the holding company is proposing to give financial assistance in connection with the acquisition of shares in the company or (as the case may be) its holding company (naming that holding company),

    (d)   whether the assistance is for the purpose of that acquisition or for reducing or discharging a liability incurred for the purpose of that acquisition,

    (e)   the name and address of the person to whom the assistance is to be given (and in the case of a company its registered office),

    (f)   the name of the person who has acquired or will acquire the shares and the number and class of the shares acquired or to be acquired,

    (g)   the principal terms on which the assistance will be given,

    (h)   the form the financial assistance will take (stating the amount of cash or value of any asset to be transferred to the person assisted), and

    (i)   the date on which the assistance is to be given.

(2)   The declaration under section 155(6) or (as the case may be) statement under section 155(6A) shall state that the directors have formed the opinion, as regards the company's initial situation immediately following the date on which the assistance is proposed to be given, that there will be no ground on which it could then be found to be unable to pay its debts; and either—

    (a)   if it is intended to commence the winding up of the company within 12 months of that date, that the company will be able to pay its debts in full within 12 months of the commencement of the winding up, or

    (b)   in any other case, that the company will be able to pay its debts as they fall due during the year immediately following that date.

(3)   In forming their opinion for purposes of subsection (2), the directors shall take into account the same liabilities (including contingent and prospective liabilities) as would be relevant under section 122 of the Insolvency Act (winding up by the court) to the question whether the company is unable to pay its debts.

(4)   The directors' statutory declaration or statement shall have annexed to it a report addressed to them by their company's auditors stating that—

    (a)   they have enquired into the state of affairs of the company, and

    (b)   they are not aware of anything to indicate that the opinion expressed by the directors in the declaration as to any of the matters mentioned in subsection (2) of this section is unreasonable in all the circumstances.

(5)   The statutory declaration or statement and auditors' report shall be delivered to the registrar of companies—

    (a)   together with a copy of any special resolution passed by the company under section 155 and delivered to the registrar in compliance with section 380, or

(b)   where no such resolution is required to be passed, within 15 days after the making of the declaration.

(6)   If a company fails to comply with subsection (5), the company and every officer of it who is in default is liable to a fine and, for continued contravention, to a daily default fine.

(7)   A director of a company who makes a statutory declaration or statement under section 155 without having reasonable grounds for the opinion expressed in it is liable to imprisonment or a fine, or both.

157. Special resolution under s 155

(1)   A special resolution required by section 155 to be passed by a company approving the giving of financial assistance must be passed on the date on which the directors of that company make the statutory declaration or statement required by that section in connection with the giving of that assistance, or within the week immediately following that date.

(2)   Where such a resolution has been passed, an application may be made to the court for the cancellation of the resolution—

(a)   by the holders of not less in the aggregate than 10 per cent in nominal value of the company's issued share capital or any class of it, or

(b)   if the company is not limited by shares, by not less than 10 per cent of the company's members;

but the application shall not be made by a person who has consented to or voted in favour of the resolution.

(3)   Subsections (3) to (10) of section 54 (litigation to cancel resolution under section 53) apply to applications under this section as to applications under section 54.

(4)   A special resolution passed by a company is not effective for purposes of section 155—

(a)   unless the declaration or statement made in compliance with subsection (6) of that section by the directors of the company, together with the auditors' report annexed to it, is available for inspection by members of the company at the meeting at which the resolution is passed,

(b)   if it is cancelled by the court on an application under this section.

158. Time for giving financial assistance under s 155

(1)   This section applies as to the time before and after which financial assistance may not be given by a company in pursuance of section 155.

(2)   Where a special resolution is required by that section to be passed approving the giving of the assistance, the assistance shall not be given before the expiry of the period of 4 weeks beginning with—

(a)   the date on which the special resolution is passed, or

(b)   where more than one such resolution is passed, the date on which the last of them is passed,

unless, as respects that resolution (or, if more than one, each of them) every member of the company which passed the resolution who is entitled to vote at general meetings of the company voted in favour of the resolution.

(3)   If application for the cancellation of any such resolution is made under section 157, the financial assistance shall not be given before the final determination of the application unless the court otherwise orders.

(4)   The assistance shall not be given after the expiry of the period of 8 weeks beginning with—

(a)   the date on which the directors of the company proposing to give the assistance made their statutory declaration or statement under section 155, or

(b)   where that company is a subsidiary and both its directors and the directors of any of its holding companies made such a declaration or statement, the date on which the earliest of the declarations or statements is made,

unless the court, on an application under section 157, otherwise orders.

159. Power to issue redeemable shares

(1)   Subject to the provisions of this Chapter, a company limited by shares or limited by guarantee and having a share capital may, if authorised to do so by its articles, issue shares which are to be redeemed or are liable to be redeemed at the option of the company or the shareholder.

(2) No redeemable shares may be issued at a time when there are no issued shares of the company which are not redeemable.

(3) Redeemable shares may not be redeemed unless they are fully paid; and the terms of redemption must provide for payment on redemption.

159A. ***Terms and manner of redemption*** [Prosp ins]

(1) Redeemable shares may not be issued unless the following conditions are satisfied as regards the terms and manner of redemption.

(2) The date on or by which, or dates between which, the shares are to be or may be redeemed must be specified in the company's articles or, if the articles so provide, fixed by the directors, and in the latter case the date or dates must be fixed before the shares are issued.

(3) Any other circumstances in which the shares are to be or may be redeemed must be specified in the company's articles.

(4) The amount payable on redemption must be specified in, or determined in accordance with, the company's articles, and in the latter case the articles must not provide for the amount to be determined by reference to any person's discretion or opinion.

(5) Any other terms and conditions of redemption shall be specified in the company's articles.

(6) Nothing in this section shall be construed as requiring a company to provide in its articles for any matter for which provision is made by this Act.

160. Financing etc of redemption

(1) Subject to the next subsection and to section 171 (private companies redeeming or purchasing own shares out of capital) and 178(4) (terms of redemption or purchase enforceable in a winding up)—

    (a) redeemable shares may only be redeemed out of distributable profits of the company or out of the proceeds of a fresh issue of shares made for the purposes of the redemption; and

    (b) any premium payable on redemption must be paid out of distributable profits of the company.

(2) If the redeemable shares were issued at a premium, any premium payable on their redemption may be paid out of the proceeds of a fresh issue of shares made for the purposes of the redemption, up to an amount equal to—

    (a) the aggregate of the premiums received by the company on the issue of the shares redeemed, or

    (b) the current amount of the company's share premium account (including any sum transferred to that account in respect of premiums on the new shares).

whichever is the less; and in that case the amount of the company's share premium account shall be reduced by a sum corresponding (or by sums in the aggregate corresponding) to the amount of any payment made by virtue of this subsection out of the proceeds of the issue of the new shares.

(3) *Subject to the following provisions of this Chapter, redemption of shares may be effected on such terms and in such manner as may be provided by the company's articles.* [Ital words prosp rep]

(4) Shares redeemed under this *section* shall be treated as cancelled on redemption, and the amount of the company's issued share capital shall be diminished by the nominal value of those shares accordingly; but the redemption of shares by a company is not to be taken as reducing the amount of the company's authorised share capital. [Italicised word prosp replaced by word 'Chapter']

(5) Without prejudice to subsection (4), where a company is about to redeem shares, it has power to issue shares up to the nominal value of the shares to be redeemed as if those shares had never been issued.

162. Power of company to purchase own shares

(1) Subject to the following provisions of this Chapter, a company limited by shares or limited by guarantee and having a share capital may, if authorised to do so by its articles, purchase its own shares (including any redeemable shares).

(2) Sections 159, 160 and 161 apply to the purchase by a company under this section of its own shares as they apply to the redemption of redeemable shares, *save that the terms and manner of purchase need not be determined by the articles as required by section 160(3).* [Ital words prosp rep]

(3)   A company may not under this section purchase its shares if as a result of the purchase there would no longer be any member of the company holding shares other than redeemable shares.

163. Definitions of 'off-market' and 'market' purchase

(1)   A purchase by a company of its own shares is 'off-market' if the shares either—

    (a)   are purchased otherwise than on a recognised investment exchange, or

    (b)   are purchased on a recognised investment exchange but are not subject to a marketing arrangement on that investment exchange.

(2)   For this purpose, a company's shares are subject to a marketing arrangement on a recognised investment exchange if either—

    (a)   they are listed under Part 6 of the Financial Services and Markets Act 2000; or

    (b)   the company has been afforded facilities for dealings in those shares to take place on that investment exchange without prior permission for individual transactions from the authority governing that investment exchange and without limit as to the time during which those facilities are to be available.

(3)   A purchase by a company of its own shares is a 'market purchase' if it is a purchase made on a recognised investment exchange, other than a purchase which is an off-market purchase by virtue of subsection (1)(b).

(4)   'Recognised investment exchange' means a recognised investment exchange other than an overseas investment exchange.

(5)   Expressions used in the definition contained in subsection (4) have the same meaning as in Part 18 of the Financial Services and Markets Act 2000.

164. Authority for off-market purchase

(1)   A company may only make an off-market purchase of its own shares in pursuance of a contract approved in advance in accordance with this section or under section 165 below.

(2)   The terms of the proposed contract must be authorised by a special resolution of the company before the contract is entered into; and the following subsections apply with respect to that authority and to resolutions conferring it.

(3)   Subject to the next subsection, the authority may be varied, revoked or from time to time renewed by special resolution of the company.

(4)   In the case of a public company, the authority conferred by the resolution must specify a date on which the authority is to expire; and in a resolution conferring or renewing authority that date must not be later than 18 months after that on which the resolution is passed.

(5)   A special resolution to confer, vary, revoke or renew authority is not effective if any member of the company holding shares to which the resolution relates exercises the voting rights carried by any of those shares in voting on the resolution and the resolution would not have been passed if he had not done so.

For the purpose—

    (a)   a member who holds shares to which the resolution relates is regarded as exercising the voting rights carried by those shares not only if he votes in respect of them on a poll on the question whether the resolution shall be passed, but also if he votes on the resolution otherwise than on a poll;

    (b)   notwithstanding anything in the company's articles, any member of the company may demand a poll on that question; and

    (c)   a vote and a demand for a poll by a person as proxy for a member are the same respectively as a vote and a demand by the member.

(6)   Such a resolution is not effective for the purposes of this section unless (if the proposed contract is in writing) a copy of the contract or (if not) a written memorandum of its terms is available for inspection by members of the company both—

    (a)   at the company's registered office for not less than 15 days ending with the date of the meeting at which the resolution is passed, and

    (b)   at the meeting itself.

A memorandum of contract terms so made available must include the names of any members holding shares to which the contract relates; and a copy of the contract so made available must have annexed to it a written memorandum specifying any such names which do not appear in the contract itself.

(7)   A company may agree to a variation of an existing contract so approved, but only if the variation is authorised by a special resolution of the company before it is agreed to; and subsections (3) to (6) above apply to the authority for a proposed variation as they apply to the authority for a proposed contract, save that a copy of the original contract or (as the case may require) a memorandum of its terms, together with any variations previously made, must also be available for inspection in accordance with subsection (6).

169. Disclosure by company of purchase of own shares

(1)   Within the period of 28 days beginning with the date on which any shares purchased by a company under this Chapter are delivered to it, the company shall deliver to the registrar of companies for registration a return in the prescribed form stating with respect to shares of each class purchased the number and nominal value of those shares and the date on which they were delivered to the company.

(2)   In the case of a public company, the return shall also state—

(a)   the aggregate amount paid by the company for the shares; and
(b)   the maximum and minimum prices paid in respect of shares of each class purchased.

(3)   Particulars of shares delivered to the company on different dates and under different contracts may be included in a single return to the registrar; and in such a case the amount required to be stated under subsection (2)(a) is the aggregate amount paid by the company for all the shares to which the return relates.

(4)   Where a company enters into a contract approved under section 164 or 165, or a contract for a purchase authorised under section 166, the company shall keep at its registered office—

(a)   if the contract is in writing, a copy of it; and
(b)   if not, a memorandum of its terms,

from the conclusion of the contract until the end of the period of 10 years beginning with the date on which the purchase of all the shares in pursuance of the contract is completed or (as the case may be) the date on which the contract otherwise determines.

(5)   Every copy and memorandum so required to be kept shall be open to inspection without charge—

(a)   by any member of the company, and
(b)   if it is a public company, by any other person.

(6)   If default is made in delivering to the registrar any return required by this section, every officer of the company who is in default is liable to a fine and, for continued contravention, to a daily default fine.

(7)   If default is made in complying with subsection (4), or if an inspection required under subsection (5) is refused, the company and every officer of it who is in default is liable to a fine and, for continued contravention, to a daily default fine.

(8)   In the case of a refusal of an inspection required under subsection (5) of a copy or memorandum, the court may by order compel an immediate inspection of it.

(9)   The obligation of a company under subsection (4) to keep a copy of any contract or (as the case may be) a memorandum of its terms applies to any variation of the contract so long as it applies to the contract.

170. The capital redemption reserve

(1)   Where under this Chapter shares of a company are redeemed or purchased wholly out of the company's profits, the amount by which the company's issued share capital is diminished in accordance with section 160(4) on cancellation of the shares redeemed or purchased shall be transferred to a reserve, called 'the capital redemption reserve'.

(2)   If the shares are redeemed or purchased wholly or partly out of the proceeds of a fresh issue and the aggregate amount of those proceeds is less than the aggregate nominal value of the shares redeemed or purchased, the amount of the difference shall be transferred to the capital redemption reserve.

(3)   But subsection (2) does not apply if the proceeds of the fresh issue are applied by the company in making a redemption or purchase of its own shares in addition to a payment out of capital under section 171.

(4)　The provisions of this Act relating to the reduction of a company's share capital apply as if the capital redemption reserve were paid-up share capital of the company, except that the reserve may be applied by the company in paying up its unissued shares to be allotted to members of the company as fully paid bonus shares.

171. Power of private companies to redeem or purchase own shares out of capital

(1)　Subject to the following provisions of this Chapter, a private company limited by shares or limited by guarantee and having a share capital may, if so authorised by its articles, make a payment in respect of the redemption or purchase under section 160 or (as the case may be) section 162, of its own shares otherwise than out of its distributable profits or the proceeds of a fresh issue of shares.

(2)　References below in this Chapter to payment out of capital are (subject to subsection (6)) to any payment so made, whether or not it would be regarded apart from this section as a payment out of capital.

(3)　The payment which may (if authorised in accordance with the following provisions of this Chapter) be made by a company out of capital in respect of the redemption or purchase of its own shares is such an amount as, taken together with—

(a)　any available profits of the company, and

(b)　the proceeds of any fresh issue of shares made for the purposes of the redemption or purchase,

is equal to the price of redemption or purchase; and the payment permissible under this subsection is referred to below in this Chapter as the permissible capital payment for the shares.

(4)　Subject to subsection (6), if the permissible capital payment for shares redeemed or purchased is less than their nominal amount, the amount of the difference shall be transferred to the company's capital redemption reserve.

(5)　Subject to subsection (6), if the permissible capital payment is greater than the nominal amount of the shares redeemed or purchased—

(a)　the amount of any capital redemption reserve, share premium account or fully paid share capital of the company, and

(b)　any amount representing unrealised profits of the company for the time being standing to the credit of any reserve maintained by the company in accordance with paragraph 34 of Schedule 4 or paragraph 34 of Schedule 8 (revaluation reserve),

may be reduced by a sum not exceeding (or by sums not in the aggregate exceeding) the amount by which the permissible capital payment exceeds the nominal amount of the shares.

(6)　Where the proceeds of a fresh issue are applied by a company in making any redemption or purchase of its own shares in addition to a payment out of capital under this section, the references in subsections (4) and (5) to the permissible capital payment are to be read as referring to the aggregate of that payment and those proceeds.

172. Availability of profits for purposes of s 171

(1)　The reference in section 171(3)(a) to available profits of the company is to the company's profits which are available for distribution (within the meaning of Part VIII; but the question whether a company has any profits so available and the amount of any such profits are to be determined for purposes of that section in accordance with the following subsections, instead of sections 270 to 275 in that Part.

(2)　Subject to the next subsection, that question is to be determined by reference to—

(a)　profits, losses, assets and liabilities,

(b)　provisions of any of the kinds mentioned in paragraphs 88 and 89 of Schedule 4 (depreciation, diminution in value of assets, retentions to meet liabilities, etc.), and

(c)　share capital and reserves (including undistributable reserves),

as stated in the relevant accounts for determining the permissible capital payment for shares.

(3)　The relevant accounts for this purpose are such accounts, prepared as at any date within the period for determining the amount of the permissible capital payment, as are necessary to enable a reasonable judgment to be made as to the amounts of any of the items mentioned in subsection (2)(a) to (c) above.

(4)　For purposes of determining the amount of the permissible capital payment for shares, the amount of the company's available profits (if any) determined in accordance with subsections (2) and (3) is treated as reduced by the amount of any distributions lawfully made by the company after the date of the relevant accounts and before the end of the period for determining the amount of that payment.

(5)   The reference in subsection (4) to distributions lawfully made by the company includes—

(a)   financial assistance lawfully given out of distributable profits in a case falling within section 154 or 155,

(b)   any payment lawfully made by the company in respect of the purchase by it of any shares in the company (except a payment lawfully made otherwise than out of distributable profits), and

(c)   a payment of any description specified in section 168(1) lawfully made by the company.

(6)   References in this section to the period for determining the amount of the permissible capital payment for shares are to the period of 3 months ending with the date on which the statutory declaration of the directors purporting to specify the amount of that payment is made in accordance with subsection (3) of the section next following.

173. Conditions for payment out of capital

(1)   Subject to any order of the court under section 177, a payment out of capital by a private company for the redemption or purchase of its own shares is not lawful unless the requirements of this and the next two sections are satisfied.

(2)   The payment out of capital must be approved by a special resolution of the company.

(3)   The company's directors must make a statutory declaration specifying the amount of the permissible capital payment for the shares in question and stating that, having made full inquiry into the affairs and prospects of the company, they have formed the opinion—

(a)   as regards its initial situation immediately following the date on which the payment out of capital is proposed to be made, that there will be no grounds on which the company could then be found unable to pay its debts, and

(b)   as regards its prospects for the year immediately following that date, that, having regard to their intentions with respect to the management of the company's business during that year and to the amount and character of the financial resources which will in their view be available to the company during that year, the company will be able to continue to carry on business as a going concern (and will accordingly be able to pay its debts as they fall due) throughout that year.

(4)   In forming their opinion for purposes of subsection(3)(a), the directors shall take into account the same liabilities (including prospective and contingent liabilities) as would be relevant under section 122 of the Insolvency Act 1986 (winding up by the court) to the question whether a company is unable to pay its debts.

(5)   The directors' statutory declaration must be in the prescribed form and contain such information with respect to the nature of the company's business as may be prescribed, and must in addition have annexed to it a report addressed to the directors by the company's auditors stating that—

(a)   they have inquired into the company's state of affairs; and

(b)   the amount specified in the declaration as the permissible capital payment for the shares in question is in their view properly determined in accordance with sections 171 and 172; and

(c)   they are not aware of anything to indicate that the opinion expressed by the directors in the declaration as to any of the matters mentioned in subsection (3) is unreasonable in all the circumstances.

(6)   A director who makes a declaration under this section without having reasonable grounds for the opinion expressed in the declaration is liable to imprisonment or a fine, or both.

174. Procedure for special resolution under s 173

(1)   The resolution required by section 173 must be passed on, or within the week immediately following, the date on which the directors make the statutory declaration required by that section; and the payment out of capital must be made no earlier than 5 nor more than 7 weeks after the date of the resolution.

(2)   The resolution is ineffective if any member of the company holding shares to which the resolution relates exercises the voting rights carried by any of those shares in voting on the resolution and the resolution would not have been passed if he had not done so.

(3)   For purposes of subsection (2), a member who holds such shares is to be regarded as exercising the voting rights carried by them in voting on the resolution not only if he votes in respect of them on a poll on the question whether the resolution shall be passed, but also if he votes on the resolution otherwise than on a poll; and, notwithstanding anything in a company's articles, any member of the company may demand a poll on that question.

(4)   The resolution is ineffective unless the statutory declaration and auditors' report required by the section are available for inspection by members of the company at the meeting at which the resolution is passed.

(5)   For purposes of this section a vote and a demand for a poll by a person as proxy for a member are the same (respectively) as a vote and demand by the member.

175. Publicity for proposed payment out of capital

(1)   Within the week immediately following the date of the resolution for payment out of capital the company must cause to be published in the Gazette a notice—

(a)   stating that the company has approved a payment out of capital for the purpose of acquiring its own shares by redemption or purchase or both (as the case may be);

(b)   specifying the amount of the permissible capital payment for the shares in question and the date of the resolution under section 173;

(c)   stating that the statutory declaration of the directors and the auditors' report required by that section are available for inspection at the company's registered office; and

(d)   stating that any creditor of the company may at any time within the 5 weeks immediately following the date of the resolution for payment out of capital apply to the court under section 176 for an order prohibiting the payment.

(2)   Within the week immediately following the date of the resolution the company must also either cause a notice to the same effect as that required by subsection (1) to be published in an appropriate national newspaper or give notice in writing to that effect to each of its creditors.

(3)   'An appropriate national newspaper' means a newspaper circulating throughout England and Wales (in the case of a company registered in England and Wales), and a newspaper circulating throughout Scotland (in the case of a company registered in Scotland).

(4)   References below in this section to the first notice date are to the day on which the company first publishes the notice required by subsection (1) or first publishes or gives the notice required by subsection (2) (whichever is the earlier).

(5)   Not later than the first notice date the company must deliver to the registrar of companies a copy of the statutory declaration of the directors and of the auditors' report required by section 173.

(6)   The statutory declaration and auditors' report—

(a)   shall be kept at the company's registered office throughout the period beginning with the first notice date and ending 5 weeks after the date of the resolution for payment out of capital, and

(b)   shall be open to the inspection of any member or creditor of the company without charge.

(7)   If an inspection required under subsection (6) is refused, the company and every officer of it who is in default is liable to a fine and, for continued contravention, to a daily default fine.

(8)   In the case of refusal of an inspection required under subsection (6) of a declaration or report, the court may by order compel an immediate inspection of that declaration or report.

176. Objections by company's members or creditors

(1)   Where a private company passes a special resolution approving for purposes of this Chapter any payment out of capital for the redemption or purchase of any of its shares—

(a)   any member of the company other than one who consented to or voted in favour of the resolution; and

(b)   any creditor of the company,

may within 5 weeks of the date on which the resolution was passed apply to the court for cancellation of the resolution.

(2)   The application may be made on behalf of the persons entitled to make it by such one or more of their number as they may appoint in writing for the purpose.

(3)   If an application is made, the company shall—

(a)   forthwith give notice in the prescribed form of that fact to the registrar of companies; and

(b)   within 15 days from the making of any order of the court on the hearing of the application, or such longer period as the court may by order direct, deliver an office copy of the order to the registrar.

(4)   A company which fails to comply with subsection (3), and any officer of it who is in default, is liable to a fine and for continued contravention, to a daily default fine.

177. Powers of court on application under s 176

(1)   On the hearing of an application under section 176 the court may, if it thinks fit, adjourn the proceedings in order that an arrangement may be made to the court's satisfaction for the purchase of the interests of dissentient members or for the protection of dissentient creditors (as the case may be); and the court may give such directions and make such orders as it thinks expedient for facilitating or carrying into effect any such arrangement.

(2)   Without prejudice to its powers under subsection (1), the court shall make an order on such terms and conditions as it thinks fit either confirming or cancelling the resolution; and, if the court confirms the resolution, it may in particular by order alter or extend any date or period of time specified in the resolution or in any provision in this Chapter which applies to the redemption or purchase of shares to which the resolution refers.

(3)   The court's order may, if the court thinks fit, provide for the purchase by the company of the shares of any of its members and for the reduction accordingly of the company's capital, and may make such alterations in the company's memorandum and articles as may be required in consequence of that provision.

(4)   If the court's order requires the company not to make any, or any specified, alteration in its memorandum or articles, the company has not then power without leave of the court to make any such alteration in breach of the requirement.

(5)   An alteration in the memorandum or articles made by virtue of an order under this section, if not made by resolution of the company, is of the same effect as if duly made by resolution; and this Act applies accordingly to the memorandum or articles as so altered.

178. Effect of company's failure to redeem or purchase

(1)   This section has effect where a company has, on or after 15th June 1982,—

    (a)   issued shares on terms that they are or are liable to be redeemed, or

    (b)   agreed to purchase any of its own shares.

(2)   The company is not liable in damages in respect of any failure on its part to redeem or purchase any of the shares.

(3)   Subsection (2) is without prejudice to any right of the holder of the shares other than his right to sue the company for damages in respect of its failure; but the court shall not grant an order for specific performance of the terms of redemption or purchase if the company shows that it is unable to meet the costs of redeeming or purchasing the shares in question out of distributable profits.

(4)   If the company is wound up and at the commencement of the winding up any of the shares have not been redeemed or purchased, the terms of redemption or purchase may be enforced against the company; and when shares are redeemed or purchased under this subsection, they are treated as cancelled.

(5)   However, subsection (4) does not apply if—

    (a)   the terms provided for the redemption or purchase to take place at a date later than that of the commencement of the winding up, or

    (b)   during the period beginning with the date on which the redemption or purchase was to have taken place and ending with the commencement of the winding up the company could not at any time have lawfully made a distribution equal in value to the price at which the shares were to have been redeemed or purchased.

(6)   There shall be paid in priority to any amount which the company is liable under subsection (4) to pay in respect of any shares—

    (a)   all other debts and liabilities of the company (other than any due to members in their character as such),

    (b)   if other shares carry rights (whether as to capital or as to income) which are preferred to the rights as to capital attaching to the first-mentioned shares, any amount due in satisfaction of those preferred rights;

but, subject to that, any such amount shall be paid in priority to any amounts due to members in satisfaction of their rights (whether as to capital or income) as members.

185. Duty of company as to issue of certificates

(1) Subject to the following provisions, every company shall—

  (a) within 2 months after the allotment of any of its shares, debentures or debenture stock, and

  (b) within 2 months after the date on which a transfer of any such shares, debentures or debenture stock is lodged with the company,

complete and have ready for delivery the certificates of all shares, the debentures and the certificates of all debenture stock allotted or transferred (unless the conditions of issue of the shares, debentures or debenture stock otherwise provide).

(2) For this purpose, 'transfer' means a transfer duly stamped and otherwise valid, or an exempt transfer within the Stock Transfer Act 1982, and does not include such a transfer as the company is for any reason entitled to refuse to register and does not register.

(3) Subsection (1) does not apply in the case of a transfer to any person where, by virtue of regulations under section 3 of the Stock Transfer Act 1982, he is not entitled to a certificate or other document of or evidencing title in respect of the securities transferred; but if in such a case the transferee—

  (a) subsequently becomes entitled to such a certificate or other document by virtue of any provision of those regulations, and

  (b) gives notice in writing of that fact to the company,

this section has effect as if the reference in subsection (1)(b) to the date of the lodging of the transfer were a reference to the date of the notice.

(4) Subsection (4A) applies in relation to a company—

  (a) of which shares or debentures are allotted to a financial institution,

  (b) of which debenture stock is allotted to a financial institution, or

  (c) with which a transfer for transferring shares, debentures or debenture stock to a financial institution is lodged.

(4A) The company is not required, in consequence of that allotment or transfer, to comply with subsection (1).

(4B) 'Financial institution' means—

  (a) a recognised clearing house acting in relation to a recognised investment exchange; or

  (b) a nominee of—

    (i) a recognised clearing house acting in that way; or

    (ii) a recognised investment exchange.

(4C) No person may be a nominee for the purposes of this section unless he is a person designated for those purposes in the rules of the recognised investment exchange in question.

(4D) Expressions used in subsections (4B) and (4C) have the same meaning as in Part 18 of the Financial Services and Markets Act 2000.

(5) If default is made in complying with subsection (1), the company and every officer of it who is in default is liable to a fine and, for continued contravention, to a daily default fine.

(6) If a company on which a notice has been served requiring it to make good any default in complying with subsection (1) fails to make good the default within 10 days after service of the notice, the court may, on the application of the person entitled to have the certificates or the debentures delivered to him, exercise the power of the following subsection.

(7) The court may make an order directing the company and any officer of it to make good the default within such time as may be specified in the order; and the order may provide that all costs of and incidental to the application shall be borne by the company or by an officer of it responsible for the default.

186. Certificate to be evidence of title

(1) A certificate under the common seal of the company specifying any shares held by a member is—

  (a) in England and Wales, prima facie evidence, and

  (b) [Applies to Scotland only.]

of his title to the shares.

196. Payment of debts out of assets subject to floating charge (England and Wales)

(1) The following applies in the case of a company registered in England and Wales, where debentures of the company are secured by a charge which, as created, was a floating charge.

(2) If possession is taken, by or on behalf of the holders of any of the debentures, of any property comprised in or subject to the charge, and the company is not at that time in course of being wound up, the company's preferential debts shall be paid out of assets coming to the hands of the person taking possession in priority to any claims for principal or interest in respect of the debentures.

(3) 'Preferential debts' means the categories of debts listed in Schedule 6 to the Insolvency Act; and for the purposes of that Schedule 'the relevant date' is the date of possession being taken as above mentioned.

(4) Payments made under this section shall be recouped, as far as may be, out of the assets of the company available for payment of general creditors.

PART VII

ACCOUNTS AND AUDIT

221. Duty to keep accounting records

(1) Every company shall keep accounting records which are sufficient to show and explain the company's transactions and are such as to—

    (a)   disclose with reasonable accuracy, at any time, the financial position of the company at that time, and

    (b)   enable the directors to ensure that any balance sheet and profit and loss account prepared under this Part complies with the requirements of this Act.

(2) The accounting records shall in particular contain—

    (a)   entries from day to day of all sums of money received and expended by the company, and the matters in respect of which the receipt and expenditure takes place, and

    (b)   a record of the assets and liabilities of the company.

(3) If the company's business involves dealing in goods, the accounting records shall contain—

    (a)   statements of stock held by the company at the end of each financial year of the company,

    (b)   all statements of stocktakings from which any such statement of stock as is mentioned in paragraph (a) has been or is to be prepared, and

    (c)   except in the case of goods sold by way of ordinary retail trade, statements of all goods sold and purchased, showing the goods and the buyers and sellers in sufficient detail to enable all these to be identified.

(4) A parent company which has a subsidiary undertaking in relation to which the above requirements do not apply shall take reasonable steps to secure that the undertaking keeps such accounting records as to enable the directors of the parent company to ensure that any balance sheet and profit and loss account prepared under this Part complies with the requirements of this Act.

(5) If a company fails to comply with any provision of this section, every officer of the company who is in default is guilty of an offence unless he shows that he acted honestly and that in the circumstances in which the company's business was carried on the default was excusable.

(6) A person guilty of an offence under this section is liable to imprisonment or a fine, or both.

222. Where and for how long records to be kept

(1) A company's accounting records shall be kept at its registered office or such other place as the directors think fit, and shall at all times be open to inspection by the company's officers.

(2) If accounting records are kept at a place outside Great Britain, accounts and returns with respect to the business dealt with in the accounting records so kept shall be sent to, and kept at, a place in Great Britain, and shall at all times be open to such inspection.

(3) The accounts and returns to be sent to Great Britain shall be such as to—

(a)   disclose with reasonable accuracy the financial position of the business in question at intervals of not more than six months, and

(b)   enable the directors to ensure that the company's balance sheet and profit and loss account comply with the requirements of this Act.

(4)   If a company fails to comply with any provision of subsections (1) to (3), every officer of the company who is in default is guilty of an offence, and liable to imprisonment or a fine or both, unless he shows that he acted honestly and that in the circumstances in which the company's business was carried on the default was excusable.

(5)   Accounting records which a company is required by section 221 to keep shall be preserved by it—

(a)   in the case of a private company, for three years from the date on which they are made, and

(b)   in the case of a public company, for six years from the date on which they are made.

This is subject to any provision contained in rules made under section 411 of the Insolvency Act 1986 (company insolvency rules).

(6)   An officer of a company is guilty of an offence, and liable to imprisonment or a fine or both, if he fails to take all reasonable steps for securing compliance by the company with subsection (5) or intentionally causes any default by the company under that subsection.

223. A company's financial year

(1)   A company's 'financial year' is determined as follows.

(2)   Its first financial year begins with the first day of its first accounting reference period and ends with the last day of that period or such other date, not more than seven days before or after the end of that period, as the directors may determine.

(3)   Subsequent financial years begin with the day immediately following the end of the company's previous financial year and end with the last day of its next accounting reference period or such other date, not more than seven days before or after the end of that period, as the directors may determine.

(4)   In relation to an undertaking which is not a company, references in this Act to its financial year are to any period in respect of which a profit and loss account of the undertaking is required to be made up (by its constitution or by the law under which it is established), whether that period is a year or not.

(5)   The directors of a parent company shall secure that, except where in their opinion there are good reasons against it, the financial year of each of its subsidiary undertakings coincides with the company's own financial year.

224. Accounting reference periods and accounting reference date

(1)   A company's accounting reference periods are determined according to its accounting reference date.

(2)   A company incorporated before 1st April 1996 may, at any time before the end of the period of nine months beginning with the date of its incorporation, by notice in the prescribed form given to the registrar specify its accounting reference date, that is, the date on which its accounting reference period ends in each calendar year.

(3)   Failing such notice, the accounting reference date of such a company is—

(a)   in the case of a company incorporated before 1st April 1990, 31st March;

(b)   in the case of a company incorporated after 1st April 1990, the last day of the month in which the anniversary of its incorporation falls.

(3A) The accounting reference date of a company incorporated on or after 1st April 1996 is the last day of the month in which the anniversary of its incorporation falls.

(4)   A company's first accounting reference period is the period of more than six months, but not more than 18 months, beginning with the date of its incorporation and ending with its accounting reference date.

(5)   Its subsequent accounting reference periods are successive periods of twelve months beginning immediately after the end of the previous accounting reference period and ending with its accounting reference date.

(6)   This section has effect subject to the provisions of section 225 relating to the alteration of accounting reference dates and the consequences of such alteration.

225. Alteration of accounting reference date

(1)   A company may by notice in the prescribed form given to the registrar specify a new accounting reference date having effect in relation to—

(a)   the company's current accounting reference period and subsequent periods; or

(b)   the company's previous accounting reference period and subsequent periods

A company's 'previous accounting reference period' means that immediately preceding its current accounting reference period.

(3)   the notice shall state whether the current or previous accounting reference period—

(a)   is to be shortened, so as to come to an end on the first occasion on which the new accounting reference date falls or fell after the beginning of the period, or

(b)   is to be extended, so as to come to an end on the second occasion on which that date falls or fell after the beginning of the period.

(4)   A notice under subsection (1) stating that the current or previous accounting reference period is to be extended is ineffective, except as mentioned below, if given less than five years after the end of an earlier accounting reference period of the company which was extended by virtue of this section.

This subsection does not apply—

(a)   to a notice given by a company which is a subsidiary undertaking or parent undertaking of another EEA undertaking if the new accounting reference date coincides with that of the other EEA undertaking or, where that undertaking is not a company, with the last day of its financial year, or

(b)   where an administration order is in force under Part II of the Insolvency Act 1986,

or where the Secretary of State directs that it should not apply, which he may do with respect to a notice which has been given or which may be given.

(5)   A notice under subsection (1) may not be given in respect of a previous accounting reference period if the period allowed for laying and delivering accounts and reports in relation to that period has already expired.

(6)   An accounting reference period may not in any case, unless an administration order is in force under Part II of the Insolvency Act 1986, be extended so as to exceed 18 months and a notice under this section is ineffective if the current or previous accounting reference period as extended in accordance with the notice would exceed that limit.

(7)   In this section 'EEA undertaking' means an undertaking established under the law of any part of the United Kingdom or the law of any other EEA State.

226. Duty to prepare individual company accounts

(1)   The directors of every company shall prepare for each financial year of the company—

(a)   a balance sheet as at the last day of the year, and

(b)   a profit and loss account.

Those accounts are referred to in this Part as the company's 'individual accounts'.

(2)   The balance sheet shall give a true and fair view of the state of affairs of the company as at the end of the financial year; and the profit and loss account shall give a true and fair view of the profit or loss of the company for the financial year.

(3)   A company's individual accounts shall comply with the provisions of Schedule 4 as to the form and content of the balance sheet and profit and loss account and additional information to be provided by way of notes to the accounts.

(4)   Where compliance with the provisions of that Schedule, and the other provisions of this Act as to the matters to be included in a company's individual accounts or in notes to those accounts, would not be sufficient to give a true and fair view, the necessary additional information shall be given in the accounts or in a note to them.

(5)   If in special circumstances compliance with any of those provisions is inconsistent with the requirement to give a true and fair view, the directors shall depart from that provision to the extent necessary to give a true and fair view.

Particulars of any such departure, the reasons for it and its effect shall be given in a note to the accounts.

233. Approval and signing of accounts

(1)   A company's annual accounts shall be approved by the board of directors and signed on behalf of the board by a director of the company.

(2)   The signature shall be on the company's balance sheet.

(3)   Every copy of the balance sheet which is laid before the company in general meeting or which is otherwise circulated, published or issued, shall state the name of the person who signed the balance sheet on behalf of the board.

(4)   The copy of the company's balance sheet which is delivered to the registrar shall be signed on behalf of the board by a director of the company.

(5)   If annual accounts are approved which do not comply with the requirements of this Act, every director of the company who is party to their approval and who knows that they do not comply or is reckless as to whether they comply is guilty of an offence and liable to a fine.

For this purpose every director of the company at the time the accounts are approved shall be taken to be a party to their approval unless he shows that he took all reasonable steps to prevent their being approved.

(6)   If a copy of the balance sheet—

    (a)   is laid before the company, or otherwise circulated, published or issued, without the balance sheet having been signed as required by this section or without the required statement of the signatory's name being included, or

    (b)   is delivered to the registrar without being signed as required by this section,

the company and every officer of it who is in default is guilty of an offence and liable to a fine.

234. Duty to prepare directors' report

(1)   The directors of a company shall for each financial year prepare a report—

    (a)   containing a fair review of the development of the business of the company and its subsidiary undertakings during the financial year and of their position at the end of it, and

    (b)   stating the amount (if any) which they recommend should be paid as dividend.

(2)   The report shall state the names of the persons who, at any time during the financial year, were directors of the company, and the principal activities of the company and its subsidiary undertakings in the course of the year and any significant change in those activities in the year.

(3)   The report shall also comply with Schedule 7 as regards the disclosure of the matters mentioned there.

(4)   In Schedule 7—

Part I relates to matters of a general nature, including changes in asset values, directors' shareholdings and other interests and contributions for political and charitable purposes,
Part II relates to the acquisition by a company of its own shares or a charge on them,
Part III relation to the employment, training and advancement of disabled persons,
Part V relates to the involvement of employees in the affairs, policy and performance of the company.
Part VI relates to the company's policy and practice on the payment of creditors.

(5)   In the case of any failure to comply with the provisions of this Part as to the preparation of a directors' report and the contents of the report, every person who was a director of the company immediately before the end of the period for laying and delivering accounts and reports for the financial year in question is guilty of an offence and liable to a fine.

(6)   In proceedings against a person for an offence under this section it is a defence for him to prove that he took all reasonable steps for securing compliance with the requirements in question.

234A.   Approval and signing of directors' report

(1)   The directors' report shall be approved by the board of directors and signed on behalf of the board by a director or the secretary of the company.

(2)   Every copy of the directors' report which is laid before the company in general meeting, or which is otherwise circulated, published or issued, shall state the name of the person who signed it on behalf of the board.

(3)   The copy of the directors' report which is delivered to the registrar shall be signed on behalf of the board by a director or the secretary of the company.

(4)   If a copy of the directors' report—

  (a)   is laid before the company, or otherwise circulated, published or issued, without the report having been signed as required by this section or without the required statement of the signatory's name being included, or

  (b)   is delivered to the registrar without being signed as required by this section,

the company and every officer of it who is in default is guilty of an offence and liable to a fine.

Quoted companies: directors' remuneration report

234B. Duty to prepare directors' remuneration report

(1)   The directors of a quoted company shall for each financial year prepare a directors' remuneration report which shall contain the information specified in Schedule 7A and comply with any requirement of that Schedule as to how information is to be set out in the report.

(2)   In Schedule 7A—

  Part 1 is introductory,
  Part 2 relates to information about remuneration committees, performance related remuneration and liabilities in respect of directors' contracts,
  Part 3 relates to detailed information about directors' remuneration (information included under Part 3 is required to be reported on by the auditors, see section 235), and
  Part 4 contains interpretative and supplementary provisions.

(3)   In the case of any failure to comply with the provisions of this Part as to the preparation of a directors' remuneration report and the contents of the report, every person who was a director of the quoted company immediately before the end of the period for laying and delivering accounts and reports for the financial year in question is guilty of an offence and liable to a fine.

(4)   In proceedings against a person for an offence under subsection (3) it is a defence for him to prove that he took all reasonable steps for securing compliance with the requirements in question.

(5)   It is the duty of any director of a company, and any person who has at any time in the preceding five years been a director of the company, to give notice to the company of such matters relating to himself as may be necessary for the purposes of Parts 2 and 3 of Schedule 7A.

(6)   A person who makes default in complying with subsection (5) commits an offence and is liable to a fine.

234C. Approval and signing of directors' remuneration report

(1)   The directors' remuneration report shall be approved by the board of directors and signed on behalf of the board by a director or the secretary of the company.

(2)   Every copy of the directors' remuneration report which is laid before the company in general meeting, or which is otherwise circulated, published or issued, shall state the name of the person who signed it on behalf of the board.

(3)   The copy of the directors' remuneration report which is delivered to the registrar shall be signed on behalf of the board by a director or the secretary of the company.

(4)   If a copy of the directors' remuneration report—

  (a)   is laid before the company, or otherwise circulated, published or issued, without the report having been signed as required by this section or without the required statement of the signatory's name being included, or

  (b)   is delivered to the registrar without being signed as required by this section,

the company and every officer of it who is in default is guilty of an offence and liable to a fine.

235. Auditors' report

(1)   A company's auditors shall make a report to the company's members on all annual accounts of the company of which copies are to be laid before the company in general meeting during their tenure of office.

(2)   The auditors' report shall state whether in the auditors' opinion the annual accounts have been properly prepared in accordance with this Act, and in particular whether a true and fair view is given—

   (a)   in the case of an individual balance sheet, of the state of affairs of the company as at the end of the financial year,

   (b)   in the case of an individual profit and loss account, of the profit or loss of the company for the financial year

   (c)   in the case of group accounts, of the state of affairs as at the end of the financial year, and the profit or loss for the financial year, of the undertakings included in the consolidation as a whole, so far as concerns members of the company.

(3)   The auditors shall consider whether the information gives in the directors' report for the financial year for which the annual accounts are prepared is consistent with those accounts; and if they are of opinion that it is not they shall state that fact in their report.

(4)   If a directors' remuneration report is prepared for the financial year for which the annual accounts are prepared the auditors shall in their report—

   (a)   report to the company's members on the auditable part of the directors' remuneration report, and

   (b)   state whether in their opinion that part of the directors' remuneration report has been properly prepared in accordance with this Act.

(5)   For the purposes of this Part, 'the auditable part' of a directors' remuneration report is the part containing the information required by Part 3 of Schedule 7A.

238. Persons entitled to receive copies of accounts and reports

(1)   A copy of each of the documents mentioned in subsection (1A), shall be sent to—

   (a)   every member of the company,

   (b)   every holder of the company's debentures, and

   (c)   every person who is entitled to receive notice of general meetings,

not less than 21 days before the date of the meeting at which copies of those documents are to be laid in accordance with section 241.

(1A) Those documents are—

   (a)   the company's annual accounts for the financial year,

   (b)   the directors' report for that financial year,

   (c)   (in the case of a quoted company) the directors' remuneration report for that financial year, and

   (d)   the auditors' report on those accounts or (in the case of a quoted company) on those accounts and the auditable part of the directors' remuneration report.

(2)   Copies need not be sent—

   (a)   to a person who is not entitled to receive notices of general meetings and of whose address the company is unaware, or

   (b)   to more than one of the joint holders of shares or debentures none of whom is entitled to receive such notices, or

   (c)   in the case of joint holders of shares or debentures some of whom are, and some not, entitled to receive such notices, to those who are not so entitled.

(3)   In the case of a company not having a share capital, copies need not be sent to anyone who is not entitled to receive notices of general meetings of the company.

(4)   If copies are sent less than 21 days before the date of the meeting, they shall, notwithstanding that fact, be deemed to have been duly sent if it is so agreed by all the members entitled to attend and vote at the meeting.

(4A) References in this section to sending to any person copies of the documents mentioned in subsection (1A) include references to using electronic communications for sending copies of those documents to such address as may for the time being be notified to the company by that person for that purpose.

(4B) For the purposes of this section copies of those documents are also to be treated as sent to a person where—

    (a)   the company and that person have agreed to his having access to the documents on a web site (instead of their being sent to him);

    (b)   the documents are documents to which that agreement applies; and

    (c)   that person is notified, in a manner for the time being agreed for the purpose between him and the company, of—

        (i)   the publication of the documents on a web site;

        (ii)   the address of that web site; and

        (iii)   the place on that web site where the documents may be accessed, and how they may be accessed.

(4C) For the purposes of this section documents treated in accordance with subsection (4B) as sent to any person are to be treated as sent to him not less than 21 days before the date of a meeting if, and only if—

    (a)   the documents are published on the web site throughout a period beginning at least 21 days before the date of the meeting and ending with the conclusion of the meeting; and

    (b)   the notification given for the purposes of paragraph (c) of that subsection is given not less than 21 days before the date of the meeting.

(4D) Nothing in subsection (4C) shall invalidate the proceedings of a meeting where—

    (a)   any documents that are required to be published as mentioned in paragraph (a) of that subsection are published for a part, but not all, of the period mentioned in that paragraph; and

    (b)   the failure to publish those documents throughout that period is wholly attributable to circumstances which it would not be reasonable to have expected the company to prevent or avoid.

(4E) A company may, notwithstanding any provision to the contrary in its articles, take advantage of any of subsections (4A) to (4D).

(5)   If default is made in complying with this section, the company and every officer of it who is in default is guilty of an offence and liable to a fine.

(6)   Where copies are sent out under this section over a period of days, references elsewhere in this Act to the day on which copies are sent out shall be construed as references to the last day of that period.

240. Requirements in connection with publication of accounts

(1)   If a company publishes any of its statutory accounts, they must be accompanied by the relevant auditors' report under section 235 or, as the case may be, the relevant report made for the purposes of section 249A(2).

(2)   A company which is required to prepare group accounts for a financial year shall not publish its statutory individual accounts for that year without also publishing with them its statutory group accounts.

(3)   If a company publishes non-statutory accounts, it shall publish with them a statement indicating—

    (a)   that they are not the company's statutory accounts,

    (b)   whether statutory accounts dealing with any financial year with which the non-statutory accounts purport to deal have been delivered to the registrar,

    (c)   whether the company's auditors have made a report under section 235 on the statutory accounts for any such financial year, and, if no such report has been made, whether the company's reporting accountant has made a report for the purposes of section 249A(2) on the statutory accounts for any such financial year, and

    (d)   whether any auditors' report so made was qualified or contained a statement under section 237(2) or (3) (accounting records or returns inadequate, accounts not agreeing with records and returns or failure to obtain necessary information and explanations) or whether any report made for the purposes of section 249A(2) was qualified;

and it shall not publish with the non-statutory accounts any auditors' report under section 235 or any report made for the purposes of section 249A(2).

(4)   For the purposes of this section a company shall be regarded as publishing a document if it publishes, issues or circulates it or otherwise makes it available for public inspection in a manner calculated to invite members of the public generally, or any class of members of the public, to read it.

(5)   References in this section to a company's statutory accounts are to its individual or group accounts for a financial year as required to be delivered to the registrar under section 242; and references to the publication by a company of 'non-statutory accounts' are to the publication of—

(a)   any balance sheet or profit and loss account relating to, or purporting to deal with, a financial year of the company, or

(b)   an account in any form purporting to be a balance sheet or profit and loss account for the group consisting of the company and its subsidiary undertakings relating to, or purporting to deal with, a financial year of the company,

otherwise than as part of the company's statutory accounts.

(6)   A company which contravenes any provision of this section, and any officer of it who is in default, is guilty of an offence and liable to a fine.

241. Accounts and reports to be laid before company in general meeting

(1)   The directors of a company shall in respect of each financial year lay before the company in general meeting copies of—

(a)   the company's annual accounts,

(b)   the directors' report,

(c)   (in the case of a quoted company) the directors' remuneration report, and

(d)   the auditors' report on those accounts or (in the case of a quoted company) on those accounts and the auditable part of the directors' remuneration report.

(2)   If the requirements of subsection (1) are not complied with before the end of the period allowed for laying and delivering accounts and reports, every person who immediately before the end of that period was a director of the company is guilty of an offence and liable to a fine and for continued contravention, to a daily default fine.

(3)   It is a defence for a person charged with such an offence to prove that he took all reasonable steps for securing that those requirements would be complied with before the end of that period.

(4)   It is not a defence to prove that the documents in question were not in fact prepared as required by this Part.

241A. Members' approval of directors' remuneration report

(1)   This section applies to every company that is a quoted company immediately before the end of a financial year.

(2)   In this section 'the meeting' means the general meeting of the company before which the company's annual accounts for the financial year are to be laid.

(3)   The company must, prior to the meeting, give to the members of the company entitled to be sent notice of the meeting notice of the intention to move at the meeting, as an ordinary resolution, a resolution approving the directors' remuneration report for the financial year.

(4)   Notice under subsection (3) shall be given to each such member in any manner permitted for the service on him of notice of the meeting.

(5)   The business that may be dealt with at the meeting includes the resolution.

(6)   The existing directors must ensure that the resolution is put to the vote of the meeting.

(7)   Subsection (5) has effect notwithstanding—

(a)   any default in complying with subsections (3) and (4);

(b)   anything in the company's articles.

(8)   No entitlement of a person to remuneration is made conditional on the resolution being passed by reason only of the provision made by this section.

(9)   In the event of default in complying with the requirements of subsections (3) and (4), every officer of the company who is in default is liable to a fine.

(10) If the resolution is not put to the vote of the meeting, each existing director is guilty of an offence and liable to a fine.

(11) If an existing director is charged with an offence under subsection (10), it is a defence for him to prove that he took all reasonable steps for securing that the resolution was put to the vote of the meeting.

(12) In this section 'existing director' means a person who, immediately before the meeting, is a director of the company.

242. Accounts and reports to be delivered to the registrar

(1) The directors of a company shall in respect of each financial year deliver to the registrar a copy of—

    (a)   the company's annual accounts,

    (b)   the directors' report,

    (c)   (in the case of a quoted company) the directors' remuneration report, and

    (d)   the auditors' report on those accounts or (in the case of a quoted company) on those accounts and the auditable part of the directors' remuneration report.

If any document comprised in those accounts or reports is in a language other than English, then, subject to section 710B(6) (delivery of certain Welsh documents without a translation), the directors shall annex to the copy of that document delivered a translation of it into English, certified in the prescribed manner to be a correct translation.

(2) If the requirements of subsection (1) are not complied with before the end of the period allowed for laying and delivering accounts and reports, every person who immediately before the end of that period was a director of the company is guilty of an offence and liable to a fine and, for continued contravention, to a daily default fine.

(3) Further, if the directors of the company fail to make good the default within 14 days after the service of a notice on them requiring compliance, the court may on the application of any member or creditor of the company or of the registrar, make an order directing the directors (or any of them) to make good the default within such time as may be specified in the order.

The court's order may provide that all costs of and incidental to the application shall be borne by the directors.

(4) It is a defence for a person charged with an offence under this section to prove that he took all reasonable steps for securing that the requirements of subsection (1) would be complied with before the end of the period allowed for laying and delivering accounts and reports.

(5) It is not a defence in any proceedings under this section to prove that the documents in question were not in fact prepared as required by this Part.

244. Period allowed for laying and delivering accounts and reports

(1) The period allowed for laying and delivering accounts and reports is—

    (a)   for a private company, 10 months after the end of the relevant accounting reference period, and

    (b)   for a public company, 7 months after the end of that period.

This is subject to the following provisions of this section.

(2) If the relevant accounting reference period is the company's first and is a period of more than 12 months, the period allowed is—

    (a)   10 months or 7 months, as the case may be, from the first anniversary of the incorporation of the company, or

    (b)   3 months from the end of the accounting reference period,

whichever last expires.

(3) Where a company carries on business, or has interests, outside the United Kingdom, the Channel Islands and the Isle of Man, the directors may, in respect of any financial year, give to the registrar before the end of the period allowed by subsection (1) or (2) a notice in the prescribed form—

    (a)   stating that the company so carries on business or has such interests, and

    (b)   claiming a 3 month extension of the period allowed for laying and delivering accounts and reports;

and upon such a notice being given the period is extended accordingly.

(4) If the relevant accounting period is treated as shortened by virtue of a notice given by the company under section 225 (alteration of accounting reference date), the period allowed for laying and delivering accounts is that

applicable in accordance with the above provisions or 3 months from the date of the notice under that section, whichever last expires.

(5)   If for any special reason the Secretary of State thinks fit he may, on an application made before the expiry of the period otherwise allowed, by notice in writing to a company extend that period by such further period as may be specified in the notice.

(6)   In this section 'the relevant accounting reference period' means the accounting reference period by reference to which the financial year for the accounts in question was determined.

246. Special provisions for small companies

(1)   Subject to section 247A, this section applies where a company qualifies as a small company in relation to a financial year.

(2)   If the company's individual accounts for the year—

(a)   comply with the provisions of Schedule 8, or

(b)   fail to comply with those provisions only in so far as they comply instead with one or more corresponding provisions of Schedule 4,

they need not comply with the provisions or, as the case may be, the remaining provisions of Schedule 4; and where advantage is taken of this subsection, references in section 226 to compliance with the provisions of Schedule 4 shall be construed accordingly.

(3)   The company's individual accounts for the year—

(a)   may give the total of the aggregates required by paragraphs (a), (c) and (d) of paragraph 1(1) of Schedule 6 (emoluments and other benefits etc of directors) instead of giving those aggregates individually; and

(b)   need not give the information required by—

(i)   paragraph 4 of Schedule 5 (financial years of subsidiary undertakings);

(ii)   paragraph 1(2)(b) of Schedule 6 (numbers of directors exercising share options and receiving shares under long term incentive schemes);

(iii)   paragraph 2 of Schedule 6 (details of highest paid director's emoluments etc); or

(iv)   paragraph 7 of Schedule 6 (excess retirement benefits of directors and past directors).

(4)   The directors' report for the year need not give the information required by—

(a)   section 234(1)(a) and (b) (fair review of business and amount to be paid as dividend);

(b)   paragraph 1(2) of Schedule 7 (statement of market value of fixed assets where substantially different from balance sheet amount);

(c)   paragraph 6 of Schedule 7 (miscellaneous disclosures); or

(d)   paragraph 11 of Schedule 7 (employee involvement).

(5)   Notwithstanding anything in section 242(1), the directors of the company need not deliver to the registrar any of the following, namely—

(a)   a copy of the company's profit and loss account for the year;

(b)   a copy of the directors' report for the year; and

(c)   if they deliver a copy of a balance sheet drawn up as at the last day of the year which complies with the requirements of Schedule 8A, a copy of the company's balance sheet drawn up as at that day.

(6)   Neither a copy of the company's accounts for the year delivered to the registrar under section 242(1), nor a copy of a balance sheet delivered to the registrar under subsection (5)(c), need give the information required by—

(a)   paragraph 4 of Schedule 5 (financial years of subsidiary undertakings);

(b)   paragraph 6 of Schedule 5 (shares of company held by subsidiary undertakings);

(c)   Part I of Schedule 6 (directors' and chairman's emoluments, pensions and compensation for loss of office); or

(d)   section 390A(3) (amount of auditors' remuneration).

(7)   The provisions of section 233 as to the signing of the copy of the balance sheet delivered to the registrar apply to a copy of a balance sheet delivered under subsection (5)(c).

(8)   Subject to subsection (9), each of the following, namely—

(a) accounts prepared in accordance with subsection (2) or (3),

(b) a report prepared in accordance with subsection (4), and

(c) a copy of accounts delivered to the registrar in accordance with subsection (5) or (6),

shall contain a statement in a prominent position on the balance sheet, in the report or, as the case may be, on the copy of the balance sheet, above the signature required by section 233, 234A or subsection (7), that they are prepared in accordance with the special provisions of this Part relating to small companies.

(9) Subsection (8) does not apply where the directors of the company have taken advantage of the exemption from audit conferred by section 249AA (dormant companies).

246A. Special provisions for medium-sized companies

(1) Subject to section 247A, this section applies where a company qualifies as a medium-sized company in relation to a financial year.

(2) The company's individual accounts for the year need not comply with the requirements of paragraph 36A of Schedule 4 (disclosure with respect to compliance with accounting standards).

(3) The company may deliver to the registrar a copy of the company's accounts for the year—

(a) which includes a profit and loss account in which the following items listed in the profit and loss account formats set out in Part I of Schedule 4 are combined as one item under the heading 'gross profit or loss'—

Items 1, 2, 3 and 6 in Formant 1;
Items 1 to 5 in Format 2;
Items A.1, B.1 and B.2 in Format 3;
Items A.1, A.2 and B.1 to B.4 in Format 4;

(b) which does not contain the information required by paragraph 55 of Schedule 4 (particulars of turnover).

(4) A copy of accounts delivered to the registrar in accordance with subsection (3) shall contain a statement in a prominent position on the copy of the balance sheet, above the signature required by section 233, that the accounts are prepared in accordance with the special provisions of this Part relating to medium-sized companies.

247. Qualification of company as small or medium-sized

(1) A company qualifies as small or medium-sized in relation to a financial year if the qualifying conditions are met—

(a) in the case of the company's first financial year, in that year, and

(b) in the case of any subsequent financial year, in that year and the preceding year.

(2) A company shall be treated as qualifying as small or medium-sized in relation to a financial year—

(a) if it so qualified in relation to the previous financial year under subsection (1) above or was treated as so qualifying under paragraph (b) below; or

(b) if it was treated as so qualifying in relation to the previous year by virtue of paragraph (a) and the qualifying conditions are met in the year in question.

(3) The qualifying conditions are met by a company in a year in which it satisfies two or more of the following requirements—

Small company

1. Turnover — Not more than £2.8 million
2. Balance sheet total — Not more than £1.4 million
3. Number of employees — Not more than 50

Medium-sized company

1. Turnover — Not more than £11.2 million
2. Balance sheet total — Not more than £5.6 million
3. Number of employees — Not more than 250.

(4) For a period which is a company's financial year but not in fact a year the maximum figures for turnover shall be proportionately adjusted.

(5) The balance sheet total means—

(a) where in the company's accounts Format 1 of the balance sheet formats set out in Part I of Schedule 4 or Part I of Schedule 8 is adopted, the aggregate of the amounts shown in the balance sheet under the headings corresponding to items A to D in that Format, and

(b) where Format 2 is adopted, the aggregate of the amounts shown under the general heading 'Assets'.

(6) The number of employees means the average number of persons employed by the company in the year (determined on a monthly basis).

That number shall be determined by applying the method of calculation prescribed by paragraph 56(2) and (3) of Schedule 4 for determining the corresponding number required to be stated in a note to the company's accounts.

247A. Cases in which special provisions do not apply

(1) Nothing in section 246 or 246A shall apply where—

(a) the company is, or was at any time within the financial year to which the accounts relate—

(i) a public company,
(ii) a person who has permission under Part 4 of the Financial Services and Markets Act 2000 to carry on one or more regulated activities, or
(iii) a person who carries on insurance market activity;

(b) the company is, or was at any time during that year, a member of an ineligible group.

(2) A group is ineligible if any of its members is—

(a) a public company or a body corporate which (not being a company) has power under its constitution to offer its shares or debentures to the public and may lawfully exercise that power,

(b) a person who has permission under Part 4 of the Financial Services and Markets Act 2000 to carry on a regulated activity, or

(c) a person who carries on an insurance market activity.

(3) A parent company shall not be treated as qualifying as a small company in relation to a financial year unless the group headed by it qualifies as a small group, and shall not be treated as qualifying as a medium-sized company in relation to a financial year unless that group qualifies as a medium-sized group (see section 249).

247B. Special auditors' report

(1) This section applies where—

(a) the directors of a company propose to deliver to the registrar copies of accounts ('abbreviated accounts') prepared in accordance with section 246(5) or (6) or 246A(3) ('the relevant provision'),

(b) the directors have not taken advantage of the exemption from audit conferred by section 249A(1) or (2) or section 249AA.

(2) If abbreviated accounts prepared in accordance with the relevant provision are delivered to the registrar, they shall be accompanied by a copy of a special report of the auditors stating that in their opinion—

(a) the company is entitled to deliver abbreviated accounts prepared in accordance with that provision, and

(b) the abbreviated accounts to be delivered are properly prepared in accordance with that provision.

(3) In such a case a copy of the auditors' report under section 235 need not be delivered, but—

(a) if that report was qualified, the special report shall set out that report in full together with any further material necessary to understand the qualification; and

(b) if that report contained a statement under—

(i) section 237(2) (accounts, records or returns inadequate or accounts not agreeing with records and returns), or

(ii) section 237(3) (failure to obtain necessary information and explanations),

the special report shall set out that statement in full.

(4)   Section 236 (signature of auditors' report) applies to a special report under this section as it applies to a report under section 235.

(5)   If abbreviated accounts prepared in accordance with the relevant provision are delivered to the registrar, references in section 240 (requirements in connection with publication of accounts) to the auditors' report under section 235 shall be read as references to the special auditors' report under this section.

249AA.   Dormant companies

(1)   Subject to section 249B(2) to (5), a company is exempt from the provisions of this Part relating to the audit of accounts in respect of a financial year if—

    (a)   it has been dormant since its formation, or

    (b)   it has been dormant since the end of the previous financial year and subsection (2) applies.

(2)   This subsection applies if the company—

    (a)   is entitled in respect of its individual accounts for the financial year in question to prepare accounts in accordance with section 246, or would be so entitled but for the application of section 247A(1)(a)(i) or (b), and

    (b)   is not required to prepare group accounts for that year.

(3)   Subsection (1) does not apply if at any time in the financial year in question the company was—

    (a)   a person who has permission under Part 4 of the Financial Services and Markets Act 2000 to carry on one or more regulated activities; or

    (b)   a person who carries on insurance market activity.

(4)   A company is 'dormant' during any period in which it has no significant accounting transaction.

(5)   'Significant accounting transaction' means a transaction which—

    (a)   is required by section 221 to be entered in the company's accounting records; but

    (b)   is not a transaction to which subsection (6) or (7) applies.

(6)   This subsection applies to a transaction arising from the taking of shares in the company by a subscriber to the memorandum as a result of an undertaking of his in the memorandum.

(7)   This subsection applies to a transaction consisting of the payment of—

    (a)   a fee to the registrar on a change of name under section 28 (change of name),

    (b)   a fee to the registrar on the re-registration of a company under Part II (re-registration as a means of altering a company's status),

    (c)   a penalty under section 242A (penalty for failure to deliver accounts), or

    (d)   a fee to the registrar for the registration of an annual return under Chapter III of Part XI.

252.   Election to dispense with laying of accounts and reports before general meeting

(1)   A private company may elect (by elective resolution in accordance with section 379A) to dispense with the laying of accounts and reports before the company in general meeting.

(2)   An election has effect in relation to the accounts and reports in respect of the financial year in which the election is made and subsequent financial years.

(3)   Whilst an election is in force, the references in the following provisions of this Act to the laying of accounts before the company in general meeting shall be read as references to the sending of copies of the accounts to members and others under section 238(1)—

    (a)   section 235(1)(accounts on which auditors are to report),

    (b)   section 270(3) and (4) (accounts by reference to which distributions are justified), and

    (c)   section 320(2)(accounts relevant for determining company's net assets for purposes of ascertaining whether approval required for certain transactions);

and the requirement in section 271(4) that the auditors' statement under that provision be laid before the company in general meeting shall be read as a requirement that it be sent to members and others along with the copies of the accounts sent to them under section 238(1).

Part II   Company

(4)   If an election under this section ceases to have effect, section 241 applies in relation to the accounts and reports in respect of the financial year in which the election ceases to have effect and subsequent financial years.

253. Right of shareholder to require laying of accounts

(1)   Where an election under section 252 is in force, the copies of the accounts and reports sent out in accordance with section 238(1)—

> (a)   shall be sent not less than 28 days before the end of the period allowed for laying and delivering accounts and reports, and
>
> (b)   shall be accompanied, in the case of a member of the company, by a notice informing him of his right to require the laying of the accounts and reports before a general meeting;

and section 238(5) (penalty for default) applies in relation to the above requirements as to the requirements contained in that section.

(2)   Before the end of the period of 28 days beginning with the day on which the accounts and reports are sent out in accordance with section 238(1), any member or auditor of the company may by notice in writing deposited at the registered office of the company require that a general meeting be held for the purpose of laying the accounts and reports before the company.

(2A)   The power of a member or auditor under subsection (2) to require the holding of a general meeting is exercisable not only by the deposit of a notice in writing but also by the transmission to the company at such address as may for the time being be specified for the purpose by or on behalf of the company of an electronic communication containing the requirement.

(3)   If the directors do not within 21 days from the date of—

> (a)   the deposit of a notice containing a requirement under subsection (2), or
>
> (b)   the receipt of such a requirement contained in an electronic communication, proceed duly to convene a meeting, the person who required the holding of the meeting may do so himself.

(4)   A meeting so convened shall not be held more than three months from that date and shall be convened in the same manner, as nearly as possible, as that in which meetings are to be convened by directors.

(5)   Where the directors do not duly convene a meeting, any reasonable expenses incurred by reason of that failure by the person who required the holding of the meeting shall be made good to him by the company, and shall be recouped by the company out of any fees, or other remuneration in respect of their services, due or to become due to such of the directors as were in default.

(6)   The directors shall be deemed not to have duly convened a meeting if they convene a meeting for a date more than 28 days after the date of the notice convening it.

PART VIII

DISTRIBUTION OF PROFIT AND ASSETS

263. Certain distributions prohibited

(1)   A company shall not make a distribution except out of profits available for the purpose.

(2)   In this Part, 'distribution' means every description of distribution of a company's assets to its members, whether in cash or otherwise, except distribution by way of—

> (a)   an issue of shares as fully or partly paid bonus shares,
>
> (b)   the redemption or purchase of any of the company's own shares out of capital (including the proceeds of any fresh issue of shares) or out of unrealised profits in accordance with Chapter VII or Part V,
>
> (c)   the reduction of share capital by extinguishing or reducing the liability of any of the members on any of the company's shares in respect of share capital not paid up, or by paying off paid up share capital, and
>
> (d)   a distribution of assets to members of the company on its winding up.

(3)   For purposes of this Part, a company's profits available for distribution are its accumulated, realised profits, so far as not previously utilised by distribution or capitalization, less its accumulated, realised losses, so far as not previously written off in a reduction or reorganisation of capital duly made.

This is subject to the provision made by sections 265 and 266 for investment and other companies.

(4)   A company shall not apply an unrealised profit in paying up debentures, or any amounts unpaid on its issued shares.

(5)   Where the directors of a company are, after making all reasonable enquiries, unable to determine whether a particular profit made before 22nd December 1980 is realised or unrealised, they may treat the profit as realised; and where after making such enquiries they are unable to determine whether a particular loss so made is realised or unrealised, they may treat the loss as unrealised.

PART IX

A COMPANY'S MANAGEMENT; DIRECTORS AND SECRETARIES; THEIR QUALIFICATIONS, DUTIES AND RESPONSIBILITIES

282. Directors

(1)   Every company registered on or after 1st November 1929 (other than a private company) shall have at least two directors.

(2)   Every company registered before that date (other than a private company) shall have at least one director.

(3)   Every private company shall have at least one director.

283. Secretary

(1)   Every company shall have a secretary.

(2)   A sole director shall not also be secretary.

(3)   Anything required or authorised to be done by or to the secretary may, if the office is vacant or there is for any other reason no secretary capable of acting, be done by or to any assistant or deputy secretary or, if there is no assistant or deputy secretary capable of acting, by or to any officer of the company authorised generally or specially in that behalf by the directors.

(4)   No company shall—

   (a)   have as secretary to the company a corporation the sole director of which is a sole director of the company;
   (b)   have as sole director of the company a corporation the sole director of which is secretary to the company.

285. Validity of acts of directors

The acts of a director or manager are valid notwithstanding any defect that may afterwards be discovered in his appointment or qualification; and this provision is not excluded by section 292(2) (void resolution to appoint).

287. Registered office

(1)   A company shall at all times have a registered office to which all communications and notices may be addressed.

(2)   On incorporation the situation of the company's registered office is that specified in the statement sent to the registrar under section 10.

(3)   The company may change the situation of its registered office from time to time by giving notice in the prescribed form to the registrar.

(4)   The change takes effect upon the notice being registered by the registrar, but until the end of the period of 14 days beginning with the date on which it is registered a person may validly serve any document on the company at its previous registered office.

(5)   For the purposes of any duty of a company—

   (a)   to keep at its registered office, or make available for public inspection there, any register, index or other document, or
   (b)   to mention the address of its registered office in any document,

a company which has given notice to the registrar of a change in the situation of its registered office may act on the change as from such date, not more than 14 days after the notice is given, as it may determine.

(6)   Where a company unavoidably ceases to perform at its registered office any such duty as is mentioned in subsection (5)(a) in circumstances in which it was not practicable to give prior notice to the registrar of a change in the situation of its registered office, but—

(a)   resumes performance of that duty at other premises as soon as practicable, and
(b)   gives notice accordingly to the registrar of a change in the situation of its registered office within 14 days of doing so,

it shall not be treated as having failed to comply with that duty.

(7)   In proceedings for an offence of failing to comply with any such duty as is mentioned in subsection (5), it is for the person charged to show that by reason of the matters referred to in that subsection or subsection (6) no offence was committed.

288. Register of directors and secretaries

(1)   Every company shall keep at its registered office a register of its directors and secretaries; and the register shall, with respect to the particulars to be contained in it of those persons, comply with sections 289 and 290 below.

(2)   The company shall, within the period of 14 days from the occurrence of—

(a)   any change among its directors or in its secretary, or
(b)   any change in the particulars contained in the register,

send to the registrar of companies a notification in the prescribed form of the change and of the date on which it occurred; and a notification of a person having become a director or secretary, or one of joint secretaries, of the company shall contain a consent, signed by that person, to act in the relevant capacity.

(3)   The register shall be open to the inspection of any member of the company without charge and of any other person on payment of such fee as may be prescribed.

(4)   If an inspection required under this section is refused, or if default is made in complying with subsection (1) or (2), the company and every officer of it who is in default is liable to a fine and, for continued contravention, to a daily default fine.

(5)   In the case of a refusal of inspection of the register, the court may by order compel an immediate inspection of it.

(5A) Where a confidentiality order made under section 723B is in force in respect of a director or secretary of a company, subsections (3) and (5) shall not apply in relation to that part of the register of the company as contains particulars of the usual residential address of that individual.

(6)   For purposes of this and the next section, a shadow director of a company is deemed a director and officer of it.

303. Resolution to remove director

(1)   A company may by ordinary resolution remove a director before the expiration of his period of office, notwithstanding anything in its articles or in any agreement between it and him.

(2)   Special notice is required of a resolution to remove a director under this section or to appoint somebody instead of a director so removed at the meeting at which he is removed.

(3)   A vacancy created by the removal of a director under this section, if not filled at the meeting at which he is removed, may be filled as a casual vacancy.

(4)   A person appointed director in place of a person removed under this section is treated, for the purpose of determining the time at which he or any other director is to retire, as if he had become director on the day on which the person in whose place he is appointed was last appointed a director.

(5)   This section is not to be taken as depriving a person removed under it of compensation or damages payable to him in respect of the termination of his appointment as director or of any appointment terminating with that as director, or as derogating from any power to remove a director which may exist apart from this section.

304. Director's right to protest removal

(1)   On receipt of notice of an intended resolution to remove a director under section 303, the company shall forthwith send a copy of the notice to the director concerned; and he (whether or not a member of the company) is entitled to be heard on the resolution at the meeting.

(2)   Where notice is given of an intended resolution to remove a director under that section, and the director concerned makes with respect to it representations in writing to the company (not exceeding a reasonable length) and requests their notification to members of the company, the company shall, unless the representations are received by it too late for it to do so—

> (a)   in any notice of the resolution given to members of the company state the fact of the representations having been made; and
> (b)   send a copy of the representations to every member of the company to whom notice of the meeting is sent (whether before or after receipt of the representations by the company).

(3)   If a copy of the representations is not sent as required by subsection (2) because received too late or because of the company's default, the director may (without prejudice to his right to be heard orally) require that the representations shall be read out at the meeting.

(4)   But copies of the representations need not be sent out and the representations need not be read out at the meeting if, on the application either of the company or of any other person who claims to be aggrieved, the court is satisfied that the rights conferred by this section are being abused to secure needless publicity for defamatory matter.

(5)   The court may order the company's costs on an application under this section to be paid in whole or in part by the director, notwithstanding that he is not a party to the application.

305. Directors' names on company correspondence, etc

(1)   A company to which this section applies shall not state, in any form, the name of any of its directors (otherwise than in the text or as a signatory) on any business letter on which the company's name appears unless it states on the letter in legible characters the name of every director of the company.

(2)   This section applies to—

> (a)   every company registered under this Act or under the former Companies Acts (except a company registered before 23rd November 1916); and
> (b)   every company incorporated outside Great Britain which has an established place of business within Great Britain, unless it had established such a place of business before that date.

(3)   If a company makes default in complying with this section, every officer of the company who is in default is liable for each offence to a fine; and for this purpose, where a corporation is an officer of the company, any officer of the corporation is deemed an officer of the company.

(4)   For the purposes of the obligation under subsection (1) to state the name of every director of the company, a person's 'name' means—

> (a)   in the case of an individual, his Christian name (or other forename) and surname; and
> (b)   in the case of a corporation or Scottish firm, its corporate or firm name.

(5)   The initial or a recognised abbreviation of a person's Christian name or other forename may be stated instead of the full Christian name or other forename.

(6)   In the case of a peer, or an individual usually known by a title, the title may be stated instead of his Christian name (or other forename) and surname or in addition to either or both of them.

(7)   In this section 'director' includes a shadow director and the reference in subsection (3) to an 'officer' shall be construed accordingly.

309. Directors to have regard to interests of employees

(1)   The matters to which the directors of a company are to have regard in the performance of their functions include the interests of the company's employees in general, as well as the interests of its members.

(2)   Accordingly, the duty imposed by this section on the directors is owed by them to the company (and the company alone) and is enforceable in the same way as any other fiduciary duty owed to a company by its directors.

(3)   This section applies to shadow directors as it does to directors.

310. Provisions exempting officers and auditors from liability

(1) This section applies to any provision, whether contained in a company's articles or in any contract with the company or otherwise for exempting any officer of the company or any person (whether an officer or not) employed by the company as auditor from, or indemnifying him against, any liability which by virtue of any rule of law would otherwise attach to him in respect of any negligence, default, breach of duty or breach of trust of which he may be guilty in relation to the company.

(2) Except as provided by the following subsection, any such provision is void.

(3) This section does not prevent a company—

> (a) from purchasing and maintaining for any such officer or auditor insurance against any such liability, or
> (b) from indemnifying any such officer or auditor against any liability incurred by him—
>
> > (i) in defending any proceedings (whether civil or criminal) in which judgment is given in his favour or he is acquitted, or
> > (ii) in connection with any application under section 144(3) or (4) (acquisition of shares by innocent nominee) or section 727 (general power to grant relief in case of honest and reasonable conduct) in which relief is granted to him by the court.

PART X

ENFORCEMENT OF FAIR DEALING BY DIRECTORS

312. Payment to director for loss of office, etc

It is not lawful for a company to make to a director of the company any payment by way of compensation for loss of office, or as consideration for or in connection with his retirement from office, without particulars of the proposed payment (including its amount) being disclosed to members of the company and the proposal being approved by the company.

316. Provisions supplementing ss 312 to 315

(1) Where in proceedings for the recovery of any payment as having, by virtue of section 313(2) or 315(1), been received by any person in trust, it is shown that—

> (a) the payment was made in pursuance of any arrangement entered into as part of the agreement for the transfer in question, or within one year before or two years after that agreement or the offer leading to it; and
> (b) the company or any person to whom the transfer was made was privy to that arrangement,

the payment is deemed, except in so far as the contrary is shown, to be one to which the provisions mentioned above in this subsection apply.

(2) If in connection with any such transfer as is mentioned in any of sections 313 to 315—

> (a) the price to be paid to a director of the company whose office is to be abolished or who is to retire from office for any shares in the company held by him is in excess of the price which could at the time have been obtained by other holders of the like shares; or
> (b) any valuable consideration is given to any such director,

the excess or the money value of the consideration (as the case may be) is deemed for the purposes of that section to have been a payment made to him by way of compensation for loss of office or as consideration for or in connection with his retirement from office.

(3) References in sections 312 to 315 to payments made to a director by way of compensation for loss of office or as consideration for or in connection with his retirement from office, do not include any bona fide payment by way of damages for breach of contract or by way of pension in respect of past services.

'Pension' here includes any superannuation allowance, superannuation gratuity or similar payment.

(4) Nothing in sections 313 to 315 prejudices the operation of any rule of law requiring disclosure to be made with respect to such payments as are there mentioned, or with respect to any other like payments made or to be made to a company's directors.

317. Directors to disclose interest in contracts

(1)   It is the duty of a director of a company who is in any way, whether directly or indirectly, interested in a contract or proposed contract with the company to declare the nature of his interest at a meeting of the directors of the company.

(2)   In the case of a proposed contract, the declaration shall be made—

(a)   at the meeting of the directors at which the question of entering into the contract is first taken into consideration; or
(b)   if the director was not at the date of that meeting interested in the proposed contract, at the next meeting of the directors held after he became so interested;

and, in a case where the director becomes interested in a contract after it is made, the declaration shall be made at the first meeting of the directors held after he becomes so interested.

(3)   For purposes of this section, a general notice given to the directors of a company by a director to the effect that—

(a)   he is a member of a specified company or firm and is to be regarded as interested in any contract which may, after the date of the notice be made with that company or firm; or
(b)   he is to be regarded as interested in any contract which may after the date of the notice be made with a specified person who is connected with him (within the meaning of section 346 below),

is deemed a sufficient declaration of interest in relation to any such contract.

(4)   However, no such notice is of effect unless either it is given at a meeting of the directors or the director takes reasonable steps to secure that it is brought up and read at the next meeting of the directors after it is given.

(5)   A reference in this section to a contract includes any transaction or arrangement (whether or not constituting a contract) made or entered into on or after 22nd December 1980.

(6)   For purposes of this section, a transaction or arrangement of a kind described in section 330 (prohibition of loans, quasi-loans etc to directors) made by a company for a director of the company or a person connected with such a director is treated (if it would not otherwise be so treated, and whether or not it is prohibited by that section) as a transaction or arrangement in which that director is interested.

(7)   A director who fails to comply with this section is liable to a fine.

(8)   This section applies to a shadow director as it applies to a director, except that a shadow director shall declare his interest, not at a meeting of the directors, but by a notice in writing to the directors which is either—

(a)   a specific notice given before the date of the meeting at which, if he had been a director, the declaration would be required by subsection (2) to be made; or
(b)   a notice which under subsection (3) falls to be treated as a sufficient declaration of that interest (or would fall to be so treated apart from subsection (4)).

(9)   Nothing in this section prejudices the operation of any rule of law restricting directors of a company from having an interest in contracts with the company.

318. Directors' service contracts to be open to inspection

(1)   Subject to the following provisions, every company shall keep at an appropriate place—

(a)   in the case of each director whose contract of service with the company is in writing, a copy of that contract;
(b)   in the case of each director whose contract of service with the company is not in writing, a written memorandum setting out its terms; and
(c)   in the case of each director who is employed under a contract of service with a subsidiary of the company, a copy of that contract or, if it is not in writing, a written memorandum setting out its terms.

(2)   All copies and memoranda kept by a company in pursuance of subsection (1) shall be kept at the same place.

(3)   The following are appropriate places for the purposes of subsection (1)—

(a)   the company's registered office;
(b)   the place where its register of members is kept (if other than its registered office);

(c)   its principal place of business, provided that is situated in that part of Great Britain in which the company is registered.

(4)   Every company shall send notice in the prescribed form to the registrar of companies of the place where copies and memoranda are kept in compliance with subsection (1), and of any change in that place, save in a case in which they have at all times been kept at the company's registered office.

(5)   Subsection (1) does not apply to a director's contract of service with the company or with a subsidiary of it if that contract required him to work wholly or mainly outside the United Kingdom; but the company shall keep a memorandum—

(a)   in the case of a contract of service with the company, giving the director's name and setting out the provisions of the contract relating to its duration;

(b)   in the case of a contract of service with a subsidiary, giving the director's name and the name and place of incorporation of the subsidiary, and setting out the provisions of the contract relating to its duration,

at the same place as copies and memoranda are kept by the company in pursuance of subsection (1).

(6)   A shadow director is treated for purposes of this section as a director.

(7)   Every copy and memorandum required by subsection (1) or (5) to be kept shall be open to inspection of any member of the company without charge.

(8)   If—

(a)   default is made in complying with subsection (1) or (5), or

(b)   an inspection required under subsection (7) is refused, or

(c)   default is made for 14 days in complying with subsection (4),

the company and every officer of it who is in default is liable to a fine and, for continued contravention, to a daily default fine.

(9)   In the case of a refusal of an inspection required under subsection (7) of a copy or memorandum, the court may by order compel an immediate inspection of it.

(10)   Subsections (1) and (5) apply to a variation of a director's contract of service as they apply to the contract.

(11)   This section does not require that there by kept a copy of, or memorandum setting out the terms of, a contract (or its variation) at a time when the unexpired portion of the term for which the contract is to be in force is less than 12 months, or at a time at which the contract can, within the next ensuing 12 months, be terminated by the company without payment of compensation.

319.   Director's contract of employment for more than 5 years

(1)   This section applies in respect of any term of an agreement whereby a director's employment with the company of which he is a director or, where he is the director of a holding company, his employment within the group is to continue, or may be continued, otherwise than at the instance of the company (whether under the original agreement or under a new agreement entered into in pursuance of it), for a period of more than 5 years during which the employment—

(a)   cannot be terminated by the company by notice; or

(b)   can be so terminated only in specified circumstances.

(2)   In any case where—

(a)   a person is or is to be employed with a company under an agreement which cannot be terminated by the company by notice or can be so terminated only in specified circumstances; and

(b)   more than 6 months before the expiration of the period for which he is or is to be so employed, the company enters into a further agreement (otherwise than in pursuance of a right conferred by or under the original agreement on the other party to it) under which he is to be employed with the company or, where he is a director of a holding company, within the group,

this section applies as if to the period for which he is to be employed under that further agreement there were added a further period equal to the unexpired period of the original agreement.

(3)   A company shall not incorporate in an agreement such a term as is mentioned in subsection (1), unless the term is first approved by a resolution of the company in general meeting and, in the case of a director of a holding company, by a resolution of that company in general meeting.

(4)   No approval is required to be given under this section by any body corporate unless it is a company within the meaning of this Act, or is registered under section 680, or if it is a wholly-owned subsidiary of any body corporate wherever incorporated.

(5)   A resolution of a company approving such a term as is mentioned in subsection (1) shall not be passed at a general meeting of the company unless a written memorandum setting out the proposed agreement incorporating the term is available for inspection by members of the company both—

(a)   at the company's registered office for not less than 15 days ending with the date of the meeting; and

(b)   at the meeting itself.

(6)   A term incorporated in an agreement in contravention of this section is, to the extent that it contravenes the section, void; and that agreement and, in a case where subsection (2) applies, the original agreement are deemed to contain a term entitling the company to terminate it at any time by the giving of reasonable notice.

(7)   In this section—

(a)   'employment' includes employment under a contract for services; and

(b)   'group', in relation to a director of a holding company, means the group which consists of that company and its subsidiaries;

and for purposes of this section a shadow director is treated as a director.

320. Substantial property transactions involving directors, etc

(1)   With the exceptions provided by the section next following, a company shall not enter into an arrangement—

(a)   whereby a director of the company or its holding company, or a person connected with such a director, acquires or is to acquire one or more non-cash assets of the requisite value from the company; or

(b)   whereby the company acquires or is to acquire one or more non-cash assets of the requisite value from such a director or a person so connected,

unless the arrangement is first approved by a resolution of the company in general meeting and, if the director or connected person is a director of its holding company or a person connected with such a director, by a resolution in general meeting of the holding company.

(2)   For this purpose a non-cash asset is of the requisite value if at the time the arrangement in question is entered into its value is not less than £2,000 but (subject to that) exceeds £100,000 or 10 per cent of the company's asset value, that is—

(a)   except in a case falling within paragraph (b) below, the value of the company's net assets determined by reference to the accounts prepared and laid under Part VII in respect of the last preceding financial year in respect of which such accounts were so laid; and

(b)   where no accounts have been so prepared and laid before that time, the amount of the company's called-up share capital.

(3)   For purposes of this section and sections 321 and 322, a shadow director is treated as a director.

321. Exceptions from s 320

(1)   No approval is required to be given under section 320 by any body corporate unless it is a company within the meaning of this Act or registered under section 680 or, if it is a wholly-owned subsidiary of any body corporate, wherever incorporated.

(2)   Section 320(1) does not apply to an arrangement for the acquisition of a non-cash asset—

(a)   if the asset is to be acquired by a holding company from any of its wholly-owned subsidiaries or from a holding company by any of its wholly-owned subsidiaries, or by one wholly-owned subsidiary of a holding company from another wholly owned subsidiary of that same holding company, or

(b)   if the arrangement is entered into by a company which is being wound up, unless the winding up in a members' voluntary winding up.

(3)   Section 320(1)(a) does not apply to an arrangement whereby a person is to acquire an asset from a company of which he is a member, if the arrangement is made with that person in his character as a member.

Part II Company

(4) Section 320(1) does not apply to a transaction on a recognised investment exchange which is effected by a director, or a person connected with him, through the agency of a person who in relation to the transaction acts as an independent broker.

For this purpose an 'independent broker' means—

(a) in relation to a transaction on behalf of a director, a person who independently of the director selects the person with whom the transaction is to be effected, and

(b) in relation to a transaction on behalf of a person connected with a director, a person who independently of that person or the director selects the person with whom the transaction is to be effected;

and 'recognised', in relation to an investment exchange, means recognised under the Financial Services and Markets Act 2000.

322. Liabilities arising from contravention of s 320

(1) An arrangement entered into by a company in contravention of section 320, and any transaction entered into in pursuance of the arrangement (whether by the company or any other person) is voidable at the instance of the company unless one or more of the conditions specified in the next subsection is satisfied.

(2) Those conditions are that—

(a) restitution of any money or other asset which is the subject-matter of the arrangement or transaction is no longer possible or the company has been indemnified in pursuance of this section by any other person for the loss or damage suffered by it; or

(b) any rights acquired bona fide for value and without actual notice of the contravention by any person who is not a party to the arrangement or transaction would be affected by its avoidance; or

(c) the arrangement is, within a reasonable period, affirmed by the company in general meeting and, if it is an arrangement for the transfer of an asset to or by a director of its holding company or a person who is connected with such a director, is so affirmed with the approval of the holding company given by a resolution in general meeting.

(3) If an arrangement is entered into with a company by a director of the company or its holding company or a person connected with him in contravention of section 320, that director and the person so connected, and any other director of the company who authorised the arrangement or any transaction entered into in pursuance of such an arrangement, is liable—

(a) to account to the company for any gain which he has made directly or indirectly by the arrangement or transaction, and

(b) (jointly and severally with any other person liable under this subsection) to indemnify the company for any loss or damage resulting from the arrangement or transaction.

(4) Subsection (3) is without prejudice to any liability imposed otherwise than by that subsection, and is subject to the following two subsections; and the liability under subsection (3) arises whether or not the arrangement or transaction entered into has been avoided in pursuance of subsection (1).

(5) If an arrangement is entered into by a company and a person connected with a director of the company or its holding company in contravention of section 320, that director is not liable under subsection (3) if he shows that he took all reasonable steps to secure the company's compliance with that section.

(6) In any case, a person so connected and any such other director as is mentioned in subsection (3) is not so liable if he shows that at the time the arrangement was entered into, he did not know the relevant circumstances constituting the contravention.

322A. Invalidity of certain transactions involving directors, etc

(1) This section applies where a company enters into a transaction to which the parties include—

(a) a director of the company or its holding company, or

(b) a person connected with such a director or a company with whom such a director is associated,

and the board of directors, in connection with the transaction, exceed any limitation on their powers under the company's constitution.

(2) The transaction is voidable at the instance of the company.

(3)   Whether or not it is avoided, any such party to the transaction as is mentioned in subsection (1)(a) or (b), and any director of the company who authorised the transaction, is liable—

(a)   to account to the company for any gain which he has made directly or indirectly by the transaction, and

(b)   to indemnify the company for any loss or damage resulting from the transaction.

(4)   Nothing in the above provisions shall be construed as excluding the operation of any other enactment or rule of law by virtue of which the transaction may be called in question or any liability to the company may arise.

(5)   The transaction ceases to be voidable if—

(a)   restitution of any money or other asset which was the subject-matter of the transaction is no longer possible, or

(b)   the company is indemnified for any loss or damage resulting from the transaction, or

(c)   rights acquired bona fide for value and without actual notice of the directors' exceeding their powers by a person who is not party to the transaction would be affected by the avoidance, or

(d)   the transaction is ratified by the company in general meeting, by ordinary or special resolution or otherwise as the case may require.

(6)   A person other than a director of the company is not liable under subsection (3) if he shows that at the time the transaction was entered into he did not know that the directors were exceeding their powers.

(7)   This section does not affect the operation of section 35A in relation to any party to the transaction not within subsection (1)(a) or (b).

But where a transaction is voidable by virtue of this section and valid by virtue of that section in favour of such a person, the court may, on the application of that person or of the company, make such order affirming, severing or setting aside the transaction, on such terms, as appear to the court to be just.

(8)   In this section 'transaction' includes any act; and the reference in subsection (1) to limitations under the company's constitution includes limitations deriving—

(a)   from a resolution of the company in general meeting or a meeting of any class of shareholders, or

(b)   from any agreement between the members of the company or of any class of shareholders.

324. Duty of director to disclose shareholdings in own company

(1)   A person who becomes a director of a company and at the time when he does so is interested in shares in, or debentures of, the company or any other body corporate, being the company's subsidiary or holding company or a subsidiary of the company's holding company, is under obligation to notify the company in writing—

(a)   of the subsistence of his interests at that time; and

(b)   of the number of shares of each class in, and the amount of debentures of each class of, the company or other such body corporate in which each interest of his subsists at that time.

(2)   A director of a company is under obligation to notify the company in writing of the occurrence, while he is a director, of any of the following events—

(a)   any event in consequence of whose occurrence he becomes, or ceases to be, interested in shares in, or debentures of, the company or any other body corporate, being the company's subsidiary or holding company or a subsidiary of the company's holding company;

(b)   the entering into by him of a contract to sell any such shares or debentures;

(c)   the assignment by him of a right granted to him by the company to subscribe for shares in, or debentures of, the company; and

(d)   the grant to him by another body corporate, being the company's subsidiary or holding company or a subsidiary of the company's holding company, of a right to subscribe for shares in, or debentures of, that other body corporate, the exercise of such a right granted to him and the assignment by him of such a right so granted;

and notification to the company must state the number or amount, and class, of shares or debentures involved.

(3)   Schedule 13 has effect in connection with subsection (1) and (2) above; and of that Schedule—

(a)   Part I contains rules for the interpretation of, and otherwise in relation to, those subsections and applies in determining, for purposes of those subsections, whether a person has an interest in shares or debentures;

(b)   Part II applies with respect to the periods within which obligations imposed by the subsections must be fulfilled; and

(c)   Part III specifies certain circumstances in which obligations arising from subsection (2) are to be treated as not discharged;

and subsections (1) and (2) are subject to any exceptions for which provision may be made by regulations made by the Secretary of State by statutory instrument.

(4)   Subsection (2) does not require the notification by a person of the occurrence of an event whose occurrence comes to his knowledge after he has ceased to be a director.

(5)   An obligation imposed by this section is treated as not discharged unless the notice by means of which it purports to be discharged is expressed to be given in fulfilment of that obligation.

(6)   This section applies to shadow directors as to directors; but nothing in it operates so as to impose an obligation with respect to shares in a body corporate which is the wholly-owned subsidiary of another body corporate.

(7)   A person who—

(a)   fails to discharge, within the proper period, an obligation to which he is subject under subsection (1) or (2), or

(b)   in purported discharge of an obligation to which he is so subject, makes to the company a statement which he knows to be false, or recklessly makes to it a statement which is false,

is guilty of an offence and liable to imprisonment or a fine, or both.

(8)   Section 732 (restriction on prosecutions) applies to an offence under this section.

325. Register of directors' interests notified under s 324

(1)   Every company shall keep a register for the purposes of section 324.

(2)   Whenever a company receives information from a director given in fulfilment of an obligation imposed on him by that section, it is under obligation to enter in the register, against the director's name, the information received and the date of the entry.

(3)   The company is also under obligation, whenever it grants to a director a right to subscribe for shares in, or debentures of, the company to enter in the register against his name—

(a)   the date on which the right is granted

(b)   the period during which, or time at which, it is exercisable,

(c)   the consideration for the grant (or, if there is no consideration, that fact), and

(d)   the description of shares or debentures involved and the number or amount of them, and the price to be paid for them (or the consideration, if otherwise than in money).

(4)   Whenever such a right as is mentioned above is exercised by a director, the company is under obligation to enter in the register against his name that fact (identifying the right), the number or amount of shares or debentures in respect of which it is exercised and, if they were registered in his name, that fact and, if not, the name or names of the person or persons in whose name or names they were registered, together (if they were registered in the names of two persons or more) with the number or amount of the shares or debentures registered in the name of each of them.

(5)   Part IV of Schedule 13 has effect with respect to the register to be kept under this section, to the way in which entries in it are to be made, to the right of inspection, and generally.

(6)   For purposes of this section, a shadow director is deemed a director.

328. Extension of s 324 to spouses and children

(1)   For the purposes of section 324—

(a)   an interest of the wife or husband of a director of a company (not being herself or himself a director of it) in shares or debentures is to be treated as the director's interest; and

(b)   the same applies to an interest of an infant son or infant daughter of a director of a company (not being himself or herself a director of it) in shares or debentures.

(2)   For those purposes—

(a) a contract, assignment or right of subscription entered into, exercised or made by, or a grant made to, the wife or husband of a director of a company (not being herself or himself a director of it) is to be treated as having been entered into, exercised or made by, or (as the case may be) as having been made to, the director; and

(b) the same applies to a contract, assignment or right of subscription entered into, exercised or made by, or grant made to, an infant son or infant daughter of a director of a company (not being himself or herself a director of it).

(3) A director of a company is under obligation to notify the company in writing of the occurrence while he or she is a director, of either of the following events, namely—

(a) the grant by the company to his (her) spouse, or to his or her infant son or infant daughter, of a right to subscribe for shares in, or debentures of, the company; and

(b) the exercise by his (her) spouse or by his or her infant son or infant daughter of such a right granted by the company to the wife, husband, son or daughter.

(4) In a notice given to the company under subsection (3) there shall be stated—

(a) in the case of the grant of a right, the like information as is required by section 324 to be stated by the director on the grant to him by another body corporate of a right to subscribe for shares in, or debentures of, that other body corporate; and

(b) in the case of the exercise of a right, the like information as is required by that section to be stated by the director on the exercise of a right granted to him by another body corporate to subscribe for shares in, or debentures of, that other body corporate.

(5) An obligation imposed by subsection (3) on a director must be fulfilled by him before the end of 5 days beginning with the day following that on which the occurrence of the event giving rise to it comes to his knowledge; but in reckoning that period of days there is disregarded any Saturday or Sunday, and any day which is a bank holiday in any part of Great Britain.

(6) A person who—

(a) fails to fulfil, within the proper period, an obligation to which he is subject under subsection (3), or

(b) in purported fulfilment of such an obligation, makes to a company a statement which he knows to be false, or recklessly makes to a company a statement which is false,

is guilty of an offence and liable to imprisonment or a fine, or both.

(7) The rules set out in Part I of Schedule 13 have effect for the interpretation of, and otherwise in relation to, subsections (1) and (2); and subsections (5), (6) and (8) of section 324 apply with any requisite modification.

(8) In this section 'son' includes step-son, 'daughter' includes step-daughter, and 'infant' means, in relation to Scotland, a person under the age of 18 years.

(9) For purposes of section 325, an obligation imposed on a director by this section is to be treated as if imposed by section 324.

330. General restriction on loans etc to directors and persons connected with them

(1) The prohibitions listed below in this section are subject to the exceptions in sections 332 to 338.

(2) A company shall not—

(a) make a loan to a director of the company or of its holding company;

(b) enter into any guarantee or provide any security in connection with a loan made by any person to such a director.

(3) A relevant company shall not—

(a) make a quasi-loan to a director of the company or of its holding company;

(b) make a loan or a quasi-loan to a person connected with such a director;

(c) enter into a guarantee or provide any security in connection with a loan or quasi-loan made by any other person for such a director or a person so connected.

(4) A relevant company shall not—

(a) enter into a credit transaction as creditor for such a director or a person so connected;

(b)   enter into any guarantee or provide any security in connection with a credit transaction made by any other person for such a director or a person so connected.

(5)   For purposes of sections 330 to 346, a shadow director is treated as a director.

(6)   A company shall not arrange for the assignment to it, or the assumption by it, of any rights, obligations or liabilities under a transaction which, if it had been entered into by the company, would have contravened subsection (2), (3) or (4); but for the purposes of sections 330 to 347 the transaction is to be treated as having been entered into on the date of the arrangement.

(7)   A company shall not take part in any arrangement whereby—

(a)   another person enters into a transaction which, if it had been entered into by the company, would have contravened any of subsections (2), (3), (4) or (6); and

(b)   that other person, in pursuance of the arrangement, has obtained or is to obtain any benefit from the company or its holding company or a subsidiary of the company or its holding company.

331. Definitions for ss 330ff

(1)   The following subsections apply for the interpretation of sections 330 to 346.

(2)   'Guarantee' includes indemnity, and cognate expressions are to be construed accordingly.

(3)   A quasi-loan is a transaction under which one party ('the creditor') agrees to pay, or pays otherwise than in pursuance of an agreement, a sum for another ('the borrower') or agrees to reimburse, or reimburses otherwise than in pursuance of an agreement, expenditure incurred by another party for another ('the borrower')—

(a)   on terms that the borrower (or a person on his behalf) will reimburse the creditor; or

(b)   in circumstances giving rise to a liability on the borrower to reimburse the creditor.

(4)   Any reference to the person to whom a quasi-loan is made is a reference to the borrower; and the liabilities of a borrower under a quasi-loan include the liabilities of any person who has agreed to reimburse the creditor on behalf of the borrower.

(6)   'Relevant company' means a company which—

(a)   is a public company, or

(b)   is a subsidiary of a public company, or

(c)   is a subsidiary of a company which has as another subsidiary a public company, or

(d)   has a subsidiary which is a public company.

(7)   A credit transaction is a transaction under which one party ('the creditor')—

(a)   supplies any goods or sells any land under a hire-purchase agreement or a conditional sale agreement;

(b)   leases or hires any land or goods in return for periodical payments;

(c)   otherwise disposes of land or supplies goods or services on the understanding that payment (whether in a lump sum or instalments or by way of periodical payments or otherwise) is to be deferred.

(8)   'Services' means anything other than goods or land.

(9)   A transaction or arrangement is made 'for' a person if—

(a)   in the case of a loan or quasi-loan, it is made to him;

(b)   in the case of a credit transaction, he is the person to whom goods or services are supplied, or land is sold or otherwise disposed of, under the transaction;

(c)   in the case of a guarantee or security, it is entered into or provided in connection with a loan or quasi-loan made to him or a credit transaction made for him;

(d)   in the case of an arrangement within subsection (6) or (7) of section 330, the transaction to which the arrangement relates was made for him; and

(e)   in the case of any other transaction or arrangement for the supply or transfer of, or of any interest in, goods, land or services, he is the person to whom the goods, land or services (or the interest) are supplied or transferred.

(10)   'Condition sale agreement' means the same as in the Consumer Credit Act 1974.

332. Short-term quasi-loans

(1)   Subsection (3) of section 330 does not prohibit a company ('the creditor') from making a quasi-loan to one of its directors or to a director of its holding company if—

(a)   the quasi-loan contains a term requiring the director or a person on his behalf to reimburse the creditor his expenditure within 2 months of its being incurred; and

(b)   the aggregate of the amount of that quasi-loan and of the amount outstanding under each relevant quasi-loan does not exceed £5,000.

(2)   A quasi-loan is relevant for this purpose if it was made to the director by virtue of this section by the creditor or its subsidiary or, where the director is a director of the creditor's holding company, any other subsidiary of that company; and 'the amount outstanding' is the amount of the outstanding liabilities of the person to whom the quasi-loan was made.

333. Inter-company loans in same group

In the case of a relevant company which is a member of a group of companies (meaning a holding company and its subsidiaries), paragraphs (b) and (c) of section 330(3) do not prohibit the company from—

(a)   making a loan or quasi-loan to another member of that group; or
(b)   entering into a guarantee or providing any security in connection with a loan or quasi-loan made by any person to another member of the group,

by reason only that a director of the group is associated with another.

334. Loans of small amounts

Without prejudice to any other provision of sections 332 to 338, paragraph (a) of section 330(2) does not prohibit a company from making a loan to a director of the company or of its holding company if the aggregate of the relevant amounts does not exceed £5,000.

335. Minor and business transactions

(1)   Section 330(4) does not prohibit a company from entering into a transaction for a person if the aggregate of the relevant amounts does not exceed £10,000.

(2)   Section 330(4) does not prohibit a company from entering into a transaction for a person if—

(a)   the transaction is entered into by the company in the ordinary course of its business; and
(b)   the value of the transaction is not greater, and the terms on which it is entered into are no more favourable, in respect of the person for whom the transaction is made, than that or those which it is reasonable to expect the company to have offered to or in respect of a person of the same financial standing but unconnected with the company.

336. Transactions at behest of holding company

The following transactions are excepted from the prohibitions of section 330—

(a)   a loan or quasi-loan by a company to its holding company, or a company entering into a guarantee or providing any security in connection with a loan or quasi-loan made by any person to its holding company;
(b)   a company, entering into a credit transaction as creditor for its holding company, or entering into a guarantee or providing any security in connection with a credit transaction made by any other person for its holding company.

337. Funding of director's expenditure on duty to company

(1)   A company is not prohibited by section 330 from doing anything to provide a director with funds to meet expenditure incurred or to be incurred by him for the purposes of the company or for the purpose of enabling him properly to perform his duties as an officer of the company.

(2)   Nor does the section prohibit a company from doing any thing to enable a director to avoid incurring such expenditure.

Part II Company

(3)   Subsections (1) and (2) apply only if one of the following conditions is satisfied—

(a)   the thing in question is done with prior approval of the company given at a general meeting at which there are disclosed all the matters mentioned in the next subsection;

(b)   that thing is done on condition that, if the approval of the company is not so given at or before the next annual general meeting, the loan is to be repaid, or any other liability arising under any such transaction discharged, within 6 months from the conclusion of that meeting;

but those subsections do not authorise a relevant company to enter into any transaction if the aggregate of the relevant amounts exceeds £20,000.

(4)   The matters to be disclosed under subsection (3)(a) are—

(a)   the purpose of the expenditure incurred or to be incurred, or which would otherwise be incurred, by the director,

(b)   the amount of the funds to be provided by the company, and

(c)   the extent of the company's liability under any transaction which is or is connected with the thing in question.

338. Loan or quasi-loan by money-lending company

(1)   There is excepted from the prohibitions in section 330—

(a)   a loan or quasi-loan made by a money-lending company to any person; or

(b)   a money-lending company entering into a guarantee in connection with any other loan or quasi-loan.

(2)   'Money-lending company' means a company whose ordinary business includes the making of loans or quasi-loans, or the giving of guarantees in connection with loans or quasi-loans.

(3)   Subsection (1) applies only if both the following conditions are satisfied—

(a)   the loan or quasi-loan in question is made by the company, or it enters into the guarantee, in the ordinary course of the company's business; and

(b)   the amount of the loan or quasi-loan, or the amount guaranteed, is not greater, and the terms of the loan, quasi-loan or guarantee are not more favourable, in the case of the person to whom the loan or quasi-loan is made or in respect of whom the guarantee is entered into, than that or those which it is reasonable to expect that company to have offered to or in respect of a person of the same financial standing but unconnected with the company.

(4)   But subsection (1) does not authorise a relevant company (unless it is a banking company) to enter into any transaction if the aggregate of the relevant amounts exceeds £100,000.

(5)   In determining that aggregate, a company which a director does not control is deemed not to be connected with him.

(6)   The condition specified in subsection (3)(b) does not of itself prevent a company from making a loan to one of its directors or a director of its holding company—

(a)   for the purpose of facilitating the purchase, for use as that director's only or main residence, of the whole or part of any dwelling-house together with any land to be occupied and enjoyed with it;

(b)   for the purpose of improving a dwelling-house or part of a dwelling-house so used or any land occupied and enjoyed with it;

(c)   in substitution for any loan made by any person and falling within paragraph (a) or (b) of this subsection,

if loans of that description are ordinarily made by the company to its employees and on terms no less favourable than those on which the transaction in question is made, and the aggregate of the relevant amounts does not exceed £100,000.

341. Civil remedies for breach of s 330

(1)   If a company enters into a transaction or arrangement in contravention of section 330, the transaction or arrangement is voidable at the instance of the company unless—

(a)   restitution of any money or any other asset which is the subject matter of the arrangement or transaction is no longer possible, or the company has been indemnified in pursuance of subsection (2)(b) below for the loss or damage suffered by it, or

(b)   any rights acquired bona fide for value and without actual notice of the contravention by a person other than the person for whom the transaction or arrangement was made would be affected by its avoidance.

(2)   Where an arrangement or transaction is made by a company for a director of the company or its holding company or a person connected with such a director in contravention of section 330, that director and the person so connected and any other director of the company who authorised the transaction or arrangement (whether or not it has been avoided in pursuance of subsection (1) is liable—

(a)   to account to the company for any gain which he has made directly or indirectly by the arrangement or transaction; and

(b)   (jointly and severally with any other person liable under this subsection) to indemnify the company for any loss or damage resulting from the arrangement or transaction.

(3)   Subsection (2) is without prejudice to any liability imposed otherwise than by that subsection, but is subject to the next two subsections.

(4)   Where an arrangement or transaction is entered into by a company and a person connected with a director of the company or its holding company in contravention of section 330, that director is not liable under subsection (2) of this section if he shows that he took all reasonable steps to secure the company's compliance with that section.

(5)   In any case, a person so connected and any such other director as is mentioned in subsection (2) is not so liable if he shows that, at the time the arrangement or transaction was entered into, he did not know the relevant circumstances constituting the contravention.

342. Criminal penalties for breach of s 330

(1)   A director of a relevant company who authorises or permits the company to enter into a transaction or arrangement knowing or having reasonable cause to believe that the company was thereby contravening section 330 is guilty of an offence.

(2)   A relevant company which enters into a transaction or arrangement for one of its directors or for a director of its holding company in contravention of section 330 is guilty of an offence.

(3)   A person who procures a relevant company to enter into a transaction or arrangement knowing or having reasonable cause to believe that the company was thereby contravening section 330 is guilty of an offence.

(4)   A person guilty of an offence under this section is liable to imprisonment or a fine, or both.

(5)   A relevant company is not guilty of an offence under subsection (2) if it shows that, at the time the transaction or arrangement was entered into, it did not know the relevant circumstances.

346. 'Connected persons', etc

(1)   This section has effect with respect to references in this Part to a person being 'connected' with a director of a company, and to a director being 'associated with' or 'controlling' a body corporate.

(2)   A person is connected with a director of a company if, but only if, he (not being himself a director of it) is—

(a)   that director's spouse, child or step-child; or
(b)   except where the context otherwise requires, a body corporate with which the director is associated; or
(c)   a person acting in his capacity as trustee of any trust the beneficiaries of which include—

(i)   the director, his spouse or any children or step-children of his, or
(ii)   a body corporate with which he is associated,

or of a trust whose terms confer a power on the trustees that may be exercised for the benefit of the director, his spouse, or any children or step-children of his, or any such body corporate; or

(d)   a person acting in his capacity as partner of that director or of any person who, by virtue of paragraph (a), (b) or (c) of this subsection, is connected with that director; or
(e)   a Scottish firm in which—

(i)   that director is a partner,
(ii)   a partner is a person who, by virtue of paragraph (a), (b) or (c) above, is connected with that director, or
(iii)   a partner is a Scottish firm in which that director is a partner or in which there is a partner who, by virtue of paragraph (a), (b) or (c) above, is connected with that director.

(3)   In subsection (2)—

   (a)   a reference to the child or step-child of any person includes an illegitimate child of his, but does not include any person who has attained the age of 18; and

   (b)   paragraph (c) does not apply to a person acting in his capacity as trustee under an employees' share scheme or a pension scheme.

(4)   A director of a company is associated with a body corporate if, but only if, he and the persons connected with him, together—

   (a)   are interested in shares comprised in the equity share capital of that body corporate of a nominal value equal to at least one-fifth of that share capital; or

   (b)   are entitled to exercise or control the exercise of more than one-fifth of the voting power at any general meeting of that body.

(5)   A director of a company is deemed to control a body corporate if, but only if—

   (a)   he or any person connected with him is interested in any part of the equity share capital of that body or is entitled to exercise or control the exercise of any part of the voting power at any general meeting of that body; and

   (b)   that director, the person connected with him and the other directors of that company, together, are interested in more than one-half of that share capital or are entitled to exercise or control the exercise of more than one-half of that voting power.

(6)   For purposes of subsections (4) and (5)—

   (a)   a body corporate with which a director is associated is not to be treated as connected with that director unless it is also connected with him by virtue of subsection (2)(c) or (d); and

   (b)   a trustee of a trust the beneficiaries of which include (or may include) a body corporate with which a director is associated is not to be treated as connected with a director by reason only of that fact.

(7)   The rules set out in Part I of Schedule 13 apply for the purposes of subsections (4) and (5).

(8)   References in those subsections to voting power the exercise of which is controlled by a director include voting power whose exercise is controlled by a body corporate controlled by him; but this is without prejudice to other provisions of subsections (4) and (5).

PART XI

COMPANY ADMINISTRATION AND PROCEDURE

348. Company name to appear outside place of business

(1)   Every company shall paint or affix, and keep painted or affixed, its name on the outside of every office or place in which its business is carried on, in a conspicuous position and in letters easily legible.

(2)   If a company does not paint or affix its name as required above, the company and every officer of it who is in default is liable to a fine; and if a company does not keep its name painted or affixed as so required, the company and every officer of it who is in default is liable to a fine and, for continued contravention, to a daily default fine.

349. Company's name to appear in its correspondence, etc

(1)   Every company shall have its name mentioned in legible characters—

   (a)   in all business letters of the company,
   (b)   in all its notices and other official publications,
   (c)   in all bills of exchange, promissory notes, endorsements, cheques and orders for money or goods purporting to be signed by or on behalf of the company, and
   (d)   in all its bills of parcels, invoices, receipts and letters of credit.

(2)   If a company fails to comply with subsection (1) it is liable to a fine.

(3)   If an officer of a company or a person on its behalf—

   (a)   issues or authorises the issue of any business letter of the company, or any notice or other official publication of the company, in which the company's name is not mentioned as required by sub-section (1), or

(b)   issues or authorises the issue of any bill of parcels, invoice, receipt or letter of credit of the company in which its name is not so mentioned,

he is liable to a fine.

(4)   If an officer of a company or a person on its behalf signs or authorises to be signed on behalf of the company any bill of exchange, promissory note, endorsement, cheque or order for money or goods in which the company's name is not mentioned as required by subsection (1), he is liable to a fine; and he is further personally liable to the holder of the bill of exchange, promissory note, cheque or order for money or goods for the amount of it (unless it is duly paid by the company).

350. Company seal

(1)   A company which has a common seal shall have its name engraved in legible characters on the seal; and if it fails to comply with this subsection it is liable to a fine.

(2)   If an officer of a company or a person on its behalf uses or authorises the use of any seal purporting to be a seal of the company on which its name is not engraved as required by subsection (1), he is liable to a fine.

351. Particulars in correspondence etc

(1)   Every company shall have the following particulars mentioned in legible characters in all business letters and order forms of the company, that is to say—

    (a)   the company's place of registration and the number with which it is registered,
    (b)   the address of its registered office,
    (c)   in the case of an investment company (as defined in section 266), the fact that it is such a company, and
    (d)   in the case of a limited company exempt from the obligation to use the word 'limited' as part of its name, the fact that it is a limited company.

(2)   If in the case of a company having a share capital there is on the stationery used for any such letters, or on the company's order forms, a reference to the amount of share capital, the reference must be to paid-up share capital.

(5)   As to contraventions of this section, the following applies—

    (a)   if a company fails to comply with subsection (1) or (2), it is liable to a fine,
    (b)   if an officer of a company or a person on its behalf issues or authorises the issue of any business letter or order form not complying with those subsections, he is liable to a fine.

352. Obligation to keep and enter up register

(1)   Every company shall keep a register of its members and enter in it the particulars required by this section.

(2)   There shall be entered in the register—

    (a)   the names and addresses of the members;
    (b)   the date on which each person was registered as a member; and
    (c)   the date at which any person ceased to be a member.

(3)   The following applies in the case of a company having a share capital—

    (a)   with the names and addresses of the members there shall be entered a statement—

        (i)   of the shares held by each member, distinguishing each share by its number (so long as the share has a number) and, where the company has more than one class of issued shares, by its class, and
        (ii)   of the amount paid or agreed to be considered as paid on the shares of each member;

    (b)   where the company has converted any of its shares into stock and given notice of the conversion to the registrar of companies, the register shall show the amount and class of stock held by each member, instead of the amount of shares and the particulars relating to shares specified in paragraph (a).

(4)   In the case of a company which does not have a share capital but has more than one class of members, there shall be entered in the register, with the names and addresses of the members, the class to which each member belongs.

(5)   If a company makes default in complying with this section, the company and every officer of it who is in default is liable to a fine and, for continued contravention, to a daily default fine.

(6)   An entry relating to a former member of the company may be removed from the register after the expiration of 20 years from the date on which he ceased to be a member.

(7)   Liability incurred by a company from the making or deletion of an entry in its register of members, or from a failure to make or delete any such entry, is not enforceable more than 20 years after the date on which the entry was made or deleted or, in the case of any such failure, the failure first occurred.

This is without prejudice to any lesser period of limitation.

359.   Power of court to rectify register

(1)   If—

(a)   the name of any person is, without sufficient cause, entered in or omitted from a company's register of members, or

(b)   default is made or unnecessary delay takes place in entering on the register the fact of any person having ceased to be a member,

the person aggrieved, or any member of the company, or the company, may apply to the court for rectification of the register.

(2)   The court may either refuse the application or may order rectification of the register and payment by the company of any damages sustained by any party aggrieved.

(3)   On such an application the court may decide any question relating to the title of a person who is a party to the application to have his name entered in or omitted from the register, whether the question arises between members or alleged members, or between members or alleged members on the one hand and the company on the other hand, and generally may decide any question necessary or expedient to be decided for rectification of the register.

(4)   In the case of a company required by this Act to send a list of its members to the registrar of companies, the court, when making an order for rectification of the register, shall by its order direct notice of the rectification to be given to the registrar.

363.   Duty to deliver annual returns

(1)   Every company shall deliver to the registrar successive annual returns each of which is made up to a date not later than the date which is from time to time the company's 'return date', that is—

(a)   the anniversary of the company's incorporation, or

(b)   if the company's last return delivered in accordance with this Chapter was made up to a different date, the anniversary of that date.

(2)   Each return shall—

(a)   be in the prescribed form,

(b)   contain the information required by or under the following provisions of this Chapter, and

(c)   be signed by a director or the secretary of the company;

and it shall be delivered to the registrar within 28 days after the date to which it is made up.

(3)   If a company fails to deliver an annual return in accordance with this Chapter before the end of the period of 28 days after a return date, the company is guilty of an offence and liable to a fine and, in the case of continued contravention, to a daily default fine.

The contravention continues until such time as an annual return made up to that return date and complying with the requirements of subsection (2) (except as to date of delivery) is delivered by the company to the registrar.

(4)   Where a company is guilty of an offence under subsection (3), every director or secretary of the company is similarly liable unless he shows that he took all reasonable steps to avoid the commission or continuation of the offence.

(5)   The references in this section to a return being delivered 'in accordance with this Chapter' are—

(a)   in relation to a return made on or after 1st October 1990, to a return with respect to which all the requirements of subsection (2) are complied with;

(b)   in relation to a return made before 1st October 1990, to a return with respect to which the formal and substantive requirements of this Chapter as it then had effect were complied with, whether or not the return was delivered in time.

366. Annual general meeting

(1)   Every company shall in each year hold a general meeting as its annual general meeting in addition to any other meetings in that year, and shall specify the meeting as such in the notices calling it.

(2)   However, so long as a company holds its first annual general meeting within 18 months of its incorporation, it need not hold it in the year of its incorporation or in the following year.

(3)   Not more than 15 months shall elapse between the date of one annual general meeting of a company and that of the next.

(4)   If default is made in holding a meeting in accordance with this section, the company and every officer of it who is in default is liable to a fine.

366A.   Election by private company to dispense with annual general meetings

(1)   A private company may elect (by elective resolution in accordance with section 379A) to dispense with the holding of annual general meetings.

(2)   An election has effect for the year in which it is made and subsequent years, but does not affect any liability already incurred by reason of default in holding an annual general meeting.

(3)   In any year in which an annual general meeting would be required to be held but for the election, and in which no such meeting has been held, any member of the company may, by notice to the company not later than three months before the end of the year, require the holding of an annual general meeting in that year.

(3A)   The power of a member under subsection (3) to require the holding of an annual general meeting is exercisable not only by the giving of a notice but also by the transmission to the company at such address as may for the time being be specified for the purpose by or on behalf of the company of an electronic communication containing the requirement.

(4)   If such a notice is given or electronic communication is transmitted, the provisions of section 366(1) and (4) apply with respect to the calling of the meeting and the consequences of default.

(5)   If the election ceases to have effect, the company is not obliged under section 366 to hold an annual general meeting in that year if, when the election ceases to have effect, less than three months of the year remains.

This does not affect any obligation of the company to hold an annual general meeting in that year in pursuance of a notice given or electronic communication transmitted under subsection (3).

(5A)   In this section, 'address' includes any number or address used for the purposes of electronic communications.

368. Extraordinary general meeting on members' requisition

(1)   The directors of a company shall, on a members' requisition, forthwith proceed duly to convene an extraordinary general meeting of the company.

This applies notwithstanding anything in the company's articles.

(2)   A members' requisition is a requisition of—

   (a)   members of the company holding at the date of the deposit of the requisition not less than one-tenth of such of the paid-up capital of the company as at that date carries the right of voting at general meetings of the company; or

   (b)   in the case of a company not having a share capital, members of it representing not less than one-tenth of the total voting rights of all the members having at the date of deposit of the requisition a right to vote at general meetings.

(3)   The requisition must state the objects of the meeting, and must be signed by the requisitionists and deposited at the registered office of the company, and may consist of several documents in like form each signed by one or more requisitionists.

(4)   If the directors do not within 21 days from the date of the deposit of the requisition proceed duly to convene a meeting, the requisitionists, or any of them representing more than one half of the total voting rights of all of them, may themselves convene a meeting, but any meeting so convened shall not be held after the expiration of 3 months from that date.

(5)   A meeting convened under this section by requisitionists shall be convened in the same manner, as nearly as possible, as that in which meetings are to be convened by directors.

(6)   Any reasonable expenses incurred by the requisitionists by reason of the failure of the directors duly to convene a meeting shall be repaid to the requisitionists by the company, and any sum so repaid shall be retained by the company out of any sums due or to become due from the company by way of fees or other remuneration in respect of their services to such of the directors as were in default.

(7)   In the case of a meeting at which a resolution is to be proposed as a special resolution, the directors are deemed not to have duly convened the meeting if they do not give the notice required for special resolutions by section 378(2).

(8)   The directors are deemed not to have duly convened a meeting if they convene a meeting for a date more than 28 days after the date of the notice convening the meeting.

369. Length of notice for calling meetings

(1)   A provision of a company's articles is void in so far as it provides for the calling of a meeting of the company (other than an adjourned meeting) by a shorter notice than—

    (a)   in the case of the annual general meeting, 21 days' notice in writing; and

    (b)   in the case of a meeting other than an annual general meeting or a meeting for the passing of a special resolution—

        (i)   7 days' notice in writing in the case of an unlimited company, and

        (ii)   otherwise, 14 days' notice in writing.

(2)   Save in so far as the articles of a company make other provision in that behalf (not being a provision avoided by subsection (1)), a meeting of the company (other than an adjourned meeting) may be called—

    (a)   in the case of the annual general meeting, by 21 days' notice in writing; and

    (b)   in the case of a meeting other than an annual general meeting or a meeting for the passing of a special resolution—

        (i)   by 7 days' notice in writing in the case of an unlimited company, and

        (ii)   otherwise, 14 days' notice in writing.

(3)   Notwithstanding that a meeting is called by shorter notice than that specified in subsection (2) or in the company's articles (as the case may be), it is deemed to have been duly called if it is so agreed—

    (a)   in the case of a meeting called as the annual general meeting, by all the members entitled to attend and vote at it; and

    (b)   otherwise, by the requisite majority.

(4)   The requisite majority for this purpose is a majority in number of the members having a right to attend and vote at the meeting, being a majority—

    (a)   together holding not less than 95 per cent in nominal value of the shares giving a right to attend and vote at the meeting; or

    (b)   in the case of a company not having a share capital, together representing not less than 95 per cent of the total voting rights at that meeting of all the members.

A private company may elect (by elective resolution in accordance with section 379A) that the above provisions shall have effect in relation to the company as if for the references to 95 per cent there were substituted references to such lesser percentage, but not less than 90 per cent, as may be specified in the resolution or subsequently determined by the company in general meeting.

(4A)   For the purposes of this section the cases in which notice in writing of a meeting is to be taken as given to a person include any case in which notice of the meeting is sent using electronic communications to such address as may for the time being be notified by that person to the company for that purpose.

(4B)   For the purposes of this section a notice in writing of a meeting is also to be treated as given to a person where—

    (a)   the company and that person have agreed that notices of meetings required to be given to that person may instead be accessed by him on a web site;

    (b)   the meeting is a meeting to which that agreement applies;

(c)   that person is notified, in a manner for the time being agreed between him and the company for the purpose, of—

   (i)   the publication of the notice on a web site;
   (ii)   the address of that web site; and
   (iii) the place on that web site where the notice may be accessed, and how it may be accessed;

   and

(d)   the notice continues to be published on that web site throughout the period beginning with the giving of that notification and ending with the conclusion of the meeting;

and for the purposes of this section a notice treated in accordance with this subsection as given to any person is to be treated as so given at the time of the notification mentioned in paragraph (c).

(4C) A notification given for the purposes of subsection (4B)(c) must—

(a)   state that it concerns a notice of a company meeting served in accordance with this Act,
(b)   specify the place, date and time of the meeting, and
(c)   state whether the meeting is to be an annual or extraordinary general meeting.

(4D) Nothing in subsection (4B) shall invalidate the proceedings of a meeting where—

(a)   any notice that is required to be published as mentioned in paragraph (d) of that subsection is published for a part, but not all, of the period mentioned in that paragraph; and
(b)   the failure to publish that notice throughout that period is wholly attributable to circumstances which it would not be reasonable to have expected the company to prevent or avoid.

(4E) A company may, notwithstanding any provision to the contrary in a company's articles, take advantage of any of subsections (4A) to (4D).

(4F) In so far as the articles of the company do not provide for notices and notifications to be served using electronic communications, the provisions of Table A (as for the time being in force) as to such service shall apply.

(4G) In this section, 'address' includes any number or address used for the purposes of electronic communications.

370. General provisions as to meetings and votes

(1)   The following provisions have effect in so far as the articles of the company do not make other provision in that behalf.

(2)   Notice of the meeting of a company shall be served on every member of it in the manner in which notices are required to be served by Table A (as for the time being in force).

(3)   Two or more members holding not less than one-tenth of the issued share capital or, if the company does not have a share capital, not less than 5 per cent in number of the members of the company may call a meeting.

(4)   Two members personally present are a quorum.

(5)   Any member elected by the members present at a meeting may be chairman of it.

(6)   In the case of a company originally having a share capital, every member has one vote in respect of each share or each £10 of stock held by him; and in any other case every member has one vote.

370A.   Quorum at meetings of the sole member

Notwithstanding any provision to the contrary in the articles of a private company limited by shares or by guarantee having only one member, one member present in person or by proxy shall be a quorum.

371. Power of court to order meeting

(1)   If for any reason it is impracticable to call a meeting of a company in any manner in which meetings of that company may be called, or to conduct the meeting in manner prescribed by the articles or this Act, the court may, either of its own motion or on the application—

(a)   of any director of the company, or
(b)   of any member of the company who would be entitled to vote at the meeting,

order a meeting to be called, held and conducted in any manner the court thinks fit.

(2)   Where such an order is made, the court may give such ancillary or consequential directions as it thinks expedient; and these may include a direction that one member of the company present in person or by proxy be deemed to constitute a meeting.

(3)   A meeting called, held and conducted in accordance with an order under subsection (1) is deemed for all purposes a meeting of the company duly called, held and conducted.

372. Proxies

(1)   Any member of a company entitled to attend and vote at a meeting of it is entitled to appoint another person (whether a member or not) as his proxy to attend and vote instead of him; and in the case of a private company a proxy appointed to attend and vote instead of a member has also the same right as the member to speak at the meeting.

(2)   But, unless the articles otherwise provide—

    (a)   subsection (1) does not apply in the case of a company not having a share capital; and

    (b)   a member of a private company is not entitled to appoint more than one proxy to attend on the same occasion; and

    (c)   a proxy is not entitled to vote except on a poll.

(2A) The appointment of a proxy may, notwithstanding any provision to the contrary in a company's articles, be contained in an electronic communication sent to such address as may be notified by or on behalf of the company for that purpose.

(2B) In so far as the articles of the company do not make other provision in that behalf, the appointment of a proxy may be contained in an electronic communication in accordance with the provisions of Table A (as for the time being in force).

(3)   In the case of a company having a share capital, in every notice calling a meeting of the company there shall appear with reasonable prominence a statement that a member entitled to attend and vote is entitled to appoint a proxy or, where that is allowed, one or more proxies to attend and vote instead of him, and that a proxy need not also be a member.

(4)   If default is made in complying with subsection (3) as respects any meeting, every officer of the company who is in default is liable to a fine.

(5)   A provision contained in a company's articles is void in so far as it would have the effect of requiring the appointment of a proxy or any document necessary to show the validity of, or otherwise relating to, the appointment of a proxy, to be received by the company or any other person more than 48 hours before a meeting or adjourned meeting in order that the appointment may be effective.

(6)   If for the purpose of any meeting of a company invitations to appoint as proxy a person or one of a number of persons specified in the invitations are issued at the company's expense to some only of the members entitled to be sent a notice of the meeting and to vote at it by proxy, then every officer of the company who knowingly and wilfully authorises or permits their issue in that manner is liable to a fine.

However, an officer is not so liable by reason only of the issue to a member at his request of a form of appointment naming the proxy, or of a list of persons willing to act as proxy, if the form or list is available on request to every member entitled to vote at the meeting by proxy.

(6A) In this section, 'address' includes any number or address used for the purposes of electronic communications.

(7)   This section applies to meetings of any class of members of a company as it applies to general meetings of the company.

373. Right to demand a poll

(1)   A provision contained in a company's articles is void in so far as it would have the effect either—

    (a)   of excluding the right to demand a poll at a general meeting on any question other than the election of the chairman of the meeting or the adjournment of the meeting; or

    (b)   of making ineffective a demand for a poll on any such question which is made either—

        (i)   by not less than 5 members having the right to vote at the meeting; or

        (ii)   by a member or members representing not less than one-tenth of the total voting rights of all the members having the right to vote at the meeting; or

(iii)   by a member or members holding shares in the company conferring a right to vote at the meeting, being shares on which an aggregate sum has been paid up equal to not less than one-tenth of the total sum paid up on all the shares conferring that right.

(2)   The appointment of a proxy to vote at a meeting of a company is deemed also to confer authority to demand or join in demanding a poll; and for the purposes of subsection (1) a demand by a person as proxy for a member is the same as a demand by the member.

374. Voting on a poll

On a poll taken at a meeting of a company or a meeting of any class of members of a company, a member entitled to more than one vote need not, if he votes, use all his votes or cast all the votes he uses in the same way.

376. Circulation of members' resolutions

(1)   Subject to the section next following, it is the duty of a company, on the requisition in writing of such number of members as is specified below and (unless the company otherwise resolves) at the expense of the requisitionists—

(a)   to give to members of the company entitled to receive notice of the next annual general meeting notice of any resolution which may properly be moved and is intended to be moved at that meeting;

(b)   to circulate to members entitled to have notice of any general meeting sent to them any statement of not more than 1,000 words with respect to the matter referred to in any proposed resolution or the business to be dealt with at that meeting.

(2)   The number of members necessary for a requisition under subsection (1) is—

(a)   any number representing not less than one-twentieth of the total voting rights of all the members having at the date of the requisition a right to vote at the meeting to which the requisition relates; or

(b)   not less than 100 members holding shares in the company on which there has been paid up an average sum, per member, of not less than £100.

(3)   Notice of any such resolution shall be given, and any such statement shall be circulated, to members of the company entitled to have notice of the meeting sent to them, by serving a copy of the resolution or statement on each such member in any manner permitted for service of notice of the meeting.

(4)   Notice of any such resolution shall be given to any other member of the company by giving notice of the general effect of the resolution in any manner permitted for giving him notice of meetings of the company.

(5)   For compliance with subsections (3) and (4), the copy must be served, or notice of the effect of the resolution be given (as the case may be) in the same manner and (so far as practicable) at the same time as notice of the meeting; and, where it is not practicable for it to be served or given at the same time, it must be served or given as soon as practicable thereafter.

(6)   The business which may be dealt with at an annual general meeting includes any resolution of which notice is given in accordance with this section; and for purposes of this subsection notice is deemed to have been so given notwithstanding the accidental omission, in giving it, of one or more members. This has effect notwithstanding anything in the company's articles.

(7)   In the event of default in complying with this section, every officer of the company who is in default is liable to a fine.

377. In certain cases, compliance with s 376 not required

(1)   A company is not bound under section 376 to give notice of a resolution or to circulate a statement unless—

(a)   a copy of the requisition signed by the requisitionists (or two or more copies which between them contain the signatures of all the requisitionists) is deposited at the registered office of the company—

(i)   in the case of a requisition requiring notice of a resolution, not less than 6 weeks before the meeting, and

(ii)   otherwise, not less than one week before the meeting; and

(b)   there is deposited or tendered with the requisition a sum reasonably sufficient to meet the company's expenses in giving effect to it.

(2)   But if, after a copy of a requisition requiring notice of a resolution has been deposited at the company's registered office, an annual general meeting is called for a date 6 weeks or less after the copy has been deposited, the copy (though not deposited within the time required by subsection(1)) is deemed properly deposited for the purposes of that subsection.

(3)   The company is also not bound under section 376 to circulate a statement if, on the application either of the company or of any other person who claims to be aggrieved, the court is satisfied that the rights conferred by that section are being abused to secure needless publicity for defamatory matter; and the court may order the company's costs on such an application to be paid in whole or in part by the requisitionists, notwithstanding that they are not parties to the application.

378. Extraordinary and special resolutions

(1)   A resolution is an extraordinary resolution when it has been passed by a majority of not less than three-fourth of such members as (being entitled to do so) vote in person or, where proxies are allowed, by proxy, at a general meeting of which notice specifying the intention to propose the resolution as an extraordinary resolution has been duly given.

(2)   A resolution is a special resolution when it has been passed by such a majority as is required for the passing of an extraordinary resolution and at a general meeting of which not less than 21 days' notice, specifying the intention to propose the resolution as a special resolution, has been duly given.

(3)   If it is so agreed by a majority in number of the members having the right to attend and vote at such a meeting, being a majority—

      (a)   together holding not less than 95 per cent in nominal value of the shares giving that right; or

      (b)   in the case of a company not having a share capital, together representing not less than 95 per cent of the total voting rights at that meeting of all the members,

a resolution may be proposed and passed as a special resolution at a meeting of which less than 21 days' notice has been given.

A private company may elect (by elective resolution in accordance with section 379A) that the above provisions shall have effect in relation to the company as if for the references to 95 per cent there were substituted references to such lesser percentage, but not less than 90 per cent, as may be specified in the resolution or subsequently determined by the company in general meeting.

(4)   At any meeting at which an extraordinary resolution or a special resolution is submitted to be passed, a declaration by the chairman that the resolution is carried is, unless a poll is demanded, conclusive evidence of the fact without proof of the number or proportion of the votes recorded in favour of or against the resolution.

(5)   In computing the majority on a poll demanded on the question that an extraordinary resolution or a special resolution be passed, reference is to be had to the number of votes cast for and against the resolution.

(6)   For purposes of this section, notice of a meeting is deemed duly given, and the meeting duly held, when the notice is given and the meeting held in the manner provided by this Act or the company's articles.

379. Resolution requiring special notice

(1)   Where by any provision of this Act special notice is required of a resolution, the resolution is not effective unless notice of the intention to move it has been given to the company at least 28 days before the meeting at which it is moved.

(2)   The company shall give its members notice of any such resolution at the same time and in the same manner as it gives notice of the meeting or, if that is not practicable, shall give them notice either by advertisement in a newspaper having an appropriate circulation or in any other mode allowed by the company's articles, at least 21 days before the meeting.

(3)   If, after notice of the intention to move such a resolution has been given to the company, a meeting is called for a date 28 days or less after the notice has been given, the notice is deemed properly given, though not given within the time required.

379A.   Elective resolution of private company

(1)   An election by a private company for the purposes of—

(a) section 80A (election as to duration of authority to allot shares),

(b) section 252 (election to dispense with laying of accounts and reports before general meeting),

(c) section 366A (election to dispense with holding of annual general meeting),

(d) section 369(4) or 378(3) (election as to majority required to authorise short notice of meeting), or

(e) section 386 (election to dispense with appointment of auditors annually),

shall be made by resolution of the company in general meeting in accordance with this section.

Such a resolution is referred to in this Act as an 'elective resolution'.

(2) An elective resolution is not effective unless—

(a) at least 21 days' notice in writing is given of the meeting, stating that an elective resolution is to be proposed and stating the terms of the resolution, and

(b) the resolution is agreed to at the meeting, in person or by proxy, by all the members entitled to attend and vote at the meeting.

(2A) An elective resolution is effective notwithstanding the fact that less than 21 days' notice in writing of the meeting is given if all the members entitled to attend and vote at the meeting so agree.

(2B) For the purposes of this section, notice in writing of the meeting is to be taken as given to a person where notice of the meeting is sent using electronic communications to such address as may for the time being be notified by that person to the company for that purpose.

(2C) For the purposes of this section a notice in writing of the meeting is also to be treated as given to a person where—

(a) the company and that person have agreed that notices of meetings required to be given to that person may instead be accessed by him on a web site;

(b) the meeting is a meeting to which that agreement applies;

(c) that person is notified, in a manner for the time being agreed between him and the company for the purpose, of—

(i) the publication of the notice on a web site;

(ii) the address of that web site; and

(iii) the place on that web site where the notice may be accessed, and how it may be accessed; and

(d) the notice continues to be published on that web site throughout the period beginning with the giving of that notification and ending with the conclusion of the meeting;

and for the purposes of this section a notice treated in accordance with this subsection as given to any person is to be treated as so given at the time of the notification mentioned in paragraph (c).

(2D) A notification given for the purposes of subsection (2C)(c) must—

(a) state that it concerns a notice of a company meeting at which an elective resolution is to be proposed, and

(b) specify the place, date and time of the meeting.

(2E) Nothing in subsection (2C) shall invalidate the proceedings of a meeting where—

(a) any notice that is required to be published as mentioned in paragraph (d) of that subsection is published for a part, but not all, of the period mentioned in that paragraph; and

(b) the failure to publish that notice throughout that period is wholly attributable to circumstances which it would not be reasonable to have expected the company to prevent or avoid.

(2F) In so far as the articles of the company do not provide for notices and notifications to be served using electronic communications, the provisions of Table A (as for the time being in force) as to such service shall apply.

(3) The company may revoke an elective resolution by passing an ordinary resolution to that effect.

(4) An elective resolution shall cease to have effect if the company is re-registered as a public company.

(5) An elective resolution may be passed or revoked in accordance with this section, and the provisions referred to in subsections (1) and (2B) to (2E) have effect, notwithstanding any contrary provision in the company's articles of association.

(5A) In this section, 'address' includes any number or address used for the purposes of electronic communications.

380. Registration, etc of resolutions and agreements

(1)   A copy of every resolution or agreement to which this section applies shall, within 15 days after it is passed or made, be forwarded to the registrar of companies and recorded by him; and it must be either a printed copy or else a copy in some other form approved by the registrar.

(2)   Where articles have been registered, a copy of every such resolution or agreement for the time being in force shall be embodied in or annexed to every copy of the articles issued after the passing of the resolution or the making of the agreement.

(3)   Where articles have not been registered, a printed copy of every such resolution or agreement shall be forwarded to any member at his request on payment of 5 pence or such less sum as the company may direct.

(4)   This section applies to—

   (a)   special resolutions;
   (b)   extraordinary resolutions;
   (bb)   an elective resolution or a resolution revoking such a resolution;
   (c)   resolutions or agreements which have been agreed to by all the members of a company but which, if not so agreed to, would not have been effective for their purpose unless (as the case may be) they had been passed as special resolutions or as extraordinary resolutions;
   (d)   resolutions or agreements which have been agreed to by all the members of some class of shareholders but which, if not so agreed to, would not have been effective for their purpose unless they had been passed by some particular majority or otherwise in some particular manner, and all resolutions or agreements which effectively bind all the members of any class of shareholders though not agreed to by all those members;
   (e)   a resolution passed by the directors of a company in compliance with a direction under section 31(2) (change of name on Secretary of State's direction);
   (f)   a resolution of a company to give, vary, revoke or renew an authority to the directors for the purposes of section 80 (allotment of relevant securities);
   (g)   a resolution of the directors passed under section 147(2) (alteration of memorandum on company ceasing to be a public company, following acquisition of its own shares);
   (h)   a resolution conferring, varying, revoking or renewing authority under section 166 (market purchase of company's own shares);
   (j)   a resolution for voluntary winding up, passed under section 84(1)(a) of the Insolvency Act;
   (k)   a resolution passed by the directors of an old public company, under section 2(1) of the Consequential Provisions Act, that the company should be re-registered as a public company;
   (l)   a resolution of the directors passed by virtue of regulation 16(2) of the Uncertificated Securities Regulations 2001 (which allows title to a company's shares to be evidenced and transferred without written instrument); and
   (m)   a resolution of a company passed by virtue of regulation 16(6) of the Uncertificated Securities Regulations 2001 (which prevents or reverses a resolution of the directors under regulation 16(2) of those Regulations).

(5)   If a company fails to comply with subsections (1) and (2B) to (2E), the company and every officer of it who is in default is liable to a fine and, for continued contravention, to a daily default fine.

(6)   If a company fails to comply with subsection (2) or (3), the company and every officer of it who is in default is liable to a fine.

(7)   For purposes of subsections (5) and (6), a liquidator of a company is deemed an officer of it.

381. Resolution passed at adjourned meeting

Where a resolution is passed at an adjourned meeting of—

   (a)   a company;
   (b)   the holders of any class of shares in a company;
   (c)   the directors of a company;

the resolution is for all purposes to be treated as having been passed on the date on which it was in fact passed, and is not to be deemed passed on any earlier date.

381A. Written resolutions of private companies

(1) Anything which in the case of a private company may be done—

    (a) by resolution of the company in general meeting, or

    (b) by resolution of a meeting of any class of members of the company,

may be done, without a meeting and without any previous notice being required, by resolution in writing signed by or on behalf of all the members of the company who at the date of the resolution would be entitled to attend and vote at such meeting.

(2) The signatures need not be on a single document provided each is on a document which accurately states the terms of the resolution.

(3) The date of the resolution means when the resolution is signed by or on behalf of the last member to sign.

(4) A resolution agreed to in accordance with this section has effect as if passed—

    (a) by the company in general meeting, or

    (b) by a meeting of the relevant class of members of the company,

as the case may be; and any reference in any enactment to a meeting at which a resolution is passed or to members voting in favour of a resolution shall be construed accordingly.

(5) Any reference in any enactment to the date of passing of a resolution is, in relation to a resolution agreed to in accordance with this section, a reference to the date of the resolution.

(6) A resolution may be agreed to in accordance with this section which would otherwise be required to be passed as a special, extraordinary or elective resolution; and any reference in any enactment to a special, extraordinary or elective resolution includes such a resolution.

(7) This section has effect subject to the exceptions specified in Part I of Schedule 15A; and in relating to certain descriptions of resolution under this section the procedural requirements of this Act have effect with the adaptations specified in Part II of that Schedule.

381B. Duty to notify auditors of proposed written resolution

(1) If a director or secretary of a company—

    (a) knows that it is proposed to seek agreement to a resolution in accordance with section 381A, and

    (b) knows the terms of the resolution,

he shall, if the company has auditors, secure that a copy of the resolution is sent to them, or that they are otherwise notified of its contents, at or before the time the resolution is supplied to a member for signature.

(2) A person who fails to comply with subsection (1) is liable to a fine.

(3) In any proceedings for an offence under this section it is a defence for the accused to prove—

    (a) that the circumstances were such that it was not practicable for him to comply with subsection (1), or

    (b) that he believed on reasonable grounds that a copy of the resolution had been sent to the company's auditors or that they had otherwise been informed of its contents.

(4) Nothing in this section affects the validity of any resolution.

381C. Written resolutions: supplementary provisions

(1) Sections 381A and 381B have effect notwithstanding any provision of the company's memorandum or articles, but do not prejudice any power conferred by any such provision.

(2) Nothing in those sections affects any enactment or rule of law as to—

    (a) things done otherwise than by passing a resolution, or

    (b) cases in which a resolution is treated as having been passed, or a person is precluded from alleging that a resolution has not been duly passed.

382. Minutes of meetings

(1)   Every company shall cause minutes of all proceedings of general meetings, all proceedings at meetings of its directors and, where there are managers, all proceedings at meetings of its managers to be entered in books kept for that purpose.

(2)   Any such minute, if purporting to be signed by the chairman of the meeting at which the proceedings were had, or by the chairman of the next succeeding meeting, is evidence of the proceedings.

(3)   Where a shadow director by means of a notice required by section 317(8) declares an interest in a contract or proposed contract, this section applies—

  (a)   if it is a specific notice under paragraph (a) of that subsection, as if the declaration had been made at the meeting there referred to, and

  (b)   otherwise, as if it had been made at the meeting of the directors next following the giving of the notice;

and the making of the declaration is in either case deemed to form part of the proceedings at the meeting.

(4)   Where minutes have been made in accordance with this section of the proceedings at any general meeting of the company or meeting of directors or managers, then, until the contrary is proved, the meeting is deemed duly held and convened, and all proceedings had at the meeting to have been duly had; and all appointments of directors, managers or liquidators are deemed valid.

(5)   If a company fails to comply with subsection (1), the company and every officer of it who is in default is liable to a fine and, for continued contravention, to a daily default fine.

382A.   Recording of written resolutions

(1)   Where a written resolution is agreed to in accordance with section 381A which has effect as if agreed by the company in general meeting, the company shall cause a record of the resolution (and of the signatures) to be entered in a book in the same way as minutes of proceedings of a general meeting of the company.

(2)   Any such record, if purporting to be signed by a director of the company or by the company secretary, is evidence of the proceedings in agreeing to the resolution; and where a record is made in accordance with this section, then, until the contrary is proved, the requirements of this Act with respect to those proceedings shall be deemed to be complied with.

(3)   Section 382(5) (penalties) applies in relation to a failure to comply with subsection (1) above as it applies in relation to a failure to comply with subsection (1) of that section; and section 383 (inspection of minute books) applies in relation to a record made in accordance with this section as it applies in relation to the minutes of a general meeting.

382B.   Recording of decisions by the sole member

(1)   Where a private company limited by shares or by guarantee has only one member and he takes any decision which may be taken by the company in general meeting and which has effect as if agreed by the company in general meeting, he shall (unless that decision is taken by way of a written resolution) provide the company with a written record of that decision.

(2)   If the sole member fails to comply with subsection (1) he shall be liable to a fine.

(3)   Failure by the sole member to comply with subsection (1) shall not affect the validity of any decision referred to in that subsection.

383. Inspection of minute books

(1)   The books containing the minutes of proceedings of any general meeting of a company held on or after 1st November 1929 shall be kept at the company's registered office, and shall be open to the inspection of any member without charge.

(3)   Any member shall be entitled on payment of such fee as may be prescribed to be furnished, within 7 days after he has made a request in that behalf to the company, with a copy of any such minutes as are referred to above.

(4)   If an inspection required under this section is refused or if a copy required under this section is not sent within the proper time, the company and every officer of it who is in default is liable in respect of each offence to a fine.

(5)   In the case of any such refusal or default, the court may by order compel an immediate inspection of the books in respect of all proceedings of general meetings, or direct that the copies required be sent to the persons requiring them.

384. Duty to appoint auditors

(1)   Every company shall appoint an auditor or auditors in accordance with this Chapter.

This is subject to section 388A (certain companies exempt from obligation to appoint auditors).

(2)   Auditors shall be appointed in accordance with section 385 (appointment at general meeting at which accounts are laid), except in the case of a private company which has elected to dispense with the laying of accounts in which case the appointment shall be made in accordance with section 385A.

(3)   References in this Chapter to the end of the time for appointing auditors are to the end of the time within which an appointment must be made under section 385(2) or 385A(2), according to whichever of those sections applies.

(4)   Sections 385 and 385A have effect subject to section 386 under which a private company may elect to dispense with the obligation to appoint auditors annually.

385. Appointment at general meeting at which accounts laid

(1)   This section applies to every public company and to a private company which has not elected to dispense with the laying of accounts.

(2)   The company shall at each general meeting at which accounts are laid, appoint an auditor or auditors to hold office from the conclusion of that meeting until the conclusion of the next general meeting at which accounts are laid.

(3)   The first auditors of the company may be appointed by the directors at any time before the first general meeting of the company at which accounts are laid; and auditors so appointed shall hold office until the conclusion of that meeting.

(4)   If the directors fail to exercise their powers under subsection (3), the powers may be exercised by the company in general meeting.

385A.   Appointment by private company which is not obliged to lay accounts

(1)   This section applies to a private company which has elected in accordance with section 252 to dispense with the laying of accounts before the company in general meeting.

(2)   Auditors shall be appointed by the company in general meeting before the end of the period of 28 days beginning with the day on which copies of the company's annual accounts for the previous financial year are sent to members under section 238 or, if notice is given under section 253(2) requiring the laying of the accounts before the company in general meeting, the conclusion of that meeting.

Auditors so appointed shall hold office from the end of that period or, as the case may be, the conclusion of that meeting until the end of the time for appointing auditors for the next financial year.

(3)   The first auditors of the company may be appointed by the directors at any time before—

(a)   the end of the period of 28 days beginning with the day on which copies of the company's first annual accounts are sent to members under section 238, or

(b)   if notice is given under section 253(2) requiring the laying of the accounts before the company in general meeting, the beginning of that meeting;

and auditors so appointed shall hold office until the end of that period or, as the case may be, the conclusion of that meeting.

(4)   If the directors fail to exercise their powers under subsection (3), the powers may be exercised by the company in general meeting.

(5)   Auditors holding office when the election is made shall, unless the company in general meeting determines otherwise, continue to hold office until the end of the time for appointing auditors for the next financial year; and auditors holding office when an election ceases to have effect shall continue to hold office until the conclusion of the next general meeting of the company at which accounts are laid.

386. Election by private company to dispense with annual appointment

(1) A private company may elect (by elective resolution in accordance with section 379A) to dispense with the obligation to appoint auditors annually.

(2) When such an election is in force the company's auditors shall be deemed to be re-appointed for each succeeding financial year on the expiry of the time for appointing auditors for that year, unless—

   (a) the directors of the company have taken advantage of the exemption conferred by section 249A or 249AA, or
   (b) a resolution has been passed under section 393 to the effect that their appointment should be brought to an end.

(3) If the election ceases to be in force, the auditors then holding office shall continue to hold office—

   (a) where section 385 then applies, until the conclusion of the next general meeting of the company at which accounts are laid;
   (b) where section 385A then applies, until the end of the time for appointing auditors for the next financial year under that section.

(4) No account shall be taken of any loss of the opportunity of further deemed re-appointment under this section in ascertaining the amount of any compensation or damages payable to an auditor on his ceasing to hold office for any reason.

389A.   Rights to information

(1) The auditors of a company have a right of access at all times to the company's books, accounts and vouchers, and are entitled to require from the company's officers such information and explanations as they think necessary for the performance of their duties as auditors.

(2) An officer of a company commits an offence if he knowingly or recklessly makes to the company's auditors a statement (whether written or oral) which—

   (a) conveys or purports to convey any information or explanations which the auditors require, or are entitled to require, as auditors of the company, and
   (b) is misleading, false or deceptive in a material particular.

A person guilty of an offence under this subsection is liable to imprisonment or a fine, or both.

(3) A subsidiary undertaking which is a body corporate incorporated in Great Britain, and the auditors of such an undertaking, shall give to the auditors of any parent company of the undertaking such information and explanations as they may reasonably require for the purposes of their duties as auditors of that company.

If a subsidiary undertaking fails to comply with this subsection, the undertaking and every officer of it who is in default is guilty of an offence and liable to a fine; and if an auditor fails without reasonable excuse to comply with this subsection he is guilty of an offence and liable to a fine.

(4) A parent company having a subsidiary undertaking which is not a body corporate incorporated in Great Britain shall, if required by its auditors to do so, take all such steps as are reasonably open to it to obtain from the subsidiary undertaking such information and explanations as they may reasonably require for the purposes of their duties as auditors of that company.

If a parent company fails to comply with this subsection, the company and every officer of it who is in default is guilty of an offence and liable to a fine.

(5) Section 734 (criminal proceedings against unincorporated bodies) applies to an offence under sub-section (3).

390. Right to attend company meetings etc

(1) A company's auditors are entitled—

   (a) to receive all notices of, and other communications relating to, any general meeting which a member of the company is entitled to receive;
   (b) to attend any general meeting of the company; and
   (c) to be heard at any general meeting which they attend on any part of the business of the meeting which concerns them as auditors.

(1A) Subsections (4A) to (4G) of section 369 (electronic communication of notices of meetings) apply for the purpose of determining whether notice of a meeting is received by the company's auditors as they apply in determining whether such a notice is given to any person.

(2)   In relation to a written resolution proposed to be agreed to by a private company in accordance with section 381A, the company's auditors are entitled—

    (a)   to receive all such communications relating to the resolution as, by virtue of any provision of Schedule 15A, are required to be supplied to a member of the company.

(3)   The right to attend or be heard at a meeting is exercisable in the case of a body corporate or partnership by an individual authorised by it in writing to act as its representative at the meeting.

390A. Remuneration of auditors

(1)   The remuneration of auditors appointed by the company in general meeting shall be fixed by the company in general meeting or in such manner as the company in general meeting may determine.

(2)   The remuneration of auditors appointed by the directors or the Secretary of State shall be fixed by the directors or the Secretary of State, as the case may be.

(3)   There shall be stated in a note to the company's annual accounts the amount of the remuneration of the company's auditors in their capacity as such.

(4)   For the purposes of this section 'remuneration' includes sums paid in respect of expenses.

(5)   This section applies in relation to benefits in kind as to payments in cash, and in relation to any such benefit references to its amount are to its estimated money value.

The nature of any such benefit shall also be disclosed.

390B. Remuneration of auditors or their associates for non-audit work

(1)   The Secretary of State may make provision by regulations for securing the disclosure of the amount of any remuneration received or receivable by a company's auditors or their associates in respect of services other than those of auditors in their capacity as such.

(2)   The regulations may—

    (a)   provide that 'remuneration' includes sums paid in respect of expenses,
    (b)   apply in relation to benefits in kind as to payments in cash, and in relation to any such benefit require disclosure of its nature and its estimated money value,
    (c)   define 'associate' in relation to an auditor,
    (d)   require the disclosure of remuneration in respect of services rendered to associated undertakings of the company, and
    (e)   define 'associated undertaking' for that purpose.

(3)   The regulations may require the auditors to disclose the relevant information in their report or require the relevant information to be disclosed in a note to the company's accounts and require the auditors to supply the directors of the company with such information as is necessary to enable that disclosure to be made.

(4)   The regulations may make different provision for different cases.

(5)   Regulations under this section shall be made by statutory instrument which shall be subject to annulment in pursuance of a resolution of either House of Parliament.

391. Removal of auditors

(1)   A company may by ordinary resolution at any time remove an auditor from office, notwithstanding anything in any agreement between it and him.

(2)   Where a resolution removing an auditor is passed at a general meeting of a company, the company shall within 14 days give notice of that fact in the prescribed form to the registrar.

If a company fails to give the notice required by this subsection, the company and every officer of it who is in default is guilty of an offence and liable to a fine and, for continued contravention, to a daily default fine.

(3)   Nothing in this section shall be taken as depriving a person removed under it of compensation or damages payable to him in respect of the termination of his appointment as auditor or of any appointment terminating with that as auditor.

(4)   An auditor of a company who has been removed has, notwithstanding his removal, the rights conferred by section 390 in relation to any general meeting of the company—

   (a)   at which his term of office would otherwise have expired, or
   (b)   at which it is proposed to fill the vacancy caused by his removal.

In such a case the references in that section to matters concerning the auditors as auditors shall be construed as references to matters concerning him as a former auditor.

391A.   Rights of auditors who are removed or not re-appointed

(1)   Special notice is required for a resolution at a general meeting of a company—

   (a)   removing an auditor before the expiration of his term of office, or
   (b)   appointing as auditor a person other than a retiring auditor.

(2)   On receipt of notice of such an intended resolution the company shall forthwith send a copy of it to the person proposed to be removed or, as the case may be, to the person proposed to be appointed and to the retiring auditor.

(3)   The auditor proposed to be removed or (as the case may be) the retiring auditor may make with respect to the intended resolution representations in writing to the company (not exceeding a reasonable length) and request their notification to members of the company.

(4)   The company shall (unless the representations are received by it too late for it to do so)—

   (a)   in any notice of the resolution given to members of the company, state the fact of the representations having been made, and
   (b)   send a copy of the representations to every member of the company to whom notice of the meeting is or has been sent.

(5)   If a copy of any such representation is not sent out as required because received too late or because of the company's default, the auditor may (without prejudice to his right to be heard orally) require that the representations be read out at the meeting.

(6)   Copies of the representations need not be sent out and the representations need not be read at the meeting if, on the application either of the company or of any other person claiming to be aggrieved, the court is satisfied that the rights conferred by this section are being abused to secure needless publicity for defamatory matter; and the court may order the company's costs on the application to be paid in whole or in part by the auditor, notwithstanding that he is not a party to the application.

392. Resignation of auditors

(1)   An auditor of a company may resign his office by depositing a notice in writing to that effect at the company's registered office.

The notice is not effective unless it is accompanied by the statement required by section 394.

(2)   An effective notice of resignation operates to bring the auditor's term of office to an end as of the date on which the notice is deposited or on such later date as may be specified in it.

(3)   The company shall within 14 days of the deposit of a notice of resignation send a copy of the notice to the registrar of companies.

If default is made in complying with this subsection, the company and every officer of it who is in default is guilty of an offence and liable to a fine and, for continued contravention, a daily default fine.

392A.   Rights of resigning auditors

(1)   This section applies where an auditor's notice of resignation is accompanied by a statement of circumstances which he considers should be brought to the attention of members or creditors of the company.

(2)   He may deposit with the notice a signed requisition calling on the directors of the company forthwith duly to convene an extraordinary general meeting of the company for the purpose of receiving and considering such explanation of the circumstances connected with his resignation as he may wish to place before the meeting.

(3)   He may request the company to circulate to its members—

(a)   before the meeting convened on his requisition, or
(b)   before any general meeting at which his term of office would otherwise have expired or at which it is proposed to fill the vacancy caused by his resignation,

a statement in writing (not exceeding a reasonable length) of the circumstances connected with his resignation.

(4)   The company shall (unless the statement is received too late for it to comply)—

(a)   in any notice of the meeting given to members of the company, state the fact of the statement having been made, and
(b)   send a copy of the statement to every member of the company to whom notice of the meeting is or has been sent.

(5)   If the directors do not within 21 days from the date of the deposit of a requisition under this section proceed duly to convene a meeting for a day not more than 28 days after the date on which the notice convening the meeting is given, every director who failed to take all reasonable steps to secure that a meeting was convened as mentioned above is guilty of an offence and liable to a fine.

(6)   If a copy of the statement mentioned above is not sent out as required because received too late or because of the company's default, the auditor may (without prejudice to his right to be heard orally) require that the statement be read out at the meeting.

(7)   Copies of a statement need not be sent out and the statement need not be read out at the meeting if, on the application either of the company or of any other person who claims to be aggrieved, the court is satisfied that the rights conferred by this section are being abused to secure needless publicity for defamatory matter; and the court may order the company's costs on such an application to be paid in whole or in part by the auditor, notwithstanding that he is not a party to the application.

(8)   An auditor who has resigned has, notwithstanding his resignation, the rights conferred by section 390 in relation to any such general meeting of the company as is mentioned in subsection (3)(a) or (b).

In such a case the references in that section to matters concerning the auditors as auditors shall be construed as references to matters concerning him as a former auditor.

394. Statement by person ceasing to hold office as auditor

(1)   Where an auditor ceases for any reason to hold office, he shall deposit at the company's registered office a statement of any circumstances connected with his ceasing to hold office which he considers should be brought to the attention of the members or creditors of the company or, if he considers that there are no such circumstances, a statement that there are none.

(2)   In the case of resignation, the statement shall be deposited along with the notice of resignation; in the case of failure to seek re-appointment, the statement shall be deposited not less than 14 days before the end of the time allowed for next appointing auditors; in any other case, the statement shall be deposited not later than the end of the period of 14 days beginning with the date on which he ceases to hold office.

(3)   If the statement is of circumstances which the auditor considers should be brought to the attention of the members or creditors of the company, the company shall within 14 days of the deposit of the statement either—

(a)   send a copy of it to every person who under section 238 is entitled to be sent copies of the accounts, or
(b)   apply to the court.

(4)   The company shall if it applies to the court notify the auditor of the application.

(5)   Unless the auditor receives notice of such an application before the end of the period of 21 days beginning with the day on which he deposited the statement, he shall within a further seven days send a copy of the statement to the registrar.

(6)   If the court is satisfied that the auditor is using the statement to secure needless publicity for defamatory matter—

(a)   it shall direct that copies of the statement need not be sent out, and
(b)   it may further order the company's costs on the application to be paid in whole or in part by the auditor, notwithstanding that he is not a party to the application;

and the company shall within 14 days of the court's decision send to the persons mentioned in subsection (3)(a) a statement setting out the effect of the order.

(7)   If the court is not so satisfied, the company shall within 14 days of the court's decision—

    (a)   send copies of the statement to the persons mentioned in subsection (3)(a), and

    (b)   notify the auditor of the court's decision;

and the auditor shall within seven days of receiving such notice send a copy of the statement to the registrar.

PART XII

REGISTRATION OF CHARGES

395. Certain charges void if not registered

(1)   Subject to the provisions of this Chapter, a charge created by a company registered in England and Wales and being a charge to which this section applies is, so far as any security on the company's property or undertaking is conferred by the charge, void against the liquidator or administrator and any creditor of the company, unless the prescribed particulars of the charge together with the instrument (if any) by which the charge is created or evidenced, are delivered to or received by the registrar of companies for registration in the manner required by this Chapter within 21 days after the date of the charge's creation.

(2)   Subsection (1) is without prejudice to any contract or obligation for repayment of the money secured by the charge; and when a charge becomes void under this section, the money secured by it immediately becomes payable.

396. Charges which have to be registered

(1)   Section 395 applies to the following charges—

    (a)   a charge for the purpose of securing any issue of debentures,

    (b)   a charge on uncalled share capital of the company,

    (c)   a charge created or evidenced by an instrument which, if executed by an individual, would require registration as a bill of sale,

    (d)   a charge on land (wherever situated) or any interest in it, but not including a charge for any rent or other periodical sum issuing out of the land,

    (e)   a charge on book debts of the company,

    (f)   a floating charge on the company's undertaking or property,

    (g)   a charge on calls made but not paid,

    (h)   a charge on a ship or aircraft, or any share in a ship,

    (j)   a charge on goodwill, or on any intellectual property.

(2)   Where a negotiable instrument has been given to secure the payment of any book debts of a company, the deposit of the instrument for the purpose of securing an advance to the company is not, for purposes of section 395, to be treated as a charge on those book debts.

(3)   The holding of debentures entitling the holder to a charge on land is not for purposes of this section deemed to be an interest in land.

(3A) The following are 'intellectual property' for the purposes of this section—

    (a)   any patent, trade mark, registered design, copyright or design right;

    (b)   any licence under or in respect of any such right.

(4)   In this Chapter, 'charge' includes mortgage.

397. Formalities of registration (debentures)

(1)   Where a series of debentures containing, or giving by reference to another instrument, any charge to the benefit of which the debenture holders of that series are entitled pari passu is created by a company, it is for purposes of section 395 sufficient if there are delivered to or received by the registrar, within 21 days after the execution of the deed containing the charge (or, if there is no such deed, after the execution of any debentures of the series), the following particulars in the prescribed form—

    (a)   the total amount secured by the whole series, and

(b)   the dates of the resolutions authorising the issue of the series and the date of the covering deed (if any) by which the security is created or defined, and

(c)   a general description of the property charged, and

(d)   the names of the trustees (if any) for the debenture holders,

together with the deed containing the charge or, if there is no such deed, one of the debentures of the series:

Provided that there shall be sent to the registrar of companies, for entry in the register, particulars in the prescribed form of the date and amount of each issue of debentures of the series, but any omission to do this does not affect the validity of any of those debentures.

(2)   Where any commission, allowance or discount has been paid or made either directly or indirectly by a company to a person in consideration of his—

(a)   subscribing or agreeing to subscribe, whether absolutely or conditionally, for debentures of the company, or

(b)   procuring or agreeing to procure subscriptions, whether absolute or conditional, for such debentures,

the particulars required to be sent for registration under section 395 shall include particulars as to the amount or rate per cent of the commission, discount or allowance so paid or made, but omission to do this does not affect the validity of the debentures issued.

(3)   The deposit of debentures as security for a debt of the company is not, for the purposes of subsection (2), treated as the issue of the debentures at a discount.

398. Verification of charge on property outside United Kingdom

(1)   In the case of a charge created out of the United Kingdom comprising property situated outside the United Kingdom, the delivery to and the receipt by the registrar of companies of a copy (verified in the prescribed manner) of the instrument by which the charge is created or evidenced has the same effect for purposes of sections 395 to 398 as the delivery and receipt of the instrument itself.

(2)   In that case, 21 days after the date on which the instrument or copy could, in due course of post (and if despatched with due diligence), have been received in the United Kingdom are substituted for the 21 days mentioned in section 395(2) (or as the case may be, section 397(1)) as the time within the particulars and instrument or copy are to be delivered to the registrar.

(3)   Where a charge is created in the United Kingdom but comprises property outside the United Kingdom, the instrument creating or purporting to create the charge may be sent for registration under section 395 notwithstanding that further proceedings may be necessary to make the charge valid or effectual according to the law of the country in which the property is situated.

(4)   Where a charge comprises property situated in Scotland or Northern Ireland and registration in the country where the property is situated is necessary to make the charge valid or effectual according to the law of that country, the delivery to and receipt by the registrar of a copy (verified in the prescribed manner) of the instrument by which the charge is created or evidenced, together with a certificate in the prescribed form stating that the charge was presented for registration in Scotland, or Northern Ireland (as the case may be) on the date on which it was so presented has, for purposes of sections 395 to 398, the same effect as the delivery and receipt of the instrument itself.

399. Company's duty to register charges it creates

(1)   It is a company's duty to send to the registrar of companies for registration the particulars of every charge created by the company and of the issues of debentures of a series requiring registration under sections 395 to 398; but registration of any such charge may be effected on the application of any person interested in it.

(2)   Where registration is effected on the application of some person other than the company, that person is entitled to recover from the company the amount of any fees properly paid by him to the registrar on the registration.

(3)   If a company fails to comply with subsection (1), then, unless the registration has been effected on the application of some other person, the company and every officer of it who is in default is liable to a fine and, for continued contravention, to a daily default fine.

400. Charges existing on property acquired

(1)   This section applies where a company registered in England and Wales acquires property which is subject to a charge of any such kind as would, if it had been created by the company after the acquisition of the property, have been required to be registered under this Chapter.

(2)   The company shall cause the prescribed particulars of the charge, together with a copy (certified in the prescribed manner to be a correct copy) of the instrument (if any) by which the charge was created or is evidenced, to be delivered to the registrar of companies for registration in manner required by this Chapter within 21 days after the date on which the acquisition is completed.

(3)   However, if the property is situated and the charge was created outside Great Britain, 21 days after the date on which the copy of the instrument could in due course of post, and if despatched with due diligence, have been received in the United Kingdom is substituted for the 21 days above-mentioned as the time within which the particulars and copy of the instrument are to be delivered to the registrar.

(4)   If default is made in complying with this section, the company and every officer of it who is in default is liable to a fine and, for continued contravention, to a daily default fine.

401. Register of charges to be kept by registrar of companies

(1)   The registrar of companies shall keep, with respect to each company, a register in the prescribed form of all the charges requiring registration under this Chapter; and he shall enter in the register with respect to such charges the following particulars—

   (a)   in the case of a charge to the benefit of which the holders of a series of debentures are entitled, the particulars specified in section 397(1),
   (b)   in the case of any other charge—

       (i)   if it is a charge created by the company, the date of its creation, and if it is a charge which was existing on property acquired by the company, the date of the acquisition of the property, and
       (ii)   the amount secured by the charge, and
       (iii) short particulars of the property charged, and
       (iv) the persons entitled to the charge.

(2)   The registrar shall give a certificate of the registration of any charge registered in pursuance of this Chapter, stating the amount secured by the charge.

The certificate—

   (a)   shall be either signed by the registrar, or authenticated by his official seal, and
   (b)   is conclusive evidence that the requirements of this Chapter as to registration have been satisfied.

(3)   The register kept in pursuance of this section shall be open to inspection by any person.

402. Endorsement of certificate on debentures

(1)   The company shall cause a copy of every certificate of registration given under section 401 to be endorsed on every debenture or certificate of debenture stock which is issued by the company, and the payment of which is secured by the charge so registered.

(2)   But this does not require a company to cause a certificate of registration of any charge so given to be endorsed on any debenture or certificate of debenture stock issued by the company before the charge was created.

(3)   If a person knowingly and wilfully authorises or permits the delivery of a debenture or certificate of debenture stock which under this section is required to have endorsed on it a copy of a certificate of registration, without the copy being so endorsed upon it, he is liable (without prejudice to any other liability) to a fine.

403. Entries of satisfaction and release

(1)   Subject to section (1A) the registrar of companies, on receipt of a statutory declaration in the prescribed form verifying, with respect to a registered charge,—

   (a)   that the debt for which the charge was given has been paid or satisfied in whole or in part, or
   (b)   that part of the property or undertaking charged has been released from the charge or has ceased to form part of the company's property or undertaking,

may enter on the register a memorandum of satisfaction in whole or in part, or of the fact that part of the property or undertaking has been released from the charge or has ceased to form part of the company's property or undertaking (as the case may be).

(1A) The registrar of companies may make any such entry as is mentioned in subsection (1) where, instead of receiving such a statutory declaration as is mentioned in that subsection, he receives a statement by a director, secretary, administrator or administrative receiver of the company which is contained in an electronic communication and that statement—

(a)   verifies the matters set out in paragraph (a) or (b) of that subsection,

(b)   contains a description of the charge,

(c)   states the date of creation of the charge and the date of its registration under this Chapter,

(d)   states the name and address of the chargee or, in the case of a debenture, trustee, and

(e)   where paragraph (b) of subsection (1) applies, contains short particulars of the property or undertaking which has been released from the charge, or which has ceased to form part of the company's property or undertaking (as the case may be).

(2)   Where the registrar enters a memorandum of satisfaction in whole, he shall if required furnish the company with a copy of it.

(2A) Any person who makes a false statement under subsection (1A) which he knows to be false or does not believe to be true is liable to imprisonment or a fine, or both.

404. Rectification of register of charges

(1)   The following applies if the court is satisfied that the omission to register a charge within the time required by this Chapter or that the omission or mis-statement of any particular with respect to any such charge or in a memorandum of satisfaction was accidental, or due to inadvertence or to some other sufficient cause, or is not of a nature to prejudice the position of creditors or shareholders of the company, or that on other grounds it is just and equitable to grant relief.

(2)   The court may, on the application of the company or a person interested, and on such terms and conditions as seem to the court just and expedient, order that the time for registration shall be extended or, as the case may be, that the omission or mis-statement shall be rectified.

405. Registration of enforcement of security

(1)   If a person obtains an order for the appointment of a receiver or manager of a company's property, or appoints such a receiver or manager under powers contained in an instrument, he shall within 7 days of the order or of the appointment under those powers, give notice of the fact to the registrar of companies; and the registrar shall enter the fact in the register of charges.

(2)   Where a person appointed receiver or manager of a company's property under powers contained in an instrument ceases to act as such receiver or manager, he shall, on so ceasing, give the registrar notice to that effect, and the registrar shall enter the fact in the register of charges.

(3)   A notice under this section shall be in the prescribed form.

(4)   If a person makes default on complying with the requirements of this section, he is liable to a fine and, for continued contravention, to a daily default fine.

406. Companies to keep copies of instruments creating charges

(1)   Every company shall cause a copy of every instrument creating a charge requiring registration under this Chapter to be kept at its registered office.

(2)   In the case of a series of uniform debentures, a copy of one debenture of the series is sufficient.

407. Company's register of charges

(1)   Every limited company shall keep at its registered office a register of charges and enter in it all charges specifically affecting property of the company and all floating charges on the company's undertaking or any of its property.

(2)   The entry shall in each case give a short description of the property charged, the amount of the charge and, except in the case of securities to bearer, the names of the persons entitled to it.

(3)   If an officer of the company knowingly and wilfully authorises or permits the omission of an entry required to be made in pursuance of this section, he is liable to a fine.

408. Right to inspect instruments which create charges, etc

(1)   The copies of instruments creating any charge requiring registration under this Chapter with the registrar of companies, and the register of charges kept in pursuance of section 407, shall be open during business hours (but subject to such reasonable restrictions as the company in general meeting may impose, so that not less than 2 hours in each day be allowed for inspection) to the inspection of any creditor or member of the company without fee.

(2)   The register of charges shall also be open to the inspection of any other person on payment of such fee, not exceeding 5 pence, for each inspection, as the company may prescribe.

(3)   If inspection of the copies referred to, or of the register, is refused, every officer of the company who is in default is liable to a fine and, for continued contravention, to a daily default fee.

(4)   If such a refusal occurs in relation to a company registered in England and Wales, the court may by order compel an immediate inspection of the copies or register.

409. Charges on property in England and Wales created by overseas company

(1)   This chapter extends to charges on property in England and Wales which are created, and to charges on property in England and Wales which is acquired, by a company (whether a company within the meaning of this Act or not) incorporated outside Great Britain which has an established place of business in England and Wales.

(2)   In relation to such a company, sections 406 and 407 apply with the substitution, for the reference to the company's registered office, of a reference to its principal place of business in England and Wales.

411. Charges on property outside United Kingdom

(1)   In the case of a charge created out of the United Kingdom comprising property situated outside the United Kingdom, the period of 21 days after the date on which the copy of the instrument creating it could (in due course of post, and if despatched with due diligence) have been received in the United Kingdom is substituted for the period of 21 days after the date of the creation of the charge as the time within which, under section 410(2), the particulars and copy are to be delivered to the registrar.

(2)   Where a charge is created in the United Kingdom but comprises property outside the United Kingdom, the copy of the instrument creating or purporting to create the charge may be sent for registration under section 410 notwithstanding that further proceedings may be necessary to make the charge valid or effectual according to the law of the country in which the property is situated.

412. Negotiable instrument to secure book debts

Where a negotiable instrument has been given to secure the payment of any book debts of a company, the deposit of the instrument for the purpose of securing an advance to the company is not, for the purposes of section 410, to be treated as a charge on those book debts.

PART XVI

FRAUDULENT TRADING BY A COMPANY

458. Punishment for fraudulent trading

If any business of a company is carried on with intent to defraud creditors of the company or creditors of any other person, or for any fraudulent purpose, every person who was knowingly a party to the carrying on of the business in that manner is liable to imprisonment or a fine, or both.

This applies whether or not the company has been, or is in the course of being, wound up.

PART XVII

PROTECTION OF COMPANY'S MEMBERS AGAINST UNFAIR PREJUDICE

459. Order on application of company member

(1)   A member of a company may apply to the court by petition for an order under this Part on the ground that the company's affairs are being or have been conducted in a manner which is unfairly prejudicial to the interests of its members generally or of some part of its members (including at least himself) or that any actual or proposed act or omission of the company (including an act or omission on its behalf) is or would be so prejudicial.

(2)   The provisions of this Part apply to a person who is not a member of a company but to whom shares in the company have been transferred or transmitted by operation of law, as those provisions apply to a member of the company; and references to a member or members are to be construed accordingly.

(3)   In this section (and so far as applicable for the purposes of this section, in section 461(2)) 'company' means any company within the meaning of this Act or any company which is not such a company but is a statutory water company within the meaning of the Water Act 1989.

461. Provisions as to petitions and orders under this Part

(1)   If the court is satisfied that a petition under this Part is well founded, it may make such order as it thinks fit for giving relief in respect of the matters complained of.

(2)   Without prejudice to the generality of subsection (1), the court's order may—

    (a)   regulate the conduct of the company's affairs in the future,

    (b)   require the company to refrain from doing or continuing an act complained of by the petitioner or to do an act which the petitioner has complained it has omitted to do,

    (c)   authorise civil proceedings to be brought in the name and on behalf of the company by such person or persons and on such terms as the court may direct,

    (d)   provide for the purchase of the shares of any members of the company by other members or by the company itself and, in the case of a purchase by the company itself, the reduction of the company's capital accordingly.

(3)   If an order under this Part requires the company not to make any, or any specified, alteration in the memorandum or articles, the company does not then have power without leave of the court to make any such alteration in breach of that requirement.

(4)   Any alteration in the company's memorandum or articles made by virtue of an order under this Part is of the same effect as if duly made by resolution of the company, and the provisions of this Act apply to the memorandum or articles as so altered accordingly.

(5)   An office copy of an order under this Part altering, or giving leave to alter, a company's memorandum or articles shall, within 14 days from the making of the order or such longer period as the court may allow, be delivered by the company to the registrar of companies for registration; and if a company makes default in complying with this subsection, the company and every officer of it who is in default is liable to a fine and, for continued contravention, to a daily default fine.

(6)   The power under section 411 of the Insolvency Act to make rules shall, so far as it relates to a winding-up petition, apply for the purposes of a petition under this Part.

PART XX

WINDING UP OF COMPANIES REGISTERED UNDER THIS ACT OR THE FORMER COMPANY ACTS

652. Registrar may strike defunct company off register

(1)   If the registrar of companies has reasonable cause to believe that a company is not carrying on business or in operation, he may send to the company by post a letter inquiring whether the company is carrying on business or in operation.

(2)   If the registrar does not within one month of sending the letter receive any answer to it, he shall within 14 days after the expiration of that month send to the company by post a registered letter referring to the first letter, and stating that no answer to it has been received, and that if an answer is not received to the second letter within

one month from its date, a notice will be published in the *Gazette* with a view to striking the company's name off the register.

(3)   If the registrar either receives an answer to the effect that the company is not carrying on business or in operation, or does not within one month after sending the second letter receiver any answer, he may publish in the *Gazette*, and send to the company by post, a notice that at the expiration of 3 months from the date of that notice the name of the company mentioned in it will, unless cause is shown to the contrary, be struck off the register and the company will be dissolved.

(4)   If, in a case where a company is being wound up, the registrar has reasonable cause to believe either that no liquidator is acting, or that the affairs of the company are fully wound up, and the returns required to be made by the liquidator have not been made for a period of 6 consecutive months, the registrar shall publish in the *Gazette* and send to the company or the liquidator (if any) a like notice as is provided in subsection (3).

(5)   At the expiration of the time mentioned in the notice the registrar may, unless cause to the contrary is previously shown by the company, strike its name off the register, and shall publish notice of this in the *Gazette*; and on the publication of that notice in the *Gazette* the company is dissolved.

(6)   However—

    (a)   the liability (if any) of every director, managing officer and member of the company continues and may be enforced as if the company had not been dissolved; and

    (b)   nothing in subsection (5) affects the power of the court to wind up a company the name of which has been struck off the register.

(7)   A notice to be sent to a liquidator under this section may be addressed to him at his last known place of business; and a letter or notice to be sent under this section to a company may be addressed to the company at its registered office or, if no office has been registered, to the care of some officer of the company.

If there is no officer of the company whose name and address are known to the registrar of companies, the letter or notice may be sent to each of the persons who subscribed the memorandum, addressed to him at the address mentioned in the memorandum.

653. Objection to striking off by person aggrieved

(1)   Subsection (2) applies if a company or any member or creditor of it feels aggrieved by the company having been struck off the register under section 652.

(2)   The court, on an application by the company or the member or creditor made before the expiration of 20 years from publication in the *Gazette* of notice under section 652, may, if satisfied that the company was at the time of the striking off carrying on business or in operation, or otherwise that it is just that the company be restored to the register, order the company's name to be restored.

(2A)   Subsections (2B) and (2D) apply if a company has been struck off the register under section 652A.

(2B)   The court, on an application by a notifiable person made before the expiration of 20 years from publication in the *Gazette* of notice under section 652A(4), may, if satisfied—

    (a)   that any duty under section 652B or 652C with respect to the giving to that person of a copy of the company's application under section 652A was not performed,

    (b)   that the making of the company's application under section 652A involved a breach of duty under section 652B(1) or (3), or

    (c)   that it is for some other reason just to do so,

order the company's name to be restored to the register.

(2C)   In subsection (2B), 'notifiable person' means a person to whom a copy of the company's application under section 652A was required to be given under section 652B or 652C.

(2D)   The court, on an application by the Secretary of State made before the expiration of 20 years from publication in the *Gazette* of notice under section 652A(4), may, if satisfied that it is in the public interest to do so, order the company's name to be restored.

(3)   On an office copy of an order under Subsection (2), (2B) or (2D) being delivered to the registrar of companies for registration the company to which the order relates is deemed to have continued in existence as if its name had not been struck off; and the court may by the order give such directions and made such provisions as seem just for

placing the company and all other persons in the same position (as nearly as may be) as if the company's name had not been struck off.

PART XXVI

INTERPRETATION

736. 'Subsidiary', 'holding company' and 'wholly-owned subsidiary'

(1)   A company is a 'subsidiary' of another company, its 'holding company', if that other company—

    (a)   holds a majority of the voting rights in it, or

    (b)   is a member of it and has the right to appoint or remove a majority of its board of directors, or

    (c)   is a member of it and controls alone, pursuant to an agreement with other shareholders or members, a majority of the voting rights in it,

or if it is a subsidiary of a company which is itself a subsidiary of that other company.

(2)   A company is a 'wholly-owned subsidiary' of another company if it has no members except that other and that other's wholly-owned subsidiaries or persons acting on behalf of that other or its wholly-owned subsidiaries.

(3)   In this section 'company' includes any body corporate.

736A.   Provisions supplementing s 736

(1)   The provisions of this section explain expressions used in section 736 and otherwise supplement that section.

(2)   In section 736(1)(a) and (c) the references to the voting rights in a company are to the rights conferred on shareholders in respect of their shares or, in the case of a company not having a share capital, on members, to vote at general meetings of the company on all, or substantially all, matters.

(3)   In section 736(1)(b) the reference to the right to appoint or remove a majority of the board of directors is to the right to appoint or remove directors holding a majority of the voting rights at meetings of the board on all, or substantially all, matters; and for the purposes of that provision—

    (a)   a company shall be treated as having the right to appoint to a directorship if—

        (i)   a person's appointment to it follows necessarily from his appointment as director of the company, or

        (ii)   the directorship is held by the company itself; and

    (b)   a right to appoint or remove which is exercisable only with the consent or concurrence of another person shall be left out of account unless no other person has a right to appoint or, as the case may be, remove in relation to that directorship.

(4)   Rights which are exercisable only in certain circumstances shall be taken into account only—

    (a)   when the circumstances have arisen, and for so long as they continue to obtain, or

    (b)   when the circumstances are within the control of the person having the rights;

and rights which are normally exercisable but are temporarily incapable of exercise shall continue to be taken into account.

(5)   Rights held by a person in a fiduciary capacity shall be treated as not held by him.

(6)   Rights held by a person as nominee for another shall be treated as held by the other; and rights shall be regarded as held as nominee for another if they are exercisable only on his instructions or with his consent or concurrence.

(7)   Rights attached to shares held by way of security shall be treated as held by the person providing the security—

    (a)   where apart from the right to exercise them for the purpose of preserving the value of the security, or of realising it, the rights are exercisable only in accordance with his instructions;

    (b)   where the shares are held in connection with the granting of loans as part of normal business activities and apart from the right to exercise them for the purpose of preserving the value of the security, or of realising it, the rights are exercisable only in his interests.

(8)   Rights shall be treated as held by a company if they are held by any of its subsidiaries; and nothing in subsection (6) or (7) shall be construed as requiring rights held by a company to be treated as held by any of its subsidiaries.

(9)   For the purposes of subsection (7) rights shall be treated as being exercisable in accordance with the instructions or in the interests of a company if they are exercisable in accordance with the instructions of or, as the case may be, in the interests of—

(a)   any subsidiary or holding company of that company, or

(b)   any subsidiary of a holding company of that company.

(10)   The voting rights in a company shall be reduced by any rights held by the company itself.

(11)   References in any provision of subsections (5) to (10) to rights held by a person include rights falling to be treated as held by him by virtue of any other provision of those subsections but not rights which by virtue of any such provision are to be treated as not held by him.

(12)   In this section 'company' includes any body corporate.

739. 'Non-cash asset'

(1)   In this Act 'non-cash asset' means any property or interest in property other than cash; and for this purpose 'cash' includes foreign currency.

(2)   A reference to the transfer or acquisition of a non-cash asset includes the creation or extinction of an estate or interest in, or a right over, any property and also the discharge of any person's liability other than a liability for a liquidated sum.

741. 'Director' and 'shadow director'

(1)   In this Act, 'director' includes any person occupying the position of director, by whatever name called.

(2)   In relation to a company, 'shadow director' means a person in accordance with whose directions or instructions the directors of the company are accustomed to act.

However, a person is not deemed a shadow director by reason only that the directors act on advice given by him in a professional capacity.

(3)   For the purposes of the following provisions of this Act, namely—

section 309 (directors' duty to have regard to interests of employees),
section 319 (directors' long-term contracts of employment),
sections 320 to 322 (substantial property transactions involving directors),
section 322B (contracts with sole members who are directors), and
sections 330 to 346 (general restrictions on power of companies to make loans, etc, to directors and others connected with them),

(being provisions under which shadow directors are treated as directors), a body corporate is not to be treated as a shadow director of any of its subsidiary companies by reason only that the directors of the subsidiary are accustomed to act in accordance with its directions or instructions.

SCHEDULE 1

Section 10

PARTICULARS OF DIRECTORS ETC TO BE CONTAINED IN STATEMENT UNDER SECTION 10

Directors

1.   Subject as provided below, the statement under section 10(2) shall contain the following particulars with respect to each person named as director—

(a)   in the case of an individual, his present name, any former name, his usual residential address, his nationality, his business occupation (if any), particulars of any other directorships held by him, or which have been held by him and his date of birth;

(b)   in the case of a corporation or Scottish firm, its corporate or firm name and registered or principal office.

2. (1) It is not necessary for the statement to contain particulars of a directorship—

    (a) which has not been held by a director at any time during the 5 years preceding the date on which the statement is delivered to the registrar,

    (b) which is held by a director in a company which—

        (i) is dormant or grouped with the company delivering the statement, and

        (ii) if he also held that directorship for any period during those 5 years, was for the whole of that period either dormant or so grouped,

    (c) which was held by a director for any period during those 5 years in a company which for the whole of that period was either dormant or grouped with the company delivering the statement.

(2) For these purposes, 'company' includes any body corporate incorporated in Great Britain; and—

    (a) section 249AA(3) applies as regards whether and when a company is or has been 'dormant', and

    (b) a company is treated as being or having been at any time grouped with another company if at that time it is or was a company of which that other is or was a wholly-owned subsidiary, or if it is or was a wholly-owned subsidiary of the other or of another company of which that other is or was a wholly-owned subsidiary.

Secretaries

3. (1) The statement shall contain the following particulars with respect to the person named as secretary or, where there are to be joint secretaries, with respect to each person named as one of them—

    (a) in the case of an individual, his present name, any former name and his usual residential address,

    (b) in the case of a corporation or a Scottish firm, its corporate or firm name and registered or principal office.

(2) However, if all the partners in a firm are joint secretaries, the name and principal office of the firm may be stated instead of the particulars otherwise required by this paragraph.

Interpretation

4. In paragraphs 1(a) and 3(1)(a) above—

    (a) 'name' means a person's Christian name (or other forename) and surname, except that in the case of a peer, or an individual usually known by a title, the title may be stated instead of his Christian name (or other forename) and surname or in addition to either or both of them; and

    (b) the reference to a former name does not include—

        (i) in the case of a peer, or an individual normally known by a British title, the name by which he was known previous to the adoption of or succession to the title, or

        (ii) in the case of any person, a former name which was changed or disused before he attained the age of 18 years or which has been changed or disused for 20 years or more, or

        (iii) in the case of a married woman, the name by which she was known previous to the marriage.

SCHEDULE 8

Section 246

FORM AND CONTENT OF ACCOUNTS PREPARED BY SMALL COMPANIES

PART I

GENERAL RULES AND FORMATS

SECTION A

GENERAL RULES

1. (1) Subject to the following provisions of this Schedule—

(a)   every balance sheet of a small company shall show the items listed in either of the balance sheet formats set out below in section B of this Part; and

(b)   every profit and loss account of a small company shall show the items listed in any one of the profit and loss account formats so set out;

in either case in the order and under the headings and sub-headings given in the format adopted.

(2) Sub-paragraph (1) above is not to be read as requiring the heading or sub-heading for any item to be distinguished by any letter or number assigned to that item in the format adopted.

2.   (1) Where in accordance with paragraph 1 a small company's balance sheet or profit and loss account for any financial year has been prepared by reference to one of the formats set out in section B below, the directors of the company shall adopt the same format in preparing the accounts for subsequent financial years of the company unless in their opinion there are special reasons for a change.

(2) Particulars of any change in the format adopted in preparing a small company's balance sheet or profit and loss account in accordance with paragraph 1 shall be disclosed, and the reasons for the change shall be explained, in a note to the accounts in which the new format is first adopted.

3.   (1) Any item required in accordance with paragraph 1 to be shown in a small company's balance sheet or profit and loss account may be shown in greater detail than required by the format adopted.

(2) A small company's balance sheet or profit and loss account may include an item representing or covering the amount of any asset or liability, income or expenditure not otherwise covered by any of the items listed in the format adopted, but the following shall not be treated as assets in any small company's balance sheet—

(a)   preliminary expenses;

(b)   expenses of and commission on any issue of shares or debentures; and

(c)   costs of research.

(3) In preparing a small company's balance sheet or profit and loss account the directors of the company shall adapt the arrangement and headings and sub-headings otherwise required by paragraph 1 in respect of items to which an Arabic number is assigned in the format adopted, in any case where the special nature of the company's business requires such adaptation.

(4) Items to which Arabic numbers are assigned in any of the formats set out in section B below may be combined in a small company's accounts for any financial year if either—

(a)   their individual amounts are not material to assessing the state of affairs or profit or loss of the company for that year; or

(b)   the combination facilitates that assessment;

but in a case within paragraph (b) the individual amounts of any items so combined shall be disclosed in a note to the accounts.

(5) Subject to paragraph 4(3) below, a heading or sub-heading corresponding to an item listed in the format adopted in preparing a small company's balance sheet or profit and loss account shall not be included if there is no amount to be shown for that item in respect of the financial year to which the balance sheet or profit and loss account relates.

(6) Every profit and loss account of a small company shall show the amount of the company's profit or loss on ordinary activities before taxation.

(7) Every profit and loss account of a small company shall show separately as additional items—

(a)   any amount set aside or proposed to be set aside to, or withdrawn or proposed to be withdrawn from, reserves;

(b)   the aggregate amount of any dividends paid and proposed.

4.   (1) In respect of every item shown in a small company's balance sheet or profit and loss account the corresponding amount for the financial year immediately preceding that to which the balance sheet or profit and loss account relates shall also be shown.

(2) Where that corresponding amount is not comparable with the amount to be shown for the item in question in respect of the financial year to which the balance sheet or profit and loss account relates, the former amount shall be adjusted and particulars of the adjustment and the reasons for it shall be disclosed in a note to the accounts.

(3) Paragraph 3(5) does not apply in any case where an amount can be shown for the item in question in respect of the financial year immediately preceding that to which the balance sheet or profit and loss account relates, and that amount shall be shown under the heading or sub-heading required by paragraph 1 for that item.

5.   Amounts in respect of items representing assets or income may not be set off against amounts in respect of items representing liabilities or expenditure (as the case may be), or vice versa.

SECTION B

THE REQUIRED FORMATS FOR ACCOUNTS

Preliminary

6.   References in this Part of this Schedule to the items listed in any of the formats set out below are to those items read together with any of the notes following the formats which apply to any of those items, and the requirement imposed by paragraph 1 to show the items listed in any such format in the order adopted in the format is subject to any provision in those notes for alternative positions for any particular items.

7.   A number in brackets following any item in any of the formats set out below is a reference to the note of that number in the notes following the formats.

8.   In the notes following the formats—

    (a)   the heading of each note gives the required heading or sub-heading for the item to which it applies and a reference to any letters and numbers assigned to that item in the formats set out below (taking a reference in the case of Format 2 of the balance sheet formats to the item listed under 'Assets' or under 'Liabilities' as the case may require); and

    (b)   references to a numbered format are to the balance sheet format or (as the case may require) to the profit and loss account format of that number set out below.

Balance Sheet Formats

Format 1

A.   Called up share capital not paid *(1)*

B.   Fixed assets

    I   Intangible assets
        1.   Goodwill *(2)*
        2.   Other intangible assets *(3)*
    II   Tangible assets
        1.   Land and buildings
        2.   Plant and machinery etc.
    III   Investments
        1.   Shares in group undertakings and participating interests
        2   Loans to group undertakings and undertakings in which the company has a participating interest
        3.   Other investments other than loans
        4.   Other investments *(4)*

C.   Current assets

    I   Stocks
        1.   Stocks
        2.   Payments on account
    II   Debtors *(5)*
        1.   Trade debtors
        2.   Amounts owed by group undertakings and undertakings in which the company has a participating interest
        3.   Other debtors
    III   Investments
        1.   Shares in group undertakings

      2.   Other investments
IV   Cash at bank and in hand

D.   Prepayments and accrued income *(6)*

E.   Creditors: amounts falling due within one year

      1.   Bank loans and overdrafts
      2.   Trade creditors
      3.   Amounts owed to group undertakings and undertakings in which the company has a participating interest
      4.   Other creditors *(7)*

F.   Net current assets (liabilities) *(8)*

G.   Total assets less current liabilities

H.   Creditors: amounts falling due after more than one year

      1.   Bank loans and overdrafts
      2.   Trade creditors
      3.   Amounts owed to group undertakings and undertakings in which the company has a participating interest
      4.   Other creditors *(7)*

I.   Provisions for liabilities and charges

J.   Accruals and deferred income *(7)*

K.   Capital and reserves

      I   Called up share capital *(9)*
      II   Share premium account
      III Revaluation reserve
      IV   Other reserves
      V   Profit and loss account

Balance Sheet Formats

Format 2

ASSETS

A.   Called up share capital not paid *(1)*

B.   Fixed assets

      I   Intangible assets
          1.   Goodwill *(2)*
          2.   Other intangible assets *(3)*
      II   Tangible assets
          1.   Land and buildings
          2.   Plant and machinery etc.
      III Investments
          1.   Shares in group undertakings and participating interests
          2.   Loans to group undertakings and undertakings in which the company has a participating interest
          3.   Other investments other than loans
          4.   Other investments *(4)*

C.   Current assets

      I   Stocks
          1.   Stocks
          2.   Payments on account
      II   Debtors *(5)*
          1.   Trade debtors

      2.   Amounts owed by group undertakings and undertakings in which the company has a participating interest

      3.   Other debtors

  III   Investments

      1.   Shares in group undertakings

      2.   Other investments

  IV   Cash at bank and in hand

D.   Prepayments and accrued income *(6)*

LIABILITIES

A.   Capital and reserves

  I   Called up share capital *(9)*

  II   Share premium account

  III   Revaluation reserve

  IV   Other reserves

  V   Profit and loss account

B.   Provisions for liabilities and charges

C.   Creditors *(10)*

      1.   Bank loans and overdrafts

      2.   Trade creditors

      3.   Amounts owed to group undertakings and undertakings in which the company has a participating interest

      4.   Other creditors *(7)*

D.   Accruals and deferred income *(7)*

Notes on the balance sheet formats

(1) Called up share capital not paid

(Formats 1 and 2, items A and C.II.3.)

This item may either be shown at item A or included under item C.II.3 in format 1 or 2.

(2) Goodwill

(Formats 1 and 2, item B.I.1.)

Amounts representing goodwill shall only be included to the extent that the goodwill was acquired for valuable consideration.

(3) Other intangible assets

(Formats 1 and 2, item B.I.2.)

Amounts in respect of concessions, patents, licences, trade marks and similar rights and assets shall only be included in a company's balance sheet under this item if either—

    (a)   the assets were acquired for valuable consideration and are not required to be shown under goodwill; or

    (b)   the assets in question were created by the company itself.

(4) Others: Other investments

(Formats 1 and 2, items B.III.4 and C.III.2.)

Where amounts in respect of own shares held are included under either of these items, the nominal value of such shares shall be shown separately.

(5) Debtors

(Formats 1 and 2, items C.II.1 to 3.)

The amount falling due after more than one year shall be shown separately for each item included under debtors unless the aggregate amount of debtors falling due after more than one year is disclosed in the notes to the accounts.

(6)   Prepayments and accrued income

(Formats 1 and 2, item D.)

This item may alternatively be included under item C.II.3 in Format 1 or 2.

(7)   Other creditors

(Format 1, items E.4, H.4 and J and Format 2, items C.4 and D.)

There shall be shown separately—

        (a)   the amount of any convertible loans, and
        (b)   the amount for creditors in respect of taxation and social security.

Payments received on account of orders shall be included in so far as they are not shown as deductions from stocks.

In Format 1, accruals and deferred income may be shown under item J or included under item E.4 or H.4, or both (as the case may require). In Format 2, accruals and deferred income may be shown under item D or within item C.4 under Liabilities.

(8)   Net current assets (liabilities)

(Format 1, item F.)

In determining the amount to be shown under this item any prepayments and accrued income shall be taken into account wherever shown.

(9)   Called up share capital

(Format 1, item K.I and Format 2, item A.I.)

The amount of allotted share capital and the amount of called up share capital which has been paid up shall be shown separately.

(10)   Creditors

(Format 2, items C.1 to 4.)

Amounts falling due within one year and after one year shall be shown separately for each of these items and for the aggregate of all of these items unless the aggregate amount of creditors falling due within one year and the aggregate amount of creditors falling due after more than one year is disclosed in the notes to the accounts.

Profit and loss account formats

Format 1

(see note (14) below)

1.   Turnover
2.   Cost of sales *(11)*
3.   Gross profit or loss
4.   Distribution costs *(11)*
5.   Administrative expenses *(11)*
6.   Other operating income
7.   Income from shares in group undertakings
8.   Income from participating interests
9.   Income from other fixed asset investments *(12)*
10. Other interest receivable and similar income *(12)*
11. Amounts written off investments
12. Interest payable and similar charges *(13)*
13. Tax on profit or loss on ordinary activities
14. Profit or loss on ordinary activities after taxation
15. Extraordinary income
16. Extraordinary charges
17. Extraordinary profit or loss

18. Tax on extraordinary profit or loss
19. Other taxes not shown under the above items
20. Profit or loss for the financial year

Profit and loss account formats

Format 2

1. Turnover
2. Change in stock of finished goods and in work in progress
3. Own work capitalised
4. Other operating income
5. (a) Raw materials and consumables
   (b) Other external charges
6. Staff costs:
   (a) wages and salaries
   (b) social security costs
   (c) other pension costs
7. (a) Depreciation and other amounts written off tangible and intangible fixed assets
   (b) Exceptional amounts written off current assets
8. Other operating charges
9. Income from shares in group undertakings
10. Income from participating interests
11. Income from other fixed asset investments *(12)*
12. Other interest receivable and similar income *(12)*
13. Amounts written off investments
14. Interest payable and similar charges *(13)*
15. Tax on profit or loss on ordinary activities
16. Profit or loss on ordinary activities after taxation
17. Extraordinary income
18. Extraordinary charges
19. Extraordinary profit or loss
20. Tax on extraordinary profit or loss
21. Other taxes not shown under the above items
22. Profit or loss for the financial year

Profit and loss account formats

Format 3

(see note (14) below)

A. Charges

   1. Cost of sales *(11)*
   2. Distribution costs *(11)*
   3. Administrative expenses *(11)*
   4. Amounts written off investments
   5. Interest payable and similar charges *(13)*
   6. Tax on profit or loss on ordinary activities
   7. Profit or loss on ordinary activities after taxation
   8. Extraordinary charges
   9. Tax on extraordinary profit or loss
   10. Other taxes not shown under the above items
   11. Profit or loss for the financial year

B. Income

   1. Turnover
   2. Other operating income
   3. Income from shares in group undertakings
   4. Income from participating interests

5. Income from other fixed asset investments *(12)*
6. Other interest receivable and similar income *(12)*
7. Profit or loss on ordinary activities after taxation
8. Extraordinary income
9. Profit or loss for the financial year

Profit and loss account formats

Format 4

A. Charges

    1. Reduction in stocks of finished goods and in work in progress
    2. (a)   Raw materials and consumables
       (b)   Other external charges
    3. Staff costs:
       (a)   wages and salaries
       (b)   social security costs
       (c)   other pension costs
    4. (a)   Depreciation and other amounts written off tangible and intangible fixed assets
       (b)   Exceptional amounts written off current assets
    5. Other operating charges
    6. Amounts written off investments
    7. Interest payable and similar charges *(13)*
    8. Tax on profit or loss on ordinary activities
    9. Profit or loss on ordinary activities after taxation
    10. Extraordinary charges
    11. Tax on extraordinary profit or loss
    12. Other taxes not shown under the above items
    13. Profit or loss for the financial year

B. Income

    1. Turnover
    2. Increase in stocks of finished goods and in work in progress
    3. Own work capitalised
    4. Other operating income
    5. Income from shares in group undertakings
    6. Income from participating interests
    7. Income from other fixed asset investments *(12)*
    8. Other interest receivable and similar income *(12)*
    9. Profit or loss on ordinary activities after taxation
    10. Extraordinary income
    11. Profit or loss for the financial year

Notes on the profit and loss account formats

(11) Cost of sales: distribution costs: administrative expenses

(Format 1, items 2, 4 and 5 and Format 3, items A.1, 2 and 3.)

These items shall be stated after taking into account any necessary provisions for depreciation or diminution in value of assets.

(12) Income from other fixed asset investments: other interest receivable and similar income

(Format 1, items 9 and 10: Format 2, items 11 and 12: Format 3, items B.5 and 6: Format 4, items B.7 and 8.)

Income and interest derived from group undertakings shall be shown separately from income and interest derived from other sources.

(13) Interest payable and similar charges

(Format 1, item 12: Format 2, item 14: Format 3, item A.5: Format 4, item A.7.)

The amount payable to group undertakings shall be shown separately.

(14) Formats 1 and 3

The amount of any provisions for depreciation and diminution in value of tangible and intangible fixed assets falling to be shown under items 7(a) and A.4(a) respectively in Formats 2 and 4 shall be disclosed in a note to the accounts in any case where the profit and loss account is prepared by reference to Format 1 or Format 3.

PART II

ACCOUNTING PRINCIPLES AND RULES

SECTION A

ACCOUNTING PRINCIPLES

Preliminary

9.   Subject to paragraph 15 below, the amounts to be included in respect of all items shown in a small company's accounts shall be determined in accordance with the principles set out in paragraphs 10 to 14.

Accounting principles

10.   The company shall be presumed to be carrying on business as a going concern.

11.   Accounting policies shall be applied consistently within the same accounts and from one financial year to the next.

12.   The amount of any item shall be determined on a prudent basis, and in particular—

(a)   only profits realised at the balance sheet date shall be included in the profit and loss account; and

(b)   all liabilities and losses which have arisen or are likely to arise in respect of the financial year to which the accounts relate or a previous financial year shall be taken into account, including those which only become apparent between the balance sheet date and the date on which it is signed on behalf of the board of directors in pursuance of section 233 of this Act.

13.   All income and charges relating to the financial year to which the accounts relate shall be taken into account, without regard to the date of receipt or payment.

14.   In determining the aggregate amount of any item the amount of each individual asset or liability that falls to be taken into account shall be determined separately.

Departure from the accounting principles

15.   If it appears to the directors of a small company that there are special reasons for departing from any of the principles stated above in preparing the company's accounts in respect of any financial year they may do so, but particulars of the departure, the reasons for it and its effect shall be given in a note to the accounts.

SECTION B

HISTORICAL COST ACCOUNTING RULES

Preliminary

16.   Subject to section C of this Part of this Schedule, the amounts to be included in respect of all items shown in a small company's account shall be determined in accordance with the rules set out in paragraphs 17 to 28.

General rules

17.   Subject to any provision for depreciation or diminution in value made in accordance with paragraph 18 or 19 the amount to be included in respect of any fixed asset shall be its purchase price or production cost.

18.   In the case of any fixed asset which has a limited useful economic life, the amount of—

(a)   its purchase price or production cost; or

(b)   where it is estimated that any such asset will have a residual value at the end of the period of its useful economic life, its purchase price or production cost less that estimated residual value;

shall be reduced by provisions for depreciation calculated to write off that amount systematically over the period of the asset's useful economic life.

19.   (1) Where a fixed asset investment of a description falling to be included under item B.III of either of the balance sheet formats set out in Part I of this Schedule has diminished in value provisions for diminution in value may be made in respect of it and the amount to be included in respect of it may be reduced accordingly; and any such provisions which are not shown in the profit and loss account shall be disclosed (either separately or in aggregate) in a note to the accounts.

(2) Provisions for diminution in value shall be made in respect of any fixed asset which has diminished in value if the reduction in its value is expected to be permanent (whether its useful economic life is limited or not), and the amount to be included in respect of it shall be reduced accordingly; and any such provisions which are not shown in the profit and loss account shall be disclosed (either separately or in aggregate) in a note to the accounts.

(3) Where the reasons for which any provision was made in accordance with sub-paragraph (1) or (2) have ceased to apply to any extent, that provision shall be written back to the extent that it is no longer necessary; and any amounts written back in accordance with this sub-paragraph which are not shown in the profit and loss account shall be disclosed (either separately or in aggregate) in a note to the accounts.

Rules for determining particular fixed asset items

20.   (1) Notwithstanding that an item in respect of 'development costs' is included under 'fixed assets' in the balance sheet formats set out in Part I of this Schedule, an amount may only be included in a small company's balance sheet in respect of development costs in special circumstances.

(2) If any amount is included in a small company's balance sheet in respect of development costs the following information shall be given in a note to the accounts—

(a)   the period over which the amount of those costs originally capitalised is being or is to be written off; and

(b)   the reasons for capitalising the development costs in question.

21.   (1) The application of paragraphs 17 to 19 in relation to goodwill (in any case where goodwill is treated as an asset) is subject to the following provisions of this paragraph.

(2) Subject to sub-paragraph (3) below, the amount of the consideration for any goodwill acquired by a small company shall be reduced by provisions for depreciation calculated to write off that amount systematically over a period chosen by the directors of the company.

(3) The period chosen shall not exceed the useful economic life of the goodwill in question.

(4) In any case where any goodwill acquired by a small company is shown or included as an asset in the company's balance sheet the period chosen for writing off the consideration for that goodwill and the reasons for choosing that period shall be disclosed in a note to the accounts.

Current assets

22.   Subject to paragraph 23, the amount to be included in respect of any current asset shall be its purchase price or production cost.

23.   (1) If the net realisable value of any current asset is lower than its purchase price or production cost the amount to be included in respect of that asset shall be the net realisable value.

(2) Where the reasons for which any provision for diminution in value was made in accordance with sub-paragraph (1) have ceased to apply to any extent, that provision shall be written back to the extent that is no longer necessary.

Excess of money owed over value received as an asset item

24.   (1) Where the amount repayable on any debt owed by a small company is greater than the value of the consideration received in the transaction giving rise to the debt, the amount of the difference may be treated as an asset.

(2) Where any such amount is so treated—

(a)   it shall be written off by reasonable amounts each year and must be completely written off before repayment of the debt; and

(b)   if the current amount is not shown as a separate item in the company's balance sheet it must be disclosed in a note to the accounts.

Assets included at a fixed amount

25.   (1) Subject to the following sub-paragraph, assets which fall to be included—

(a)   amongst the fixed assets of a small company under the item 'tangible assets'; or

(b)   amongst the current assets of a small company under the item 'raw materials and consumables';

may be included at a fixed quantity and value.

(2) Sub-paragraph (1) applied to assets of a kind which are constantly being replaced, where—

(a)   their overall value is not material to assessing the company's state of affairs; and

(b)   their quantity, value and composition are not subject to material variation.

Determination of purchase price or production cost

26.   (1) The purchase price of an asset shall be determined by adding to the actual price paid any expenses incidental to its acquisition.

(2) The production cost of an asset shall be determined by adding to the purchase price of the raw materials and consumables used the amount of the costs incurred by the company which are directly attributable to the production of the asset.

(3) In addition, there may be included in the production cost of an asset—

(a)   a reasonable proportion of the costs incurred by the company which are only indirectly attributable to the production of that asset, but only to the extent that they relate to the period of production; and

(b)   interest on capital borrowed to finance the production of that asset, to the extent that it accrues in respect of the period of production;

provided, however, in a case within paragraph (b) above, that the inclusion of the interest in determining the cost of that asset and the amount of the interest so included is disclosed in a note to the accounts.

(4) In the case of current assets distribution costs may not be included in production costs.

27.   (1) Subject to the qualification mentioned below, the purchase price or production cost of—

(a)   any assets which fall to be included under any item shown in a small company's balance sheet under the general item 'stocks'; and

(b)   any assets which are fungible assets (including investments);

may be determined by the application of any of the methods mentioned in sub-paragraph (2) below in relation to any such assets of the same class.

The method chosen must be one which appears to the directors to be appropriate in the circumstances of the company.

(2) Those methods are—

(a)   the method known as 'first in, first out' (FIFO);

(b)   the method known as 'last in, first out' (LIFO);

(c)   a weighted average price; and

(d)   any other method similar to any of the methods mentioned above.

(3) For the purposes of this paragraph, assets of any description shall be regarded as fungible if assets of that description are substantially indistinguishable one from another.

Substitution of original stated amount where price or cost unknown

28.   Where there is no record of the purchase price or production cost of any asset of a small company or of any price, expenses or costs relevant for determining its purchase price or production cost in accordance with paragraph 26, or any such record cannot be obtained without unreasonable expense or delay, its purchase price or production cost shall be taken for the purposes of paragraphs 17 to 23 to be the value ascribed to it in the earliest available record of its value made on or after its acquisition or production by the company.

SECTION C

ALTERNATIVE ACCOUNTING RULES

Preliminary

29. (1) The rules set out in section B are referred to below in this Schedule as the historical cost accounting rules.

(2) Those rules, with the omission of paragraph 16, 21 and 25 to 28, are referred to below in this Part of this Schedule as the depreciation rules; and references below in this Schedule to the historical cost accounting rules do not include the depreciation rules as they apply by virtue of paragraph 32.

30. Subject to paragraphs 32 to 34, the amounts to be included in respect of assets of any description mentioned in paragraph 31 may be determined on any basis so mentioned.

Alternative accounting rules

31. (1) Intangible fixed assets, other than goodwill, may be included at their current cost.

(2) Tangible fixed assets may be included at a market value determined as at the date of their last valuation or at their current cost.

(3) Investments of any description falling to be included under item B.III of either of the balance sheet formats set out in Part I of this Schedule may be included either—

(a) at a market value determined as at the date of their last valuation; or

(b) at a value determined on any basis which appears to the directors to be appropriate in the circumstances of the company;

but in the latter case particulars of the method of valuation adopted and of the reasons for adopting it shall be disclosed in a note to the accounts.

(4) Investments of any description falling to be included under item C.III of either of the balance sheet formats set out in Part I of this Schedule may be included at their current cost.

(5) Stocks may be included at their current cost.

Application of the depreciation rules

32. (1) Where the value of any asset of a small company is determined on any basis mentioned in paragraph 31, that value shall be, or (as the case may require) be the starting point for determining, the amount to be included in respect of that asset in the company's accounts, instead of its purchase price or production cost or any value previously so determined for that asset; and the depreciation rules shall apply accordingly in relation to any such asset with the substitution for any reference to its purchase price or production cost of a reference to the value most recently determined for that asset on any basis mentioned in paragraph 31.

(2) The amount of any provision for depreciation required in the case of any fixed asset by paragraph 18 or 19 as it applies by virtue of sub-paragraph (1) is referred to below in this paragraph as the adjusted amount, and the amount of any provision which would be required by that paragraph in the case of that asset according to the historical cost accounting rules is referred to as the historical cost amount.

(3) Where sub-paragraph (1) applies in the case of any fixed asset the amount of any provision for depreciation in respect of that asset—

(a) included in any item shown in the profit and loss account in respect of amounts written off assets of the description in question; or

(b) taken into account in stating any item so shown which is required by note *(11)* of the notes on the profit and loss account formats set out in Part I of this Schedule to be stated after taking into account any necessary provision for depreciation or diminution in value of assets included under it;

may be the historical cost amount instead of the adjusted amount, provided that the amount of any difference between the two is shown separately in the profit and loss account or in a note to the accounts.

Additional information to be provided in case of departure from historical cost accounting rules

33.   (1) This paragraph applies where the amounts to be included in respect of assets covered by any items shown in a small company's accounts have been determined on any basis mentioned in paragraph 31.

(2) The items affected and the basis of valuation adopted in determining the amounts of the assets in question in the case of each such item shall be disclosed in a note to the accounts.

(3) In the case of each balance sheet item affected (except stocks) either—

(a)   the comparable amounts determined according to the historical cost accounting rules; or
(b)   the difference between those amounts and the corresponding amounts actually shown in the balance sheet in respect of that item;

shall be shown separately in the balance sheet or in a note to the accounts.

(4) In sub-paragraph (3) above, references in relation to any item to the comparable amounts determined as there mentioned are references to—

(a)   the aggregate amount which would be required to be shown in respect of that item if the amounts to be included in respect of all the assets covered by that item were determined according to the historical cost accounting rules; and
(b)   the aggregate amount of the cumulative provisions for depreciation or diminution in value which would be permitted or required in determining those amounts according to those rules.

Revaluation reserve

34.   (1) With respect to any determination of the value of an asset of a small company on any basis mentioned in paragraph 31, the amount of any profit or loss arising from that determination (after allowing, where appropriate, for any provisions for depreciation or diminution in value made otherwise than by reference to the value so determined and any adjustments of any such provisions made in the light of that determination) shall be credited or (as the case may be) debited to a separate reserve ('the revaluation reserve').

(2) The amount of the revaluation reserve shall be shown in the company's balance sheet under a separate sub-heading in the position given for the item 'revaluation reserve' in Format 1 or 2 of the balance sheet formats set out in Part I of this Schedule, but need not be shown under that name.

(3) An amount may be transferred—

(a)   from the revaluation reserve—
(i)   to the profit and loss account, if the amount was previously charged to that account or represents realised profit, or
(ii)   on capitalisation,
(b)   to or from the revaluation reserve in respect of the taxation relating to any profit or loss credited or debited to the reserve;

and the revaluation reserve shall be reduced to the extent that the amounts transferred to it are no longer necessary for the purposes of the valuation method used.

(4) In sub-paragraph (3)(a)(ii) 'capitalisation', in relation to an amount standing to the credit of the revaluation reserve, means applying it in wholly or partly paying up unissued shares in the company to be allotted to members of the company as fully or partly paid shares.

(5) The revaluation reserve shall not be reduced except as mentioned in this paragraph.

(6) The treatment for taxation purposes of amounts credited or debited to the revaluation reserve shall be disclosed in a note to the accounts.

PART III

NOTES TO THE ACCOUNTS

Preliminary

35.   Any information required in the case of any small company by the following provisions of this Part of this Schedule shall (if not given in the company's accounts) be given by way of a note to those accounts.

Disclosure of accounting policies

36.   The accounting policies adopted by the company in determining the amounts to be included in respect of items shown in the balance sheet and in determining the profit or loss of the company shall be stated (including such policies with respect to the depreciation and diminution in value of assets).

37.   Paragraphs 38 to 47 require information which either supplements the information given with respect to any particular items shown in the balance sheet or is otherwise relevant to assessing the company's state of affairs in the light of the information so given.

Share capital and debentures

38.   (1) The following information shall be given with respect to the company's share capital—

(a)   The authorised share capital; and

(b)   where shares of more than one class have been allotted, the number and aggregate nominal value of shares of each class allotted.

(2) In the case of any part of the allotted share capital that consists of redeemable shares, the following information shall be given—

(a)   the earliest and latest dates on which the company has power to redeem those shares;

(b)   whether those shares must be redeemed in any event or are liable to be redeemed at the option of the company or of the shareholder; and

(c)   whether any (and, if so, what) premium is payable on redemption.

39.   If the company has allotted any shares during the financial year, the following information shall be given—

(a)   the classes of shares allotted; and

(b)   as respects each class of shares, the number allotted, their aggregate nominal value, and the consideration received by the company for the allotment.

Fixed assets

40.   (1) In respect of each item which is or would but for paragraph 3(4)(b) be shown under the general item 'fixed assets' in the company's balance sheet the following information shall be given—

(a)   the appropriate amounts in respect of that item as at the date of the beginning of the financial year and as at the balance sheet date respectively;

(b)   the effect on any amount shown in the balance sheet in respect of that item of—
(i)   any revision on the amount in respect of any assets included under that item made during that year on any basis mentioned in paragraph 31;
(ii)   acquisitions during that year of any assets;
(iii) disposals during that year of any assets; and
(iv)   any transfers of assets of the company to and from that item during that year.

(2) The reference in sub-paragraph (1)(a) to the appropriate amounts in respect of any item as at any date there mentioned is a reference to amounts representing the aggregate amounts determined, as at that date, in respect of assets falling to be included under that item on either of the following bases, that is to say—

(a)   on the basis of purchase price or production cost (determined in accordance with paragraphs 26 and 27); or

(b)   on any basis mentioned in paragraph 31,

(leaving out of account in either case any provisions for depreciation or diminution in value).

(3) In respect of each item within sub-paragraph (1)—

(a)   the cumulative amount of provisions for depreciation or diminution in value of assets included under that item as at each date mentioned in sub-paragraph (1)(a);

(b)   the amount of any such provisions made in respect of the financial year;

(c)   the amount of any adjustments made in respect of any such provisions during that year in consequence of the disposal of any assets; and

(d)   the amount of any other adjustments made in respect of any such provisions during that year; shall also be stated.

41.   Where any fixed assets of the company (other than listed investments) are included under any item shown in the company's balance sheet at an amount determined on any basis mentioned in paragraph 31, the following information shall be given—

(a)   the years (so far as they are known to the directors) in which the assets were severally valued and the several values; and

(b)   in the case of assets that have been valued during the financial year, the names of the persons who valued them or particulars of their qualifications for doing so and (whichever is stated) the bases of valuation used by them.

42.   (1) In respect of the amount of each item which is or would but for paragraph 3(4)(b) be shown in the company's balance sheet under the general item 'investments' (whether as fixed assets or as current assets) there shall be stated how much of that amount is ascribable to listed investments.

(2) Where the amount of any listed investments is stated for any item in accordance with sub-paragraph (1), the following amounts shall also be stated—

(a)   the aggregate market value of those investments where it differs from the amount so stated; and

(b)   both the market value and the stock exchange value of any investments of which the former value is, for the purposes of the accounts, taken as being higher than the latter.

Reserves and provisions

43.   (1) Where any amount is transferred—

(a)   to or from any reserves; or

(b)   to any provisions for liabilities and charges; or

(c)   from any provision for liabilities and charges otherwise than for the purpose for which the provision was established;

and the reserves or provisions are or would but for paragraph 3(4)(b) be shown as separate items in the company's balance sheet, the information mentioned in the following sub-paragraph shall be given in respect of the aggregate of reserves or provisions included in the same item.

(2) That information is—

(a)   the amount of the reserves or provisions as at the date of the beginning of the financial year and as at the balance sheet date respectively;

(b)   any amounts transferred to or from the reserves or provisions during that year; and

(c)   the source and application respectively of any amounts so transferred.

(3) Particulars shall be given of each provision included in the item 'other provisions' in the company's balance sheet in any case where the amount of that provision is material.

Details of indebtedness

44.   (1) For the aggregate of all items shown under 'creditors' in the company's balance sheet there shall be stated the aggregate of the following amounts, that is to say—

(a)   the amount of any debts included under 'creditors' which are payable or repayable otherwise than by instalments and fall due for payment or repayment after the end of the period of five years beginning with the day next following the end of the financial year; and

(b)   in the case of any debts so included which are payable or repayable by instalments, the amount of any instalments which fall due for repayment after the end of that period.

(2) In respect of each item shown under 'creditors' in the company's balance sheet there shall be stated the aggregate amount of any debts included under that item in respect of which any security has been given by the company.

(3) References above in this paragraph to an item shown under 'creditors' in the company's balance sheet include references, where amounts falling due to creditors within one year and after more than one year are distinguished in the balance sheet—

(a)   in a case within sub-paragraph (1), to an item shown under the latter of those categories; and

(b)   in a case within sub-paragraph (2), to an item shown under either of those categories;

and references to items shown under 'creditors' include references to items which would but for paragraph 3(4)(b) be shown under that heading.

45. If any fixed cumulative dividends on the company's shares are in arrear, there shall be stated—

    (a)   the amount of the arrears; and

    (b)   the period for which the dividends or, if there is more than one class, each class of them are in arrear.

Guarantees and other financial commitments

46.   (1) Particulars shall be given of any charge on the assets of the company to secure the liabilities of any other person, including, where practicable, the amount secured.

    (2) The following information shall be given with respect to any other contingent liability not provided for—

    (a)   the amount or estimated amount of that liability;

    (b)   its legal nature; and

    (c)   whether any valuable security has been provided by the company in connection with that liability and if so, what.

    (3) There shall be stated, where practicable, the aggregate amount or estimated amount of contracts for capital expenditure, so far as not provided for.

    (4) Particulars shall be given of—

    (a)   any pension commitments included under any provision shown in the company's balance sheet; and

    (b)   and such commitments for which no provision has been made;

and where any such commitment relates wholly or partly to pensions payable to past directors of the company separate particulars shall be given of that commitment so far as it relates to such pensions.

    (5) Particulars shall also be given of any other financial commitments which—

    (a)   have not been provided for; and

    (b)   are relevant to assessing the company's state of affairs.

    (6) Commitments within any of sub-paragraphs (1) to (5) which are undertaken on behalf of or for the benefit of—

    (a)   any parent undertaking or fellow subsidiary undertaking, or

    (b)   any subsidiary undertaking of the company;

shall be stated separately from the other commitments within that sub-paragraph, and commitments within paragraph (a) shall also be stated separately from those within paragraph (b).

Miscellaneous matters

47.   Particulars shall be given of any case where the purchase price or production cost of any asset is for the first time determined under paragraph 28.

Information supplementing the profit and loss account

48.   Paragraphs 49 and 50 require information which either supplements the information given with respect to any particular items shown in the profit and loss account or otherwise provides particulars of income or expenditure of the company or of circumstances affecting the items shown in the profit and loss account.

Particulars of turnover

49.   (1) If the company has supplied geographical markets outside the United Kingdom during the financial year in question, there shall be stated the percentage of its turnover that, in the opinion of the directors, is attributable to those markets.

    (2) In analysing for the purposes of this paragraph the source of turnover, the directors of the company shall have regard to the manner in which the company's activities are organised.

Miscellaneous matters

50.   (1) Where any amount relating to any preceding financial year is included in any item in the profit and loss account, the effect shall be stated.

    (2) Particulars shall be given of any extraordinary income or charges arising in the financial year.

(3) The effect shall be stated of any transactions that are exceptional by virtue of size or incidence though they fall within the ordinary activities of the company.

General

51. (1) Where sums originally denominated in foreign currencies have been brought into account under any items shown in the balance sheet or profit and loss account, the basis on which those sums have been translated into sterling shall be stated.

(2) Subject to the following sub-paragraph, in respect of every item stated in a note to the accounts the corresponding amount for the financial year immediately preceding that to which the accounts relate shall also be stated and where the corresponding amount is not comparable, it shall be adjusted and particulars of the adjustment and the reasons for it shall be given.

(3) Sub-paragraph (2) does not apply in relation to any amounts stated by virtue of any of the following provisions of this Act—

(a) paragraph 13 of Schedule 4A (details of accounting treatment of acquisitions),
(b) paragraphs 2, 8(3), 16, 21(1)(d), 22(4) and (5), 24(3) and (4) and 27(3) and (4) of Schedule 5 (shareholdings in other undertakings),
(c) Part II and III of Schedule 6 (loans and other dealings in favour of directors and others), and
(d) paragraphs 40 and 43 above (fixed assets and reserves and provisions).

Dormant companies acting as agents

51A. Where the directors of a company take advantage of the exemption conferred by section 249AA, and the company has during the financial year in question acted as an agent for any person, the fact that it has so acted must be stated.

PART IV

INTERPRETATION OF SCHEDULE

52. The following paragraphs apply for the purposes of this Schedule and its interpretation.

Historical cost accounting rules

53. References to the historical cost accounting rules shall be read in accordance with paragraph 29.

Listed investments

54. (1) 'Listed investment' means an investment as respects which there has been granted a listing on—

(a) a recognised investment exchange other than an overseas investment exchange; or
(b) a stock exchange of repute outside Great Britain.

(2) 'Recognised investment exchange' and 'overseas investment exchange' have the meaning given in Part 18 of the Financial Services and Markets Act 2000.

Loans

55. A loan is treated as falling due for repayment, and an instalment of a loan is treated as falling due for payment, on the earliest date on which the lender could require payment or (as the case may be) payment, if he exercised all options and rights available to him.

Materiality

56. Amounts which in the particular context of any provision of this Schedule are not material may be disregarded for the purposes of that provision.

Provisions

57. (1) References to provisions for depreciation or diminution in value of assets are to any amount written off by way of providing for depreciation or diminution in value of assets.

(2) Any reference in the profit and loss account formats set out in Part I of this Schedule to the depreciation of, or amounts written off, assets of any description is to any provision for depreciation or diminution in value of assets of that description.

58.   References to provisions for liabilities or changes are to any amount retained as reasonably necessary for the purpose of providing for any liability or loss which is either likely to be incurred, or certain to be incurred but uncertain as to amount or as to the date on which it will arise.

Staff costs

59.   (1) 'Social security costs' means any contributions by the company to any state social security or pension scheme, fund or arrangement.

(2) 'Pension costs' includes any costs incurred by the company in respect of any pension scheme established for the purpose of providing pensions for persons currently or formerly employed by the company, any sums set aside for the future payment of pensions directly by the company to current or former employees and any pensions paid directly to such persons without having first been set aside.

(3) Any amount stated in respect of the item 'social security costs' or in respect of the item 'wages and salaries' in the company's profit and loss account shall be determined by reference to payments made or costs incurred in respect of all persons employed by the company during the financial year under contracts of service.

SCHEDULE 8A

FORM AND CONTENT OF ABBREVIATED ACCOUNTS OF SMALL COMPANIES DELIVERED TO REGISTRAR

PART I

BALANCE SHEET FORMATS

1.   A small company may deliver to the registrar a copy of the balance sheet showing the items listed in either of the balance sheet formats set out in paragraph 2 below in the order and under the headings and sub-headings given in the format adopted, but in other respects corresponding to the full balance sheet.

2.   The formats referred to in paragraph 1 are as follows—

Balance Sheet Formats

Format 1

A.   Called up share capital not paid

B.   Fixed assets
    I   Intangible assets
    II   Tangible assets
    III   Investments

C.   Current assets
    I   Stocks
    II   Debtors *(1)*
    III   Investments
    IV   Cash at bank and in hand

D.   Prepayments and accrued income

E.   Creditors: amounts falling due within one year

F.   Net current assets (liabilities)

G.   Total assets less current liabilities

H.   Creditors: amounts falling due after more than one year

I.   Provisions for liabilities and charges

J.   Accruals and deferred income

K.   Capital and reserves
    I   Called up share capital
    II   Share premium account

III   Revaluation reserve

IV   Other reserves

V   Profit and loss account

Balance Sheet Formats

Format 2

ASSETS

A.   Called up share capital not paid

B.   Fixed assets
    I   Intangible assets
    II   Tangible assets
    III   Investments

C.   Current assets
    I   Stocks
    II   Debtors *(1)*
    III   Investments
    IV   Cash at bank and in hand

D.   Prepayments and accrued income

LIABILITIES

A.   Capital and reserves
    I   Called up share capital
    II   Share premium account
    III   Revaluation reserve
    IV   Other reserves
    V   Profit and loss account

B.   Provisions for liabilities and charges

C.   Creditors *(2)*

D.   Accruals and deferred income

Notes on the balance sheet formats

(1) Debtors

(Formats 1 and 2, item C.II.)

The aggregate amount of debtors falling due after more than one year shall be shown separately, unless it is disclosed in the notes to the accounts.

(2) Creditors

(Formats 2, Liabilities item C.)

The aggregate amount of creditors falling due within one year and of creditors falling due after more than one year shall be shown separately, unless it is disclosed in the notes to the accounts.

PART III

NOTES TO THE ACCOUNTS

Preliminary

3.   Any information required in the case of any small company by the following provisions of this Part of this Schedule shall (if not given in the company's accounts) be given by way of a note to those accounts.

Disclosure of accounting policies

4.   The accounting policies adopted by the company in determining the amounts to be included in respect of items shown in the balance sheet and in determining the profit or loss of the company shall be stated (including such policies with respect to the depreciation and diminution in value of assets).

Information supplementing the balance sheet

Share capital and debentures

5.   (1) The following information shall be given with respect to the company's share capital—

   (a)   the authorised share capital; and
   (b)   where shares of more than one class have been allotted, the number and aggregate nominal value of shares of each class allotted.

   (2) In the case of any part of the allotted share capital that consists of redeemable shares, the following information shall be given—

   (a)   the earliest and latest dates on which the company has power to redeem those shares;
   (b)   whether those shares must be redeemed in any event or are liable to be redeemed at the option of the company or of the shareholder; and
   (c)   whether any (and, if so, what) premium is payable on redemption.

6.   If the company has allotted any shares during the financial year, the following information shall be given—

   (a)   the classes of shares allotted; and
   (b)   as respects each class of shares, the number allotted, their aggregate nominal value, and the consideration received by the company for the allotment.

Fixed assets

7.   (1) In respect of each item to which a letter or Roman number is assigned under the general item 'fixed assets' in the company's balance sheet the following information shall be given—

   (a)   the appropriate amounts in respect of that item as at the date of the beginning of the financial year and as at the balance sheet date respectively;
   (b)   the effect on any amount shown in the balance sheet in respect of that item of—
      (i)   any revision of the amount in respect of any assets included under that item made during that year on any basis mentioned in paragraph 31 of Schedule 8;
      (ii)   acquisitions during that year of any assets;
      (iii) disposals during that year of any assets; and
      (iv)   any transfers of assets of the company to and from that item during that year.

   (2) The reference in sub-paragraph (1)(a) to the appropriate amounts in respect of any item as at any date there mentioned is a reference to amounts representing the aggregate amounts determined, as at that date, in respect of assets falling to be included under that item on either of the following bases, that is to say—

   (a)   on the basis of purchase price or production cost (determined in accordance with paragraphs 26 and 27 of Schedule 8); or
   (b)   on any basis mentioned in paragraph 31 of that Schedule,

(leaving out of account in either case any provisions for depreciation or diminution in value).

   (3) In respect of each item within sub-paragraph (1)—

   (a)   the cumulative amount of provision for depreciation or diminution in value of assets included under that item as at each date mentioned in sub-paragraph (1)(a);
   (b)   the amount of any such provisions made in respect of the financial year;
   (c)   the amount of any adjustments made in respect of any such provisions during that year in consequence of the disposal of any assets; and
   (d)   the amount of any other adjustments made in respect of any such provisions during that year;

shall also be stated.

Details of indebtedness

8.   (1) For the aggregate of all items shown under 'creditors' in the company's balance sheet there shall be stated the aggregate of the following amounts, that is to say—

(a)   the amount of any debts included under 'creditors' which are payable or repayable otherwise than by instalments and fall due for payment or repayment after the end of the period of five years beginning with the day next following the end of the financial year; and

(b)   in the case of any debts so included which are payable or repayable by instalments, the amount of any instalments which fall due for payment after the end of that period.

(2) In respect of each item shown under 'creditors' in the company's balance sheet there shall be stated the aggregate amount of any debts included under that item, in respect of which any security has been given by the company.

General

9.   (1) Where sums originally denominated in foreign currencies have been brought into account under any items shown in the balance sheet or profit and loss account, the basis on which those sums have been translated into sterling shall be stated.

(2) Subject to the following sub-paragraph, in respect of every item required to be stated in a note to the accounts by or under any provision of this Act, the corresponding amount for the financial year immediately preceding that to which the accounts relate shall also be stated and where the corresponding amount is not comparable, it shall be adjusted and particulars of the adjustment and the reasons for it shall be given.

(3) Sub-paragraph (2) does not apply in relation to any amounts stated by virtue of any of the following provisions of this Act—

(a)   paragraph 13 of Schedule 4A (details of accounting treatment of acquisitions),

(b)   paragraphs 2, 8(3), 16, 21(1)(d), 22(4) and (5), 24(3) and (4) and 27(3) and (4) of Schedule 5 (shareholdings in other undertakings),

(c)   Parts II and III of Schedule 6 (loans and other dealings in favour of directors and others), and

(d)   paragraph 7 above (fixed assets).

Dormant companies acting as agents

9A.   Where the directors of a company take advantage of the exemption conferred by section 249AA, and the company has during the financial year in question acted as an agent for any person, the fact that it has so acted must be stated.

SCHEDULE 13

Sections 324, 325, 326, 328 and 346

PROVISIONS SUPPLEMENTING AND INTERPRETING SECTIONS 324–328

PART I

RULES FOR INTERPRETATION OF THE SECTIONS AND ALSO SECTION 346(4) AND (5)

1.   (1) A reference to an interest in shares or debentures is to be read as including any interest of any kind whatsoever in shares or debentures.

(2) Accordingly, there are to be disregarded any restraints or restrictions to which the exercise of any right attached to the interest is or may be subject.

2.   Where property is held on trust and any interest in shares or debentures is comprised in the property, any beneficiary of the trust who (apart from this paragraph) does not have an interest in the shares or debentures is to be taken as having such an interest; but this paragraph is without prejudice to the following provisions of this Part of this Schedule.

3.   (1) A person is taken to have an interest in shares or debentures if—

(a)   he enters into a contract for their purchase by him (whether for cash or other consideration), or

(b)   not being the registered holder, he is entitled to exercise any right conferred by the holding of the shares or debentures, or is entitled to control the exercise of any such right.

(2) For purposes of sub-paragraph (1)(b), a person is taken to be entitled to exercise or control the exercise of a right conferred by the holding of shares or debentures if he—

(a)   has a right (whether subject to conditions or not) the exercise of which would make him so entitled, or

(b)   is under an obligation (whether or not so subject) the fulfilment of which would make him so entitled.

(3) A person is not by virtue of sub-paragraph (1)(b) taken to be interested in shares or debentures by reason only that he—

(a)   has been appointed a proxy to vote at a specified meeting of a company or of any class of its members and at any adjournment of that meeting, or

(b)   has been appointed by a corporation to act as its representative at any meeting of a company or of any class of its members.

4.   A person is taken to be interested in shares or debentures if a body corporate is interested in them and—

(a)   that body corporate or its directors are accustomed to act in accordance with his directions or instructions, or

(b)   he is entitled to exercise or control the exercise of one-third or more of the voting power at general meetings of that body corporate.

As this paragraph applies for the purposes of section 346(4) and (5), 'more than one-half' is substituted for 'one-third or more'.

5.   Where a person is entitled to exercise or control the exercise of one-third or more of the voting power at general meetings of a body corporate, and that body corporate is entitled to exercise or control the exercise of any of the voting power at general meetings of another body corporate ('the effective voting power'), then, for purposes of paragraph 4(b), the effective voting power is taken to be exercisable by that person.

As this paragraph applies for the purposes of section 346(4) and (5), 'more than one-half' is substituted for 'one-third or more'.

6.   (1) A person is taken to have an interest in shares or debentures if, otherwise than by virtue of having an interest under a trust—

(a)   he has a right to call for delivery of the shares or debentures to himself or to his order, or

(b)   he has a right to acquire an interest in shares or debentures or is under an obligation to take an interest in shares or debentures;

whether in any case the right or obligation is conditional or absolute.

(2) Rights or obligations to subscribe for shares or debentures are not to be taken, for purposes of sub-paragraph (1), to be rights to acquire, or obligations to take, an interest in shares or debentures.

This is without prejudice to paragraph 1.

7.   Persons having a joint interest are deemed each of them to have that interest.

8.   It is immaterial that shares or debentures in which a person has an interest are unidentifiable.

9.   So long as a person is entitled to receive, during the lifetime of himself or another, income from trust property comprising shares or debentures, an interest in the shares or debentures in reversion or remainder or (as regards Scotland) in fee, are to be disregarded.

10.   A person is to be treated as uninterested in shares or debentures if, and so long as, he holds them under the law in force in England and Wales as a bare trustee or as a custodian trustee, or under the law in force in Scotland, as a simple trustee.

11.   (1) There is to be disregarded an interest of a person subsisting by virtue of—

(a)   any unit trust scheme which is an authorised unit trust scheme;

(b)   a scheme made under section 22 or 22A of the Charities Act 1960 or section 24 or 25 of the Charities Act 1993, section 11 of the Trustee Investments Act 1961 or section 1 of the Administration of Justice Act 1965; or

(c)   the scheme set out in the Schedule to the Church Funds Investment Measure 1958.

(2) 'Unit trust scheme' and 'authorised unit trust scheme' have the meaning given in section 237 of the Financial Services and Markets Act 2000.

12. There is to be disregarded any interest—

(a) of the Church of Scotland General Trustees or of the Church of Scotland Trust in shares or debentures held by them;

(b) of any other person in shares or debentures held by those Trustees or that Trust otherwise than as simple trustees.

'The Church of Scotland General Trustees' are the body incorporated by the order confirmed by the Church of Scotland (General Trustees) Order Confirmation Act 1921; and 'the Church of Scotland Trust' is the body incorporated by the order confirmed by the Church of Scotland Trust Order Confirmation Act 1932.

13. Delivery to a person's order of shares or debentures in fulfilment of a contract for the purchase of them by him or in satisfaction of a right of his to call for their delivery, or failure to deliver shares or debentures in accordance with the terms of such a contract or on which such a right falls to be satisfied, is deemed to constitute an event in consequence of the occurrence of which he ceases to be interested in them, and so is the lapse of a person's right to call for delivery of shares or debentures.

PART II

PERIODS WITHIN WHICH OBLIGATIONS IMPOSED BY SECTION 324 MUST BE FULFILLED

14. (1) An obligation imposed on a person by section 324(1) to notify an interest must, if he knows of the existence of the interest on the day on which he becomes a director, be fulfilled before the expiration of the period of 5 days beginning with the day following that day.

(2) Otherwise, the obligation must be fulfilled before the expiration of the period of 5 days beginning with the day following that in which the existence of the interest comes to his knowledge.

15. (1) An obligation imposed on a person by section 324(2) to notify the occurrence of an event must, if at the time at which the event occurs he knows of its occurrence and of the fact that its occurrence gives rise to the obligation, be fulfilled before the expiration of the period of 5 days beginning with the day following that on which the event occurs.

(2) Otherwise, the obligation must be fulfilled before the expiration of a period of 5 days beginning with the day following that on which the fact that the occurrence of the event gives rise to the obligation comes to his knowledge.

16. In reckoning, for purposes of paragraphs 14 and 15, any period of days, a day that is a Saturday or Sunday, or a bank holiday in any part of Great Britain, is to be disregarded.

PART III

CIRCUMSTANCES IN WHICH OBLIGATION IMPOSED BY SECTION 324 IS NOT DISCHARGED

17. (1) Where an event of whose occurrence a director is, by virtue of section 324(2)(a), under obligation to notify a company consists of his entering into a contract for the purchase by him of shares or debentures, the obligation is not discharged in the absence of inclusion in the notice of a statement of the price to be paid by him under the contract.

(2) An obligation imposed on a director by section 324(2)(b) is not discharged in the absence of inclusion in the notice of the price to be received by him under the contract.

18. (1) An obligation imposed on a director by virtue of section 324(2)(c) to notify a company is not discharged in the absence of inclusion in the notice of a statement of the consideration for the assignment (or, if it be the case that there is no consideration, that fact).

(2) Where an event of whose occurrence a director is, by virtue of section 324(2)(d), under obligation to notify a company consists in his assigning a right, the obligation is not discharged in the absence of inclusion in the notice of a similar statement.

19. (1) Where an event of whose occurrence a director is, by virtue of section 324(2)(d), under obligation to notify a company consists in the grant to him of a right to subscribe for shares or debentures, the obligation is not discharged in the absence of inclusion in the notice of a statement of—

(a) the date on which the right was granted,

(b) the period during which or the time at which the right is exercisable,

(c) the consideration for the grant (or, if it be the case that there is no consideration, that fact), and

(d) the price to be paid for the shares or debentures.

(2) Where an event of whose occurrence a director is, by section 324(2)(d), under obligation to notify a company consists in the exercise of a right granted to him to subscribe for shares or debentures, the obligation is not discharged in the absence of inclusion in the notice of a statement of—

(a) the number of shares or amount of debentures in respect of which the right was exercised, and

(b) if it be the case that they were registered in his name, that fact, and, if not, the name or names of the person or persons in whose name or names they were registered, together (if they were registered in the names of 2 persons or more) with the number or amount registered in the name of each of them.

20. In this Part, a reference to price paid or received includes any consideration other than money.

PART IV

PROVISIONS WITH RESPECT TO REGISTER OF DIRECTORS' INTERESTS TO BE KEPT UNDER SECTION 325

21. The register must be so made up that the entries in it against the several names appear in chronological order.

22. An obligation imposed by section 325(2) to (4) must be fulfilled before the expiration of the period of 3 days beginning with the day after that on which the obligation arises; but in reckoning that period, a day which is a Saturday or Sunday or a bank holiday in any part of Great Britain is to be disregarded.

23. The nature and extent of an interest recorded in the register of a director in any shares or debentures shall, if he so requires, be recorded in the register.

24. The company is not, by virtue of anything done for the purposes of section 325 or this part of this Schedule, affected with notice of, or put upon enquiry as to, the rights of any person in relation to any shares or debentures.

25. The register shall—

(a) if the company's register of members is kept at its registered office, be kept there;

(b) if the company's register of members is not so kept, be kept at the company's registered office or at the place where its register of members is kept;

and shall be open to the inspection of any member of the company without charge and of any other person on payment of such fee as may be prescribed.

26. (1) Any member of the company or other person may require a copy of the register, or of any part of it, on payment of such fee as may be prescribed.

(2) The company shall cause any copy so required by a person to be sent to him within the period of 10 days beginning with the day after that on which the requirement is received by the company.

27. The company shall send notice in the prescribed form to the registrar of companies of the place where the register is kept and of any change in that place, save in a case in which it has at all times been kept at its registered office.

28. Unless the register is in such a form as to constitute in itself an index, the company shall keep an index of the names inscribed in it, which shall—

(a) in respect of each name, contain a sufficient indication to enable the information entered against it to be readily found; and

(b) be kept at the same place as the register;

and the company shall, within 14 days after the date on which a name is entered in the register, make any necessary alteration in the index.

29. The register shall be produced at the commencement of the company's annual general meeting and remain open and accessible during the continuance of the meeting to any person attending the meeting.

SCHEDULE 15A

Section 381A(7)

WRITTEN RESOLUTIONS OF PRIVATE COMPANIES

PART I

EXCEPTIONS

1. Section 381A does not apply to—

(a) a resolution under section 303 removing a director before the expiration of his period of office, or

(b) a resolution under section 391 removing an auditor before the expiration of his term of office.

PART II

ADAPTATION OF PROCEDURAL REQUIREMENTS

INTRODUCTORY

2. (1) In this Part of this Schedule (which adapts certain requirements of this Act in relation to proceedings under section 381A)—

(a) a 'written resolution' means a resolution agreed to, or proposed to be agreed to, in accordance with that section, and

(b) a 'relevant member' means a member by whom, or on whose behalf, the resolution is required to be signed in accordance with that section.

(2) A written resolution is not effective if any of the requirements of this Part of this Schedule is not complied with.

Section 95 (disapplication of pre-emption rights)

3. (1) The following adaptations have effect in relation to a written resolution under section 95(2) (disapplication of pre-emption rights), or renewing a resolution under that provision.

(2) So much of section 95(5) as requires the circulation of a written statement by the directors with a notice of meeting does not apply, but such a statement must be supplied to each relevant member at or before the time at which the resolution is supplied to him for signature.

(3) Section 95(6) (offences) applies in relation to the inclusion in any such statement of matter which is misleading, false or deceptive in a material particular.

Section 155 (financial assistance for purchase of company's own shares or those of holding company)

4. In relation to a written resolution giving approval under section 155(4) or (5) (financial assistance for purchase of company's own shares or those of holding company), section 157(4)(a) (documents to be available at meeting) does not apply, but the documents referred to in that provision must be supplied to each relevant member at or before the time at which the resolution is supplied to him for signature.

Sections 164, 165 and 167 (authority for off-market purchase or contingent purchase contract of company's own shares)

5. (1) The following adaptations have effect in relation to a written resolution—

(a) conferring authority to make an off-market purchase of the company's own shares under section 164(2),

(b) conferring authority to vary a contract for an off-market purchase of the company's own shares under section 164(7), or

(c) varying, revoking or renewing any such authority under section 164(3).

(2) Section 164(5) (resolution ineffective if passed by exercise of voting rights by member holding shares to which the resolution relates) does not apply; but for the purposes of section 381A(1) a member holding shares to which the resolution relates shall not be regarded as a member who would be entitled to attend and vote.

(3) Section 164(6) (documents to be available at company's registered office and at meeting) does not apply, but the documents referred to in that provision and, where that provision applies by virtue of section 164(7), the further documents referred to in that provision must be supplied to each relevant member at or before the time at which the resolution is supplied to him for signature.

(4) The above adaptations also have effect in relation to a written resolution in relation to which the provisions of section 164(3) to (7) apply by virtue of—

(a)   section 165(2) (authority for contingent purchase contract), or

(b)   section 167(2) (approval of release of rights under contract approved under section 164 or 165).

Section 173 (approval for payment out of capital)

6.   (1) The following adaptations have effect in relation to a written resolution giving approval under section 173(2)(redemption or purchase of company's own shares out of capital).

(2) Section 174(2) (resolution ineffective if passed by exercise of voting rights by member holding shares to which the resolution relates) does not apply; but for the purposes of section 381A(1) a member holding shares to which the resolution relates shall not be regarded as a member who would be entitled to attend and vote.

(3) Section 174(4) (documents to be available at meeting) does not apply, but the documents referred to in that provision must be supplied to each relevant member at or before the time at which the resolution is supplied to him for signature.

Section 319 (approval of director's service contract)

7.   In relation to a written resolution approving any such term as is mentioned in section 319(1) (director's contract of employment for more than five years), section 319(5) (documents to be available at company's registered office and at meeting) does not apply, but the documents referred to in that provision must be supplied to each relevant member at or before the time at which the resolution is supplied to him for signature.

Section 337 (funding of director's expenditure in performing his duties)

8.   In relation to a written resolution giving approval under section 337(3)(a)(funding a director's expenditure in performing his duties), the requirement of that provision that certain matters be disclosed at the meeting at which the resolution is passed does not apply, but those matters must be disclosed to each relevant member at or before the time at which the resolution is supplied to him for signature.

Table A as prescribed by Companies (Tables A to F) Regulations 1985, SI 1985/805

Regulations for Management of a Company Limited by Shares

INTERPRETATION

1.   In these regulations

'the Act' means the Companies Act 1985 including any statutory modification or re-enactment thereof for the time being in force.
'the articles' means the articles of the company.
'clear days' in relation to the period of a notice means that period excluding the day when the notice is given or deemed to be given and the day for which it is given or on which it is to take effect.
'communication' means the same as in the Electronic Communications Act 2000.
'electronic communication' means the same as in the Electronic Communications Act 2000.
'executed' includes any mode of execution.
'office' means the registered office of the company.
'the holder' in relation to shares means the member whose name is entered in the register of members as the holder of the shares.
'the seal' means the common seal of the company.
'secretary' means the secretary of the company or any other person appointed to perform the duties of the secretary of the company, including a joint, assistant or deputy secretary.
'the United Kingdom' means Great Britain and Northern Ireland.

Unless the context otherwise requires, words or expressions contained in these regulations bear the same meaning as in the Act but excluding any statutory modification thereof not in force when these regulations become binding on the company.

SHARE CAPITAL

2.   Subject to the provisions of the Act and without prejudice to any rights attached to any existing shares, any share may be issued with such rights or restrictions as the company may by ordinary resolution determine.

3.   Subject to the provisions of the Act, shares may be issued which are to be redeemed or are to be liable to be redeemed at the option of the company or the holder on such terms and in such manner as may be provided by the articles.

4.   The company may exercise the powers of paying commissions conferred by the Act. Subject to the provisions of the Act, any such commission may be satisfied by the payment of cash or by the allotment of fully or partly paid shares or partly in one way and partly in the other.

5.   Except as required by law, no person shall be recognised by the company as holding any share upon any trust and (except as otherwise provided by the articles or by law) the company shall not be bound by or recognise any interest in any share except an absolute right to the entirety thereof in the holder.

SHARE CERTIFICATES

6.   Every member, upon becoming the holder of any shares, shall be entitled without payment to one certificate for all the shares of each class held by him (and, upon transferring a part of his holding of shares of any class, to a certificate for the balance of such holding) or several certificates each for one or more of his shares upon payment for every certificate after the first of such reasonable sum as the directors may determine. Every certificate shall be sealed with the seal and shall specify the number, class and distinguishing numbers (if any) of the shares to which it relates and the amount or respective amounts paid up thereon. The company shall not be bound to issue more than one certificate for shares held jointly by several persons and delivery of a certificate to one joint holder shall be sufficient delivery to all of them.

7.   If a share certificate is defaced, worn-out, lost or destroyed, it may be renewed on such terms (if any) as to evidence and indemnity and payment of the expenses reasonably incurred by the company in investigating evidence as the directors may determine but otherwise free of charge, and (in the case of defacement or wearing-out) on delivery up of the old certificate.

LIEN

8.   The company shall have a first and paramount lien on every share (not being a fully paid share) for all moneys (whether presently payable or not) payable at a fixed time or called in respect of that share. The directors may at any time declare any share to be wholly or in part exempt from the provisions of this regulation. The company's lien on a share shall extend to any amount payable in respect of it.

9.   The company may sell in such manner as the directors determine any shares on which the company has a lien if a sum in respect of which the lien exists is presently payable and is not paid within fourteen clear days after notice has been given to the holder of the share or to the person entitled to it in consequence of the death or bankruptcy of the holder, demanding payment and stating that if the notice is not complied with the shares may be sold.

10.   To give effect to a sale the directors may authorise some person to execute an instrument of transfer of the shares sold to, or in accordance with the directions of, the purchaser. The title of the transferee to the shares shall not be affected by any irregularity in or invalidity of the proceedings in reference to the sale.

11.   The net proceeds of the sale, after payment of the costs, shall be applied in payment of so much of the sum for which the lien exists as is presently payable, and any residue shall (upon surrender to the company for cancellation of the certificate for the shares sold and subject to a like lien for any moneys not presently payable as existed upon the shares before the sale) be paid to the person entitled to the shares at the date of the sale.

CALLS ON SHARES AND FORFEITURE

12.   Subject to the terms of allotment, the directors may make calls upon the members in respect of any moneys unpaid on their shares (whether in respect of nominal value or premium) and each member shall (subject to receiving at least fourteen clear days' notice specifying when and where payment is to be made) pay to the company as required by the notice the amount called on his shares. A call may be required to be paid by instalments. A call may, before receipt by the company of any sum due thereunder, be revoked in whole or part and payment of a call may be postponed in whole or part. A person upon whom a call is made shall remain liable for calls made upon him notwithstanding the subsequent transfer of the shares in respect whereof the call was made.

13.   A call shall be deemed to have been made at the time when the resolution of the directors authorising the call was passed.

14.   The joint holders of a share shall be jointly and severally liable to pay all calls in respect thereof.

15.   If a call remains unpaid after it has become due and payable the person from whom it is due and payable shall pay interest on the amount unpaid from the day it became due and payable until it is paid at the rate fixed by the terms of allotment of the share or in the notice of the call or, if no rate is fixed, at the appropriate rate (as defined by the Act) but the directors may waive payment of the interest wholly or in part.

16.   An amount payable in respect of a share on allotment or at any fixed date, whether in respect of nominal value or premium or as an instalment of a call, shall be deemed to be a call and if it is not paid the provisions of the articles shall apply as if that amount has become due and payable by virtue of a call.

17.   Subject to the terms of the allotment, the directors may make arrangements on the issue of shares for a difference between the holders in the amounts and times of payment of calls on their shares.

18.   If a call remains unpaid after it has become due and payable the directors may give to the person from whom it is due not less than fourteen clear days' notice requiring payment of the amount unpaid together with any interest which may have accrued. The notice shall name the place where payment is to be made and shall state that if the notice is not complied with the shares in respect of which the call was made will be liable to be forfeited.

19.   If the notice is not complied with any share in respect of which it was given may, before the payment required by the notice has been made, be forfeited by a resolution of the directors and the forfeiture shall include all dividends or other moneys payable in respect of the forfeited shares and not paid before the forfeiture.

20.   Subject to the provisions of the Act, a forfeited share may be sold, re-allotted or otherwise disposed of on such terms and in such manner as the directors determine either to the person who was before the forfeiture the holder or to any other person and at any time before sale, re-allotment or other disposition, the forfeiture may be cancelled on such terms as the directors think fit. Where for the purposes of its disposal a forfeited share is to be transferred to any person the directors may authorise some person to execute an instrument of transfer of the share to that person.

21.   A person any of whose shares have been forfeited shall cease to be a member in respect of them and shall surrender to the company for cancellation the certificate for the shares forfeited but shall remain liable to the

company for all moneys which at the date of forfeiture were presently payable by him to the company in respect of those shares with interest at the rate at which interest was payable on those moneys before the forfeiture or, if no interest was so payable, at the appropriate rate (as defined in the Act) from the date of forfeiture until payment but the directors may waive payment wholly or in part or enforce payment without any allowance for the value of the shares at the time of forfeiture or for any consideration received on their disposal.

22.   A statutory declaration by a director or the secretary that a share has been forfeited on a specified date shall be conclusive evidence of the facts stated in it as against all persons claiming to be entitled to the share and the declaration shall (subject to the execution of an instrument of transfer if necessary) constitute a good title to the share and the person to whom the share is disposed of shall not be bound to see to the application of the consideration, if any, nor shall his title to the share be affected by any irregularity in or invalidity of the proceedings in reference to the forfeiture or disposal of the share.

TRANSFER OF SHARES

23.   The instrument of transfer of a share may be in any usual form or in any other form which the directors may approve and shall be executed by or on behalf of the transferor and, unless the share is fully paid, by or on behalf of the transferee.

24.   The directors may refuse to register the transfer of a share which is not fully paid to a person of whom they do not approve and they may refuse to register the transfer of a share on which the company has a lien. They may also refuse to register a transfer unless—

(a)   it is lodged at the office or at such other place as the directors may appoint and is accompanied by the certificate for the shares to which it relates and such other evidence as the directors may reasonably require to show the right of the transferor to make the transfer;

(b)   it is in respect of only one class of shares; and

(c)   it is in favour of not more than four transferees.

25.   If the directors refuse to register a transfer of a share, they shall within two months after the date on which the transfer was lodged with the company send to the transferee notice of the refusal.

26.   The registration of transfers of shares or of transfers of any class of shares may be suspended at such times and for such periods (not exceeding thirty days in any year) as the directors may determine.

27.   No fee shall be charged for the registration of any instrument of transfer or other document relating to or affecting the title to any share.

28.   The company shall be entitled to retain any instrument of transfer which is registered, but any instrument of transfer which the directors refuse to register shall be returned to the person lodging it when notice of the refusal is given.

TRANSMISSION OF SHARES

29.   If a member dies the survivor or survivors where he was a joint holder, and his personal representatives where he was a sole holder or the only survivor of joint holders, shall be the only person recognised by the company as having any title to his interest; but nothing herein contained shall release the estate of a deceased member from any liability in respect of any share which had been jointly held by him.

30.   A person becoming entitled to a share in consequence of the death or bankruptcy of a member may, upon such evidence being produced as the directors may properly require, elect either to become the holder of the share or to have some person nominated by him registered as the transferee. If he elects to become the holder he shall give notice to the company to that effect. If he elects to have another person registered he shall execute an instrument of transfer of the share to that person. All the articles relating to the transfer of shares shall apply to the notice or instrument of transfer as if it were an instrument of transfer executed by the member and the death or bankruptcy of the member had not occurred.

31.   A person becoming entitled to a share in consequence of the death or bankruptcy of a member shall have the rights to which he would be entitled if he were the holder of the share, except that he shall not, before being registered as the holder of the share, be entitled in respect of it to attend or vote at any meeting of the company or at any separate meeting of the holders of any class of shares in the company.

ALTERATION OF SHARE CAPITAL

32.   The company may by ordinary resolution—

(a)   increase its share capital by new shares of such amount as the resolution prescribes;

(b)   consolidate and divide all or any of its share capital into shares of larger amount than its existing shares;

(c)   subject to the provisions of the Act, sub-divide its shares, or any of them, into shares of smaller amount and the resolution may determine that, as between the shares resulting from the sub-division, any of them may have any preference or advantage as compared with the others; and

(d)   cancel shares which, at the date of the passing of the resolution, have not been taken or agreed to be taken by any person and diminish the amount of its share capital by the amount of the shares so cancelled.

33.   Whenever as a result of a consolidation of shares any members would become entitled to fractions of a share, the directors may, on behalf of those members, sell the shares representing the fractions for the best price reasonably obtainable to any person (including, subject to the provisions of the Act, the company) and distribute the net proceeds of sale in due proportion among those members, and the directors may authorise some person to execute an instrument of transfer of the shares to, or in accordance with the directions of, the purchaser. The transferee shall not be bound to see to the application of the purchase money nor shall his title to the shares be affected by any irregularity in or invalidity of the proceedings in reference to the sale.

34.   Subject to the provisions of the Act, the company may by special resolution reduce its share capital, any capital redemption reserve and any share premium account in any way.

PURCHASE OF OWN SHARES

35.   Subject to the provisions of the Act, the company may purchase its own shares (including any redeemable shares) and, if it is a private company, make a payment in respect of the redemption or purchase of its own shares otherwise than out of distributable profits of the company or the proceeds of a fresh issue of shares.

GENERAL MEETINGS

36.   All general meetings other than annual general meetings shall be called extraordinary general meetings.

37.   The directors may call general meetings and, on the requisition of members pursuant to the provisions of the Act, shall forthwith proceed to convene an extraordinary general meeting for a date not later than eight weeks after receipt of the requisition. If there are not within the United Kingdom sufficient directors to call a general meeting, any director or any member of the company may call a general meeting.

NOTICE OF GENERAL MEETINGS

38.   An annual general meeting and an extraordinary general meeting called for the passing of a special resolution or a resolution appointing a person as a director shall be called by at least twenty-one clear days' notice. All other extraordinary general meetings shall be called by at least fourteen clear days' notice but a general meeting may be called by shorter notice if it is so agreed:

(a)   in the case of an annual general meeting, by all the members entitled to attend and vote thereat; and

(b)   in the case of any other meeting by a majority in number of the members having a right to attend and vote being a majority together holding not less than ninety-five per cent in nominal value of the shares giving that right.

The notice shall specify the time and place of the meeting and the general nature of the business to be transacted and, in the case of an annual general meeting, shall specify the meeting as such.

Subject to the provisions of the articles and to any restrictions imposed on any shares, the notice shall be given to all the members, to all persons entitled to a share in consequence of the death or bankruptcy of a member and to the directors and auditors.

39.   The accidental omission to give notice of a meeting to, or the non-receipt of notice of a meeting by, any person entitled to receive notice shall not invalidate the proceedings at the meeting.

PROCEEDINGS AT GENERAL MEETINGS

40.   No business shall be transacted at any meeting unless a quorum is present. Two persons entitled to vote upon the business to be transacted, each being a member or a proxy for a member or a duly authorised representative of a corporation, shall be a quorum.

41. If such a quorum is not present within half an hour from the time appointed for the meeting, or if during a meeting such a quorum ceases to be present, the meeting shall stand adjourned to the same day in the next week at the same time and place or to such time and place as the directors may determine.

42. The chairman, if any, of the board of directors or in his absence some other director nominated by the directors shall preside as chairman of the meeting, but if neither the chairman nor such other director (if any) be present within fifteen minutes after the time appointed for holding the meeting and willing to act, the directors present shall elect one of their number to be chairman and, if there is only one director present and willing to act, he shall be chairman.

43. If no director is willing to act as chairman, or if no director is present within fifteen minutes after the time appointed for holding the meeting, the members present and entitled to vote shall choose one of their number to be chairman.

44. A director shall, notwithstanding that he is not a member, be entitled to attend and speak at any general meeting and at any separate meeting of the holders of any class of shares in the company.

45. The chairman may, with the consent of a meeting at which a quorum is present (and shall if so directed by the meeting), adjourn the meeting from time to time and from place to place, but no business shall be transacted at an adjourned meeting other than business which might properly have been transacted at the meeting had the adjournment not taken place. When a meeting is adjourned for fourteen days or more, at least seven clear days' notice shall be given specifying the time and place of the adjourned meeting and the general nature of the business to be transacted. Otherwise it shall not be necessary to give any such notice.

46. A resolution put to the vote of a meeting shall be decided on a show of hands unless before, or on the declaration of the result of, the show of hands a poll is duly demanded. Subject to the provisions of the Act, a poll may be demanded—

    (a) by the chairman; or

    (b) by at least two members having the right to vote at the meeting; or

    (c) by a member or members representing not less than one-tenth of the total voting rights of all the members having the right to vote at the meeting; or

    (d) by a member or members holding shares conferring a right to vote at the meeting being shares on which an aggregate sum has been paid up equal to not less than one-tenth of the total sum paid up on all the shares conferring that right;

and demand by a person as proxy for a member shall be the same as a demand by the member.

47. Unless a poll is duly demanded a declaration by the chairman that a resolution has been carried or carried unanimously, or by a particular majority, or lost, or not carried by a particular majority and an entry to that effect in the minutes of the meeting shall be conclusive evidence of the fact without proof of the number or proportion of the votes recorded in favour of or against the resolution.

48. The demand for a poll may, before the poll is taken, be withdrawn but only with the consent of the chairman and a demand so withdrawn shall not be taken to have invalidated the result of a show of hands declared before the demand was made.

49. A poll shall be taken as the chairman directs and he may appoint scrutineers (who need not be members) and fix a time and place for declaring the result of the poll. The result of the poll shall be deemed to be the resolution of the meeting at which the poll was demanded.

50. In the case of an equality of votes, whether on a show of hands or on a poll, the chairman shall be entitled to a casting vote in addition to any other vote he may have.

51. A poll demanded on the election of a chairman or on a question of adjournment shall be taken forthwith. A poll demanded on any other question shall be taken either forthwith or at such time and place as the chairman directs not being more than thirty days after the poll is demanded. The demand for a poll shall not prevent the continuance of a meeting for the transaction of any business other than the question on which the poll was demanded. If a poll is demanded before the declaration of the result of a show of hands and the demand is duly withdrawn, the meeting shall continue as if the demand had not been made.

52. No notice need be given of a poll not taken forthwith if the time and place at which it is to be taken are announced at the meeting at which it is demanded. In any other case at least seven clear days' notice shall be given specifying the time and place at which the poll is to be taken.

53.   A resolution in writing executed by or on behalf of each member who would have been entitled to vote upon it if it had been proposed at a general meeting at which he was present shall be as effectual as if it had been passed at a general meeting duly convened and held and may consist of several instruments in the like form each executed by or on behalf of one or more members.

VOTES OF MEMBERS

54.   Subject to any rights or restrictions attached to any shares, on a show of hands every member who (being an individual) is present in person or (being a corporation) is present by a duly authorised representative, not being himself a member entitled to vote, shall have one vote and on a poll every member shall have one vote for every share of which he is the holder.

55.   In the case of joint holders the vote of the senior who tenders a vote, whether in person or by proxy, shall be accepted to the exclusion of the votes of the other joint holders; and seniority shall be determined by the order in which the names of the holders stand in the register of member.

56.   A member in respect of whom an order has been made by any court having jurisdiction (whether in the United Kingdom or elsewhere) in matters concerning mental disorder may vote, whether on a show of hands or on a poll, by his receiver, curator bonis or other person authorised in that behalf appointed by that court, and any such receiver, curator bonis or other person may, on a poll, vote by proxy. Evidence to the satisfaction of the directors of the authority of the person claiming to exercise the right to vote shall be deposited at the office, or at such other place as is specified in accordance with the articles for the deposit of instruments of proxy, not less than 48 hours before the time appointed for holding the meeting or adjourned meeting at which the right to vote is to be exercised and in default the right to vote shall not be exercisable.

57.   No member shall vote at any general meeting or at any separate meeting of the holders of any class of shares in the company, either in person or by proxy, in respect of any shares held by him unless all moneys presently payable by him in respect of that share have been paid.

58.   No objection shall be raised to the qualification of any voter except at the meeting or adjourned meeting at which the vote objected to is tendered, and every vote not disallowed at the meeting shall be valid. Any objection made in due time shall be referred to the chairman whose decision shall be final and conclusive.

59.   On a poll votes may be given either personally or by proxy. A member may appoint more than one proxy to attend on the same occasion.

60.   The appointment of a proxy shall be executed by or on behalf of the appointor and shall be in the following form (or in a form as near thereto as circumstances allow or in any other form which is usual or which the directors may approve)—

'   PLC/Limited

    I/We,   , of   , being a member/members of the above-named company, hereby appoint   of   ,
or failing him,   of   ,
as my/our proxy to vote in my/our names[s] and on my/our behalf at the annual/ extraordinary general meeting of the company to be held on   19   , and at any adjournment thereof.

Signed on   19   .'

61.   Where it is desired to afford members an opportunity of instructing the proxy how he shall act the appointment of a proxy shall be in the following form (or in a form as near thereto as circumstances allow or in any other form which is usual or which the directors may approve)—

                              PLC/Limited

    I/We   , of   , being a member/members of the of above-named company,
hereby   appoint   of
    , or failing him   of
                                  , as my/our proxy to vote in my/our name[s]
and on my/our behalf at the annual/extraordinary general meeting of the company, to be held on
           19   , and at any adjournment thereof.

This form is to be used in respect of the resolutions mentioned below as follows:

Resolution No. 1 *for *against
Resolution No. 2 *for *against

*Strike out whichever is not desired.

Unless otherwise instructed, the proxy may vote as he thinks fit or abstain from voting.

Signed this   day of   19   .'

62.   The appointment of a proxy and any authority under which it is executed or a copy of such authority certified notarially or in some other way approved by the directors may—

(a)   in the case of an instrument in writing be deposited at the office or at such other place within the United Kingdom as is specified in the notice convening the meeting or in any instrument of proxy sent out by the company in relation to the meeting not less than 48 hours before the time for holding the meeting or adjourned meeting at which the person named in the instrument proposes to vote; or

(aa)   in the case of an appointment contained in an electronic communication, where an address has been specified for the purpose of receiving electronic communications—

(i)   in the notice convening the meeting, or

(ii)   in any instrument of proxy sent out by the company in relation to the meeting, or

(iii) in any invitation contained in an electronic communication to appoint a proxy issued by the company in relation to the meeting,

be received at such address not less than 48 hours before the time for holding the meeting or adjourned meeting at which the person named in the appointment proposes to vote;

(b)   in the case of a poll taken more than 48 hours after it is demanded, be deposited or received as aforesaid after the poll has been demanded and not less than 24 hours before the time appointed for the taking of the poll; or

(c)   where the poll is not taken forthwith but is taken not more than 48 hours after it was demanded, be delivered at the meeting at which the poll was demanded to the chairman or to the secretary or to any director;

and an appointment of proxy which is not deposited, delivered or received in a manner so permitted shall be invalid. In this regulation and the next, 'address', in relation to electronic communications, includes any number or address used for the purposes of such communications.

63.   A vote given or poll demanded by proxy or by the duly authorised representative of a corporation shall be valid notwithstanding the previous determination of the authority of the person voting or demanding a poll unless notice of the determination was received by the company at the office or at such other place at which the instrument of proxy was duly deposited or, where the appointment of the proxy was contained in an electronic communication, at the address at which such appointment was duly received before the commencement of the meeting or adjourned meeting at which the vote is given or the poll demanded or (in the case of a poll taken otherwise than on the same day as the meeting or adjourned meeting) the time appointed for taking the poll.

NUMBER OF DIRECTORS

64.   Unless otherwise determined by ordinary resolution, the number of directors (other than alternate directors) shall not be subject to any maximum but shall be not less than two.

ALTERNATE DIRECTORS

65.   Any director (other than an alternate director) may appoint any other director, or any other person approved by resolution of the directors and willing to act, to be an alternate director and may remove from office an alternate director so appointed by him.

66.   An alternate director shall be entitled to receive notice of all meetings of directors and of all meetings of committees of directors of which his appointor is a member, to attend and vote at any such meeting at which the director appointing him is not personally present, and generally to perform all the functions of his appointor as a director in his absence but shall not be entitled to receive any remuneration from the company for his services as an alternate director. But it shall not be necessary to give notice of such a meeting to an alternate director who is absent from the United Kingdom.

67.   An alternate director shall cease to be an alternate director if his appointor ceases to be a director; but, if a director retires by rotation or otherwise but is reappointed or deemed to have been reappointed at the meeting at which he retires, any appointment of an alternate director made by him which was in force immediately prior to his retirement shall continue after his reappointment.

68.   Any appointment or removal of an alternate director shall be by notice to the company signed by the director making or revoking the appointment or in any other manner approved by the directors.

69.   Save as otherwise provided in the articles, an alternate director shall be deemed for all purposes to be a director and shall alone be responsible for his own acts and defaults and he shall not be deemed to be the agent of the director appointing him.

POWERS OF DIRECTORS

70.   Subject to the provisions of the Act, the memorandum and the articles and to any directions given by special resolution, the business of the company shall be managed by the directors who may exercise all the powers of the company. No alteration of the memorandum or articles and no such direction shall invalidate any prior act of the directors which would have been valid if that alteration had not been made or that direction had not been given. The powers given by this regulation shall not be limited by any special power given to the directors by the articles and a meeting of directors at which a quorum is present may exercise all powers exercisable by the directors.

71.   The directors may, by power of attorney or otherwise, appoint any person to be the agent of the company for such purposes and on such conditions as they determine, including authority for the agent to delegate all or any of his powers.

DELEGATION OF DIRECTORS' POWERS

72.   The directors may delegate any of their powers to any committee consisting of one or more directors. They may also delegate to any managing director or any director holding any other executive office such of their powers as they consider desirable to be exercised by him. Any such delegation may be made subject to any conditions the directors may impose, and either collaterally with or to the exclusion of their own powers and may be revoked or altered. Subject to any such conditions, the proceedings of a committee with two or more members shall be governed by the articles regulating the proceedings of directors so far as they are capable of applying.

APPOINTMENT AND RETIREMENT OF DIRECTORS

73.   At the first annual general meeting all the directors shall retire from office, and at every subsequent annual general meeting one-third of the directors who are subject to retirement by rotation or, if their number is not three or a multiple of three, the number nearest to one-third shall retire from office; but, if there is only one director who is subject to retirement by rotation, he shall retire.

74.   Subject to the provisions of the Act, the directors to retire by rotation shall be those who have been longest in office since their last appointment or reappointment, but as between persons who became or were last reappointed directors on the same day those to retire shall (unless they otherwise agree among themselves) be determined by lot.

75.   If the company, at the meeting at which a director retires by rotation, does not fill the vacancy the retiring director shall, if willing to act, be deemed to have been reappointed unless at the meeting it is resolved not to fill the vacancy or unless a resolution for the reappointment of the director is put to the meeting and lost.

76.   No person other than a director retiring by rotation shall be appointed or reappointed a director at any general meeting unless—

(a)   he is recommended by the directors; or

(b)   not less than fourteen nor more than thirty-five clear days before the date appointed for the meeting, notice executed by a member qualified to vote at the meeting has been given to the company of the intention to propose that person for appointment or reappointment stating the particulars which would, if he were so appointed or reappointed, be required to be included in the company's register of directors together with notice executed by that person of his willingness to be appointed or reappointed.

77.   Not less than seven nor more than twenty-eight clear days before the date appointed for holding a general meeting notice shall be given to all who are entitled to receive notice of the meeting of any person (other than a director retiring by rotation at the meeting) who is recommended by the directors for appointment or reappointment as a director at the meeting or in respect of whom notice has been duly given to the company of the intention to

propose him at the meeting for appointment or reappointment as a director. The notice shall give the particulars of that person which would, if he were so appointed or re-appointed, be required to be included in the company's register of directors.

78.   Subject as aforesaid, the company may by ordinary resolution appoint a person who is willing to act to be a director either to fill a vacancy or as an additional director and may also determine the rotation in which any additional directors are to retire.

79.   The directors may appoint a person who is willing to act to be a director, either to fill a vacancy or as an additional director, provided that the appointment does not cause the number of directors to exceed any number fixed by or in accordance with the articles as the maximum number of directors. A director so appointed shall hold office only until the next following annual general meeting and shall not be taken into account in determining the directors who are to retire by rotation at the meeting. If not reappointed at such annual general meeting, he shall vacate office at the conclusion thereof.

80.   Subject as aforesaid, a director who retires at an annual general meeting may, if willing to act, be reappointed. If he is not reappointed, he shall retain office until the meeting appoints someone in his place, or if it does not do so, until the end of the meeting.

DISQUALIFICATION AND REMOVAL OF DIRECTORS

81.   The office of a director shall be vacated if—

(a)   he ceases to be a director by virtue of any provision of the Act or he becomes prohibited by law from being a director; or

(b)   he becomes bankrupt or makes any arrangement or composition with his creditors generally; or

(c)   he is, or may be, suffering from mental disorder and either—

(i)   he is admitted to hospital in pursuance of an application for admission for treatment under the Mental Health Act 1983 or, in Scotland, an application for admission under the Mental Health (Scotland) Act 1960, or

(ii)   an order is made by a court having jurisdiction (whether in the United Kingdom or elsewhere) in matters concerning mental disorder for his detention or for the appointment of a receiver, curator bonis or other person to exercise powers with respect to his property or affairs; or

(d)   he resigns his office by notice to the company; or

(e)   he shall for more than six consecutive months have been absent without permission of the directors from meetings of directors held during that period and the directors resolve that his office be vacated.

REMUNERATION OF DIRECTORS

82.   The directors shall be entitled to such remuneration as the company may by ordinary resolution determine and, unless the resolution provides otherwise, the remuneration shall be deemed to accrue from day to day.

DIRECTORS' EXPENSES

83.   The directors may be paid all travelling, hotel, and other expenses properly incurred by them in connection with their attendance at meetings of directors or committees of directors or general meetings or separate meetings of the holders of any class of shares or of debentures of the company or otherwise in connection with the discharge of their duties.

DIRECTORS' APPOINTMENTS AND INTERESTS

84.   Subject to the provisions of the Act, the directors may appoint one or more of their number to the office of managing director or to any other executive office under the company and may enter into an agreement or arrangement with any director for his employment by the company or for the provision by him of any services outside the scope of the ordinary duties of a director. Any such appointment, agreement or arrangement may be made upon such terms as the directors determine and they may remunerate any such director for his services as they think fit. Any appointment of a director to an executive office shall terminate if he ceases to be a director but without prejudice to any claim to damages for breach of the contract of service between the director and the company. A managing director and a director holding any other executive office shall not be subject to retirement by rotation.

85.   Subject to the provision of the Act, and provided that he has disclosed to the directors the nature and extent of any material interest of his, a director notwithstanding his office—

   (a)   may be a party to, or otherwise interested in, any transaction or arrangement with the company or in which the company is otherwise interested;

   (b)   may be a director or other officer of, or employed by, or a party to any transaction or arrangement with, or otherwise interested in, any body corporate promoted by the company or in which the company is otherwise interested; and

   (c)   shall not, by reason of his office, be accountable to the company for any benefit which he derives from any such office or employment or from any such transaction or arrangement or from any interest in any such body corporate and no such transaction or arrangement shall be liable to be avoided on the ground of any such interest or benefit.

86.   For the purposes of regulation 85—

   (a)   a general notice given to the directors that a director is to be regarded as having an interest of the nature and extent specified in the notice in any transaction or arrangement in which a specified person or class of persons is interested shall be deemed to be a disclosure that the director has an interest in any such transaction of the nature and extent so specified; and

   (b)   an interest of which a director has no knowledge and of which it is unreasonable to expect him to have knowledge shall not be treated as an interest of his.

DIRECTORS' GRATUITIES AND PENSIONS

87.   The directors may provide benefits, whether by the payment of gratuities or pensions or by insurance or otherwise, for any director who has held but no longer holds any executive office or employment with the company or with any body corporate which is or has been a subsidiary, and for any member of his family (including a spouse and a former spouse) or any person who is or was dependent on him, and may (as well before as after he ceases to hold such office or employment) contribute to any fund and pay premiums for the purchase or provision of any such benefit.

PROCEEDINGS OF DIRECTORS

88.   Subject to the provisions of the articles, the directors may regulate their proceedings as they think fit. A director may, and the secretary at the request of a director shall, call a meeting of the directors. It shall not be necessary to give notice of a meeting to a director who is absent from the United Kingdom. Questions arising at a meeting shall be decided by a majority of votes. In the case of an equality of votes, the chairman shall have a second or casting vote. A director who is also an alternate director shall be entitled in the absence of his appointor to a separate vote on behalf of his appointor in addition to his own vote.

89.   The quorum for the transaction of the business of the directors may be fixed by the directors and unless so fixed at any other number shall be two. A person who holds office only as an alternate director shall, if his appointor is not present, be counted in the quorum.

90.   The continuing directors or a sole continuing director may act notwithstanding any vacancies in their number, but, if the number of directors is less than the number fixed as a quorum, the continuing directors or director may act only for the purpose of filling vacancies or of calling a general meeting.

91.   The directors may appoint one of their number to be the chairman of the board of directors and may at any time remove him from that office. Unless he is unwilling to do so, the director so appointed shall preside at every meeting of directors at which he is present. But if there is no director holding that office, or if the director holding it is unwilling to preside or is not present within five minutes after the time appointed for the meeting, the directors present may appoint one of their number to be chairman of the meeting.

92.   All acts done by a meeting of directors, or of a committee of directors, or by a person acting as a director shall, notwithstanding that it be afterwards discovered that there was a defect in the appointment of any director or that any of them were disqualified from holding office, or had vacated office, or were not entitled to vote, be as valid as if every such person had been duly appointed and was qualified and had continued to be director and had been entitled to vote.

93.   A resolution in writing signed by all the directors entitled to receive notice of a meeting of directors or of a committee of directors shall be as valid and effectual as if it had been passed at a meeting of directors or (as the case may be) a committee of directors duly convened and held and may consist of several documents in the like form each signed by one or more directors; but a resolution signed by an alternate director need not also be signed by his appointor and, if it is signed by a director who has appointed an alternate director, it need not be signed by the alternate director in that capacity.

94.   Save as otherwise provided by the articles, a director shall not vote at a meeting of directors or of a committee of directors on any resolution concerning a matter in which he has, directly or indirectly, an interest or duty which is material and which conflicts or may conflict with the interests of the company unless his interest or duty arises only because the case falls within one or more of the following paragraphs—

(a)   the resolution relates to the giving to him of a guarantee, security, or indemnity in respect of money lent to, or an obligation incurred by him for the benefit of, the company or any of its subsidiaries;

(b)   the resolution relates to the giving to a third party of a guarantee, security, or indemnity in respect of an obligation of the company or any of its subsidiaries for which the director has assumed responsibility in whole or part and whether alone or jointly with others under a guarantee or indemnity or by the giving of security;

(c)   his interest arises by virtue of his subscribing or agreeing to subscribe for any shares, debentures or other securities of the company or any of its subsidiaries, or by virtue of his being, or intending to become, a participant in the underwriting or sub-underwriting of an offer of any such shares, debentures, or other securities by the company or any of its subsidiaries for subscription, purchase or exchange;

(d)   the resolution relates in any way to a retirement benefits scheme which has been approved, or is conditional upon approval, by the Board of Inland Revenue for taxation purposes.

For the purposes of this regulation, an interest of a person who is, for any purpose of the Act (excluding any statutory modification thereof not in force when this regulation becomes binding on the company), connected with a director shall be treated as an interest of the director and, in relation to an alternate director, an interest of his appointor shall be treated as an interest of the alternate director without prejudice to any interest which the alternate director has otherwise.

95.   A director shall not be counted in the quorum present at a meeting in relation to a resolution on which he is not entitled to vote.

96.   The company may by ordinary resolution suspend or relax to any extent, either generally or in respect of any particular matter, any provision of the articles prohibiting a director from voting at a meeting of directors or of a committee of directors.

97.   Where proposals are under consideration concerning the appointment of two or more directors to offices or employments with the company or any body corporate in which the company is interested the proposals may be divided and considered in relation to each director separately and (provided he is not for another reason precluded from voting) each of the directors concerned shall be entitled to vote and be counted in the quorum in respect of each resolution except that concerning his own appointment.

98.   If a question arises at a meeting of directors or of a committee of directors as to the right of a director to vote, the question may, before the conclusion of the meeting, be referred to the chairman of the meeting and his ruling in relation any director other than himself shall be final and conclusive.

SECRETARY

99.   Subject to the provisions of the Act, the secretary shall be appointed by the directors for such term, at such remuneration and upon such conditions as they may think fit; and any secretary so appointed may be removed by them.

MINUTES

100.   The directors shall cause minutes to be made in books kept for the purpose—

(a)   of all appointments of officers made by the directors; and

(b)   of all proceedings at meetings of the company, of the holders of any class of shares in the company, and of the directors, and of committees of directors, including the names of the directors present at each such meeting.

THE SEAL

101.   The seal shall only be used by the authority of the directors or of a committee of directors authorised by the directors. The directors may determine who shall sign any instrument to which the seal is affixed and unless otherwise so determined it shall be signed by a director and by the secretary or by a second director.

DIVIDENDS

102. Subject to the provisions of the Act, the company may by ordinary resolution declare dividends in accordance with the respective rights of the members, but no dividend shall exceed the amount recommended by the directors.

103. Subject to the provisions of the Act, the directors may pay interim dividends if it appears to them that they are justified by the profits of the company available for distribution. If the share capital is divided into different classes, the directors may pay interim dividends on shares which confer deferred or non-preferred rights with regard to dividend as well as on shares which confer preferential rights with regard to dividend, but no interim dividend shall be paid on shares carrying deferred or non-preferred rights if, at the time of payment, any preferential dividend is in arrear. The directors may also pay at intervals settled by them any dividend payable at a fixed rate if it appears to them that the profits available for distribution justify the payment. Provided the directors act in good faith they shall not incur any liability to the holders of shares conferring preferred rights for any loss they may suffer by the lawful payment of an interim dividend on any shares having deferred or non-preferred rights.

104. Except as otherwise provided by the rights attached to shares, all dividends shall be declared and paid according to the amounts paid up on the shares on which the dividend is paid. All dividends shall be apportioned and paid proportionately to the amounts paid up on the shares during any portion or portions of the period in respect of which the dividend is paid; but, if any share is issued on terms providing that it shall rank for dividend as from a particular date, that share shall rank for dividend accordingly.

105. A general meeting declaring a dividend may, upon the recommendation of the directors, direct that it shall be satisfied wholly or partly by the distribution of assets and, where any difficulty arises in regard to the distribution, the directors may settle the same and in particular may issue fractional certificates and fix the value for distribution of any assets and may determine that cash shall be paid to any member upon the footing of the value so fixed in order to adjust the rights of members and may vest any assets in trustees.

106. Any dividend or other moneys payable in respect of a share may be paid by cheque sent by post to the registered address of the person entitle or, if two or more persons are the holders of the share or are jointly entitled to it by reason of the death or bankruptcy of the holder, to the registered address of that one of those persons who is first named in the register of members or to such person and to such address as the person or persons entitled may in writing direct. Every cheque shall be made payable to the order of the person or persons entitled or to such other person as the person or persons entitled may in writing direct and payment of the cheque shall be a good discharge to the company. Any joint holder or other person jointly entitled to a share as aforesaid may give receipts for any dividend or other moneys payable in respect of the share.

107. No dividend or other moneys payable in respect of a share shall bear interest against the company unless otherwise provided by the rights attached to the share.

108. Any dividend which has remained unclaimed for twelve years from the date when it became due for payment shall, if the directors so resolve, be forfeited and cease to remain owing by the company.

ACCOUNTS

109. No member shall (as such) have any right of inspecting any accounting records or other book or document of the company except as conferred by statute or authorised by the directors or by ordinary resolution of the company.

CAPITALISATION OF PROFITS

110. The directors may with the authority of an ordinary resolution of the company—

    (a)   subject as hereinafter provided, resolve to capitalise any undivided profits of the company not required for paying any preferential dividend (whether or not they are available for distribution) or any sum standing to the credit of the company's share premium account or capital redemption reserve;

    (b)   appropriate the sum resolved to be capitalised to the members who would have been entitled to it if it were distributed by way of dividend and in the same proportions and apply such sum on their behalf either in or towards paying up the amounts, if any, for the time being unpaid on any shares held by them respectively, or in paying up in full unissued shares or debentures of the company of a nominal amount equal to that sum, and allot the shares or debentures credited as fully paid to those members, or as they may direct, in those proportions, or partly in one way and partly in the other: but the share premium account, the capital redemption reserve, and any profits which are not available for distribution may, for the purposes of this regulation, only be applied in paying up unissued shares to be allotted to members credited as fully paid;

(c) make such provision by the issue of fractional certificates or by payment in cash or otherwise as they determine in the case of shares or debentures becoming distributable under this regulation in fractions; and

(d) authorise any person to enter on behalf of all the members concerned into an agreement with the company providing for the allotment to them respectively, credited as fully paid, of any shares or debentures to which they are entitled upon such capitalisation, any agreement made under such authority being binding on all such members.

NOTICES

111. Any notice to be given to or by any person pursuant to the articles (other than a notice calling a meeting of the directors) shall be in writing or shall be given using electronic communications to an address for the time being notified for that purpose to the person giving the notice.

In this regulation, 'address', in relation to electronic communications, includes any number or address used for the purposes of such communications.

112. The company may give any notice to a member either personally or by sending it by post in a prepaid envelope addressed to the member at his registered address or by leaving it at that address or by giving it using electronic communications to an address for the time being notified to the company by the member. In the case of joint holders of a share, all notices shall be given to the joint holder and notice so given shall be sufficient notice to all the joint holders. A member whose registered address is not within the United Kingdom and who gives to the company an address within the United Kingdom at which notices may be given to him, or an address to which notices may be sent using electronic communications, shall be entitled to have notices given to him at that address, but otherwise no such member shall be entitled to receive any notice from the company.

In this regulation and the next, 'address', in relation to electronic communications, includes any number or address used for the purposes of such communications.

113. A member present, either in person or by proxy, at any meeting of the company or of the holders of any class of shares in the company shall be deemed to have received notice of the meeting and, where requisite, of the purposes for which it was called.

114. Every person who becomes entitled to a share shall be bound by any notice in respect of that share which, before his name is entered in the register of members, has been duly given to a person from whom he derives his title.

115. Proof that an envelope containing a notice was properly addressed, prepaid and posted shall be conclusive evidence that the notice was given. Proof that a notice contained in an electronic communication was sent in accordance with guidance issued by the Institute of Chartered Secretaries and Administrators shall be conclusive evidence that the notice was given. A notice shall be deemed to be given at the expiration of 48 hours after the envelope containing it was posted or, in the case of a notice contained in an electronic communication, at the expiration of 48 hours after the time it was sent.

116. A notice may be given by the company to the persons entitled to a share in consequence of the death or bankruptcy of a member by sending or delivering it, in any manner authorised by the articles for the giving of notice to a member, addressed to them by name, or by the title of representatives of the deceased, or trustee of the bankrupt or by any like description at the address, if any, within the United Kingdom supplied for that purpose by the persons claiming to be so entitled. Until such an address has been supplied, a notice may be given in any manner in which it might have been given if the death or bankruptcy had not occurred.

WINDING UP

117. If the company is wound up, the liquidator may, with the sanction of an extraordinary resolution of the company and any other sanction required by the Act, divide among the members in specie the whole or any part of the assets of the company and may, for that purpose, value any assets and determine how the division shall be carried out as between the members or different classes of members. The liquidator may, with the like sanction, vest the whole or any part of the assets in trustees upon such trusts for the benefit of the members as he with the like sanction determines, but no member shall be compelled to accept any assets upon which there is a liability.

INDEMNITY

118. Subject to the provisions of the Act but without prejudice to any indemnity to which a director may otherwise be entitled, every director or other officer or auditor of the company shall be indemnified out of the assets of the

company against any liability incurred by him in defending any proceedings, whether civil or criminal, in which judgment is given in his favour or in which he is acquitted or in connection with any application in which relief is granted to him by the court from liability for negligence, default, breach of duty or breach of trust in relation to the affairs of the company.

Table B as prescribed by Companies (Tables A to F) Regulations 1985, SI 1985/805

A PRIVATE COMPANY LIMITED BY SHARES

MEMORANDUM OF ASSOCIATION

1.   The company's name is 'The South Wales Motor Transport Company cyfyngedig'.

2.   The company's registered office is to be situated in Wales.

3.   The company's objects are the carriage of passengers and goods in motor vehicles between such places as the company may from time to time determine and the doing of all such other things as are incidental or conducive to the attainment of that object.

4.   The liability of the members is limited.

5.   The company's share capital is £50,000 divided into 50,000 shares of £1 each.

We, the subscribers to this memorandum of association, wish to be formed into a company pursuant to this memorandum; and we agree to take the number of shares shown opposite our respective names.

Names and Addresses of Subscribers	Number of shares taken by each Subscriber
1. Thomas Jones, 138 Mountfield Street, Tredegar	1
2. Mary Evans, 19 Merthyr Road, Aberystwyth	1
	Total shares taken 2

Dated   19   .

Witness to the above signatures.

Anne Brown, 'Woodlands', Fieldside Road, Bryn Mawr.

Part II Company

Company Directors Disqualification Act 1986

1. Disqualification orders: general

(1) In the circumstances specified below in this Act a court may, and under section 6 shall, make against a person a disqualification order, that is to say an order that for a period specified in the order—

    (a) he shall not be a director of a company, act as receiver of a company's property or in any way, whether directly or indirectly, be concerned or take part in the promotion, formation or management of a company unless (in each case) he has the leave of the court, and

    (b) he shall not act as an insolvency practitioner.

(2) In each section of this Act which gives to a court power or, as the case may be, imposes on it the duty to make a disqualification order there is specified the maximum (and, in section 6, the minimum) period of disqualification which may or (as the case may be) must be imposed by means of the order and, unless the court otherwise orders, the period of disqualification so imposed shall begin at the end of the period of 21 days beginning with the date of the order.

(3) Where a disqualification order is made against a person who is already subject to such an order or to a disqualification undertaking, the periods specified in those orders or, as the case may be, in the order and the undertaking shall run concurrently.

(4) A disqualification order may be made on grounds which are or include matters other than criminal convictions, notwithstanding that the person in respect of whom it is to be made may be criminally liable in respect of those matters.

1A. Disqualification undertakings: general

(1) In the circumstances specified in sections 7 and 8 the Secretary of State may accept a disqualification undertaking, that is to say an undertaking by any person that, for a period specified in the undertaking, the person—

    (a) will not be a director of a company, act as receiver of a company's property or in any way, whether directly or indirectly, be concerned or take part in the promotion, formation or management of a company unless (in each case) he has the leave of a court, and

    (b) will not act as an insolvency practitioner.

(2) The maximum period which may be specified in a disqualification undertaking is 15 years; and the minimum period which may be specified in a disqualification undertaking under section 7 is two years.

(3) Where a disqualification undertaking by a person who is already subject to such an undertaking or to a disqualification order is accepted, the periods specified in those undertakings or (as the case may be) the undertaking and the order shall run concurrently.

(4) In determining whether to accept a disqualification undertaking by any person, the Secretary of State may take account of matters other than criminal convictions, notwithstanding that the person may be criminally liable in respect of those matters.

2. Disqualification on conviction of indictable offence

(1) The court may make a disqualification order against a person where he is convicted of an indictable offence (whether on indictment or summarily) in connection with the promotion, formation, management, liquidation or striking off of a company, with the receivership of a company's property or with his being an administrative receiver of a company.

(2) 'The court' for this purpose means—

    (a) any court having jurisdiction to wind up the company in relation to which the offence was committed, or

    (b) the court by or before which the person is convicted of the offence, or

    (c) in the case of a summary conviction in England and Wales, any other magistrates' court acting for the same petty sessions area;

and for the purposes of this section the definition of 'indictable offence' in Schedule 1 to the Interpretation Act 1978 applies for Scotland as it does for England and Wales.

(3) The maximum period of disqualification under this section is—

(a)   where the disqualification order is made by a court of summary jurisdiction, 5 years, and

(b)   in any other case, 15 years.

3.   Disqualification for persistent breaches of companies legislation

(1)   The court may make a disqualification order against a person where it appears to it that he has been persistently in default in relation to provisions of the companies legislation requiring any return, account or other document to be filed with, delivered or sent, or notice of any matter to be given, to the registrar of companies.

(2)   On an application to the court for an order to be made under this section, the fact that a person has been persistently in default in relation to such provisions as are mentioned above may (without prejudice to its proof in any other manner) be conclusively proved by showing that in the 5 years ending with the date of the application he has been adjudged guilty (whether or not on the same occasion) of three or more defaults in relation to those provisions.

(3)   A person is to be treated under subsection (2) as being adjudged guilty of a default in relation to any provision of that legislation if—

(a)   he is convicted (whether on indictment or summarily) of an offence consisting in a contravention of or failure to comply with that provision (whether on his own part or on the part of any company), or

(b)   a default order is made against him, that is to say an order under any of the following provisions—

(i)   section 242(4) of the Companies Act (order requiring delivery of company accounts).

(ia)   section 245B of that Act (order requiring preparation of revised accounts).

(ii)   section 713 of that Act (enforcement of company's duty to make returns),

(iii)   section 41 of the Insolvency Act (enforcement of receiver's or manager's duty to make returns), or

(iv)   section 170 of that act (corresponding provision for liquidator in winding up),

in respect of any such contravention of or failure to comply with that provision (whether on his own part or on the part of any company).

(4)   In this section 'the court' means any court having jurisdiction to wind up any of the companies in relation to which the offence or other default has been or is alleged to have been committed.

(5)   The maximum period of disqualification under this section is 5 years.

4.   Disqualification for fraud, etc in winding up

(1)   The court may make a disqualification order against a person if, in the course of the winding up of a company, it appears that he—

(a)   has been guilty of an offence for which he is liable (whether he has been convicted or not) under section 458 of the Companies Act (fraudulent trading), or

(b)   has otherwise been guilty, while an officer or liquidator of the company receiver of the company's property or administrative receiver of the company, of any fraud in relation to the company or of any breach of his duty as such officer, liquidator, receiver or administrative receiver.

(2)   In this section 'the court' means any court having jurisdiction to wind up any of the companies in relation to which the offence or other default has been or is alleged to have been committed; and 'officer' includes a shadow director.

(3)   The maximum period of disqualification under this section is 15 years.

5.   Disqualification on summary conviction

(1)   An offence counting for the purposes of this section is one of which a person is convicted (either on indictment or summarily) in consequence of a contravention of, or failure to comply with, any provision of the companies legislation requiring a return, account or other document to be filed with, delivered or sent, or notice of any matter to be given, to the registrar of companies (whether the contravention or failure is on the person's own part or on the part of any company).

(2)   Where a person is convicted of a summary offence counting for those purposes, the court by which he is convicted (or, in England and Wales, any other magistrates' court acting for the same petty sessions area) may make a disqualification order against him if the circumstances specified in the next subsection are present.

(3)   Those circumstances are that, during the 5 years ending with the date of the conviction, the person has had made against him, or has been convicted of, in total not less than 3 default orders and offences counting for the purposes of this section; and those offences may include that of which he is convicted as mentioned in sub-section (2) and any other offence of which he is convicted on the same occasion.

(4)   For the purposes of this section—

    (a)   the definition of 'summary offence' in Schedule 1 to the Interpretation Act 1978 applies for Scotland as for England and Wales, and

    (b)   'default order' means the same as in section 3(3)(b).

(5)   The maximum period of disqualification under this section is 5 years.

6.   Duty of court to disqualify unfit directors of insolvent companies

(1)   The court shall make a disqualification order against a person in any case where, on an application under this section, it is satisfied—

    (a)   that he is or has been a director of a company which has at any time become insolvent (whether while he was a director or subsequently), and

    (b)   that his conduct as a director of that company (either taken alone or taken together with his conduct as a director of any other company or companies) makes him unfit to be concerned in the management of a company.

(2)   For the purposes of this section and the next, a company becomes insolvent if—

    (a)   the company goes into liquidation at a time when its assets are insufficient for the payment of its debts and other liabilities and the expenses of the winding up,

    (b)   an administration order is made in relation to the company, or

    (c)   an administrative receiver of the company is appointed;

and references to a person's conduct as a director of any company or companies include, where that company or any of those companies has become insolvent, that person's conduct in relation to any matter connected with or arising out of the insolvency of that company.

(3)   In this section and section 7(2), 'the court' means—

    (a)   where the company in question is being or has been wound up by the court, that court,

    (b)   where the company in question is being or has been wound up voluntarily, any court which has or (as the case may be) had jurisdiction to wind it up,

    (c)   where neither of the preceding paragraphs applies but an administration order has at any time been made, or an administrative receiver has at any time been appointed, in relation to the company in question, any court which has jurisdiction to wind it up.

(3A)   Sections 117 and 120 of the Insolvency Act 1986 (jurisdiction) shall apply for the purposes of subsection (3) as if the references in the definitions of 'registered office' to the presentation of the petition for winding up were references—

    (a)   in a case within paragraph (b) of that subsection, to the passing of the resolution for voluntary winding up,

    (b)   in a case within paragraph (c) of that subsection, to the making of the administration order or (as the case may be) the appointment of the administrative receiver.

(3B)   Nothing in subsection (3) invalidates any proceedings by reason of their being taken in the wrong court; and proceedings—

    (a)   for or in connection with a disqualification order under this section, or

    (b)   in connection with a disqualification undertaking accepted under section 7,

may be retained in the court in which the proceedings were commenced, although it may not be the court in which they ought to have been commenced.

(3C)   In this section and section 7, 'director' includes a shadow director.

(4)   Under this section the minimum period of disqualification is 2 years, and the maximum period is 15 years.

9.   Matters for determining unfitness of directors

(1)   Where it falls to a court to determine whether a person's conduct as a director of any particular company or companies makes him unfit to be concerned in the management of a company, the court shall, as respects his conduct as a director of that company or, as the case may be, each of those companies, have regard in particular—

    (a)   to the matters mentioned in Part I of Schedule 1 to this Act, and

    (b)   where the company has become insolvent, to the matters mentioned in Part II of that Schedule;

and references in that Schedule to the director and the company are to be read accordingly.

(1A)   In determining whether he may accept a disqualification undertaking from any person the Secretary of State shall, as respects the person's conduct as a director of any company concerned, have regard in particular—

    (a)   to the matters mentioned in Part I of Schedule 1 to this Act, and

    (b)   where the company has become insolvent, to the matters mentioned in Part II of that Schedule;

and references in that Schedule to the director and the company are to be read accordingly.

(2)   Section 6(2) applies for the purposes of this section and Schedule 1 as it applies for the purposes of sections 6 and 7 and in this section and that Schedule 'director' includes a shadow director.

(3)   Subject to the next subsection, any reference in Schedule 1 to an enactment contained in the Companies Act or the Insolvency Act includes, in relation to any time before the coming into force of that enactment, the corresponding enactment in force at that time.

(4)   The Secretary of State may by order modify any of the provisions of Schedule 1; and such an order may contain such transitional provisions as may appear to the Secretary of State necessary or expedient.

(5)   The power to make orders under this section is exercisable by statutory instrument subject to annulment in pursuance of a resolution of either House of Parliament.

10.   Participation in wrongful trading

(1)   Where the court makes a declaration under section 213 or 214 of the Insolvency Act that a person is liable to make a contribution to a company's assets, then, whether or not an application for such an order is made by any person, the court may, if it thinks fit, also make a disqualification order against the person to whom the declaration relates.

(2)   The maximum period of disqualification under this section is 15 years.

11.   Undischarged bankrupts

(1)   It is an offence for a person who is an undischarged bankrupt to act as director of, or directly or indirectly to take part in or be concerned in the promotion, formation or management of, a company, except with the leave of the court.

(2)   'The court' for this purpose is the court by which the person was adjudged bankrupt or, in Scotland, sequestration of his estates was awarded.

(3)   In England and Wales, the leave of the court shall not be given unless notice of intention to apply for it has been served on the official receiver; and it is the latter's duty, if he is of opinion that it is contrary to the public interest that the application should be granted, to attend on the hearing of the application and oppose it.

12.   Failure to pay under county court administration order

(1)   The following has effect where a court under section 429 of the Insolvency Act revokes an administration order under Part VI of the County Courts Act 1984.

(2)   A person to whom that section applies by virtue of the order under section 429(2)(b) shall not, except with the leave of the court which made the order, act as director or liquidator of, or directly or indirectly take part or be concerned in the promotion, formation or management of, a company.

SCHEDULE 1

Section 9

MATTERS FOR DETERMINING UNFITNESS OF DIRECTORS

PART I

MATTERS APPLICABLE IN ALL CASES

1.   Any misfeasance or breach of any fiduciary or other duty by the director in relation to the company.

2.   Any misapplication or retention by the director of, or any conduct by the director giving rise to an obligation to account for, any money or other property of the company.

3.   The extent of the director's responsibility for the company entering into any transaction liable to be set aside under Part XVI of the Insolvency Act (provisions against debt avoidance).

4.   The extent of the director's responsibility for any failure by the company to comply with any of the following provisions of the Companies Act, namely—

   (a)   section 221 (companies to keep accounting records);
   (b)   section 222 (where and for how long records to be kept);
   (c)   section 288 (register of directors and secretaries);
   (d)   section 352 (obligation to keep and enter up register of members);
   (e)   section 353 (location of register of members);
   (f)   section 363 (duty of company to make annual returns); and
   (h)   sections 399 and 415 (company's duty to register charges it creates).

5.   The extent of the director's responsibility for any failure by the directors of the company to comply with—

   (a)   section 226 or 227 of the Companies Act (duty to prepare annual accounts); or
   (b)   section 233 of that Act (approval and signature of accounts).

5A.   In the application of this Part of this Schedule in relation to any person who is a director of an open-ended investment company, any reference to a provision of the Companies Act is to be taken to be a reference to the corresponding provision of the Open-Ended Investment Companies Regulations 2001 or of any rules made under regulation 6 of those Regulations (Financial Services Authority rules).

PART II

MATTERS APPLICABLE WHERE COMPANY HAS BECOME INSOLVENT

6.   The extent of the director's responsibility for the causes of the company becoming insolvent.

7.   The extent of the director's responsibility for any failure by the company to supply any goods or services which have been paid for (in whole or in part).

8.   The extent of the director's responsibility for the company entering into any transaction or giving any preference, being a transaction or preference—

   (a)   liable to be set aside under section 127 or sections 238 to 240 of the Insolvency Act, or
   (b)   challengeable under section 242 or 243 of that Act or under any rule of law in Scotland.

9.   The extent of the director's responsibility for any failure by the directors of the company to comply with section 98 of the Insolvency Act (duty to call creditors' meeting in creditors' voluntary winding up).

10.   Any failure by the director to comply with any obligation imposed on him by or under any of the following provisions of the Insolvency Act—

   (a)   section 22 (company's statement of affairs in administration);
   (b)   section 47 (statement of affairs to administrative receiver);
   (c)   section 66 (statement of affairs in Scottish receivership);
   (d)   section 99 (directors' duty to attend meeting; statement of affairs in creditors' voluntary winding up);
   (e)   section 131 (statement of affairs in winding up by the court);
   (f)   section 234 (duty of anyone with company property to deliver it up);
   (g)   section 235 (duty to co-operate with liquidator, etc).

PART III

TAXATION

At the time of going to press, the Finance Bill 2003 has yet to complete its passage through Parliament. Those sections of the legislation that appear in Part III: Taxation should therefore be checked with reference to the Finance Act 2003 once it has received Royal Assent.

Inheritance Tax Act 1984

PART IV

CLOSE COMPANIES

PART I

GENERAL

1. Charge on transfers

Inheritance tax shall be charged on the value transferred by a chargeable transfer.

2. Chargeable transfers and exempt transfers

(1)   A chargeable transfer is a transfer of value which is made by an individual but is not (by virtue of Part II of this Act or any other enactment) an exempt transfer.

(2)   A transfer of value made by an individual and exempt only to a limited extent—

(a)   is, if all the value transferred by it is within the limit, an exempt transfer, and

(b)   is, if that value is partly within and partly outside the limit, a chargeable transfer of so much of that value as is outside the limit as well as an exempt transfer of so much of that value as is within the limit.

(3)   Except where the context otherwise requires, references in this Act to chargeable transfers, to their making or to the values transferred by them shall be construed as including references to occasions on which tax is chargeable under Chapter III of Part III of this Act (apart from section 79), to their occurrence or to the amounts on which tax is then chargeable.

3. Transfers of value

(1)   Subject to the following provisions of this Part of this Act, a transfer of value is a disposition made by a person (the transferor) as a result of which the value of his estate immediately after the disposition is less than it would be but for the disposition; and the amount by which it is less is the value transferred by the transfer.

(2)   For the purposes of subsection (1) above no account shall be taken of the value of excluded property which ceases to form part of a person's estate as a result of a disposition.

(3)   Where the value of a person's estate is diminished and that of another person's estate, or of settled property in which no interest in possession subsists, is increased by the first-mentioned person's omission to exercise a right, he shall be treated for the purposes of this section as having made a disposition at the time (or latest time) when he could have exercised the right, unless it is shown that the omission was not deliberate.

(4)   Except as otherwise provided, references in this Act to a transfer of value made, or made by any person, include references to events on the happening of which tax is chargeable as if a transfer of value had been made, or, as the case may be, had been made by that person; and 'transferor' shall be construed accordingly.

3A. Potentially exempt transfers

(1)   Any reference in this Act to a potentially exempt transfer is a reference to a transfer of value—

(a)   which is made by an individual on or after 18th March 1986; and

(b)   which, apart from this section, would be a chargeable transfer (or to the extent to which, apart from this section, it would be such a transfer); and

(c)   to the extent that it constitutes either a gift to another individual or a gift into an accumulation and maintenance trust or a disabled trust;

but this subsection has effect subject to any provision of this Act which provides that a disposition (or transfer of value) of a particular description is not a potentially exempt transfer.

(2)   Subject to subsection (6) below, a transfer of value falls within subsection (1)(c) above, as a gift to another individual—

(a)   to the extent that the value transferred is attributable to property which, by virtue of the transfer, becomes comprised in the estate of that other individual, or

(b)   so far as that value is not attributable to property which becomes comprised in the estate of another person, to the extent that, by virtue of the transfer, the estate of that other individual is increased.

(3)   Subject to subsection (6) below, a transfer of value falls within subsection (1)(c) above, as a gift into an accumulation and maintenance trust or a disabled trust, to the extent that the value transferred is attributable to property which, by virtue of the transfer, becomes settled property to which section 71 or 89 of this Act applies.

(4)   A potentially exempt transfer which is made seven years or more before the death of the transferor is an exempt transfer and any other potentially exempt transfer is a chargeable transfer.

(5)   During the period beginning on the date of a potentially exempt transfer and ending immediately before—

(a)   the seventh anniversary of that date, or
(b)   if it is earlier, the death of the transferor,

it shall be assumed for the purposes of this Act that the transfer will prove to be an exempt transfer.

(6)   Where, under any provision of this Act other than section 52, tax is in any circumstances to be charged as if a transfer of value had been made, that transfer shall be taken to be a transfer which is not a potentially exempt transfer.

(7)   In the application of this section to an event on the happening of which tax is chargeable under section 52 below, the reference in subsection (1)(a) above to the individual by whom the transfer of value is made is a reference to the person who, by virtue of section 3(4) above, is treated as the transferor.

4.   Transfers on death

(1)   On the death of any person tax shall be charged as if, immediately before his death, he had made a transfer of value and the value transferred by it had been equal to the value of his estate immediately before his death.

(2)   For the purposes of this section, where it cannot be known which of two or more persons who have died survived the other or others they shall be assumed to have died at the same instant.

5.   Meaning of estate

(1)   For the purposes of this Act a person's estate is the aggregate of all the property to which he is beneficially entitled, except that the estate of a person immediately before his death does not include excluded property.

(2)   A person who has a general power which enables him, or would if he were sui juris enable him, to dispose of any property other than settled property, or to charge money on any property other than settled property, shall be treated as beneficially entitled to the property or money; and for this purpose 'general power' means a power or authority enabling the person by whom it is exercisable to appoint or dispose of property as he thinks fit.

(3)   In determining the value of a person's estate at any time his liabilities at that time shall be taken into account, except as otherwise provided by this Act.

(4)   The liabilities to be taken into account in determining the value of a transferor's estate immediately after a transfer of value include his liability for inheritance tax on the value transferred but not his liability (if any) for any other tax or duty resulting from the transfer.

(5)   Except in the case of a liability imposed by law, a liability incurred by a transferor shall be taken into account only to the extent that it was incurred for a consideration in money or money's worth.

PART II

EXEMPT TRANSFERS

18.   Transfers between spouses

(1)   A transfer of value is an exempt transfer to the extent that the value transferred is attributable to property which becomes comprised in the estate of the transferor's spouse or, so far as the value transferred is not so attributable, to the extent that that estate is increased.

(2)   If, immediately before the transfer, the transferor but not the transferor's spouse is domiciled in the United Kingdom the value in respect of which the transfer is exempt (calculated as a value on which no tax is chargeable) shall not exceed £55,000 less any amount previously taken into account for the purposes of the exemption conferred by this section.

(3)   Subsection (1) above shall not apply in relation to property if the testamentary or other disposition by which it is given—

(a)   takes effect on the termination after the transfer of value of any interest or period, or

(b)   depends on a condition which is not satisfied within twelve months after the transfer;

but paragraph (a) above shall not have effect by reason only that the property is given to a spouse only if he survives the other spouse for a specified period.

(4)   For the purposes of this section, property is given to a person if it becomes his property or is held on trust for him.

19.   Annual exemption

(1)   Transfers of value made by a transferor in any one year are exempt to the extent that the values transferred by them (calculated as values on which no tax is chargeable) do not exceed £3,000.

(2)   Where those values fall short of £3,000, the amount by which they fall short shall, in relation to the next following year, be added to the £3,000 mentioned in subsection (1) above.

(3)   Where those values exceed £3,000, the excess—

(a)   shall, as between transfers made on different days, be attributed so far as possible to a later rather than an earlier transfer, and

(b)   shall, as between transfers made on the same day, be attributed to them in proportion to the values transferred by them.

(3A)   A transfer of value which is a potentially exempt transfer—

(a)   shall in the first instance be left out of account for the purposes of subsections (1) to (3) above; and

(b)   if it proves to be a chargeable transfer, shall for the purposes of those subsections be taken into account as if, in the year in which it was made, it was made later than any transfer of value which was not a potentially exempt transfer.

(4)   In this section 'year' means period of twelve months ending with 5th April.

(5)   Section 3(4) above shall not apply for the purposes of this section (but without prejudice to sections 57 and 94(5) below).

20.   Small gifts

(1)   Transfers of value made by a transferor in any one year by outright gifts to any one person are exempt if the values transferred by them (calculated as values on which no tax is chargeable) do not exceed £250.

(2)   In this section 'year' means period of twelve months ending with 5th April.

(3)   Section 3(4) above shall not apply for the purposes of this section.

21.   Normal expenditure out of income

(1)   A transfer of value is an exempt transfer if, or to the extent that, it is shown—

(a)   that it was made as part of the normal expenditure of the transferor, and

(b)   that (taking one year with another) it was made out of his income, and

(c)   that, after allowing for all transfers of value forming part of his normal expenditure, the transferor was left with sufficient income to maintain his usual standard of living.

(2)   A payment of a premium on a policy of insurance on the transferor's life, or a gift of money or money's worth applied, directly or indirectly, in payment of such a premium, shall not for the purposes of this section be regarded as part of his normal expenditure if, when the insurance was made or at any earlier or later time, an annuity was purchased on his life, unless it is shown that—

(a)   the purchase of the annuity, and

(b)   the making or any variation of the insurance or of any prior insurance for which the first-mentioned insurance was directly or indirectly substituted,

were not associated operations.

(3)   So much of a purchased life annuity (within the meaning of section 657 of the Taxes Act 1988) as is, for the purposes of the provisions of the Tax Acts relating to income tax on annuities and other annual payments, treated as the capital element contained in the annuity, shall not be regarded as part of the transferor's income for the purposes of this section.

(4)   Subsection (3) above shall not apply to annuities purchased before 13th November 1974.

(5)   Section 3(4) above shall not apply for the purposes of this section.

22.   Gifts in consideration of marriage

(1)   Transfers of value made by gifts in consideration of marriage are exempt to the extent that the values transferred by such transfers made by any one transferor in respect of any one marriage (calculated as values on which no tax is chargeable) do not exceed—

(a)   in the case of gifts within subsection (2) below by a parent of a party to the marriage, £5,000,

(b)   in the case of other gifts within subsection (2) below, £2,500, and

(c)   in any other case £1,000;

any excess being attributed to the transfers in proportion to the values transferred.

(2)   A gift is within this subsection if—

(a)   it is an outright gift to a child or remoter descendant of the transferor or

(b)   the transferor is a parent or remoter ancestor of either party to the marriage, and either the gift is an outright gift to the other party to the marriage or the property comprised in the gift is settled by the gift, or

(c)   the transferor is a party to the marriage, and either the gift is an outright gift to the other party to the marriage or the property comprised in the gift is settled by the gift;

and in this section 'child' includes an illegitimate child, an adopted child and a step-child and 'parent', 'descendant' and 'ancestor' shall be construed accordingly.

(3)   A disposition which is an outright gift shall not be treated for the purposes of this section as a gift made in consideration of marriage if, or in so far as, it is a gift to a person other than a party to the marriage.

(4)   A disposition which is not an outright gift shall not be treated for the purposes of this section as a gift made in consideration of marriage if the persons who are or may become entitled to any benefit under the disposition include any person other than—

(a)   the parties to the marriage, issue of the marriage, or a wife or husband of any such issue;

(b)   persons becoming entitled on the failure of trusts for any such issue under which trust property would (subject only to any power of appointment to a person falling within paragraph (a) or (c) of this subsection) vest indefeasibly on the attainment of a specified age or either on the attainment of such an age or on some earlier event, or persons becoming entitled (subject as aforesaid) on the failure of any limitation in tail;

(c)   a subsequent wife or husband of a party to the marriage, or any issue, or the wife or husband of any issue, of a subsequent marriage of either party;

(d)   persons becoming entitled under such trusts, subsisting under the law of England and Wales or of Northern Ireland, as are specified in   of the Trustee Act 1925 or section 34(1) of the Trustee Act (Northern Ireland) 1958 (protective trusts), the principal beneficiary being a person falling within paragraph (a) or (c) of this subsection, or under such trusts, modified by the enlargement, as respects any period during which there is no such issue as aforesaid in existence, of the class of potential beneficiaries specified in paragraph (ii) of the said section 33(1) or paragraph (b) of the said section 34(1);

(e)   persons becoming entitled under trusts subsisting under the law of Scotland and corresponding with such trusts as are mentioned in paragraph (d) above;

(f)   as respects a reasonable amount of remuneration, the trustees of the settlement.

(5)   References in subsection (4) above to issue shall apply as if any person legitimated by a marriage, or adopted by the husband and wife jointly, were included among the issue of that marriage.

(6)   Section 3(4) above shall not apply for the purposes of this section (but without prejudice to section 57 below).

23. Gifts to charities

(1) Transfers of value are exempt to the extent that the values transferred by them are attributable to property which is given to charities.

(2) Subsection (1) above shall not apply in relation to property if the testamentary or other disposition by which it is given—

  (a) takes effect on the termination after the transfer of value of any interest or period, or
  (b) depends on a condition which is not satisfied within twelve months after the transfer, or
  (c) is defeasible;

and for this purpose any disposition which has not been defeated at a time twelve months after the transfer of value and is not defeasible after that time shall be treated as not being defeasible (whether or not it was capable of being defeated before that time).

(3) Subsection (1) above shall not apply in relation to property which is an interest in other property if—

  (a) that interest is less than the donor's, or
  (b) the property is given for a limited period;

and for this purpose any question whether an interest is less than the donor's shall be decided as at a time twelve months after the transfer of value.

(4) Subsection (1) above shall not apply in relation to any property if—

  (a) the property is land or a building and is given subject to an interest reserved or created by the donor which entitles him, his spouse or a person connected with him to possession of, or to occupy, the whole or any part of the land or building rent-free or at a rent less than might be expected to be obtained in a transaction at arm's length between persons not connected with each other, or
  (b) the property is not land or a building and is given subject to an interest reserved or created by the donor other than—

    (i) an interest created by him for full consideration in money or money's worth, or
    (ii) an interest which does not substantially affect the enjoyment of the property by the person or body to whom it is given;

and for this purpose any question whether property is given subject to an interest shall be decided as at a time twelve months after the transfer of value.

(5) Subsection (1) above shall not apply in relation to property if it or any part of it may become applicable for purposes other than charitable purposes or those of a body mentioned in section 24 or 25 below or, where it is land, of a body mentioned in section 24A below.

(6) For the purposes of this section property is given to charities if it becomes the property of charities or is held on trust for charitable purposes only, and 'donor' shall be construed accordingly.

PART IV

CLOSE COMPANIES

94. Charge on participators

(1) Subject to the following provisions of this Part of this Act, where a close company makes a transfer of value, tax shall be charged as if each individual to whom an amount is apportioned under this section had made a transfer of value of such amount as after deduction of tax (if any) would be equal to the amount so apportioned, less the amount (if any) by which the value of his estate is more than it would be but for the company's transfer; but for this purpose his estate shall be treated as not including any rights or interests in the company.

(2) For the purposes of subsection (1) above the value transferred by the company's transfer of value shall be apportioned among the participators according to their respective rights and interests in the company immediately before the transfer, and any amount so apportioned to a close company shall be further apportioned among its participators, and so on; but—

  (a) so much of that value as is attributable to any payment or transfer of assets to any person which falls to be taken into account in computing that person's profits or gains or losses for the purposes of income tax or corporation tax (or would fall to be so taken into account but for section 208 of the Taxes Act 1988) shall not be apportioned, and

 (b) if any amount which would otherwise be apportioned to an individual who is domiciled outside the United Kingdom is attributable to the value of any property outside the United Kingdom, that amount shall not be apportioned.

(3) In determining for the purposes of this section whether a disposition made by a close company is a transfer of value or what value is transferred by such a transfer no account shall be taken of the surrender by the company, in pursuance of section 240 or 402 of the Taxes Act 1988, of any relief or of the benefit of any amount of advance corporation tax paid by it.

(4) Where the amount apportioned to a person under this section is 5 per cent or less of the value transferred by the company's transfer of value then, notwithstanding section 3(4) above, tax chargeable under subsection (1) above shall be left out of account in determining, with respect to any time after the company's transfer, what previous transfers of value he has made.

(5) References in section 19 above to transfers of value made by a transferor and to the values transferred by them (calculated as there mentioned) shall be treated as including references to apportionments made to a person under this section and to the amounts for the tax on which (if charged) he would be liable.

PART V

MISCELLANEOUS RELIEFS

103. Preliminary

(1) In this Chapter references to a transfer of value include references to an occasion on which tax is chargeable under Chapter III of Part III of this Act (apart from section 79), and

 (a) references to the value transferred by a transfer of value include references to the amount on which tax is then chargeable, and

 (b) references to the transferor include references to the trustees of the settlement concerned.

(2) For the purposes of this Chapter a company and all its subsidiaries are members of a group, and 'holding company' and 'subsidiary' have the meanings given by section 736 of the Companies Act 1985.

(3) In this Chapter 'business' includes a business carried on in the exercise of a profession or vocation, but does not include a business carried on otherwise than for gain.

104. The relief

(1) Where the whole or part of the value transferred by a transfer of value is attributable to the value of any relevant business property, the whole or that part of the value transferred shall be treated as reduced—

 (a) in the case of property falling within section 105(1)(a)(b) or (bb) below, by 100 per cent;

 (b) in the case of other relevant business property, by 50 per cent;

but subject to the following provisions of this Chapter.

(2) For the purposes of this section, the value transferred by a transfer of value shall be calculated as a value on which no tax is chargeable.

105. Relevant business property

(1) Subject to the following provisions of this section and to sections 106, 108, 112(3) and 113 below, in this Chapter 'relevant business property' means, in relation to any transfer of value,—

 (a) property consisting of a business or interest in a business;

 (b) securities of a company which are unquoted and which (either by themselves or together with other such securities owned by the transferor and any unquoted shares so owned) gave the transferor control of the company immediately before the transfer;

 (bb) any unquoted shares in a company;

 (cc) shares in or securities of a company which are quoted and which (either by themselves or together with other such shares or securities owned by the transferor) gave the transferor control of the company immediately before the transfer;

(d) any land or building, machinery or plant which, immediately before the transfer, was used wholly or mainly for the purposes of a business carried on by a company of which the transferor then had control or by a partnership of which he then was a partner; and

(e) any land or building, machinery or plant which, immediately before the transfer, was used wholly or mainly for the purposes of a business carried on by the transferor and was settled property in which he was then beneficially entitled to an interest in possession.

(1ZA)   In subsection (1) above 'quoted', in relation to any shares or securities, means listed on a recognised stock exchange and 'unquoted', in relation to any shares or securities, means not so listed.

(2)   Shares in or securities of a company do not fall within subsection (1)(cc) above if—

(a) they would not have been sufficient, without other property, to give the transferor control of the company immediately before the transfer, and

(b) their value is taken by virtue of section 176 below to be less than the value previously determined.

(3)   A business or interest in a business, or shares in or securities of a company, are not relevant business property if the business or, as the case may be, the business carried on by the company consists wholly or mainly of one or more of the following, that is to say, dealing in securities, stocks or shares, land or buildings or making or holding investments.

(4)   Subsection (3) above—

(a) does not apply to any property if the business concerned is wholly that of a market maker or is that of a discount house and (in either case) is carried on in the United Kingdom, and

(b) does not apply to shares in or securities of a company if the business of the company consists wholly or mainly in being a holding company of one or more companies whose business does not fall within that subsection.

(5)   Shares in or securities of a company are not relevant business property in relation to a transfer of value if at the time of the transfer a winding-up order has been made in respect of the company or the company has passed a resolution for voluntary winding-up or is otherwise in process of liquidation, unless the business of the company is to continue to be carried on after a reconstruction or amalgamation and the reconstruction or amalgamation either is the purpose of the winding-up or liquidation or takes place not later than one year after the transfer of value.

(6)   Land, a building, machinery or plant owned by the transferor and used wholly or mainly for the purposes of a business carried on as mentioned in subsection (1)(d) or (e) above is not relevant business property in relation to a transfer of value, unless the business or the transferor's interest in it is, or shares or securities of the company carrying on the business immediately before the transfer are, relevant business property in relation to the transfer.

(7)   In this section 'market maker' means a person who—

(a) holds himself out at all normal times in compliance with the rules of The Stock Exchange as willing to buy and sell securities, stocks or shares at a price specified by him, and

(b) is recognised as doing so by the Council of The Stock Exchange.

106. Minimum period of ownership

Property is not relevant business property in relation to a transfer of value unless it was owned by the transferor throughout the two years immediately preceding the transfer.

107. Replacements

(1)   Property shall be treated as satisfying the condition in section 106 above if—

(a) it replaced other property and it, that other property and any property directly or indirectly replaced by that other property were owned by the transferor for periods which together comprised at least two years falling within the five years immediately preceding the transfer of value, and

(b) any other property concerned was such that, had the transfer of value been made immediately before it was replaced, it would (apart from section 106) have been relevant business property in relation to the transfer.

(2)   In a case falling within subsection (1) above relief under this Chapter shall not exceed what it would have been had the replacement or any one or more of the replacements not been made.

(3)   For the purposes of subsection (2) above changes resulting from the formation, alteration or dissolution of a partnership, or from the acquisition of a business by a company controlled by the former owner of the business, shall be disregarded.

(4)   Without prejudice to subsection (1) above, where any shares falling within section 105(1)(bb) above which are owned by the transferor immediately before the transfer would under any of the provisions of sections 126 to 136 of the 1992 Act be identified with other shares previously owned by him his period of ownership of the first-mentioned shares shall be treated for the purposes of section 106 above as including his period of ownership of the other shares.

108. Successions

For the purposes of sections 106 and 107 above, where the transferor became entitled to any property on the death of another person—

  (a)   he shall be deemed to have owned it from the date of the death, and
  (b)   if that other person was his spouse he shall also be deemed to have owned it for any period during which the spouse owned it.

109. Successive transfers

(1)   Where—

  (a)   the whole or part of the value transferred by a transfer of value (in this section referred to as the earlier transfer) was eligible for relief under this Chapter (or would have been so eligible if such relief had been capable of being given in respect of transfers of value made at that time), and
  (b)   the whole or part of the property which, in relation to the earlier transfer, was relevant business property became, through the earlier transfer, the property of the person or of the spouse of the person who is the transferor in relation to a subsequent transfer of value, and
  (c)   that property or part, or any property directly or indirectly replacing it, would (apart from section 106 above) have been relevant business property in relation to the subsequent transfer of value, and
  (d)   either the earlier transfer was, or the subsequent transfer of value is, a transfer made on the death of the transferor,

the property which would have been relevant business property but for section 106 above shall be relevant business property notwithstanding that section.

(2)   Where the property which, by virtue of subsection (1) above, is relevant business property replaced the property or part referred to in paragraph (c) of that subsection, relief under this Chapter shall not exceed what it would have been had the replacement or any one or more of the replacements not been made, but section 107(3) above shall apply with the necessary modifications for the purposes of this subsection.

(3)   Where, under the earlier transfer, the amount of the value transferred which was attributable to the property or part referred to in subsection (1)(c) above was part only of its value, a like part only of the value which (apart from this subsection) would fall to be reduced under this Chapter by virtue of this section shall be so reduced.

113. Contracts for sale

Where any property would be relevant business property in relation to a transfer of value but a binding contract for its sale has been entered into at the time of the transfer, it is not relevant business property in relation to the transfer unless—

  (a)   the property is a business or interest in a business and the sale is to a company which is to carry on the business and is made in consideration wholly or mainly of shares in or securities of that company, or
  (b)   the property is shares in or securities of a company and the sale is made for the purpose of reconstruction or amalgamation.

113A.   Transfers within seven years before death of transferor

(1)   Where any part of the value transferred by a potentially exempt transfer which proves to be a chargeable transfer would (apart from this section) be reduced in accordance with the preceding provisions of this Chapter, it shall not be so reduced unless the conditions in subsection (3) below are satisfied.

(2)   Where—

(a)   any part of the value transferred by any chargeable transfer, other than a potentially exempt transfer, is reduced in accordance with the preceding provisions of this Chapter, and

(b)   the transfer is made within seven years of the death of the transferor,

then, unless the conditions in subsection (3) below are satisfied, the additional tax chargeable by reason of the death shall be calculated as if the value transferred had not been so reduced.

(3)   The conditions referred to in subsections (1) and (2) above are—

(a)   that the original property was owned by the transferee throughout the period beginning with the date of the chargeable transfer and ending with the death of the transferor; and

(b)   except to the extent that the original property consists of shares or securities to which subsection (3A) below applies, that, in relation to a notional transfer of value made by the transferee immediately before the death, the original property would (apart from section 106 above) be relevant business property.

(3A)   This subsection applies to shares or securities—

(a)   which were quoted at the time of the chargeable transfer referred to in subsection (1) or (2) above; or

(b)   which fell within paragraph (b) or (bb) of section 105(1) above in relation to that transfer and were unquoted throughout the period referred to in subsection (3)(a) above.

(3B)   In subsection (3A) above 'quoted', in relation to any shares or securities, means listed on a recognised stock exchange and 'unquoted', in relation to any shares or securities, means not so listed.

(4)   If the transferee has died before the transferor, the reference in subsection (3) above to the death of the transferor shall have effect as a reference to the death of the transferee.

(5)   If the conditions in subsection (3) above are satisfied only with respect to part of the original property, then,—

(a)   in a case falling within subsection (1) above, only a proportionate part of so much of the value transferred as is attributable to the original property shall be reduced in accordance with the preceding provisions of this Chapter, and

(b)   in a case falling within subsection (2) above, the additional tax shall be calculated as if only a proportionate part of so much of the value transferred as was attributable to the original property had been so reduced.

(6)   Where any shares owned by the transferee immediately before the death in question—

(a)   would under any of the provisions of sections 126 to 136 of the 1992 Act be identified with the original property (or part of it), or

(b)   were issued to him in consideration of the transfer of a business or interest in a business consisting of the original property (or part of it),

they shall be treated for the purposes of this section as if they were the original property (or that part of it).

(7)   This section has effect subject to section 113B below.

(7A)   The provisions of this Chapter for the reduction of value transferred shall be disregarded in any determination for the purposes of this section of whether there is a potentially exempt or chargeable transfer in any case.

(8)   In this section—

'the original property' means the property which was relevant business property in relation to the chargeable transfer referred to in subsection (1) or subsection (2) above; and

'the transferee' means the person whose property the original property became on that chargeable transfer or, where on the transfer the original property became or remained settled property in which no qualifying interest in possession (within the meaning of Chapter III of Part III of this Act) subsists, the trustees of the settlement.

113B. Application of section 113A to replacement property

(1)   Subject to subsection (2) below, this section applies where—

(a)   the transferee has disposed of all or part of the original property before the death of the transferor; and

(b)   the whole of the consideration received by him for the disposal has been applied by him in acquiring other property (in this section referred to as 'the replacement property').

(2)   This section does not apply unless—

(a)   the replacement property is acquired, or a binding contract for its acquisition is entered into, within the allowed period after the disposal of the original property (or, as the case may be, the part concerned); and

(b)   the disposal and acquisition are both made in transactions at arm's length or on terms such as might be expected to be included in a transaction at arm's length.

(3)   Where this section applies, the conditions in section 113A(3) above shall be taken to be satisfied in relation to the original property (or, as the case may be, the part concerned) if—

(a)   the replacement property is owned by the transferee immediately before the death of the transferor; and

(b)   throughout the period beginning with the date of the chargeable transfer and ending with the death (disregarding any period between the disposal and acquisition) either the original property or the replacement property was owned by the transferee; and

(c)   in relation to a notional transfer of value made by the transferee immediately before the death, the replacement property would (apart from section 106 above) be relevant business property.

(4)   If the transferee has died before the transferor, any reference in subsections (1) to (3) above to the death of the transferor shall have effect as a reference to the death of the transferee.

(5)   In any case where—

(a)   all or part of the original property has been disposed of before the death of the transferor or is excluded by section 113 above from being relevant business property in relation to the notional transfer of value referred to in section 113A(3)(b) above, and

(b)   the replacement property is acquired, or a binding contract for its acquisition is entered into, after the death of the transferor but within the allowed period after the disposal of the original property or part, and

(c)   the transferor dies before the transferee,

subsection (3) above shall have effect with the omission of paragraph (a), and as if any reference to a time immediately before the death of the transferor or to the death were a reference to the time when the replacement property is acquired.

(6)   Section 113A(6) above shall have effect in relation to the replacement property as it has effect in relation to the original property.

(7)   Where a binding contract for the disposal of any property is entered into at any time before the disposal of the property, the disposal shall be regarded for the purposes of subsections (2)(a) and (5)(b) above as taking place at that time.

(8)   In this section 'the original property' and 'the transferee' have the same meaning as in section 113A above and 'allowed period' means the period of three years or such longer period as the Board may allow.

115. Preliminary

(1)   In this Chapter references to a transfer of value include references to an occasion on which tax is chargeable under Chapter III of Part III of this Act (apart from section 79) and—

(a)   references to the value transferred by a transfer of value include references to the amount on which tax is then chargeable, and

(b)   references to the transferor include references to the trustees of the settlement concerned.

(2)   In this Chapter 'agricultural property' means agricultural land or pasture and includes woodland and any building used in connection with the intensive rearing of livestock or fish if the woodland or building is occupied with agricultural land or pasture and the occupation is ancillary to that of the agricultural land or pasture; and also includes such cottages, farm buildings and farmhouses, together with the land occupied with them, as are of a character appropriate to the property.

(3)   For the purposes of this Chapter the agricultural value of any agricultural property shall be taken to be the value which would be the value of the property if the property were subject to a perpetual covenant prohibiting its use otherwise than as agricultural property.

(4)   For the purposes of this Chapter the breeding and rearing of horses on a stud farm and the grazing of horses in connection with those activities shall be taken to be agriculture and any buildings used in connection with those activities to be farm buildings.

(5)　This Chapter applies to agricultural property only if it is in the United Kingdom, the Channel Islands or the Isle of Man.

116. The relief

(1)　Where the whole or part of the value transferred by a transfer of value is attributable to the agricultural value of agricultural property, the whole or that part of the value transferred shall be treated as reduced by the appropriate percentage, but subject to the following provisions of this Chapter.

(2)　The appropriate percentage is 100 per cent if—

(a)　the interest of the transferor in the property immediately before the transfer carries the right to vacant possession or the right to obtain it within the next twelve months, or

(b)　the transferor has been beneficially entitled to that interest since before 10th March 1981 and the conditions set out in subsection (3) below are satisfied; or

(c)　the interest of the transferor in the property immediately before the transfer does not carry either of the rights mentioned in paragraph (a) above because the property is let on a tenancy beginning on or after 1st September 1995;

and, subject to subsection (4) below, it is 50 per cent in any other case.

(3)　The conditions referred to in subsection (2)(b) above are—

(a)　that if the transferor had disposed of his interest by a transfer of value immediately before 10th March 1981 and duly made a claim under paragraph 1 of Schedule 8 to the Finance Act 1975, the value transferred would have been computed in accordance with paragraph 2 of that Schedule and relief would not have been limited by paragraph 5 of that Schedule (restriction to £250,000 or one thousand acres); and

(b)　that the transferor's interest did not at any time during the period beginning with 10th March 1981 and ending with the date of the transfer carry a right mentioned in subsection (2)(a) above, and did not fail to do so by reason of any act or deliberate omission of the transferor during that period.

(4)　Where the appropriate percentage would be 100 per cent but for a limitation on relief that would have been imposed (as mentioned in subsection (3)(a) above) by paragraph 5 of Schedule 8 to the Finance Act 1975, the appropriate percentage shall be 100 per cent in relation to a part of the value transferred equal to the amount which would have attracted relief under that Schedule and 50 per cent in relation to the remainder.

(5)　In determining for the purposes of subsections (3)(a) and (4) above whether or to what extent relief under Schedule 8 to the Finance Act 1975 would have been limited by paragraph 5 of that Schedule, that paragraph shall be construed as if references to relief given under that Schedule in respect of previous chargeable transfers included references to—

(a)　relief given under this Chapter by virtue of subsection (2)(b) or (4) above, and

(b)　relief given under Schedule 14 to the Finance Act 1981 by virtue of paragraph 2(2)(b) or (4) of that Schedule,

in respect of previous chargeable transfers made on or after 10th March 1981.

(5A)　Where, in consequence of the death on or after 1st September 1995 of the tenant or, as the case may be, the last surviving tenant of any property, the tenancy—

(a)　becomes vested in a person, as a result of his being a person beneficially entitled under the deceased tenant's will or other testamentary writing or on his intestacy, and

(b)　is or becomes binding on the landlord and that person as landlord and tenant respectively,

subsection (2)(c) above shall have effect as if the tenancy so vested had been a tenancy beginning on the date of the death.

(5B)　Where in consequence of the death on or after 1st September 1995 of the tenant or, as the case may be, the last surviving tenant of any property, a tenancy of the property or of any property comprising the whole or part of it—

(a)　is obtained by a person under or by virtue of an enactment, or

(b)　is granted to a person in circumstances such that he is already entitled under or by virtue of an enactment to obtain such a tenancy, but one which takes effect on a later date, or

(c)   is granted to a person who is or has become the only or only remaining applicant, or the only or only remaining person eligible to apply, under a particular enactment for such a tenancy in the particular case,

subsection (2)(c) above shall have effect as if the tenancy so obtained or granted had been a tenancy beginning on the date of the death.

(5C) Subsection (5B) above does not apply in relation to property situate in Scotland.

(5D) If, in a case where the transferor dies on or after 1st September 1995,—

(a)   the tenant of any property has, before the death, given notice of intention to retire in favour of a new tenant, and

(b)   the tenant's retirement in favour of the new tenant takes place after the death but not more than thirty months after the giving of the notice,

subsection (2)(c) above shall have effect as if the tenancy granted or assigned to the new tenant had been a tenancy beginning immediately before the transfer of value which the transferor is treated by section 4(1) above as making immediately before his death.

(5E) In subsection (5D) above and this subsection—

'the new tenant' means—

(a)   the person or persons identified in a notice of intention to retire in favour of a new tenant as the person or persons who it is desired should become the tenant of the property to which that notice relates; or

(b)   the survivor or survivors of the persons so identified, whether alone or with any other person or persons;

'notice of intention to retire in favour of a new tenant' means, in the case of any property, a notice or other written intimation given to the landlord by the tenant, or (in the case of a joint tenancy or tenancy in common) all of the tenants, of the property indicating, in whatever terms, his or their wish that one or more persons identified in the notice or intimation should become the tenant of the property;

'the retiring tenant's tenancy' means the tenancy of the person or persons giving the notice of intention to retire in favour of a new tenant;

'the tenant's retirement in favour of the new tenant' means—

(a)   the assignment, or (in Scotland) assignation, of the retiring tenant's tenancy to the new tenant in circumstances such that the tenancy is or becomes binding on the landlord and the new tenant as landlord and tenant respectively; or

(b)   the grant of a tenancy of the property which is the subject of the retiring tenant's tenancy, or of any property comprising the whole or part of that property, to the new tenant and the acceptance of that tenancy by him;

and, except in Scotland, 'grant' and 'acceptance' in paragraph (b) above respectively include the deemed grant, and the deemed acceptance, of a tenancy under or by virtue of any enactment.

(6)   For the purposes of this Chapter the interest of one of two or more joint tenants or tenants in common (or, in Scotland, joint owners or owners in common) shall be taken to carry a right referred to in subsection (2)(a) above if the interests of all of them together carry that right.

(7)   For the purposes of this section, the value transferred by a transfer of value shall be calculated as a value on which no tax is chargeable.

117. Minimum period of occupation or ownership

Subject to the following provisions of this Chapter, section 116 above does not apply to any agricultural property unless—

(a)   it was occupied by the transferor for the purposes of agriculture throughout the period of two years ending with the date of the transfer, or

(b)   it was owned by him throughout the period of seven years ending with that date and was throughout that period occupied (by him or another) for the purposes of agriculture.

118. Replacements

(1) Where the agricultural property occupied by the transferor on the date of the transfer replaced other agricultural property, the condition stated in section 117(a) above shall be treated as satisfied if it, the other property and any agricultural property directly or indirectly replaced by the other property were occupied by the transferor for the purposes of agriculture for periods which together comprised at least two years falling within the five years ending with that date.

(2) Where the agricultural property owned by the transferor on the date of the transfer replaced other agricultural property, the condition stated in section 117(b) above shall be treated as satisfied if it, the other property and any agricultural property directly or indirectly replaced by the other property were, for periods which together comprised at least seven years falling within the ten years ending with that date, both owned by the transferor and occupied (by him or another) for the purposes of agriculture.

(3) In a case falling within subsection (1) or (2) above relief under this Chapter shall not exceed what it would have been had the replacement or any one or more of the replacements not been made.

(4) For the purposes of subsection (3) above changes resulting from the formation, alteration or dissolution of a partnership shall be disregarded.

119. Occupation by company or partnership

(1) For the purposes of sections 117 and 118 above, occupation by a company which is controlled by the transferor shall be treated as occupation by the transferor.

(2) For the purposes of sections 117 and 118 above, occupation of any property by a Scottish partnership shall, notwithstanding section 4(2) of the Partnership Act 1890, be treated as occupation of it by the partners.

120. Successions

(1) For the purposes of section 117 above, where the transferor became entitled to any property on the death of another person—

    (a)   he shall be deemed to have owned it (and, if he subsequently occupies it, to have occupied it) from the date of the death, and

    (b)   if that other person was his spouse he shall also be deemed to have occupied it for the purposes of agriculture for any period for which it was so occupied by his spouse, and to have owned it for any period for which his spouse owned it.

(2) Where the transferor became entitled to his interest on the death of his spouse on or after 10th March 1981—

    (a)   he shall for the purposes of section 116(2)(b) above be deemed to have been beneficially entitled to it for any period for which his spouse was beneficially entitled to it;

    (b)   the condition set out in section 116(3)(a) shall be taken to be satisfied if and only if it is satisfied in relation to his spouse; and

    (c)   the condition set out in section 116(3)(b) shall be taken to be satisfied only if it is satisfied both in relation to him and in relation to his spouse.

121. Successive transfers

(1) Where—

    (a)   the whole or part of the value transferred by a transfer of value (in this section referred to as the earlier transfer) was eligible for relief under this Chapter (or would have been so eligible if such relief had been capable of being given in respect of transfers of value made at that time), and

    (b)   the whole or part of the property which, in relation to the earlier transfer, was or would have been eligible for relief became, through the earlier transfer, the property of the person (or of the spouse of the person) who is the transferor in relation to a subsequent transfer of value and is at the time of the subsequent transfer occupied for the purposes of agriculture either by that person or by the personal representative of the transferor in relation to the earlier transfer, and

    (c)   that property or part or any property directly or indirectly replacing it would (apart from section 117 above) have been eligible for relief in relation to the subsequent transfer of value, and

    (d)   either the earlier transfer was, or the subsequent transfer of value is, a transfer made on the death of the transferor, the property which would have been eligible for relief but for section 117 above shall be eligible for relief notwithstanding that section.

(2)   Where the property which, by virtue of subsection (1) above, is eligible for relief replaced the property or part referred to in paragraph (c) of that subsection, relief under this Chapter shall not exceed what it would have been had the replacement or any one or more of the replacements not been made, but section 118(4) above shall apply for the purposes of this subsection as it applies for the purposes of section 118(3).

(3)   Where, under the earlier transfer the amount of the value transferred which was attributable to the property or part referred to in subsection (1)(c) above was part only of its value, a like part only of the value which (apart from this subsection) would fall to be reduced under this Chapter by virtue of this section shall be so reduced.

PART VIII

ADMINISTRATION AND COLLECTION

227. Payment by instalments – land, shares and businesses

(1)   Where any of the tax payable on the value transferred by a chargeable transfer is attributable to the value of qualifying property and—

(a)   the transfer is made on death, or
(b)   the tax so attributable is borne by the person benefiting from the transfer, or
(c)   the transfer is made under Part III of this Act and the property concerned continues to be comprised in the settlement,

the tax so attributable may, if the person paying it by notice in writing to the Board so elects, be paid by ten equal yearly instalments.

(1A)   Subsection (1) above does not apply to

(a)   tax payable on the value transferred by a potentially exempt transfer which proves to be a chargeable transfer, or
(b)   additional tax becoming payable on the value transferred by any chargeable transfer by reason of the transferor's death within seven years of the transfer,

except to the extent that the tax is attributable to the value of property which satisfies one of the conditions specified in subsection (1C) below and, in the case of property consisting of unquoted shares on unquoted securities, the further condition specified in section 228 (3A) below.

(1AA)   In subsection (1A) above, 'unquoted', in relation to any shares or securities, means not listed on a recognised stock exchange.

(1B)   In this section 'the transferee' means the person whose property the qualifying property became on the transfer or, where on the transfer the qualifying property became comprised in a settlement in which no qualifying interest in possession (within the meaning of Chapter III of Part III of this Act) subsists, the trustees of the settlement.

(1C)   The conditions referred to in subsection (1A) above are—

(a)   that the property was owned by the transferee throughout the period beginning with the date of the chargeable transfer and ending with the death of the transferor (or, if earlier, the death of the transferee), or
(b)   that for the purposes of determining the tax, or additional tax, due by reason of the death of the transferor, the value of the property is reduced in accordance with the provisions of Chapter I or Chapter II of Part V of this Act by virtue of section 113B or section 124B above.

(2)   In this section 'qualifying property' means—

(a)   land of any description, wherever situated;
(b)   shares or securities to which section 228 below applies;
(c)   a business or an interest in a business.

(3)   The first of the instalments referred to in subsection (1) above shall be payable—

(a)   if the chargeable transfer was made on death, six months after the end of the month in which the death occurred, and
(b)   in any other case, at the time when the tax would be due if it were not payable by instalments;

and interest under section 233 below on the unpaid portion of the tax shall be added to each instalment and paid accordingly, except as otherwise provided in section 234 below.

(4)   Notwithstanding the making of an election under this section, the tax for the time being unpaid, with interest to the time of payment, may be paid at any time; and if at any time (whether before or after the date when the first instalment is payable) the whole or any part of the property concerned is sold, the tax unpaid (or, in the case of a sale of part, the proportionate part of that tax) shall become payable forthwith (or, if the sale precedes the date when the first instalment is payable, on that date) together with any interest accrued under section 233 below.

(5)   References in subsection (4) above to the sale of property shall have effect—

(a)   in a case within subsection (1)(b) above other than a case within subsection (1A) above where the transferee dies before the transferor, as if they included references to any chargeable transfer in which the value transferred is wholly or partly attributable to the value of the property, other than a transfer made on death, and

(b)   in a case within subsection (1)(c) above, as references to the property ceasing to be comprised in the settlement.

(6)   For the purposes of subsection (4) above—

(a)   the sale of an interest or part of an interest in a business shall be treated as a sale of part of the business, and

(b)   the payment, under a partnership agreement or otherwise, of a sum in satisfaction of the whole or part of an interest in a business otherwise than on a sale shall be treated as a sale of the interest or part at the time of payment.

(7)   For the purposes of this section—

(a)   the value of a business or of an interest in a business shall be taken to be its net value;

(b)   the net value of a business is the value of the assets used in the business (including goodwill) reduced by the aggregate amount of any liabilities incurred for the purposes of the business;

(c)   in ascertaining the net value of an interest in a business, no regard shall be had to assets or liabilities other than those by reference to which the net value of the business would have fallen to be ascertained if the tax had been attributable to the entire business; and

(d)   'business' includes a business carried on in the exercise of a profession or vocation, but does not include a business carried on otherwise than for gain.

228. Shares, etc within section 227

(1)   This section applies—

(a)   to shares or securities of a company which immediately before the chargeable transfer gave control of the company—

(i)   in the case of a transfer on death, to the deceased,

(ii)   in the case of a transfer under Chapter III of Part III of this Act, to the trustee, and

(iii)   in any other case, to the transferor;

(b)   to shares or securities of a company which do not fall under paragraph (a) above and are unquoted, if the chargeable transfer is made on death and the condition stated in subsection (2) below is satisfied;

(c)   to shares or securities of a company which do not fall under paragraph (a) above and are unquoted, if the Board are satisfied that the tax attributable to their value cannot be paid in one sum without undue hardship (assuming, in the case of a chargeable transfer made otherwise than on death, that the shares or securities would be retained by the persons liable to pay the tax);

(d)   to shares of a company which do not fall under paragraph (a) above and are unquoted, if the conditions stated in subsection (3) below are satisfied.

(2)   The condition mentioned in subsection (1)(b) above is that not less than 20 per cent of so much of the tax chargeable on the value transferred as is tax for which the person paying the tax attributable as mentioned in section 227(1) above is liable (in the same capacity) consists of tax attributable to the value of the shares or securities or such other tax (if any) as may by virtue of section 227 be paid by instalments.

(3)   The conditions mentioned in subsection (1)(d) above are that so much of the value transferred (calculated, if the transfer is not made on death, as if no tax were chargeable on it) as is attributable to the shares exceeds £20,000 and that either—

(a)   the nominal value of the shares is not less than 10 per cent of the nominal value of all the shares of the company at the time of the transfer, or

(b)   the shares are ordinary shares and their nominal value is not less than 10 per cent. of the nominal value of all ordinary shares of the company at that time.

(3A) The further condition referred to in section 227(1A) above is that the shares or securities remained unquoted throughout the period beginning with the date of the chargeable transfer and ending with the death of the transferor (or, if earlier, the death of the transferee).

(4)   In this section 'ordinary shares' means shares which carry either—

(a)   a right to dividends not restricted to dividends at a fixed rate, or

(b)   a right to conversion into shares carrying such a right as is mentioned in paragraph (a) above.

(5)   In this section 'unquoted', in relation to any shares or securities, means not listed on a recognised stock exchange.

PART IX

MISCELLANEOUS AND SUPPLEMENTARY

268. Associated operations

(1)   In this Act 'associated operations' means, subject to subsection (2) below, any two or more operations of any kind, being—

(a)   operations which affect the same property, or one of which affects some property and the other or others of which affect property which represents, whether directly or indirectly, that property, or income arising from that property, or any property representing accumulations of any such income, or

(b)   any two operations of which one is effected with reference to the other, or with a view to enabling the other to be effected or facilitating its being effected, and any further operation having a like relation to any of those two, and so on,

whether those operations are effected by the same person or different persons, and whether or not they are simultaneous; and 'operation' includes an omission.

(2)   The granting of a lease for full consideration in money or money's worth shall not be taken to be associated with any operation effected more than three years after the grant, and no operation effected on or after 27th March 1974 shall be taken to be associated with an operation effected before that date.

(3)   Where a transfer of value is made by associated operations carried out at different times it shall be treated as made at the time of the last of them; but where any one or more of the earlier operations also constitute a transfer of value made by the same transferor, the value transferred by the earlier operations shall be treated as reducing the value transferred by all the operations taken together, except to the extent that the transfer constituted by the earlier operations but not that made by all the operations taken together is exempt under section 18 above.

269. Control of company

(1)   For the purposes of this Act a person has control of a company at any time if he then has the control of powers of voting on all questions affecting the company as a whole which if exercised would yield a majority of the votes capable of being exercised on them.

(2)   For the purposes of this Act shares or securities shall be deemed to give a person control of a company if, together with any shares or securities which are related property within the meaning of section 161 above, they would be sufficient to give him control of the company (as defined in subsection (1) above).

(3)   Where shares or securities are comprised in a settlement, any powers of voting which they give to the trustees of the settlement shall for the purposes of subsection (1) above be deemed to be given to the person beneficially entitled in possession to the shares or securities (except in a case where no individual is so entitled).

(4)   Where a company has shares or securities of any class giving powers of voting limited to either or both of—

(a)   the question of winding up the company, and

(b)   any question primarily affecting shares or securities of that class,

the reference in subsection (1) above to all questions affecting the company as a whole shall have effect as a reference to all such questions except any in relation to which those powers are capable of being exercised.

270. Connected persons

For the purposes of this Act any question whether a person is connected with another shall be determined as, for the purposes of the 1992 Act, it falls to be determined under section 286 of that Act, but as if in that section 'relative' included uncle, aunt, nephew and niece and 'settlement', 'settlor' and 'trustee' had the same meanings as in this Act.

Part III Taxation

Income and Corporation Taxes Act 1988

PART I

THE CHARGE TO TAX

1.   The charge to income tax

(1)   Income tax shall be charged in accordance with the provisions of the Income Tax Acts in respect of all property, profits or gains respectively described or comprised in the Schedules, A, D, E and F, set out in sections 15 to 20 or which in accordance with the Income Tax Acts are to be brought into charge to tax under any of those Schedules or otherwise.

[(1)   Income tax is charged in accordance with the Income Tax Acts on—

    (a)   all amounts which, under those Acts, are charged to tax under any of Schedules A, D and F (set out in sections 15, 18 and 20),

    (b)   all amounts which are charged to tax under any of the following provisions of ITEPA 2003—

        (i)   Part 2 (employment income),
        (ii)   Part 9 (pension income), and
        (iii)   Part 10 (social security income), and

    (c)   any other amounts which, under the Income Tax Acts, are charged to income tax.]

(2)   Where any Act enacts that income tax shall be charged for any year, income tax shall be charged for that year—

    (aa)   in respect of so much of an individual's total income as does not exceed £1,920, at such rate as Parliament may determine to be the starting rate for that year;

    (a)   in respect of any income which does not fall within paragraph (aa) above or paragraph (b) below, at such rate as Parliament may determine to be the basic rate for that year;

    (b)   in respect of so much of an individual's total income as exceeds £29,900 at such higher rate as Parliament may determine;

but this subsection has effect subject to any provision of the Income Tax Acts providing for income tax to be charged at a different rate in certain cases.

(2A)   The amount up to which an individual's income is by virtue of subsection (2) above chargeable for any year at the starting rate shall be known as the starting rate limit.

(3)   The amount up to which an individual's income is by virtue of subsection (2) above chargeable for any year at the starting rate or the basic rate shall be known as the basic rate limit.

(4)   If the retail prices index for the month of September preceding a year of assessment is higher than it was for the previous September, then, unless Parliament otherwise determines, subsection (2) above shall apply for that year as if for each of the amounts specified in that subsection as it applied for the previous year (whether by virtue of this subsection or otherwise) there were substituted an amount arrived at by increasing the amount for the previous year by the same percentage as the percentage increase in the retail prices index and—

    (a)   if the result in the case of the amount specified in subsection (2)(aa) above is not a multiple of £10, rounding it up to the nearest amount which is such a multiple, and

    (b)   if the result in the case of the amount specified in subsection (2)(b) above is not a multiple of £100, rounding it up to the nearest amount which is such a multiple.

(5A)   Subsection (4) above shall not require any change to be made in the amounts deductible or repayable under *section 203* [PAYE regulations] during the period beginning with 6th April and ending with 17th June in the year of assessment.

(6)   The Treasury shall before each year of assessment make an order specifying the amounts which by virtue of subsection (4) above will be treated as specified for that year in subsection (2) above.

(6A)   Where income tax at the basic rate has been borne on income chargeable at the starting rate any necessary repayment of tax shall be made on the making of a claim.

(7)   Part VII contains general provisions relating to the taxation of income of individuals.

Note: for 2003/04, the amounts specified by the Treasury pursuant to s 1(6) for use in s 1(2) are – £1,960 for s 1(2)(aa) and £30,500 for s 1(2)(b).

Note: Sub-section (1) in square brackets substituted for sub-section (1) in italics, and in sub-section (5A) words in square brackets substituted for words in italics by Income Tax (Earnings and Pensions) Act 2003, s 722, Sch 6, Pt 1, paras 1, 2(1)–(3), for the purposes of income tax for the year 2003–04 and subsequent years of assessment, and for the purposes of corporation tax for accounting periods ending after 5 April 2003.

1A. Application of lower rate to income from savings and distributions

(1)   Subject to sections 496(2), 686 and 720(5), so much of any person's total income for any year of assessment as—

   (a)   comprises income to which this section applies, and
   (b)   in the case of an individual, is not

      (i)   savings income falling within section 1(2)(aa), or
      (ii)   income falling within section 1(2)(b),

shall, by virtue of this section, be charged for that year at the rate applicable in accordance with subsection (1A) below, instead of at the rate otherwise applicable to it in accordance with section 1(2)(aa) and (a).

(1AA)   In subsection (1)(b)(i) above 'savings income' means income to which this section applies other than—

   (a)   income chargeable under Schedule F, or
   (b)   equivalent foreign income falling within subsection (3)(b) below and chargeable under Case V of Schedule D.

(1A)   The rate applicable in accordance with this subsection is—

   (a)   in the case of income chargeable under Schedule F, the Schedule F ordinary rate;
   (b)   in the case of equivalent foreign income falling within subsection (3)(b) below and chargeable under Case V of Schedule D, the Schedule F ordinary rate; and
   (c)   in the case of any other income, the lower rate.

(1B)   In relation to any year of assessment for which income tax is charged the lower rate is 20 per cent or such other rate as Parliament may determine.

(2)   Subject to subsection (4) below, this section applies to the following income—

   (a)   any income chargeable under Case III of Schedule D other than—

      (i)   relevant annuities and other annual payments that are not interest; and
      (ii)   amounts so chargeable by virtue of section 119;

   (aa)   any amount chargeable to tax under Case VI of Schedule D by virtue of section 714, 716 or 723;
   (b)   any income chargeable under Schedule F; and
   (c)   subject to subsection (4) below, any equivalent foreign income.

(3)   The income which is equivalent foreign income for the purposes of this section is any income chargeable under Case IV or V of Schedule D which—

   (a)   is equivalent to a description of income falling within subsection (2)(a) above but arises from securities or other possessions out of the United Kingdom; or
   (b)   consists in any such dividend or other distribution of a company not resident in the United Kingdom as would be chargeable under Schedule F if the company were resident in the United Kingdom.

(4)   This section does not apply to—

   (a)   any income chargeable under Case IV or V of Schedule D which is such that section 65(5)(a) or (b) provides for the tax to be computed on the full amount of sums received in the United Kingdom; or
   (b)   any amounts deemed by virtue of section 695(4)(b) or 696(6) to be income chargeable under Case IV of Schedule D

(5)   For the purposes of subsection (1)(b) above and any other provisions of the Income Tax Acts—

   (a)   so much of any person's income as comprises income to which this section applies shall be treated as the highest part of his income; and
   (b)   so much of that part as consists of—

> (i)   income chargeable under Schedule F (if any), and
>
> (ii) equivalent foreign income falling within subsection (3)(b) above and chargeable under Case V of Schedule D (if any),

shall be treated as the highest part of that part.

(6)   Subsection (5) above shall have effect subject to section 833(3) but shall otherwise have effect notwithstanding any provision requiring income of any description to be treated for the purposes of the Income Tax Acts (other than section 550) as the highest part of a person's income.

(6A)   Where income tax at the basic rate has been borne on income chargeable at the lower rate any necessary repayment of tax shall be made on the making of a claim.

(7)   In this section 'relevant annuity' means any annuity other than a purchased life annuity to which section 656 applies or to which that section would apply but for section 657(2)(a).

1B.   Rates of tax applicable to Schedule F income etc

(1)   In the case of so much of an individual's income which consists of—

> (a)   income chargeable under Schedule F (if any), and
>
> (b)   equivalent foreign income falling within section 1A(3)(b) and chargeable under Case V of Schedule D (if any),

as is income falling within section 1(2)(b), income tax shall, by virtue of this subsection, be charged at the Schedule F upper rate, instead of at the rate otherwise applicable to it in accordance with section 1(2)(b).

(2)   In relation to any year of assessment for which income tax is charged—

> (a)   the Schedule F ordinary rate is 10 per cent, and
>
> (b)   the Schedule F upper rate is 32.5 per cent,

or, in either case, such other rate as Parliament may determine.

8.   General scheme of corporation tax

(1)   Subject to any exceptions provided for by the Corporation Tax Acts, a company shall be chargeable to corporation tax on all its profits wherever arising.

(2)   A company shall be chargeable to corporation tax on profits accruing for its benefit under any trust, or arising under any partnership, in any case in which it would be so chargeable if the profits accrued to it directly; and a company shall be chargeable to corporation tax on profits arising in the winding up of the company, but shall not otherwise be chargeable to corporation tax on profits accruing to it in a fiduciary or representative capacity except as respects its own beneficial interest (if any) in those profits.

(3)   Corporation tax for any financial year shall be charged on profits arising in that year; but assessments to corporation tax shall be made on a company by reference to accounting periods, and the amount chargeable (after making all proper deductions) of the profits arising in an accounting period shall, where necessary, be apportioned between the financial years in which the accounting period falls.

In relation to accounting periods ending after such day, not being earlier than 31st March 1992, as the Treasury may by order appoint for the purposes of this subsection, this subsection shall have effect with the substitution for 'assessments to corporation tax shall be made on a company' of 'corporation tax shall be computed and chargeable (and any assessments shall accordingly be made)'.

9.   Computation of income: application of income tax principles

(1)   Except as otherwise provided by the Tax Acts, the amount of any income shall for purposes of corporation tax be computed in accordance with income tax principles, all questions as to the amounts which are or are not to be taken into account as income, or in computing income, or charged to tax as a person's income, or as to the time when any such amount is to be treated as arising, being determined in accordance with income tax law and practice as if accounting periods were years of assessment.

(2)   For the purposes of this section 'income tax law' means, in relation to any accounting period, the law applying, for the year of assessment in which the period ends, to the charge on individuals of income tax, except that it does not include such of the enactments of the Income Tax Acts as make special provision for individuals in relation to matters referred to in subsection (1) above.

(3)   Accordingly, for purposes of corporation tax, income shall be computed, and the assessment shall be made, under the like Schedules and Cases as apply for purposes of income tax [—

(a)   Schedules A, D and F, and the Cases of those Schedules, as they apply for purposes of income tax, and

(b)   the following provisions of ITEPA 2003 (which impose charges to income tax)—

(i)   Part 2 (employment income),

(ii)   Part 9 (pension income), and

(iii)   Part 10 (social security income)],

and in accordance with the provisions applicable to those Schedules and Cases [and those Parts], but (subject to the provisions of the Corporation Tax Acts) the amounts so computed for the several sources of income, if more than one, together with any amount to be included in respect of chargeable gains, shall be aggregated to arrive at the total profits.

(4)   Without prejudice to the generality of subsection (1) above, any provision of the Income Tax Acts which confers an exemption from income tax, or which provides for a person to be charged to income tax on any amount (whether expressed to be income or not, and whether an actual amount or not), shall, except as otherwise provided, have the like effect for purposes of corporation tax.

(5)   Where, by virtue of this section or otherwise, any enactment applies both to income tax and to corporation tax—

(a)   it shall not be affected in its operation by the fact that they are distinct taxes but, so far as is consistent with the Corporation Tax Acts, shall apply in relation to income tax and corporation tax as if they were one tax, so that, in particular, a matter which in a case involving two individuals is relevant for both of them in relation to income tax shall in a like case involving an individual and a company be relevant for him in relation to that tax and for it in relation to corporation tax; and

(b)   for that purpose references in any such enactment to a relief from or charge to income tax, or to a specified provision of the Income Tax Acts shall, in the absence of or subject to any express adaptation, be construed as being or including a reference to any corresponding relief from or charge to corporation tax, or to any corresponding provision of the Corporation Tax Acts.

(6)   The provisions of the Income Tax Acts applied by this section do not include sections 1 to 5, 60 to 69, Part VII or sections 348 to 350 of this Act; and nothing in this section shall be taken to mean that income arising in any period is to be computed by reference to any other period (except in so far as this results from apportioning to different parts of a period income of the whole period).

Note: In sub-section (3), words in italics substituted by words in square brackets by Income Tax (Earnings and Pensions) Act 2003, s 722, Sch 6, Pt 1, paras 1, 4, for the purposes of income tax for the year 2003–04 and subsequent years of assessment, and for the purposes of corporation tax for accounting periods ending after 5 April 2003.

15.   Schedule A

(1)   The Schedule referred to as Schedule A is as follows—

SCHEDULE A

1.— (1) Tax is charged under this Schedule on the annual profits arising from a business carried on for the exploitation, as a source of rents or other receipts, of any estate, interest or rights in or over land in the United Kingdom.

(2)   To the extent that any transaction is entered into for the exploitation, as a source of rents or other receipts, of any estate, interest or rights in or over land in the United Kingdom, it is taken to be entered into in the course of such a business.

(3)   All businesses and transactions carried on or entered into by a particular person or partnership, so far as they are businesses or transactions the profits of which are chargeable to tax under this Schedule, are treated for the purposes of this Schedule as, or as entered into in the course of carrying on, a single business.

There are qualifications to this rule in the case of—

(a)   companies not resident in the United Kingdom (see subsection (1A) below); and

(b)   insurance companies (see sections 432AA and 441B(2A)).

(4)   The receipts referred to in the expression 'as a source of rents or other receipts' include—

    (a)   payments in respect of a licence to occupy or otherwise to use land or the exercise of any other right over land, and

    (b)   rentcharges, ground annuals and feu duties and other annual payments reserved in respect of, or charged on or issuing out of, the land.

2.— (1) This Schedule does not apply to profits arising from the occupation of land.

(2)   This Schedule does not apply to—

    (a)   profits charged to tax under Case I of Schedule D under—

        section 53(1) (farming and market gardening), or
        section 55 (mines, quarries and other concerns);

    (b)   receipts or expenses taken into account as trading receipts or expenses under section 98 (tied premises);

    (c)   rent charged to tax under Schedule D under—

        section 119 (rent, etc. payable in connection with mines, quarries and other concerns), or
        section 120(1) (certain rent, etc. payable in respect of electric line wayleaves).

(3)   The profits of a Schedule A business carried on by a company shall be computed without regard to items giving rise to—

credits or debits within Chapter II of Part IV of the Finance Act 1996 (loan relationships), or
credits or debits within Schedule 26 to the Finance Act 2002 (derivative contracts).

This Schedule does not affect the operation of those provisions.

3.— (1) For the purposes of this Schedule a right to use a caravan or houseboat, where the use to which the caravan or houseboat may be put in pursuance of the right is confined to use at a single location in the United Kingdom, is treated as a right deriving from an estate or interest in land in the United Kingdom.

(2)   In sub-paragraph (1)—

'caravan' has the meaning given by section 29(1) of the Caravan Sites and Control of Development Act 1960; and
'houseboat' means a boat or similar structure designed or adapted for use as a place of human habitation.

4.— (1) In the case of a furnished letting, any sum payable for the use of furniture shall be taken into account in computing the profits chargeable to tax under this Schedule in the same way as rent.

Expenses in connection with the provision of furniture shall similarly be taken into account in the same way as expenses in connection with the premises.

(2)   A furnished letting means where—

    (a)   a sum is payable in respect of the use of premises, and

    (b)   the tenant or other person entitled to the use of the premises is also entitled, in connection with that use, to the use of furniture.

(3)   This paragraph does not apply if the receipts and expenses are taken into account in computing the profits of a trade consisting in, or involving, making furniture available for use in premises.

(4)   In this paragraph—

    (a)   any reference to a sum includes the value of consideration other than money, and references to a sum being payable shall be construed accordingly; and

    (b)   'premises' includes a caravan or houseboat within the meaning of paragraph 3.

(1A) In the case of a company which is not resident in the United Kingdom—

    (a)   businesses carried on and transactions entered into by it the profits of which are within the charge to corporation tax under Schedule A, and

    (b)   businesses carried on and transactions entered into by it the profits of which are within the charge to income tax under Schedule A,

are treated as separate Schedule A businesses.

(4)   Part II contains further provisions relating to the charge of tax under Schedule A.

18.   Schedule D

(1)   The Schedule referred to as Schedule D is as follows—

SCHEDULE D

Tax under this Schedule shall be charged in respect of—

(a)   the annual profits or gains arising or accruing—

   (i)   to any person residing in the United Kingdom from any kind of property whatever, whether situated in the United Kingdom or elsewhere, and

   (ii)   to any person residing in the United Kingdom from any trade, profession or vocation, whether carried on in the United Kingdom or elsewhere, and

   (iii)   to any person, whether a Commonwealth citizen or not, although not resident in the United Kingdom from any property whatever in the United Kingdom or from any trade, profession or vocation exercised within the United Kingdom, and

(b)   all interest of money, annuities and other annual profits or gains not charged under Schedule A *or E* [or under ITEPA 2003 as employment income, pension income or social security income], and not specially exempted from tax.

(2)   Tax under Schedule D shall be charged under the Cases set out in subsection (3) below, and subject to and in accordance with the provisions of the Tax acts applicable to those Cases respectively.

(3)   The Cases are—

Case I: tax in respect of any trade carried on in the United Kingdom or elsewhere but not contained in Schedule A;

Case II: tax in respect of any profession or vocation not contained in any other Schedule;

Case: III: tax in respect of—

   (a)   any interest of money, whether yearly or otherwise, or any annuity or other annual payment, whether such payment is payable within or out of the United Kingdom, either as a charge on any property of the person paying the same by virtue of any deed or will or otherwise, or as a reservation out of it, or as a personal debt or obligation by virtue of any contract, or whether the same is received and payable half-yearly or at any shorter or more distant periods, but not including any payment chargeable under Schedule A, and

   (b)   all discounts, and

   (c)   income from securities which is payable out of the public revenue of the United Kingdom or Northern Ireland;

Case IV: tax in respect of income arising from securities out of the United Kingdom;

Case V: tax in respect of income arising from professions out of the United Kingdom not being *income consisting of emoluments of any office or employment* [employment income, pension income or social security income on which tax is charged under ITEPA 2003];

Case VI: tax in respect of any annual profits or gains not falling under any other Case of Schedule D and not charged by virtue of Schedule A *or E* [or by virtue of ITEPA 2003 as employment income, pension income or social security income].

(3A) For the purposes of corporation tax subsection (3) above shall have effect as if the following Case were substituted for Cases III and IV, that is to say—

'Case III: tax in respect of—

   (a)   profits and gains which, as profits and gains arising from loan relationships, are to be treated as chargeable under this Case by virtue of Chapter II of Part IV of the Finance Act 1996;

   (b)   any annuity or other annual payment which—

      (i)   is payable (whether inside or outside the United Kingdom and whether annually or at shorter or longer intervals) in respect of anything other than a loan relationship; and

(ii)   is not a payment chargeable under Schedule A;

(c)   any discount arising otherwise than in respect of a loan relationship;'

and as if Case V did not include tax in respect of any income falling within paragraph (a) of the substituted Case III.

(3B) The references in Case IV of Schedule D to income arising from securities out of the United Kingdom, and in Case V of Schedule D to income arising from possessions out of the United Kingdom, shall be taken, in the case of relevant foreign holdings, to include references to the following—

(a)   any proceeds of such a sale or other realisation of coupons for foreign dividends as is effected by a bank in the United Kingdom which pays the proceeds over or carries them into an account;

(b)   any proceeds of a sale of such coupons to a dealer in coupons in the United Kingdom by a person who is not a bank or another dealer in coupons.

(3C) In this section 'relevant foreign holdings' means—

(a)   any securities issued by or on behalf of a government or a public or local authority in a country outside the United Kingdom; or

(b)   any shares or securities issued by or on behalf of a body of persons not resident in the United Kingdom;

and 'securities' here includes loan stock and similar securities.

(3D) In this section 'foreign dividends' means—

(a)   in relation to relevant foreign holdings falling within subsection (3C)(a) above, interest or annual payments payable out of the revenue of the government or authority in question; and

(b)   in relation to relevant foreign holdings falling within subsection (3C)(b) above, any dividends, interest or annual payments payable in respect of the holdings in question.

(3E) In this section—

(a)   'bank' has the meaning given by section 840A; and

(b)   references to coupons include, in relation to any foreign dividends, warrants for and bills of exchange purporting to be drawn or made in payment of those dividends.

(4) The provisions of Schedule D and of subsection (2) above are without prejudice to any other provision of the Tax Acts directing tax to be charged under Schedule D or under one or other of the Cases set out in subsection (3) above, and tax directed to be so charged shall be charged accordingly.

(5) Parts III and IV contain further provisions relating to the charge to tax under Schedule D.

Note: In sub-sections (1) and (3), words in italics substituted by words in square brackets by Income Tax (Earnings and Pensions) Act 2003, s 722, Sch 6, Pt 1, paras 1, 5, for the purposes of income tax for the year 2003–04 and subsequent years of assessment, and for the purposes of corporation tax for accounting periods ending after 5 April 2003.

20.   Schedule F

(1) The Schedule referred to as Schedule F is as follows—

SCHEDULE F

1. Subject to section 95(1A)(a), income tax under this Schedule shall be chargeable for any year of assessment in respect of all dividends and other distributions in that year of a company resident in the United Kingdom which are not specially excluded from income tax, and for the purposes of income tax all such distributions shall be regarded as income however they fall to be dealt with in the hands of the recipient.

2. For the purposes of this Schedule and all other purposes of the Tax Acts (other than section 95(1) of this Act and section 219(4A) of the Finance Act 1994) any such distribution in respect of which a person is entitled to a tax credit shall be treated as representing income equal to the aggregate of the amount or value of that distribution and the amount of that credit, and income tax under this Schedule shall accordingly be charged on that aggregate.

(2) Except as provided by section 171 of the Finance Act 1993 or section 219 of the Finance Act 1994 (underwriters), no distribution which is chargeable under Schedule F shall be chargeable under any other provision of the Income Tax Acts.

(3) Part VI contains further provisions relating to company distributions and tax credits.

PART IV

PROVISIONS RELATING TO THE SCHEDULE D CHARGE

60. Assessment on current year basis

(1) Subject to subsection (2) below and section 63A, income tax shall be charged under Cases I and II of Schedule D on the full amount of the profits of the year of assessment.

(2) Where, in the case of a trade, profession or vocation, a basis period for the year of assessment is given by subsection (3) below or sections 61 to 63, the profits of that period shall be taken to be the profits of the year.

(3) Subject to sections 61 to 63, the basis period for a year of assessment is as follows—

    (a) if the year is the first year of assessment in which there is an accounting date which falls not less than 12 months after the commencement date, the period of 12 months ending with that accounting date; and

    (b) if there is a basis period for the immediately preceding year and that basis period is not given by section 61, the period of 12 months beginning immediately after the end of that basis period.

(4) In the case of a person who, if he had not died, would under the provisions of this section and sections 61 to 63A have become chargeable to income tax for any year, the tax which would have been so chargeable—

    (a) shall be assessed and charged on his personal representatives, and

    (b) shall be a debt due from and payable out of his estate.

(5) In this section and sections 61 to 63—

'accounting date', in relation to a year of assessment, means a date in the year to which accounts are made up or, where there are two or more such dates, the latest of those dates;

'the commencement date' and 'the commencement year' mean respectively the date on which and the year of assessment in which the trade, profession or vocation is set up and commenced.

61. Basis of assessment at commencement

(1) Notwithstanding anything in section 60, where the year of assessment is the commencement year, the computation of the profits chargeable to income tax under Case I or II of Schedule D shall be made on the profits or gains arising in the year.

(2) Subject to section 63, where the year of assessment is the year next following the commencement year and—

    (a) there is an accounting date in the year and the period beginning with the commencement date and ending with the accounting date is a period of less than 12 months; or

    (b) the basis period for the year would, apart from this subsection, be given by section 62(2) and the period beginning with the commencement date and ending with the new date in the year is a period of less than 12 months,

the basis period for the year is the period of 12 months beginning with the commencement date.

(3) In this section 'the new date' has the same meaning as in section 62.

62. Change of basis period

(1) Subsection (2) below applies where, in the case of a trade, profession or vocation—

    (a) an accounting change, that is, a change from one accounting date ('the old date') to another ('the new date'), is made or treated as made in a year of assessment; and

    (b) either section 62A applies or the year of assessment is the year next following or next but one following the commencement year.

(2) The basis period for the year of assessment is as follows—

    (a) if the year is the year next following the commencement year or the relevant period is a period of less than 12 months, the period of 12 months ending with the new date in the year; and

    (b) if the relevant period is a period of more than 12 months, that period;

and in this subsection 'the relevant period' means the period beginning immediately after the end of the basis period for the preceding year and ending with the new date in the year.

(3)   Where subsection (2) above does not apply as respects an accounting change made or treated as made in a year of assessment ('the first year'), this section and section 62A shall have effect in relation to the next following year ('the second year') as if the change had not been made or treated as made.

(4)   As a consequence of subsection (3) above—

(a)   an accounting change shall be treated as made in the second year if the date or, as the case may be, the latest date in that year to which accounts are made up is a date other than the date of the end of the basis period for the first year; and

(b)   no such change shall be treated as made in the second year if that date is the date of the end of that period.

(5)   For the purposes of this section an accounting change is made in the first year of assessment in which accounts are not made up to the old date, or accounts are made up to the new date, or both.

62A. Conditions for such a change

(1)   This section applies in relation to an accounting change if the following are fulfilled, namely—

(a)   the first and second conditions mentioned below, and
(b)   either the third or the fourth condition so mentioned.

(2)   The first condition is that the first accounting period ending with the new date does not exceed 18 months.

(3)   The second condition—

(a)   in the case of a trade, profession or vocation carried on by an individual, that notice of the accounting change is given to an officer of the Board in a return under section 8 of the Management Act on or before the day on which that return is required to be made and delivered under that section;

(b)   in the case of a trade, profession or vocation carried on by persons in partnership, that notice of the accounting change is given to an officer of the Board in a return under section 12AA of that Act on or before the day specified in relation to that return under subsection (2) or (3) of that section.

(4)   The third condition is that no accounting change as respects which section 62(2) has applied has been made or treated as made in any of the five years immediately preceding the year of assessment.

(5)   The fourth condition is that—

(a)   the notice required by the second condition sets out the reasons for which the change is made; and

(b)   either the officer is satisfied that the change is made for bona fide commercial reasons or he does not, within 60 days of receiving the notice, give notice to the person carrying on the trade, profession or vocation that he is not so satisfied.

(6)   An appeal may be brought against the giving of a notice under subsection (5)(b) above within the period of 30 days beginning with the date on which the notice is given.

(7)   Subject to subsection (8) below, the provisions of the Management Act relating to appeals shall have effect in relation to an appeal under subsection (6) above as they have effect in relation to an appeal against an assessment to tax.

(8)   On an appeal under subsection (6) above section 50(6) to (8) of the Management Act shall not apply but the Commissioners may—

(a)   if they are satisfied that the change is made for bona fide commercial reasons, set the notice under subsection (5)(b) above aside; or

(b)   if they are not so satisfied, confirm that notice.

(9)   Obtaining a tax advantage shall not be regarded as a bona fide commercial reason for the purposes of subsections (5) and (8) above.

(10) In this section—

(a)   'accounting period' means a period for which accounts are made up, and
(b)   expressions which are also used in section 62 have the same meanings as in that section.

Part III Taxation

63. Basis of assessment on discontinuance

Where a trade, profession or vocation is permanently discontinued in a year of assessment other than the commencement year, the basis period for the year shall be the period beginning—

    (a)   where the year is the year next following the commencement year, immediately after the end of the commencement year, and

    (b)   in any other case, immediately after the end of the basis period for the preceding year of assessment,

and (in either case) ending with the date on which the trade, profession or vocation is permanently discontinued.

63A. Overlap profits and overlap losses

(1)   Where, in the case of any trade, profession or vocation, the basis period for a year of assessment is given by section 62(2)(b), a deduction shall be made in computing the profits of that year of an amount equal to that given by the formula in subsection (2) below.

(2)   The formula referred to in subsection (1) above is—

$$A \times \frac{B - C}{D}$$

where—

    $A =$ the aggregate of any overlap profits less the aggregate of any amounts previouslu deducted under subsection (1) above;

    $B =$ the number of days in the basis period;

    $C =$ the number of days in the year of assessment;

    $D =$ the aggregate of the overlap periods of any overlap profits less the aggregate number of days given by the variable 'B – C' in any previous applications of this subsection.

(3)   Where, in the case of any trade, profession or vocation, the basis period for a year of assessment is given by section 63, a deduction shall be made in computing the profits of that year of an amount equal to—

    (a)   the aggregate of any overlap profits, less

    (b)   the aggregate of any amounts deducted under subsection (1) above.

(4)   Where, in the case of any trade, profession or vocation, an amount of a loss would, apart from this subsection, fall to be included in the computations for two successive years of assessment, that amount shall not be included in the computation for the second of those years.

(5)   In this section—

'overlap profit' means an amount of profits which, by virtue of sections 60 to 62, is included in the computations for two successive years of assessment; and

'overlap period', in relation to an overlap profit, means the number of days in the period in which the overlap profit arose.

74. General rules as to deductions not allowable

(1)   Subject to the provisions of the Tax acts, in computing the amount of the profits to be charged under Case I or Case II of Schedule D, no sum shall be deducted in respect of—

    (a)   any disbursements or expenses, not being money wholly and exclusively laid out or expended for the purposes of the trade, profession or vocation;

    (b)   any disbursements or expenses of maintenance of the parties, their families or establishments, or any sums expended for any other domestic or private purposes distinct from the purposes of the trade, profession or vocation;

    (c)   the rent of the whole or any part of any dwelling-house or domestic offices, except any such part as is used for the purposes of the trade, profession or vocation, and where any such part is so used, the sum so deducted shall not, unless in any particular case it appears that having regard to all the circumstances some greater sum ought to be deducted, exceed two-thirds of the rent bona fide paid for that dwelling-house or those offices;

(d) any sum expended for repairs of premises occupied, or for the supply, repairs or alterations of any implements, utensils or articles employed, for the purposes of the trade, profession or vocation, beyond the sum actually expended for those purposes;

(e) any loss not connected with or arising out of the trade, profession or vocation;

(f) any capital withdrawn from, or any sum employed or intended to be employed as capital in, the trade, profession or vocation, but so that this paragraph shall not be treated as disallowing the deduction of any interest;

(g) any capital employed in improvements of premises occupied for the purposes of the trade, profession or vocation;

(h) any interest which might have been made if any such sums as aforesaid had been laid out at interest;

(j) any debts, except—

    (i) a bad debt;

    (ii) a debt or part of a debt released by the creditor wholly and exclusively for the purposes of his trade, profession or vocation as part of a relevant arrangement or compromise; and

    (iii) a doubtful debt to the extent estimated to be bad, meaning, in the case of the bankruptcy or insolvency of the debtor, the debt except to the extent that any amount may reasonably be expected to be received on the debt;

(k) any average loss beyond the actual amount of loss after adjustment;

(l) any sum recoverable under an insurance or contract of indemnity;

(m) any annuity or other annual payment (other than interest) payable out of the profits or gains;

(n) any interest paid to a person not resident in the United Kingdom if and so far as it is interest at more than a reasonable commercial rate;

(o) any interest in so far as the payment of that interest is or would be, otherwise than by virtue of section 375(2), either—

    (i) a payment of interest to which section 369 applies, or

    (ii) a payment of interest to which that section would apply but for section 373(5);

(p) any royalty or other sum paid in respect of the user of a patent.

(2) In paragraph (j) of subsection (1) above 'relevant arrangement or compromise' means—

(a) a voluntary arrangement which has taken effect under or by virtue of the Insolvency Act 1986 or the Insolvency (Northern Ireland) Order 1989; or

(b) a compromise or arrangement which has taken effect under section 425 of the Companies Act 1985 or Article 418 of the Companies (Northern Ireland) Order 1986.

113. Effect, for income tax, of change in ownership of trade, profession or vocation

(1) Where there is a change in the persons engaged in carrying on any trade, profession or vocation chargeable under Case I or II of Schedule D, then, subject to the provisions of this section, the amount of the profits of the trade, profession or vocation on which income tax is chargeable for any year of assessment and the persons on whom it is chargeable, shall be determined as if the trade, profession or vocation had been permanently discontinued, and a new one set up and commenced, at the date of the change.

(2) Where—

(a) there is such a change as is mentioned in subsection (1) above, and

(b) a person engaged in carrying on the trade, profession or vocation immediately before the change continues to be so engaged immediately after it,

subsection (1) above shall not apply to treat the trade, profession or vocation as discontinued or a new one as set up and commenced.

(6) In the case of the death of a person who, if he had not died, would under the provisions of this section have become chargeable to tax for any year, the tax which would have been so chargeable shall be assessed and charged upon his executors or administrators, and shall be a debt due from and payable out of his estate.

(7) For the purposes of this section, a change in the personal representatives of any person, or in the trustees of any trust, shall not be treated as a change in the persons engaged in the carrying on of any trade, profession or vocation carried on by those personal representatives or trustees as such.

PART VI

COMPANY DISTRIBUTIONS, TAX CREDITS ETC

219. Purchase by unquoted trading company of own shares

(1)   References in the Corporation Tax Acts to distributors of a company shall not include references to a payment made by a company on the redemption, repayment or purchase of its own shares if the company is an unquoted trading company or the unquoted holding company of a trading group and either—

    (a)   the redemption, repayment or purchase is made wholly or mainly for the purpose of benefiting a trade carried on by the company or by any of its 75 per cent subsidiaries, and does not form part of a scheme or arrangement the main purpose or one of the main purposes of which is—

        (i)   to enable the owner of the shares to participate in the profits of the company without receiving a dividend, or
        (ii)   the avoidance of tax; and

    the conditions specified in sections 220 to 224, so far as applicable, are satisfied in relation to the owner of the shares; or

    (b)   the whole or substantially the whole of the payment (apart from any sum applied in paying capital gains tax charged on the redemption, repayment or purchase) is applied by the person to whom it is made in discharging a liability of his for inheritance tax charged on a death and is so applied within the period of two years after the death;

and in sections 220 to 224—

    'the purchase' means the redemption, repayment or purchase referred to in subsection (1)(a) above; and
    'the vendor' means the owner of the shares at the time it is made.

(2)   Where, apart from this subsection, a payment falls within subsection (1)(b) above, subsection (1) above shall not apply to the extent that the liability in question could without undue hardship have been discharged otherwise than through the redemption, repayment or purchase of shares in the company or another unquoted company which is a trading company or the holding company of a trading group.

220. Conditions as to residence and period of ownership

(1)   The vendor must be resident and ordinarily resident in the United Kingdom in the year of assessment in which the purchase is made and if the shares are held through a nominee the nominee must also be so resident and ordinarily resident.

(2)   The residence and ordinary residence of trustees shall be determined for the purposes of this section as they are determined under section 69 of the 1992 Act for the purposes of that Act.

(3)   The residence and ordinary residence of personal representatives shall be taken for the purposes of this section to be the same as the residence and ordinary residence of the deceased immediately before his death.

(4)   The references in this section to a person's ordinary residence shall be disregarded in the case of a company.

(5)   The shares must have been owned by the vendor throughout the period of five years ending with the date of the purchase.

(6)   If at any time during that period the shares were transferred to the vendor by a person who was then his spouse living with him then, unless that person is alive at the date of the purchase but is no longer the vendor's spouse living with him, any period during which the shares were owned by that person shall be treated for the purposes of subsection (5) above as a period of ownership by the vendor.

(7)   Where the vendor became entitled to the shares under the will or on the intestacy of a previous owner or is the personal representative of a previous owner—

    (a)   any period during which the shares were owned by the previous owner or his personal representatives shall be treated for the purposes of subsection (5) above as a period of ownership by the vendor, and
    (b)   that subsection shall have effect as if it referred to three years instead of five.

(8)   In determining whether the condition in subsection (5) above is satisfied in a case where the vendor acquired shares of the same class at different times—

(a) shares acquired earlier shall be taken into account before shares acquired later, and

(b) any previous disposal by him of shares of that class shall be assumed to be a disposal of shares acquired later rather than of shares acquired earlier.

(9) If for the purposes of capital gains tax the time when shares were acquired would be determined under any provision of Chapter II of Part IV of the 1992 Act (reorganisation of share capital, conversion of securities, etc.) then, unless the shares were allotted for payment or were comprised in share capital to which section 249 applies, it shall be determined in the same way for the purposes of this section.

221. Reduction of vendor's interest as shareholder

(1) If immediately after the purchase the vendor owns shares in the company, then, subject to section 224, the vendor's interest as a shareholder must be substantially reduced.

(2) If immediately after the purchase any associate of the vendor owns shares in the company then, subject to section 224, the combined interests as shareholders of the vendor and his associates must be substantially reduced.

(3) The question whether the combined interests as shareholders of the vendor and his associates are substantially reduced shall be determined in the same way as is (under the following subsections) the question whether a vendor's interest as a shareholder is substantially reduced, except that the vendor shall be assumed to have the interests of his associates as well as his own.

(4) Subject to subsection (5) below, the vendor's interest as a shareholder shall be taken to be substantially reduced if and only if the total nominal value of the shares owned by him immediately after the purchase, expressed as a fraction of the issued share capital of the company at that time, does not exceed 75 per cent of the corresponding fraction immediately before the purchase.

(5) The vendor's interest as a shareholder shall not be taken to be substantially reduced where—

(a) he would, if the company distributed all its profits available for distribution immediately after the purchase, be entitled to a share of those profits, and

(b) that share, expressed as a fraction of the total of those profits, exceeds 75 per cent of the corresponding fraction immediately before the purchase.

(6) In determining for the purposes of subsection (5) above the division of profits among the persons entitled to them, a person entitled to periodic distributions calculated by reference to fixed rates or amounts shall be regarded as entitled to a distribution of the amount or maximum amount to which he would be entitled for a year.

(7) In subsection (5) above 'profits available for distribution' has the same meaning as it has for the purposes of Part VIII of the Companies Act 1985, except that for the purposes of that subsection the amount of the profits available for distribution (whether immediately before or immediately after the purchase) shall be treated as increased—

(a) in the case of every company, by £100, and

(b) in the case of a company from which any person is entitled to periodic distributions of the kind mentioned in subsection (6) above, by a further amount equal to that required to make the distribution to which he is entitled in accordance with that subsection;

and where the aggregate of the sums payable by the company on the purchase and on any contemporaneous redemption, repayment or purchase of other shares of the company exceeds the amount of the profits available for distribution immediately before the purchase, that amount shall be treated as further increased by an amount equal to the excess.

(8) References in this section to entitlement are, except in the case of trustees and personal representatives, references to beneficial entitlement.

222. Conditions applicable where purchasing company is member of group

(1) Subject to section 224, where the company making the purchase is immediately before the purchase a member of a group and—

(a) immediately after the purchase the vendor owns shares in one or more other members of the group (whether or not he then owns shares in the company making the purchase), or

(b) immediately after the purchase the vendor owns shares in the company making the purchase and immediately before the purchase he owned shares in one or more other members of the group, the vendor's interest as a shareholder in the group must be substantially reduced.

(2) In subsections (5) to (7) below 'relevant company' means the company making the purchase and any other member of the group in which the vendor owns shares immediately before or immediately after the purchase, but subject to subsection (4) below.

(3) Subject to section 224, where the company making the purchase is immediately before the purchase a member of a group and at that time an associate of the vendor owns shares in any member of the group, the combined interests as shareholders in the group of the vendor and his associates must be substantially reduced.

(4) The question whether the combined interests as shareholders in the group of the vendor and his associates are substantially reduced shall be determined in the same way as is (under the following subsections) the question whether a vendor's interest as a shareholder in a group is substantially reduced, except that the vendor shall be assumed to have the interests of his associates as well as his own (and references in subsections (5) to (7) below to a relevant company shall be construed accordingly).

(5) The vendor's interest as a shareholder in the group shall be ascertained by—

    (a) expressing the total nominal value of the shares owned by him in each relevant company as a fraction of the issued share capital of the company,

    (b) adding together the fractions so obtained, and

    (c) dividing the result by the number of relevant companies (including any in which he owns no shares).

(6) Subject to subsection (7) below, the vendor's interest as a shareholder in the group shall be taken to be substantially reduced if and only if it does not exceed 75 per cent of the corresponding interest immediately before the purchase.

(7) The vendor's interest as a shareholder in the group shall not be taken to be substantially reduced if—

    (a) he would, if every member of the group distributed all its profits available for distribution immediately after the purchase (including any profits received by it on a distribution by another member), be entitled to a share of the profits of one or more of them, and

    (b) that share, or the aggregate of those shares, expressed as a fraction of the aggregate of the profits available for distribution of every member of the group which is—

        (i) a relevant company, or

        (ii) a 51 per cent subsidiary of a relevant company,

    exceeds 75 per cent of the corresponding fraction immediately before the purchase.

(8) Subsections (6) and (7) of section 221 shall apply for the purposes of subsection (7) above as they apply for the purposes of subsection (5) of that section.

(9) Subject to the following subsections, in this section 'group' means a company which has one or more 51 per cent subsidiaries, but is not itself a 51 per cent subsidiary of any other company, together with those subsidiaries.

(10) Where the whole or a significant part of the business carried on by an unquoted company ('the successor company') was previously carried on by—

    (a) the company making the purchase, or

    (b) a company which is (apart from this subsection) a member of a group to which the company making the purchase belongs,

the successor company and any company of which it is a 51 per cent subsidiary shall be treated as being a member of the same group as the company making the purchase (whether or not, apart from this subsection, the company making the purchase is a member of a group).

(11) Subsection (10) above shall not apply if the successor company first carried on the business there referred to more than three years before the time of the purchase.

(12) For the purposes of this section a company which has ceased to be a 51 per cent subsidiary of another company before the time of the purchase shall be treated as continuing to be such a subsidiary if at that time there exist arrangements under which it could again become such a subsidiary.

223. Other conditions

(1) Subject to section 224, the vendor must not immediately after the purchase be connected with the company making the purchase or with any company which is a member of the same group as that company.

In this subsection 'group' has the same meaning as it has for the purposes of section 222.

(2)   Subject to section 224, the purchase must not be part of a scheme or arrangement which is designed or likely to result in the vendor or any associate of his having interests in any company such that, if he had those interests immediately after the purchase, any of the conditions in sections 221 and 222 and subsection (1) above could not be satisfied.

(3)   A transaction occurring within one year after the purchase shall be deemed for the purposes of subsection (2) above to be part of a scheme or arrangement of which the purchase is also part.

224. Relaxation of conditions in certain cases

Where—

(a)   any of the conditions in section 221 to 223 which are applicable are not satisfied in relation to the vendor, but

(b)   he proposed or agreed to the purchase in order that the condition in section 221(2) or 222(3) could be satisfied in respect of the redemption, repayment or purchase of shares owned by a person of whom he is an associate,

then, to the extent that that result is produced by virtue of the purchase, section 219(1)(a) shall have effect as if the conditions in sections 221 to 223 were satisfied in relation to the vendor.

225. Advance clearance of payments by Board

(1)   A payment made by a company on the redemption, repayment or purchase of its own shares shall be deemed—

(a)   to be one to which section 219 applies if, before it is made, the Board have on the application of the company notified the company that they are satisfied that the section will apply; and

(b)   to be one to which section 219 does not apply if, before it is made, the Board have on the application of the company notified the company that they are satisfied that the section will not apply.

(2)   An application under this section shall be in writing and shall contain particulars of the relevant transactions; and the Board may, within 30 days of the receipt of the application or of any further particulars previously required under this subsection, by notice require the applicant to furnish further particulars for the purpose of enabling the Board to make their decision.

(3)   If a notice under subsection (2) above is not complied with within 30 days or such longer period as the Board may allow, the Board need not proceed further on the application.

(4)   The Board shall notify their decision to the applicant within 30 days of receiving the application or, if they give a notice under subsection (2) above, within 30 days of the notice being complied with.

(5)   If particulars furnished under this section do not fully and accurately disclose all facts and circumstances material for the decision of the Board, any resulting notification by the Board shall be void.

226. Returns and information

(1)   A company which treats a payment made by it as one to which section 219 applies shall within 60 days after making the payment make a return to the inspector giving particulars of the payment and of the circumstances by reason of which that section is regarded as applying to it.

(2)   Where a company treats a payment made by it as one to which section 219(1)(a) applies, any person connected with the company who knows of any such scheme or arrangement affecting the payment as is mentioned in section 223(2) shall, within 60 days after he first knows of both the payment and the scheme or arrangement, give a notice to the inspector containing particulars of the scheme or arrangement.

(3)   Where the inspector has reason to believe that a payment treated by the company making it as one to which section 219(1)(a) applies may form part of a scheme or arrangement of the kind referred to therein or in section 223(2), he may by notice require the company or any person who is connected with the company to furnish him within such time, not being less than 60 days, as may be specified in the notice with—

(a)   a declaration in writing stating whether or not, according to information which the company or that person has or can reasonably obtain, any such scheme or arrangement exists or has existed, and

(b) such other information as the inspector may reasonably require for the purposes of the provision in question and the company or that person has or can reasonably obtain.

(4) The recipient of a payment treated by the company making it as one to which section 219 applies, and any person on whose behalf such a payment is received, shall if so required by the inspector state whether the payment received by him or on his behalf is received on behalf of any person other than himself and, of so, the name and address of that person.

227. Associated persons

(1) Any question whether a person is an associate of another in relation to a company shall be determined for the purposes of sections 219 to 226 and 228 in accordance with the following provisions of this section.

(2) A husband and wife living together are associates of one another, a person under the age of 18 is an associate of his parents, and his parents are his associates.

(3) A person connected with a company is an associate of the company and of any company controlled by it, and the company and any company controlled by it are his associates.

(4) Where a person connected with one company has control of another company, the second company is an associate of the first.

(5) Where shares in a company are held by trustees (other than bare trustees) then in relation to that company, but subject to subsection (8) below, the trustees are associates of—

(a) any person who directly or indirectly provided property to the trustees or has made a reciprocal arrangement for another to do so,

(b) any person who is, by virtue of subsection (2) above, an associate of a person within paragraph (a) above, and

(c) any person who is or may become beneficially entitled to a significant interest in the shares;

and any such person is an associate of the trustees.

(6) Where shares in a company are comprised in the estate of a deceased person, then in relation to that company the deceased's personal representatives are associates of any person who is or may become beneficially entitled to a significant interest in the shares, and any such person is an associate of the personal representatives.

(7) Where one person is accustomed to act on the directions of another in relation to the affairs of a company, then in relation to that company the two persons are associates of one another.

(8) Subsection (5) above shall not apply to shares held on trusts which—

(a) relate exclusively to an exempt approved scheme as defined in Chapter I of Part XIV, or

(b) are exclusively for the benefit of the employees, or the employees and directors, of the company referred to in that subsection or of companies in a group to which that company belongs, or their dependants (and are not wholly or mainly for the benefit of directors or their relatives);

and for the purposes of this subsection 'group' means a company which has one or more 51 per cent subsidiaries, together with those subsidiaries.

(9) For the purposes of subsections (5) and (6) above a person's interest is significant if its value exceeds 5 per cent of the value of all the property held on the trusts or, as the case may be, comprised in the estate concerned, excluding any property in which he is not and cannot become beneficially entitled to an interest.

228. Connected persons

(1) Any question whether a person is connected with a company shall be determined for the purposes of sections 219 to 227 in accordance with the following provisions of this section.

(2) A person is connected with a company if he directly or indirectly possesses or is entitled to acquire more than 30 per cent of—

(a) the issued ordinary share capital of the company, or

(b) the loan capital and issued share capital of the company, or

(c) the voting power in the company.

(3) Where a person—

(a) acquired or became entitled to acquire loan capital of a company in the ordinary course of a business carried on by him, being a business which includes the lending of money, and

(b) takes no part in the management or conduct of the company,

his interest in that loan capital shall be disregarded for the purposes of subsection (2) above.

(4) A person is connected with a company if he directly or indirectly possesses or is entitled to acquire such rights as would, in the event of the winding up of the company or in any other circumstances, entitle him to receive more than 30 per cent of the assets of the company which would then be available for distribution to equity holders of the company; and for the purposes of this subsection—

(a) the persons who are equity holders of the company, and

(b) the percentage of the assets of the company to which a person would be entitled,

shall be determined in accordance with paragraphs 1 and 3 of Schedule 18, taking references in paragraph 3 to the first company as references to an equity holder and references to a winding up as including references to any other circumstances in which assets of the company are available for distribution to its equity holders.

(5) A person is connected with a company if he has control of it.

(6) References in this section to the loan capital of a company are references to any debt incurred by the company—

(a) for any money borrowed or capital assets acquired by the company, or

(b) for any right to receive income created in favour of the company, or

(c) for consideration the value of which to the company was (at the time when the debt was incurred) substantially less than the amount of the debt (including any premium thereon).

(7) For the purposes of this section a person shall be treated as entitled to acquire anything which he is entitled to acquire at a future date or will at a future date be entitled to acquire.

(8) For the purposes of this section a person shall be assumed to have the rights or powers of his associates as well as his own.

229. Other interpretative provisions

(1) In sections 219 to 228—

'control' has the meaning given by section 840;

'holding company' means a company whose business (disregarding any trade carried on by it) consists wholly or mainly of the holding of shares or securities of one or more companies which are its 75 per cent subsidiaries;

'personal representatives' means persons responsible for administering the estate of a deceased person;

'quoted company' means a company whose shares (or any class of whose shares) are listed in the official list of a stock exchange;

'shares' includes stock;

'trade' does not include dealing in shares, securities, land or futures and 'trading activities' shall be construed accordingly;

'trading company' means a company whose business consists wholly or mainly of the carrying on of a trade or trades;

'trading group' means a group the business of whose members, taken together, consists wholly or mainly of the carrying on of a trade or trades, and for this purpose group means a company which has one or more 75 per cent subsidiaries together with those subsidiaries; and

'unquoted company' means a company which is neither a quoted company nor a 51 per cent subsidiary of a quoted company.

(2) References in sections 219 to 228 to the owner of shares are references to the beneficial owner except where the shares are held on trusts (other than bare trusts) or are comprised in the estate of a deceased person, and in such a case are references to the trustees or, as the case may be, to the deceased's personal representatives.

(3) References in sections 219 to 228 to a payment made by a company include references to anything else that is, or would but for section 219 be, a distribution.

PART VII

GENERAL PROVISIONS RELATING TO TAXATION OF INCOME OF INDIVIDUALS

338. Charges on income deducted from total profits

(1)   Charges on income are allowed as deductions from a company's total profits in computing the corporation tax chargeable for an accounting period.

(2)   They are deducted from the company's total profits for the period as reduced by any other relief from tax other than group relief.

(3)   The amount of the deduction is limited to the amount that reduces the company's total profits for the period to nil.

(4)   Except as otherwise provided, a deduction is allowed only in respect of payments made by the company in the accounting period concerned.

(5)   The above provisions are subject to any express exceptions in the Corporation Tax Acts.

338A.   Meaning of 'charges on income'

(1)   This section defines what payments or other amounts are 'charges on income' for the purposes of corporation tax.

This section has effect subject to any express exceptions in the Corporation Tax Acts.

(2)   Subject to the following provisions of this section, the following (and only the following) are charges on income—

    (a)   annuities or other annual payments that meet the conditions specified in section 338B;
    (b)   qualifying donations within the meaning of section 339 (qualifying donations to charity);
    (c)   amounts allowed as charges on income under section 587B(2)(a)(ii) (gifts of shares etc to charity).

(3)   No payment that is deductible in computing profits or any description of profits for the purposes of corporation tax shall be treated as a charge on income.

(4)   No payment shall be treated as a charge on income if (without being so deductible) it is—

    (a)   an annuity payable by an insurance company, or
    (b)   an annuity or other annual payment payable by a company wholly or partly in satisfaction of any claim under an insurance policy in relation to which the company is the insurer.

In paragraph (a) 'insurance company' has the same meaning as in Chapter 1 of Part 12.

338B.   Charges on income: annuities or other annual payments

(1)   An annuity or other annual payment is a charge on income if—

    (a)   the requirements specified in subsection (2) are met, and
    (b)   it is not excluded from being a charge on income for the purposes of corporation tax—

        (i)   by any of the following provisions of this section, or
        (ii)   by any other provision of the Corporation Tax Acts.

(2)   The requirements are that the payment—

    (a)   is made under a liability incurred for a valuable and sufficient consideration,
    (b)   is not charged to capital,
    (c)   is ultimately borne by the company, and
    (d)   in the case of a company not resident in the United Kingdom, is incurred wholly and exclusively for the purposes of a trade which is or is to be carried on by it in the United Kingdom through a branch or agency.

(3)   An annuity or other annual payment made to a person not resident in the United Kingdom shall be treated as a charge on income only if the following conditions are met.

(4)   The conditions are that the company making the payment is resident in the United Kingdom and that either—

- (a) the company deducts tax from the payment in accordance with section 349, and accounts under Schedule 16 for the tax so deducted, or
- (b) the person beneficially entitled to the income in respect of which the payment is made is a company that is not resident in the United Kingdom but which carries on a trade in the United Kingdom through a branch or agency and the payment falls to be brought into account in computing the chargeable profits (within the meaning given by section 11(2) of that company), or
- (c) the payment is one payable out of income brought into charge to tax under Case V of Schedule D.

(5) An annuity or other annual payment is not a charge on income if—

- (a) it is payable in respect of the company's loan relationships, or
- (b) it is a royalty to which Schedule 29 to the Finance Act 2002 applies (intangible fixed assets).

(6) Nothing in this section prevents an annuity or other annual payment from being a charge on income if it is a qualifying donation (within the meaning of section 339).

PART IX

ANNUAL PAYMENTS AND INTEREST

348. Payments out of profits or gains brought into charge to income tax: deduction of tax

(1) Subject to any provision to the contrary in the Income Tax Acts, where any annuity or other annual payment *charged with tax under Case III of Schedule D* [to which this subsection applies], not being interest, is payable wholly out of profits or gains brought into charge to income tax—

- (a) the whole of the profits or gains shall be assessed and charged with income tax on the person liable to the annuity or other annual payment, without distinguishing the annuity or other annual payment; and
- (b) the person liable to make the payment, whether out of the profits or gains charged with income tax or out of any annual payment liable to deduction, or from which a deduction has been made, shall be entitled on making the payment to deduct and retain out of it a sum representing the amount of income tax thereon; and
- (c) the person to whom the payment is made shall allow the deduction on receipt of the residue of the payment, and the person making the deduction shall be acquitted and discharged of so much money as is represented by the deduction, as if that sum had been actually paid; and
- (d) the deduction shall be treated as income tax paid by the person to whom the payment is made.

[(1A) Subsection (1) applies to any annuity or other annual payment, not being interest—

- (a) which is charged with tax under Case III of Schedule D,
- (b) which is charged with tax under Part 9 of ITEPA 2003 (pension income) because section 605 of that Act applies to it (retirement annuity contracts: annuities), or
- (c) which arises from a source in the United Kingdom and is charged with tax under Part 9 of ITEPA 2003 because section 609, 610 or 611 of that Act applies to it (certain employment-related annuities).]

(2) Subject to any provision to the contrary in the Income Tax Acts, where—

- (a) any royalty or other sum paid in respect of the user of a patent;

is paid wholly out of profits or gains brought into charge to income tax, the person making the payment shall be entitled on making the payment to deduct and retain out of it a sum representing the amount of the income tax thereon.

(3) This section does not apply to any payment to which section 687 applies or to any payment which is a qualifying donation for the purposes of section 25 of the Finance Act 1990.

Note: In sub-section (1), words in square brackets substituted for words in italics, and sub-section (1A) in square brackets inserted by Income Tax (Earnings and Pensions) Act 2003, s 722, Sch 6, Pt 1, paras 1, 50(1)-(3), for the purposes of income tax for the year 2003–04 and subsequent years of assessment, and for the purposes of corporation tax for accounting periods ending after 5 April 2003.

353. General provision

(1) Where a person pays interest in any year of assessment, that person, if he makes a claim to the relief, shall for that year of assessment be entitled (subject to sections 359 to 368) to relief in accordance with this section in respect

of so much (if any) of the amount of that interest as is eligible for relief under this section by virtue of sections 359 to 365.

(1A) Where a person is entitled for any year of assessment to relief under this section in respect of any amount of interest which—

(a) is eligible for that relief by virtue of section 365,

that relief shall consist in an income tax reduction for that year calculated by reference to that amount.

(1B) Where a person is entitled for any year of assessment to relief under this section in respect of any amount of interest which—

(a) is eligible for that relief otherwise than by virtue of section 365,

that relief shall consist (subject to sections 237(5)(b) and 355(4)) in a deduction or set-off of that amount from or against that person's income for that year.

(1E) Where any person is entitled for any year of assessment to relief under this section in respect of any amount of interest which is eligible for that relief partly as mentioned in subsection (1A) above and partly as mentioned in subsection (1B) above, that amount of interest shall be apportioned between the cases to which each of those subsections applies without regard to what parts of the total amount borrowed remain outstanding but according to—

(a) the proportions of the total amount borrowed which were applied for different purposes;

and subsection (1A) or (1B) above shall apply accordingly in relation to the interest apportioned to the case to which that subsection applies.

(1F) Where any person is entitled under this section for any year of assessment to an income tax reduction calculated by reference to an amount of interest, the amount of that person's liability for that year to income tax on his total income shall be the amount to which he would have been liable apart from this section less whichever is the smaller of—

(a) the amount equal to the applicable percentage of that amount of interest; and
(b) the amount which reduces his liability to nil.

(1G) In subsection (1F) above 'the applicable percentage' means 23 per cent.

(1H) In determining for the purposes of subsection (1F) above the amount of income tax to which a person would be liable apart from any income tax reduction under this section, no account shall be taken of—

(a) any income tax reduction under Chapter I of Part VII or section 347B;
(b) any relief by way of a reduction of liability to tax which is given in accordance with any arrangements having effect by virtue of section 788 or by way of a credit under section 790(1); or
(c) any tax at the basic rate on so much of that person's income as is income the income tax of which he is entitled to charge against any other person or to deduct, retain or satisfy out of any payment.

(2) This section does not apply to a payment of relevant loan interest to which section 369 applies.

(3) Relief under this section shall not be given in respect of—

(a) interest on a debt incurred by overdrawing an account or by debiting the account of any person as the holder of a credit card or under similar arrangements; or
(b) where interest is paid at a rate in excess of a reasonable commercial rate, so much of the interest as represents the excess.

359. Loan to buy machinery or plant

(1) Where an individual is a member of a partnership which, under section 264 of the Capital Allowances Act, is entitled to a capital allowance or liable to a balancing charge for any period of account in respect of plant or machinery belonging to the individual, any interest paid by him in that period of account on a loan to defray money applied as capital expenditure on the provision of that plant or machinery is eligible for relief under section 353, except interest falling due and payable more than three years after the end of the period of account in which the debt was incurred.

(2) Where the machinery or plant is in use partly for the purposes of the trade, profession or vocation carried on by the partnership and partly for other purposes, such part only of the interest is eligible for relief under section 353

as is just and reasonable to attribute to the purposes of the trade, profession or vocation, having regard to all the relevant circumstances and, in particular, to the extent of the use for those other purposes.

(3)   Where the holder of an office or employment—

    (a)   is under Part 2 of the Capital Allowances Act entitled to a capital allowance or liable to a balancing charge, (or would be so entitled or liable but for some contribution made by the employer), for any year of assessment in respect of plant or machinery belonging to him and in use for the purposes of the office or employment; and

    (b)   pays interest in that year on a loan to defray money applied as capital expenditure on the provision of that plant or machinery;

the interest so paid is eligible for relief under section 353 unless it is interest falling due and payable more than three years after the end of the year of assessment in which the debt was incurred.

(4)   Where the machinery or plant is in use partly for the purposes of the office or employment and partly for other purposes, such part only of the interest is eligible for relief under section 353 as it is just and reasonable to attribute to the purposes of the office or employment, having regard to all the relevant circumstances and, in particular, to the extent of the use for those other purposes.

360. Loan to buy interest in close company

(1)   Subject to the following provisions of this section and sections 361 to 364, interest is eligible for relief under section 353 if it is interest on a loan to an individual to defray money applied—

    (a)   in acquiring any part of the ordinary share capital of a close company complying with section 13A(2); or

    (b)   in lending money to such a close company which is used wholly and exclusively for the purposes of the business of the company or of any associated company of it which is a close company satisfying any of those conditions; or

    (c)   in paying off another loan interest on which would have been eligible for relief under section 353 had the loan not been paid off (on the assumption, if the loan was free of interest, that it carried interest);

and either the conditions stated in subsection (2) below or those stated in subsection (3) below are satisfied.

(2)   The conditions first referred to in subsection (1) above are—

    (a)   that, when the interest is paid, the company continues to comply with section 13A(2) and the individual has a material interest in the company; and

    (b)   that he shows that in the period from the application of the proceeds of the loan to the payment of the interest he has not recovered any capital from the company, apart from any amount taken into account under section 363(1); and

    (c)   that, if the company exists wholly or mainly for the purpose of holding investments or other property, no property held by the company is used as a residence by the individual;

but the condition in paragraph (c) above shall not apply in a case where the individual has worked for the greater part of his time in the actual management or conduct of the business of the company, or of an associated company of the company.

(3)   The conditions secondly referred to in subsection (1) above are—

    (a)   that, when the interest is paid, the company continues to comply with section 13A(2) and the individual holds any part of the ordinary share capital of the company; and

    (b)   that in the period from the application of the proceeds of the loan to the payment of the interest the individual has worked for the greater part of his time in the actual management or conduct of the company or of an associated company of the company; and

    (c)   that he shows in the period from the application of the proceeds of the loan to the payment of the interest he has not recovered any capital from the company, apart from any amount taken into account under section 363(1).

(3A)   Interest shall not be eligible for relief under section 353 by virtue of paragraph (a) of subsection (1) above in respect of shares acquired on or after 14th March 1989 if at any time the person by whom they are acquired, or that person's husband or wife, makes a claim for relief in respect of them under Chapter III of Part VII or makes a claim in respect of them under Schedule 5B to the 1992 Act.

Part III Taxation

(4)   Subject to section 360A, in this section expressions to which a meaning is assigned by Part XI have that meaning.

360A.   Meaning of 'material interest' in section 360

(1)   For the purposes of section 360(2)(a) an individual shall be treated as having a material interest in a company if he, either on his own or with one or more associates, or if any associate of his with or without such other associates,—

(a)   is the beneficial owner of, or able, directly or through the medium of other companies, or by any other indirect means to control, more than 5 per cent of the ordinary share capital of the company, or

(b)   possesses, or is entitled to acquire, such rights as would, in the event of the winding-up of the company or in any other circumstances, give an entitlement to receive more than 5 per cent of the assets which would then be available for distribution among the participators.

(2)   Subject to the following provisions of this section, in subsection (1) above 'associate', in relation to an individual, means—

(a)   any relative or partner of the individual;

(b)   the trustee or trustees of a settlement in relation to which the individual is, or any relative of his (living or dead) is or was, a settlor ('settlement' and 'settlor' having the same meaning as in Chapter IA of Part XV (see section 660G(1) and (2)); and

(c)   where the individual is interested in any shares or obligations of the company which are subject to any trust, or are part of the estate of a deceased person, the trustee or trustees of the settlement concerned or, as the case may be, the personal representative of the deceased.

(3)   In relation to any loan made after 5th April 1987, there shall be disregarded for the purposes of subsection (2)(c) above—

(a)   the interest of the trustees of an approved profit sharing scheme (within the meaning of section 187) in any shares which are held by them in accordance with the scheme and have not yet been appropriated to an individual; and

(b)   any rights exercisable by those trustees by virtue of that interest.

(4)   In relation to any loan made on or after the day on which the Finance Act 1989 was passed, where the individual has an interest in shares or obligations of the company as a beneficiary of an employee benefit trust, the trustees shall not be regarded as associates of his by reason only of that interest unless subsection (6) below applies in relation to him.

(5)   In subsection (4) above 'employee benefit trust' has the same meaning as in paragraph 7 of Schedule 8, except that in its application for this purpose paragraph 7(5)(b) shall have effect as if it referred to the day on which the Finance Act 1989 was passed instead of to 14th March 1989.

(6)   This subsection applies in relation to an individual if at any time on or after the day on which the Finance Act 1989 was passed—

(a)   the individual, either on his own or with any one or more of his associates, or

(b)   any associate of his, with or without other such associates,

has been the beneficial owner of, or able (directly or through the medium of other companies or by any other indirect means) to control, more than 5 per cent of the ordinary share capital of the company.

(7)   Sub-paragraphs (9) to (12) of paragraph 7 of Schedule 8 shall apply for the purposes of subsection (6) above in relation to an individual as they apply for the purposes of that paragraph in relation to an employee.

(8)   In relation to any loan made before 14th November 1986, where the individual is interested in any shares or obligations of the company which are subject to any trust, or are part of the estate of a deceased person, subsection (2)(c) above shall have effect as if for the reference to the trustee or trustees of the settlement concerned or, as the case may be, the personal representative of the deceased there were substituted a reference to any person (other than the individual) interested in the settlement or estate, but subject to subsection (9) below.

(9)   Subsection (8) above shall not apply so as to make an individual an associate as being entitled or eligible to benefit under a trust—

(a)   if the trust relates exclusively to an exempt approved scheme as defined in section 592, or

(b)   if the trust is exclusively for the benefit of the employees, or the employees and directors, of the company or their dependants (and not wholly or mainly for the benefit of directors or their relatives), and the individual in question is not (and could not as a result of the operation of the trust become), either on his own or with his relatives, the beneficial owner of more than 5 per cent of the ordinary share capital of the company;

and in applying paragraph (b) above any charitable trusts which may arise on the failure or determination of other trusts shall be disregarded.

(10)   In this section 'participator' has the meaning given by section 417(1) and 'relative' means husband or wife, parent or remoter forebear, child or remoter issue or brother or sister.

PART X

LOSS RELIEF AND GROUP RELIEF

362. Loan to buy into partnership

(1)   Subject to sections 363 to 365, interest is eligible for relief under section 353 if it is interest on a loan to an individual to defray money applied—

(a)   in purchasing a share in a partnership; or

(b)   in contributing money to a partnership by way of capital or premium, or in advancing money to a partnership, where the money contributed or advanced is used wholly for the purposes of the trade, profession or vocation carried on by the partnership; or

(c)   in paying off another loan interest on which would have been eligible for relief under that section had the loan not been paid off (on the assumption, if the loan was free of interest, that it carried interest);

and the conditions stated in subsection (2) below are satisfied.

(2)   The conditions referred to in subsection (1) above are—

(a)   that, throughout the period from the application of the proceeds of the loan until the interest was paid, the individual has been a member of the partnership otherwise than—

(i)   as a limited partner in a limited partnership registered under the Limited Partnerships Act 1907, or

(ii)   as a member of an investment LLP; and

(b)   that he shows that in that period he has not recovered any capital from the partnership, apart from any amount taken into account under section 363(1).

363. Provisions supplementary to sections 360 to 362

(1)   If at any time after the application of the proceeds of the loan the individual has recovered any amount of capital from the close company, co-operative, employee-controlled company or partnership without using that amount in repayment of the loan, he shall be treated for the purposes of sections 353, 360, 361 and 362 as if he had at that time repaid that amount out of the loan, so that out of the interest otherwise eligible for relief (or, where section 367(4) applies, out of the proportion so eligible) and payable for any period after that time there shall be deducted an amount equal to interest on the amount of capital so recovered.

(2)   The individual shall be treated as having recovered an amount of capital from the close company, co-operative, employee-controlled company or partnership if—

(a)   he receives consideration of that amount or value for the sale, exchange or assignment of any part of the ordinary share capital of the company or of his share or shares in the co-operative or of his interest in the partnership, or of any consideration of that amount or value by way of repayment of any part of that ordinary share capital or of his share or shares in the co-operative; or

(b)   the close company, co-operative, employee-controlled company or partnership repays that amount of a loan or advance from him or the partnership returns that amount of capital to him; or

(c)   he receives consideration of that amount or value for assigning any debt due to him from the close company, co-operative, employee-controlled company or partnership;

and where a sale or assignment is not a bargain made at arm's length, the sale or assignment shall be deemed to be for a consideration of an amount equal to the market value of what is disposed of.

(3)   In the application of this section to Scotland for the word 'assignment' wherever it occurs there shall be substituted the word 'assignation'.

(4)   Section 360, or, as the case may be, 361(2) or (4) or 362(2) and subsections (1) to (3) above, shall apply to a loan within section 360(1)(c), 361(1)(c) or (3)(b) or 362(1)(c) as if it, and any loan it replaces, were one loan, and so that—

(a)   references to the application of the proceeds of the loan were references to the application of the proceeds of the original loan; and

(b)   any restriction under subsection (1) above which applies to any loan which has been replaced shall apply to the loan which replaces it.

(5)   In this section and sections 361 and 362—

'co-operative' means a common ownership enterprise or a co-operative enterprise as defined in section 2 of the Industrial Common Ownership Act 1976; and

'subsidiary' has the same meaning as for the purposes of section 2 of that Act.

380. Set-off against general income

(1)   Where in any year of assessment any person sustains a loss in any trade, profession, vocation or employment carried on by him either solely or in partnership, he may, by notice given within twelve months from the 31st January next following that year, make a claim for relief from income tax on—

(a)   so much of his income for that year as is equal to the amount of the loss or, where it is less than that amount, the whole of that income; or

(b)   so much of his income for the last preceding year as is equal to that amount or where it is less than that amount, the whole of that income;

but relief shall not be given for the loss or the same part of the loss both under paragraph (a) and under paragraph (b) above.

(2)   Any relief claimed under paragraph (a) of subsection (1) above in respect of any income shall be given in priority to any relief claimed in respect of that income under paragraph (b) of that subsection.

381. Further relief for individuals for losses in early years of trade

(1)   Where an individual carrying on a trade sustains a loss in the trade in—

(a)   the year of assessment in which it is first carried on by him; or

(b)   any of the next three years of assessment;

he may, by notice given on or before the first anniversary of the 31st January next following the year of assessment in which the loss is sustained, make a claim for relief under this section.

(2)   Subject to section 492 and this section, relief shall be given under subsection (1) above from income tax on so much of the claimant's income as is equal to the amount of the loss or, where it is less than that amount, the whole of that income, being income for the three years of assessment last preceding that in which the loss is sustained, taking income for an earlier year before income for a later year.

(3)   Relief shall not be given for the same loss or the same portion of a loss both under subsection (1) above and under any other provision of the Income Tax Acts.

(4)   Relief shall not be given under subsection (1) above in respect of a loss sustained in any period unless the trade was carried on throughout that period on a commercial basis and in such a way that profits in the trade (or, where the carrying on of the trade forms part of a larger undertaking, in the undertaking as a whole) could reasonably be expected to be realised in that period or within a reasonable time thereafter.

(5)   Relief shall not be given under subsection (1) above in respect of a loss sustained by an individual in a trade if—

(a)   at the time when it is first carried on by him he is married to and living with another individual who has previously carried on the trade; and

(b)   the loss is sustained in a year of assessment later than the third year of assessment after that in which the trade was first carried on by the other individual.

(7)   This section applies, with the necessary modifications, in relation to a profession or vocation as it applies in relation to a trade.

382. Provisions supplementary to sections 380 and 381

(3)   Subject to subsection (4) below, for the purposes of sections 380 and 381, the amount of a loss sustained in a trade, profession or vocation shall be computed in like manner and in respect of the same period as the profits arising or accruing from the trade, profession or vocation are computed under the provisions of the Income Tax Acts applicable to Case I or II of Schedule D.

(4)   An amount of a loss which, apart from this subsection, would fall to be included in the computations for two successive years of assessment shall not be included in the computation for the second of those years.

384. Restrictions on right of set-off

(1)   Subject to subsection (2) below, a loss shall not be available for relief under section 380 unless, for the year of assessment in which the loss is claimed to have been sustained, the trade was being carried on on a commercial basis and with a view to the realisation of profits in the trade or, where the carrying on of the trade formed part of a larger undertaking in the undertaking as a whole.

(2)   Subsection (1) above shall not apply to a loss made, by any person in the exercise of functions conferred by or under any enactment (including an enactment contained in a local or private Act).

(3)   Where during a year of assessment there is a change in the manner in which a trade is being carried on, it shall be treated for the purposes of this section as having been carried on throughout the year in the way in which it was being carried on by the end of the year.

(4)   Subject to subsection (5) below, where a trade is (or falls to be treated as being) carried on for a part only of a year of assessment by reason of its being (or falling to be treated as being) set up and commenced, or discontinued, or both, in that year, subsections (1) to (3) above shall have effect in relation to the trade as regards that part of that year as if any reference to the manner of carrying on the trade for or by the end of that year were a reference to the manner of carrying it on for or by the end of that part of that year.

(6)   There shall be disregarded for the purposes of sections 380 and 381 so much of any loss as derives from any allowances made to an individual under Part 2 of the Capital Allowances Act in respect of expenditure incurred on the provision of plant or machinery for leasing in the course of a trade unless—

    (a)   the trade is carried on by him (alone or in partnership) for a continuous period of at least six months in, or beginning or ending in, the year of assessment in which the loss was sustained; and

    (b)   he devotes substantially the whole of his time to carrying it on (alone or in partnership) throughout that year or if it is set up or permanently discontinued (or both) in that year, for a continuous period of at least six months beginning or ending in that year.

(7)   Subsection (6) above shall apply also to expenditure incurred by an individual on the provision for the purposes of a trade carried on by him (alone or in partnership) of an asset which is not to be leased if payments in the nature of royalties or licence fees are to accrue from rights granted by him in connection with that asset.

(8)   Where relief has been given in a case to which subsection (6) above applies it shall be withdrawn by the making of an assessment under Case VI of Schedule D.

(9)   Where at any time a trade is carried on so as to afford a reasonable expectation of profit, it shall be treated for the purposes of subsection (1) above as being carried on at that time with a view to the realisation of profits.

(10) Subsections (1) to (5) and (9) above—

    (a)   apply to professions and vocations as they apply to trades, with references to a commercial basis construed accordingly; and

    (b)   have effect without prejudice to section 397.

(11) Expressions used in subsections (6) to (8) and in Part 2 of the Capital Allowances Act have same meaning in those subsections as in that Part; and those subsections are without prejudice to section 384A.

384A.   Restriction of set-off of allowances against general income

(1)   Relief shall not be given to an individual under sections 380 and 381 by reference to a first-year allowance under Part 2 of the Capital Allowances Act (plant and machinery allowances) in the circumstances specified in

subsection (2) or (4) below.

(2)   The circumstances are that the allowance is in respect of expenditure incurred on the provision of plant or machinery for leasing in the course of a qualifying activity and—

(a)   at the time when the expenditure was incurred, the qualifying activity was carried on by the individual in question in partnership with a company (with or without other partners), or

(b)   a scheme has been effected or arrangements have been made (whether before or after that time) with a view to the qualifying activity being so carried on by that individual.

(3)   For the purposes of subsection (2) above letting a ship on charter shall be regarded as leasing it if, apart from this subsection, it would not be so regarded.

(4)   The circumstances are that the allowance is made in connection with—

(a)   a qualifying activity which at the time when the expenditure was incurred was carried on by the individual in partnership or which has subsequently been carried on by him in partnership or transferred to a person who was connected with him, or

(b)   an asset which after that time has been transferred by the individual to a person who was connected with him or, at a price lower than its market value, to any other person,

and the condition in subsection (5) below is met.

(5)   The condition is that a scheme has been effected or arrangements have been made (whether before or after the time referred to in subsection (4) above) such that the sole or main benefit that might be expected to accrue to the individual from the transaction under which the expenditure was incurred was the obtaining of a reduction in tax liability by means of relief under sections 380 and 381.

(6)   Where relief has been given in circumstances in which subsection (1) applies it shall be withdrawn by the making of an assessment under Case VI of Schedule D.

(7)   Section 839 (how to tell whether persons are connected) applies for the purposes of subsection (4) above.

(8)   Expressions used in this section and in Part 2 of the Capital Allowances Act have the same meaning as in that Part.

385. Carry-forward against subsequent profits

(1)   Where a person has, in any trade, profession or vocation carried on by him either alone or in partnership, sustained a loss (to be computed as mentioned in subsections (3) and (4) of section 382) in respect of which relief has not been wholly given either under section 380 or any provision of the Income Tax Acts—

(a)   he may make a claim requiring that any part of the loss for which relief has not been so given shall be set off for the purposes of income tax against the income of the trade, profession or vocation for subsequent years of assessment; and

(b)   where he makes such a claim, the income from the trade profession or vocation in any subsequent year of assessment shall be treated as reduced by that part of the loss, or by so much of that part as cannot, on that claim, be relieved against such income of an earlier year of assessment.

(4)   Where in any year of assessment relief cannot be given, or cannot be wholly given, in respect of a loss carried forward under this section because the amount of the profits of the trade assessed under Case I of Schedule D for that year is insufficient, any interest or dividends being interest or dividends—

(a)   on investments arising in that year, and

(b)   which would fall to be taken into account as trading receipts in computing the profits of the trade for the purposes of assessment under that Case but for the fact that they have been subjected to tax under other provisions of the Income Tax Acts,

shall be treated for the purposes of the application of this section as if they were profits on which the person carrying on the trade was assessed under that Case in respect of that trade for that year of assessment, and relief shall be given accordingly by repayment or otherwise.

(7)   In so far as relief in respect of any loss has been given to any person under this section, that person shall not be entitled to claim relief in respect of that loss under any other provision of the Income Tax Acts.

386. Carry-forward where business transferred to a company

(1) Where—

    (a)   a business carried on by any individual, or any individuals in partnership, has been transferred to a company in consideration solely or mainly of the allotment of shares in the company to that individual or those individuals; and

    (b)   in the case of any individual to whom, or to whose nominee or nominees, shares have been so allotted, his total income for any year of assessment throughout which he is the beneficial owner of the shares, and throughout which the company carries on the business, includes any income derived by him from the company, whether by way of dividends on those shares or otherwise;

then, subject to subsection (2) below, section 385 (except subsection (5)) shall apply as if the income so derived were profits on which that individual was assessed under Schedule D in respect of that business for that year.

(2) Where under section 385 as applied by subsection (1) above a loss falls to be deducted from or set-off against any income for any year of assessment, the deduction or set-off shall be made in the first place against that part, if any, of the income in respect of which the individual has been, or is liable to be, assessed to tax for that year.

(3) This section, in its application to the year of assessment in which a business is transferred, shall have effect as if, for the reference in subsection (1)(b) to the year of assessment throughout which the individual is the beneficial owner of the shares and the business is carried on by the company, there were substituted a reference to the period from the date of the transfer to the following 5th April.

388. Carry-back of terminal losses

(1) Where a trade, profession or vocation is permanently discontinued in the year 1988-89 or any later year, and any person then carrying it on, either alone or in partnership, has sustained therein a loss to which this section applies ('a terminal loss'), that person may, subject to the provisions of this section and of section 389, make a claim requiring that the amount of the terminal loss shall, as far as may be, be deducted from or set off against the amount of profits on which he has been charged to income tax under Schedule D in respect of the trade, profession or vocation for the year of assessment in which the discontinuance occurs and the three years last proceeding it; and there shall be made all such reductions of assessments or repayments of tax as may be necessary to give effect to the claim.

(2) Relief shall not be given in respect of the same matter both under this section and under some other provision of the Income Tax Acts.

(3) Any relief under this section shall be given as far as possible from the assessment for a later rather than an earlier year.

(4) Where—

    (a)   a claim under this section is made in respect of a terminal loss sustained in a trade, and

    (b)   relief cannot be given, or cannot be wholly given, against the profits of the trade charged to income tax under Schedule D for any year because the amount of those profits is insufficient,

any relevant interest or dividends arising in that year shall be treated for the purposes of the application of this section as if they were profits on which the person carrying on the trade was assessed under Case I of Schedule D in respect of that trade for that year of assessment, and relief shall be given accordingly by repayment or otherwise.

For the purposes of this subsection 'any relevant interest or dividends' means interest or dividends which would fall to be taken into account as trading receipts in computing the profits of the trade for the purpose of assessment under Case I of Schedule D but for the fact that they have been subjected to tax under other provisions of the Income Tax Acts.

(5) The profits on which a person or partnership has been charged to income tax for any year of assessment shall be treated for the purposes of any relief under this section from the assessment for that year as reduced by the amount of those profits applied in making any payment from which income tax was deducted, but was not accounted for because the payment was made out of profits or gains brought into charge to income tax; and the like reduction shall be made in the amount of the terminal loss for which relief may be given under this section from the assessments for earlier years unless the payment was one which, if not made out of profits or gains brought into charge to income tax—

    (a)   could have been assessed to income tax under section 350, and

    (b)   if so assessed, could have been treated as a loss by virtue of section 387.

(6)   The question whether a person has sustained any and, if so, what terminal loss in a trade, profession or vocation shall be determined for the purposes of this section by taking the amounts (if any) of the following, in so far as they have not otherwise been taken into account so as to reduce or relieve any charge to tax—

> (a)   the loss sustained by him in the trade, profession or vocation in the year of assessment in which it is permanently discontinued;
>
> (c)   the loss sustained by him in the trade, profession or vocation in the part of the preceding year of assessment beginning 12 months before the discontinuance;

(7)   For the purposes of paragraphs (a) and (c) of that subsection the amount of a loss shall, subject to the provisions of this section, be computed in the same way as profits under the provisions of the Income Tax Acts applicable to Cases I and II of Schedule D.

393. Losses other than terminal losses

(1)   Where in any accounting period a company carrying on a trade incurs a loss in the trade, the loss shall be set off for the purposes of corporation tax against any trading income from the trade in succeeding accounting periods; and (so long as the company continues to carry on the trade) its trading income from the trade in any succeeding accounting period shall then be treated as reduced by the amount of the loss, or by so much of that amount as cannot, under this subsection or on a claim (if made) under section 393A(1) be relieved against income or profits of an earlier accounting period.

(7)   The amount of a loss incurred in a trade in an accounting period shall be computed for the purposes of this section in the same way as trading income from the trade in that period would have been computed.

(8)   For the purposes of this section 'trading income' means, in relation to any trade, the income which falls or would fall to be included in respect of the trade in the total profits of the company; but where—

> (a)   in an accounting period a company incurs a loss in a trade in respect of which it is within the charge to corporation tax under Case I or V of Schedule D, and
>
> (b)   in any later accounting period to which the loss or any part of it is carried forward under subsection (1) above relief in respect thereof cannot be given, or cannot wholly be given, because the amount of the trading income of the trade is insufficient,

any interest or dividends on investments which would fall to be taken into account as trading receipts in computing that trading income but for the fact that they have been subjected to tax under other provisions shall be treated for the purposes of subsection (1) above as if they were trading income of the trade.

(9)   Where in an accounting period the charges on income paid by a company—

> (a)   exceed the amount of the profits against which they are deductible, and
>
> (b)   include payments made wholly and exclusively for the purposes of a trade carried on by the company,

then, up to the amount of that excess or of those payments, whichever is the less, the charges on income so paid shall in computing a loss for the purposes of subsection (1) above be deductible as if they were trading expenses of the trade.

(10)   In this section references to a company carrying on a trade refer to the company carrying it on so as to be within the charge to corporation tax in respect of it.

393A.   Losses: set off against profits of the same, or an earlier, accounting period

(1)   Subject to section 492(3), where in any accounting period ending on or after 1st April 1991 a company carrying on a trade incurs a loss in the trade, then, subject to subsection (3) below, the company may make a claim requiring that the loss be set off for the purposes of corporation tax against profits (of whatever description)—

> (a)   of that accounting period, and
>
> (b)   if the company was then carrying on the trade and the claim so requires, of preceding accounting periods falling wholly or partly within the period specified in subsection (2) below;

and, subject to that subsection and to any relief for an earlier loss, the profits of any of those accounting periods shall then be treated as reduced by the amount of the loss, or by so much of that amount as cannot be relieved under this subsection against profits of a later accounting period.

(2)   The period referred to in paragraph (b) of subsection (1) above is (subject to subsection (2A) below) the period of twelve months immediately preceding the accounting period in which the loss is incurred; but the amount of the

reduction that may be made under that subsection in the profits of an accounting period falling partly before the beginning of that period shall not exceed a part of those profits proportionate to the part of the accounting period falling within that period.

(2A) This section shall have effect in relation to any loss to which this subsection applies as if, in subsection (2) above, the words 'three years' were substituted for the words 'twelve months'.

(2B) Where a company ceases to carry on a trade at any time, subsection (2A) above applies to the following—

    (a)   the whole of any loss incurred in that trade by that company in an accounting period beginning twelve months or less before that time; and

    (b)   the part of any loss incurred in that trade by that company in an accounting period ending, but not beginning, in that twelve months which is proportionate to the part of that accounting period falling within those twelve months.

(2C) Where—

    (a)   a loss is incurred by a company in a ring fence trade carried on by that company, and

    (b)   the accounting period in which the loss is incurred is an accounting period for which an allowance under section 164 of the Capital Allowances Act (abandonment expenditure incurred before cessation of ring fence trade) is made to that company,

subsection (2A) above applies to so much of the amount of that loss not falling within subsection (2B) above as does not exceed the amount of that allowance.

(3)   Subsection (1) above shall not apply to trades falling within Case V of Schedule D; and a loss incurred in a trade in any accounting period shall not be relieved under that subsection unless—

    (a)   the trade is one carried on in the exercise of functions conferred by or under any enactment (including an enactment contained in a local or private Act), or

    (b)   for that accounting period the trade was being carried on on a commercial basis and with a view to the realisation of gain in the trade or in any larger undertaking of which the trade formed part;

but this subsection is without prejudice to section 397.

(4)   For the purposes of subsection (3) above—

    (a)   where at any time a trade is carried on so as to afford a reasonable expectation of gain, it shall be treated as being carried on at that time with a view to the realisation of gain; and

    (b)   where in an accounting period there is a change in the manner in which a trade is being carried on, it shall be treated as having throughout the accounting period been carried on in the way in which it was being carried on by the end of that period.

(7)   Subject to subsection (7A) below, where a company ceases to carry on a trade, subsection (9) of section 393 shall apply in computing for the purposes of this section a loss in the trade in an accounting period ending with the cessation, or ending at any time in the twelve months immediately preceding the cessation, as it applies in computing a loss in an accounting period for the purposes of subsection (1) of that section.

(7A) For the purposes of this section where—

    (a)   subsection (7) above has effect for computing the loss for any accounting period, and

    (b)   that accounting period is one beginning before the beginning of the twelve months mentioned in that subsection,

the part of that loss that is not the part falling within subsection (2B)(b) above shall be treated as reduced (without any corresponding increase in the part of the loss that does fall within subsection (2B)(b) above) by an amount equal to so much of the aggregate of the charges on income treated as expenses by virtue of subsection (7) above as is proportionate to the part of the accounting period that does not fall within those twelve months.

(8)   Relief shall not be given by virtue of subsection (1)(b) above in respect of a loss incurred in a trade so as to interfere with any relief under section 338 in respect of payments made wholly and exclusively for the purposes of that trade.

(9)   For the purposes of this section—

    (a)   the amount of a loss incurred in a trade in an accounting period shall be computed in the same way as trading income from the trade in that period would have been computed;

(b)   'trading income' means, in relation to any trade, the income which falls or would fall to be included in respect of the trade in the total profits of the company; and

(c)   references to a company carrying on a trade refer to the company carrying it on so as to be within the charge to corporation tax in respect of it.

(10)   A claim under subsection (1) above may only be made within the period of two years immediately following the accounting period in which the loss is incurred or within such further period as the Board may allow.

(11)   In any case where—

(a)   by virtue of section 165 of the Capital Allowances Act (abandonment expenditure within 3 years of ceasing ring fence trade) the qualifying expenditure of the company for the chargeable period related to the cessation of its ring fence trade is treated as increased by any amount, or

(b)   by virtue of section 416 of that Act (expenditure on restoration within 3 years of ceasing to trade) any expenditure is treated as qualifying expenditure incurred by the company on the last day of trading,

then, in relation to any claim under subsection (1) above to the extent that it relates to an increase falling within paragraph (a) above or to expenditure falling within paragraph (b) above, subsection (10) above shall have effect with the substitution of 'five years' for 'two years'.

(12)   In this section 'ring fence trade' has the same meaning as in section 162 of the Capital Allowances Act.

PART XI

CLOSE COMPANIES

414. Close companies

(1)   For the purposes of the Tax acts, a 'close company' is one which is under the control of five or fewer participators, or of participators who are directors, except that the expression does not apply—

(a)   to a company not resident in the United Kingdom;

(b)   to a registered industrial and provident society within the meaning of section 486(12) or to a building society;

(c)   to a company controlled by or on behalf of the Crown, and not otherwise a close company; or

(d)   to a company falling within section 415 or subsection (5) below.

(2)   Subject to section 415 and subsection (5) below, a company resident in the United Kingdom (but not falling within subsection (1)(b) above) is also a close company if five or fewer participators, or participators who are directors, together possess or are entitled to acquire—

(a)   such rights as would, in the event of the winding-up of the company ('the relevant company') on the basis set out in subsection (2A) below, entitle them to receive the greater part of the assets of the relevant company which would then be available for distribution among the participators, or

(b)   such rights as would in that event so entitle them if any rights which any of them or any other person has as a loan creditor (in relation to the relevant company or any other company) were disregarded.

(2A)   In the notional winding-up of the relevant company, the part of the assets available for distribution among the participators which any person is entitled to receive is the aggregate of—

(a)   any part of those assets which he would be entitled to receive in the event of the winding-up of the company, and

(b)   any part of those assets which he would be entitled to receive if—

(i)   any other company which is a participator in the relevant company and is entitled to receive any assets in the notional winding-up were also wound up on the basis set out in this subsection, and

(ii)   the part of the assets of the relevant company to which the other company is entitled were distributed among the participators in the other company in proportion to their respective entitlement to the assets of the other company available for distribution among the participators.

(2B)   In the application of subsection (2A) above to the notional winding-up of the other company and to any further notional winding-up required by paragraph (b) of that subsection (or by any further application of that paragraph), references to the 'the relevant company' shall have effect as references to the company concerned.

(2C) In ascertaining under subsection (2) above whether five or fewer participators, or participators who are directors, together possess or are entitled to acquire rights such as are mentioned in paragraph (a) or (b) of that subsection—

    (a)   a person shall be treated as a participator in or director of the relevant company if he is a participator in or director of any other company which would be entitled to receive assets in the notional winding-up of the relevant company on the basis set out in subsection (2A) above, and

    (b)   except in the application of subsection (2A) above, no account shall be taken of a participator which is a company unless the company possesses or is entitled to acquire the rights in a fiduciary or representative capacity.

(2D) Subsections (4) to (6) of section 416 apply for the purposes of subsections (2) and (2A) above as they apply for the purposes of subsection (2) of that section.

(4)   For the purposes of this section—

    (a)   a company is to be treated as controlled by or on behalf of the Crown if, but only if, it is under the control of the Crown or of persons acting on behalf of the Crown, independently of any other person, and

    (b)   where a company is so controlled, it shall not be treated as being otherwise a close company unless it can be treated as a close company as being under the control of persons acting independently of the Crown.

(5)   A company is not to be treated as a close company—

    (a)   if—

        (i)   it is controlled by a company which is not a close company, or by two or more companies none of which is a close company; and

        (ii)   it cannot be treated as a close company except by taking as one of the five or fewer participators requisite for its being so treated a company which is not a close company;

    (b)   if it cannot be treated as a close company except by virtue of paragraph (a) of subsection (2) above or paragraph (c) of section 416(2) and it would not be a close company if the references in those paragraphs to participators did not include loan creditors who are companies other than close companies.

(6)   References in subsection (5) above to a close company shall be treated as applying to any company which, if resident in the United Kingdom, would be a close company.

(7)   If shares in any company ('the first company') are held on trust for an exempt approved scheme as defined in section 592, then, unless the scheme is established wholly or mainly for the benefit of persons who are, or are dependants of, directors or employees or past directors or employees of—

    (a)   the first company; or

    (b)   an associated company of the first company; or

    (c)   a company which is under the control of any director or associate of a director of the first company or of two or more persons each of whom is such a director or associate; or

    (d)   a close company;

the persons holding the shares shall, for the purposes of subsection (5) above, be deemed to be the beneficial owners of the shares and, in that capacity, to be a company which is not a close company.

416. Meaning of 'associated company' and 'control'

(1)   For the purposes of this Part, a company is to be treated as another's 'associated company' at a given time if, at that time or at any other time within one year previously, one of the two has control of the other, or both are under the control of the same person or persons.

(2)   For the purposes of this Part, a person shall be taken to have control of a company if he exercises, or is able to exercise or is entitled to acquire, direct or indirect control over the company's affairs, and in particular, but without prejudice to the generality of the preceding words, if he possesses or is entitled to acquire—

    (a)   the greater part of the share capital or issued share capital of the company or of the voting power in the company; or

(b)   such part of the issued share capital of the company as would, if the whole of the income of the company were in fact distributed among the participators (without regard to any rights which he or any other person has as a loan creditor), entitle him to receive the greater part of the amount so distributed; or

(c)   such rights as would, in the event of the winding-up of the company or in any other circumstances, entitle him to receive the greater part of the assets of the company which would then be available for distribution among the participators.

(3)   Where two or more persons together satisfy any of the conditions of subsection (2) above, they shall be taken to have control of the company.

(4)   For the purposes of subsection (2) above a person shall be treated as entitled to acquire anything which he is entitled to acquire at a future date, or will at a future date be entitled to acquire.

(5)   For the purposes of subsections (2) and (3) above, there shall be attributed to any person any rights or powers of a nominee for him, that is to say, any rights or powers which another person possesses on his behalf or may be required to exercise on his direction or behalf.

(6)   For the purposes of subsections (2) and (3) above, there may also be attributed to any person all the rights and powers of any company of which he has, or he and associates of his have, control or any two or more such companies, or of any associate of his or of any two or more associates of his, including those attributed to a company or associate under subsection (5) above, but not those attributed to an associate under this subsection; and such attributions shall be made under this subsection as will result in the company being treated as under the control of five or fewer participators if it can be so treated.

417. Meaning of 'participator', 'associate', 'director' and 'loan creditor'

(1)   For the purposes of this Part, a 'participator' is, in relation to any company, a person having a share or interest in the capital or income of the company, and, without prejudice to the generality of the preceding words, includes—

(a)   any person who possesses, or is entitled to acquire, share capital or voting rights in the company;

(b)   any loan creditor of the company;

(c)   any person who possesses, or is entitled to acquire, a right to receive or participate in distributions of the company (construing 'distributions' without regard to section 418) or any amounts payable by the company (in cash or in kind) to loan creditors by way of premium on redemption; and

(d)   any person who is entitled to secure that income or assets (whether present or future) of the company will be applied directly or indirectly for his benefit.

In this subsection references to being entitled to do anything apply where a person is presently entitled to do it at a future date, or will at a future date be entitled to do it.

(2)   The provisions of subsection (1) above are without prejudice to any particular provision of this Part requiring a participator in one company to be treated as being also a participator in another company.

(3)   For the purposes of this Part 'associate' means, in relation to a participator—

(a)   any relative or partner of the participator;

(b)   the trustee or trustees of any settlement in relation to which the participator is, or any relative of his (living or dead) is or was, a settlor ('settlement' and 'settlor' having here the same meaning as in Chapter IA of Part XV (see section 660G(1) and (2)); and

(c)   where the participator is interested in any shares or obligations of the company which are subject to any trust, or are part of the estate of a deceased person—

(i)   the trustee or trustees of the settlement concerned or, as the case may be, the personal representatives of the deceased; and

(ii)   if the participator is a company, any other company interested in those shares or obligations;

and has a corresponding meaning in relation to a person other than a participator.

(4)   In subsection (3) above 'relative' means husband or wife, parent or remoter forebear, child or remoter issue, or brother or sister.

(5)   For the purposes of this Part 'director' includes any person occupying the position of director by whatever name called, any person in accordance with whose directions or instructions the directors are accustomed to act, and any person who—

(a)   is a manager of the company or otherwise concerned in the management of the company's trade or business, and

(b)   is, either on his own or with one or more associates, the beneficial owner of, or able, directly or through the medium of other companies or by any other indirect means, to control 20 per cent or over of the ordinary share capital of the company.

(6)   In subsection (5)(b) above the expression 'either on his own or with one or more associates' requires a person to be treated as owning or, as the case may be, controlling what any associate owns or controls, even if he does not own or control share capital on his own.

(7)   Subject to subsection (9) below, for the purposes of this Part 'loan creditor', in relation to a company, means a creditor in respect of any debt incurred by the company—

(a)   for any money borrowed or capital assets acquired by the company; or

(b)   for any right to receive income created in favour of the company; or

(c)   for consideration the value of which to the company was (at the time when the debt was incurred) substantially less than the amount of the debt (including any premium thereon);

or in respect of any redeemable loan capital issued by the company.

(8)   Subject to subsection (9) below, a person who is not the creditor in respect of any debt or loan capital to which subsection (7) above applies but nevertheless has a beneficial interest therein shall, to the extent of that interest, be treated for the purposes of this Part as a loan creditor in respect of that debt or loan capital.

(9)   A person carrying on a business of banking shall not be deemed to be a loan creditor in respect of any loan capital or debt issued or incurred by the company for money lent by him to the company in the ordinary course of that business.

419. Loans to participators etc

(1)   Subject to the following provisions of this section and section 420, where a close company, otherwise than in the ordinary course of a business carried on by it which includes the lending of money, makes any loan or advances any money to an individual who is a participator in the company or an associate of a participator, there shall be assessed on and recoverable from the company, as if it were an amount of corporation tax chargeable on the company for the accounting period in which the loan or advance is made, an amount equal to 25 per cent of the amount of the loan or advance.

In relation to a loan or advance made in an accounting period ending after the day, not being earlier than 31st March 1992, appointed by order by the Treasury for the purpose of this provision, this subsection shall have effect with the substitution for 'assessed on and recoverable' of 'due'.

(2)   For the purposes of this section the cases in which a close company is to be regarded as making a loan to any person include a case where—

(a)   that person incurs a debt to the close company; or

(b)   a debt due from that person to a third party is assigned to the close company;

and then the close company shall be regarded as making a loan of an amount equal to the debt.

(3)   Tax due by virtue of this section in relation to any loan or advance shall be due and payable in accordance with Section 59D of the Management Act on the day following the expiry of nine months from the end of the accounting period in which the loan or advance was made.

(4)   Where a close company has made a loan or advance which gave rise to a charge to tax on the company under subsection (1) above and

(a)   the loan or advance or any part of it is repaid to the company, or

(b)   the whole or part of the debt in respect of the loan or advance is released or written off,

relief shall be given from that tax, or a proportionate part of it.

Relief under this subsection shall be given on a claim, which must be made within six years from the end of the financial year in which the repayment is made or the release or writing off occurs.

(4A) Where—

(a)   the repayment of the whole or any part of a loan or advance occurs on or after the day on which tax by virtue of this section becomes due in relation to that loan or advance, or

(b)   the release or writing off of the whole or any part of the debt in respect of a loan or advance occurs on or after the day on which tax by virtue of this section becomes due in relation to that loan or advance,

relief in respect of the repayment, release or writing off shall not be given under subsection (4) above at any time before the expiry of nine months from the end of the accounting period in which the repayment, release or writing off occurred.

(4B)   Schedule 1A to the Taxes Management Act 1970 (claims and elections not included in return) applies to a claim for relief under subsection (4) above unless—

(a)   the claim is included (by amendment or otherwise) in the return for the period in which the loan or advance was made, and

(b)   the relief may be given at the time the claim is made.

(5)   Where, under arrangements made by any person otherwise than in the ordinary course of a business carried on by him—

(a)   a close company makes a loan or advance which, apart from this subsection, does not give rise to any charge on the company under subsection (1) above, and

(b)   some person other than the close company makes a payment or transfers property to, or releases or satisfies (in whole or in part) a liability of, an individual who is a participator in the company or an associate of a participator,

then, unless in respect of the matter referred to in paragraph (b) above there falls to be included in the total income of the participator or associate an amount not less than the loan or advance, this section shall apply as if the loan or advance had been made to him.

(6)   In subsection (1) and (5)(b) above the references to an individual shall apply also to a company receiving the loan or advance in a fiduciary or representative capacity.

(7)   For the purposes of this section any participator in a company which controls another company shall be treated as being also a participator in that other company.

420. Exceptions from section 419

(1)   Section 419(2)(a) shall not apply to a debt incurred for the supply by the close company of goods or services in the ordinary course of its trade or business unless the credit given exceeds six months or is longer than that normally given to the company's customers.

(2)   Section 419(1) shall not apply to a loan made to a director or employee of a close company, or of an associated company of the close company, if—

(a)   neither the amount of the loan, nor that amount when taken together with any other outstanding loans which—

(i)   were made by the close company or any of its associated companies to the borrower; and

(ii)   if made before 31st March 1971, were made for the purpose of purchasing a dwelling which was or was to be the borrower's only or main residence;

exceeds £15,000 and the outstanding loans falling within sub-paragraph (ii) above do not together exceed £10,000; and

(b)   the borrower works full-time for the close company or any of its associated companies; and

(c)   the borrower does not have a material interest in the close company or in any associated company of the close company;

but if the borrower acquires such a material interest at a time when the whole or part of any such loan made after 30th March 1971 remains outstanding the close company shall be regarded as making to him at that time a loan of an amount equal to the sum outstanding.

Section 168(11) shall apply for the purpose of determining whether a person has, for the purpose of this subsection, a material interest in a company, but with the omission of the words following '417(3)'.

421. Taxation of borrower when loan under section 419 released etc

(1)   Subject to the following provisions of this section, where a company is assessed or liable to be assessed under section 419 in respect of a loan or advance and releases or writes off the whole or part of the debt in respect of it, then—

(a) for the purpose of computing the total income of the person to whom the loan or advance was made, a sum equal to the amount so released or written off shall be treated as income received by him after deduction of income tax at the Schedule F ordinary rate from a corresponding gross amount;

(b) no repayment of income tax shall be made in respect of that income and no assessment shall be made on him in respect of income tax at the Schedule F ordinary rate on that income;

(c) the income included by virtue of paragraph (a) above in his total income shall be treated (without prejudice to paragraph (b) above) as if it were income to which section 1A applies by virtue of subsection (2)(b) of that section, but notwithstanding the preceding provisions of this subsection, shall be treated for the purposes of sections 348 and 349(1) as not brought into charge to income tax;

(d) for the purpose of determining whether any or what amount of tax is, by virtue of paragraph (a) above, to be taken into account as having been deducted from a gross amount in the case of an individual whose total income is reduced by any deductions so much only of that gross amount shall be taken into account as is part of his total income as so reduced.

(2)   If the loan or advance referred to in subsection (1) above was made to a person who has since died, or to trustees of a trust which has come to an end, this section, instead of applying to the person to whom it was made, shall apply to the person from whom the debt is due at the time of release or writing off (and if it is due from him as personal representative, within the meaning of Part XVI, the amount treated as received by him shall accordingly be included for the purposes of that Part in the aggregate income of the estate) and subsection (1) above shall apply accordingly with the necessary modifications.

(3)   This section shall not have effect in relation to a loan or advance made to a person if any sum falls in respect of the loan or advance to be included in his income by virtue of section 677, except so far as the amounts released or written off exceeds the sums previously falling to be so included (without the addition for income tax provided for by subsection (6) of that section).

(4)   This section shall be construed as one with section 419.

PART XIX

SUPPLEMENTAL

838. Subsidiaries

(1)   For the purposes of the Tax Acts a body corporate shall be deemed to be—

(a) a '51 per cent subsidiary' of another body corporate if and so long as more than 50 per cent of its ordinary share capital is owned directly or indirectly by that other body corporate;

(b) a '75 per cent subsidiary' of another body corporate if and so long as not less than 75 per cent of its ordinary share capital is owned directly or indirectly by that other body corporate;

(c) a '90 per cent subsidiary' of another body corporate if and so long as not less than 90 per cent of its ordinary share capital is owned directly by that other body corporate.

(2)   In subsection (1)(a) and (b) above 'owned directly or indirectly' by a body corporate means owned, whether directly or through another body corporate or other bodies corporate or partly directly and partly through another body corporate or other bodies corporate.

(3)   In this section references to ownership shall be construed as references to beneficial ownership.

(4)   For the purposes of this section the amount of ordinary share capital of one body corporate owned by a second body corporate through another body corporate or other bodies corporate, or partly directly and partly through another body corporate or other bodies corporate, shall be determined in accordance with the following provisions of this section.

(5)   Where, in the case of a number of bodies corporate, the first directly owns ordinary share capital of the second and the second directly owns ordinary share capital of the third, then for the purposes of this section, the first shall be deemed to own ordinary share capital of the third through the second, and, if the third directly owns ordinary share capital of a fourth, the first shall be deemed to own ordinary share capital of the fourth through the second and third, and the second shall be deemed to own ordinary share capital of the fourth through the third and so on.

(6)   In this section—

(a) any number of bodies corporate of which the first directly owns ordinary share capital of the next and the next directly owns ordinary share capital of the next but one, and so on, and, if they are more than three, any three or more of them, are referred to as 'a series';

    (b)   in any series—
        (i)   that body corporate which owns ordinary share capital of another through the remainder is referred to as the 'first owner';
        (ii) that other body corporate the ordinary share capital of which is so owned is referred to as 'the last owned body corporate';
        (iii) the remainder, if one only, is referred to as 'an intermediary' and, if more than one, are referred to as 'a chain of intermediaries';
    (c)   a body corporate in a series which directly owns ordinary share capital of another body corporate in the series is referred to as 'an owner'; and
    (d)   any two bodies corporate in a series of which one owns ordinary share capital of the other directly, and not through one or more of the other bodies corporate in the series, are referred to as being directly related to one another.

(7)   Where every owner in a series owns the whole of the ordinary share capital of the body corporate to which it is directly related, the first owner shall be deemed to own through the intermediary or chain of intermediaries the whole of the ordinary share capital of the last owned body corporate.

(8)   Where one of the owners in a series owns a fraction of the ordinary share capital of the body corporate to which it is directly related, and every other owner in the series owns the whole of the ordinary share capital of the body corporate to which it is directly related, the first owner shall be deemed to own that fraction of the ordinary share capital of the last owned body corporate through the intermediary or chain of intermediaries.

(9)   Where—

    (a)   each of two or more of the owners in a series owns a fraction, and every other owner in the series owns the whole, of the ordinary share capital of the body corporate to which it is directly related; or
    (b)   every owner in a series owns a fraction of the ordinary share capital of the body corporate to which it is directly related;

the first owner shall be deemed to own through the intermediary or chain of intermediaries such fraction of the ordinary share capital of the last owned body corporate as results from the multiplication of those fractions.

(10) Where the first owner in any series owns a fraction of the ordinary share capital of the last owned body corporate in that series through the intermediary or chain of intermediaries in that series, and also owns another fraction or other fractions of the ordinary share capital of the last owned body corporate, either—

    (a)   directly, or
    (b)   through an intermediary or intermediaries which is not a member or are not members of that series, or
    (c)   through a chain or chains of intermediaries of which one or some or all are not members of that series, or
    (d)   in a case where the series consists of more than three bodies corporate, through an intermediary or intermediaries which is a member or are members of the series, or through a chain or chains of intermediaries consisting of some but not all of the bodies corporate of which the chain of intermediaries in the series consists;

then, for the purpose of ascertaining the amount of the ordinary share capital of the last owned body corporate owned by the first owner, all those fractions shall be aggregated and the first owner shall be deemed to own the sum of those fractions.

839. Connected persons

(1)   For the purposes of, and subject to, the provisions of the Tax Acts which apply this section, any question whether a person is connected with another shall be determined in accordance with the following provisions of this section (any provision that one person is connected with another being taken to mean that they are connected with one another).

(2)   A person is connected with an individual if that person is the individual's wife or husband, or is a relative, or the wife or husband of a relative, of the individual or of the individual's wife or husband.

(3)   A person, in his capacity as trustee of a settlement, is connected with—

    (a)   any individual who in relation to the settlement is a settlor,
    (b)   any person who is connected with such an individual, and
    (c)   any body corporate which is connected with that settlement.

In this subsection 'settlement' and 'settlor' have the same meaning as in Chapter IA of Part XV (see section 660G(1) and (2)).

(3A) For the purpose of subsection (3) above a body corporate is connected with a settlement if—

    (a)   it is a close company (or only not a close company because it is not resident in the United Kingdom) and the participators include the trustees of the settlement; or

    (b)   it is controlled (within the meaning of section 840) by a company falling within paragraph (a) above.

(4)   Except in relation to acquisitions or disposals of partnership assets pursuant to bona fide commercial arrangements, a person is connected with any person with whom he is in partnership, and with the wife or husband or relative of any individual with whom he is in partnership.

(5)   A company is connected with another company—

    (a)   if the same person has control of both, or a person has control of one and persons connected with him, or he and persons connected with him, have control of the other; or

    (b)   if a group of two or more persons has control of each company, and the groups either consist of the same persons or could be regarded as consisting of the same persons by treating (in one or more cases) a member of either group as replaced by a person with whom he is connected.

(6)   A company is connected with another person if that person has control of it or if that person and persons connected with him together have control of it.

(7)   Any two or more persons acting together to secure or exercise control of a company shall be treated in relation to that company as connected with one another and with any person acting on the directions of any of them to secure or exercise control of the company.

(8)   In this section—

'company' includes any body corporate or unincorporated association, but does not include a partnership, and this section shall apply in relation to any unit trust scheme as if the scheme were a company and as if the rights of the unit holders were shares in the company;
'control' shall be construed in accordance with section 416; and
'relative' means brother, sister, ancestor or lineal descendant.

840. Meaning of 'control' in certain contexts

(1)   For the purposes of, and subject to, the provisions of the Tax Acts which apply this section, 'control', in relation to a body corporate, means the power of a person to secure—

    (a)   by means of the holding of shares or the possession of voting power in or in relation to that or any other body corporate; or

    (b)   by virtue of any powers conferred by the articles of association or other document regulating that or any other body corporate,

that the affairs of the first-mentioned body corporate are conducted in accordance with the wishes of that person, and, in relation to a partnership, means the right to a share of more than one-half of the assets, or of more than one-half of the income, of the partnership.

Finance Act 1991

72. Deduction of trading losses

(1)   Where under section 380 of the Taxes Act 1988 (set-off of trading losses against general income) a person makes a claim for relief for a year of assessment in respect of an amount ('the trading loss') which is available for relief under that section, he may in the notice by which the claim is made make a claim under this subsection for the relevant amount for the year to be determined.

(2)   The relevant amount for the year is so much of the trading loss as—

    (a)   cannot be set off against the claimant's income for the year, and

    (b)   has not already been taken into account for the purpose of giving relief (under section 380 or this section or otherwise) for any other year.

(3)   Where the claim under subsection (1) above is finally determined, the relevant amount for the year shall be treated for the purposes of capital gains tax as an allowable loss accruing to the claimant in the year; but the preceding provisions of this subsection shall not apply to so much of the relevant amount as exceeds the maximum amount.

(4)   The maximum amount is the amount on which the claimant would be chargeable to capital gains tax for the year, disregarding sections 2A (taper relief) and 3(1) (annual exempt amount) of the Taxation of Chargeable Gains Act 1992 and the effect of this section.

(5)   In ascertaining the maximum amount, no account shall be taken of any event—

    (a)   occurring after the date on which the claim under subsection (1) above is finally determined, and

    (b)   in consequence of which the amount referred to in subsection (4) above is reduced by virtue of any enactment relating to capital gains tax.

(6)   An amount treated as an allowable loss by virtue of this section shall not be allowed as a deduction from chargeable gains accruing to a person in any year of assessment beginning after he has ceased to carry on the trade, profession, vocation or employment in which the relevant trading loss was sustained.

(7)   For the purposes of this section, the claim under subsection (1) above shall not be deemed to be finally determined until the relevant amount for the year can no longer be varied, whether by the Commissioners on appeal or on the order of any court.

(8)   References in sections 382(3), and 385(1) of the Taxes Act 1988 to relief under section 380 of that Act shall be construed as including references to relief under this section.

(9)   This section shall apply in relation to losses sustained in the year 1991–92 and subsequent years of assessment.

Part III Taxation

Taxation of Chargeable Gains Act 1992

PART I

CAPITAL GAINS TAX AND CORPORATION TAX ON CHARGEABLE GAINS

1.   The charge to tax

(1)   Tax shall be charged in accordance with this Act in respect of capital gains, that is to say chargeable gains computed in accordance with this Act and accruing to a person on the disposal of assets.

(2)   Companies shall be chargeable to corporation tax in respect of chargeable gains accruing to them in accordance with section 6 of the Taxes Act and the other provisions of the Corporation Tax Acts.

(3)   Without prejudice to subsection (2), capital gains tax shall be charged for all years of assessment in accordance with the following provisions of this Act.

2.   Persons and gains chargeable to capital gains tax, and allowable losses

(1)   Subject to any exceptions provided by this Act, and without prejudice to sections 10 and 276, a person shall be chargeable to capital gains tax in respect of chargeable gains accruing to him in a year of assessment during any part of which he is resident in the United Kingdom, or during which he is ordinarily resident in the United Kingdom.

(2)   Capital gains tax shall be charged on the total amount of chargeable gains accruing to the person chargeable in the year of assessment, after deducting—

    (a)   any allowable losses accruing to that person in that year of assessment, and

    (b)   so far as they have not been allowed as a deduction from chargeable gains accruing in any previous year of assessment, any allowable losses accruing to that person in any previous year of assessment (not earlier than the year 1965–66).

(3)   Except as provided by section 62, an allowable loss accruing in a year of assessment shall not be allowable as a deduction from chargeable gains accruing in any earlier year of assessment, and relief shall not be given under this Act more than once in respect of any loss or part of a loss, and shall not be given under this Act if and so far as relief has been or may be given in respect of it under the Income Tax Acts.

(4)   Where any amount is treated by virtue of any of sections 77, 86, 87 and 89(2) (read, where applicable, with section 10A) as an amount of chargeable gains accruing to any person in any year of assessment—

    (a)   that amount shall be disregarded for the purposes of subsection (2) above; and

    (b)   the amount on which that person shall be charged to capital gains tax for that year (instead of being the amount given by that subsection) shall be the sum of the amounts specified in subsection (5) below.

(5)   Those amounts are—

    (a)   the amount which after—

        (i)   making any deductions for which subsection (2) provides, and

        (ii)   applying any reduction in respect of taper relief under section 2A,

    is the amount given for the year of assessment by the application of that subsection in accordance with subsection (4)(a) above; and

    (b)   every amount which is treated by virtue of sections 77, 86, 87 and 89(2) (read, where applicable, with section 10A) as an amount of chargeable gains accruing to the person in question in that year.

2A.   Taper relief

(1)   This section applies where, for any year of assessment—

    (a)   there is, in any person's case, an excess of the total amount referred to in subsection (2) of section 2 over the amounts falling to be deducted from that amount in accordance with that subsection; and

    (b)   the excess is or includes an amount representing the whole or a part of any chargeable gain that is eligible for taper relief.

(2)   The amount on which capital gains tax is taken to be charged by virtue of section 2(2) shall be reduced to the amount computed by—

(a)   applying taper relief to so much of every chargeable gain eligible for that relief as is represented in the excess;

(b)   aggregating the results; and

(c)   adding to the aggregate of the results so much of every chargeable gain not eligible for taper relief as is represented in the excess.

(3)   Subject to the following provisions of this Act, a chargeable gain is eligible for taper relief if—

(a)   it is a gain on the disposal of a business asset with a qualifying holding period of at least one year; or

(b)   it is a gain on the disposal of a non-business asset with a qualifying holding period of at least three years.

(4)   Where taper relief falls to be applied to the whole or any part of a gain on the disposal of a business or non-business asset, that relief shall be applied by multiplying the amount of that gain or part of a gain by the percentage given by the table in subsection (5) below for the number of whole years in the qualifying holding period of that asset.

(5)   That table is as follows—

Gains on disposals of business assets		Gains on disposals of non-business assets	
Number of whole years in qualifying holding period	Percentage of gain chargeable	Number of whole years in qualifying holding period	Percentage of gain chargeable
1	50	—	—
2 or more	25	—	—
		3	95
		4	90
		5	85
		6	80
		7	75
		8	70
		9	65
		10 or more	60

(6)   The extent to which the whole or any part of a gain on the disposal of a business or non-business asset is to be treated as represented in the excess mentioned in subsection (1) above shall be determined by treating deductions made in accordance with section 2(2)(a) and (b) as set against chargeable gains in such order as results in the largest reduction under this section of the amount charged to capital gains tax under section 2.

(7)   Schedule A1 shall have effect for the purposes of this section.

(8)   The qualifying holding period of an asset for the purposes of this section is—

(a)   in the case of a business asset, the period after 5th April 1998 for which the asset had been held at the time of its disposal;

(b)   in the case of a non-business asset where—

(i)   the time which, for the purposes of paragraph 2 of Schedule A1, is the time when the asset is taken to have been acquired by the person making the disposal is a time before 17th March 1998, and

(ii)   there is no period which by virtue of paragraph 12 of that Schedule does not count for the purposes of taper relief,

the period mentioned in paragraph (a) plus one year;

(c)   in the case of any other non-business asset, the period mentioned in paragraph (a).

This subsection is subject to paragraph 2(4) of Schedule A1 and paragraph 3 of Schedule 5BA.

3.   Annual exempt amount

(1)   An individual shall not be chargeable to capital gains tax in respect of so much of his taxable amount for any year of assessment as does not exceed the exempt amount for the year.

(2)   Subject to subsection (3) below, the exempt amount for any year of assessment shall be £7,700.

(3)   If the retail prices index for the month of September preceding a year of assessment is higher than it was for the previous September, then, unless Parliament otherwise determines, subsection (2) above shall have effect for that year as if for the amount specified in that subsection as it applied for the previous year (whether by virtue of this subsection or otherwise) there were substituted an amount arrived at by increasing the amount for the previous year by the same percentage as the percentage increase in the retail prices index and, if the result is not a multiple of £100, rounding it up to the nearest amount which is such a multiple.

(4)   The Treasury shall, before each year of assessment, make an order specifying the amount which by virtue of this section is the exempt amount for that year.

(5)   For the purposes of this section an individual's taxable amount for any year of assessment is the amount which, after—

(a)   making every deduction for which section 2(2) provides,
(b)   applying any reduction in respect of taper relief under section 2A, and
(c)   adding any amounts falling to be added by virtue of section 2(5)(b),

is (apart from this section) the amount for that year on which that individual is chargeable to capital gains tax in accordance with section 2.

(5A)   Where, in the case of any individual, the amount of the adjusted net gains for any year of assessment is equal to or less than the exempt amount for that year, no deduction shall be made for that year in respect of—

(a)   any allowable losses carried forward from a previous year; or
(b)   any allowable losses carried back from a subsequent year in which the individual dies.

(5B)   Where, in the case of any individual, the amount of the adjusted net gains for any year of assessment exceeds the exempt amount for the year, the deductions made for that year in respect of allowable losses falling within subsection (5A)(a) or (b) above shall not be greater than the excess.

(5C)   In subsections (5A) and (5B) above the references, in relation to any individual's case, to the adjusted net gains for any year are references to the amount given in his case by—

(a)   taking the amount for that year from which the deductions for which section 2(2)(a) and (b) provides are to be made;
(b)   deducting only the amounts falling to be deducted in accordance with section 2(2)(a); and
(c)   in a year in which any amount falls to be brought into account by virtue of section 2(5)(b), adding whichever is the smaller of the exempt amount for that year and the amount falling to be so brought into account.

(6)   Where in a year of assessment—

(a)   the amount of chargeable gains accruing to an individual does not exceed the exempt amount for the year, and
(b)   the aggregate amount or value of the consideration for all the disposals of assets made by him (other than disposals gains accruing on which are not chargeable gains) does not exceed an amount equal to twice the exempt amount for the year,

a statement to the effect of paragraphs (a) and (b) above shall, unless the inspector otherwise requires, be sufficient compliance with any notice under section 8 of the Management Act requiring the individual to make a return of the chargeable gains accruing to him in that year.

(7)   For the year of assessment in which an individual dies and for the next 2 following years, subsections (1) to (6) above shall apply to his personal representatives as they apply to an individual.

(8)   Schedule 1 shall have effect as respects the application of this section to trustees.

PART V

TRANSFER OF BUSINESS ASSETS

152. Roll-over relief

(1)   If the consideration which a person carrying on a trade obtains for the disposal of, or of his interest in, assets ('the old assets') used, and used only, for the purposes of the trade throughout the period of ownership is applied by him in acquiring other assets, or an interest in other assets ('the new assets') which on the acquisition are taken into use, and used only, for the purposes of the trade, and the old assets and new assets are within the classes of

assets listed in section 155, then the person carrying on the trade shall, on making a claim as respects the consideration which has been so applied, be treated for the purposes of this Act—

(a)   as if the consideration for the disposal of, or of the interest in, the old assets were (if otherwise of a greater amount or value) of such amount as would secure that on the disposal neither a gain nor a loss accrues to him, and

(b)   as if the amount or value of the consideration for the acquisition of, or of the interest in, the new assets were reduced by the excess of the amount or value of the actual consideration for the disposal of, or of the interest in, the old assets over the amount of the consideration which he is treated as receiving under paragraph (a) above,

but neither paragraph (a) nor paragraph (b) above shall affect the treatment for the purposes of this Act of the other party to the transaction involving the old assets, or of the other party to the transaction involving the new assets.

(2)   Where subsection (1)(a) above applies to exclude a gain which, in consequence of Schedule 2, is not all chargeable gain, the amount of the reduction to be made under subsection (1)(b) above shall be the amount of the chargeable gain, and not the whole amount of the gain.

(3)   Subject to subsection (4) below, this section shall only apply if the acquisition of, or of the interest in, the new assets takes place, or an unconditional contract for the acquisition is entered into, in the period beginning 12 months before and ending 3 years after the disposal of, or of the interest in, the old assets, or at such earlier or later time as the Board may by notice allow.

(4)   Where an unconditional contract for the acquisition is so entered into, this section may be applied on a provisional basis without waiting to ascertain whether the new assets, or the interest in the new assets, is acquired in pursuance of the contract, and, when that fact is ascertained, all necessary adjustments shall be made by making or amending assessments or by repayment or discharge of tax, and shall be so made notwithstanding any limitation on the time within which assessments or amendments may be made.

(5)   This section shall not apply unless the acquisition of, or of the interest in, the new assets was made for the purpose of their use in the trade, and not wholly or partly for the purpose of realising a gain from the disposal of, or of the interest in, the new assets.

(6)   If, over the period of ownership or any substantial part of the period of ownership, part of a building or structure is, and part is not, used for the purposes of a trade, this section shall apply as if the part so used, with any land occupied for purposes ancillary to the occupation and use of that part of the building or structure, were a separate asset, and subject to any necessary apportionments of consideration for an acquisition or disposal of, or of an interest in, the building or structure and other land.

(7)   If the old assets were not used for the purposes of the trade throughout the period of ownership this section shall apply as if a part of the asset representing its use for the purposes of the trade having regard to the time and extent to which it was, and was not, used for those purposes, were a separate asset which had been wholly used for the purposes of the trade, and this subsection shall apply in relation to that part subject to any necessary apportionment of consideration for an acquisition or disposal of, or of the interest in, the asset.

(8)   This section shall apply in relation to a person who, either successively or at the same time, carries on 2 or more trades as if both or all of them were a single trade.

(9)   In this section 'period of ownership' does not include any period before 31st March 1982.

(10)   The provisions of this Act fixing the amount of the consideration deemed to be given for the acquisition or disposal of assets shall be applied before this section is applied.

(11)   Without prejudice to section 52(4), where consideration is given for the acquisition or disposal of assets some or part of which are assets in relation to which a claim under this section applies, and some or part of which are not, the consideration shall be apportioned in such manner as is just and reasonable.

153. Assets only partly replaced

(1)   Section 152(1) shall not apply if part only of the amount or value of the consideration for the disposal of, or of the interest in, the old assets is applied as described in that subsection, but if all of the amount or value of the consideration except for a part which is less than the amount of the gain (whether all chargeable gain or not) accruing on the disposal of, or of the interest in, the old assets is so applied, then the person carrying on the trade, on making a claim as respects the consideration which has been so applied, shall be treated for the purposes of this Act—

(a) as if the amount of the gain so accruing were reduced to the amount of the said part (and, if not all chargeable gain, with a proportionate reduction in the amount of the chargeable gain), and

(b) as if the amount or value of the consideration for the acquisition of, or of the interest in, the new assets were reduced by the amount by which the gain is reduced (or as the case may be the amount by which the chargeable gain is proportionately reduced) under paragraph (a) of this subsection,

but neither paragraph (a) nor paragraph (b) above shall affect the treatment for the purposes of this Act of the other party to the transaction involving the old assets, or of the other party to the transaction involving the new assets.

153A. Provisional application of sections 152 and 153

(1) This section applies where a person carrying on a trade who for a consideration disposes of, or of his interest in, any assets ('the old assets') declares, in his return for the chargeable period in which the disposal takes place—

(a) that the whole or any specified part of the consideration will be applied in the acquisition of, or of an interest in, other assets ('the new assets') which on the acquisition will be taken into use, and used only, for the purposes of the trade;

(b) that the acquisition will take place as mentioned in subsection (3) of section 152; and

(c) that the new assets will be within the classes listed in section 155.

(2) Until the declaration ceases to have effect, section 152 or, as the case may be, section 153 shall apply as if the acquisition had taken place and the person had made a claim under that section.

(3) The declaration shall cease to have effect as follows—

(a) if and to the extent that it is withdrawn before the relevant day, or is superseded before that day by a valid claim made under section 152 or 153, on the day on which it is so withdrawn or superseded; and

(b) if and to the extent that it is not so withdrawn or superseded, on the relevant day.

(4) On the declaration ceasing to have effect in whole or in part, all necessary adjustments—

(a) shall be made by making or amending assessments or by repayment or discharge of tax; and

(b) shall be so made notwithstanding any limitation on the time within which assessments or amendments may be made.

(5) In this section 'the relevant day' means—

(a) in relation to capital gains tax, the third anniversary of the 31st January next following the year of assessment in which the disposal of, or of the interest in, the old assets took place;

(b) in relation to corporation tax, the fourth anniversary of the last day of the accounting period in which that disposal took place.

(6) Subsections (6), (8), (10) and (11) of section 152 shall apply for the purposes of this section as they apply for the purposes of that section.

154. New assets which are depreciating assets

(1) Sections 152, 153 and 229 shall have effect subject to the provisions of this section in which—

(a) the 'held-over gain' means the amount by which, under those sections, and apart from the provisions of this section, any chargeable gain on one asset ('asset No. 1') is reduced, with a corresponding reduction of the expenditure allowable in respect of another asset ('asset No. 2'), and

(b) any reference to a gain of any amount being carried forward to any asset is a reference to a reduction of that amount in a chargeable gain coupled with a reduction of the same amount in expenditure allowable in respect of that asset.

(2) If asset No. 2 is a depreciating asset, the held-over gain shall not be carried forward, but the claimant shall be treated as if so much of the chargeable gain on asset No. 1 as is equal to the held-over gain did not accrue until—

(a) the claimant disposes of asset No. 2, or

(b) he ceases to use asset No. 2 for the purposes of a trade carried on by him, or

(c) the expiration of a period of 10 years beginning with the acquisition of asset No. 2,

whichever event comes first.

(3) Where section 229 has effect subject to the provisions of this section, subsection (2)(b) above shall have effect as if it read—

'(b) section 232(3) applies as regards asset No. 2 (whether or not by virtue of section 232(5)), or'.

(4) If, in the circumstances specified in subsection (5) below, the claimant acquires an asset ('asset No. 3') which is not a depreciating asset, and claims under section 152 or 153—

(a) the gain held-over from asset No. 1 shall be carried forward to asset No. 3, and

(b) the claim which applies to asset No. 2 shall be treated as withdrawn (so that subsection (2) above does not apply).

(5) The circumstances are that asset No. 3 is acquired not later than the time when the chargeable gain postponed under subsection (2) above would accrue and, assuming—

(a) that the consideration for asset No. 1 was applied in acquiring asset No. 3, and

(b) that the time between the disposal of asset No. 1 and the acquisition of asset No. 3 was within the time limited by section 152(3),

the whole amount of the postponed gain could be carried forward from asset No. 1 to asset No. 3; and the claim under subsection (4) above shall be accepted as if those assumptions were true.

(6) If part only of the postponed gain could be carried forward from asset No. 1 to asset No. 3, and the claimant so requires, that and the other part of the postponed gain shall be treated as derived from 2 separate assets, so that, on that claim—

(a) subsection (4) above applies to the first-mentioned part, and

(b) the other part remains subject to subsection (2) above.

(7) For the purposes of this section, an asset is a depreciating asset at any time if—

(a) at that time it is a wasting asset, as defined in section 44, or

(b) within the period of 10 years beginning at that time it will become a wasting asset (so defined).

155. Relevant classes of assets

The classes of assets for the purposes of section 152(1) are as follows.

CLASS 1

Assets within Heads A and B below.

Head A

1. Any building or part of a building and any permanent or semi-permanent structure in the nature of a building, occupied (as well as used) only for the purposes of the trade.

2. Any land occupied (as well as used) only for the purposes of the trade.

Head A has effect subject to section 156.

Head B

Fixed plant or machinery which does not from part of a building or of a permanent or semi-permanent structure in the nature of a building.

CLASS 2

Ships aircraft and hovercraft ('hovercraft' having the same meaning as in the Hovercraft Act 1968).

CLASS 3

Satellites, space stations and spacecraft (including launch vehicles).

CLASS 4

Goodwill

CLASS 5

Milk quotas (that is, rights to sell dairy produce without being liable to pay milk levy or to deliver dairy produce without being liable to pay a contribution to milk levy) and potato quotas (that is, rights to produce potatoes without being liable to pay more than the ordinary contribution to the Potato Marketing Board's fund).

CLASS 6

Ewe and suckler cow premium quotas (that is, rights in respect of any ewes or suckler cows to receive payments by way of any subsidy entitlement to which is determined by reference to limits contained in a Community instrument).

CLASS 7

Fish quota (that is, an allocation of quota to catch fish stocks, which derives from the Total Allowable Catches set in pursuance of Article 8(4) of Council Regulation (EEC) No 3760/92 and under annual Council Regulations made in accordance with that Article, or under any replacement Community Instruments.

CLASS 8

Assets within heads A and B below.

Head A

Rights of a member of Lloyd's under a syndicate within the meaning of Chapter III of Part II of the Finance Act 1993.

Head B

An asset which a member of Lloyd's is treated as having acquired by virtue of section 82 of the Finance Act 1999.

156. Assets of Class 1

(1)   This section has effect as respect head A of Class 1 in section 155.

(2)   Head A shall not apply where the trade is a trade—

   (a)   of dealing in or developing land, or
   (b)   of providing services for the occupier of land in which the person carrying on the trade has an estate or interest.

(3)   Where the trade is a trade of dealing in or developing land, but a profit on the sale of any land held for the purposes of the trade would not form part of the trading profits, then, as regards that land, the trade shall be treated for the purposes of subsection (2)(a) above as if it were not a trade of dealing in or developing land.

(4)   Where section 98 of the Taxes Act applies (tied premises: receipts and expenses treated as those of trade), the trader shall be treated, to the extent that the conditions in subsection (1) of that section are met in relation to premises, as occupying as well as using the premises for the purposes of the trade.

156A.   Cessation of trade by limited liability partnership

(1)   Where, immediately before the time of cessation of trade, a member of a limited liability partnership holds an asset, or an interest in an asset, acquired by him for a consideration treated as reduced under section 152 or 153, he shall be treated as if a chargeable gain equal to the amount of the reduction accrued to him immediately before that time.

(2)   Where, as a result of section 154(2), a chargeable gain on the disposal of an asset, or an interest in an asset, by a member of a limited liability partnership has not accrued before the time of cessation of trade, the member shall be treated as if the chargeable gain accrued immediately before that time.

(3)   In this section 'the time of cessation of trade', in relation to a limited liability partnership, means the time when section 59A(1) ceases to apply in relation to the limited liability partnership.

157. Trade carried on by personal company: business assets dealt with by individual

In relation to a case where—

   (a)   the person disposing of, or of his interest in, the old assets and acquiring the new assets, or an interest in them, is an individual, and
   (b)   the trade or trades in question are carried on not by that individual but by a company which, both at the time of the disposal and at the time of the acquisition referred to in paragraph (a) above, is his personal company, that is to say, a company the voting rights in which are exercisable, as to not less than 5 per cent, by him,

any reference in sections 152 to 156 to the person carrying on the trade (or the 2 or more trades) includes a reference to that individual.

158. Activities other than trades, and interpretation

(1)   Sections 152 to 157 shall apply with the necessary modifications—

(a)   in relation to the discharge of the functions of a public authority, and

(b)   in relation to the occupation of woodlands where the woodlands are managed by the occupier on a commercial basis and with a view to the realisation of profits, and

(c)   in relation to a profession, vocation, office or employment, and

(d)   in relation to such of the activities of a body of persons whose activities are carried on otherwise than for profit and are wholly or mainly directed to the protection or promotion of the interests of its members in the carrying on of their trade or profession as are so directed, and

(e)   in relation to the activities of an unincorporated association or other body chargeable to corporation tax, being a body not established for profit whose activities are wholly or mainly carried on otherwise than for profit, but in the case of assets within head A of class 1 only if they are both occupied and used by the body, and in the case of other assets only if they are used by the body,

as they apply in relation to a trade.

(2)   In sections 152 to 157 and this section the expressions 'trade' 'profession', 'vocation', 'office' and 'employment' have the same meanings as in the Income Tax Acts, but not so as to apply the provisions of the Income Tax Acts as to the circumstances in which, on a change in the persons carrying on a trade, a trade is to be regarded as discontinued, or as set up and commenced.

(3)   Sections 152 to 157 and this section shall be construed as one.

162. Roll-over relief on transfer of business

(1)   This section shall apply for the purposes of this Act where a person who is not a company transfers to a company a business as a going concern, together with the whole assets of the business, or together with the whole of those assets other than cash, and the business is so transferred wholly or partly in exchange for shares issued by the company to the person transferring the business.

Any shares so received by the transferor in exchange for the business are referred to below as 'the new assets'.

(2)   The amount determined under subsection (4) below shall be deducted from the aggregate of the chargeable gains less allowable losses ('the amount of the gain on the old assets').

(3)   For the purpose of computing any chargeable gain accruing on the disposal of any new asset—

(a)   the amount determined under subsection (4) below shall be apportioned between the new assets as a whole, and

(b)   the sums allowable as a deduction under section 38(1)(a) shall be reduced by the amount apportioned to the new asset under paragraph (a) above;

and if the shares which comprise the new assets are not all of the same class, the apportionment between the shares under paragraph (a) above shall be in accordance with their market values at the time they were acquired by the transferor.

(4)   The amount referred to in subsections (2) and (3)(a) above shall not exceed the cost of the new assets but, subject to that, it shall be the fraction—

$$\frac{A}{B}$$

of the amount of the gain on the old assets where—

'A' is the cost of the new assets, and

'B' is the value of the whole of the consideration received by the transferor in exchange for the business;

and for the purposes of this subsection 'the cost of the new assets' means any sums which would be allowable as a deduction under section 38(1)(a) if the new assets were disposed of as a whole in circumstances giving rise to a chargeable gain.

(5)   References in this section to the business, in relation to shares or consideration received in exchange for the business, include references to such assets of the business as are referred to in subsection (1) above.

165. Relief for gifts of business assets

(1)   If—

    (a)   an individual ('the transferor') makes a disposal otherwise than under a bargain at arm's length of an asset within subsection (2) below, and

    (b)   a claim for relief under this section is made by the transferor and the person who acquires the asset ('the transferee') or, where the trustees of a settlement are the transferee, by the transferor alone,

then, subject to subsection (3) and sections 166, 167 and 169, subsection (4) below shall apply in relation to the disposal.

(2)   An asset is within this subsection if—

    (a)   it is, or is an interest in, an asset used for the proposes of a trade, profession or vocation carried on by—

        (i)   the transferor, or

        (ii)   his personal company, or

        (iii)   a member of a trading group of which the holding company is his personal company, or

    (b)   it consists of shares or securities of a trading company, or of the holding company of a trading group, where—

        (i)   the shares or securities are not listed on a recognised stock exchange, or

        (ii)   the trading company or holding company is the transferor's personal company.

(3)   Subsection (4) below does not apply in relation to a disposal if—

    (a), (b) ...

    (c)   in the case of a disposal of qualifying corporate bonds, a gain is deemed to accrue by virtue of section 116(10)(b), or

    (d)   subsection (3) of section 260 applies in relation to the disposal (or would apply if a claim for relief were duly made under that section).

(4)   Where a claim for relief is made under this section in respect of a disposal—

    (a)   the amount of any chargeable gain which, apart from this section, would accrue to the transferor on the disposal, and

    (b)   the amount of the consideration for which apart from this section, the transferee would be regarded for the purposes of capital gains tax as having acquired the asset or, as the case may be, the shares or securities,

shall each be reduced by an amount equal to the held-over gain on the disposal.

(5)   Part I of Schedule 7 shall have effect for extending the relief provided for by virtue of subsections (1) to (4) above in the case of agricultural property and for applying it in relation to settled property.

(6)   Subject to Part II of Schedule 7 and subsection (7) below, the reference in subsection (4) above to the held-over gain on a disposal is a reference to the chargeable gain which would have accrued on that disposal apart from subsection (4) above ..., and in subsection (7) below that chargeable gain is referred to as the unrelieved gain on the disposal.

(7)   In any case where—

    (a)   there is actual consideration (as opposed to the consideration equal to the market value which is deemed to be given by virtue of section 17(1) for a disposal in respect of which a claim for relief is made under this section, and

    (b)   that actual consideration exceeds the sums allowable as a deduction under section 38,

the held-over gain on the disposal shall be the amount by which the unrelieved gain on the disposal exceeds the excess referred to in paragraph (b) above.

(8)   Subject to subsection (9) below, in this section and Schedule 7—

[(a) 'personal company', in relation to an individual, means a company the voting rights in which are exercisable, as to not less than 5 per cent, by that individual;

(aa) 'holding company', 'trading company' and 'trading group' have the meanings given by paragraph 22 of Schedule A1; and]

(b) 'trade', 'profession' and 'vocation' have the same meaning as in the Income Tax Acts.

(9) In this section and Schedule 7 and in determining whether a company is a trading company for the purposes of this section and that Schedule, the expression 'trade' shall be taken to include the occupation of woodlands where the woodlands are managed by the occupier on a commercial basis and with a view to the realisation of profits.

(10) Where a disposal after 13th March 1989, in respect of which a claim is made under this section, is (or proves to be) a chargeable transfer for inheritance tax purposes, there shall be allowed as a deduction in computing (for capital gains tax purposes) the chargeable gain accruing to the transferee on the disposal of the asset in question an amount equal to whichever is the lesser of—

(a) the inheritance tax attributable to the value of the asset, and

(b) the amount of the chargeable gain as computed apart from this subsection,

and, in the case of a disposal which, being a potentially exempt transfer, proves to be a chargeable transfer, all necessary adjustments shall be made, whether by the discharge or repayment of capital gains tax or otherwise.

(11) Where an amount of inheritance tax—

(a) falls to be redetermined in consequence of the transferor's death within 7 years of making the chargeable transfer in question, or

(b) is otherwise varied,

after it has been taken into account under subsection (10) above, all necessary adjustments shall be made, whether by the making of an assessment to capital gains tax or by the discharge or repayment of such tax.

PART VI

COMPANIES, OIL, INSURANCE ETC

170. Interpretation of sections 171 to 181

(1) This section has effect for the interpretation of sections 171 to 181 except in so far as the context otherwise requires, and in those sections—

(a) 'profits' means income and chargeable gains, and

(b) 'trade' includes 'vocation', and includes also an office or employment.

Until 6th April 1993 paragraph (b) shall have effect with the addition at the end of the words 'or the occupation of woodlands in any context in which the expression is applied to that in the Income Tax Acts'.

(2) Except as otherwise provided—

(b) subsections (3) to (6) below apply to determine whether companies form a group and, where they do, which is the principal company of the group;

(c) in applying the definition of '75 per cent subsidiary' in section 838 of the Taxes Act any share capital of a registered industrial and provident society shall be treated as ordinary share capital; and

(d) 'group' and 'subsidiary' shall be construed with any necessary modifications where applied to a company incorporated under the law of a country outside the United Kingdom.

(3) Subject to subsections (4) to (6) below—

(a) a company (referred to below and in sections 171 to 181 as the 'principal company of the group') and all its 75 per cent subsidiaries form a group and, if any of those subsidiaries have 75 per cent subsidiaries, the group includes them and their 75 per cent subsidiaries, and so on, but

(b) a group does not include any company (other than the principal company of the group) that is not an effective 51 per cent subsidiary of the principal company of the group.

(4) A company cannot be the principal company of a group if it is itself a 75 per cent subsidiary of another company.

(5) Where a company ('the subsidiary') is a 75 per cent subsidiary of another company but those companies are prevented from being members of the same group by subsection (3)(b) above, the subsidiary may, where the

requirements of subsection (3) above are satisfied, itself be the principal company of another group notwithstanding subsection (4) above unless this subsection enables a further company to be the principal company of a group of which the subsidiary would be a member.

(6)   A company cannot be a member of more than one group; but where, apart from this subsection, a company would be a member of 2 or more groups (the principal company of each group being referred to below as the 'head of a group'), it is a member only of that group, if any, of which it would be a member under one of the following tests (applying earlier tests in preference to later tests)—

    (a)   it is a member of the group it would be a member of if, in applying subsection (3)(b) above, there were left out of account any amount to which a head of a group is or would be beneficially entitled of any profits available for distribution to equity holders of a head of another group or of any assets of a head of another group available for distribution to its equity holders on a winding-up,

    (b)   it is a member of the group the head of which is beneficially entitled to a percentage of profits available for distribution to equity holders of the company that is greater than the percentage of those profits to which any other head of a group is so entitled,

    (c)   it is a member of the group the head of which would be beneficially entitled to a percentage of any assets of the company available for distribution to its equity holders on a winding-up that is greater than the percentage of those assets to which any other head of a group would be so entitled,

    (d)   it is a member of the group the head of which owns directly or indirectly a percentage of the company's ordinary share capital that is greater than the percentage of that capital owned directly or indirectly by any other head of a group (interpreting this paragraph as if it were included in section 838(1)(a) of the Taxes Act).

(7)   For the purposes of this section and sections 171 to 181, a company ('the subsidiary') is an effective 51 per cent subsidiary of another company ('the parent') at any time if and only if—

    (a)   the parent is beneficially entitled to more than 50 per cent of any profits available for distribution to equity holders of the subsidiary; and

    (b)   the parent would be beneficially entitled to more than 50 per cent of any assets of the subsidiary available for distribution to its equity holders on a winding-up.

(8)   Schedule 18 to the Taxes Act (group relief: equity holders and profits or assets available for distribution) shall apply for the purposes of subsections (6) and (7) above as if the references to subsection (7) of section 413 of that Act were references to subsections (6) and (7) above and as if, in paragraph 1(4), the words from 'but' to the end and paragraphs 5(3) and 5B to 5E and 7(1)(b) were omitted.

(9)   For the purposes of this section and sections 171 to 181, references to a company apply only to—

    (a)   a company within the meaning of the Companies Act 1985 or the corresponding enactment in Northern Ireland, and

    (b)   a company (other than a limited liability partnership) which is constituted under any other Act or a Royal Charter or letters patent or is formed under the law of a country or territory outside the United Kingdom, and

    (c)   a registered industrial and provident society within the meaning of section 486 of the Taxes Act; and

  (cc)   an incorporated friendly society within the meaning of the Friendly Societies Act 1992; and

    (d)   a building society.

(10)   For the purposes of this section and sections 171 to 181, a group remains the same group so long as the same company remains the principal company of the group, and if at any time the principal company of a group becomes a member of another group, the first group and the other group shall be regarded as the same, and the question whether or not a company has ceased to be a member of a group shall be determined accordingly.

(11)   For the purposes of this section and sections 171 to 181, the passing of a resolution or the making of an order, or any other act, for the winding-up of a member of a group of companies shall not be regarded as the occasion of that or any other company ceasing to be a member of the group.

(12)   Sections 171 to 181, except in so far as they relate to recovery of tax, shall also have effect in relation to bodies from time to time established by or under any enactment for the carrying on of any industry or part of an industry, or of any undertaking, under national ownership or control as if they were companies within the meaning of those sections, and as if any such bodies charged with related functions (and in particular the Boards and Holding Company established under the Transport Act 1962 and the new authorities within the meaning of the Transport Act 1968 established under that Act of 1968) and subsidiaries of any of them formed a group, and as if also any 2 or more such bodies charged at different times with the same or related functions were members of a group.

(13) Subsection (12) shall have effect subject to any enactment by virtue of which property, rights, liabilities or activities of one such body fall to be treated for corporation tax as those of another, including in particular any such enactment in Chapter VI of Part XII of the Taxes Act.

(14) Sections 171 to 181, except in so far as they relate to recovery of tax, shall also have effect in relation to the Executive for a designated area within the meaning of section 9(1) of the Transport Act 1968 as if that Executive were a company within the meaning of those sections.

PART VIII

SUPPLEMENTAL

281. Payments by instalments of tax on gifts

(1) Subsection (2) below applies where—

    (a) the whole or any part of any assets to which this section applies is disposed of by way of gift or is deemed to be disposed of under section 71(1) or 72(1), and

    (b) the disposal is one—

        (i) to which neither section 165(4) nor section 260(3) applies (or would apply if a claim were duly made), or

        (ii) to which either of those sections does apply but on which the held-over gain (within the meaning of the section applying) is less than the chargeable gain which would have accrued on that disposal apart from that section.

(2) Where this subsection applies, the capital gains tax chargeable on a gain accruing on the disposal may, if the person paying it by notice to the inspector so elects, be paid by 10 equal yearly instalments.

(3) The assets to which this section applies are—

    (a) land or an estate or interest in land,

    (b) any shares or securities of a company which, immediately before the disposal, gave control of the company to the person by whom the disposal was made or deemed to be made, and

    (c) any shares or securities of a company not falling under paragraph (b) above and not listed on a recognised stock exchange nor dealt in on the Unlisted Securities Market.

(4) Where tax is payable by instalments by virtue of this section, the first instalment shall be due on the day on which the tax would be payable apart from this section.

(5) Subject to the following provisions of this section—

    (a) tax payable by instalments by virtue of this section carries interest in accordance with Part IX of the Management Act as that Part applies where no election is made under subsection (2) above, and

    (b) the interest on the unpaid portion of the tax shall be added to each instalment and paid accordingly.

(6) Tax payable by instalments by virtue of this section which is for the time being unpaid, with interest (determined in accordance with subsection (5)(a) above) to the date of payment, may be paid at any time.

(7) Tax which apart from this subsection would be payable by instalments by virtue of this section and which is for the time being unpaid, with interest (determined in accordance with subsection (5)(a) above as if the tax were tax payable by instalments by virtue of this section) to the date of payment, shall become due and payable immediately if—

    (a) the disposal was by way of gift to a person connected with the donor or was deemed to be made under section 71(1) or 72(1), and

    (b) the assets are disposed of for valuable consideration under a subsequent disposal (whether or not the subsequent disposal is made by the person who acquired them under the first disposal).

286. Connected persons: interpretation

(1) Any question whether a person is connected with another shall for the purposes of this Act be determined in accordance with the following subsections of this section (any provision that one person is connected with another being taken to mean that they are connected with one another).

(2) A person is connected with an individual if that person is the individual's husband or wife, or is a relative, or the husband or wife of a relative, of the individual or of the individual's husband or wife.

(3)   A person, in his capacity as trustee of a settlement, is connected with—

    (a)   any individual who in relation to the settlement is a settlor,

    (b)   any person who is connected with such an individual, and

    (c)   any body corporate which is connected with that settlement.

In this subsection 'settlement' and 'settlor' have the same meaning as in Chapter IA of Part XV of the Taxes Act (see section 660G(1) and (2) of that Act).

(3A)   For the purpose of subsection (3) above a body corporate is connected with a settlement if—

    (a)   it is a close company (or only not a close company because it is not resident in the United Kingdom) and the participators include the trustees of the settlement; or

    (b)   it is controlled (within the meaning of section 840 of the Taxes Act) by a company falling within paragraph (a) above.

(4)   Except in relation to acquisitions or disposals of partnership assets pursuant to bona fide commercial arrangements, a person is connected with any person with whom he is in partnership, and with the husband or wife or a relative of any individual with whom he is in partnership.

(5)   A company is connected with another company—

    (a)   if the same person has control of both, or a person has control of one and persons connected with him, or he and persons connected with him, have control of the other, or

    (b)   if a group or of two or more persons has control of each company, and the groups either consist of the same persons or could be regarded as consisting of the same persons by treating (in one or more cases) a member of either group as replaced by a person with whom he is connected.

(6)   A company is connected with another person, if that person has control of it or if that person and persons connected with him together have control of it.

(7)   Any 2 or more persons acting together to secure or exercise control of a company shall be treated in relation to that company as connected with one another and with any person acting on the directions of any of them to secure or exercise control of the company.

(8)   In this section 'relative' means brother, sister, ancestor or lineal descendant.

SCHEDULE A1

APPLICATION OF TAPER RELIEF

Introductory

1.— (1) Section 2A shall be construed subject to and in accordance with this Schedule.

(2)   The different provisions of this Schedule have effect for construing the other provisions of this Schedule, as well as for construing section 2A.

Period for which an asset is held and relevant period of ownership

2.— (1) In relation to any gain on the disposal of a business or non-business asset, the period after 5th April 1998 for which the asset had been held at the time of its disposal is the period which—

    (a)   begins with whichever is the later of 6th April 1998 and the time when the asset disposed of was acquired by the person making the disposal; and

    (b)   ends with the time of the disposal on which the gain accrued.

(2)   Where an asset is disposed of, its relevant period of ownership is whichever is the shorter of—

    (a)   the period after 5th April 1998 for which the asset had been held at the time of its disposal; and

    (b)   the period of ten years ending with that time.

(3)   The following shall be disregarded for determining when a person is to be treated for the purposes of this paragraph as having acquired an asset, that is to say—

    (a)   so much of section 73(1)(b) as treats the asset as acquired at a date before 6th April 1965; and

    (b)   sections 239(2)(b), 257(2)(b) and 259(2)(b).

(4)   Where the period after 5th April 1998 for which an asset had been held at the time of its disposal includes any period which, in accordance with any of paragraphs 10 to 12 below or paragraph 4 of Schedule 5BA, is a period that does not count for the purposes of taper relief—

    (a)   the qualifying holding period of the asset shall be treated for the purposes of section 2A as reduced by the length of the period that does not count or, as the case may be, of the aggregate of the periods that do not count; and

    (b)   the period that does not count or, as the case may be, every such period—

        (i)   shall be left out of account in computing for the purposes of sub-paragraph (2) above the period of ten years ending with the time of the asset's disposal; and

        (ii)   shall be assumed not to be comprised in the asset's relevant period of ownership.

(5)   Sub-paragraphs (1) to (3) above have effect subject to the provisions of paragraphs 13 to 19 below.

Rules for determining whether a gain is a gain on the disposal of a business asset or non-business asset

3.— (1) Subject to the following provisions of this Schedule, a chargeable gain accruing to any person on the disposal of any asset is a gain on the disposal of a business asset if that asset was a business asset throughout its relevant period of ownership.

(2)   Where—

    (a)   a chargeable gain accrues to any person on the disposal of any asset,

    (b)   that gain does not accrue on the disposal of an asset that was a business asset throughout its relevant period of ownership, and

    (c)   that asset has been a business asset throughout one or more periods comprising part of its relevant period of ownership,

a part of that gain shall be taken to be a gain on the disposal of a business asset and, in accordance with sub-paragraph (4) below, the remainder shall be taken to be a gain on the disposal of a non-business asset.

(3)   Subject to the following provisions of this Schedule, where sub-paragraph (2) above applies, the part of the chargeable gain accruing on the disposal of the asset that shall be taken to be a gain on the disposal of a business asset is the part of it that bears the same proportion to the whole of the gain as is borne to the whole of its relevant period of ownership by the aggregate of the periods which—

    (a)   are comprised in its relevant period of ownership, and

    (b)   are periods throughout which the asset is to be taken (after applying paragraphs 8 and 9 below) to have been a business asset.

(4)   So much of any chargeable gain accruing to any person on the disposal of any asset as is not a gain on the disposal of a business asset shall be taken to be a gain on the disposal of a non-business asset.

(5)   Where, by virtue of sub-paragraphs (2) to (4) above, a gain on the disposal of a business asset accrues on the same disposal as a gain on the disposal of a non-business asset—

    (a)   the two gains shall be treated for the purposes of taper relief as separate gains accruing on separate disposals of separate assets; but

    (b)   the periods after 5th April 1998 for which each of the assets shall be taken to have been held at the time of their disposal shall be the same and shall be determined without reference to the length of the periods mentioned in sub-paragraph (3)(a) and (b) above.

Conditions for shares to qualify as business assets

4.— (1) This paragraph applies, in the case of the disposal of any asset, for determining (subject to the following provisions of this Schedule) whether the asset was a business asset at a time before its disposal when it consisted of, or of an interest in, any shares in a company ('the relevant company').

(2)   Where the disposal is made by an individual, the asset was a business asset at that time if at that time the relevant company was a qualifying company by reference to that individual.

(3)   Where the disposal is made by the trustees of a settlement, the asset was a business asset at that time if at that time the relevant company was a qualifying company by reference to the trustees of that settlement.

(4)   Where the disposal is made by an individual's personal representatives, the asset was a business asset at that time if at that time the relevant company was a qualifying company by reference to the personal representatives.

(5)   Where the disposal is made by an individual who acquired the asset as legatee (as defined in section 64) and that time is not a time when the asset was a business asset by virtue of sub-paragraph (2) above, the asset shall be taken to have been a business asset at that time if at that time—

(a)   it was held by the personal representatives of the deceased; and
(b)   the relevant company was a qualifying company by reference to the personal representatives.

Conditions for other assets to qualify as business assets

5.— (1) This paragraph applies, in the case of the disposal of any asset, for determining (subject to the following provisions of this Schedule) whether the asset was a business asset at a time before its disposal when it was neither shares in a company nor an interest in shares in a company.

(2)   Where the disposal is made by an individual, the asset was a business asset at that time if at that time it was being used, wholly or partly, for purposes falling within one or more of the following paragraphs—

(a)   the purposes of a trade carried on at that time by that individual or by a partnership of which that individual was at that time a member;
(b)   the purposes of any trade carried on by a company which at that time was a qualifying company by reference to that individual;
(c)   the purposes of any trade carried on by a company which at that time was a member of a trading group the holding company of which was at that time a qualifying company by reference to that individual;
(d)   the purposes of any office or employment held by that individual with a person carrying on a trade.

(3)   Where the disposal is made by the trustees of a settlement, the asset was a business asset at that time if at that time it was being used, wholly or partly, for purposes falling within one or more of the following paragraphs—

(a)   the purposes of a trade carried on by the trustees of the settlement or by a partnership whose members at that time included—

(i)   the trustees of the settlement; or
(ii)   any one or more of the persons who at that time were the trustees of the settlement (so far as acting in their capacity as such trustees);

(b)   the purposes of a trade carried on at that time by an eligible beneficiary or by a partnership of which an eligible beneficiary was at that time a member;
(c)   the purposes of any trade carried on by a company which at that time was a qualifying company by reference to the trustees of the settlement or an eligible beneficiary;
(d)   the purposes of any trade carried on by a company which at that time was a member of a trading group the holding company of which was at that time a qualifying company by reference to the trustees of the settlement or an eligible beneficiary;
(e)   the purposes of any office or employment held by an eligible beneficiary with a person carrying on a trade.

(4)   Where the disposal is made by an individual's personal representatives, the asset was a business asset at that time if at that time it was being used, wholly or partly, for purposes falling within one or more of the following paragraphs—

(a)   the purposes of a trade carried on by the deceased's personal representatives;
(b)   the purposes of any trade carried on by a company which at that time was a qualifying company by reference to the deceased's personal representatives;
(c)   the purposes of any trade carried on by a company which at that time was a member of a trading group the holding company of which was at that time a qualifying company by reference to the deceased's personal representatives.

(5)   Where the disposal is made by an individual who acquired the asset as legatee (as defined in section 64) and that time is not a time when the asset was a business asset by virtue of sub-paragraph (2) above, the asset shall be taken to have been a business asset at that time if at that time it was—

(a)   being held by the personal representatives of the deceased, and
(b)   being used, wholly or partly, for purposes falling within one or more of paragraphs (a) to (c) of sub-paragraph (4) above.

Companies which are qualifying companies

6.— (1) A company shall be taken to have been a qualifying company by reference to an individual at any time when—

  (a)   the company was a trading company or the holding company of a trading group, and

  (b)   one or more of the following conditions was met—

    (i)   the company was unlisted,

    (ii)   the individual was an officer or employee of the company, or of a company having a relevant connection with it, or

    (iii) the voting rights in the company were exercisable, as to not less than 5%, by the individual.

(1A) A company shall also be taken to have been a qualifying company by reference to an individual at any time when—

  (a)   the company was a non-trading company or the holding company of a non-trading group,

  (b)   the individual was an officer or employee of the company, or of a company having a relevant connection with it, and

  (c)   the individual did not have a material interest in the company or in any company which at that time had control of the company.

(2)   A company shall be taken to have been a qualifying company by reference to the trustees of a settlement at any time when—

  (a)   the company was a trading company or the holding company of a trading group, and

  (b)   one or more of the following conditions was met—

    (i)   the company was unlisted,

    (ii)   an eligible beneficiary was an officer or employee of the company, or of a company having a relevant connection with it, or

    (iii) the voting rights in the company were exercisable, as to not less than 5%, by the trustees.

(2A) A company shall also be taken to have been a qualifying company by reference to the trustees of a settlement at any time when—

  (a)   the company was a non-trading company or the holding company of a non-trading group,

  (b)   an eligible beneficiary was an officer or employee of the company, or of a company having a relevant connection with it, and

  (c)   the trustees of the settlement did not have a material interest in the company or in any company which at that time had control of the company.

(3)   A company shall be taken to have been a qualifying company by reference to an individual's personal representatives at any time when—

  (a)   the company was a trading company or the holding company of a trading group, and

  (b)   one or more of the following conditions was met—

    (i)   the company was unlisted, or

    (ii)   the voting rights in the company were exercisable, as to not less than 5%, by the personal representatives.

(4)   For the purposes of this paragraph an individual shall be regarded as having a material interest in a company if—

  (a)   the individual,

  (b)   the individual together with one or more persons connected with him, or

  (c)   any person connected with the individual, with or without any such persons,

has a material interest in the company.

(5)   For the purposes of this paragraph the trustees of a settlement shall be regarded as having a material interest in a company if—

  (a)   the trustees of the settlement,

  (b)   the trustees of the settlement together with one or more persons connected with them, or

  (c)   any person connected with the trustees of the settlement, with or without any other such persons,

has a material interest in the company.

(6)   In this paragraph, 'company' does not include a unit trust scheme, notwithstanding anything in section 99.

(7)   This paragraph is supplemented by paragraph 6A below (meaning of 'material interest').

Meaning of 'material interest'

6A.— (1) For the purposes of paragraph 6 above, a material interest in a company means possession of, or the ability to control (directly or through the medium of other companies or by any other indirect means),—

(a)   more than 10% of the issued shares in the company of any particular class,

(b)   more than 10% of the voting rights in the company,

(c)   such rights as would, if the whole of the income of the company were distributed among the participators (without regard to any rights of any person as a loan creditor) give an entitlement to receive more than 10% of the amount distributed, or

(d)   such rights as would, in the event of the winding up of the company or in any other circumstances, give an entitlement to receive more than 10% of the assets of the company which would then be available for distribution among the participators.

(2)   For the purposes of sub-paragraph (1) above a right to acquire shares or rights (however arising) shall be treated as a right to control them.

(3)   A person shall be treated for the purposes of this paragraph as having a right to acquire any shares or rights —

(a)   which he is entitled to acquire at a future date, or

(b)   which he will at a future date be entitled to acquire.

(4)   Where—

(a)   in the case of any shares or rights, an entitlement falling within sub-paragraph (3)(a) or (b) above is conferred on a person by a contract, but

(b)   the contract is conditional,

the person shall be treated for the purposes of this paragraph as having a right to acquire the shares or rights as from the time at which the contract is made.

(5)   In any case where—

(a)   the shares of any particular class attributed to a person consist of or include shares which he or another person has a right to acquire, and

(b)   the circumstances are such that if the right were to be exercised the shares acquired would be shares which were previously unissued and which the company is contractually bound to issue in the event of the exercise of the right,

then in determining at any time prior to the exercise of the right whether the number of shares of that class attributed to the person exceeds a particular percentage of the issued shares of that class, the number of issued shares of that class shall be taken to be increased by the number of unissued shares referred to in paragraph (b) above.

(6)   The references in sub-paragraph (5) above to the shares of any particular class attributed to a person are to the shares which in accordance with sub-paragraph (1)(a) above fall to be brought into account in his case to determine whether their number exceeds a particular percentage of the issued shares of the company of that class.

(7)   Sub-paragraphs (5) and (6) above shall apply, with the necessary modifications, in relation to—

(a)   voting rights in the company (and attribution of such rights to a person in accordance with sub-paragraph (1)(b) above),

(b)   rights which would, if the whole of the income of the company were distributed among the participators (without regard to any rights of any person as a loan creditor) give an entitlement to receive any of the amount distributed (and attribution of such rights to a person in accordance with sub-paragraph (1)(c) above), and

(d)   rights which would, in the event of the winding up of the company or in any other circumstances, give an entitlement to receive any of the assets of the company which would then be available for distribution among the participators (and attribution of such rights to a person in accordance with sub-paragraph (1)(d) above),

as they apply in relation to shares of any particular class (and their attribution to a person in accordance with sub-paragraph (1)(a) above).

(8)   For the purposes of this paragraph, 'participator' and 'loan creditor' have the meaning given by section 417 of the Taxes Act.

Persons who are eligible beneficiaries

7.— (1) An eligible beneficiary, in relation to an asset comprised in a settlement and a time, is any individual having at that time a relevant interest in possession under the settlement in either—

(a)   the whole of the settled property; or

(b)   a part of the settled property that is or includes that asset.

(2)   In this paragraph 'relevant interest in possession', in relation to property comprised in a settlement, means any interest in possession under that settlement other than—

(a)   a right under that settlement to receive an annuity; or

(b)   a fixed-term entitlement.

(3)   In sub-paragraph (2) above 'fixed-term entitlement', in relation to property comprised in a settlement, means any interest under that settlement which is limited to a term that is fixed and is not a term at the end of which the person with that interest will become entitled to the property.

Cases where there are non-qualifying beneficiaries

8.— (1) This paragraph applies in the case of a disposal of an asset by the trustees of a settlement where the asset's relevant period of ownership is or includes a period ('a sharing period') throughout which—

(a)   the asset was a business asset by reference to one or more eligible beneficiaries;

(b)   the asset would not otherwise have been a business asset; and

(c)   there is a non-qualifying part of the relevant income, or there would be if there were any relevant income for that period.

(2)   The period throughout which the asset disposed of is to be taken to have been a business asset shall be determined as if the relevant fraction of every sharing period were a period throughout which the asset was not a business asset.

(3)   In sub-paragraph (2) above 'the relevant fraction', in relation to any sharing period, means the fraction which represents the proportion of relevant income for that period which is, or (if there were such income) would be, a non-qualifying part of that income.

(4)   Where a sharing period is a period in which the proportion mentioned in sub-paragraph (3) above has been different at different times, this paragraph shall require a separate relevant fraction to be determined for, and applied to, each part of that period for which there is a different proportion.

(5)   For the purposes of this paragraph the non-qualifying part of any relevant income for any period is so much of that income for that period as is or, as the case may be, would be—

(a)   income to which no eligible beneficiary has any entitlement; or

(b)   income to which a non-qualifying eligible beneficiary has an entitlement.

(6)   In sub-paragraph (5) above 'non-qualifying eligible beneficiary', in relation to a period, means an eligible beneficiary who is not a beneficiary by reference to whom (if he were the only beneficiary) the asset disposed of would be a business asset throughout that period.

(7)   In this paragraph 'relevant income' means income from the part of the settled property comprising the asset disposed of.

Cases where an asset is used at the same time for different purposes

9.— (1) This paragraph applies in the case of a disposal by any person of an asset where the asset's relevant period of ownership is or includes a period ('a mixed-use period') throughout which the asset—

(a)   was a business asset by reference to its use for purposes mentioned in paragraph 5(2) to (5) above; but

(b)   was, at the same time, being put to a non-qualifying use.

(2)   The period throughout which the asset disposed of is to be taken to have been a business asset shall be determined as if the relevant fraction of every mixed-use period were a period throughout which the asset was not a business asset.

(3)   In sub-paragraph (2) above 'the relevant fraction', in relation to any mixed-use period, means the fraction which represents the proportion of the use of the asset during that period that was a non-qualifying use.

(4)   Where both this paragraph and paragraph 8 above apply in relation to the whole or any part of a period—

    (a)   effect shall be given to that paragraph first; and

    (b)   further reductions by virtue of this paragraph in the period for which the asset disposed of is taken to have been a business asset shall be made in respect of only the relevant part of any non-qualifying use.

(5)   In sub-paragraph (4) above the reference to the relevant part of any non-qualifying use is a reference to the proportion of that use which is not a use to which a non-qualifying part of any relevant income is attributable.

(6)   Where a mixed-use period is a period in which—

    (a)   the proportion mentioned in sub-paragraph (3) above has been different at different times, or

    (b)   different attributions have to be made for the purposes of sub-paragraphs (4) and (5) above for different parts of the period,

this paragraph shall require a separate relevant fraction to be determined for, and applied to, each part of the period for which there is a different proportion or attribution.

(7)   In this paragraph—

'non-qualifying use', in relation to an asset, means any use of the asset for purposes which are not purposes in respect of which the asset would fall to be treated as a business asset at the time of its use; and

'non-qualifying part' and 'relevant income' have the same meanings as in paragraph 8 above.

Periods of limited exposure to fluctuations in value not to count

10.— (1) Where, in the case of any asset disposed of ('the relevant asset'), the period after 5th April 1998 for which that asset had been held at the time of its disposal is or includes a period during which—

    (a)   the person making the disposal, or

    (b)   a relevant predecessor of his,

had limited exposure to fluctuations in the value of the asset, the period during which that person or predecessor had that limited exposure shall not count for the purposes of taper relief.

(2)   The times when a person shall be taken for the purposes of this paragraph to have had such limited exposure in the case of the relevant asset shall be all the times while he held that asset when a transaction entered into at any time by him, or by a relevant predecessor of his, had the effect that he—

    (a)   was not exposed, or not exposed to any substantial extent, to the risk of loss from fluctuations in the value of the relevant asset; and

    (b)   was not able to enjoy, or to enjoy to any substantial extent, any opportunities to benefit from such fluctuations.

(3)   The transactions referred to in sub-paragraph (2) above do not include—

    (a)   any insurance policy which the person in question might reasonably have been expected to enter into and which is insurance against the loss of the relevant asset or against damage to it, or against both; or

    (b)   any transaction having effect in relation to fluctuations in the value of the relevant asset so far only as they are fluctuations resulting from fluctuations in the value of foreign currencies.

(4)   In this paragraph 'relevant predecessor'—

    (a)   in relation to a person disposing of an asset, means any person other than the person disposing of it who held that asset at a time falling in the period which is taken to be the whole period for which it had been held at the time of its disposal; and

    (b)   in relation to a relevant predecessor of a person disposing of an asset, means any other relevant predecessor of that person.

(5)   In sub-paragraph (4) above, the reference, in relation to an asset, to the whole period for which it had been held at the time of its disposal is a reference to the period that would be given for that asset by paragraph 2(1) above if, in paragraph (a), the words 'whichever is the later of 6th April 1998 and' were omitted.

Periods of share ownership not to count if company is not active

11A.— (1) Where there is a disposal of an asset consisting of shares in a company, any period after 5th April 1998 during which the asset consisted of shares in a company that—

(a)   was a close company, and

(b)   was not active,

shall not count for the purposes of taper relief.

(2)   Subject to the following provisions of this paragraph, a company is regarded as active at any time when—

(a)   it is carrying on a business of any description,

(b)   it is preparing to carry on a business of any description, or

(c)   it or another person is winding up the affairs of a business of any description that it has ceased to carry on.

(3)   In sub-paragraph (2) above—

(a)   references to a business include a business that is not conducted on a commercial basis or with a view to the realisation of a profit, and

(b)   references to carrying on a business include holding assets and managing them.

(4)   For the purposes of this paragraph a company is not regarded as active by reason only of its doing all or any of the following—

(a)   holding money (in any currency) in cash or on deposit;

(b)   holding other assets whose total value is insignificant;

(c)   holding shares in or debentures of a company that is not active;

(d)   making loans to an associated company or to a participator or an associate of a participator;

(e)   carrying out administrative functions in order to comply with requirements of the Companies Act 1985 or the Companies (Northern Ireland) Order 1986 or other regulatory requirements.

(5)   Notwithstanding anything in sub-paragraphs (2) to (4) above a company shall be treated as active for the purposes of this paragraph if—

(a)   it is the holding company of a group of companies that contains at least one active company, or

(b)   it has a qualifying shareholding in a joint venture company or is the holding company of a group of companies any member of which has a qualifying shareholding in a joint venture company.

(6)   In this paragraph 'associated company' has the meaning given by section 416 of the Taxes Act and 'participator' and 'associate' have the meaning given by section 417 of that Act.

(7)   Any reference in this paragraph to shares in or debentures of a company includes an interest in, or option in respect of, shares in or debentures of a company.

Periods of share ownership not to count in a case of value shifting

12.— (1) This paragraph applies (subject to sub-paragraph (4) below) where—

(a)   there is a disposal of an asset consisting of shares in a close company, and

(b)   at least one relevant shift of value involving that asset has occurred between the relevant time and the time of the disposal.

(2)   So much of the period after 5th April 1998 for which the asset had been held at the time of its disposal as falls before the time, or latest time, in that period at which there was a relevant shift of value involving that asset shall not count for the purposes of taper relief.

(3)   For the purposes of this paragraph a relevant shift of value involving any asset shall be taken to have occurred whenever—

(a)   a person having control of a close company exercised his control of that company so that value passed into that asset out of a relevant holding; or

(b)   effect was given to any other transaction by virtue of which value passed into that asset out of a relevant holding.

(4)   A relevant shift of value involving an asset shall be disregarded for the purposes of this paragraph if—

(a)   that shift of value is one in which the value passing into that asset out of the relevant holding is insignificant; or

(b)   that shift of value took place at a time when the qualifying holding period of the relevant holding was at least as long as the qualifying holding period of that asset.

(5)   In sub-paragraphs (3) and (4) above the references to a relevant holding shall be construed, in relation to any case in which value has passed out of one asset into another asset consisting of shares in a company, as a reference to any holding by—

(a)   the person who, following the exercise of control or other transaction by virtue of which the value has passed, held the other asset, or

(b)   a person connected with him,

of any shares in that company or in a company under the control of the same person or persons as that company.

(6)   For the purposes of sub-paragraph (4)(b) above the reference to the qualifying holding period of a holding or other asset at the time when a shift of value takes place shall be taken to be what, in relation to a disposal at that time of that holding or other asset by the person then entitled to dispose of it, would be taken to have been its qualifying holding period for the purposes of section 2A.

(7)   In this paragraph references to shares in a company include references to rights over a company.

(8)   In this paragraph 'the relevant time', in relation to the disposal of an asset consisting of shares in a company, means the beginning of the period after 5th April 1998 for which that asset had been held at the time of its disposal.

Rules for options

13.— (1) This paragraph applies where by virtue of section 144—

(a)   the grant of an option and the transaction entered into by the grantor in fulfilment of his obligations under the option, or

(b)   the acquisition of an option and the transaction entered into by the person exercising the option,

fall to be treated as one transaction.

(2)   The time of the disposal of any asset disposed of in pursuance of the transaction shall be the time of the following disposal—

(a)   if the option binds the grantor to sell, the disposal made in fulfilment of the grantor's obligations under the option;

(b)   if the option binds the grantor to buy, the disposal made to the grantor in consequence of the exercise of the option.

(3)   The time of the acquisition of any asset acquired in pursuance of the option, or in consequence of its exercise, shall be the time of the exercise of the option.

(4)   Any question whether the asset disposed of or acquired was a business asset at any time shall be determined by reference to the asset to which the option related, and not the option.

Further rules for assets derived from other assets

14.— (1) This paragraph applies if, in a case where—

(a)   assets have merged,

(b)   an asset has divided or otherwise changed its nature, or

(c)   different rights or interests in or over any asset have been created or extinguished at different times,

the value of any asset disposed of is derived (through one or more successive events falling within paragraphs (a) to (c) above but not otherwise) from one or more other assets acquired into the same ownership at a time before the acquisition of the asset disposed of.

(2)   The asset disposed of shall be deemed for the purposes of this Schedule to have been acquired at the earliest time at which any asset from which its value is derived was acquired into the same ownership.

(3)   Any determination of whether the asset disposed of was a business asset at a time when another asset from which its value is derived was in the ownership of the person making the disposal shall be made as if that other asset were the asset disposed of or, as the case may be, were comprised in it.

Special rules for assets transferred between spouses

15.— (1) This paragraph applies where a person ('the transferring spouse') has disposed of any asset to another ('the transferee spouse') by a disposal falling within section 58(1).

(2)   Paragraph 2 above shall have effect in relation to any subsequent disposal of the asset as if the time when the transferee spouse acquired the asset were the time when the transferring spouse acquired it.

(3)   Where for the purposes of paragraph 2 above the transferring spouse would be treated—

(a)   in a case where there has been one or more previous disposals falling within section 58(1), by virtue of sub-paragraph (2) above, or by virtue of that sub-paragraph together with any other provision of this Schedule, or

(b)   in a case where there has not been such a previous disposal, by virtue of such another provision,

as having acquired the asset at a time other than the time when the transferring spouse did acquire it, the reference in that sub-paragraph to the time when the transferring spouse acquired it shall be read as a reference to the time when for the purposes of that paragraph the transferring spouse is treated as having acquired it.

(4)   Where there is a disposal by the transferee spouse, any question whether the asset was a business asset at a time before that disposal shall be determined as if—

(a)   in relation to times when the asset was held by the transferring spouse, references in paragraph 5(2) above to the individual by whom the disposal is made included references to the transferring spouse; and

(b)   the reference in paragraph 5(5) above to the acquisition of the asset as a legatee by the individual by whom the disposal is made included a reference to its acquisition as a legatee by the transferring spouse.

(5)   Where, in the case of any asset, there has been more than one transfer falling within section 58(1) during the period after 5th April 1998 for which the transferee spouse has held it at the time of that spouse's disposal of that asset, sub-paragraph (4) above shall have effect as if a reference, in relation to any time, to the transferring spouse were a reference to the individual who was the transferring spouse in relation to the next disposal falling within section 58(1) to have been made after that time.

Special rules for postponed gains

16.— (1) Sub-paragraph (3) below applies where the whole or any part of any gain which—

(a)   would (but for any provision of this Act) have accrued on the disposal of any asset, or

(b)   would have accrued on any disposal assumed under any enactment to have been made at any time,

falls by virtue of an enactment mentioned in sub-paragraph (2) below to be treated as accruing on or after 6th April 1998 at a time (whether or not the time of a subsequent disposal) which falls after the time of the actual or assumed disposal mentioned in paragraph (a) or (b) above ('the charged disposal').

(2)   Those enactments are—

(a)   section 10A,
(b)   section 116(10),
(c)   section 134,
(d)   section 154(2) or (4),
(e)   Schedule 5B or 5C, or
(f)   paragraph 27 of Schedule 15 to the Finance Act 1996 (qualifying indexed securities).

(3)   In relation to the gain or part of a gain that is treated as accruing after the time of the charged disposal—

(a)   references in this Schedule (except this sub-paragraph) to the disposal on which the gain or part accrues are references to the charged disposal; and

(b)   references in this Schedule to the asset disposed of by that disposal are references to the asset that was or would have been disposed of by the charged disposal;

and, accordingly, the end of the period after 5th April 1998 for which that asset had been held at the time of the disposal on which that gain or part accrues shall be deemed to have been the time of the charged disposal.

(4)   In relation to any gain that is treated by virtue of—

(a)   subsection (1) of section 12, or
(b)   subsection (2) of section 279,

as accruing after the time of the disposal from which it accrues, references in this Schedule to the disposal on which the gain accrues, to the asset disposed of on that disposal and to the time of that disposal shall be construed disregarding that subsection.

(5)   It shall be immaterial for the purposes of this paragraph—

    (a)   that the time of the charged disposal or, as the case may be, the time of the actual disposal from which the gain accrues was before 6th April 1998; and

    (b)   that the time at which the charged disposal is treated as accruing is postponed on more than one occasion under an enactment specified in sub-paragraph (2) above.

Special rule for property settled by a company

17.— (1) No part of any chargeable gain accruing to the trustees of a settlement on the disposal of any asset shall be treated as a gain on the disposal of a business asset if—

    (a)   the settlor is a company, and

    (b)   that company has an interest in the settlement at the time of the disposal.

(2)   Subject to the following provisions of this paragraph, a company which is a settlor in relation to any settlement shall be regarded as having an interest in a settlement if—

    (a)   any property which may at any time be comprised in the settlement, or any derived property is, or will or may become, payable to or applicable for the benefit of that company or an associated company; or

    (b)   that company or an associated company enjoys a benefit deriving directly or indirectly from any property which is comprised in the settlement or any derived property.

(3)   This paragraph does not apply unless the settlor or an associated company is within the charge to corporation tax in respect of chargeable gains for the accounting period in which the chargeable gain accrues.

(5)   For the purposes of this paragraph a company is to be treated as another's associated company at any time if at that time, or at another time within one year previously—

    (a)   one of them has had control of the other; or

    (b)   both have been under the control of the same person or persons.

(6)   In this paragraph 'settlor' has the meaning given by section 660G(1) and (2) of the Taxes Act.

(7)   This paragraph has effect subject to paragraph 20 below.

Special rules for assets acquired in the reconstruction of mutual businesses etc

18.— (1) Where—

    (a)   shares in a company have been issued under any arrangements for the issue of shares in that company in respect of the interests of the members of a mutual company; and

    (b)   a person to whom shares were issued under those arrangements falls by virtue of subsection (2)(a) of section 136 to be treated as having exchanged interests of his as a member of the mutual company for shares issued under those arrangements,

paragraph 2 above shall have effect (notwithstanding that section) as if the time of that person's acquisition of the shares were the time when they were issued to him.

(2)   Where—

    (a)   a registered friendly society has been incorporated under the Friendly Societies Act 1992, and

    (b)   there has been a change under Schedule 4 to that Act as a result of which a member of the registered society, or of a branch of the registered society, has become a member of the incorporated society or of a branch of the incorporated society,

paragraph 2 above shall have effect (notwithstanding anything in section 217B) in relation to the interests and rights in the incorporated society, or the branch of the incorporated society, which that person had immediately after the change, as if the time of their acquisition by him were the time of the change.

(3)   In this paragraph—

'the incorporated society', in relation to the incorporation of a registered friendly society, means the society after incorporation;
'insurance company' means an undertaking carrying on the business of effecting or carrying out contracts of insurance and, for the purposes of this definition, 'contract of insurance' has the meaning given by Article 3(1) of the Financial Services and Markets Act 2000 (Regulated Activities) Order 2001;

'mutual company' means—

> (a)   a mutual insurance company; or
> (b)   a company of another description carrying on a business on a mutual basis;

'mutual insurance company' means any insurance company carrying on a business without having a share capital;

'the registered society', in relation to the incorporation of a registered friendly society, means the society before incorporation.

Special rule for ancillary trust funds

19.— (1) Use of an asset as part of an ancillary trust fund of a member of Lloyd's—

> (a)   shall not be regarded as a use in respect of which the asset is to be treated as a business asset at any time; but
> (b)   shall be disregarded in any determination for the purposes of paragraph 9 above of whether it was being put to a non-qualifying use at the same time as it was being used for purposes mentioned in paragraph 5(2) to (5) above.

(2)   In this section 'ancillary trust fund' has the same meaning as in Chapter III of Part II of the Finance Act 1993.

General rules for settlements

20.— (1) Where, in the case of any settlement, the settled property originates from more than one settlor, this Schedule shall have effect as if there were a separate and distinct settlement for the property originating from each settlor, and references in this Schedule to an eligible beneficiary shall be construed accordingly.

(2)   Subsections (1) to (5) of section 79 apply for the purposes of this paragraph as they apply for the purposes of that section.

General rule for apportionments under this Schedule

21.— Where any apportionment falls to be made for the purposes of this Schedule it shall be made—

> (a)   on a just and reasonable basis; and
> (b)   on the assumption that an amount falling to be apportioned by reference to any period arose or accrued at the same rate throughout the period over which it falls to be treated as having arisen or accrued.

Interpretation of Schedule

22.— (1) In this Schedule—

'51 per cent. subsidiary' has the meaning given by section 838 of the Taxes Act;
'commercial association of companies' means a company together with such of its associated companies (within the meaning of section 416 of the Taxes Act) as carry on businesses which are of such a nature that the businesses of the company and the associated companies, taken together, may be reasonably considered to make up a single composite undertaking;
'eligible beneficiary' shall be construed in accordance with paragraphs 7 and 20 above;
'group of companies' means a company which has one or more 51 per cent subsidiaries, together with those subsidiaries;
'holding company' means a company that has one or more 51 per cent subsidiaries;
'interest in shares' means an interest as a co-owner (whether the shares are owned jointly or in common, and whether or not the interests of the co-owners are equal), and 'interest in debentures', in relation to any debentures, has a corresponding meaning;
'joint venture company' has the meaning given by paragraph 23(2) below;
'non-trading company' means a company which is not a trading company;
'non-trading group' means a group of trading companies which is not a trading group;
'office' and 'employment' have the same meanings as in the Income Tax Acts;
'ordinary share capital' has the meaning given by section 832(1) of the Taxes Act;
'qualifying company' shall be construed in accordance with paragraph 6 above;
'qualifying shareholding', in relation to a joint venture company, has the meaning given by paragraph 23(3) below;
'relevant period of ownership' shall be construed in accordance with paragraph 2 above;
'shares', in relation to a company, includes—

> (a)   any securities of that company, and

      (b)   any debentures of that company that are deemed, by virtue of section 251(6), to be securities for the purposes of that section;

'trade' means (subject to section 241(3)) anything which—

      (a)   is a trade, profession or vocation, within the meaning of the Income Tax Acts; and
      (b)   is conducted on a commercial basis and with a view to the realisation of profits;

'trading company' has the meaning given by paragraph 22A below;

'trading group' has the meaning given by paragraph 22B below;

'transaction' includes any agreement, arrangement or understanding, whether or not legally enforceable, and a series of transactions.

'unlisted company' means a company—

      (a)   none of whose shares is listed on a recognised stock exchange, and
      (b)   which is not a 51 per cent subsidiary of a company whose shares, or any class of whose shares, is so listed;

(2)   For the purposes of this Schedule one company has a relevant connection with another company at any time when they are both members of the same group of companies or of the same commercial association of companies.

(3)   References in this Schedule to the acquisition of an asset that was provided, rather than acquired, by the person disposing of it are references to its provision.

(4)   References in this Schedule, in relation to a part disposal, to the asset disposed of are references to the asset of which there is a part disposal.

Meaning of 'trading company'

22A.— (1) In this Schedule 'trading company' means a company carrying on trading activities whose activities do not include to a substantial extent activities other than trading activities.

(2)   For the purposes of sub-paragraph (1) above 'trading activities' means activities carried on by the company—

      (a)   in the course of, or for the purposes of, a trade being carried on by it,
      (b)   for the purposes of a trade that it is preparing to carry on,
      (c)   with a view to its acquiring or starting to carry on a trade, or
      (d)   with a view to its acquiring a significant interest in the share capital of another company that—

            (i)   is a trading company or the holding company of a trading group, and
            (ii)   if the acquiring company is a member of a group of companies, is not a member of that group.

(3)   Activities do not qualify as trading activities under sub-paragraph (2)(c) or (d) above unless the acquisition is made, or (as the case may be) the company starts to carry on the trade, as soon as is reasonably practicable in the circumstances.

(4)   The reference in sub-paragraph (2)(d) above to the acquisition of a significant interest in the share capital of another company is to an acquisition of ordinary share capital in the other company—

      (a)   such as would make that company a 51 per cent subsidiary of the acquiring company, or
      (b)   such as would give the acquiring company a qualifying shareholding in a joint venture company without making the two companies members of the same group of companies.

Meaning of 'trading group'

22B.— (1) In this Schedule 'trading group' means a group of companies—

      (a)   one or more of whose members carry on trading activities, and
      (b)   the activities of whose members, taken together, do not include to a substantial extent activities other than trading activities.

(2)   For the purposes of sub-paragraph (1) above 'trading activities' means activities carried on by a member of the group—

      (a)   in the course of, or for the purposes of, a trade being carried on by any member of the group,
      (b)   for the purposes of a trade that any member of the group is preparing to carry on,
      (c)   with a view to any member of the group acquiring or starting to carry on a trade, or

(d)   with a view to any member of the group acquiring a significant interest in the share capital of another company that—

   (i)   is a trading company or the holding company of a trading group, and
   (ii)   is not a member of the same group of companies as the acquiring company.

(3)   Activities do not qualify as trading activities under sub-paragraph (2)(c) or (d) above unless the acquisition is made, or (as the case may be) the group member in question starts to carry on the trade, as soon as is reasonably practicable in the circumstances.

(4)   The reference in sub-paragraph (2)(d) above to the acquisition of a significant interest in the share capital of another company is to an acquisition of ordinary share capital in the other company—

(a)   such as would make that company a member of the same group of companies as the acquiring company, or

(b)   such as would give the acquiring company a qualifying shareholding in a joint venture company without making the joint venture companies a member of the same group of companies as the acquiring company.

(5)   For the purposes of this paragraph the activities of the members of the group shall be treated as one business (with the result that activities are disregarded to the extent that they are intra-group activities).

Qualifying shareholdings in joint venture companies

23.— (1) This Schedule has effect subject to the following provisions where a company ('the investing company') has a qualifying shareholding in a joint venture company.

(2)   For the purposes of this Schedule a company is a 'joint venture company' if, and only if—

(a)   it is a trading company or the holding company of a trading group, and
(b)   75% or more of its ordinary share capital (in aggregate) is held by not more than five persons.

For the purposes of paragraph (b) above the shareholdings of members of a group of companies shall be treated as held by a single company.

(3)   For the purposes of this Schedule a company has a 'qualifying shareholding' in a joint venture company if —

(a)   it holds 10% or more of the ordinary share capital of the joint venture company, or
(b)   it is a member of a group of companies, it holds ordinary share capital of the joint venture company and the members of the group between them hold 10% or more of that share capital.

(4)   For the purpose of determining whether the investing company is a trading company—

(a)   any holding by it of shares in the joint venture company shall be disregarded, and
(b)   it shall be treated as carrying on an appropriate proportion—

   (i)   of the activities of the joint venture company, or
   (ii)   where the joint venture company is the holding company of a trading group, of the activities of that group.

(6)   For the purpose of determining whether a group of companies is a trading group—

(a)   every holding of shares in the joint venture company by a member of the group having a qualifying shareholding in that company shall be disregarded, and
(b)   each member of the group having such a qualifying shareholding shall be treated as carrying on an appropriate proportion of the activities—

   (i)   of the joint venture company, or
   (ii)   where the joint venture company is the holding company of a trading group, of that group.

This sub-paragraph does not apply if the joint venture company is a member of the group.

(7)   In sub-paragraphs (4)(b) and (6)(b) above 'an appropriate proportion' means a proportion corresponding to the percentage of the ordinary share capital of the joint venture company held by the investing company or, as the case may be, by the group member concerned.

(7A) For the purposes of this paragraph the activities of a joint venture company that is a holding company and its 51 per cent subsidiaries shall be treated as a single business (so that activities are disregarded to the extent that they are intra-group activities).

Joint enterprise companies: relevant connection

24.— (1) This Schedule has effect subject to sub-paragraph (5) below in any case where a company ('the investing company') has a qualifying shareholding in a joint enterprise company.

(2)   For the purposes of this paragraph, a company is 'joint enterprise company' if, and only if, 75% or more of its ordinary share capital (in aggregate) is held by not more than five persons.

(3)   For the purposes of sub-paragraph (2) above the shareholdings of members of a group of companies shall be treated as held by a single company.

(4)   For the purposes of this paragraph a company has a 'qualifying shareholding' in a joint enterprise company if—

    (a)   it holds 10% or more of the ordinary share capital of the joint enterprise company, or

    (b)   it is a member of a group of companies, it holds ordinary share capital of the joint enterprise company and the members of the group between them hold 10% or more of that share capital.

(5)   The following shall be treated as having a relevant connection with each other—

    (a)   the investing company;

    (b)   the joint enterprise company;

    (c)   any company having a relevant connection with the investing company;

    (d)   any company having a relevant connection with the joint enterprise company by virtue of being—

        (i)   a 51 per cent subsidiary of that company, or

        (ii)   a member of the same commercial association of companies.

SCHEDULE 7

RELIEF FOR GIFTS OF BUSINESS ASSETS

PART I

AGRICULTURAL PROPERTY AND SETTLED PROPERTY

Agricultural property

1.— (1) This paragraph applies where—

    (a)   there is a disposal of an asset which is, or is an interest in, agricultural property within the meaning of Chapter II of Part V of the Inheritance Tax Act 1984 (inheritance tax relief for agricultural property), and

    (b)   apart from this paragraph, the disposal would not fall within section 165(1) by reason only that the agricultural property is not used for the purposes of a trade carried on as mentioned in section 165(2)(a).

(2)   Where this paragraph applies, section 165(1) shall apply in relation to the disposal if the circumstances are such that a reduction in respect of the asset—

    (a)   is made under Chapter II of Part V of the Inheritance Tax Act 1984 in relation to a chargeable transfer taking place on the occasion of the disposal, or

    (b)   would be so made if there were a chargeable transfer on that occasion, or

    (c)   would be so made but for section 124A of that Act (assuming, where there is no chargeable transfer on that occasion, that there were).

Settled property

2.— (1) If—

    (a)   the trustees of a settlement make a disposal otherwise than under a bargain at arm's length of an asset within sub-paragraph (2) below, and

(b)   a claim for relief under section 165 is made by the trustees and the person who acquires the asset ('the transferee') or, where the trustees of a settlement are also the transferee, by the trustees making the disposal alone,

then, subject to sections 165(3), 166, 167 and 169, section 165(4) shall apply in relation to the disposal.

(2)   An asset is within this sub-paragraph if—

(a)   it is, or is an interest in, an asset used for the purposes of a trade, profession or vocation carried on by—

(i)   the trustees making the disposal, or

(ii)   a beneficiary who had an interest in possession in the settled property immediately before the disposal, or

(b)   it consists of shares or securities of a trading company, or of the holding company of a trading group, where—

(i)   the shares or securities are not listed on a recognised stock exchange, or

(ii)   not less than 25 per cent of the voting rights exercisable by shareholders of the company in general meeting are exercisable by the trustees at the time of the disposal.

(3)   Where section 165(4) applies by virtue of this paragraph, references to the trustees shall be substituted for the references in section 165(4)(a) to the transferor; and where it applies in relation to a disposal which is deemed to occur by virtue of section 71(1) or 72(1) section 165(7) shall not apply.

3.— (1) This paragraph applies where—

(a)   there is a disposal of an asset which is, or is an interest in, agricultural property within the meaning of Chapter II of Part V of the Inheritance Tax Act 1984, and

(b)   apart from this paragraph, the disposal would not fall within paragraph 2(1)(a) above by reason only that the agricultural property is not used for the purposes of a trade as mentioned in paragraph 2(2)(a) above.

(2)   Where this paragraph applies paragraph 2(1) above shall apply in relation to the disposal if the circumstances are such that a reduction in respect of the asset—

(a)   is made under Chapter II of Part V of the Inheritance Tax Act 1984 in relation to a chargeable transfer taking place on the occasion of the disposal, or

(b)   would be so made if there were a chargeable transfer on that occasion, or

(c)   would be so made but for section 124A of that Act (assuming, where there is no chargeable transfer on that occasion, that there were).

PART II

REDUCTIONS IN HELD-OVER GAIN

Application and interpretation

4.— (1) The provisions of this Part of this Schedule apply in cases where a claim for relief is made under section 165.

(2)   In this Part of this Schedule—

(a)   'the principal provision' means section 165(2), or, as the case may require, sub-paragraph (2) of paragraph 2 above,

(b)   'shares' includes securities,

(c)   'the transferor' has the same meaning as in section 165 except that, in a case where paragraph 2 above applies, it refers to the trustees mentioned in that paragraph, and

(d)   'unrelieved gain', in relation to a disposal, has the same meaning as in section 165(7).

(3)   In this Part of this Schedule—

(a)   any reference to a disposal of an asset is a reference to a disposal which falls within subsection (1) of section 165 by virtue of subsection (2)(a) of that section or, as the case may be, falls within sub-paragraph (1) of paragraph 2 above by virtue of sub-paragraph (2)(a) of that paragraph, and

(b)   any reference to a disposal of shares is a reference to a disposal which falls within subsection (1) of section 165 by virtue of subsection (2)(b) of that section or, as the case may be, falls within sub-paragraph (1) of paragraph 2 above by virtue of sub-paragraph (2)(b) of that paragraph.

(4)   In relation to a disposal of an asset or of shares, any reference in the following provisions of this Part of this Schedule to the held-over gain is a reference to the held-over gain on that disposal as determined under subsection (6) or, where it applies, subsection (7) of section 165.

Reductions peculiar to disposals of assets

5.— (1) If, in the case of a disposal of an asset, the asset was not used for the purposes of the trade, profession or vocation referred to in paragraph (a) of the principal provision throughout the period of its ownership by the transferor, the amount of the held-over gain shall be reduced by multiplying it by the fraction—

$$\frac{A}{B}$$

where—

A is the number of days in that period of ownership during which the asset was so used, and
B is the number of days in that period.

(2)   This paragraph shall not apply where the circumstances are such that a reduction in respect of the asset—

   (a)   is made under Chapter II of Part V of the Inheritance Tax Act 1984 in relation to a chargeable transfer taking place on the occasion of the disposal, or
   (b)   would be so made if there were a chargeable transfer on that occasion, or
   (c)   would be so made but for section 124A of that Act (assuming, where there is no chargeable transfer on that occasion, that there were).

6.— (1) If, in the case of a disposal of an asset, the asset is a building or structure and, over the period of its ownership by the transferor or any substantial part of that period, part of the building or structure was, and part was not, used for the purposes of the trade, profession or vocation referred to in paragraph (a) of the principal provision, there shall be determined the fraction of the unrelieved gain on the disposal which it is just and reasonable to apportion to the part of the asset which was so used, and the amount of the held-over gain (as reduced, if appropriate, under paragraph 5 above) shall be reduced by multiplying it by that fraction.

(2)   This paragraph shall not apply where the circumstances are such that a reduction in respect of the asset—

   (a)   is made under Chapter II of Part V of the Inheritance Tax Act 1984 in relation to a chargeable transfer taking place on the occasion of the disposal, or
   (b)   would be so made if there were a chargeable transfer on that occasion, or
   (c)   would be so made but for section 124A of that Act (assuming, where there is no chargeable transfer on that occasion, that there were).

Reduction peculiar to disposal of shares

7.— (1) If in the case of a disposal of shares assets which are not business assets are included in the chargeable assets of the company whose shares are disposed of, or, where that company is the holding company of a trading group, in the group's chargeable assets, and either—

   (a)   at any time within the period of 12 months before the disposal not less than 25 per cent of the voting rights exercisable by shareholders of the company in general meeting are exercisable by the transferor, or
   (b)   the transferor is an individual and, at any time within that period, the company is his personal company,

the amount of the held-over gain shall be reduced by multiplying it by the fraction—

$$\frac{A}{B}$$

where—

A is the market value on the date of the disposal of those chargeable assets of the company or of the group which are business assets, and
B is the market value on that date of all the chargeable assets of the company, or as the case may be of

the group.

(2)   For the purposes of this paragraph—

    (a)   an asset is a business asset in relation to a company or a group if it is or is an interest in an asset used for the purposes of a trade, profession or vocation carried on by the company, or as the case may be by a member of the group; and

    (b)   an asset is a chargeable asset in relation to a company or a group at any time if, on a disposal at that time, a gain accruing to the company, or as the case may be to a member of the group, would be a chargeable gain.

(3)   Where the shares disposed of are shares of the holding company of a trading group, then for the purposes of this paragraph—

    (a)   the holding by one member of the group of the ordinary share capital of another member shall not count as a chargeable asset, and

    (b)   if the whole of the ordinary share capital of a 51 per cent subsidiary of the holding company is not owned directly or indirectly by that company, the value of the chargeable assets of the subsidiary shall be taken to be reduced by multiplying it by the fraction—

$$\frac{A}{B}$$

where—

        A is the amount of the ordinary share capital of the subsidiary owned directly or indirectly by the holding company, and
        B is the whole of that share capital.

(4)   Expressions used in sub-paragraph (3) above have the same meanings as in section 838 of the Taxes Act.

Capital Allowances Act 2001

CHAPTER 4

FIRST-YEAR QUALIFYING EXPENDITURE

Types of expenditure which may qualify for first-year allowances

44.   Expenditure incurred by small or medium-sized enterprises

(1)   Expenditure is first-year qualifying expenditure if—

    (a)   it is incurred by a small or medium-sized enterprise, and

    (b)   it is not excluded by subsection (2) or section 46 (general exclusions).

(2)   Long-life asset expenditure is not first-year qualifying expenditure under subsection (1).

45.   ICT expenditure incurred by small enterprises

(1)   Expenditure is first-year qualifying expenditure if—

    (a)   it is incurred on or before 31st March 2003,

    (b)   it is incurred by a small enterprise,

    (c)   it is expenditure on information and communications technology, and

    (d)   it is not excluded by section 46 (general exclusions).

(2)   'Expenditure on information and communications technology' means expenditure on items within any of the following classes.

Class A. Computers and associated equipment

This class covers—

    (a)   computers,

    (b)   peripheral devices designed to be used by being connected to or inserted in a computer,

    (c)   equipment (including cabling) for use primarily to provide a data connection between—

        (i)   one computer and another, or

        (ii)   a computer and a data communications network, and

    (d)   dedicated electrical systems for computers.

For this purpose 'computer' does not include computerised control or management systems or other systems that are part of a larger system whose principal function is not processing or storing information.

Class B. Other qualifying equipment

This class covers—

    (a)   wireless application protocol telephones,

    (b)   third generation mobile telephones,

    (c)   devices designed to be used by being connected to a television set and capable of receiving and transmitting information from and to data networks, and

    (d)   other devices—

        (i)   substantially similar to those within paragraphs (a), (b) and (c), and

        (ii)   capable of receiving and transmitting information from and to data networks.

This is subject to any order under subsection (3).

Class C. Software

This class covers the right to use or otherwise deal with software for the purposes of any equipment within Class A or B.

(3)   The Treasury may make provision by order—

    (a)   further defining the kinds of equipment within Class B, or

    (b)   adding further kinds of equipment to that class.

45A. Expenditure on energy-saving plant or machinery

(1)   Expenditure is first-year qualifying expenditure if—

    (a)   it is expenditure on energy-saving plant or machinery that is unused and not second-hand,

    (b)   it is incurred on or after 1st April 2001, and

    (c)   it is not excluded by section 46 (general exclusions).

(2)   Energy-saving plant or machinery means plant or machinery in relation to which the following conditions are met—

    (a)   when the expenditure is incurred, or

    (b)   when the contract for the provision of the plant or machinery is entered into.

(3)   The conditions are that the plant or machinery—

    (a)   is of a description specified by Treasury order, and

    (b)   meets the energy-saving criteria specified by Treasury order for plant or machinery of that description.

(4)   Any such order may make provision by reference to any technology list, or product list, issued by the Secretary of State (whether before or after the coming into force of this section).

45B. Certification of energy-saving plant and machinery

(1)   The Treasury may by order provide that, in such cases as may be specified in the order, no section 45A allowance may be made unless a relevant certificate of energy efficiency is in force.

A 'section 45A allowance' means a first-year allowance in respect of expenditure that is first-year qualifying expenditure under section 45A.

(2)   A certificate of energy efficiency is one certifying that—

    (a)   particular plant or machinery, or

    (b)   plant or machinery constructed to a particular design,

meets the energy-saving criteria specified in relation to that description of plant or machinery by order under section 45A.

(3)   A relevant certificate of energy efficiency means one issued—

    (a)   by the Secretary of State or a person authorised by the Secretary of State;

    (b)   in the case of plant or machinery used or for use in Scotland, by the Scottish Ministers or a person authorised by them;

    (c)   in the case of plant or machinery used or for use in Wales, by the National Assembly for Wales or a person authorised by it;

    (d)   in the case of plant or machinery used or for use in Northern Ireland, by the Department of Enterprise, Trade and Investment in Northern Ireland or a person authorised by it.

(4)   If a certificate of energy efficiency is revoked—

    (a)   the certificate is to be treated for the purposes of this section as if it had never been issued, and

    (b)   all such assessments and adjustments of assessments are to be made as are necessary as a result of the revocation.

(5)   If a person who has made a tax return becomes aware that, as a result of the revocation of a certificate of energy efficiency after the return was made, the return has become incorrect, he must give notice to the Inland Revenue specifying how the return needs to be amended.

(6)   The notice must be given within 3 months beginning with the day on which the person first became aware that anything in the tax return had become incorrect because of the revocation of the certificate.

45C. Energy-saving components of plant or machinery

(1) This section applies for the purpose of apportioning expenditure incurred on plant or machinery if one or more components of the plant or machinery (but not all of it) is of a description specified by Treasury order under section 45A(3).

(2) If—

    (a)   only one of the components is of such a description, and

    (b)   an amount is specified by the order in respect of that component,

the part of the expenditure that is section 45A expenditure must not exceed that amount.

(3) If—

    (a)   more than one of the components is of such a description, and

    (b)   an amount is specified by the order in respect of each of those components,

the part of the expenditure that is section 45A expenditure must not exceed the total of those amounts.

(4) If the expenditure is treated under this Act as incurred in instalments, the proportion of each instalment that is section 45A expenditure is the same as the proportion of the whole of the expenditure that is section 45A expenditure.

(5) If this section applies, the expenditure is not apportioned under section 562(3) (apportionment where property sold with other property).

(6) In this section 'section 45A expenditure' means expenditure that is first-year qualifying expenditure under section 45A.

45D. Expenditure on cars with low carbon dioxide emissions

(1) Expenditure is first-year qualifying expenditure if—

    (a)   it is incurred in the period beginning with 17th April 2002 and ending with 31st March 2008,

    (b)   it is expenditure on a car which is first registered on or after 17th April 2002 and which is unused and not second-hand,

    (c)   the car—

        (i)   is an electrically-propelled car, or

        (ii)   is a car with low CO_2 emissions, and

    (d)   the expenditure is not excluded by section 46 (general exclusions).

(2) For the purposes of this section a car with low CO_2 emissions is a car which satisfies the conditions in subsections (3) and (4).

(3) The first condition is that, when the car is first registered, it is so registered on the basis of an EC certificate of conformity, or a UK approval certificate, that specifies—

    (a)   in the case of a car other than a bi-fuel car, a CO_2 emissions figure in terms of grams per kilometre driven, or

    (b)   in the case of a bi-fuel car, separate CO_2 emissions figures in terms of grams per kilometre driven for different fuels.

(4) The second condition is that the applicable CO_2 emissions figure in the case of the car does not exceed 120 grams per kilometre driven.

(5) For the purposes of subsection (4) the applicable CO_2 emissions figure in the case of a car other than a bi-fuel car is—

    (a)   where the EC certificate of conformity or UK approval certificate specifies only one CO_2 emissions figure, that figure, and

    (b)   where the certificate specifies more than one CO_2 emissions figure, the figure specified as the CO_2 emissions (combined) figure.

(6) For the purposes of subsection (4) the applicable CO_2 emissions figure in the case of a bi-fuel car is—

    (a)   where the EC certificate of conformity or UK approval certificate specifies more than one CO_2 emissions figure in relation to each fuel, the lowest CO_2 emissions (combined) figure specified, and

(b)   in any other case, the lowest CO2 figure specified by the certificate.

(7)   The Treasury may by order amend the amount from time to time specified in subsection (4).

(8)   In this section any reference to a car—

(a)   includes a reference to a mechanically propelled road vehicle of a type commonly used as a hackney carriage, but

(b)   does not include a reference to a motorcycle.

(9)   For the purposes of this section, a car is an electrically-propelled car only if—

(a)   it is propelled solely by electrical power, and

(b)   that power is derived from—

(i)   a source external to the vehicle, or

(ii)   an electrical storage battery which is not connected to any source of power when the vehicle is in motion.

(10)   In this section—

'bi-fuel car' means a car which is capable of being propelled by—

(a)   petrol and road fuel gas, or

(b)   diesel and road fuel gas;

'car' has the meaning given by section 81 (extended meaning of 'car');
'diesel' means any diesel fuel within the definition in Article 2 of Directive 98/70/EC of the European Parliament and of the Council;
'EC certificate of conformity' means a certificate of conformity issued by a manufacturer under any provision of the law of a Member State implementing Article 6 of Council Directive 70/156/EEC, as amended;
'petrol' has the meaning given by Article 2 of Directive 98/70/EC of the European Parliament and of the Council;
'road fuel gas' has the same meaning as in section 168AB of ICTA;
'UK approval certificate' means a certificate issued under—

(a)   section 58(1) or (4) of the Road Traffic Act 1988, or

(b)   Article 31A(4) or (5) of the Road Traffic (Northern Ireland) Order 1981.

45E.   Expenditure on plant or machinery for gas refuelling station

(1)   Expenditure is first-year qualifying expenditure if—

(a)   it is incurred in the period beginning with 17th April 2002 and ending with 31st March 2008,

(b)   it is expenditure on plant or machinery for a gas refuelling station where the plant or machinery is unused and not second-hand, and

(c)   it is not excluded by section 46 (general exclusions).

(2)   For the purposes of this section expenditure on plant or machinery for a gas refuelling station is expenditure on plant or machinery installed at a gas refuelling station for use solely for or in connection with refuelling vehicles with natural gas or hydrogen fuel.

(3)   For the purposes of subsection (2) the plant or machinery which is for use for or in connection with refuelling vehicles with natural gas or hydrogen fuel includes—

(a)   any storage tank for natural gas or hydrogen fuel,

(b)   any compressor, pump, control or meter used for or in connection with refuelling vehicles with natural gas or hydrogen fuel, and

(c)   any equipment for dispensing natural gas or hydrogen fuel to the fuel tank of a vehicle.

(4)   For the purposes of this section—

'gas refuelling station' means any premises, or that part of any premises, where vehicles are refuelled with natural gas or hydrogen fuel;
'hydrogen fuel' means a fuel consisting of gaseous or cryogenic liquid hydrogen which is used for propelling vehicles; and
'vehicle' means a mechanically propelled road vehicle.

45F. Expenditure on plant and machinery for use wholly in a ring fence trade

(1)   Expenditure is first-year qualifying expenditure if—

   (a)   it is incurred on or after 17th April 2002,
   (b)   it is incurred by a company,
   (c)   it is incurred on the provision of plant or machinery for use wholly for the purposes of a ring fence trade, and
   (d)   it is not excluded by section 46 (general exclusions).

(2)   This section is subject to section 45G (plant or machinery used for less than five years in a ring fence trade).

(3)   In this section 'ring fence trade' means a ring fence trade in respect of which tax is chargeable under section 501A of the Taxes Act 1988 (supplementary charge in respect of ring fence trades).

45G. Plant or machinery used for less than five years in a ring fence trade

(1)   Expenditure incurred by a company on the provision of plant or machinery is to be treated as never having been first-year qualifying expenditure under section 45F if the plant or machinery—

   (a)   is at no time in the relevant period used in a ring fence trade carried on by the company or a company connected with it, or
   (b)   is at any time in the relevant period used for a purpose other than that of a ring fence trade carried on by the company or a company connected with it.

(2)   For the purposes of this section 'the relevant period' means whichever of the following periods, beginning with the incurring of the expenditure, first ends, namely—

   (a)   the period ending with the fifth anniversary of the incurring of the expenditure, or
   (b)   the period ending with the day preceding the first occasion on which the plant or machinery, after becoming owned by the company which incurred the expenditure, is not owned by a company which is either that company or a company connected with it.

(3)   All such assessments and adjustments of assessments are to be made as are necessary to give effect to subsection (1).

(4)   If a person who has made a return becomes aware that, after making it, anything in it has become incorrect because of the operation of this section, he must give notice to the Inland Revenue specifying how the return needs to be amended.

(5)   The notice must be given within 3 months beginning with the day on which the person first became aware that anything in the return had become incorrect because of the operation of this section.

(6)   In this section 'ring fence trade' has the same meaning as in section 45F.

46. General exclusions applying to sections 40, 44 and 45

(1)   Expenditure within any of the general exclusions in subsection (2) is not first-year qualifying expenditure under—

section 40	(expenditure incurred for Northern Ireland purposes by small or medium-sized enterprises),
section 44	(expenditure incurred by small or medium-sized enterprises),
section 45	(ICT expenditure incurred by small enterprises),
section 45A	(expenditure on energy-saving plant or machinery),
section 45D	(expenditure on cars with low CO2 emissions),
section 45E	(expenditure on plant or machinery for gas refuelling station), or
section 45F	(expenditure on plant and machinery for use wholly in a ring fence trade).

(2)   The general exclusions are—

   General exclusion 1
   The expenditure is incurred in the chargeable period in which the qualifying activity is permanently discontinued.

General exclusion 2
The expenditure is incurred on the provision of a car (as defined by section 81).

General exclusion 3
The expenditure is of the kind described in section 94 (ships).

General exclusion 4
The expenditure is of the kind described in section 95 (railway assets).

General exclusion 5
The expenditure would be long-life asset expenditure but for paragraph 20 of Schedule 3 (transitional provisions).

General exclusion 6
The expenditure is on the provision of plant or machinery for leasing (whether in the course of a trade or otherwise).
For this purpose, the letting of a ship on charter, or of any other asset on hire, is to be regarded as leasing (whether or not it would otherwise be so regarded).

General exclusion 7
The circumstances of the incurring of the expenditure are that—

(a)   the provision of the plant or machinery on which the expenditure is incurred is connected with a change in the nature or conduct of a trade or business carried on by a person other than the person incurring the expenditure, and

(b)   the obtaining of a first-year allowance is the main benefit, or one of the main benefits, which could reasonably be expected to arise from the making of the change.

General exclusion 8
Either of the following sections applies—

section 13 (use for qualifying activity of plant or machinery provided for other purposes);
section 14 (use for qualifying activity of plant or machinery which is a gift).

This is subject to section 161 (pre-trading expenditure on mineral exploration and access).

(3)   Subsection (1) is subject to the following provisions of this section.

(4)   General exclusion 2 does not prevent expenditure being first-year qualifying expenditure under section 45D.

(5)   General exclusion 6 does not prevent expenditure being first-year qualifying expenditure under section 45A, 45D or 45E.

Expenditure of small or medium-sized enterprises

47.   Expenditure of small or medium-sized enterprises: companies

(1)   Use this section to decide whether expenditure incurred by a company is, for the purposes of this Chapter, incurred by—

(a)   a small or medium-sized enterprise, or
(b)   a small enterprise.

(2)   The expenditure is incurred by a small or medium-sized enterprise if the company—

(a)   qualifies (or is treated as qualifying) as small or medium-sized under the relevant companies legislation in relation to the financial year of the company in which the expenditure is incurred, and
(b)   is not a member of a large group at the time when the expenditure is incurred.

(3)   The expenditure is incurred by a small enterprise if the company—

(a)   qualifies (or is treated as qualifying) as small under the relevant companies legislation in relation to the financial year of the company in which the expenditure is incurred, and
(b)   is not a member of a large or medium-sized group at the time when the expenditure is incurred.

(4)   Except in the case of a company formed and registered in Northern Ireland—

(a)   'the relevant companies legislation' means section 247 of the Companies Act 1985, and

(b) 'financial year' has the same meaning as in Part VII of the 1985 Act.

(5) In the case of such a company—

(a) 'the relevant companies legislation' means Article 255 of the Companies (Northern Ireland) Order 1986, and

(b) 'financial year' has the same meaning as in Part VIII of the 1986 Order.

(6) 'Company' means—

(a) a company, or an overseas company, within the meaning of the 1985 Act, or

(b) a company, or a Part XXIII company, within the meaning of the 1986 Order.

CHAPTER 5

ALLOWANCES AND CHARGES

First-year allowances

52. First-year allowances

(1) A person is entitled to a first-year allowance in respect of first-year qualifying expenditure if—

(a) the expenditure is incurred in a chargeable period to which this Act applies, and

(b) the person owns the plant or machinery at some time during that chargeable period.

(2) Any first-year allowance is made for the chargeable period in which the first-year qualifying expenditure is incurred.

(3) The amount of the allowance is a percentage of the first-year qualifying expenditure in respect of which the allowance is made, as shown in the Table—

Table

AMOUNT OF FIRST-YEAR ALLOWANCES

Type of first year qualifying enterprise	*Amount*
Expenditure qualifying under section 40 (expenditure incurred for Northern Ireland purposes by small or medium-sized enterprises)	100%;
Expenditure qualifying under section 44 (expenditure incurred by small or medium-sized enterprises)	40%;
Expenditure qualifying under section 45 (ICT expenditure incurred by small enterprises	100%
Expenditure qualifying under section 45A (expenditure on energy-saving plant or machinery	100%

(4) A person who is entitled to a first-year allowance may claim the allowance in respect of the whole or a part of the first-year qualifying expenditure.

(5) Subsection (1) needs to be read with section 236 (first-year allowances in respect of additional VAT liabilities) and is subject to—

section 205 (reduction of first-year allowance if plant or machinery provided partly for purposes other than those of qualifying activity),

section 210 (reduction of first-year allowance if it appears that a partial depreciation subsidy is or will be payable), and

sections 217, 223 and 241 (anti-avoidance: no first-year allowance in certain cases).

Part III Taxation

Pooling

53. Pooling of qualifying expenditure

(1)   Qualifying expenditure has to be pooled for the purpose of determining a person's entitlement to writing-down allowances and balancing allowances and liability to balancing charges.

(2)   If a person carries on more than one qualifying activity, expenditure relating to the different activities must not be allocated to the same pool.

54. The different kinds of pools

(1)   There are single asset pools, class pools and the main pool.

(2)   A single asset pool may not contain expenditure relating to more than one asset.

(3)   The following provide for qualifying expenditure to be allocated to a single asset pool—

section 74 (car above the cost threshold);
section 86 (short-life asset);
section 127 (ship);
section 206 (plant or machinery provided or used partly for purposes other than those of qualifying activity);
section 211 (payment of partial depreciation subsidy);
section 538 (contribution allowances: plant and machinery).

(4)   A class pool is a pool which may contain expenditure relating to more than one asset.

(5)   The following provide for qualifying expenditure to be allocated to a class pool—

section 101 (long-life assets);
section 107 (overseas leasing).

(6)   Qualifying expenditure may be allocated to the main pool only if it does not fall to be allocated to a single asset pool or a class pool.

Writing-down and balancing allowances and balancing charges

55. Determination of entitlement or liability

(1)   Whether a person is entitled to a writing-down allowance or a balancing allowance, or liable to a balancing charge, for a chargeable period is determined separately for each pool of qualifying expenditure and depends on—

(a)   the available qualifying expenditure in that pool for that period ('AQE'), and
(b)   the total of any disposal receipts to be brought into account in that pool for that period ('TDR').

(2)   If AQE exceeds TDR, the person is entitled to a writing-down allowance or a balancing allowance for the period.

(3)   If TDR exceeds AQE, the person is liable to a balancing charge for the period.

(4)   The entitlement under subsection (2) is to a writing-down allowance except for the final chargeable period when it is to a balancing allowance.

(5)   The final chargeable period is given by section 65.

(6)   Subsection (2) is subject to section 110(1) (overseas leasing: allowances prohibited in certain cases).

56. Amount of allowances and charges

(1)   The amount of the writing-down allowance to which a person is entitled for a chargeable period is 25%; of the amount by which AQE exceeds TDR.

(2)   Subsection (1) is subject to—

(a)   section 102 (long-life asset expenditure: 6%;), and
(b)   section 109 (overseas leasing: 10%;).

(3)   If the chargeable period is more or less than a year, the amount is proportionately increased or reduced.

(4)   If the qualifying activity has been carried on for part only of the chargeable period, the amount is proportionately reduced.

(5)   A person claiming a writing-down allowance may require the allowance to be reduced to a specified amount.

(6)   The amount of the balancing charge to which a person is liable for a chargeable period is the amount by which TDR exceeds AQE.

(7)   The amount of the balancing allowance to which a person is entitled for the final chargeable period is the amount by which AQE exceeds TDR.

Available qualifying expenditure

57. Available qualifying expenditure

(1)   The general rule is that a person's available qualifying expenditure in a pool for a chargeable period consists of—

    (a)   any qualifying expenditure allocated to the pool for that period in accordance with section 58, and

    (b)   any unrelieved qualifying expenditure carried forward in the pool from the previous chargeable period under section 59.

(2)   A person's available qualifying expenditure in a pool for a chargeable period also includes any amount allocated to the pool for that period under—

section 26(3) (net costs of demolition);
section 86(2) or 87(2) (allocation of expenditure in short-life asset pool);
section 111(3) (overseas leasing: standard recovery mechanism);
section 129(1), 132(2), 133(3) or 137 (provisions relating to operation of single ship pool and deferment of balancing charges in respect of ships);
section 161C(2) (decommissioning expenditure incurred by person carrying on trade of oil extraction);
section 165(3) (abandonment expenditure incurred after cessation of ring fence trade);
section 206(3) (plant or machinery used partly for purposes other than those of the qualifying activity);
section 211(4) (partial depreciation subsidy paid).

(3)   A person's available qualifying expenditure does not include any expenditure excluded by—

section 8(4) or 9(1) (rules against double relief);
section 166(2) (transfers of interests in oil fields: anti-avoidance);
section 185(2), 186(2) or 187(2) (restrictions where other claims made in respect of fixture);
section 218(1), 224(1), 228(2), 242(2), or 243(2) (general anti-avoidance provisions).

(4)   Subsection (1) is also subject to section 220 (allocation to chargeable periods of expenditure incurred on plant or machinery for leasing under finance lease).

58.   Initial allocation of qualifying expenditure to pools

(1)   The following rules apply to the allocation of a person's qualifying expenditure to the appropriate pool.

(2)   An amount of qualifying expenditure is not to be allocated to a pool for a chargeable period if that amount has been taken into account in determining the person's available qualifying expenditure for an earlier chargeable period.

(3)   Qualifying expenditure is not to be allocated to a pool for a chargeable period before that in which the expenditure is incurred.

(4)   Qualifying expenditure is not to be allocated to a pool for a chargeable period unless the person owns the plant or machinery at some time in that period.

(5)   If a first-year allowance is made in respect of an amount of first-year qualifying expenditure—

    (a)   subject to subsection (6), none of that amount is to be allocated to a pool for the chargeable period in which the expenditure is incurred, and

    (b)   the amount that may be allocated to a pool for any chargeable period is limited to the balance left after deducting the first-year allowance.

(6)   If—

(a)   a first-year allowance is made in respect of an amount of first-year qualifying expenditure,

(b)   a disposal event occurs in respect of the plant or machinery in any chargeable period, and

(c)   none of the balance left after deducting the first-year allowance has been allocated to a pool for an earlier chargeable period,

the balance (or some of it) must be allocated to a pool for the chargeable period in which the disposal event occurs.

(7)   Subsection (6) applies even if the balance is nil (because of a 100%; first-year allowance).

(8)   'The appropriate pool' means whichever pool is applicable under the provisions of this Part apart from this section.

59. Unrelieved qualifying expenditure

(1)   A person has unrelieved qualifying expenditure to carry forward from a chargeable period if for that period AQE exceeds TDR.

(2)   The amount of the unrelieved qualifying expenditure is—

(a)   the excess less the writing-down allowance made for the period, or

(b)   if no writing-down allowance is claimed for the period, the excess.

(3)   No amount may be carried forward as unrelieved qualifying expenditure from the final chargeable period.

266. Election where predecessor and successor are connected persons

(1)   This section applies if a person ('the successor') succeeds to a qualifying activity which was until that time carried on by another person ('the predecessor') and—

(a)   the two persons are connected with each other,

(b)   each of them is within the charge to tax on the profits of the qualifying activity, and

(c)   the successor is not a dual resident investing company.

(2)   If this section applies, the predecessor and the successor may jointly elect for the provisions of section 267 to have effect.

(3)   The election may be made whether or not any plant or machinery has actually been sold or transferred.

(4)   The election must be made by notice to the Inland Revenue within 2 years after the date on which the succession takes effect.

(5)   For the purposes of this section, the predecessor and the successor are connected with each other if any of the following conditions is met—

(a)   they would be treated as connected persons under section 839 of ICTA;

(b)   one of them is a partnership and the other has the right to a share in that partnership;

(c)   one of them is a body corporate and the other has control over that body;

(d)   both of them are partnerships and another person has the right to a share in both of them;

(e)   both of them are bodies corporate, or one of them is a partnership and the other is a body corporate, and (in either case) another person has control over both of them.

(6)   In subsection (5) any reference to a right to a share in a partnership is to be read as a reference to a right to a share of the assets or income of the partnership.

(7)   Sections 104, 108 and 265 (disposal value of long-life assets, effect of disposal to connected person on overseas leasing pool and general provisions about successions) do not apply if an election is made under this section.

(8)   This section does not apply if section 561 applies (transfer of UK trade to a company in another member State).

267. Effect of election

(1)   If an election is made under section 266, the following provisions have effect.

(2)   For the purposes of making allowances and charges under this Part, relevant plant or machinery is treated as sold by the predecessor to the successor—

(a) when the succession takes place, and

(b) at a price which gives rise to neither a balancing allowance nor a balancing charge.

(3) 'Relevant plant or machinery' means any plant or machinery which—

(a) immediately before the succession, was owned by the predecessor, and was either in use or provided and available for use for the purposes of the qualifying activity, and

(b) immediately after the succession, is owned by the successor, and is either in use or provided and available for use for the purposes of the qualifying activity.

(4) Allowances and charges are to be made under this Part to or on the successor as if everything done to or by the predecessor had been done to or by the successor.

(5) All such assessments and adjustments of assessments are to be made as are necessary to give effect to the election.

PART 3

INDUSTRIAL BUILDINGS ALLOWANCES

CHAPTER 1

INTRODUCTION

271. Industrial buildings allowances

(1) Allowances are available under this Part if—

(a) expenditure has been incurred on the construction of a building or structure,

(b) the building or structure is (or, in the case of an initial allowance, is to be)—

(i) in use for the purposes of a qualifying trade,

(ii) a qualifying hotel,

(iii) a qualifying sports pavilion, or

(iv) in relation to qualifying enterprise zone expenditure, a commercial building or structure, and

(c) the expenditure incurred on the construction of the building or structure, or other expenditure, is qualifying expenditure.

(2) In the rest of this Part—

(a) 'building' is short for 'building or structure', and

(b) 'industrial building' means, subject to Chapter 2 (which defines terms used in subsection (1)(b) etc), a building or structure which is within subsection (1)(b).

(3) Allowances under this Part are made to the person who for the time being has the relevant interest in the building (see Chapter 3) in relation to the qualifying expenditure (see Chapter 4).

272. Expenditure on the construction of a building

(1) For the purposes of this Part, expenditure on the construction of a building does not include expenditure on the acquisition of land or rights in or over land.

(2) This Part has effect in relation to capital expenditure incurred by a person on repairs to a part of a building as if it were capital expenditure on the construction of that part of the building for the first time.

(3) For the purposes of subsection (2), expenditure incurred for the purposes of a trade on repairs to a building is to be treated as capital expenditure if it is not expenditure that would be allowed to be deducted in calculating the profits of the trade for tax purposes.

273. Preparation of sites for plant or machinery

(1) Subsection (2) applies if—

(a) capital expenditure is or has been incurred in preparing, cutting, tunnelling or levelling land for the purposes of preparing the land as a site for the installation of plant or machinery, and

(b)   no allowance could (apart from this section) be made in respect of that expenditure under this Part or Part 2 (plant and machinery allowances).

(2)   This Part has effect in relation to the expenditure as if—

(a)   the purpose of incurring the expenditure were to prepare the land as a site for the construction of a building, and

(b)   the installed plant or machinery were a building.

CHAPTER 2

INDUSTRIAL BUILDINGS

Buildings in use for the purposes of a qualifying trade

274. Trades and undertakings which are 'qualifying trades'

(1)   'Qualifying trade' means—

(a)   a trade of a kind described in Table A, or

(b)   an undertaking of a kind described in Table B, if the undertaking is carried on by way of trade.

Table A

TRADES WHICH ARE 'QUALIFYING TRADES'

1	*Manufacturing*	A trade consisting of manufacturing goods or materials.
2	*Processing*	A trade consisting of subjecting goods or materials to a process.
		This includes (subject to section 276(3)) maintaining or repairing goods or materials.
3	*Storage*	A trade consisting of storing goods or materials—

      (a)   which are to be used in the manufacture of other goods or materials,

      (b)   which are to be subjected, in the course of a trade, to a process,

      (c)   which, having been manufactured or produced or subjected,in the course of a trade, to a process, have not yet been delivered to any purchaser, or

      (d)   on their arrival in the United Kingdom from a place outside the United Kingdom.

4	*Agricultural contracting*	A trade consisting of—

      (a)   ploughing or cultivating land occupied by another,

      (b)   carrying out any other agricultural operation on land occupied by another, or

      (c)   threshing another's crops.

For this purpose 'crops' includes vegetable produce.

5	*Working foreign plantations*	A trade consisting of working land outside the United Kingdom used for—

      (a)   growing and harvesting crops,

      (b)   husbandry, or

      (c)   forestry.

For this purpose 'crops' includes vegetable produce and 'harvesting crops' includes the collection of vegetable produce (however effected).

6	*Fishing*	A trade consisting of catching or taking fish or shellfish.
7	*Mineral extraction*	A trade consisting of working a source of mineral deposits. 'Mineral deposits' includes any natural deposits capable of being lifted or extracted from the earth, and for this purpose geothermal energy is to be treated as a natural deposit. 'Source of mineral deposits' includes a mine, an oil well and a source of geothermal energy.

Table B

UNDERTAKINGS WHICH ARE 'QUALIFYING TRADES' IF CARRIED ON BY WAY OF TRADE

1	*Electricity*	An undertaking for the generation, transformation, conversion, transmission or distribution of electrical energy.
2	*Water*	An undertaking for the supply of water for public consumption.
3	*Hydraulic power*	An undertaking for the supply of hydraulic power.
4	*Sewerage*	An undertaking for the provision of sewerage services within the meaning of the Water Industry Act 1991 (c 56).
5	*Transport*	A transport undertaking.
6	*Highway undertakings*	A highway undertaking, that is, so much of any undertaking relating to the design, building, financing and operation of roads as is carried on—

(a)   for the purposes of, or

(b)   in connection with,

the exploitation of highway concessions.

7	*Tunnels*	A tunnel undertaking.
8	*Bridges*	A bridge undertaking.
9	*Inland navigation*	An inland navigation undertaking.
10	*Docks*	A dock undertaking.

A dock includes—

(a)   any harbour, and

(b)   any wharf, pier, jetty or other works in or at which vessels can ship or unship merchandise or passengers,

other than a pier or jetty primarily used for recreation.

(2)   Item 6 of Table B needs to be read with Chapter 9 (application of this Part to highway undertakings).

275. Building used for welfare of workers

A building is in use for the purposes of a qualifying trade if it is—

(a)   provided by the person carrying on the qualifying trade for the welfare of workers employed in that qualifying trade, and

(b)   in use for the welfare of such workers.

276. Parts of trades and undertakings

(1)   Sections 274 and 275 apply in relation to part of a trade or undertaking as they apply in relation to a trade or undertaking.

But this is subject to subsections (2) and (3).

(2)   If—

(a)   a building is in use for the purpose of a trade or undertaking, and

(b)   part only of the trade or undertaking is a qualifying trade,

the building is in use for the purposes of the qualifying trade only if it is in use for the purposes of that part of the trade or undertaking.

(3)   Maintaining or repairing goods or materials is not a qualifying trade if—

(a)   the goods or materials are employed in a trade or undertaking,

(b)   the maintenance or repair is carried out by the person employing the goods or materials, and

(c)   the trade or undertaking is not itself a qualifying trade.

277. Exclusion of dwelling-houses, retail shops, showrooms, hotels and offices etc

(1)   A building is not in use for the purposes of a qualifying trade if it is in use as, or as part of, or for any purpose ancillary to the purposes of—

(a)   a dwelling-house;

(b)   a retail shop, or premises of a similar character where a retail trade or business (including repair work) is carried on;

(c)   a showroom;

(d)   a hotel;

(e)   an office.

(2)   Subsection (3) is about buildings constructed for occupation by, or for the welfare of persons employed—

(a)   on, or in connection with, working land outside the United Kingdom which is used as described in item 5 of Table A in section 274 (foreign plantations), or

(b)   at, or in connection with, working a source of mineral deposits as defined in item 7 of Table A (mineral extraction).

(3)   Subsection (1) does not apply to a building which this subsection is about if the building—

(a)   is likely to be of little or no value to the person carrying on the trade when the land or source is no longer worked, or

(b)   will cease to be owned by that person on the ending of a foreign concession under which the land or source is worked.

(4)   'Foreign concession' means a right or privilege granted by the government of, or any municipality or other authority in, a territory outside the United Kingdom.

(5)   Subsection (1) is subject to section 283 (non-industrial part of building disregarded).

278. Building used by more than one licensee

A building used by more than one licensee of the same person is not in use for the purposes of a qualifying trade unless each licensee uses it, or the part to which the licence relates, for the purposes of a qualifying trade.

CHAPTER 6

WRITING-DOWN ALLOWANCES

309. Entitlement to writing-down allowance

(1)   A person is entitled to a writing-down allowance for a chargeable period if—

(a)   qualifying expenditure has been incurred on a building,

(b)   at the end of that chargeable period, the person is entitled to the relevant interest in the building in relation to that expenditure, and

(c)   at the end of that chargeable period, the building is an industrial building.

(2)   A person claiming a writing-down allowance may require the allowance to be reduced to a specified amount.

310. Basic rule for calculating amount of allowance

(1)   The basic rule is that the writing-down allowance for a chargeable period is—

(a)   in the case of qualifying enterprise zone expenditure, 25%; of the expenditure, and

(b)   in the case of other qualifying expenditure, 4%; of the expenditure.

(2)   The allowance is proportionately increased or reduced if the chargeable period is more or less than a year.

(3)   This basic rule does not apply if section 311 applies.

311. Calculation of allowance after sale of relevant interest

(1)   If a relevant event occurs, the writing-down allowance for any chargeable period ending after the event is—

$$RQE \times \frac{A}{B}$$

where—

> RQE is the amount of the residue of qualifying expenditure immediately after the event,
> A is the length of the chargeable period, and
> B is the length of the period from the date of the event to the end of the period of 25 years beginning with the day on which the building was first used.

(2)   On any later relevant event, the writing-down allowance is further adjusted in accordance with this section.

(3)   'Relevant event' means—

    (a)   a sale of the relevant interest in the building which is a balancing event to which section 314 applies, or

    (b)   an event which is a relevant event for the purposes of this section under section 347 or 349 (additional VAT liabilities and rebates).

312. Allowance limited to residue of qualifying expenditure

(1)   The amount of the writing-down allowance for a chargeable period is limited to the residue of qualifying expenditure.

(2)   For this purpose the residue is ascertained immediately before writing off the writing-down allowance at the end of the chargeable period.

313. Meaning of 'the residue of qualifying expenditure'

The residue of qualifying expenditure is the qualifying expenditure that has not yet been written off in accordance with Chapter 8.

Income Tax (Earnings and Pensions) Act 2003

PART 1

OVERVIEW

1.   Overview of contents of this Act

(1)   This Act imposes charges to income tax on—

    (a)   employment income (see Parts 2 to 7),

    (b)   pension income (see Part 9), and

    (c)   social security income (see Part 10).

(2) Those charges to tax have effect for the purposes of section 1(1) of ICTA (the general charge to income tax).

(3) This Act also—

    (a)   confers certain reliefs in respect of liabilities of former employees (see Part 8),

    (b)   provides for the assessment, collection and recovery of income tax in respect of employment, pension or social security income that is PAYE income (see Part 11), and

    (c)   allows deductions to be made from such income in respect of payroll giving (see Part 12).

PART 2

EMPLOYMENT INCOME: CHARGE TO TAX

CHAPTER 1

INTRODUCTION

3.   Structure of employment income Parts

(1)   The structure of the employment income Parts is as follows—

this Part imposes the charge to tax on employment income, and sets out—

    (a)   how the amount charged to tax for a tax year is to be calculated, and

    (b)   who is liable for the tax charged;

Part 3 sets out what are earnings and provides for amounts to be treated as earnings;

Part 4 deals with exemptions from the charge to tax under this Part (and, in some cases, from other charges to tax);

Part 5 deals with deductions from taxable earnings;

Part 6 deals with employment income other than earnings or share-related income; and

Part 7 deals with share-related income and exemptions.

(2)   In this Act 'the employment income Parts' means this Part and Parts 3 to 7.

4.   'Employment' for the purposes of the employment income Parts

(1)   In the employment income Parts 'employment' includes in particular—

    (a)   any employment under a contract of service,

    (b)   any employment under a contract of apprenticeship, and

    (c)   any employment in the service of the Crown.

(2)   In those Parts 'employed', 'employee' and 'employer' have corresponding meanings.

5.   Application to offices and office-holders

(1)   The provisions of the employment income Parts that are expressed to apply to employments apply equally to offices, unless otherwise indicated.

(2)   In those provisions as they apply to an office—

    (a)   references to being employed are to being the holder of the office;
    (b)   'employee' means the office-holder;
    (c)   'employer' means the person under whom the office-holder holds office.

(3)   In the employment income Parts 'office' includes in particular any position which has an existence independent of the person who holds it and may be filled by successive holders.

CHAPTER 2

TAX ON EMPLOYMENT INCOME

6.   Nature of charge to tax on employment income

(1)   The charge to tax on employment income under this Part is a charge to tax on—

    (a)   general earnings, and
    (b)   specific employment income.

The meaning of 'employment income', 'general earnings' and 'specific employment income' is given in section 7.

(2)   The amount of general earnings or specific employment income which is charged to tax in a particular tax year is set out in section 9.

(3)   The rules in Chapters 4 and 5 of this Part, which are concerned with—

    (a)   the residence and domicile of an employee in a tax year, and
    (b)   the tax year in which amounts are received or remitted to the United Kingdom,

apply for the purposes of the charge to tax on general earnings but not that on specific employment income.

(4)   The person who is liable for any tax charged on employment income is set out in section 13.

(5)   Employment income is not charged to tax under this Part if it is within the charge to tax under Case I of Schedule D by virtue of section 314(1) of ICTA (divers and diving supervisors).

7.   Meaning of 'employment income', 'general earnings' and 'specific employment income'

(1)   This section gives the meaning for the purposes of the Tax Acts of 'employment income', 'general earnings' and 'specific employment income'.

(2)   'Employment income' means—

    (a)   earnings within Chapter 1 of Part 3,
    (b)   any amount treated as earnings (see subsection (5)), or
    (c)   any amount which counts as employment income (see subsection (6)).

(3)   'General earnings' means—

    (a)   earnings within Chapter 1 of Part 3, or
    (b)   any amount treated as earnings (see subsection (5)),

excluding in each case any exempt income.

(4)   'Specific employment income' means any amount which counts as employment income (see subsection (6)), excluding any exempt income.

(5)   Subsection (2)(b) or (3)(b) refers to any amount treated as earnings under—

    (a)   Chapters 7 and 8 of this Part (application of provisions to agency workers and workers under arrangements made by intermediaries),
    (b)   Chapters 2 to 11 of Part 3 (the benefits code),
    (c)   Chapter 12 of Part 3 (payments treated as earnings), or
    (d)   section 262 of CAA 2001 (balancing charges to be given effect by treating them as earnings).

(6)   Subsection (2)(c) or (4) refers to any amount which counts as employment income by virtue of—

    (a)   Part 6 (income which is not earnings or share-related),

(b)   Part 7 (share-related income and exemptions), or

(c)   any other enactment.

8.   Meaning of 'exempt income'

For the purposes of the employment income Parts, an amount of employment income within paragraph (a), (b) or (c) of section 7(2) is 'exempt income' if, as a result of any exemption in Part 4 or elsewhere, no liability to income tax arises in respect of it as such an amount.

CHAPTER 3

OPERATION OF TAX CHARGE

9.   Amount of employment income charged to tax

(1)   The amount of employment income which is charged to tax under this Part for a particular tax year is as follows.

(2)   In the case of general earnings, the amount charged is the net taxable earnings from an employment in the year.

(3)   That amount is calculated under section 11 by reference to any taxable earnings from the employment in the year (see section 10(2)).

(4)   In the case of specific employment income, the amount charged is the net taxable specific income from an employment for the year.

(5)   That amount is calculated under section 12 by reference to any taxable specific income from the employment for the year (see section 10(3)).

(6)   Accordingly, no amount of employment income is charged to tax under this Part for a particular tax year unless—

(a)   in the case of general earnings, they are taxable earnings from an employment in that year, or

(b)   in the case of specific employment income, it is taxable specific income from an employment for that year.

10.   Meaning of 'taxable earnings' and 'taxable specific income'

(1)   This section explains what is meant by 'taxable earnings' and 'taxable specific income' in the employment income Parts.

(2)   'Taxable earnings' from an employment in a tax year are to be determined in accordance with—

(a)   Chapter 4 of this Part (rules applying to employees resident, ordinarily resident and domiciled in the UK), or

(b)   Chapter 5 of this Part (rules applying to employees resident, ordinarily resident or domiciled outside the UK).

(3)   'Taxable specific income' from an employment for a tax year means the full amount of any specific employment income which, by virtue of Part 6 or 7 or any other enactment, counts as employment income for that year in respect of the employment.

13.   Person liable for tax

(1)   The person liable for any tax on employment income under this Part is the taxable person mentioned in subsection (2) or (3).

This is subject to subsection (4).

(2)   If the tax is on general earnings, 'the taxable person' is the person to whose employment the earnings relate.

(3)   If the tax is on specific employment income, 'the taxable person' is the person in relation to whom the income is, by virtue of Part 6 or 7 or any other enactment, to count as employment income.

(4)   If the tax is on general earnings received, or remitted to the United Kingdom, after the death of the person to whose employment the earnings relate, the person's personal representatives are liable for the tax.

(5)　In that event the tax is accordingly to be assessed on the personal representatives and is a debt due from and payable out of the estate.

PART 3

EMPLOYMENT INCOME: EARNINGS AND BENEFITS ETC TREATED AS EARNINGS

CHAPTER 1

EARNINGS

62.　Earnings

(1)　This section explains what is meant by 'earnings' in the employment income Parts.

(2)　In those Parts 'earnings', in relation to an employment, means—

    (a)　any salary, wages or fee,

    (b)　any gratuity or other profit or incidental benefit of any kind obtained by the employee if it is money or money's worth, or

    (c)　anything else that constitutes an emolument of the employment.

(3)　For the purposes of subsection (2) 'money's worth' means something that is—

    (a)　of direct monetary value to the employee, or

    (b)　capable of being converted into money or something of direct monetary value to the employee.

(4)　Subsection (1) does not affect the operation of statutory provisions that provide for amounts to be treated as earnings (and see section 721(7)).

CHAPTER 10

TAXABLE BENEFITS: RESIDUAL LIABILITY TO CHARGE

Introduction

201.　Employment-related benefits

(1)　This Chapter applies to employment-related benefits.

(2)　In this Chapter—

    'benefit' means a benefit or facility of any kind;
    'employment-related benefit' means a benefit, other than an excluded benefit, which is provided in a tax year—

    (a)　for an employee, or

    (b)　for a member of an employee's family or household,

    by reason of the employment.

    For the definition of 'excluded benefit' see section 202.

(3)　A benefit provided by an employer is to be regarded as provided by reason of the employment unless—

    (a)　the employer is an individual, and

    (b)　the provision is made in the normal course of the employer's domestic, family or personal relationships.

(4)　For the purposes of this Chapter it does not matter whether the employment is held at the time when the benefit is provided so long as it is held at some point in the tax year in which the benefit is provided.

(5)　References in this Chapter to an employee accordingly include a prospective or former employee.

202.　Excluded benefits

(1)　A benefit is an 'excluded benefit' for the purposes of this Chapter if—

(a)   any of Chapters 3 to 9 of the benefits code applies to the benefit,

(b)   any of those Chapters would apply to the benefit but for an exception, or

(c)   the benefit consists in the right to receive, or the prospect of receiving, sums treated as earnings under section 221 (payments where employee absent because of sickness or disability).

(2)   In this section 'exception', in relation to the application of a Chapter of the benefits code to a benefit, means any enactment in the Chapter which provides that the Chapter does not apply to the benefit.

But for this purpose section 86 (transport vouchers under pre-26th March 1982 arrangements) is not an exception.

Cash equivalent of benefit treated as earnings

203. Cash equivalent of benefit treated as earnings

(1)   The cash equivalent of an employment-related benefit is to be treated as earnings from the employment for the tax year in which it is provided.

(2)   The cash equivalent of an employment-related benefit is the cost of the benefit less any part of that cost made good by the employee to the persons providing the benefit.

(3)   The cost of an employment-related benefit is determined in accordance with section 204 unless—

(a)   section 205 provides that the cost is to be determined in accordance with that section, or

(b)   section 206 provides that the cost is to be determined in accordance with that section.

Determination of the cost of the benefit

204. Cost of the benefit: basic rule

The cost of an employment-related benefit is the expense incurred in or in connection with provision of the benefit (including a proper proportion of any expense relating partly to provision of the benefit and partly to other matters).

205. Cost of the benefit: asset made available without transfer

(1)   The cost of an employment-related benefit ('the taxable benefit') is determined in accordance with this section if—

(a)   the benefit consists in—

(i)   an asset being placed at the disposal of the employee, or at the disposal of a member of the employee's family or household, for the employee's or member's use, or

(ii)   an asset being used wholly or partly for the purposes of the employee or a member of the employee's family or household, and

(b)   there is no transfer of the property in the asset.

(2)   The cost of the taxable benefit is the higher of—

(a)   the annual value of the use of the asset, and

(b)   the annual amount of the sums, if any, paid by those providing the benefit by way of rent or hire charge for the asset,

together with the amount of any additional expense.

(3)   For the purposes of subsection (2), the annual value of the use of an asset is—

(a)   in the case of land, its annual rental value;

(b)   in any other case, 20% of the market value of the asset at the time when those providing the taxable benefit first applied the asset in the provision of an employment-related benefit (whether or not the person provided with that benefit is also the person provided with the taxable benefit).

If those providing the taxable benefit first applied the asset in the provision of an employment-related benefit before 6th April 1980, paragraph (b) is to be read as if the reference to 20% were a reference to 10%.

(4)   In this section 'additional expense' means the expense incurred in or in connection with provision of the taxable benefit (including a proper proportion of any expense relating partly to provision of the benefit and partly to other matters), other than—

    (a)   the expense of acquiring or producing the asset incurred by the person to whom the asset belongs, and

    (b)   any rent or hire charge payable for the asset by those providing the asset.

CHAPTER 11

TAXABLE BENEFITS: EXCLUSION OF LOWER-PAID EMPLOYMENTS FROM PARTS OF BENEFITS CODE

Introduction

216. Provisions not applicable to lower-paid employments

(1)   The Chapters of the benefits code listed in subsection (4) do not apply to an employment in relation to a tax year if—

    (a)   it is lower-paid employment in relation to that year (see section 217), and

    (b)   condition A or B is met.

(2)   Condition A is that the employee is not employed as a director of a company.

(3)   Condition B is that the employee is employed as a director of a company but has no material interest in the company and either—

    (a)   the employment is as a full-time working director, or

    (b)   the company is non-profit-making or is established for charitable purposes only.

'Non-profit-making' means that the company does not carry on a trade and its functions do not consist wholly or mainly in the holding of investments or other property.

(4)   The Chapters referred to in subsection (1) are—

    Chapter 3 (taxable benefits: expenses payments);
    Chapter 6 (taxable benefits: cars, vans and related benefits);
    Chapter 7 (taxable benefits: loans);
    Chapter 8 (taxable benefits: notional loans in respect of acquisitions of shares);
    Chapter 9 (taxable benefits: disposals of shares for more than market value);
    Chapter 10 (taxable benefits: residual liability to charge).

(5)   Subsection (1)—

    (a)   means that in any of those Chapters a reference to an employee does not include an employee whose employment is within the exclusion in that subsection, if the context is such that the reference is to an employee in relation to whom the Chapter applies, but

    (b)   does not restrict the meaning of references to employees in other contexts.

(6)   Subsection (1) has effect subject to—

    section 188(2) (discharge of loan: where employment becomes lower-paid),
    section 195(3) (discharge of notional loan: where employment becomes lower-paid),
    section 199(4) (disposal for more than market value: where employment becomes lower-paid), and
    section 220 (employment in two or more related employments).

What is lower-paid employment

217. Meaning of 'lower-paid employment'

(1)   For the purposes of this Chapter an employment is 'lower-paid employment' in relation to a tax year if the earnings rate for the employment for the year (calculated under section 218) is less than £8,500.

(2)   Subsection (1) is subject to section 220 (employment in two or more related employments).

PART 4

EMPLOYMENT INCOME: EXEMPTIONS

CHAPTER 9

EXEMPTIONS: PENSION PROVISION

307. Death or retirement benefit provision

(1) No liability to income tax arises by virtue of Chapter 10 of Part 3 (taxable benefits: residual liability to charge) in respect of provision made by an employee's employer for a retirement or death benefit.

(2) In subsection (1) 'retirement or death benefit' means a pension, annuity, lump sum, gratuity or other similar benefit which will be paid or given to the employee or a member of the employee's family or household in the event of the employee's retirement or death.

308. Exemption of contributions to approved personal pension arrangements

(1) No liability to income tax arises in respect of earnings where an employer makes contributions under approved personal pension arrangements made by an employee.

(2) In this section 'approved' and 'personal pension arrangements' have the meaning given by section 630(1) of ICTA.

CHAPTER 10

EXEMPTIONS: TERMINATION OF EMPLOYMENT

Redundancy payments

309. Limited exemptions for statutory redundancy payments

(1) No liability to income tax in respect of earnings arises by virtue of a redundancy payment or an approved contractual payment, except where subsection (2) applies.

(2) Where an approved contractual payment exceeds the amount which would have been due if a redundancy payment had been payable, the excess is liable to income tax.

(3) No liability to income tax in respect of employment income other than earnings arises by virtue of a redundancy payment or an approved contractual payment, except where it does so by virtue of Chapter 3 of Part 6 (payments and benefits on termination of employment etc).

(4) For the purposes of this section—

  (a) a statutory payment in respect of a redundancy payment is to be treated as paid on account of the redundancy payment, and
  (b) a statutory payment in respect of an approved contractual payment is to be treated as paid on account of the approved contractual payment.

(5) In this section—

  'approved contractual payment means a payment to a person on the termination of the person's employment under an agreement in respect of which an order is in force under section 157 of ERA 1996 or Article 192 of ER(NI)O 1996,
  'redundancy payment' means a redundancy payment under Part 11 of ERA 1996 or Part 12 of ER(NI)O 1996, and
  'statutory payment' means a payment under section 167(1) of ERA 1996 or Article 202(1) of ER(NI)O 1996.

(6) In subsection (5) 'employment', in relation to a person, has the meaning given in section 230(5) of ERA 1996 or Article 3(5) of ER(NI)O 1996.

PART 5

EMPLOYMENT INCOME: DEDUCTIONS ALLOWED FROM EARNINGS

CHAPTER 2

DEDUCTIONS FOR EMPLOYEE'S EXPENSES

General rule for deduction of employee's expenses

336. Deductions for expenses: the general rule

(1)   The general rule is that a deduction from earnings is allowed for an amount if—

    (a)   the employee is obliged to incur and pay it as holder of the employment, and
    (b)   the amount is incurred wholly, exclusively and necessarily in the performance of the duties of the employment.

(2)   The following provisions of this Chapter contain additional rules allowing deductions for particular kinds of expenses and rules preventing particular kinds of deductions.

(3)   No deduction is allowed under this section for an amount that is deductible under sections 337 to 342 (travel expenses).

PART 6

EMPLOYMENT INCOME: INCOME WHICH IS NOT EARNINGS OR SHARE-RELATED

CHAPTER 3

PAYMENTS AND BENEFITS ON TERMINATION OF EMPLOYMENT ETC

Preliminary

401. Application of this Chapter

(1)   This Chapter applies to payments and other benefits which are received directly or indirectly in consideration or in consequence of, or otherwise in connection with—

    (a)   the termination of a person's employment,
    (b)   a change in the duties of a person's employment, or
    (c)   a change in the earnings from a person's employment,

by the person, or the person's spouse, blood relative, dependant or personal representatives.

(2)   Subsection (1) is subject to subsection (3) and sections 405 to 413 (exceptions for certain payments and benefits).

(3)   This Chapter does not apply to any payment or other benefit chargeable to income tax apart from this Chapter.

(4)   For the purposes of this Chapter—

    (a)   a payment or other benefit which is provided on behalf of, or to the order of, the employee or former employee is treated as received by the employee or former employee, and
    (b)   in relation to a payment or other benefit—

        (i)   any reference to the employee or former employee is to the person mentioned in subsection (1), and
        (ii)   any reference to the employer or former employer is to be read accordingly.

402. Meaning of 'benefit'

(1)   In this Chapter 'benefit' includes anything in respect of which, were it received for performance of the duties of the employment, an amount—

(a)   would be taxable earnings from the employment, or
(b)   would be such earnings apart from an earnings-only exemption.

This is subject to subsections (2) to (4).

(2)   In this Chapter 'benefit' does not include a benefit received in connection with the termination of a person's employment that is a benefit which, were it received for performance of the duties of the employment, would fall within—

(a)   section 239(4) (exemption of benefits connected with taxable cars and vans and exempt heavy goods vehicles), so far as that section applies to a benefit connected with a car or van,
(b)   section 269 (exemption where benefits or money obtained in connection with taxable car or van or exempt heavy goods vehicle),
(c)   section 319 (mobile telephones), or
(d)   section 320 (limited exemption for computer equipment).

(3)   In this Chapter 'benefit' does not include a benefit received in connection with any change in the duties of, or earnings from, a person's employment to the extent that it is a benefit which, were it received for performance of the duties of the employment, would fall within section 271(1) (limited exemption of removal benefits and expenses).

(4)   The right to receive a payment or benefit is not itself a benefit for the purposes of this Chapter.

Payments and benefits treated as employment income

403. Charge on payment or other benefit

(1)   The amount of a payment or benefit to which this Chapter applies counts as employment income of the employee or former employee for the relevant tax year if and to the extent that it exceeds the £30,000 threshold.

(2)   In this section 'the relevant tax year' means the tax year in which the payment or other benefit is received.

(3)   For the purposes of this Chapter—

(a)   a cash benefit is treated as received—

(i)   when it is paid or a payment is made on account of it, or
(ii)   when the recipient becomes entitled to require payment of or on account of it, and

(b)   a non-cash benefit is treated as received when it is used or enjoyed.

(4)   For the purposes of this Chapter the amount of a payment or benefit in respect of an employee or former employee exceeds the £30,000 threshold if and to the extent that, when it is aggregated with other such payments or benefits to which this Chapter applies, it exceeds £30,000 according to the rules in section 404 (how the £30,000 threshold applies).

(5)   If it is received after the death of the employee or former employee—

(a)   the amount of a payment or benefit to which this Chapter applies counts as the employment income of the personal representatives for the relevant year if or to the extent that it exceeds £30,000 according to the rules in section 404, and
(b)   the tax is accordingly to be assessed and charged on them and is a debt due from and payable out of the estate.

(6)   In this Chapter references to the taxable person are to the person in relation to whom subsection (1) or (5) provides for an amount to count as employment income.

PART IV

INSOLVENCY

Insolvency Act 1986

PART I

COMPANY VOLUNTARY ARRANGEMENTS

1. Those who may propose an arrangement

(1)   The directors of a company (other than one for which an administration order is in force, or which is being wound up) may make a proposal under this Part to the company and to its creditors for a composition in satisfaction of its debts or a scheme of arrangement of its affairs (from hereon referred to, in either case, as a 'voluntary arrangement').

(2)   A proposal under this Part is one which provides for some person ('the nominee') to act in relation to the voluntary arrangement either as trustee or otherwise for the purpose of supervising its implementation; and the nominee must be a person who is qualified to act as an insolvency practitioner or authorised to act as nominee, in relation to the voluntary arrangement.

(3)   Such a proposal may also be made—

   (a)   where an administration order is in force in relation to the company, by the administrator, and
   (b)   where the company is being wound up, by the liquidator.

(4) In this Part a reference to a company includes a reference to a company in relation to which a proposal for a voluntary arrangement may be made by virtue of Article 3 of the EC Regulation.

1A.   Moratorium

(1)   Where the directors of an eligible company intend to make a proposal for a voluntary arrangement, they may take steps to obtain a moratorium for the company.

(2)   The provisions of Schedule A1 to this Act have effect with respect to—

   (a)   companies eligible for a moratorium under this section,
   (b)   the procedure for obtaining such a moratorium,
   (c)   the effects of such a moratorium, and
   (d)   the procedure applicable (in place of sections 2 to 6 and 7) in relation to the approval and implementation of a voluntary arrangement where such a moratorium is or has been in force.

2.   Procedure where nominee is not the liquidator or administrator

(1)   This section applies where the nominee under section 1 is not the liquidator or administrator of the company and the directors do not propose to take steps to obtain a moratorium under section 1A for the company.

(2)   The nominee shall, within 28 days (or such longer period as the court may allow) after he is given notice of the proposal for a voluntary arrangement, submit a report to the court stating—

   (a)   whether, in his opinion, the proposed voluntary arrangement has a reasonable prospect of being approved and implemented,
   (aa)   whether, in his opinion, meetings of the company and of its creditors should be summoned to consider the proposal, and
   (b)   if in his opinion such meetings should be summoned, the date on which, and time and place at which, he proposed the meetings should be held.

(3)   For the purposes of enabling the nominee to prepare his report, the person intending to make the proposal shall submit to the nominee—

   (a)   a document setting out the terms of the proposed voluntary arrangement, and
   (b)   a statement of the company's affairs containing—

      (i)   such particulars of its creditors and of its debts and other liabilities and of its assets as may be prescribed, and
      (ii)   such other information as may be prescribed.

(4)   The court may—

    (a)   on an application made by the person intending to make the proposal, in a case where the nominee has failed to submit the report required by this section or has died, or

    (b)   on an application made by that person or the nominee, in a case where it is impracticable or inappropriate for the nominee to continue to act as such,

direct that the nominee be replaced as such by another person qualified to act as an insolvency practitioner, or authorised to act as nominee, in relation to the voluntary arrangement.

3.   Summoning of meetings

(1)   Where the nominee under section 1 is not the liquidator or administrator, and it has been reported to the court that such meetings as are mentioned in section 2(2) should be summoned, the person making the report shall (unless the court otherwise directs) summon those meetings for the time, date and place proposed in the report.

(2)   Where the nominee is the liquidator or administrator, he shall summon meetings of the company and of its creditors to consider the proposal for such a time, date and place as he thinks fit.

(3)   The persons to be summoned to a creditors' meeting under this section are every creditor of the company of whose claim and address the person summoning the meeting is aware.

4.   Decisions of meetings

(1)   The meetings summoned under section 3 shall decide whether to approve the proposed voluntary arrangement (with or without modifications).

(2)   The modifications may include one conferring the functions proposed to be conferred on the nominee on another person qualified to act as an insolvency practitioner or authorised to act as nominee, in relation to the voluntary arrangement.

But they shall not include any modification by virtue of which the proposal ceases to be a proposal such as is mentioned in section 1.

(3)   A meeting so summoned shall not approve any proposal or modification which affects the right of a secured creditor of the company to enforce his security, except with the concurrence of the creditor concerned.

(4)   Subject as follows, a meeting so summoned shall not approve any proposal or modification under which—

    (a)   any preferential debt of the company is to be paid otherwise than in priority to such of its debts as are not preferential debts, or

    (b)   a preferential creditor of the company is to be paid an amount in respect of a preferential debt that bears to that debt a smaller proportion than is borne to another preferential debt by the amount that is to be paid in respect of that other debt.

However, the meeting may approve such a proposal or modification with the concurrence of the preferential creditor concerned.

(5)   Subject as above, each of the meetings shall be conducted in accordance with the rules.

(6)   After the conclusion of either meeting in accordance with the rules, the chairman of the meeting shall report the result of the meeting to the court, and, immediately after reporting to the court, shall give notice of the result of the meeting to such persons as may be prescribed.

(7)   References in this section to preferential debts and preferential creditors are to be read in accordance with section 386 in Part XII of this Act.

4A.   Approval of arrangement

(1)   This section applies to a decision, under section 4, with respect to the approval of a proposed voluntary arrangement.

(2)   The decision has effect if, in accordance with the rules—

    (a)   it has been taken by both meetings summoned under section 3, or

    (b)   (subject to any order made under subsection (4)) it has been taken by the creditors' meeting summoned under that section.

(3)   If the decision taken by the creditors' meeting differs from that taken by the company meeting, a member of the company may apply to the court.

(4)   An application under subsection (3) shall not be made after the end of the period of 28 days beginning with—

  (a)   the day on which the decision was taken by the creditors' meeting, or
  (b)   where the decision of the company meeting was taken on a later day, that day.

(5)   Where a member of a regulated company, within the meaning given by paragraph 44 of Schedule A1, applies to the court under subsection (3), the Financial Services Authority is entitled to be heard on the application.

(6)   On an application under subsection (3), the court may—

  (a)   order the decision of the company meeting to have effect instead of the decision of the creditors' meeting, or
  (b)   make such other order as it thinks fit.

5.   Effect of approval

(1)   This section applies where a decision approving a voluntary arrangement has effect under section 4A.

(2)   The voluntary arrangement—

  (a)   takes effect as if made by the company at the creditors' meeting, and
  (b)   binds every person who in accordance with the rules—

    (i)   was entitled to vote at that meeting (whether or not he was present or represented at it), or
    (ii)   would have been so entitled if he had had notice of it,

    as if he were a party to the voluntary arrangement.

(2A) If—

  (a)   when the arrangement ceases to have effect any amount payable under the arrangement to a person bound by virtue of subsection (2)(b)(ii) has not been paid, and
  (b)   the arrangement did not come to an end prematurely,

the company shall at that time become liable to pay to that person the amount payable under the arrangement.

(3)   Subject as follows, if the company is being wound up or an administration order is in force, the court may do one or both of the following, namely—

  (a)   by order stay or sist all proceedings in the winding up or discharge the administration order;
  (b)   give such directions with respect to the conduct of the winding up or the administration as it thinks appropriate for facilitating the implementation of the voluntary arrangement.

(4)   The court shall not make an order under subsection (3)(a)—

  (a)   at any time before the end of the period of 28 days beginning with the first day on which each of the reports required by section 4(6) has been made to the court, or
  (b)   at any time when an application under the next section or an appeal in respect of such an application is pending, or at any time in the period within which such an appeal may be brought.

6.   Challenge of decisions

(1)   Subject to this section, an application to the court may be made, by any of the persons specified below, on one or both of the following grounds, namely—

  (a)   that a voluntary arrangement which has effect under section 4A unfairly prejudices the interests of a creditor, member or contributory of the company;
  (aa) a person who would have been entitled, in accordance with the rules, to vote at the creditors' meeting if he had had notice of it;
  (b)   that there has been some material irregularity at or in relation to either of the meetings.

(2)   The persons who may apply under this section are—

  (a)   a person entitled, in accordance with the rules, to vote at either of the meetings;

    (aa)   a person who would have been entitled, in accordance with the rules, to vote at the creditors' meeting if he had had notice of it;

    (b)   the nominee or any person who has replaced him under section 2(4) or 4(2); and

    (c)   if the company is being wound up or an administration order is in force, the liquidator or administrator.

(3)   An application under this section shall not be made—

    (a)   after the end of the period of 28 days beginning with the first day on which each of the reports required by section 4(6) has been made to the court or

    (b)   in the case of a person who was not given notice of the creditors' meeting, after the end of the period of 28 days beginning with the day on which he became aware that the meeting had taken place,

but (subject to that) an application made by a person within subsection (2)(aa) on the ground that the voluntary arrangement prejudices his interests may be made after the arrangement has ceased to have effect, unless it came to an end prematurely.

(4)   Where on such an application the court is satisfied as to either of the grounds mentioned in subsection (1), it may do one or both of the following, namely—

    (a)   revoke or suspend any decision approving the voluntary arrangement which has effect under section 4A or, in a case falling within subsection (1)(b), any decision taken by the meeting in question which has effect under that section;

    (b)   give a direction to any person for the summoning of further meetings to consider any revised proposal the person who made the original proposal may make or, in a case falling within subsection (1)(b), a further company or (as the case may be) creditors' meeting to reconsider the original proposal.

(5)   Where at any time after giving a direction under subsection (4)(b) for the summoning of meetings to consider a revised proposal the court is satisfied that the person who made the original proposal does not intend to submit a revised proposal, the court shall revoke the direction and revoke or suspend any decision approving the voluntary arrangement which has effect under section 4A.

(6)   In a case where the court, on an application under this section with respect to any meeting—

    (a)   gives a direction under subsection (4)(b), or

    (b)   revokes or suspends an approval under subsection (4)(a) or (5),

the court may give such supplemental directions as it thinks fit and, in particular, directions with respect to things done under the voluntary arrangement since it took effect.

(7)   Except in pursuance of the preceding provisions of this section, a decision taken at a meeting summoned under section 3 is not invalidated by any irregularity at or in relation to the meeting.

6A. False representations, etc

(1)   If, for the purpose of obtaining the approval of the members or creditors of a company to a proposal for a voluntary arrangement, a person who is an officer of the company—

    (a)   makes any false representation, or

    (b)   fraudulently does, or omits to do, anything,

he commits an offence.

(2)   Subsection (1) applies even if the proposal is not approved.

(3)   For purposes of this section 'officer' includes a shadow director.

(4)   A person guilty of an offence under this section is liable to imprisonment or a fine, or both.

7. Implementation of proposal

(1)   This section applies where a voluntary arrangement has effect under section 4A.

(2)   The person who is for the time being carrying out in relation to the voluntary arrangement the functions conferred—

    (a)   on the nominee by virtue of the approval given at one or both of the meetings summoned under section 3, or

    (b)   by virtue of section 2(4) or 4(2) on a person other than the nominee, shall be known as the supervisor of the voluntary arrangement.

(3)   If any of the company's creditors or any other person is dissatisfied by any act, omission or decision of the supervisor, he may apply to the court; and on the application the court may—

    (a)   confirm, reverse or modify any act or decision of the supervisor,

    (b)   give him directions, or

    (c)   make such other order as it thinks fit.

(4)   The supervisor—

    (a)   may apply to the court for directions in relation to any particular matter arising under the voluntary arrangement, and

    (b)   is included among the persons who may apply to the court for the winding up of the company or for an administration order to be made in relation to it.

(5)   The court may, whenever—

    (a)   it is expedient to appoint a person to carry out the functions of the supervisor, and

    (b)   it is inexpedient, difficult or impracticable for an appointment to be made without the assistance of the court,

make an order appointing a person who is qualified to act as an insolvency practitioner or authorised to act as supervisor, in relation to the voluntary arrangement, either in substitution for the existing supervisor or to fill a vacancy.

(6)   The power conferred by subsection (5) is exercisable so as to increase the number of persons exercising the functions of supervisor or, where there is more than one person exercising those functions, so as to replace one or more of those persons.

7A.   Prosecution of delinquent officers of company

(1)   This section applies where a moratorium under section 1A has been obtained for a company or the approval of a voluntary arrangement in relation to a company has taken effect under section 4A or paragraph 36 of Schedule A1.

(2)   If it appears to the nominee or supervisor that any past or present officer of the company has been guilty of any offence in connection with the moratorium or, as the case may be, voluntary arrangement for which he is criminally liable, the nominee or supervisor shall forthwith—

    (a)   report the matter to the appropriate authority, and

    (b)   provide the appropriate authority with such information and give the authority such access to and facilities for inspecting and taking copies of documents (being information or documents in the possession or under the control of the nominee or supervisor and relating to the matter in question) as the authority requires.

In this subsection, 'the appropriate authority' means—

    (i)   in the case of a company registered in England and Wales, the Secretary of State, and

    (ii)   in the case of a company registered in Scotland, the Lord Advocate.

(3)   Where a report is made to the Secretary of State under subsection (2), he may, for the purpose of investigating the matter reported to him and such other matters relating to the affairs of the company as appear to him to require investigation, exercise any of the powers which are exercisable by inspectors appointed under section 431 or 432 of the Companies Act to investigate a company's affairs.

(4)   For the purpose of such an investigation any obligation imposed on a person by any provision of the Companies Act to produce documents or give information to, or otherwise to assist, inspectors so appointed is to be regarded as an obligation similarly to assist the Secretary of State in his investigation.

(5)   An answer given by a person to a question put to him in exercise of the powers conferred by subsection (3) may be used in evidence against him.

(6)   However, in criminal proceedings in which that person is charged with an offence to which this subsection applies—

    (a)   no evidence relating to the answer may be adduced, and

    (b)   no question relating to it may be asked,

Part IV   Insolvency

by or on behalf of the prosecution, unless evidence relating to it is adduced, or a question relating to it is asked, in the proceedings by or on behalf of that person.

(7)   Subsection (6) applies to any offence other than—

    (a)   an offence under section 2 or 5 of the Perjury Act 1911 (false statements made on oath otherwise than in judicial proceedings or made otherwise than on oath), or

    (b)   an offence under section 44(1) or (2) of the Criminal Law (Consolidation) (Scotland) Act 1995 (false statements made on oath or otherwise than on oath).

(8)   Where a prosecuting authority institutes criminal proceedings following any report under subsection (2), the nominee or supervisor, and every officer and agent of the company past and present (other than the defendant or defender), shall give the authority all assistance in connection with the prosecution which he is reasonably able to give.

For this purpose—

    'agent' includes any banker or solicitor of the company and any person employed by the company as auditor, whether that person is or is not an officer of the company,

    'prosecuting authority' means the Director of Public Prosecutions, the Lord Advocate or the Secretary of State.

(9)   The court may, on the application of the prosecuting authority, direct any person referred to in subsection (8) to comply with that subsection if he has failed to do so.

7B.   Arrangements coming to an end prematurely

For the purposes of this Part, a voluntary arrangement the approval of which has taken effect under section 4A or paragraph 36 of Schedule A1 comes to an end prematurely if, when it ceases to have effect, it has not been fully implemented in respect of all persons bound by the arrangement by virtue of section 5(2)(b)(i) or, as the case may be, paragraph 37(2)(b)(i) of Schedule A1.

PART II

ADMINISTRATION ORDERS

8.   Power of court to make order

(1)   Subject to this section, if the court—

    (a)   is satisfied that a company is or is likely to become unable to pay its debts (within the meaning given to that expression by section 123 of this Act), and

    (b)   considers that the making of an order under this section would be likely to achieve one or more of the purposes mentioned below,

the court may make an administration order in relation to the company.

(1A)   For the purposes of a petition presented by the Financial Services Authority alone or together with any other party, an authorised deposit taker who defaults in an obligation to pay any sum due and payable in respect of a relevant deposit is deemed to be unable to pay its debts as mentioned in subsection (1).

(1B)   In subsection (1A)—

    (a)   'authorised deposit taker' means a person who has permission under Part 4 of the Financial Services and Markets Act 2000 to accept deposits, but excludes a person who has such permission only for the purpose of carrying on another regulated activity in accordance with that permission; and

    (b)   'relevant deposit' must be read with—

        (i)   section 22 of the Financial Services and Markets Act 2000,

        (ii)   any relevant order under that section, and

        (iii)   Schedule 2 to that Act,

    but any restriction on the meaning of deposit which arises from the identity of the person making it is to be disregarded.

(2)   An administration order is an order directing that during the period for which the order is in force, the affairs, business and property of the company shall be managed by a person ('the administrator') appointed for the purpose by the court.

(3)   The purposes for whose achievement an administration order may be made are—

    (a)   the survival of the company, and the whole, or any part of its undertaking, as a going concern;

    (b)   the approval of a voluntary arrangement under Part I;

    (c)   the sanctioning under section 425 of the Companies Act of a compromise or arrangement between the company and any such persons as are mentioned in that section; and

    (d)   a more advantageous realisation of the company's assets than would be effected on a winding up;

and the order shall specify the purpose or purposes for which it is made.

(4)   An administration order shall not be made in relation to a company after it has gone into liquidation.

(5)   An administration order shall not be made against a company if—

    (a)   it effects or carries out contracts of insurance, but is not—

        (i)   exempt from the general prohibition, within the meaning of section 19 of the Financial Services and Markets Act 2000, in relation to effecting or carrying out contracts of insurance, or

        (ii)   an authorised deposit taker within the meaning given by subsection (1B), and effecting or carrying out contracts of insurance in the course of a banking business;

    (b)   it continues to have a liability in respect of a deposit which was held by it in accordance with the Banking Act 1979 or the Banking Act 1987, but is not an authorised deposit taker, within the meaning given by subsection (1B).

(6)   Subsection (5)(a) must be read with—

    (a)   section 22 of the Financial Services and Markets Act 2000;

    (b)   any relevant order under that section; and

    (c)   Schedule 2 to that Act.

(7)   In this Part a reference to a company includes a reference to a company in relation to which an administration order may be made by virtue of Article 3 of the EC Regulation.

9.   Application for order

(1)   An application to the court for an administration order shall be by petition presented either by the company or the directors, or by a creditor or creditors (including any contingent or prospective creditor or creditors), or by a justices' chief executive in the exercise of the power conferred by section 87A of the Magistrates' Court Act 1980 (enforcement of fines imposed on companies), or by all or any of those parties, together or separately.

(2)   Where a petition is presented to the court—

    (a)   notice of the petition shall be given forthwith to any person who has appointed, or is or may be entitled to appoint, an administrative receiver of the company and to such other persons as may be prescribed, and

    (b)   the petition shall not be withdrawn except with the leave of the court.

(3)   Where the court is satisfied that there is an administrative receiver of the company, the court shall dismiss the petition unless it is also satisfied either—

    (a)   that the person by whom or on whose behalf the receiver was appointed has consented to the making of the order, or

    (b)   that, if an administration order were made, any security by virtue of which the receiver was appointed would—

        (i)   be void against the administrator to any extent by virtue of the provisions of Part XII of the Companies Act 1985 (registration of company charges).
             [Para (b) (i)–(iii) renumbered (ii)–(iv); prosp sub not yet in force.]

        (ii)   be liable to be released or discharged under sections 238 to 240 in Part VI (transactions at an undervalue and preferences),

        (iii)   be avoided under section 245 in that Part (avoidance of floating charges), or

        (iv)   [Applies to Scotland only]

(4)   Subject to subsection (3), on hearing a petition the court may dismiss it, or adjourn the hearing conditionally or unconditionally, or make an interim order or any other order that it thinks fit.

(5)   Without prejudice to the generality of subsection (4), an interim order under that subsection may restrict the exercise of any powers of the directors or of the company (whether by reference to the consent of the court or of a person qualified to act as an insolvency practitioner in relation to the company, or otherwise).

10.   Effect of application

(1)   During the period beginning with the presentation of a petition for an administration order and ending with the making of such an order or the dismissal of the petition—

    (a)   no resolution may be passed or order made for the winding up of the company;

    (aa)   no landlord or other person to whom rent is payable may exercise any right of forfeiture by peaceable re-entry in relation to premises let to the company in respect of a failure by the company to comply with any term or condition of its tenancy of such premises, except with the leave of the court and subject to such terms as the court may impose;

    (b)   no steps may be taken to enforce any security over the company's property, or to repossess goods in the company's possession under any hire-purchase agreement, except with the leave of the court and subject to such terms as the court may impose; and

    (c)   no other proceedings and no execution or other legal process may be commenced or continued, and no distress may be levied, against the company or its property except with the leave of the court and subject to such terms as aforesaid.

(2)   Nothing in subsection (1) requires the leave of the court—

    (a)   for the presentation of a petition for the winding up of the company,

    (b)   for the appointment of an administrative receiver of the company, or

    (c)   for the carrying out by such a receiver (whenever appointed) of any of his functions.

(3)   Where—

    (a)   a petition for an administration order is presented at a time when there is an administrative receiver of the company, and

    (b)   the person by or on whose behalf the receiver was appointed has not consented to the making of the order,

the period mentioned in subsection (1) is deemed not to begin unless and until that person so consents.

(4)   References in this section and the next to hire-purchase agreements include conditional sale agreements, chattel leasing agreements and retention of title agreements.

(5)   [Applies to Scotland only]

11.   Effect of order

(1)   On the making of an administration order—

    (a)   any petition for the winding up of the company shall be dismissed, and

    (b)   any administrative receiver of the company shall vacate office.

(2)   Where an administration order has been made, any receiver of part of the company's property shall vacate office on being required to do so by the administrator.

(3)   During the period for which an administration order is in force—

    (a)   no resolution may be passed or order made for the winding up the company;

    (b)   no administrative receiver of the company may be appointed;

    (ba)   no landlord or other person to whom rent is payable may exercise any right of forfeiture by peaceable re-entry in relation to premises let to the company in respect of a failure by the company to comply with any term or condition of its tenancy of such premises, except with the consent of the administrator or the leave of the court and subject (where the court gives leave) to such terms as the court may impose;

    (c)   no other steps may be taken to enforce any security over the company's property, or to repossess goods in the company's possession under any hire-purchase agreement, except with the consent of the administrator or the leave of the court and subject (where the court gives leave) to such terms as the court may impose; and

(d) no other proceedings and no execution or other legal process may be commenced or continued, and no distress may be levied, against the company or its property except with the consent of the administrator or the leave of the court and subject (where the court gives leave) to such terms as aforesaid.

(4) Where at any time an administrative receiver of the company has vacated office under subsection (1)(b), or a receiver of part of the company's property has vacated office under subsection (2)—

(a) his remuneration and any expenses properly incurred by him, and

(b) any indemnity to which he is entitled out of the assets of the company,

shall be charged on and (subject to subsection (3) above) paid out of any property of the company which was in his custody or under his control at that time in priority to any security held by the person by or on whose behalf he was appointed.

(5) Neither an administrative receiver who vacates office under subsection (1)(b) nor a receiver who vacates office under subsection (2) is required on or after so vacating office to take any steps for the purpose of complying with any duty imposed on him by section 40 or 59 of this Act (duty to pay preferential creditors).

12. Notification of order

(1) Every invoice, order for goods or business letter which, at a time when an administration order is in force in relation to a company, is issued by or on behalf of the company or the administrator, being a document on or in which the company's name appears, shall also contain the administrator's name and a statement that the affairs, business and property of the company are being managed by the administrator.

(2) If default is made in complying with this section, the company and any of the following persons who without reasonable excuse authorises or permits the default, namely, the administrator and any officer of the company, is liable to a fine.

13. Appointment of administrator

(1) The administrator of a company shall be appointed either by the administration order or by an order under the next subsection.

(2) If a vacancy occurs by death, resignation or otherwise in the office of the administrator, the court may by order fill the vacancy.

(3) An application for an order under subsection (2) may be made—

(a) by any continuing administrator of the company; or

(b) where there is no such administrator, by a creditors' committee established under section 26 below; or

(c) where there is no such administrator and no such committee, by the company or the directors or by any creditor or creditors of the company.

14. General powers

(1) The administrator of a company—

(a) may do all such things as may be necessary for the management of the affairs, business and property of the company, and

(b) without prejudice to the generality of paragraph (a), has the powers specified in Schedule 1 to this Act;

and in the application of that Schedule to the administrator of a company the words 'he' and 'him' refer to the administrator.

(2) The administrator also has power—

(a) to remove any director of the company and to appoint any person to be a director of it, whether to fill a vacancy or otherwise, and

(b) to call any meeting of the members or creditors of the company.

(3) The administrator may apply to the court for directions in relation to any particular matter arising in connection with the carrying out of his functions.

(4) Any power conferred on the company or its officers, whether by this Act or the Companies Act or by the memorandum or articles of association, which could be exercised in such a way as to interfere with the exercise by

the administrator of his powers is not exercisable except with the consent of the administrator, which may be given either generally or in relation to particular cases.

(5)   In exercising his powers the administrator is deemed to act as the company's agent.

(6)   A person dealing with the administrator in good faith and for value is not concerned to inquire whether the administrator is acting within his powers.

17.   General duties

(1)   The administrator of a company shall, on his appointment, take into his custody or under his control all the property to which the company is or appears to be entitled.

(2)   The administrator shall manage the affairs, business and property of the company—

(a)   at any time before proposals have been approved (with or without modifications) under section 24 below, in accordance with any directions given by the court, and

(b)   at any time after proposals have been so approved, in accordance with those proposals as from time to time revised, whether by him or a predecessor of his.

(3)   The administrator shall summon a meeting of the company's creditors if—

(a)   he is requested, in accordance with the rules, to do so by one-tenth, in value, of the company's creditors, or

(b)   he is directed to do so by the court.

18.   Discharge or variation of administration order

(1)   The administrator of a company may at any time apply to the court for the administration order to be discharged, or to be varied so as to specify an additional purpose.

(2)   The administrator shall make an application under this section if—

(a)   it appears to him that the purpose or each of the purposes specified in the order either has been achieved or is incapable of achievement, or

(b)   he is required to do so by a meeting of the company's creditors summoned for the purpose in accordance with the rules.

(3)   On the hearing of an application under this section, the court may by order discharge or vary the administration order and make such consequential provision as it thinks fit, or adjourn the hearing conditionally or unconditionally, or make an interim order or any other order it thinks fit.

(4)   Where the administration order is discharged or varied the administrator shall, within 14 days after the making of the order effecting the discharge or variation, send an office copy of that order to the registrar of companies.

(5)   If the administrator without reasonable excuse fails to comply with subsection (4), he is liable to a fine and, for continued contravention, to a daily default fine.

20.   Release of administrator

(1)   A person who has ceased to be the administrator of a company has his release with effect from the following time, that is to say—

(a)   in the case of a person who has died, the time at which notice is given to the court in accordance with the rules that he has ceased to hold office;

(b)   in any other case, such time as the court may determine.

(2)   Where a person has his release under this section, he is, with effect from the time specified above, discharged from all liability both in respect of acts or omissions of his in the administration and otherwise in relation to his conduct as administrator.

(3)   However, nothing in this section prevents the exercise, in relation to a person who has had his release as above, of the court's powers under section 212 in Chapter X of Part IV (summary remedy against delinquent directors, liquidators, etc).

23. Statement of proposals

(1)   Where an administration order has been made, the administrator shall, within 3 months (or such longer period as the court may allow) after the making of the order—

    (a)   send to the registrar of companies and (so far as he is aware of their addresses) to all creditors a statement of his proposals for achieving the purpose or purposes specified in the order, and

    (b)   lay a copy of the statement before a meeting of the company's creditors summoned for the purpose on not less than 14 days' notice.

(2)   The administrator shall also, within 3 months (or such longer period as the court may allow) after the making of the order, either—

    (a)   send a copy of the statement (so far as he is aware of their addresses) to all members of the company, or

    (b)   publish in the prescribed manner a notice stating an address to which members of the company should write for copies of the statement to be sent to them free of charge.

(3)   If the administrator without reasonable excuse fails to comply with this section, he is liable to a fine and, for continued contravention, to a daily default fine.

24. Consideration of proposals by creditors' meeting

(1)   A meeting of creditors summoned under section 23 shall decide whether to approve the administrator's proposals.

(2)   The meeting may approve the proposals with modifications, but shall not do so unless the administrator consents to each modification.

(3)   Subject as above, the meeting shall be conducted in accordance with the rules.

(4)   After the conclusion of the meeting in accordance with the rules, the administrator shall report the result of the meeting to the court and shall give notice of that result to the registrar of companies and to such persons as may be prescribed.

(5)   If a report is given to the court under subsection (4) that the meeting has declined to approve the administrator's proposals (with or without modifications), the court may by order discharge the administration order and make such consequential provision as it thinks fit, or adjourn the hearing conditionally or unconditionally, or make an interim order or any other order that it thinks fit.

(6)   Where the administration order is discharged, the administrator shall, within 14 days after the making of the order effecting the discharge, send an office copy of that order to the registrar of companies.

(7)   If the administrator without reasonable excuse fails to comply with subsection (6), he is liable to a fine and, for continued contravention, to a daily default fine.

25. Approval of substantial revisions

(1)   This section applies where—

    (a)   proposals have been approved (with or without modifications) under section 24, and

    (b)   the administrator proposes to make revisions of those proposals which appear to him substantial.

(2)   The administrator shall—

    (a)   send to all creditors of the company (so far as he is aware of their addresses) a statement in the prescribed form of his proposed revisions, and

    (b)   lay a copy of the statement before a meeting of the company's creditors summoned for the purpose on not less than 14 days' notice;

and he shall not make the proposed revisions unless they are approved by the meeting.

(3)   The administrator shall also either—

    (a)   send a copy of the statement (so far as he is aware of their addresses) to all members of the company, or

    (b)   publish in the prescribed manner a notice stating an address to which members of the company should write for copies of the statement to be sent to them free of charge.

(4)   The meeting of creditors may approve the proposed revisions with modifications, but shall not do so unless the administrator consents to each modification.

(5)   Subject as above, the meeting shall be conducted in accordance with the rules.

(6)   After the conclusion of the meeting in accordance with the rules, the administrator shall give notice of the result of the meeting to the registrar of companies and to such persons as may be prescribed.

26.   Creditors' committee

(1)   Where a meeting of creditors summoned under section 23 has approved the administrator's proposals (with or without modifications), the meeting may, if it thinks fit, establish a committee ('the creditors' committee') to exercise the functions conferred on it by or under this Act.

(2)   If such a committee is established, the committee may, on giving not less than 7 days' notice, require the administrator to attend before it at any reasonable time and furnish it with such information relating to the carrying out of his functions as it may reasonably require.

27.   Protection of interests of creditors and members

(1)   At any time when an administration order is in force, a creditor or member of the company may apply to the court by petition for an order under this section on the ground—

   (a)   that the company's affairs, business and property are being or have been managed by the administrator in a manner which is unfairly prejudicial to the interests of its creditors or members generally, or of some part of its creditors or members (including at least himself), or
   (b)   that any actual or proposed act or omission of the administrator is or would be so prejudicial.

(2)   On an application for an order under this section the court may, subject as follows, make such order as it thinks fit for giving relief in respect of the matters complained of, or adjourn the hearing conditionally or unconditionally, or make an interim order or any other order that it thinks fit.

(3)   An order under this section shall not prejudice or prevent—

   (a)   the implementation of a voluntary arrangement approved under section 4 in [Ital words prosp rep] Part I, or any compromise or arrangement sanctioned under section 425 of the Companies Act; or
   (b)   where the application for the order was made more than 28 days after the approval of any proposals or revised proposals under section 24 or 25, the implementation of those proposals or revised proposals.

(4)   Subject as above, an order under this section may in particular—

   (a)   regulate the future management by the administrator of the company's affairs, business and property;
   (b)   require the administrator to refrain from doing or continuing an act complained of by the petitioner, or to do an act which the petitioner has complained he has omitted to do;
   (c)   require the summoning of a meeting of creditors or members for the purpose of considering such matters as the court may direct;
   (d)   discharge the administration order and make such consequential provision as the court thinks fit.

(5)   Nothing in section 15 or 16 is to be taken as prejudicing applications to the court under this section.

(6)   Where the administration order is discharged, the administrator shall, within 14 days after the making of the order effecting the discharge, send an office copy of that order to the registrar of companies; and if without reasonable excuse he fails to comply with this subsection, he is liable to a fine and, for continued contravention, to a daily default fine.

PART III

RECEIVERSHIP

29.   Definitions

(1)   It is hereby declared that, except where the context otherwise requires—

   (a)   any reference in the Companies Act or this Act to a receiver or manager of the property of a company, or to a receiver of it, includes a receiver or manager, or (as the case may be) a receiver of part only of that property and a receiver only of the income arising from the property or from part of it; and

(b) any reference in the Companies Act or this Act to the appointment of a receiver or manager under powers contained in an instrument includes an appointment made under powers which, by virtue of any enactment, are implied in and have effect as if contained in an instrument.

(2) In this Chapter 'administrative receiver' means—

(a) a receiver or manager of the whole (or substantially the whole) of a company's property appointed by or on behalf of the holders of any debentures of the company secured by a charge which, as created, was a floating charge, or by such a charge and one or more other securities; or

(b) a person who would be such a receiver or manager but for the appointment of some other person as the receiver of part of the company's property.

31. Disqualification of undischarged bankrupt

If a person being an undischarged bankrupt acts as receiver or manager of the property of a company on behalf of debenture holders, he is liable to imprisonment or a fine, or both.

This does not apply to a receiver or manager acting under an appointment made by the court.

33. Time from which appointment is effective

(1) The appointment of a person as a receiver or manager of a company's property under powers contained in an instrument—

(a) is of no effect unless it is accepted by that person before the end of the business day next following that on which the instrument of appointment is received by him or on his behalf, and

(b) subject to this, is deemed to be made at the time at which the instrument of appointment is so received.

(2) This section applies to the appointment of two or more persons as joint receivers or managers of a company's property under powers contained in an instrument, subject to such modifications as may be prescribed by the rules.

40. Payment of debts out of assets subject to floating charge

(1) The following applies, in the case of a company, where a receiver is appointed on behalf of the holders of any debentures of the company secured by a charge which, as created, was a floating charge.

(2) If the company is not at the time in course of being wound up, its preferential debts (within the meaning given to that expression by section 386 in Part XII) shall be paid out of the assets coming to the hands of the receiver in priority to any claims for principal or interest in respect of the debentures.

(3) Payments made under this section shall be recouped, as far as may be, out of the assets of the company available for payment of general creditors.

42. General powers

(1) The powers conferred on the administrative receiver of a company by the debentures by virtue of which he was appointed are deemed to include (except in so far as they are inconsistent with any of the provisions of those debentures) the powers specified in Schedule 1 to this Act.

(2) In the application of Schedule 1 to the administrative receiver of a company—

(a) the words 'he' and 'him' refer to the administrative receiver, and

(b) references to the property of the company are to the property of which he is or, but for the appointment of some other person as the receiver of part of the company's property, would be the receiver or manager.

(3) A person dealing with the administrative receiver in good faith and for value is not concerned to inquire whether the receiver is acting within his powers.

44. Agency and liability for contracts

(1) The administrative receiver of a company—

(a) is deemed to be the company's agent, unless and until the company goes into liquidation;

(b) is personally liable on any contract entered into by him in the carrying out of his functions (except in so far as the contract otherwise provides) and, to the extent of any qualifying liability, on any contract of employment adopted by him in the carrying out of those functions; and

(c)   is entitled in respect of that liability to an indemnity out of the assets of the company.

(2)   For the purposes of subsection (1)(b) the administrative receiver is not to be taken to have adopted a contract of employment by reason of anything done or omitted to be done within 14 days after his appointment.

(2A)   For the purposes of subsection (1)(b), a liability under a contract of employment is a qualifying liability if—

(a)   it is a liability to pay a sum by way of wages or salary or contribution to an occupational pension scheme,
(b)   it is incurred while the administrative receiver is in office, and
(c)   it is in respect of services rendered wholly or partly after the adoption of the contract.

(2B)   Where a sum payable in respect of a liability which is a qualifying liability for the purposes of subsection (1)(b) is payable in respect of services rendered partly before and partly after the adoption of the contract, liability under subsection (1)(b) shall only extend to so much of the sum as is payable in respect of services rendered after the adoption of the contract.

(2C)   For the purposes of subsections (2A) and (2B)—

(a)   wages or salary payable in respect of a period of holiday or absence from work through sickness or other good cause are deemed to be wages or (as the case may be) salary in respect of services rendered in that period, and
(b)   a sum payable in lieu of holiday is deemed to be wages or (as the case may be) salary in respect of services rendered in the period by reference to which the holiday entitlement arose.

(2D)   In subsection (2C)(a), the reference to wages or salary payable in respect of a period of holiday includes any sums which, if they had been paid, would have been treated for the purposes of the enactments relating to social security as earnings in respect of that period.

(3)   This section does not limit any right to indemnity which the administrative receiver would have apart from it, nor limit his liability on contracts entered into or adopted without authority, nor confer any right to indemnity in respect of that liability.

46.   Information to be given by administrative receiver

(1)   Where an administrative receiver is appointed, he shall—

(a)   forthwith send to the company and publish in the prescribed manner a notice of his appointment, and
(b)   within 28 days after his appointment, unless the court otherwise directs, send such a notice to all the creditors of the company (so far as he is aware of their addresses).

(2)   This section and the next do not apply in relation to the appointment of an administrative receiver to act—

(a)   with an existing administrative receiver, or
(b)   in place of an administrative receiver dying or ceasing to act,

except that, where they apply to an administrative receiver who dies or ceases to act before they have been fully complied with, the references in this section and the next to the administrative receiver include (subject to the next subsection) his successor and any continuing administrative receiver.

(3)   If the company is being wound up, this section and the next apply notwithstanding that the administrative receiver and the liquidator are the same person, but with any necessary modifications arising from that fact.

(4)   If the administrative receiver without reasonable excuse fails to comply with this section, he is liable to a fine and, for continued contravention, to a daily default fine.

48.   Report by administrative receiver

(1)   Where an administrative receiver is appointed, he shall, within 3 months (or such longer period as the court may allow) after his appointment, send to the registrar of companies, to any trustees for secured creditors of the company and (so far as he is aware of their addresses) to all such creditors a report as to the following matters, namely—

(a)   the events leading up to his appointment, so far as he is aware of them;
(b)   the disposal or proposed disposal by him of any property of the company and the carrying on or proposed carrying on by him of any business of the company;

(c) the amounts of principal and interest payable to the debenture holders by whom or on whose behalf he was appointed and the amounts payable to preferential creditors; and

(d) the amount (if any) likely to be available for the payment of other creditors.

(2) The administrative receiver shall also, within 3 months (or such longer period as the court may allow) after his appointment, either—

(a) send a copy of the report (so far as he is aware of their addresses) to all unsecured creditors of the company; or

(b) publish in the prescribed manner a notice stating an address to which unsecured creditors of the company should write for copies of the report to be sent to them free of charge,

and (in either case), unless the court otherwise directs, lay a copy of the report before a meeting of the company's unsecured creditors summoned for the purpose on not less than 14 days' notice.

(3) The court shall not give a direction under subsection (2) unless—

(a) the report states the intention of the administrative receiver to apply for the direction, and

(b) a copy of the report is sent to the persons mentioned in paragraph (a) of that subsection, or a notice is published as mentioned in paragraph (b) of that subsection, not less than 14 days before the hearing of the application.

(4) Where the company has gone or goes into liquidation, the administrative receiver—

(a) shall, within 7 days after his compliance with subsection (1) or, if later, the nomination or appointment of the liquidator, send a copy of the report to the liquidator, and

(b) where he does so within the time limited for compliance with subsection (2), is not required to comply with that subsection.

(5) A report under this section shall include a summary of the statement of affairs made out and submitted to the administrative receiver under section 47 and of his comments (if any) upon it.

(6) Nothing in this section is to be taken as requiring any such report to include any information the disclosure of which would seriously prejudice the carrying out by the administrative receiver of his functions.

(7) Section 46(2) applies for the purposes of this section also.

(8) If the administrative receiver without reasonable excuse fails to comply with this section, he is liable to a fine and, for continued contravention, to a daily default fine.

72A. *Floating charge holder not to appoint administrative receiver*

(1) The holder of a qualifying floating charge in respect of a company's property may not appoint an administrative receiver of the company.

(2) In Scotland, the holder of a qualifying floating charge in respect of a company's property may not appoint or apply to the court for the appointment of a receiver who on appointment would be an administrative receiver of property of the company.

(3) In subsections (1) and (2)—

> *'holder of a qualifying floating charge in respect of a company's property' has the same meaning as in paragraph 14 of Schedule B1 to this Act, and*
> *'administrative receiver' has the meaning given by section 251.*

(4) This section applies—

(a) to a floating charge created on or after a date appointed by the Secretary of State by order made by statutory instrument, and

(b) in spite of any provision of an agreement or instrument which purports to empower a person to appoint an administrative receiver (by whatever name).

(5) An order under subsection (4)(a) may—

(a) make provision which applies generally or only for a specified purpose;

(b) make different provision for different purposes;

(c) make transitional provision.

(6) This section is subject to the exceptions specified in sections 72B to 72G.

Part IV Insolvency

Note: Section in italics prosp ins Enterprise Act 2002, s 250(1)

72B. First exception: capital market

(1)   Section 72A does not prevent the appointment of an administrative receiver in pursuance of an agreement which is or forms part of a capital market arrangement if—

> *(a)   a party incurs or, when the agreement was entered into was expected to incur, a debt of at least £50 million under the arrangement, and*
> *(b)   the arrangement involves the issue of a capital market investment.*

(2)   In subsection (1)—

> *'capital market arrangement' means an arrangement of a kind described in paragraph 1 of Schedule 2A, and*
> *'capital market investment' means an investment of a kind described in paragraph 2 or 3 of that Schedule.*

Note: Section in italics prosp ins Enterprise Act 2002, s 250(1)

72C. Second exception: public-private partnership

(1)   Section 72A does not prevent the appointment of an administrative receiver of a project company of a project which—

> *(a)   is a public-private partnership project, and*
> *(b)   includes step-in rights.*

(2)   In this section 'public-private partnership project' means a project—

> *(a)   the resources for which are provided partly by one or more public bodies and partly by one or more private persons, or*
> *(b)   which is designed wholly or mainly for the purpose of assisting a public body to discharge a function.*

(3)   In this section—

> *'step-in rights' has the meaning given by paragraph 6 of Schedule 2A, and*
> *'project company' has the meaning given by paragraph 7 of that Schedule.*

Note: Section in italics prosp ins Enterprise Act 2002, s 250(1)

72D. Third exception: utilities

(1)   Section 72A does not prevent the appointment of an administrative receiver of a project company of a project which—

> *(a)   is a utility project, and*
> *(b)   includes step-in rights.*

(2)   In this section—

> *(a)   'utility project' means a project designed wholly or mainly for the purpose of a regulated business,*
> *(b)   'regulated business' means a business of a kind listed in paragraph 10 of Schedule 2A,*
> *(c)   'step-in rights' has the meaning given by paragraph 6 of that Schedule, and*
> *(d)   'project company' has the meaning given by paragraph 7 of that Schedule.*

Note: Section in italics prosp ins Enterprise Act 2002, s 250(1)

72E. Fourth exception: project finance

(1)   Section 72A does not prevent the appointment of an administrative receiver of a project company of a project which—

> *(a)   is a financed project, and*
> *(b)   includes step-in rights.*

(2)   In this section—

> *(a)   a project is 'financed' if under an agreement relating to the project a project company incurs, or when the agreement is entered into is expected to incur, a debt of at least £50 million for the purposes of carrying out the project,*

(b) *'project company' has the meaning given by paragraph 7 of Schedule 2A, and*

(c) *'step-in rights' has the meaning given by paragraph 6 of that Schedule.*

Note: Section in italics prosp ins Enterprise Act 2002, s 250(1)

72F. Fifth exception: financial market

Section 72A does not prevent the appointment of an administrative receiver of a company by virtue of—

(a) *a market charge within the meaning of section 173 of the Companies Act 1989,*

(b) *a system-charge within the meaning of the Financial Markets and Insolvency Regulations 1996,*

(c) *a collateral security charge within the meaning of the Financial Markets and Insolvency (Settlement Finality) Regulations 1999.*

Note: Section in italics prosp ins Enterprise Act 2002, s 250(1)

72G Sixth exception: registered social landlord

Section 72A does not prevent the appointment of an administrative receiver of a company which is registered as a social landlord under Part 1 of the Housing Act 1996 or under Part 3 of the Housing (Scotland) Act 2001.

Note: Section in italics prosp ins Enterprise Act 2002, s 250(1)

72H. Sections 72A to 72G: supplementary

(1) Schedule 2A (which supplements sections 72B to 72G) shall have effect.

(2) The Secretary of State may by order—

(a) insert into this Act provision creating an additional exception to section 72A(1) or (2);

(b) provide for a provision of this Act which creates an exception to section 72A(1) or (2) to cease to have effect;

(c) amend section 72A in consequence of provision made under paragraph (a) or (b);

(d) amend any of sections 72B to 72G;

(e) amend Schedule 2A.

(3) An order under subsection (2) must be made by statutory instrument.

(4) An order under subsection (2) may make—

(a) provision which applies generally or only for a specified purpose;

(b) different provision for different purposes;

(c) consequential or supplementary provision;

(d) transitional provision.

(5) An order under subsection (2)—

(a) in the case of an order under subsection (2)(e), shall be subject to annulment in pursuance of a resolution of either House of Parliament,

(b) in the case of an order under subsection (2)(d) varying the sum specified in section 72B(1)(a) or 72E(2)(a) (whether or not the order also makes consequential or transitional provision), shall be subject to annulment in pursuance of a resolution of either House of Parliament, and

(c) in the case of any other order under subsection (2)(a) to (d), may not be made unless a draft has been laid before and approved by resolution of each House of Parliament.

Note: Sub-section in italics prosp ins Enterprise Act 2002, s 250(1)

PART IV

WINDING UP OF COMPANIES REGISTERED UNDER THE COMPANIES ACTS

73. Alternative modes of winding up

(1) The winding up of a company, within the meaning given to that expression by section 735 of the Companies Act may be either voluntary (Chapters II, III, IV and V in this Part) or by the court (Chapter VI).

(2) This Chapter, and Chapters VII to X, relate to winding up generally, except where otherwise stated.

Contributories

74.   Liability as contributories of present and past members

(1)   When a company is wound up, every present and past member is liable to contribute to its assets to any amount sufficient for payment of its debts and liabilities, and the expenses of the winding up, and for the adjustment of the rights of the contributories among themselves.

(2)   This is subject as follows—

(a)   a past member is not liable to contribute if he has ceased to be a member for one year or more before the commencement of the winding up;

(b)   a past member is not liable to contribute in respect of any debt or liability of the company contracted after he ceased to be a member;

(c)   a past member is not liable to contribute, unless it appears to the court that the existing members are unable to satisfy the contributions required to be made by them in pursuance of the Companies Act and this Act;

(d)   in the case of a company limited by shares, no contribution is required from any member exceeding the amount (if any) unpaid on the shares in respect of which he is liable as a present or past member;

(e)   nothing in the Companies Act or this Act invalidates any provision contained in a policy of insurance or other contract whereby the liability of individual members on the policy or contract is restricted, or whereby the funds of the company are alone made liable in respect of the policy or contract;

(f)   a sum due to any member of the company (in his character of a member) by way of dividends, profits or otherwise is not deemed to be a debt of the company, payable to that member in a case of competition between himself and any other creditor not a member of the company, but any such sum may be taken into account for the purpose of the final adjustment of the rights of the contributories among themselves.

(3)   In the case of a company limited by guarantee, no contribution is required from any member exceeding the amount undertaken to be contributed by him to the company's assets in the event of its being wound up; but if it is a company with a share capital, every member of it is liable (in addition to the amount so undertaken to be contributed to the assets), to contribute to the extent of any sums unpaid on shares held by him.

84.   Circumstances in which company may be wound up voluntarily

(1)   A company may be wound up voluntarily—

(a)   when the period (if any) fixed for the duration of the company by the articles expires, or the event (if any) occurs, on the occurrence of which the articles provide that the company is to be dissolved, and the company in general meeting has passed a resolution requiring it to be wound up voluntarily;

(b)   if the company resolves by special resolution that it be wound up voluntarily;

(c)   if the company resolves by extraordinary resolution to the effect that it cannot by reason of its liabilities continue its business, and that it is advisable to wind up.

(2)   In this Act the expression 'a resolution for voluntary winding up' means a resolution passed under any of the paragraphs of subsection (1).

(3)   A resolution passed under paragraph (a) of subsection (1), as well as a special resolution under paragraph (b) and an extraordinary resolution under paragraph (c), is subject to section 380 of the Companies Act (copy of resolution to be forwarded to registrar of companies within 15 days).

85.   Notice of resolution to wind up

(1)   When a company has passed a resolution for voluntary winding up, it shall, within 14 days after the passing of the resolution, give notice of the resolution by advertisement in the Gazette.

(2)   If default is made in complying with this section, the company and every officer of it who is in default is liable to a fine and, for continued contravention, to a daily default fine.

For purposes of this subsection the liquidator is deemed an officer of the company.

86.   Commencement of winding up

A voluntary winding up is deemed to commence at the time of the passing of the resolution for voluntary winding up.

87. Effect on business and status of company

(1)   In case of a voluntary winding up, the company shall from the commencement of the winding up cease to carry on its business, except so far as may be required for its beneficial winding up.

(2)   However, the corporate state and corporate powers of the company, notwithstanding anything to the contrary in its articles, continue until the company is dissolved.

88. Avoidance of share transfers etc after winding-up resolution

Any transfer of shares, not being a transfer made to or with the sanction of the liquidator, and any alteration in the status of the company's members, made after the commencement of a voluntary winding up, is void.

89. Statutory declaration of solvency

(1)   Where it is proposed to wind up a company voluntarily, the directors (or, in the case of a company having more than two directors, the majority of them) may at a directors' meeting made a statutory declaration to the effect that they have made a full inquiry into the company's affairs and that, having done so, they have formed the opinion that the company will be able to pay its debts in full, together with interest at the official rate (as defined in section 251), within such period, not exceeding 12 months from the commencement of the winding up, as may be specified in the declaration.

(2)   Such a declaration by the directors has no effect for purposes of this Act unless—

  (a)   it is made within the 5 weeks immediately preceding the date of the passing of the resolution for winding up, or on that date but before the passing of the resolution, and
  (b)   it embodies a statement of the company's assets and liabilities as at the latest practicable date before the making of the declaration.

(3)   The declaration shall be delivered to the registrar of companies before the expiration of 15 days immediately following the date on which the resolution for winding up is passed.

(4)   A director making a declaration under this section without having reasonable grounds for the opinion that the company will be able to pay its debts in full, together with interest at the official rate, within the period specified is liable to imprisonment or a fine, or both.

(5)   If the company is wound up in pursuance of a resolution passed within 5 weeks after the making of the declaration, and its debts (together with interest at the official rate) are not paid or provided for in full within the period specified, it is to be presumed (unless the contrary is shown) that the director did not have reasonable grounds for his opinion.

(6)   If a declaration required by subsection (3) to be delivered to the registrar is not so delivered with the time prescribed by that subsection, the company and every officer in default is liable to a fine and, for continued contravention, to a daily default fine.

90. Distinction between 'members' and 'creditors' voluntary winding up

A winding up in the case of which a directors' statutory declaration under section 89 had been made is a 'members' voluntary winding up'; and a winding up in the case of which such a declaration has not been made is a 'creditors' voluntary winding up'.

CHAPTER III

MEMBERS' VOLUNTARY WINDING UP

91. Appointment of liquidator

(1)   In a members' voluntary winding up, the company in general meeting shall appoint one or more liquidators for the purpose of winding up the company's affairs and distributing its assets.

(2)   On the appointment of a liquidator all the powers of the directors cease, except so far as the company in general meeting or the liquidator sanctions their continuance.

92. Power to fill vacancy in office of liquidator

(1)   If a vacancy occurs by death, resignation or otherwise in the office of liquidator appointed by the company, the company in general meeting may, subject to any arrangement with its creditors, fill the vacancy.

(2)   For that purpose a general meeting may be convened by any contributory or, if there were more liquidators than one, by the continuing liquidators.

(3)   The meeting shall be held in manner provided by this Act or by the articles, or in such manner as may, on application by any contributory or by the continuing liquidators, be determined by the court.

93. General company meeting at each year's end

(1)   Subject to sections 96 and 102, in the event of the winding up continuing for more than one year, the liquidator shall summon a general meeting of the company at the end of the first year from the commencement of the winding up, and of each succeeding year, or at the first convenient date within 3 months from the end of the year or such longer period as the Secretary of State may allow.

(2)   The liquidator shall lay before the meeting an account of his acts and dealings, and of the conduct of the winding up, during the preceding year.

(3)   If the liquidator fails to comply with this section, he is liable to a fine.

94. Final meeting prior to dissolution

(1)   As soon as the company's affairs are fully wound up, the liquidator shall make up an account of the winding up, showing how it has been conducted and the company's property has been disposed of, and thereupon shall call a general meeting of the company for the purpose of laying before it the account, and giving an explanation of it.

(2)   The meeting shall be called by advertisement in the *Gazette*, specifying its time, place and object and published at least one month before the meeting.

(3)   Within one week after the meeting, the liquidator shall send to the registrar of companies a copy of the account, and shall make a return to him of the holding of the meeting and of its date.

(4)   If the copy is not sent or the return is not made in accordance with subsection (3), the liquidator is liable to a fine and, for continued contravention, to a daily default fine.

(5)   If a quorum is not present at the meeting, the liquidator shall, in lieu of the return mentioned above, make a return that the meeting was duly summoned and that no quorum was present; and upon such a return being made, the provisions of subsection (3) as to making of the return are deemed complied with.

(6)   If the liquidator fails to call a general meeting of the company as required by subsection (1), he is liable to a fine.

95. Effect of company's insolvency

(1)   This section applies where the liquidator is of the opinion that the company will be unable to pay its debts in full (together with interest at the official rate) within the period stated in the directors' declaration under section 89.

(2)   The liquidator shall—

(a)   summon a meeting of creditors for a day not later than the 28th day after the day on which he formed that opinion;

(b)   send notices of the creditors' meeting to the creditors by post not less than 7 days before the day on which that meeting is to be held;

(c)   cause notice of the creditors' meeting to be advertised once in the *Gazette* and once at least in 2 newspapers circulating in the relevant locality (that is to say the locality in which the company's principal place of business in Great Britain was situated during the relevant period); and

(d)   during the period before the day on which the creditors' meeting is to be held, furnish creditors free of charge with such information concerning the affairs of the company as they may reasonably require;

and the notice of the creditors' meeting shall state the duty imposed by paragraph (d) above.

(3)   The liquidator shall also—

(a)   make out a statement in the prescribed form as to the affairs of the company;

(b)   lay that statement before the creditors' meeting; and

    (c)   attend and preside at that meeting.

(4)   The statement as to the affairs of the company shall be verified by affidavit by the liquidator and shall show—

    (a)   particulars of the company's assets, debts and liabilities:
    (b)   the names and addresses of the company's creditors;
    (c)   the securities held by them respectively;
    (d)   the dates when the securities were respectively given; and
    (e)   such further or other information as may be prescribed.

(5)   Where the company's principal place of business in Great Britain was situated in different localities at different times during the relevant period, the duty imposed by subsection (2)(c) applies separately in relation to each of those localities.

(6)   Where the company had no place of business in Great Britain during the relevant period, references in subsections (2)(c) and (5) to the company's principal place of business in Great Britain are replaced by references to its registered office.

(7)   In this section 'the relevant period' means the period of 6 months immediately preceding the day on which were sent the notices summoning the company meeting at which it was resolved that the company be wound up voluntarily.

(8)   If the liquidator without reasonable excuse fails to comply with this section, he is liable to a fine.

96.   Conversion to creditors' voluntary winding up

As from the day on which the creditors' meeting is held under section 95, this Act has effect as if—

    (a)   the directors' declaration under section 89 had not been made; and
    (b)   the creditors' meeting and the company meeting at which it was resolved that the company be wound up voluntarily were the meetings mentioned in section 98 in the next Chapter;

and accordingly the winding up becomes a creditors' voluntary winding up.

CHAPTER IV

CREDITORS' VOLUNTARY WINDING UP

97.   Application of this Chapter

(1)   Subject as follows, this Chapter applies in relation to a creditors' voluntary winding up.

(2)   Sections 98 and 99 do not apply where, under section 96 in Chapter III, a members' voluntary winding up has become a creditors' voluntary winding up.

98.   Meeting of creditors

(1)   The company shall—

    (a)   cause a meeting of its creditors to be summoned for a day not later than the 14th day after the day on which there is to be held the company meeting at which the resolution for voluntary winding up is to be proposed;
    (b)   cause the notices of the creditors' meeting to be sent by post to the creditors not less than 7 days before the day on which that meeting is to be held; and
    (c)   cause notice of the creditors' meeting to be advertised once in the *Gazette* and once at least in two newspapers circulating in the relevant locality (that is to say the locality in which the company's principal place of business in Great Britain was situated during the relevant period).

(2)   The notice of the creditors' meeting shall state either—

    (a)   the name and address of a person qualified to act as an insolvency practitioner in relation to the company who, during the period before the day on which that meeting is to be held, will furnish creditors free of charge with such information concerning the company's affairs as they may reasonably require; or

(b)   a place in the relevant locality where, on the two business days falling next before the day on which that meeting is to be held, a list of the names and addresses of the company's creditors will be available for inspection free of charge.

(3)   Where the company's principal place of business in Great Britain was situated in different localities at different times during the relevant period, the duties imposed by subsections (1)(c) and (2)(b) above apply separately in relation to each of those localities.

(4)   Where the company had no place of business in Great Britain during the relevant period, references in subsections (1)(c) and (3) to the company's principal place of business in Great Britain are replaced by references to its registered office.

(5)   In this section 'the relevant period' means the period of 6 months immediately preceding the day on which were sent the notices summoning the company meeting at which it was resolved that the company be wound up voluntarily.

(6)   If the company without reasonable excuse fails to comply with subsection (1) or (2), it is guilty of an offence and liable to a fine.

99.   Directors to lay statement of affairs before creditors

(1)   The directors of the company shall—

(a)   make out a statement in the prescribed form as to the affairs of the company;
(b)   cause that statement to be laid before the creditors' meeting under section 98; and
(c)   appoint one of their number to preside at that meeting;

and it is the duty of the director so appointed to attend the meeting and preside over it.

(2)   The statement as to the affairs of the company shall be verified by affidavit by some or all of the directors and shall show—

(a)   particulars of the company's assets, debts and liabilities;
(b)   the names and addresses of the company's creditors;
(c)   the securities held by them respectively;
(d)   the dates when the securities were respectively given; and
(e)   such further or other information as may be prescribed.

(3)   If—

(a)   the directors without reasonable excuse fail to comply with subsection (1) or (2); or
(b)   any director without reasonable excuse fails to comply with subsection (1), so far as requiring him to attend and preside at the creditors' meeting,

the directors are or (as the case may be) the director is guilty of an offence and liable to a fine.

100. Appointment of liquidator

(1)   The creditors and the company at their respective meetings mentioned in section 98 may nominate a person to be liquidator for the purpose of winding up the company's affairs and distributing its assets.

(2)   The liquidator shall be the person nominated by the creditors or, where no person has been so nominated, the person (if any) nominated by the company.

(3)   In the case of different persons being nominated, any director, member or creditor of the company may, within 7 days after the date on which the nomination was made by the creditors, apply to the court for an order either—

(a)   directing that the person nominated as liquidator by the company shall be liquidator instead of or jointly with the person nominated by the creditors, or
(b)   appointing some other person to be liquidator instead of the person nominated by the creditors.

101. Appointment of liquidation committee

(1)   The creditors at the meeting to be held under section 98 or at any subsequent meeting may, if they think fit, appoint a committee ('the liquidation committee') of not more than 5 persons to exercise the functions conferred on it by or under this Act.

(2)   If such a committee is appointed, the company may, either at the meeting at which the resolution for voluntary winding up is passed or at any time subsequently in general meeting, appoint such number of persons as they think fit to act as members of the committee, not exceeding 5.

(3)   However, the creditors may, if they think fit, resolve that all or any of the persons so appointed by the company ought not to be members of the liquidation committee; and if the creditors so resolve—

(a)   the persons mentioned in the resolution are not then, unless the court otherwise directs, qualified to act as members of the committee; and

(b)   on any application to the court under this provision the court may, if it thinks fit, appoint other persons to act as such members in place of the persons mentioned in the resolution.

(4)   In Scotland, the liquidation committee has, in addition to the powers and duties conferred and imposed on it by this Act, such of the powers and duties of commissioners on a bankrupt estate as may be conferred and imposed on liquidation committees by the rules.

102. Creditors' meeting where winding up converted under s 96

Where, in the case of a winding up which was, under section 96 in Chapter III, converted to a creditors' voluntary winding up, a creditors' meeting is held in accordance with section 95, any appointment made or committee established by that meeting is deemed to have been made or established by a meeting held in accordance with section 98 in this Chapter.

103. Cesser of directors' powers

On the appointment of a liquidator, all the powers of the directors cease, except so far as the liquidation committee (or, if there is no such committee, the creditors) sanction their continuance.

106. Final meeting prior to dissolution

(1)   As soon as the company's affairs are fully wound up, the liquidator shall make up an account of the winding up, showing how it has been conducted and the company's property has been disposed of, and thereupon shall call a general meeting of the company and a meeting of the creditors for the purpose of laying the account before the meetings and giving an explanation of it.

(2)   Each such meeting shall be called by advertisement in the *Gazette* specifying the time, place and object of the meeting, and published at least one month before it.

(3)   Within one week after the date of the meetings (or, if they are not held on the same date, after the date of the later one) the liquidator shall send to the registrar of companies a copy of the account, and shall make a return to him of the holding of the meetings and of their dates.

(4)   If the copy is not sent or the return is not made in accordance with subsection (3), the liquidator is liable to a fine and, for continued contravention, to a daily default fine.

(5)   However, if a quorum is not present at either such meeting, the liquidator shall, in lieu of the return required by subsection (3), make a return that the meeting was duly summoned and that no quorum was present; and upon such return being made the provisions of that subsection as to the making of the return are, in respect of that meeting, deemed complied with.

(6)   If the liquidator fails to call a general meeting of the company or a meeting of the creditors as required by this section, he is liable to a fine.

CHAPTER V

PROVISIONS APPLYING TO BOTH KINDS OF VOLUNTARY WINDING UP

107. Distribution of company's property

Subject to the provisions of this Act as to preferential payments, the company's property in a voluntary winding up shall on the winding up be applied in satisfaction of the company's liabilities pari passu and, subject to that application, shall (unless the articles otherwise provide) be distributed among the members according to their rights and interests in the company.

109. Notice by liquidator of his appointment

(1)   The liquidator shall, within 14 days after his appointment, publish in the *Gazette* and deliver to the registrar of companies for registration a notice of his appointment in the form prescribed by statutory instrument made by the Secretary of State.

(2)   If the liquidator fails to comply with this section, he is liable to a fine and, for continued contravention, to a daily default fine.

122. Circumstances in which company may be wound up by the court

(1)   A company may be wound up by the court if—

(a)   the company has by special resolution resolved that the company be wound up by the court,

(b)   being a public company which was registered as such on its original incorporation, the company has not been issued with a certificate under section 117 of the Companies Act (public company share capital requirements) and more than a year has expired since it was so registered,

(c)   it is an old public company, within the meaning of the Consequential Provisions Act,

(d)   the company does not commence its business within a year from its incorporation or suspends its business for a whole year,

(e)   except in the case of a private company limited by shares or by guarantee, the number of members is reduced below 2,

(f)   the company is unable to pay its debts,

(fa) at the time at which a moratorium for the company under section 1A comes to an end, no voluntary arrangement approved under Part I has effect in relation to the company,

(g)   the court is of the opinion that it is just and equitable that the company should be wound up.

(2)   [Applies only to companies registered in Scotland.]

For this purpose a creditor's security is deemed to be in jeopardy if the Court is satisfied that events have occurred or are about to occur which render it unreasonable in the creditor's interests that the company should retain power to dispose of the property which is subject to the floating charge.

123. Definition of inability to pay debts

(1)   A company is deemed unable to pay its debts—

(a)   if a creditor (by assignment or otherwise) to whom the company is indebted in a sum exceeding £750 then due has served on the company, by leaving it at the company's registered office, a written demand (in the prescribed form) requiring the company to pay the sum so due and the company has for 3 weeks thereafter neglected to pay the sum or to secure or compound for it to the reasonable satisfaction of the creditor, or

(b)   if, in England and Wales, execution or other process issued on a judgment, decree or order of any court in favour of a creditor of the company is returned unsatisfied in whole or in part, or

(c)   [Applies to Scotland only]

(d)   if, in Northern Ireland, a certificate of unenforceability has been granted in respect of a judgment against the company, or

(e)   if it is proved to the satisfaction of the court that the company is unable to pay its debts as they fall due.

(2)   A company is also deemed unable to pay its debts if it is proved to the satisfaction of the court that the value of the company's assets is less than the amount of its liabilities, taking into account its contingent and prospective liabilities.

(3)   The money sum for the time being specified in subsection (1)(a) is subject to increase or reduction by order under section 416 in Part XV.

124. Application for winding up

(1)   Subject to the provisions of this section, an application to the court for the winding up of a company shall be by petition presented either by the company, or the directors, or by any creditor or creditors (including any contingent or prospective creditor or creditors), contributory or contributories, or by a liquidator (within the meaning of Article 2(b) of the EC Regulation) appointed in proceedings by virtue of Article 3(1) of the EC Regulation or a temporary administrator (within the meaning of Article 38 of the EC Regulation) or by the justices'

chief executive in the exercise of the power conferred by section 87A of the Magistrates' Courts Act 1980 (enforcement of fines imposed on companies), or by all or any of those parties, together or separately.

(2) Except as mentioned below, a contributory is not entitled to present a winding-up petition unless either—

(a) the number of members is reduced below 2, or

(b) the shares in respect of which he is a contributory, or some of them, either were originally allotted to him, or have been held by him, and registered in his name, for at least 6 months during the 18 months before the commencement of the winding up, or have devolved on him through the death of a former holder.

(3) A person who is liable under section 76 to contribute to a company's assets in the event of its being wound up may petition on either of the grounds set out in section 122(1)(f) and (g), and subsection (2) above does not then apply; but unless the person is a contributory otherwise than under section 76, he may not in his character as contributory petition on any other ground.

(3A) A winding-up petition on the ground set out in section 122(1)(fa) may only be presented by one or more creditors.

This subsection is deemed included in Chapter VII of Part V of the Companies Act (redeemable shares; purchase by a company of its own shares) for the purposes of the Secretary of State's power to make regulations under section 179 of that Act.

(4) A winding-up petition may be presented by the Secretary of State—

(a) if the ground of the petition is that in section 122(1)(b) or (c), or

(b) in a case falling within section 124A below.

(5) Where a company is being wound up voluntarily in England and Wales, a winding-up petition may be presented by the official receiver attached to the court as well as by any other person authorised in that behalf under the other provisions of this section; but the court shall not make a winding-up order on the petition unless it is satisfied that the voluntary winding up cannot be continued with due regard to the interests of the creditors or contributories.

124A. Petition for winding up on grounds of public interest

(1) Where it appears to the Secretary of State from—

(a) any report made or information obtained under Part XIV of the Companies Act 1985 (company investigations, &c.),

(b) any report made by inspectors under—

(i) section 167, 168, 169 or 284 of the Financial Services and Markets Act 2000, or

(ii) where the company is an open-ended investment company (within the meaning of that Act), regulations made as a result of section 262(2)(k) of that Act;

(bb) any information or documents obtained under section 165, 171, 172, 173 or 175 of that Act,

(c) any information obtained under section 2 of the Criminal Justice Act 1987 or section 52 of the Criminal Justice (Scotland) Act 1987 (fraud investigations), or

(d) any information obtained under section 83 of the Companies Act 1989 (powers exercisable for purpose of assisting overseas regulatory authorities),

that it is expedient in the public interest that a company should be wound up, he may present a petition for it to be wound up if the court thinks it just and equitable for it to be so.

(2) This section does not apply if the company is already being wound up by the court.

125. Powers of court on hearing of petition

(1) On hearing a winding-up petition the court may dismiss it, or adjourn the hearing conditionally or unconditionally, or make an interim order, or any other order that it thinks fit; but the court shall not refuse to make a winding-up order on the ground only that the company's assets have been mortgaged to an amount equal to or in excess of those assets, or that the company has no assets.

(2) If the petition is presented by members of the company as contributories on the ground that it is just and equitable that the company should be wound up, the court, if it is of opinion—

(a)   that the petitioners are entitled to relief either by winding up the company or by some other means, and

(b)   that in the absence of any other remedy it would be just and equitable that the company should be wound up,

shall make a winding-up order; but this does not apply if the court is also of the opinion both that some other remedy is available to the petitioners and that they are acting unreasonably in seeking to have the company wound up instead of pursuing that other remedy.

126. Power to stay or restrain proceedings against company

(1)   At any time after the presentation of a winding-up petition, and before a winding-up order has been made, the company, or any creditor or contributory, may—

(a)   where any action or proceeding against the company is pending in the High Court or Court of Appeal in England and Wales or Northern Ireland, apply to the court in which the action or proceeding is pending for a stay of proceedings therein, and

(b)   where any other action or proceeding is pending against the company, apply to the court having jurisdiction to wind up the company to restrain further proceedings in the action or proceeding;

and the court to which application is so made may (as the case may be) stay, sist or restrain the proceedings accordingly on such terms as it thinks fit.

(2)   In the case of a company registered under section 680 of the Companies Act (pre-1862 companies; companies formed under legislation other than the Companies Acts) or the previous corresponding legislation, where the application to stay, sist or restrain is by a creditor, this section extends to actions and proceedings against any contributory of the company.

127. Avoidance of property dispositions etc

In a winding up by the court, any disposition of the company's property, and any transfer of shares, or alteration in the status of the company's members, made after the commencement of the winding up is, unless the court otherwise orders, void.

132. Investigation by official receiver

(1)   Where a winding-up order is made by the court in England and Wales, it is the duty of the official receiver to investigate—

(a)   if the company has failed, the causes of the failure; and

(b)   generally, the promotion, formation, business, dealings and affairs of the company,

and to make such report (if any) to the court as he thinks fit.

(2)   The report is, in any proceedings, prima facie evidence of the facts stated in it.

133. Public examination of officers

(1)   Where a company is being wound up by the court, the official receiver or, in Scotland, the liquidator may at any time before the dissolution of the company apply to the court for the public examination of any person who—

(a)   is or has been an officer of the company; or

(b)   has acted as liquidator or administrator of the company or as receiver or manager or, in Scotland, receiver of its property; or

(c)   not being a person falling within paragraph (a) or (b), is or has been concerned, or has taken part, in the promotion, formation or management of the company.

(2)   Unless the court otherwise orders, the official receiver or, in Scotland, the liquidator shall make an application under subsection (1) if he is requested in accordance with the rules to do so by—

(a)   one-half, in value, of the company's creditors; or

(b)   three-quarters, in value, of the company's contributories.

(3)   On an application under subsection (1), the court shall direct that a public examination of the person to whom the application relates shall be held on a day appointed by the court; and that person shall attend on that day and be publicly examined as to the promotion, formation or management of the company or as to the conduct of its business and affairs, or his conduct or dealings in relation to the company.

(4)　The following may take part in the public examination of a person under this section and may question that person concerning the matters mentioned in subsection (3), namely—

    (a)　the official receiver;

    (b)　the liquidator of the company;

    (c)　any person who has been appointed as special manager of the company's property or business;

    (d)　any creditor of the company who has tendered a proof or, in Scotland, submitted a claim in the winding up;

    (e)　any contributory of the company.

136. Functions of official receiver in relation to office of liquidator

(1)　The following provisions of this section have effect, subject to section 140 below, on a winding-up order being made by the court in England and Wales.

(2)　The official receiver, by virtue of his office, becomes the liquidator of the company and continues in office until another person becomes liquidator under the provisions of this Part.

(3)　The official receiver is, by virtue of his office, the liquidator during any vacancy.

(4)　At any time when he is the liquidator of the company, the official receiver may summon separate meetings of the company's creditors and contributories for the purpose of choosing a person to be liquidator of the company in place of the official receiver.

(5)　It is the duty of the official receiver—

    (a)　as soon as practicable in the period of 12 weeks beginning with the day on which the winding-up order was made, to decide whether to exercise his power under subsection (4) to summon meetings, and

    (b)　if in pursuance of paragraph (a) he decides not to exercise that power, to give notice of his decision, before the end of that period, to the court and to the company's creditors and contributories, and

    (c)　(whether or not he has decided to exercise that power) to exercise his power to summon meetings under subsection (4) if he is at any time requested, in accordance with the rules, to do so by one-quarter, in value, of the company's creditors; and accordingly, where the duty imposed by paragraph (c) arises before the official receiver has performed a duty imposed by paragraph (a) or (b), he is not required to perform the latter duty.

(6)　A notice given under subsection (5)(b) to the company's creditors shall contain an explanation of the creditors' power under subsection (5)(c) to require the official receiver to summon meetings of the company's creditors and contributories.

146. Duty to summon final meeting

(1)　Subject to the next subsection, if it appears to the liquidator of a company which is being wound by the court that the winding up of the company is for practical purposes complete and the liquidator is not the official receiver, the liquidator shall summon a final general meeting of the company's creditors which—

    (a)　shall receive the liquidator's report of the winding up, and

    (b)　shall determine whether the liquidator should have his release under section 174 in Chapter VII of this Part.

(2)　The liquidator may, if he thinks fit, give the notice summoning the final general meeting at the same time as giving notice of any final distribution of the company's property but, if summoned for an earlier date, that meeting shall be adjourned (and, if necessary, further adjourned) until a date on which the liquidator is able to report to the meeting that the winding up of the company is for practical purposes complete.

(3)　In the carrying out of his functions in the winding up it is the duty of the liquidator to retain sufficient sums from the company's property to cover the expenses of summoning and holding the meeting required by this section.

165. Voluntary winding up

(1)　This section has effect where a company is being wound up voluntarily, but subject to section 166 below in the case of a creditors' voluntary winding up.

(2)　The liquidator may—

(a) in the case of a members' voluntary winding up, with the sanction of an extraordinary resolution of the company, and

(b) in the case of a creditors' voluntary winding up, with the sanction of the court or the liquidation committee (or, if there is no such committee, a meeting of the company's creditors),

exercise any of the powers specified in Part I of Schedule 4 to this Act (payment of debts, compromise of claims, etc).

(3) The liquidator may, without sanction, exercise either of the powers specified in Part II of that Schedule (institution and defence of proceedings; carrying on the business of the company) and any of the general powers specified in Part III of that Schedule.

(4) The liquidator may—

(a) exercise the court's power of settling a list of contributories (which list is prima facie evidence of the liability of the persons named in it to be contributories),

(b) exercise the court's power of making calls,

(c) summon general meetings of the company for the purpose of obtaining its sanction by special or extraordinary resolution or for any other purpose he may think fit.

(5) The liquidator shall pay the company's debts and adjust the rights of the contributories among themselves.

(6) Where the liquidator in exercise of the powers conferred on him by this Act disposes of any property of the company to a person who is connected with the company (within the meaning of section 249 in Part VII), he shall, if there is for the time being a liquidation committee, give notice to the committee of that exercise of his powers.

166. Creditors' voluntary winding up

(1) This section applies where, in the case of a creditors' voluntary winding up, a liquidator has been nominated by the company.

(2) The powers conferred on the liquidator by section 165 shall not be exercised, except with the sanction of the court, during the period before the holding of the creditors' meeting under section 98 in Chapter IV.

(3) Subsection (2) does not apply in relation to the power of the liquidator—

(a) to take into his custody or under his control all the property to which the company is or appears to be entitled;

(b) to dispose of perishable goods and other goods the value of which is likely to diminish if they are not immediately disposed of; and

(c) to do all such other things as may be necessary for the protection of the company's assets.

(4) The liquidator shall attend the creditors' meeting held under section 98 and shall report to the meeting on any exercise by him of his powers (whether or not under this section or under section 112 or 165).

(5) If default is made—

(a) by the company in complying with subsection (1) or (2) of section 98, or

(b) by the directors in complying with subsection (1) or (2) of section 99,

the liquidator shall, within 7 days of the relevant day, apply to the court for directions as to the manner in which that default is to be remedied.

(6) 'The relevant day' means the day on which the liquidator was nominated by the company or the day on which he first became aware of the default, whichever is the later.

(7) If the liquidator without reasonable excuse fails to comply with this section, he is liable to a fine.

167. Winding up by the court

(1) Where a company is being wound up by the court, the liquidator may—

(a) with the sanction of the court or the liquidation committee, exercise any of the powers specified in Parts I and II of Schedule 4 to this Act (payment of debts; compromise of claims, etc; institution and defence of proceedings; carrying on of the business of the company), and

(b) with or without that sanction, exercise any of the general powers specified in Part III of that Schedule.

(2)   Where the liquidator (not being the official receiver), in exercise of the powers conferred on him by this Act—

  (a)   disposes of any property of the company to a person who is connected with the company (within the meaning of section 249 in part VII), or

  (b)   employs a solicitor to assist him in the carrying out of his functions,

he shall, if there is for the time being a liquidation committee, give notice to the committee of that exercise of his powers.

(3)   The exercise by the liquidator in a winding up by the court of the powers conferred by this section is subject to the control of the court, and any creditor or contributory may apply to the court with respect to any exercise or proposed exercise of any of those powers.

175. Preferential debts (general provision)

(1)   In a winding up the company's preferential debts (within the meaning given by section 386 in Part XII) shall be paid in priority to all other debts.

(2)   Preferential debts—

  (a)   rank equally among themselves after the expenses of the winding up and shall be paid in full, unless the assets are insufficient to meet them, in which case they abate in equal proportions; and

  (b)   so far as the assets of the company available for payment of general creditors are insufficient to meet them, have priority over the claims of holders of debentures secured by, or holders of, any floating charge created by the company, and shall be paid accordingly out of any property comprised in or subject to that charge.

178. Power to disclaim onerous property

(1)   This and the next two sections apply to a company that is being wound up in England and Wales.

(2)   Subject as follows, the liquidator may, by the giving of the prescribed notice, disclaim any onerous property and may do so notwithstanding that he has taken possession of it, endeavoured to sell it, or otherwise exercised rights of ownership in relation to it.

(3)   The following is onerous property for the purposes of this section—

  (a)   any unprofitable contract, and

  (b)   any other property of the company which is unsaleable or not readily saleable or is such that it may give rise to a liability to pay money or perform any other onerous act.

(4)   A disclaimer under this section—

  (a)   operates so as to determine, as from the date of the disclaimer, the rights, interests and liabilities of the company in or in respect of the property disclaimed; but

  (b)   does not, except so far as is necessary for the purpose of releasing the company form any liability, affect the rights or liabilities of any other person.

(5)   A notice of disclaimer shall not be given under this section in respect of any property if—

  (a)   a person interested in the property has applied in writing to the liquidator or one of his predecessors as liquidator requiring the liquidator or that predecessor to decide whether he will disclaim or not, and

  (b)   the period of 28 days beginning with the day on which that application was made, or such longer period as the court may allow, has expired without a notice of disclaimer having been given under this section in respect of that property.

(6)   Any person sustaining loss or damage in consequence of the operation of a disclaimer under this section is deemed a creditor of the company to the extent of the loss or damage and accordingly may prove for the loss or damage in the winding up.

212. Summary remedy against delinquent directors, liquidators, etc

(1)   This section applies if in the course of the winding up of a company it appears that a person who—

  (a)   is or has been an officer of the company,

  (b)   has acted as liquidator, administrator or administrative receiver of the company, or

(c) not being a person falling within paragraph (a) or (b), is or has been concerned, or has taken part, in the promotion, formation or management of the company,

has misapplied or retained, or become accountable for, any money or other property of the company, or been guilty of any misfeasance or breach of any fiduciary or other duty in relation to the company.

(2) The reference in subsection (1) to any misfeasance or breach of any fiduciary or other duty in relation to the company includes, in the case of a person who has acted as liquidator or administrator of the company, any misfeasance or breach of any fiduciary or other duty in connection with the carrying out of his functions as liquidator or administrator of the company.

(3) The court may, on the application of the official receiver or the liquidator, or of any creditor or contributory, examine into the conduct of the person falling within subsection (1) and compel him—

(a) to repay, restore or account for the money or property or any part of it, with interest at such rate as the court thinks just, or

(b) to contribute such sum to the company's assets by way of compensation in respect of the misfeasance or breach of fiduciary or other duty as the court thinks just.

(4) The power to make an application under subsection (3) in relation to a person who has acted as liquidator or administrator of the company is not exercisable, except with the leave of the court, after that person has had his release.

(5) The power of a contributory to make an application under subsection (3) is not exercisable except with the leave of the court, but is exercisable notwithstanding that he will not benefit from any order the court may make on the application.

213. Fraudulent trading

(1) If in the course of the winding up of a company it appears that any business of the company has been carried on with intent to defraud creditors of the company or creditors of any other person, or for any fraudulent purpose, the following has effect.

(2) The court, on the application of the liquidator may declare that any persons who were knowingly parties to the carrying on of the business in the manner above-mentioned are to be liable to make such contributions (if any) to the company's assets as the court thinks proper.

214. Wrongful trading

(1) Subject to subsection (3) below, if in the course of the winding up of a company it appears that subsection (2) of this section applies in relation to a person who is or has been a director of the company, the court, on the application of the liquidator, may declare that that person is to be liable to make such contribution (if any) to the company's assets as the court thinks proper.

(2) This subsection applies in relation to a person if—

(a) the company has gone into insolvent liquidation,

(b) at some time before the commencement of the winding up of the company, that person knew or ought to have concluded that there was no reasonable prospect that the company would avoid going into insolvent liquidation, and

(c) that person was a director of the company at that time;

but the court shall not make a declaration under this section in any case where the time mentioned in paragraph (b) above was before 28th April 1986.

(3) The court shall not make a declaration under this section with respect to any person if it is satisfied that after the condition specified in subsection (2)(b) was first satisfied in relation to him that person took every step with a view to minimising the potential loss to the company's creditors as (assuming him to have known that there was no reasonable prospect that the company would avoid going into insolvent liquidation) he ought to have taken.

(4) For the purposes of subsections (2) and (3), the facts which a director of a company ought to know or ascertain, the conclusions which he ought to reach and the steps which he ought to take are those which would be known or ascertained, or reached or taken, by a reasonably diligent person having both—

(a) the general knowledge, skill and experience that may reasonably be expected of a person carrying out the same functions as are carried out by that director in relation to the company, and

(b) the general knowledge, skill and experience that the director has.

(5) The reference in subsection (4) to the functions carried out in relation to a company by a director of the company includes any functions which he does not carry out but which have been entrusted to him.

(6) For the purposes of this section a company goes into insolvent liquidation if it goes into liquidation at a time when its assets are insufficient for the payment of its debts and other liabilities and the expenses of the winding up.

(7) In this section 'director' includes a shadow director.

(8) This section is without prejudice to section 213.

215. Proceedings under ss 213–214

(1) On the hearing of an application under section 213, or 214, the liquidator may himself give evidence or call witnesses.

(2) Where under either section the court makes a declaration, it may give such further directions as it thinks proper for giving effect to the declaration; and in particular, the court may—

(a) provide for the liability of any person under the declaration to be a charge on any debt or obligation due from the company to him, or on any mortgage or charge or any interest in a mortgage or charge on assets of the company held by or vested in him, or any person on his behalf, or any person claiming as assignee from or through the person liable or any person acting on his behalf, and

(b) from time to time make such further order as may be necessary for enforcing any charge imposed under this subsection.

(3) For the purposes of subsection (2), 'assignee'—

(a) includes a person to whom or in whose favour, by the directions of the person made liable, the debt, obligation, mortgage or charge was created, issued or transferred or the interest created, but

(b) does not include an assignee for valuable consideration (not including consideration by way of marriage) given in good faith and without notice of any of the matters on the ground of which the declaration is made.

(4) Where the court makes a declaration under either section in relation to a person who is a creditor of the company, it may direct that the whole or any part of any debt owed by the company to that person and any interest thereon shall rank in priority after all other debts owed by the company and after any interest on those debts.

(5) Sections 213 and 214 have effect notwithstanding that the person concerned may be criminally liable in respect of matters on the ground of which the declaration under the section is to be made.

216. Restriction on re-use of company names

(1) This section applies to a person where a company ('the liquidating company') has gone into insolvent liquidation on or after the appointed day and he was a director or shadow director of the company at any time in the period of 12 months, ending with the day before it went into liquidation.

(2) For the purposes of this section, a name is a prohibited name in relation to such a person if—

(a) it is a name by which the liquidating company was known at any time in that period of 12 months, or

(b) it is a name which is so similar to a name falling within paragraph (a) as to suggest an association with that company.

(3) Except with leave of the court or in such circumstances as may be prescribed, a person to whom this section applies shall not at any time in the period of 5 years beginning with the day on which the liquidating company went into liquidation—

(a) be a director of any other company that is known by a prohibited name, or

(b) in any way, whether directly or indirectly, be concerned or take part in the promotion, formation or management of any such company, or

(c) in any way, whether directly or indirectly, be concerned or take part in the carrying on of a business carried on (otherwise than by a company) under a prohibited name.

(4) If a person acts in contravention of this section, he is liable to imprisonment or a fine, or both.

(5)   In subsection (3) 'the court' means any court having jurisdiction to wind up companies; and on an application for leave under that subsection, the Secretary of State or the official receiver may appear and call the attention of the court to any matters which seem to him to be relevant.

(6)   References in this section, in relation to any time, to a name by which a company is known are to the name of the company at that time or to any name under which the company carries on business at that time.

(7)   For the purposes of this section a company goes into insolvent liquidation if it goes into liquidation at a time when its assets are insufficient for the payment of its debts and other liabilities and the expenses of the winding up.

(8)   In this section 'company' includes a company which may be wound up under Part V of this Act.

217. Personal liability for debts, following contravention of s 216

(1)   A person is personally responsible for all the relevant debts of a company if at any time—

    (a)   in contravention of section 216, he is involved in the management of the company, or

    (b)   as a person who is involved in the management of the company, he acts or is willing to act on instructions given (without the leave of the court) by a person whom he knows at that time to be in contravention in relation to the company of section 216.

(2)   Where a person is personally responsible under this section for the relevant debts of a company, he is jointly and severally liable in respect of those debts with the company and any other person who, whether under this section or otherwise, is so liable.

(3)   For the purposes of this section the relevant debts of a company are—

    (a)   in relation to a person who is personally responsible under paragraph (a) of subsection (1), such debts and other liabilities of the company as are incurred at a time when that person was involved in the management of the company, and

    (b)   in relation to a person who is personally responsible under paragraph (b) of that subsection, such debts and other liabilities of the company as are incurred at a time when that person was acting or was willing to act on instructions given as mentioned in that paragraph.

(4)   For the purposes of this section, a person is involved in the management of a company if he is a director of the company or if he is concerned, whether directly or indirectly, or takes part, in the management of the company.

(5)   For the purposes of this section a person who, as a person involved in the management of a company, has at any time acted on instructions given (without the leave of the court) by a person whom he knew at that time to be in contravention in relation to the company of section 216 is presumed, unless the contrary is shown, to have been willing at any time thereafter to act on any instructions given by that person.

(6)   In this section 'company' includes a company which may be wound up under Part V.

Investigation and prosecution of malpractice

218. Prosecution of delinquent officers and members of company

(1)   If it appears to the court in the course of a winding up by the court that any past or present officer, or any member, of the company has been guilty of any offence in relation to the company for which he is criminally liable, the court may (either on the application of a person interested in the winding up or of its own motion) direct the liquidator to refer the matter—

    (a)   in the case of a winding up in England and Wales, to the Secretary of State, and

    (b)   in the case of a winding up in Scotland, to the Lord Advocate.

(3)   If in the case of a winding up by the court in England and Wales it appears to the liquidator, not being the official receiver, that any past or present officer of the company, or any member of it, has been guilty of an offence in relation to the company for which he is criminally liable, the liquidator shall report the matter to the official receiver.

(4)   If it appears to the liquidator in the course of a voluntary winding up that any past or present officer of the company, or any member of it, has been guilty of an offence in relation to the company for which he is criminally liable, he shall forthwith report the matter—

    (a)   in the case of a winding up in England and Wales, to the Secretary of State, and

(b)   in the case of a winding up in Scotland, to the Lord Advocate,

and shall furnish to the Secretary of State or (as the case may be) the Lord Advocate such information and give to him such access to and facilities for inspecting and taking copies of documents (being information or documents in the possession or under the control of the liquidator and relating to the matter in question) as the Secretary of State or (as the case may be) the Lord Advocate requires.

(5)   Where a report is made to the Secretary of State under subsection (4) he may, for the purpose of investigating the matter reported to him and such other matters relating to the affairs of the company as appear to him to require investigation, exercise any of the powers which are exercisable by inspectors appointed under section 431 or 432 of the Companies Act to investigate a company's affairs.

(6)   If it appears to the court in the course of a voluntary winding up that—

(a)   any past or present officer of the company, or any member of it, has been guilty as above-mentioned, and

(b)   no report with respect to the matter has been made by the liquidator under subsection (4),

the court may (on the application of any person interested in the winding up or of its own motion) direct the liquidator to make such a report.

On a report being made accordingly, this section has effect as though the report had been made in pursuance of subsection (4).

219. Obligations arising under s 218

(1)   For the purpose of an investigation by the Secretary of State in consequence of a report made to him under section 218(4), any obligation imposed on a person by any provision of the Companies Act to produce documents or give information to, or otherwise to assist, inspectors appointed as mentioned in section 218(5) is to be regarded as an obligation similarly to assist the Secretary of State in his investigation.

(2)   An answer given by a person to a question put to him in exercise of the powers conferred by section 218(5) may be used in evidence against him.

(2A)   However, in criminal proceedings in which that person is charged with an offence to which this subsection applies—

(a)   no evidence relating to the answer may be adduced, and

(b)   no question relating to it may be asked,

by or on behalf of the prosecution, unless evidence relating to it is adduced, or a question relating to it is asked, in the proceedings by or on behalf of that person.

(2B)   Subsection (2A) applies to any offence other than—

(a)   an offence under section 2 or 5 of the Perjury Act 1911 (false statements made on oath otherwise than in judicial proceedings or made otherwise than on oath), or

(b)   an offence under section 44(1) or (2) of the Criminal Law (Consolidation) (Scotland) Act 1995 (false statements made on oath or otherwise than on oath).

(3)   Where criminal proceedings are instituted by the Director of Public Prosecutions, the Lord Advocate or the Secretary of State following any report or reference under section 218, it is the duty of the liquidator and every officer and agent of the company past and present (other than the defendant or defender) to give to the Director of Public Prosecutions, the Lord Advocate or the Secretary of State (as the case may be) all assistance in connection with the prosecution which he is reasonably able to give.

For this purpose 'agent' includes any banker or solicitor of the company and any person employed by the company as auditor, whether that person is or is not an officer of the company.

(4)   If a person fails or neglects to give assistance in the manner required by subsection (3), the court may, on the application of the Director of Public Prosecutions, the Lord Advocate or the Secretary of State (as the case may be) direct the person to comply with that subsection; and if the application is made with respect to a liquidator, the court may (unless it appears that the failure or neglect to comply was due to the liquidator not having in his hands sufficient assets of the company to enable him to do so) direct that the costs shall be borne by the liquidator personally.

Part IV Insolvency

PART VI

MISCELLANEOUS PROVISIONS APPLYING TO COMPANIES WHICH ARE INSOLVENT OR IN LIQUIDATION

238. Transactions at an undervalue (England and Wales)

(1)   This section applies in the case of a company where—

    (a)   an administration order is made in relation to the company, or

    (b)   the company goes into liquidation;

and 'the office-holder' means the administrator or the liquidator, as the case may be.

(2)   Where the company has at a relevant time (defined in section 240) entered into a transaction with any person at an undervalue, the office-holder may apply to the court for an order under this section.

(3)   Subject as follows, the court shall, on such an application, make such order as it thinks fit for restoring the position to what it would have been if the company had not entered into that transaction.

(4)   For the purposes of this section and section 241, a company enters into a transaction with a person at an undervalue if—

    (a)   the company makes a gift to that person or otherwise enters into a transaction with that person on terms that provide for the company to receive no consideration, or

    (b)   the company enters into a transaction with that person for a consideration the value of which, in money or money's worth, is significantly less than the value, in money or money's worth, of the consideration provided by the company.

(5)   The court shall not make an order under this section in respect of a transaction at an undervalue if it is satisfied—

    (a)   that the company which entered into the transaction did so in good faith and for the purpose of carrying on its business, and

    (b)   that at the time it did so there were reasonable grounds for believing that the transaction would benefit the company.

239. Preferences (England and Wales)

(1)   This section applies as does section 238.

(2)   Where the company has at a relevant time (defined in the next section) given a preference to any person, the office-holder may apply to the court for an order under this section.

(3)   Subject as follows, the court shall, on such an application, make such order as it thinks fit for restoring the position to what it would have been if the company had not given that preference.

(4)   For the purposes of this section and section 241, a company gives a preference to a person if—

    (a)   that person is one of the company's creditors or a surety or guarantor for any of the company's debts or other liabilities, and

    (b)   the company does anything or suffers anything to be done which (in either case) has the effect of putting that person into a position which, in the event of the company going into insolvent liquidation, will be better that the position he would have been in if that thing had not been done.

(5)   The court shall not make an order under this section in respect of a preference given to any person unless the company which gave the preference was influenced in deciding to give it by a desire to produce in relation to that person the effect mentioned in subsection (4)(b).

(6)   A company which has given a preference to a person connected with the company (otherwise than by reason only of being its employee) at the time the preference was given is presumed, unless the contrary is shown, to have been influenced in deciding to give it by such a desire as is mentioned in subsection (5).

(7)   The fact that something has been done in pursuance of the order of a court does not, without more, prevent the doing or suffering of that thing from constituting the giving of a preference.

240. 'Relevant time' under ss 238, 239

(1) Subject to the next subsection, the time at which a company enters into a transaction at an undervalue or gives a preference is a relevant time if the transaction is entered into, or the preference given—

(a) in the case of a transaction at an undervalue or of a preference which is given to a person who is connected with the company (otherwise than by reason only of being its employee), at a time in the period of 2 years ending with the onset of insolvency (which expression is defined below),

(b) in the case of a preference which is not such a transaction and is not so given, at a time in the period of 6 months ending with the onset of insolvency, and

(c) in either case, at a time between the presentation of a petition for the making of an administration order in relation to the company and the making of such an order on that petition.

(2) Where a company enters into a transaction at an under-value or gives a preference at a time mentioned in subsection (1)(a) or (b), that time is not a relevant time for the purposes of section 238 or 239 unless the company—

(a) is at that time unable to pay its debts within the meaning of section 123 in Chapter VI of Part IV, or

(b) becomes unable to pay its debts within the meaning of that section in consequence of the transaction or preference;

but the requirements of this subsection are presumed to be satisfied, unless the contrary is shown, in relation to any transaction at an undervalue which is entered into by a company with a person who is connected with the company.

(3) For the purposes of subsection (1), the onset of insolvency is—

(a) in a case where section 238 or 239 applies by reason of the making of an administration order or of a company going into liquidation immediately upon the discharge of an administration order, the date of the presentation of the petition on which the administration order was made,

(aa) in a case where section 238 or 239 applies by reason of a company going into liquidation following conversion of administration into winding up by virtue of Article 37 of the EC Regulation, the date of the presentation of the petition on which the administration order was made, and

(b) in a case where the section applies by reason of a company going into liquidation at any other time, the date of the commencement of the winding up.

241. Orders under ss 238, 239

(1) Without prejudice to the generality of sections 238(3) and 239(3), an order under either of those sections with respect to a transaction or preference entered into or given by a company may (subject to the next subsection)—

(a) require any property transferred as part of the transaction, or in connection with the giving of the preference, to be vested in the company,

(b) require any property to be so vested if it represents in any person's hands the application either of the proceeds of sale of property so transferred or of money so transferred,

(c) release or discharge (in whole or in part) any security given by the company,

(d) require any person to pay, in respect of benefits received by him from the company, such sums to the office-holder as the court may direct,

(e) provide for any surety or guarantor whose obligations to any person were released or discharged (in whole or in part) under the transaction, or by the giving of the preference, to be under such new or revived obligations to that person as the court thinks appropriate,

(f) provide for security to be provided for the discharge of any obligation imposed by or arising under the order, for such an obligation to be charged on any property and for the security or charge to have the same priority as a security or charge released or discharged (in whole or in part) under the transaction or by the giving of the preference, and

(g) provide for the extent to which any person whose property is vested by the order in the company, or on whom obligations are imposed by the order, is to be able to prove in the winding up of the company for debts or other liabilities which arose from, or were released or discharged (in whole or in part) under or by, the transaction or the giving of the preference.

(2) An order under section 238 or 239 may affect the property of, or impose any obligation on, any person whether or not he is the person with whom the company in question entered into the transaction or (as the case may be) the person to whom the preference was given; but such an order—

    (a)   shall not prejudice any interest in property which was acquired from a person other than the company and was acquired in good faith and for value or prejudice any interest deriving from such an interest, and

    (b)   shall not require a person who received a benefit from the transaction or preference in good faith and for value to pay a sum to the office-holder, except where that person was a party to the transaction or the payment is to be in respect of a preference given to that person at a time when he was a creditor of the company.

(2A) Where a person has acquired an interest in property from a person other than the company in question, or has received a benefit from the transaction or preference, and at the time of that acquisition or receipt—

    (a)   he had notice of the relevant surrounding circumstances and of the relevant proceedings, or

    (b)   he was connected with, or was an associate of, either the company in question or the person with whom that company entered into the transaction or to whom that company gave the preference,

then, unless the contrary is shown, it shall be presumed for the purposes of paragraph (a) or (as the case may be) paragraph (b) of subsection (2) that the interest was acquired or the benefit was received otherwise than in good faith.

(3)   For the purposes of subsection (2A)(a), the relevant surrounding circumstances are (as the case may require)—

    (a)   the fact that the company in question entered into the transaction at an undervalue; or

    (b)   the circumstances which amounted to the giving of the preference by the company in question;

and subsections (3A) to (3C) have effect to determine whether, for those purposes, a person has notice of the relevant proceedings.

(3A) In a case where section 238 or 239 applies by reason of the making of an administration order, a person has notice of the relevant proceedings if he has notice—

    (a)   of the fact that the petition on which the administration order is made has been presented; or

    (b)   of the fact that the administration order has been made.

(3B) In a case where section 238 or 239 applies by reason of the company in question going into liquidation immediately upon the discharge of an administration order, a person has notice of the relevant proceedings if he has notice—

    (a)   of the fact that the petition on which the administration order is made has been presented;

    (b)   of the fact that the administration order has been made; or

    (c)   of the fact that the company has gone into liquidation.

(3C) In a case where section 238 or 239 applies by reason of the company in question going into liquidation at any other time, a person has notice of the relevant proceedings if he has notice—

    (a)   where the company goes into liquidation on the making of a winding-up order, of the fact that the petition on which the winding-up order is made has been presented or of the fact that the company has gone into liquidation;

    (b)   in any other case, of the fact that the company has gone into liquidation.

(4)   The provisions of sections 238 to 241 apply without prejudice to the availability of any other remedy, even in relation to a transaction or preference which the company had no power to enter into or give.

242. Gratuitous alienations (Scotland)

(1)   Where this subsection applies and—

    (a)   the winding up of a company has commenced, an alienation by the company is challengeable by—

        (i)   any creditor who is a creditor by virtue of a debt incurred on or before the date of such commencement, or

        (ii)   the liquidator;

    (b)   an administration order is in force in relation to a company, an alienation by the company is challengeable by the administrator.

(2)   Subsection (1) applies where—

(a) by the alienation, whether before or after 1 April 1986 (the coming into force of section 75 of the Bankruptcy (Scotland) Act 1985), any part of the company's property is transferred or any claim or right of the company is discharged or renounced, and

(b) the alienation takes place on a relevant day.

(3) For the purposes of subsection (2)(b), the day on which an alienation takes place is the day on which it becomes completely effectual; and in that subsection 'relevant day' means, if the alienation has the effect of favouring—

(a) a person who is an associate (within the meaning of the Bankruptcy (Scotland) Act 1985) of the company, a day not earlier than 5 years before the date on which—

   (i) the winding up of the company commences, or
   (ii) as the case may be, the administration order is made; or

(b) any other person, a day not earlier than 2 years before that date.

(4) On a challenge being brought under subsection (1), the court shall grant decree of reduction or for such restoration of property to the company's assets or other redress as may be appropriate; but the court shall not grant such a decree if that person seeking to uphold the alienation establishes—

(a) that immediately, or at any other time, after the alienation the company's assets were greater than its liabilities, or

(b) that the alienation was made for adequate consideration, or

(c) that the alienation—

   (i) was a birthday, Christmas or other conventional gift, or
   (ii) was a gift made, for a charitable purpose, to a person who is not an associate of the company,

which, having regard to all the circumstances, it was reasonable for the company to make:

Provided that this subsection is without prejudice to any right or interest acquired in good faith and for value from or through the transferee in the alienation.

(5) In subsection (4) above, 'charitable purpose' means any charitable, benevolent or philanthropic purpose, whether or not it is charitable within the meaning of any rule of law.

(6) For the purposes of the foregoing provisions of this section, an alienation in implementation of a prior obligation is deemed to be one for which there was no consideration or no adequate consideration to the extent that the prior obligation was undertaken for no consideration or no adequate consideration.

(7) A liquidator and an administrator have the same right as a creditor has under any rule of law to challenge an alienation of a company made for no consideration or no adequate consideration.

(8) This section applies to Scotland only.

243. Unfair preferences (Scotland)

(1) Subject to subsection (2) below, subsection (4) below applies to a transaction entered into by a company, whether before or after 1 April 1986, which has the effect of creating a preference in favour of a creditor to the prejudice of the general body of creditors, being a preference created not earlier than 6 months before the commencement of the winding up of the company or the making of an administration order in relation to the company.

(2) Subsection (4) below does not apply to any of the following transactions—

(a) a transaction in the ordinary course of trade or business;

(b) a payment in cash for a debt which when it was paid had become payable, unless the transaction was collusive with the purpose of prejudicing the general body of creditors;

(c) a transaction whereby the parties to it undertake reciprocal obligations (whether the performance by the parties of their respective obligations occurs at the same time or at different times) unless the transaction was collusive as aforesaid;

(d) the granting of a mandate by a company authorising an arrestee to pay over the arrested funds or part thereof to the arrester where—

   (i) there has been a decree for payment or a warrant for summary diligence, and

(ii)   the decree or warrant has been preceded by an arrestment on the dependence of the action or followed by an arrestment in execution.

(3)   For the purposes of subsection (1) above, the day on which a preference was created is the day on which the preference became completely effectual.

(4)   A transaction to which this subsection applies is challengeable by—

(a)   in the case of a winding up—

(i)   any creditor who is a creditor by virtue of a debt incurred on or before the date of commencement of the winding up, or
(ii)   the liquidator; and

(b)   in the case of an administration order, the administrator.

(5)   On a challenge being brought under subsection (4) above, the court, if satisfied that the transaction challenged is a transaction to which this section applies, shall grant decree of reduction or for such restoration of property to the company's assets or other redress as may be appropriate:

Provided that this subsection is without prejudice to any right or interest acquired in good faith and for value from or through the creditor in whose favour the preference was created.

(6)   A liquidator and an administrator have the same right as a creditor has under any rule of law to challenge a preference created by a debtor.

(7)   This section applies to Scotland only.

244. Extortionate credit transactions

(1)   This section applies as does section 238, and where the company is, or has been, a party to a transaction for, or involving, the provision of credit to the company.

(2)   The court may, on the application of the office-holder, make an order with respect to the transaction if the transaction is or was extortionate and was entered into in the period of 3 years ending with the day on which the administration order was made or (as the case may be) the company went into liquidation.

(3)   For the purposes of this section a transaction is extortionate if, having regard to the risk accepted by the person providing the credit—

(a)   the terms of it are or were such as to require grossly exorbitant payments to be made (whether unconditionally or in certain contingencies) in respect of the provision of the credit, or
(b)   it otherwise grossly contravened ordinary principles of fair dealing;

and it shall be presumed, unless the contrary is proved, that a transaction with respect to which an application is made under this section is or, as the case may be, was extortionate.

(4)   An order under this section with respect to any transaction may contain such one or more of the following as the court thinks fit, that is to say—

(a)   provision setting aside the whole or part of any obligation created by the transaction,
(b)   provision otherwise varying the terms of the transaction or varying the terms on which any security for the purposes of the transaction is held,
(c)   provision requiring any person who is or was a party to the transaction to pay to the office-holder any sums paid to that person, by virtue of the transaction, by the company,
(d)   provision requiring any person to surrender to the office-holder any property held by him as security for the purposes of the transaction,
(e)   provision directing accounts to be taken between any persons.

(5)   The powers conferred by this section are exercisable in relation to any transaction concurrently with any powers exercisable in relation to that transaction as a transaction at an undervalue or under section 242 (gratuitous alienations in Scotland).

245. Avoidance of certain floating charges

(1)   This section applies as does section 238, but applies to Scotland as well as to England and Wales.

(2)   Subject as follows, a floating charge on the company's undertaking or property created at a relevant time is invalid except to the extent of the aggregate of—

    (a)   the value of so much of the consideration for the creation of the charge as consists of money paid, or goods or services supplied, to the company at the same time as, or after, the creation of the charge,

    (b)   the value of so much of that consideration as consists of the discharge or reduction, at the same time as, or after, the creation of the charge, of any debt of the company, and

    (c)   the amount of such interest (if any) as is payable on the amount falling within paragraph (a) or (b) in pursuance of any agreement under which the money was so paid, the goods or services were so supplied or the debt was so discharged or reduced.

(3)   Subject to the next subsection, the time at which a floating charge is created by a company is a relevant time for the purposes of this section if the charge is created—

    (a)   in the case of a charge which is created in favour of a person who is connected with the company, at a time in the period of 2 years ending with the onset of insolvency,

    (b)   in the case of a charge which is created in favour of any other person, at a time in the period of 12 months ending with the onset of insolvency, or

    (c)   in either case, at a time between the presentation of a petition for the making of an administration order in relation to the company and the making of such an order on that petition.

(4)   Where a company creates a floating charge at a time mentioned in subsection (3)(b) and the person in favour of whom the charge is created is not connected with the company, that time is not a relevant time for the purposes of this section unless the company—

    (a)   is at that time unable to pay its debts within the meaning of section 123 in Chapter VI of Part VI, or

    (b)   becomes unable to pay its debts within the meaning of that section in consequence of the transaction under which the charge is created.

(5)   For the purposes of subsection (3), the onset of insolvency is—

    (a)   in a case where this section applies by reason of the making of an administration order, the date of the presentation of the petition on which the order was made, and

    (b)   in a case where this section applies by reason of a company going into liquidation, the date of the commencement of the winding up.

(6)   For the purposes of subsection (2)(a) the value of any goods or services supplied by way of consideration for a floating charge is the amount in money which at the time they were supplied could reasonably have been expected to be obtained for supplying the goods or services in the ordinary course of business and on the same terms (apart from the consideration) as those on which they were supplied to the company.

PART VII

INTERPRETATION FOR FIRST GROUP OF PARTS

247. 'Insolvency' and 'go into liquidation'

(1)   In this Group of Parts, except in so far as the context otherwise requires, 'insolvency', in relation to a company, includes the approval of a voluntary arrangement under Part I, the making of an administration order or the appointment of an administrative receiver.

(2)   For the purposes of any provision in this Group of Parts, a company goes into liquidation if it passes a resolution for voluntary winding up or an order for its winding up is made by the court at a time when it has not already gone into liquidation by passing such a resolution.

(3)   The reference to a resolution for voluntary winding up in subsection (2) includes a resolution deemed to occur by virtue of an order made following conversion of a voluntary arrangement or administration into winding up under Article 37 of the EC Regulation.

248. 'Secured creditor' etc

In this Group of Parts, except in so far as the context otherwise requires—

    (a)   'secured creditor', in relation to a company, means a creditor of the company who holds in respect of his debt a security over property of the company, and 'unsecured creditor' is to be read accordingly; and

    (b)   'security' means—

(i) in relation to England and Wales, any mortgage, charge, lien or other security, and

(ii) in relation to Scotland, any security (whether heritable or moveable), any floating charge and any right of lien or preference and any right of retention (other than a right of compensation or set off).

249. 'Connected' with a company

For the purposes of any provision in this Group of Parts, a person is connected with a company if—

(a) he is a director or shadow director of the company or an associate of such a director or shadow director, or

(b) he is an associate of the company;

and 'associate' has the meaning given by section 435 in Part XVIII of this Act.

252. Interim order of court

(1) In the circumstances specified below, the court may in the case of a debtor (being an individual) make an interim order under this section.

(2) An interim order has the effect that, during the period for which it is in force—

(a) no bankruptcy petition relating to the debtor may be presented or proceeded with,

(aa) no landlord or other person to whom rent is payable may exercise any right of forfeiture by peaceable re-entry in relation to premises let to the debtor in respect of a failure by the debtor to comply with any term or condition of his tenancy of such premises, except with the leave of the court, and

(b) no other proceedings, and no execution or other legal process, may be commenced or continued and no distress may be levied against the debtor or his property except with the leave of the court.

253. Application for interim order

(1) Application to the court for an interim order may be made where the debtor intends to make a proposal under this Part, that is, a proposal to his creditors for a composition in satisfaction of his debts or a scheme of arrangement of his affairs (from here on referred to, in either case, as a 'voluntary arrangement').

(2) The proposal must provide for some person ('the nominee') to act in relation to the voluntary arrangement either as trustee or otherwise for the purpose of supervising its implementation and the nominee must be a person who is qualified to act as an insolvency practitioner, or authorised to act as nominee, in relation to the voluntary arrangement.

(3) Subject as follows, the application may be made—

(a) if the debtor is an undischarged bankrupt, by the debtor, the trustee of his estate, or the official receiver, and

(b) in any other case, by the debtor.

(4) An application shall not be made under subsection (3)(a) unless the debtor has given notice of the proposal to the official receiver and, if there is one, the trustee of his estate.

(5) An application shall not be made while a bankruptcy petition presented by the debtor is pending, if the court has, under section 273 below, appointed an insolvency practitioner to inquire into the debtor's affairs and report.

254. Effect of application

(1) At any time when an application under section 253 for an interim order is pending—

(a) no landlord or other person to whom rent is payable may exercise any right of forfeiture by peaceable re-entry in relation to premises let to the debtor in respect of a failure by the debtor to comply with any term or condition of his tenancy of such premises, except with the leave of the court, and

(b) the court may forbid the levying of any distress on the debtor's property or its subsequent sale, or both, and stay any action, execution or other legal process against the property or person of the debtor.

(2) Any court in which proceedings are pending against an individual may, on proof that an application under that section has been made in respect of that individual, either stay the proceedings or allow them to continue on such terms as it thinks fit.

255. Cases in which interim order can be made

(1)   The court shall not make an interim order on an application under section 253 unless it is satisfied—

(a)   that the debtor intends to make a proposal under this Part;

(b)   that on the day of the making of the application the debtor was an undischarged bankrupt or was able to petition for his own bankruptcy;

(c)   that no previous application has been made by the debtor for an interim order in the period of 12 months ending with that day; and

(d)   that the nominee under the debtor's proposal is willing to act in relation to the proposal.

(2)   The court may make an order if it thinks that it would be appropriate to do so for the purpose of facilitating the consideration and implementation of the debtor's proposal.

(3)   Where the debtor is an undischarged bankrupt, the interim order may contain provision as to the conduct of the bankruptcy, and the administration of the bankrupt's estate, during the period for which the order is in force.

(4)   Subject as follows, the provision contained in an interim order by virtue of subsection (3) may include provision staying proceedings in the bankruptcy or modifying any provision in this Group of Parts, and any provision of the rules in their application to the debtor's bankruptcy.

(5)   An interim order shall not, in relation to a bankrupt, make provision relaxing or removing any of the requirements of provisions in this Group of Parts, or of the rules, unless the court is satisfied that that provision is unlikely to result in any significant diminution in, or in the value of, the debtor's estate for the purposes of the bankruptcy.

(6)   Subject to the following provisions of this Part, an interim order made on an application under section 253 ceases to have effect at the end of the period of 14 days beginning with the day after the making of the order.

256. Nominee's report on debtor's proposal

(1)   Where an interim order has been made on an application under section 253, the nominee shall, before the order ceases to have effect, submit a report to the court stating—

(a)   whether, in his opinion, the voluntary arrangement which the debtor is proposing has a reasonable prospect of being approved and implemented,

(aa)   whether, in his opinion, a meeting of the debtor's creditors should be summoned to consider the debtor's proposal, and

(b)   if in his opinion such a meeting should be summoned, the date on which, and time and place at which, he proposes the meeting should be held.

(2)   For the purpose of enabling the nominee to prepare his report the debtor shall submit to the nominee—

(a)   a document setting out the terms of the voluntary arrangement which the debtor is proposing, and

(b)   a statement of his affairs containing—

(i)   such particulars of his creditors and of his debts and other liabilities and of his assets as may be prescribed, and

(ii)   such other information as may be prescribed.

(3)   The court may—

(a)   on an application made by the debtor in a case where the nominee has failed to submit the report required by this section or has died, or

(b)   on an application made by the debtor or the nominee in a case where it is impracticable or inappropriate for the nominee to continue to act as such,

direct that the nominee shall be replaced as such by another person qualified to act as an insolvency practitioner, or authorised to act as nominee, in relation to the voluntary arrangement.

(3A) The court may, on an application made by the debtor in a case where the nominee has failed to submit the report required by this section, direct that the interim order shall continue, or (if it has ceased to have effect) be renewed, for such further period as the court may specify in the direction.

(4)   The court may, on the application of the nominee, extend the period for which the interim order has effect so as to enable the nominee to have more time to prepare his report.

(5)   If the court is satisfied on receiving the nominee's report that a meeting of the debtor's creditors should be summoned to consider the debtor's proposal, the court shall direct that the period for which the interim order has effect shall be extended, for such further period as it may specify in the direction, for the purpose of enabling the debtor's proposal to be considered by his creditors in accordance with the following provisions of this Part.

(6)   The court may discharge the interim order if it is satisfied, on the application of the nominee—

  (a)   that the debtor has failed to comply with his obligations under subsection (2), or
  (b)   that for any other reason it would be inappropriate for a meeting of the debtor's creditors to be summoned to consider the debtor's proposal.

Procedure where no interim order made

256A.   Debtor's proposal and nominee's report

(1)   This section applies where a debtor (being an individual)—

  (a)   intends to make a proposal under this Part (but an interim order has not been made in relation to the proposal and no application for such an order is pending), and
  (b)   if he is an undischarged bankrupt, has given notice of the proposal to the official receiver and, if there is one, the trustee of his estate,

unless a bankruptcy petition presented by the debtor is pending and the court has, under section 273, appointed an insolvency practitioner to inquire into the debtor's affairs and report.

(2)   For the purpose of enabling the nominee to prepare a report to the court, the debtor shall submit to the nominee—

  (a)   a document setting out the terms of the voluntary arrangement which the debtor is proposing, and
  (b)   a statement of his affairs containing—

    (i)   such particulars of his creditors and of his debts and other liabilities and of his assets as may be prescribed, and
    (ii)   such other information as may be prescribed.

(3)   If the nominee is of the opinion that the debtor is an undischarged bankrupt, or is able to petition for his own bankruptcy, the nominee shall, within 14 days (or such longer period as the court may allow) after receiving the document and statement mentioned in subsection (2), submit a report to the court stating—

  (a)   whether, in his opinion, the voluntary arrangement which the debtor is proposing has a reasonable prospect of being approved and implemented,
  (b)   whether, in his opinion, a meeting of the debtor's creditors should be summoned to consider the debtor's proposal, and
  (c)   if in his opinion such a meeting should be summoned, the date on which, and time and place at which, he proposes the meeting should be held.

(4) The court may—

  (a)   on an application made by the debtor in a case where the nominee has failed to submit the report required by this section or has died, or
  (b)   on an application made by the debtor or the nominee in a case where it is impracticable or inappropriate for the nominee to continue to act as such,

direct that the nominee shall be replaced as such by another person qualified to act as an insolvency practitioner, or authorised to act as nominee, in relation to the voluntary arrangement.

(5)   The court may, on an application made by the nominee, extend the period within which the nominee is to submit his report.

257. Summoning of creditors' meeting

(1)   Where it has been reported to the court under section 256 or 256A that a meeting of the debtor's creditors should be summoned, the nominee (or his replacement under section 256(3) or 256A(4)) shall, unless the court otherwise directs, summon that meeting for the time, date and place proposed in his report.

(2)   The persons to be summoned to the meeting are every creditor of the debtor of whose claim and address the person summoning the meeting is aware.

(3)   For this purpose the creditors of a debtor who is an undischarged bankrupt include—

    (a)   every person who is a creditor of the bankrupt in respect of a bankruptcy debt, and

    (b)   every person who would be such a creditor if the bankruptcy had commenced on the day on which notice of the meeting is given.

258. Decisions of creditors' meeting

(1)   A creditors' meeting summoned under section 257 shall decide whether to approve the proposed voluntary arrangement.

(2)   The meeting may approve the proposed voluntary arrangement with modifications, but shall not do so unless the debtor consents to each modification.

(3)   The modifications subject to which the proposed voluntary arrangement may be approved may include one conferring the functions proposed to be conferred on the nominee on another person qualified to act as an insolvency practitioner or authorised to act as nominee, in relation to the voluntary arrangement.

But they shall not include any modification by virtue of which the proposal ceases to be a proposal under this Part.

(4)   The meeting shall not approve any proposal or modification which affects the right of a secured creditor of the debtor to enforce his security, except with the concurrence of the creditor concerned.

(5)   Subject as follows, the meeting shall not approve any proposal or modification under which—

    (a)   any preferential debt of the debtor is to be paid otherwise than in priority to such of his debts as are not preferential debts, or

    (b)   a preferential creditor of the debtor is to be paid an amount in respect of a preferential debt that bears to that debt a smaller proportion than is borne to another preferential debt by the amount that is to be paid in respect of that other debt.

However, the meeting may approve such a proposal or modification with the concurrence of the preferential creditor concerned.

(6)   Subject as above, the meeting shall be conducted in accordance with the rules.

(7)   In this section 'preferential debt' has the meaning given by section 386 in Part XII; and 'preferential creditor' is to be construed accordingly.

259. Report of decisions to court

(1)   After the conclusion in accordance with the rules of the meeting summoned under section 257, the chairman of the meeting shall report the result of it to the court and, immediately after so reporting, shall give notice of the result of the meeting to such persons as may be prescribed.

(2)   If the report is that the meeting has declined (with or without modifications) to approve the debtor's proposal, the court may discharge any interim order which is in force in relation to the debtor.

260. Effect of approval

(1)   This section has effect where the meeting summoned under section 257 approves the proposed voluntary arrangement (with or without modifications).

(2)   The approved arrangement—

    (a)   takes effect as if made by the debtor at the meeting, and

    (b)   binds every person who in accordance with the rules—

(i)   was entitled to vote at the meeting (whether or not he was present or represented at it), or

(ii)   would have been so entitled if he had had notice of it,

as if he were a party to the arrangement.

(2A) If—

(a)   when the arrangement ceases to have effect any amount payable under the arrangement to a person bound by virtue of subsection (2)(b)(ii) has not been paid, and

(b)   the arrangement did not come to an end prematurely,

the debtor shall at that time become liable to pay to that person the amount payable under the arrangement.

(3)   The Deeds of Arrangement Act 1914 does not apply to the approved voluntary arrangement.

(4)   Any interim order in force in relation to the debtor immediately before the end of the period of 28 days beginning with the day on which the report with respect to the creditors' meeting was made to the court under section 259 ceases to have effect at the end of that period.

This subsection applies except to such extent as the court may direct for the purposes of any application under section 262 below.

(5)   Where proceedings on a bankruptcy petition have been stayed by an interim order which ceases to have effect under subsection (4), that petition is deemed, unless the court otherwise orders, to have been dismissed.

261. Effect where debtor an undischarged bankrupt

(1)   Subject as follows, where the creditors' meeting summoned under section 257 approves the proposed voluntary arrangement (with or without modifications) and the debtor is an undischarged bankrupt, the court may do one or both of the following, namely—

(a)   annul the bankruptcy order by which he was adjudged bankrupt;

(b)   give such directions with respect to the conduct of the bankruptcy and the administration of the bankrupt's estate as it thinks appropriate for facilitating the implementation of the approved voluntary arrangement.

(2)   The court shall not annul a bankruptcy order under subsection (1)—

(a)   at any time before the end of the period of 28 days beginning with the day on which the report of the creditors' meeting was made to the court under section 259, or

(b)   at any time when an application under section 262 below, or an appeal in respect of such an application, is pending or at any time in the period within which such an appeal may be brought.

262. Challenge of meeting's decision

(1)   Subject to this section, an application to the court may be made, by any of the persons specified below, on one or both of the following grounds, namely—

(a)   that a voluntary arrangement approved by a creditors' meeting summoned under section 257 unfairly prejudices the interests of a creditor of the debtor;

(b)   that there has been some material irregularity at or in relation to such a meeting.

(2)   The persons who may apply under this section are—

(a)   the debtor;

(b)   a person who—

(i)   was entitled, in accordance with the rules, to vote at the creditors' meeting, or

(ii)   would have been so entitled if he had had notice of it;

(c)   the nominee (or his replacement under section 256(3), 256A(4) or 258(3)); and

(d)   if the debtor is an undischarged bankrupt, the trustee of his estate or the official receiver.

(3)   An application under this section shall not be made—

(a)   after the end of the period of 28 days beginning with the day on which the report of the creditors' meeting was made to the court under section 259 or

(b)   in the case of a person who was not given notice of the creditors' meeting, after the end of the period of 28 days beginning with the day on which he became aware that the meeting had taken place, but (subject to that) an application made by a person within subsection (2)(b)(ii) on the ground that the arrangement prejudices his interests may be made after the arrangement has ceased to have effect, unless it has come to an end prematurely.

(4)   Where on an application under this section the court is satisfied as to either of the grounds mentioned in subsection (1), it may do one or both of the following, namely—

    (a)   revoke or suspend any approval given by the meeting;
    (b)   give a direction to any person for the summoning of a further meeting of the debtor's creditors to consider any revised proposal he may make or, in a case falling within subsection (1)(b), to reconsider his original proposal.

(5)   Where at any time after giving a direction under subsection (4)(b) for the summoning of a meeting to consider a revised proposal the court is satisfied that the debtor does not intend to submit such a proposal, the court shall revoke the direction and revoke or suspend any approval given at the previous meeting.

(6)   Where the court gives a direction under subsection (4)(b), it may also give a direction continuing or, as the case may require, renewing, for such period as may be specified in the direction, the effect in relation to the debtor of any interim order.

(7)   In any case where the court, on an application made under this section with respect to a creditors' meeting, gives a direction under subsection (4)(b) or revokes or suspends an approval under subsection (4)(a) or (5), the court may give such supplemental directions as it thinks fit and, in particular, directions with respect to—

    (a)   things done since the meeting under any voluntary arrangement approved by the meeting, and
    (b)   such things done since the meeting as could not have been done if an interim order had been in force in relation to the debtor when they were done.

(8)   Except in pursuance of the preceding provisions of this section, an approval given at a creditors' meeting summoned under section 257 is not invalidated by any irregularity at or in relation to the meeting.

262A.   False representations etc

(1)   If for the purpose of obtaining the approval of his creditors to a proposal for a voluntary arrangement, the debtor—

    (a)   makes any false representation, or
    (b)   fraudulently does, or omits to do, anything,

he commits an offence.

(2)   Subsection (1) applies even if the proposal is not approved.

(3)   A person guilty of an offence under this section is liable to imprisonment or a fine, or both.

262B.   Prosecution of delinquent debtors

(1)   This section applies where a voluntary arrangement approved by a creditors' meeting summoned under section 257 has taken effect.

(2)   If it appears to the nominee or supervisor that the debtor has been guilty of any offence in connection with the arrangement for which he is criminally liable, he shall forthwith—

    (a)   report the matter to the Secretary of State, and
    (b)   provide the Secretary of State with such information and give the Secretary of State such access to and facilities for inspecting and taking copies of documents (being information or documents in his possession or under his control and relating to the matter in question) as the Secretary of State requires.

(3)   Where a prosecuting authority institutes criminal proceedings following any report under subsection (2), the nominee or, as the case may be, supervisor shall give the authority all assistance in connection with the prosecution which he is reasonably able to give.

For this purpose, 'prosecuting authority' means the Director of Public Prosecutions or the Secretary of State.

(4)   The court may, on the application of the prosecuting authority, direct a nominee or supervisor to comply with subsection (3) if he has failed to do so.

Part IV Insolvency

262C.   Arrangements coming to an end prematurely

For the purposes of this Part, a voluntary arrangement approved by a creditors' meeting summoned under section 257 comes to an end prematurely if, when it ceases to have effect, it has not been fully implemented in respect of all persons bound by the arrangement by virtue of section 260(2)(b)(i).

263. Implementation and supervision of approved voluntary arrangement

(1)   This section applies where a voluntary arrangement approved by a creditors' meeting summoned under section 257 has taken effect.

(2)   The person who is for the time being carrying out, in relation to the voluntary arrangement, the functions conferred by virtue of the approval on the nominee (or his replacement under section 256(3), 256A(4) or 258(3)) shall be known as the supervisor of the voluntary arrangement.

(3)   If the debtor, any of his creditors or any other person is dissatisfied by any act, omission or decision of the supervisor, he may apply to the court; and on such an application the court may—

    (a)   confirm, reverse or modify any act or decision of the supervisor,
    (b)   give him directions, or
    (c)   make such other order as it thinks fit.

(4)   The supervisor may apply to the court for directions in relation to any particular matter arising under the voluntary arrangement.

(5)   The court may, whenever—

    (a)   it is expedient to appoint a person to carry out the functions of the supervisor, and
    (b)   it is inexpedient, difficult or impracticable for an appointment to be made without the assistance of the court,

make an order appointing a person who is qualified to act as an insolvency practitioner [or authorised to act as supervisor, in relation to the voluntary arrangement], either in substitution for the existing supervisor or to fill a vacancy.

This is without prejudice to section 41(2) of the Trustee Act 1925 (power of court to appoint trustees of deeds of arrangement).

(6)   The power conferred by subsection (5) is exercisable so as to increase the number of persons exercising the functions of the supervisor or, where there is more than one person exercising those functions, so as to replace one or more of those persons.

263A.   Availability

Section 263B applies where an individual debtor intends to make a proposal to his creditors for a voluntary arrangement and—

    (a)   the debtor is an undischarged bankrupt,
    (b)   the official receiver is specified in the proposal as the nominee in relation to the voluntary arrangement, and
    (c)   no interim order is applied for under section 253.

Note: Section in italics prosp ins Enterprise Act 2002, s 264(1), Sch 22, para 2.

263B.   Decision

(1)   The debtor may submit to the official receiver—

    (a)   a document setting out the terms of the voluntary arrangement which the debtor is proposing, and
    (b)   a statement of his affairs containing such particulars as may be prescribed of his creditors, debts, other liabilities and assets and such other information as may be prescribed.

(2)   If the official receiver thinks that the voluntary arrangement proposed has a reasonable prospect of being approved and implemented, he may make arrangements for inviting creditors to decide whether to approve it.

(3)   For the purposes of subsection (2) a person is a 'creditor' only if—

    (a)   he is a creditor of the debtor in respect of a bankruptcy debt, and

(b)   the official receiver is aware of his claim and his address.

(4)   *Arrangements made under subsection (2)—*

(a)   *must include the provision to each creditor of a copy of the proposed voluntary arrangement,*

(b)   *must include the provision to each creditor of information about the criteria by reference to which the official receiver will determine whether the creditors approve or reject the proposed voluntary arrangement, and*

(c)   *may not include an opportunity for modifications to the proposed voluntary arrangement to be suggested or made.*

(5)   *Where a debtor submits documents to the official receiver under subsection (1) no application under section 253 for an interim order may be made in respect of the debtor until the official receiver has—*

(a)   *made arrangements as described in subsection (2), or*

(b)   *informed the debtor that he does not intend to make arrangements (whether because he does not think the voluntary arrangement has a reasonable prospect of being approved and implemented or because he declines to act).*

Note: Section in italics prosp ins Enterprise Act 2002, s 264(1), Sch 22, para 2.

263C.   Result

As soon as is reasonably practicable after the implementation of arrangements under section 263B(2) the official receiver shall report to the court whether the proposed voluntary arrangement has been approved or rejected.

Note: Section in italics prosp ins Enterprise Act 2002, s 264(1), Sch 22, para 2.

263D.   Approval of voluntary arrangement

(1)   *This section applies where the official receiver reports to the court under section 263C that a proposed voluntary arrangement has been approved.*

(2)   *The voluntary arrangement—*

(a)   *takes effect,*

(b)   *binds the debtor, and*

(c)   *binds every person who was entitled to participate in the arrangements made under section 263B(2).*

(3)   *The court shall annul the bankruptcy order in respect of the debtor on an application made by the official receiver.*

(4)   *An application under subsection (3) may not be made—*

(a)   *during the period specified in section 263F(3) during which the voluntary arrangement can be challenged by application under section 263F(2),*

(b)   *while an application under that section is pending, or*

(c)   *while an appeal in respect of an application under that section is pending or may be brought.*

(5)   *The court may give such directions about the conduct of the bankruptcy and the administration of the bankrupt's estate as it thinks appropriate for facilitating the implementation of the approved voluntary arrangement.*

(6)   *The Deeds of Arrangement Act 1914 does not apply to the voluntary arrangement.*

(7)   *A reference in this Act or another enactment to a voluntary arrangement approved under this Part includes a reference to a voluntary arrangement which has effect by virtue of this section.*

Note: Section in italics prosp ins Enterprise Act 2002, s 264(1), Sch 22, para 2.

263E.   Implementation

Section 263 shall apply to a voluntary arrangement which has effect by virtue of section 263D(2) as it applies to a voluntary arrangement approved by a creditors' meeting.

Note: Section in italics prosp ins Enterprise Act 2002, s 264(1), Sch 22, para 2.

263F. *Revocation*

(1)   The court may make an order revoking a voluntary arrangement which has effect by virtue of section 263D(2) on the ground—

    (a)   that it unfairly prejudices the interests of a creditor of the debtor, or

    (b)   that a material irregularity occurred in relation to the arrangements made under section 263B(2).

(2)   An order under subsection (1) may be made only on the application of—

    (a)   the debtor,

    (b)   a person who was entitled to participate in the arrangements made under section 263B(2),

    (c)   the trustee of the bankrupt's estate, or

    (d)   the official receiver.

(3)   An application under subsection (2) may not be made after the end of the period of 28 days beginning with the date on which the official receiver makes his report to the court under section 263C.

(4)   But a creditor who was not made aware of the arrangements under section 263B(2) at the time when they were made may make an application under subsection (2) during the period of 28 days beginning with the date on which he becomes aware of the voluntary arrangement.

Note: Section in italics prosp ins Enterprise Act 2002, s 264(1), Sch 22, para 2.

263G *Offences*

(1)   Section 262A shall have effect in relation to obtaining approval to a proposal for a voluntary arrangement under section 263D.

(2)   Section 262B shall have effect in relation to a voluntary arrangement which has effect by virtue of section 263D(2) (for which purposes the words 'by a creditors' meeting summoned under section 257' shall be disregarded).

Note: Section in italics prosp ins Enterprise Act 2002, s 264(1), Sch 22, para 2.

264. **Who may present a bankruptcy petition**

(1)   A petition for a bankruptcy order to be made against an individual may be presented to the court in accordance with the following provisions of this Part—

    (a)   by one of the individual's creditors or jointly by more than one of them,

    (b)   by the individual himself,

    (ba)   by a temporary administrator (within the meaning of Article 38 of the EC Regulation),

    (bb)   by a liquidator (within the meaning of Article 2(b) of the EC Regulation) appointed in proceedings by virtue of Article 3(1) of the EC Regulation,

    (c)   by the supervisor of, or any person (other than the individual) who is for the time being bound by, a voluntary arrangement proposed by the individual and approved under Part VIII, *or*

    (d)   *where a criminal bankruptcy order has been made against the individual, by the Official Petitioner or by any person specified in the order in pursuance of section 39(3)(b) of the Powers of Criminal Courts Act 1973.* [Ital words prosp rep]

(2)   Subject to those provisions, the court may make a bankruptcy order on any such petition.

265. **Conditions to be satisfied in respect of debtor**

(1)   A bankruptcy petition shall not be presented to the court under section 264(1)(a) or (b) unless the debtor—

    (a)   is domiciled in England and Wales,

    (b)   is personally present in England and Wales on the day on which the petition is presented, or

    (c)   at any time in the period of 3 years ending with that day—

        (i)   has been ordinarily resident, or has had a place of residence, in England and Wales, or

        (ii)   has carried on business in England and Wales.

(2)   The reference in subsection (1)(c) to an individual carrying on business includes—

    (a)   the carrying on of business by a firm or partnership of which the individual is a member, and

    (b)   the carrying on of business by an agent or manager for the individual or for such a firm or partnership.

(3)   This section is subject to Article 3 of the EC Regulation.

PART IX

BANKRUPTCY

266. Other preliminary conditions

(1)   Where a bankruptcy petition relating to an individual is presented by a person who is entitled to present a petition under two or more paragraphs of section 264(1), the petition is to be treated for the purposes of this Part as a petition under such one of those paragraphs as may be specified in the petition.

(2)   A bankruptcy petition shall not be withdrawn without the leave of the court.

(3)   The court has a general power, if it appears to it to do so on the grounds that there has been a contravention of the rules or for any other reason, to dismiss a bankruptcy petition or to stay proceedings on such a petition; and, where it stays proceedings on a petition, it may do so on such terms and conditions as it thinks fit.

(4)   Without prejudice to subsection (3), where a petition under section 264(1)(a), (b) or (c) in respect of an individual is pending at a time when a criminal bankruptcy order is made against him, or is presented after such an order has been so made, the court may on the application of the Official Petitioner dismiss the petition if it appears to it appropriate to do so. [Ital words prosp rep]

267. Grounds of creditor's petition

(1)   A creditor's petition must be in respect of one or more debts owed by the debtor, and the petitioning creditor or each of the petitioning creditors must be a person to whom the debt or (as the case may be) at least one of the debts is owed.

(2)   Subject to the next three sections, a creditor's petition may be presented to the court in respect of a debt or debts only if, at the time the petition is presented—

    (a)   the amount of the debt, or the aggregate amount of the debts, is equal to or exceeds the bankruptcy level,

    (b)   the debt, or each of the debts, is for a liquidated sum payable to the petitioning creditor, or one or more of the petitioning creditors, either immediately or at some certain, future time, and is unsecured,

    (c)   the debt, or each of the debts, is a debt which the debtor appears either to be unable to pay or to have no reasonable prospect of being able to pay, and

    (d)   there is no outstanding application to set aside a statutory demand served (under section 268 below) in respect of the debt or any of the debts.

(3)   A debt is not to be regarded for the purposes of subsection (2) as a debt for a liquidated sum by reason only that the amount of the debt is specified in a criminal bankruptcy order. [Ital words prosp rep]

(4)   'The bankruptcy level' is £750; but the Secretary of State may by order in a statutory instrument substitute any amount specified in the order for that amount or (as the case may be) for the amount which by virtue of such an order is for the time being the amount of the bankruptcy level.

(5)   An order shall not be made under subsection (4) unless a draft of it has been laid before, and approved by a resolution of, each House of Parliament.

268. Definition of 'inability to pay', etc; the statutory demand

(1)   For the purposes of section 267(2)(c), the debtor appears to be unable to pay a debt if, but only if, the debt is payable immediately and either—

    (a)   the petitioning creditor to whom the debt is owed has served on the debtor a demand (known as 'the statutory demand') in the prescribed form requiring him to pay the debt or to secure or compound for it to the satisfaction of the creditor, at least 3 weeks have elapsed since the demand was served and the demand has been neither complied with nor set aside in accordance with the rules, or

    (b)   execution or other process issued in respect of the debt on a judgment or order of any court in favour of the petitioning creditor, or one or more of the petitioning creditors to whom the debt is owed, has been returned unsatisfied in whole or in part.

(2)   For the purposes of section 267(2)(c) the debtor appears to have no reasonable prospect of being able to pay a debt if, but only if, the debt is not immediately payable and—

    (a)   the petitioning creditor to whom it is owed has served on the debtor a demand (also known as 'the statutory demand') in the prescribed form requiring him to establish to the satisfaction of the creditor that there is a reasonable prospect that the debtor will be able to pay the debt when it falls due,

    (b)   at least 3 weeks have elapsed since the demand was served, and

    (c)   the demand has been neither complied with nor set aside in accordance with the rules.

269. Creditor with security

(1)   A debt which is the debt, or one of the debts, in respect of which a creditor's petition is presented need not be unsecured if either—

    (a)   the petition contains a statement by the person having the right to enforce the security that he is willing, in the event of a bankruptcy order being made, to give up his security for the benefit of all the bankrupt's creditors, or

    (b)   the petition is expressed not to be made in respect of the secured part of the debt and contains a statement by that person of the estimated value at the date of the petition of the security for the secured part of the debt.

(2)   In a case falling within subsection (1)(b) the secured and unsecured parts of the debt are to be treated for the purposes of sections 267 to 270 as separate debts.

270. Expedited petition

In the case of a creditor's petition presented wholly or partly in respect of a debt which is the subject of a statutory demand under section 268, the petition may be presented before the end of the 3-week period there mentioned if there is a serious possibility that the debtor's property or the value of any of his property will be significantly diminished during that period and the petition contains a statement to that effect.

271. Proceedings on creditor's petition

(1)   The court shall not make a bankruptcy order on a creditor's petition unless it is satisfied that the debt, or one of the debts, in respect of which the petition was presented is either—

    (a)   a debt which, having been payable at the date of the petition or having since become payable, has been neither paid nor secured or compounded for, or

    (b)   a debt which the debtor has no reasonable prospect of being able to pay when it falls due.

(2)   In a case in which the petition contains such a statement as is required by section 270, the court shall not make a bankruptcy order until at least 3 weeks have elapsed since the service of any statutory demand under section 268.

(3)   The court may dismiss the petition if it is satisfied that the debtor is able to pay all his debts or is satisfied—

    (a)   that the debtor has made an offer to secure or compound for a debt in respect of which the petition is presented,

    (b)   that the acceptance of that offer would have required the dismissal of the petition, and

    (c)   that the offer has been unreasonably refused;

and, in determining for the purposes of this subsection whether the debtor is able to pay all his debts, the court shall take into account his contingent and prospective liabilities.

(4)   In determining for the purposes of this section what constitutes a reasonable prospect that a debtor will be able to pay a debt when it falls due, it is to be assumed that the prospect given by the facts and other matters known to the creditor at the time he entered into the transaction resulting in the debt was a reasonable prospect.

(5)   Nothing in sections 267 to 271 prejudices the power of the court, in accordance with the rules, to authorise a creditor's petition to be amended by the omission of any creditor or debt and to be proceeded with as if things done for the purposes of those sections had been done only by or in relation to the remaining creditors or debts.

272. Grounds of debtor's petition

(1)   A debtor's petition may be presented to the court only on the grounds that the debtor is unable to pay his debts.

(2)   The petition shall be accompanied by a statement of the debtor's affairs containing—

    (a)   such particulars of the debtor's creditors and of his debts and other liabilities and of his assets as may be prescribed, and

(b)   such other information as may be prescribed.

273. Appointment of insolvency practitioner by the court

(1)   Subject to the next section, on the hearing of a debtor's petition the court shall not make a bankruptcy order if it appears to the court—

(a)   that if a bankruptcy order were made the aggregate amount of the bankruptcy debts, so far as unsecured, would be less than the small bankruptcies level,

(b)   that if a bankruptcy order were made, the value of the bankrupt's estate would be equal to or more than the minimum amount,

(c)   that within the period of 5 years ending with the presentation of the petition the debtor has neither been adjudged bankrupt nor made a composition with his creditors in satisfaction of his debts or a scheme of arrangement of his affairs, and

(d)   that it would be appropriate to appoint a person to prepare a report under section 274.

'The minimum amount' and 'the small bankruptcies level' mean such amounts as may for the time being be prescribed for the purposes of this section.

(2)   Where on the hearing of the petition, it appears to the court as mentioned in subsection (1), the court shall appoint a person who is qualified to act as an insolvency practitioner in relation to the debtor—

(a)   to prepare a report under the next section, and

(b)   subject to section 258(3) in Part VIII, to act in relation to any voluntary arrangement to which the report relates either as trustee or otherwise for the purpose of supervising its implementation.

274. Action on report of insolvency practitioner

(1)   A person appointed under section 273 shall inquire into the debtor's affairs and, within such period as the court may direct, shall submit a report to the court stating whether the debtor is willing, for the purposes of Part VIII, to make a proposal for a voluntary arrangement.

(2)   A report which states that the debtor is willing as above mentioned shall also state—

(a)   whether, in the opinion of the person making the report, a meeting of the debtor's creditors should be summoned to consider the proposal, and

(b)   if in that person's opinion such a meeting should be summoned, the date on which, and time and place at which, he proposes the meeting should be held.

(3)   On considering a report under this section the court may—

(a)   without any application, make an interim order under section 252, if it thinks that it is appropriate to do so for the purpose of facilitating the consideration and implementation of the debtor's proposal, or

(b)   if it thinks it would be inappropriate to make such an order, make a bankruptcy order.

(4)   An interim order made by virtue of this section ceases to have effect at the end of such period as the court may specify for the purpose of enabling the debtor's proposal to be considered by his creditors in accordance with the applicable provisions of Part VIII.

(5)   Where it has been reported to the court under this section that a meeting of the debtor's creditors should be summoned, the person making the report shall, unless the court otherwise directs, summon that meeting for the time, date and place proposed in his report.

The meeting is then deemed to have been summoned under section 257 in Part VIII, and subsections (2) and (3) of that section, and sections 258 to 263 apply accordingly.

275. Summary administration

(1)   Where on the hearing of a debtor's the court makes a bankruptcy order and the case is as specified in the next subsection, the court shall, if it appears to it appropriate to do so, issue a certificate for the summary administration of the bankrupt's estate.

(2)   That case is where it appears to the court—

(a)   that if a bankruptcy order were made the aggregate amount of the bankruptcy debts so far as unsecured would be less than the small bankruptcies level (within the meaning given by section 273), and

(b)   that within the period of 5 years ending with the presentation of the petition the debtor has neither been adjudged bankrupt nor made a composition with his creditors in satisfaction of his debts or a scheme of arrangement of his affairs,

whether the bankruptcy order is made because it does not appear to the court as mentioned in section 273(1)(b) or (d), or it is made because the court thinks it would be inappropriate to make an interim order under section 252.

(3)   The court may at any time revoke a certificate issued under this section if it appears to it that, on any grounds existing at the time the certificate was issued, the certificate ought not to have been issued.

278. Commencement and continuance

The bankruptcy of an individual against whom a bankruptcy order has been made—

(a)   commences with the day on which the order is made, and

(b)   continues until the individual is discharged under the following provisions of this Chapter.

279. Duration

(1)   Subject as follows, a bankrupt is discharged from bankruptcy—

(a)   in the case of an individual who was adjudged bankrupt on a petition under section 264(1)(d) or who had been an undischarged bankrupt at any time in the period of 15 years ending with the commencement of the bankruptcy, by an order of the court under the section next following, and

(b)   in any other case, by the expiration of the relevant period under this section.

(2)   That period is as follows—

(a)   where a certificate for the summary administration of the bankrupt's estate has been issued and is not revoked before the bankrupt's discharge, the period of 2 years beginning with the commencement of the bankruptcy, and

(b)   in any other case, the period of 3 years beginning with the commencement of the bankruptcy.

(3)   Where the court is satisfied on the application of the official receiver that an undischarged bankrupt in relation to whom subsection (1)(b) applies has failed or is failing to comply with any of his obligations under this Part, the court may order that the relevant period under this section shall cease to run for such period, or until the fulfilment of such conditions (including a condition requiring the court to be satisfied as to any matter), as may be specified in the order.

(4)   This section is without prejudice to any power of the court to annul a bankruptcy order.

280. Discharge by order of the court

(1)   An application for an order of the court discharging an individual from bankruptcy in a case falling within section 279(1)(a) may be made by the bankrupt at any time after the end of the period of 5 years beginning with the commencement of the bankruptcy.

(2)   On an application under this section the court may—

(a)   refuse to discharge the bankrupt from bankruptcy,

(b)   make an order discharging him absolutely, or

(c)   make an order discharging him subject to such conditions with respect to any income which may subsequently become due to him, or with respect to property devolving upon him, or acquired by him, after his discharge, as may be specified in the order.

(3)   The court may provide for an order falling within subsection (2)(b) or (c) to have immediate effect or to have its effect suspended for such period, or until the fulfilment of such conditions (including a condition requiring the court to be satisfied as to any matter), as may be specified in the order.

281. Effect of discharge

(1)   Subject as follows, where a bankrupt is discharged, the discharge releases him from all the bankruptcy debts, but has no effect—

(a)   on the functions (so far as they remain to be carried out) of the trustee of his estate, or

(b)   on the operation, for the purposes of the carrying out of those functions, of the provisions of this Part;

and, in particular, discharge does not affect the right of any creditor of the bankrupt to prove in the bankruptcy for any debt from which the bankrupt is released.

(2)   Discharge does not affect the right of any secured creditor of the bankrupt to enforce his security for the payment of a debt from which the bankrupt is released.

(3)   Discharge does not release the bankrupt from any bankruptcy debt which he incurred in respect of, or forbearance in respect of which was secured by means of, any fraud or fraudulent breach of trust to which he was a party.

(4)   Discharge does not release the bankrupt from any liability in respect of a fine imposed for an offence or from any liability under a recognisance except, in the case of a penalty imposed for an offence under an enactment relating to the public revenue or of a recognisance, with the consent of the Treasury.

(4A)   In subsection (4) the reference to a fine includes a reference to a confiscation order under Part 2, 3 or 4 of the Proceeds of Crime Act 2002.

(5)   Discharge does not, except to such extent and on such conditions as the court may direct, release the bankrupt from any bankruptcy debt which—

   (a)   consists in a liability to pay damages for negligence, nuisance or breach of a statutory, contractual or other duty, or to pay damages by virtue of Part I of the Consumer Protection Act 1987, being in either case damages in respect of personal injuries to any person, or

   (b)   arises under any order made in family proceedings or under a maintenance assessment made under the Child Support Act 1991.

(6)   Discharge does not release the bankrupt from such other bankruptcy debts, not being debts provable in his bankruptcy, as are prescribed.

(7)   Discharge does not release any person other than the bankrupt from any liability (whether as partner or co-trustee of the bankrupt or otherwise) from which the bankrupt is released by the discharge, or from any liability as surety for the bankrupt or as a person in the nature of such a surety.

(8)   In this section—

   'family proceedings' means—

   (a)   family proceedings within the meaning of the Magistrates' Courts Act 1980 and any proceedings which would be such proceedings but for section 65(1)(ii) of that Act (proceedings for variation of order for periodical payments); and

   (b)   family proceedings within the meaning of Part V of the Matrimonial and Family Proceedings Act 1984;

   'fine' means the same as in the Magistrates' Courts Act 1980; and

   'personal injuries' includes death and any disease or other impairment of a person's physical or mental condition.

281A.   *Post-discharge restrictions*

Schedule 4A to this Act (bankruptcy restrictions order and bankruptcy restrictions undertaking) shall have effect.

Note: Section in italics prosp ins Enterprise Act 2002, s 260.

282.   Court's power to annul bankruptcy order

(1)   The court may annul a bankruptcy order if it at any time appears to the court—

   (a)   that, on the grounds existing at the time the order was made, the order ought not to have been made, or

   (b)   that, to the extent required by the rules, the bankruptcy debts and the expenses of the bankruptcy have all, since the making of the order, been either paid or secured for to the satisfaction of the court.

(2)   The court may annul a bankruptcy order made against an individual on a petition under paragraph (a), (b) or (c) of section 264(1) if it at any time appears to the court, on an application by the Official Petitioner—

   (a)   that the petition was pending at a time when a criminal bankruptcy order was made against the individual or was presented after such an order was so made, and

   (b)   no appeal is pending (within the meaning of section 277) against the individual's conviction of any offence by virtue of which the criminal bankruptcy order was made;

and the court shall annul a bankruptcy order made on a petition under section 264(1)(d) if it at any time appears to the court that the criminal bankruptcy order on which the petition was based had been rescinded in consequence of an appeal. [Ital words prosp rep]

(3)   The court may annul a bankruptcy order whether or not the bankrupt has been discharged from the bankruptcy.

(4)   Where the court annuls a bankruptcy order (whether under this section or under section 261 in Part VIII)—

    (a)   any sale or other disposition of property, payment made or other thing duly done, under any provision in this Group of Parts, by or under the authority of the official receiver or a trustee of the bankrupt's estate or by the court is valid, but

    (b)   if any of the bankrupt's estate is then vested, under any such provision, in such a trustee, it shall vest in such person as the court may appoint or, in default of any such appointment, revert to the bankrupt on such terms (if any) as the court may direct;

and the court may include in its order such supplemental provisions as may be authorised by the rules.

(5)   In determining for the purposes of section 279 whether a person was an undischarged bankrupt at any time, any time when he was a bankrupt by virtue of an order that was subsequently annulled is to be disregarded.

283.   Definition of bankrupt's estate

(1)   Subject as follows, a bankrupt's estate for the purposes of any of this Group of Parts comprises—

    (a)   all property belonging to or vested in the bankrupt at the commencement of the bankruptcy, and

    (b)   any property which by virtue of any of the following provisions of this Part is comprised in that estate or is treated as falling within the preceding paragraph.

(2)   Subsection (1) does not apply to—

    (a)   such tools, books, vehicles and other items of equipment as are necessary to the bankrupt for use personally by him in his employment, business or vocation;

    (b)   such clothing, bedding, furniture, household equipment and provisions as are necessary for satisfying the basic domestic needs of the bankrupt and his family.

This subsection is subject to section 308 in Chapter IV (certain excluded property reclaimable by trustee).

(3)   Subsection (1) does not apply to—

    (a)   property held by the bankrupt on trust for any other person, or

    (b)   the right of nomination to a vacant ecclesiastical benefice.

(3A) Subject to section 308A in Chapter IV, subsection(1) does not apply to—

    (a)   a tenancy which is an assured tenancy or an assured agricultural occupancy, within the meaning of Part I of the Housing Act 1988, and the terms of which inhibit an assignment as mentioned in section 127(5) of the Rent Act 1977, or

    (b)   a protected tenancy, within the meaning of the Rent Act 1977, in respect of which, by virtue of any provision of Part IX of that Act, no premium can lawfully be required as a condition of assignment, or

    (c)   a tenancy of a dwelling-house by virtue of which the bankrupt is, within the meaning of the Rent (Agriculture) Act 1976, a protected occupier of the dwelling-house, and the terms of which inhibit an assignment as mentioned in section 127(5) of the Rent Act 1977, or

    (d)   a secure tenancy, within the meaning of Part IV of the Housing Act 1985, which is not capable of being assigned, except in the cases mentioned in section 91(3) of that Act.

(4)   References in any of this group of Parts to property, in relation to a bankrupt, include references to any power exercisable by him over or in respect of property except in so far as the power is exercisable over or in respect of property not for the time being comprised in the bankrupt's estate and—

    (a)   is so exercisable at a time after either the official receiver has had his release in respect of that estate under section 299(2) in Chapter III or a meeting summoned by the trustee of that estate under section 331 in Chapter IV has been held, or

    (b)   cannot be so exercised for the benefit of the bankrupt;

and a power exercisable over or in respect of property is deemed for the purposes of any of this Group of Parts to vest in the person entitled to exercise it at the time of the transaction or event by virtue of which it is exercisable by that person (whether or not it becomes so exercisable at that time).

(5)   For the purposes of any such provision in this Group of Parts, property comprised in a bankrupt's estate is so comprised subject to the rights of any person other than the bankrupt (whether as a secured creditor of the bankrupt or otherwise) in relation thereto, but disregarding—

(a)   any rights in relation to which a statement such as is required by section 269(1)(a) was made in the petition on which the bankrupt was adjudged bankrupt, and

(b)   any rights which have been otherwise given up in accordance with the rules.

(6)   This section has effect subject to the provisions of any enactment not contained in this Act under which any property is to be excluded from a bankrupt's estate.

283A.   *Bankrupt's home ceasing to form part of estate*

(1)   This section applies where property comprised in the bankrupt's estate consists of an interest in a dwelling-house which at the date of the bankruptcy was the sole or principal residence of—

(a)   the bankrupt,

(b)   the bankrupt's spouse, or

(c)   a former spouse of the bankrupt.

(2)   At the end of the period of three years beginning with the date of the bankruptcy the interest mentioned in subsection (1) shall—

(a)   cease to be comprised in the bankrupt's estate, and

(b)   vest in the bankrupt (without conveyance, assignment or transfer).

(3)   Subsection (2) shall not apply if during the period mentioned in that subsection—

(a)   the trustee realises the interest mentioned in subsection (1),

(b)   the trustee applies for an order for sale in respect of the dwelling-house,

(c)   the trustee applies for an order for possession of the dwelling-house,

(d)   the trustee applies for an order under section 313 in Chapter IV in respect of that interest, or

(e)   the trustee and the bankrupt agree that the bankrupt shall incur a specified liability to his estate (with or without the addition of interest from the date of the agreement) in consideration of which the interest mentioned in subsection (1) shall cease to form part of the estate.

(4)   Where an application of a kind described in subsection (3)(b) to (d) is made during the period mentioned in subsection (2) and is dismissed, unless the court orders otherwise the interest to which the application relates shall on the dismissal of the application—

(a)   cease to be comprised in the bankrupt's estate, and

(b)   vest in the bankrupt (without conveyance, assignment or transfer).

(5)   If the bankrupt does not inform the trustee or the official receiver of his interest in a property before the end of the period of three months beginning with the date of the bankruptcy, the period of three years mentioned in subsection (2)—

(a)   shall not begin with the date of the bankruptcy, but

(b)   shall begin with the date on which the trustee or official receiver becomes aware of the bankrupt's interest.

(6)   The court may substitute for the period of three years mentioned in subsection (2) a longer period—

(a)   in prescribed circumstances, and

(b)   in such other circumstances as the court thinks appropriate.

(7)   The rules may make provision for this section to have effect with the substitution of a shorter period for the period of three years mentioned in subsection (2) in specified circumstances (which may be described by reference to action to be taken by a trustee in bankruptcy).

(8)   The rules may also, in particular, make provision—

(a)   requiring or enabling the trustee of a bankrupt's estate to give notice that this section applies or does not apply;

(b)   about the effect of a notice under paragraph (a);

(c)   requiring the trustee of a bankrupt's estate to make an application to the Chief Land Registrar.

(9)   Rules under subsection (8)(b) may, in particular—

(a)   *disapply this section;*

(b)   *enable a court to disapply this section;*

(c)   *make provision in consequence of a disapplication of this section;*

(d)   *enable a court to make provision in consequence of a disapplication of this section;*

(e)   *make provision (which may include provision conferring jurisdiction on a court or tribunal) about compensation.*

Note: Section in italics prosp ins Enterprise Act 2002, s 261(1).

284. Restrictions on dispositions of property

(1)   Where a person is adjudged bankrupt, any disposition of property made by that person in the period to which this section applies is void except to the extent that it is or was made with the consent of the court, or is or was subsequently ratified by the court.

(2)   Subsection (1) applies to a payment (whether in cash or otherwise) as it applies to a disposition of property and, accordingly, where any payment is void by virtue of that subsection, the person paid shall hold the sum paid for the bankrupt as part of his estate.

(3)   This section applies to the period beginning with the day of the presentation of the petition for the bankruptcy order and ending with the vesting, under Chapter IV of this Part, of the bankrupt's estate in a trustee.

(4)   The preceding provisions of this section do not give a remedy against any person—

(a)   In respect of any property or payment which he received before the commencement of the bankruptcy in good faith, for value and without notice that the petition had been presented, or

(b)   in respect of any interest in property which derives from an interest in respect of which there is, by virtue of this subsection, no remedy.

(5)   Where after the commencement of his bankruptcy the bankrupt has incurred a debt to a banker or other person by reason of the making of a payment which is void under this section, that debt is deemed for the purposes of any of this Group of Parts to have been incurred before the commencement of the bankruptcy unless—

(a)   that banker or person had notice of the bankruptcy before the debt was incurred, or

(b)   it is not reasonably practicable for the amount of the payment to be recovered from the person to whom it was made.

(6)   A disposition of property is void under this section notwithstanding that the property is not or, as the case may be, would not be comprised in the bankrupt's estate; but nothing in this section affects any disposition made by a person of property held by him on trust for any other person.

289. Investigatory duties of official receiver

(1)   Subject to subsection (5) below, it is the duty of the official receiver to investigate the conduct and affairs of every bankrupt and to make such report (if any) to the court as he thinks fit.

(2)   Where an application is made by the bankrupt under section 280 for his discharge from bankruptcy, it is the duty of the official receiver to make a report to the court with respect to the prescribed matters; and the court shall consider that report before determining what order (if any) to make under that section.

(3)   A report by the official receiver under this section shall, in any proceedings, be prima facie evidence of the facts stated in it.

(4)   In subsection (1) the reference to the conduct and affairs of a bankrupt includes his conduct and affairs before the making of the order by which he was adjudged bankrupt.

(5)   Where a certificate for the summary administration of the bankrupt's estate is for the time being in force, the official receiver shall carry out an investigation under subsection (1) only if he thinks fit.

306. Vesting of bankrupt's estate in trustee

(1)   The bankrupt's estate shall vest in the trustee immediately on his appointment taking effect or, in the case of the official receiver, on his becoming trustee.

(2)   Where any property which is, or is to be, comprised in the bankrupt's estate vests in the trustee (whether under this section or under any other provision of this Part), it shall so vest without any conveyance, assignment or transfer.

306A.   Property subject to restraint order

(1)   This section applies where—

    (a)   property is excluded from the bankrupt's estate by virtue of section 417(2)(a) of the Proceeds of Crime Act 2002 (property subject to a restraint order),

    (b)   an order under section 50, 52, 128, 198 or 200 of that Act has not been made in respect of the property, and

    (c)   the restraint order is discharged.

(2)   On the discharge of the restraint order the property vests in the trustee as part of the bankrupt's estate.

(3)   But subsection (2) does not apply to the proceeds of property realised by a management receiver under section 49(2)(d) or 197(2)(d) of that Act (realisation of property to meet receiver's remuneration and expenses).

306B.   Property in respect of which receivership or administration order made

(1)   This section applies where—

    (a)   property is excluded from the bankrupt's estate by virtue of section 417(2)(b), (c) or (d) of the Proceeds of Crime Act 2002 (property in respect of which an order for the appointment of a receiver or administrator under certain provisions of that Act is in force),

    (b)   a confiscation order is made under section 6, 92 or 156 of that Act,

    (c)   the amount payable under the confiscation order is fully paid, and

    (d)   any of the property remains in the hands of the receiver or administrator (as the case may be).

(2)   The property vests in the trustee as part of the bankrupt's estate.

306C.   Property subject to certain orders where confiscation order discharged or quashed

(1)   This section applies where—

    (a)   property is excluded from the bankrupt's estate by virtue of section 417(2)(a), (b), (c) or (d) of the Proceeds of Crime Act 2002 (property in respect of which a restraint order or an order for the appointment of a receiver or administrator under that Act is in force),

    (b)   a confiscation order is made under section 6, 92 or 156 of that Act, and

    (c)   the confiscation order is discharged under section 30, 114 or 180 of that Act (as the case may be) or quashed under that Act or in pursuance of any enactment relating to appeals against conviction or sentence.

(2)   Any such property in the hands of a receiver appointed under Part 2 or 4 of that Act or an administrator appointed under Part 3 of that Act vests in the trustee as part of the bankrupt's estate.

(3)   But subsection (2) does not apply to the proceeds of property realised by a management receiver under section 49(2)(d) or 197(2)(d) of that Act (realisation of property to meet receiver's remuneration and expenses).

307. After-acquired property

(1)   Subject to this section and section 309, the trustee may by notice in writing claim for the bankrupt's estate any property which has been acquired by, or has devolved upon, the bankrupt since the commencement of the bankruptcy.

(2)   A notice under this section shall not be served in respect of—

    (a)   any property falling within subsection (2) or (3) of section 283 in Chapter II,

    (b)   any property which by virtue of any other enactment is excluded from the bankrupt's estate, or

    (c)   without prejudice to section 280(2)(c) (order of court on application for discharge), any property which is acquired by, or devolves upon, the bankrupt after his discharge.

(3)   Subject to the next subsection, upon the service on the bankrupt of a notice under this section the property to which the notice relates shall vest in the trustee as part of the bankrupt's estate; and the trustee's title to that property has relation back to the time at which the property was acquired by, or devolved upon, the bankrupt.

(4)   Where, whether before or after service of a notice under this section—

    (a)   a person acquires property in good faith, for value and without notice of the bankruptcy, or

    (b)   a banker enters into a transaction in good faith and without such notice, the trustee is not in respect of that property or transaction entitled by virtue of this section to any remedy against that person or banker, or any person whose title to any property derives from that person or banker.

(5)   References in this section to property do not include any property which, as part of the bankrupt's income, may be the subject of an income payments order under section 310.

308. Vesting in trustee of certain items of excess value

(1)   Subject to the next section, where—

(a)   property is excluded by virtue of section 283(2) (tools of trade, household effects, etc.) from the bankrupt's estate, and

(b)   it appears to the trustee that the realisable value of the whole or any part of that property exceeds the cost of a reasonable replacement for that property or that part of it,

the trustee may by notice in writing claim that property or, as the case may be, that part of it for the bankrupt's estate.

(2)   Upon the service on the bankrupt of a notice under this section, the property to which the notice relates vests in the trustee as part of the bankrupt's estate; and, except against a purchaser in good faith, for value and without notice of the bankruptcy, the trustee's title to that property has relation back to the commencement of the bankruptcy.

(3)   The trustee shall apply funds comprised in the estate to the purchase by or on behalf of the bankrupt of a reasonable replacement for any property vested in the trustee under this section; and the duty imposed by this subsection has priority over the obligation of the trustee to distribute the estate.

(4)   For the purposes of this section property is a reasonable replacement for other property if it is reasonably adequate for meeting the needs met by the other property.

308A.   Vesting in trustee of certain tenancies

Upon the service on the bankrupt by the trustee of a notice in writing under this section, any tenancy—

(a)   which is excluded by virtue of section 283(3A) from the bankrupt's estate, and

(b)   to which the notice relates,

vests in the trustee as part of the bankrupt's estate; and, except against a purchaser in good faith, for value and without notice of the bankruptcy, the trustee's title to that tenancy has relation back to the commencement of the bankruptcy.

309. Time-limit for notice under s 307 or 308

(1)   Except with the leave of the court, a notice shall not be served—

(a)   under section 307, after the end of the period of 42 days beginning with the day on which it first came to the knowledge of the trustee that the property in question had been acquired by, or had devolved upon, the bankrupt;

(b)   under section 308 or section 308A after the end of the period of 42 days beginning with the day on which the property or tenancy in question first came to the knowledge of the trustee.

(2)   For the purposes of this section—

(a)   anything which comes to the knowledge of the trustee is deemed in relation to any successor of his as trustee to have come to the knowledge of the successor at the same time; and

(b)   anything which comes (otherwise than under paragraph (a)) to the knowledge of the person before he is the trustee is deemed to come to his knowledge on his appointment taking effect or, in the case of the official receiver, on his becoming trustee.

310. Income payments orders

(1)   The court may, on the application of the trustee, make an order ('an income payments order') claiming for the bankrupt's estate so much of the income of the bankrupt during the period for which the order is in force as may be specified in the order.

(2)   The court shall not make an income payments order the effect of which would be to reduce the income of the bankrupt when taken together with any payments to which subsection (8) applies below what appears to the court to be necessary for meeting the reasonable domestic needs of the bankrupt and his family.

(3)   An income payments order shall, in respect of any payment of income to which it is to apply, either—

(a)   require the bankrupt to pay the trustee an amount equal to so much of that payment as is claimed by the order, or

(b)   require the person making the payment to pay so much of it as is so claimed to the trustee, instead of to the bankrupt.

(4)   Where the court makes an income payments order it may, if it thinks fit, discharge or vary any attachment of earnings order that is for the time being in force to secure payments by the bankrupt.

(5)   Sums received by the trustee under an income payments order form part of the bankrupt's estate.

(6)   An income payments order shall not be made after the discharge of the bankrupt, and if made before, shall not have effect after his discharge except—

(a)   in the case of a discharge under section 279(1)(a) (order of court), by virtue of a condition imposed by the court under section 280(2)(c) (income, etc after discharge), or

(b)   in the case of a discharge under section 279(1)(b) (expiration of relevant period), by virtue of a provision of the order requiring it to continue in force for a period ending after the discharge but no later than 3 years after the making of the order.

(7)   For the purposes of this section the income of the bankrupt comprises every payment in the nature of income which is from time to time made to him or to which he from time to time becomes entitled, including any payment in respect of the carrying on of any business or in respect of any office or employment and (despite anything in section 11 or 12 of the Welfare Reform and Pensions Act 1999) any payment under a pension sheme but excluding any payment to which subsection (8) applies.

(8)   This section applies to—

(a)   payments by way of guaranteed minimum pension; and

(b)   payments giving effect to the bankrupt's protected rights as a member of a pension scheme.

(9)   In this section, 'guaranteed minimum pension' and 'protected rights' have the same meaning as in the Pension Schemes Act 1993.

310A.   *Income payments agreement*

(1)   In this section 'income payments agreement' means a written agreement between a bankrupt and his trustee or between a bankrupt and the official receiver which provides—

(a)   that the bankrupt is to pay to the trustee or the official receiver an amount equal to a specified part or proportion of the bankrupt's income for a specified period, or

(b)   that a third person is to pay to the trustee or the official receiver a specified proportion of money due to the bankrupt by way of income for a specified period.

(2)   A provision of an income payments agreement of a kind specified in subsection (1)(a) or (b) may be enforced as if it were a provision of an income payments order.

(3)   While an income payments agreement is in force the court may, on the application of the bankrupt, his trustee or the official receiver, discharge or vary an attachment of earnings order that is for the time being in force to secure payments by the bankrupt.

(4)   The following provisions of section 310 shall apply to an income payments agreement as they apply to an income payments order—

(a)   subsection (5) (receipts to form part of estate), and

(b)   subsections (7) to (9) (meaning of income).

(5)   An income payments agreement must specify the period during which it is to have effect; and that period—

(a)   may end after the discharge of the bankrupt, but

(b)   may not end after the period of three years beginning with the date on which the agreement is made.

(6)   An income payments agreement may (subject to subsection (5)(b)) be varied—

(a)   by written agreement between the parties, or

(b)   by the court on an application made by the bankrupt, the trustee or the official receiver.

(7)   The court—

> (a)   *may not vary an income payments agreement so as to include provision of a kind which could not be*
>   *included in an income payments order, and*
>
> (b)   *shall grant an application to vary an income payments agreement if and to the extent that the court*
>   *thinks variation necessary to avoid the effect mentioned in section 310(2).*

Note: Section in italics prosp ins Enterprise Act 2002, s 260.

313A.   Low value home: application for sale, possession or charge

(1)   This section applies where—

> (a)   *property comprised in the bankrupt's estate consists of an interest in a dwelling-house which at the date*
>   *of the bankruptcy was the sole or principal residence of—*
>
> > (i)   *the bankrupt,*
> > (ii)   *the bankrupt's spouse, or*
> > (iii) *a former spouse of the bankrupt, and*
>
> (b)   *the trustee applies for an order for the sale of the property, for an order for possession of the property*
>   *or for an order under section 313 in respect of the property.*

(2)   The court shall dismiss the application if the value of the interest is below the amount prescribed for the
purposes of this subsection.

(3)   In determining the value of an interest for the purposes of this section the court shall disregard any matter
which it is required to disregard by the order which prescribes the amount for the purposes of subsection (2).

Note: Section in italics prosp ins Enterprise Act 2002, s 260.

314. Powers of trustee

(1)   The trustee may—

> (a)   with the permission of the creditors' committee or the court, exercise any of the powers specified in
>   Part I of Schedule 5 to this Act, and
> (b)   without that permission, exercise any of the general powers specified in Part II of that Schedule.

(2)   With the permission of the creditors' committee or the court, the trustee may appoint the bankrupt—

> (a)   to superintend the management of his estate or any part of it,
> (b)   to carry on his business (if any) for the benefit of his creditors, or
> (c)   in any other respect to assist in administering the estate in such manner and on such terms as the trustee
>   may direct.

(3)   A permission given for the purposes of subsection (1)(a) or (2) shall not be a general permission but shall
relate to a particular proposed exercise of the power in question; and a person dealing with the trustee in good faith
and for value is not to be concerned to enquire whether any permission required in either case has been given.

(4)   Where the trustee has done anything without the permission required by subsection (1)(a) or (2), the court or
the creditors' committee may, for the purpose of enabling him to meet his expenses out of the bankrupt's estate,
ratify what the trustee has done.

But the committee shall not do so unless it is satisfied that the trustee has acted in a case of urgency and has sought
its ratification without undue delay.

(5)   Part III of Schedule 5 to this Act has effect with respect to the things which the trustee is able to do for the
purposes of, or in connection with, the exercise of any of his powers under any of this Group of Parts.

(6)   Where the trustee (not being the official receiver) in exercise of the powers conferred on him by any provision
in this Group of Parts—

> (a)   disposes of any property comprised in the bankrupt's estate to an associate of the bankrupt, or
> (b)   employs a solicitor,

he shall, if there is for the time being a creditors' committee, give notice to the committee of that exercise of his
powers.

(7)   Without prejudice to the generality of subsection (5) and Part III of Schedule 5, the trustee may, if he thinks
fit, at any time summon a general meeting of the bankrupt's creditors.

Subject to the preceding provisions in this Group of Parts, he shall summon such a meeting if he is requested to do so by a creditor of the bankrupt and the request is made with the concurrence of not less than one-tenth, in value, of the bankrupt's creditors (including the creditor making the request).

(8)   Nothing in this Act is to be construed as restricting the capacity of the trustee to exercise any of his powers outside England and Wales.

CHAPTER V

EFFECT OF BANKRUPTCY ON CERTAIN RIGHTS, TRANSACTIONS, ETC

Rights under trusts of land

335A.   Rights under trusts of land

(1)   Any application by a trustee of a bankrupt's estate under section 14 of the Trusts of Land and Appointment of Trustees Act 1996 (powers of court in relation to trusts of land) for an order under that section for the sale of land shall be made to the court having jurisdiction in relation to the bankruptcy.

(2)   On such an application the court shall make such order as it thinks just and reasonable having regard to—

    (a)   the interests of the bankrupt's creditors;
    (b)   where the application is made in respect of land which includes a dwelling house which is or has been the home of the bankrupt or the bankrupt's spouse or former spouse—

        (i)   the conduct of the spouse or former spouse, so far as contributing to the bankruptcy,
        (ii)   the needs and financial resources of the spouse or former spouse, and
        (iii)   the needs of any children; and

    (c)   all the circumstances of the case other than the needs of the bankrupt.

(3)   Where such an application is made after the end of the period of one year beginning with the first vesting under Chapter IV of this Part of the bankrupt's estate in a trustee, the court shall assume, unless the circumstances of the case are exceptional, that the interests of the bankrupt's creditors outweigh all other considerations.

(4)   The powers conferred on the court by this section are exercisable on an application whether it is made before or after the commencement of this section.

336.   Rights of occupation etc of bankrupt's spouse

(1)   Nothing occurring in the initial period of the bankruptcy (that is to say, the period beginning with the day of the presentation of the petition for the bankruptcy order and ending with the vesting of the bankrupt's estate in a trustee) is to be taken as having given rise to any matrimonial home rights under Part IV of the Family Law Act 1996 in relation to a dwelling house comprised in the bankrupt's estate.

(2)   Where a spouse's matrimonial home rights under the Act of 1996 are a charge on the estate or interest of the other spouse, or of trustees for the other spouse, and the other spouse is adjudged bankrupt—

    (a)   the charge continues to subsist notwithstanding the bankruptcy and, subject to the provisions of that Act, binds the trustee of the bankrupt's estate and persons deriving title under that trustee, and
    (b)   any application for an order under section 33 of that Act shall be made to the court having jurisdiction in relation to the bankruptcy.

(4)   On such an application as is mentioned in subsection (2) the court shall make such order under section 33 of the Act of 1996 as it thinks just and reasonable having regard to—

    (a)   the interests of the bankrupt's creditors,
    (b)   the conduct of the spouse or former spouse, so far as contributing to the bankruptcy,
    (c)   the needs and financial resources of the spouse or former spouse,
    (d)   the needs of any children, and
    (e)   all the circumstances of the case other than the needs of the bankrupt.

(5)   Where such an application is made after the end of the period of one year beginning with the first vesting under Chapter IV of this Part of the bankrupt's estate in a trustee, the court shall assume, unless the circumstances of the case are exceptional, that the interests of the bankrupt's creditors outweigh all other considerations.

337. Rights of occupation of bankrupt

(1)   This section applies where—

(a)   a person who is entitled to occupy a dwelling house by virtue of a beneficial estate or interest is adjudged bankrupt, and

(b)   any persons under the age of 18 with whom that person had at some time occupied that dwelling house had their home with that person at the time when the bankruptcy petition was presented and at the commencement of the bankruptcy.

(2)   Whether or not the bankrupt's spouse (if any) has matrimonial home rights under Part IV of the Family Law Act 1996—

(a)   the bankrupt has the following rights as against the trustee of his estate—

(i)   if in occupation, a right not to be evicted or excluded from the dwelling house or any part of it, except with the leave of the court,

(ii)   if not in occupation, a right with the leave of the court to enter into and occupy the dwelling house, and

(b)   the bankrupt's rights are a charge, having the like priority as an equitable interest created immediately before the commencement of the bankruptcy, on so much of his estate or interest in the dwelling house as vests in the trustee.

(3)   The Act of 1996 has effect, with the necessary modifications, as if—

(a)   the rights conferred by paragraph (a) of subsection (2) were matrimonial home rights under that Act,

(b)   any application for such leave as is mentioned in that paragraph were an application for an order under section 33 of that Act, and

(c)   any charge under paragraph (b) of that subsection on the estate or interest of the trustee were a charge under that Act on the estate or interest of a spouse.

(4)   Any application for leave such as is mentioned in subsection (2)(a) or otherwise by virtue of this section for an order under section 33 of the Act of 1996 shall be made to the court having jurisdiction in relation to the bankruptcy.

(5)   On such an application the court shall make such order under section 33 of the Act of 1996 as it thinks just and reasonable having regard to the interests of the creditors, to the bankrupt's financial resources, to the needs of the children and to all the circumstances of the case other than the needs of the bankrupt.

(6)   Where such an application is made after the end of the period of one year beginning with the first vesting (under Chapter IV of this Part) of the bankrupt's estate in a trustee, the court shall assume, unless the circumstances of the case are exceptional, that the interests of the bankrupt's creditors outweigh all other considerations.

338. Payments in respect of premises occupied by bankrupt

Where any premises comprised in a bankrupt's estate are occupied by him (whether by virtue of the preceding section or otherwise) on condition that he makes payments towards satisfying any liability arising under a mortgage of the premises or otherwise towards the outgoings of the premises, the bankrupt does not, by virtue of those payments, acquire any interest in the premises.

339. Transactions at an undervalue

(1)   Subject as follows in this section and sections 341 and 342, where an individual is adjudged bankrupt and he has at a relevant time (defined in section 341) entered into a transaction with any person at an undervalue, the trustee of the bankrupt's estate may apply to the court for an order under this section.

(2)   The court shall, on such an application, make such order as it thinks fit for restoring the position to what it would have been if that individual had not entered into that transaction.

(3)   For the purposes of this section and sections 341 and 342, an individual enters into a transaction with a person at an undervalue if—

(a)   he makes a gift to that person or he otherwise enters into a transaction with that person on terms that provide for him to receive no consideration,

(b)   he enters into a transaction with that person in consideration of marriage, or

(c) he enters into a transaction with that person for a consideration the value of which, in money or money's worth, is significantly less than the value, in money or money's worth, of the consideration provided by the individual.

340. Preferences

(1) Subject as follows in this and the next two sections, where an individual is adjudged bankrupt and he has at a relevant time (defined in section 341) given a preference to any person, the trustee of the bankrupt's estate may apply to the court for an order under this section.

(2) The court shall, on such an application, make such order as it thinks fit for restoring the position to what it would have been if that individual had not given that preference.

(3) For the purposes of this and the next two sections, an individual gives a preference to a person if—

(a) that person is one of the individual's creditors or a surety or guarantor for any of his debts or other liabilities, and

(b) the individual does anything or suffers anything to be done which (in either case) has the effect of putting that person into a position which, in the event of the individual's bankruptcy, will be better than the position he would have been in if that thing had not been done.

(4) The court shall not make an order under this section in respect of a preference given to any person unless the individual who gave the preference was influenced in deciding to give it by a desire to produce in relation to that person the effect mentioned in subsection (3)(b) above.

(5) An individual who has given a preference to a person who, at the time the preference was given, was an associate of his (otherwise than by reason only of being his employee) is presumed, unless the contrary is shown, to have been influenced in deciding to give it by such a desire as is mentioned in subsection (4).

(6) The fact that something has been done in pursuance of the order of a court does not, without more, prevent the doing or suffering of that thing from constituting the giving of a preference.

341. 'Relevant time' under ss 339, 340

(1) Subject as follows, the time at which an individual enters into a transaction at an undervalue or gives a preference is a relevant time if the transaction is entered into or the preference given—

(a) in the case of a transaction at an undervalue, at a time in the period of 5 years ending with the day of the presentation of the bankruptcy petition on which the individual is adjudged bankrupt,

(b) in the case of a preference which is not a transaction at an undervalue and is given to a person who is an associate of the individual (otherwise than by reason only of being his employee), at a time in the period of 2 years ending with that day, and

(c) in any other case of a preference which is not a transaction at an undervalue, at a time in the period of 6 months ending with that day.

(2) Where an individual enters into a transaction at an undervalue or gives a preference at a time mentioned in paragraph (a), (b) or (c) of subsection (1) (not being, in the case of a transaction at an undervalue, a time less than 2 years before the end of the period mentioned in paragraph (a)), that time is not a relevant time for the purposes of sections 339 and 340 unless the individual—

(a) is insolvent at that time, or

(b) becomes insolvent in consequence of the transaction or preference;

but the requirements of this subsection are presumed to be satisfied, unless the contrary is shown, in relation to any transaction at an undervalue which is entered into by an individual with a person who is an associate of his (otherwise than by reason only of being his employee).

(3) For the purposes of subsection (2), an individual is insolvent if—

(a) he is unable to pay his debts as they fall due, or

(b) the value of his assets is less than the amount of his liabilities, taking into account his contingent and prospective liabilities.

(4) A transaction entered into or preference given by a person who is subsequently adjudged bankrupt on a petition under section 264(1)(d) (criminal bankruptcy) is to be treated as having been entered into or given at a relevant time for the purposes of sections 339 and 340 if it was entered into or given at any time on or after the date

specified for the purposes of this subsection in the criminal bankruptcy order on which the petition was based. [Ital words prosp rep]

(5)   No order shall be made under section 339 or 340 by virtue of subsection (4) of this section where an appeal is pending (within the meaning of section 277) against the individual's conviction of any offence by virtue of which the criminal bankruptcy order was made. [Ital words prosp rep]

342. Orders under ss 339, 340

(1)   Without prejudice to the generality of section 339(2) or 340(2), an order under either of those sections with respect to a transaction or preference entered into or given by an individual who is subsequently adjudged bankrupt may (subject as follows)—

(a)   require any property transferred as part of the transaction, or in connection with the giving of the preference, to be vested in the trustee of the bankrupt's estate as part of that estate;

(b)   require any property to be so vested if it represents in any person's hands the application either of the proceeds of sale of property so transferred or of money so transferred;

(c)   release or discharge (in whole or in part) any security given by the individual;

(d)   require any person to pay, in respect of benefits received by him from the individual, such sums to the trustee of his estate as the court may direct;

(e)   provide for any surety or guarantor whose obligations to any person were released or discharged (in whole or in part) under the transaction or by the giving of the preference to be under such new or revived obligations to that person as the court thinks appropriate;

(f)   provide for security to be provided for the discharge of any obligation imposed by or arising under the order, for such an obligation to be charged on any property and for the security or charge to have the same priority as a security or charge released or discharged (in whole or in part) under the transaction or by the giving of the preference; and

(g)   provide for the extent to which any person whose property is vested by the order in the trustee of the bankrupt's estate, or on whom obligations are imposed by the order, is to be able to prove in the bankruptcy for debts or other liabilities which arose from, or were released or discharged (in whole or in part) under or by, the transaction or the giving of the preference.

(2)   An order under section 339 or 340 may affect the property of, or impose any obligation on, any person whether or not he is the person with whom the individual in question entered into the transaction or, as the case may be, the person to whom the preference was given; but such an order—

(a)   shall not prejudice any interest in property which was acquired from a person other than that individual and was acquired in good faith and for value or prejudice any interest deriving from such an interest, and

(b)   shall not require a person who received a benefit from the transaction or preference in good faith and for value to pay a sum to the trustee of the bankrupt's estate, except where he was a party to the transaction or the payment is to be in respect of a preference given to that person at a time when he was a creditor of that individual.

(2A) Where a person has acquired an interest in property from a person other than the individual in question, or has received a benefit from the transaction or preference, and at the time of that acquisition or receipt—

(a)   he had notice of the relevant surrounding circumstances and of the relevant proceedings, or

(b)   he was an associate of, or was connected with, either the individual in question or the person with whom that individual entered into the transaction or to whom that individual gave the preference,

then, unless the contrary is shown, it shall be presumed for the purposes of paragraph (a) or (as the case may be) paragraph (b) of subsection (2) that the interest was acquired or the benefit was received otherwise than in good faith.

(3)   Any sums required to be paid to the trustee in accordance with an order under section 339 or 340 shall be comprised in the bankrupt's estate.

(4)   For the purposes of subsection (2A)(a), the relevant surrounding circumstances are (as the case may require)—

(a)   the fact that the individual in question entered into the transaction at an undervalue; or

(b)   the circumstances which amounted to the giving of the preference by the individual in question.

(5)   For the purposes of subsection (2A)(a), a person has notice of the relevant proceedings if he has notice—

(a)   of the fact that the petition on which the individual in question is adjudged bankrupt has been presented; or

(b)   of the fact that the individual in question has been adjudged bankrupt.

(6)   Section 249 in Part VII of this Act shall apply for the purposes of subsection (2A)(b) as it applies for the purposes of the first Group of Parts.

342A.   Recovery of excessive pension contributions

(1)   Where an individual who is adjudged bankrupt—

(a)   has rights under an approved pension arrangement, or

(b)   has excluded rights under an unapproved pension arrangement,

the trustee of the bankrupt's estate may apply to the court for an order under this section.

(2)   If the court is satisfied—

(a)   that the rights under the arrangement are to any extent, and whether directly or indirectly, the fruits of relevant contributions, and

(b)   that the making of any of the relevant contributions ('the excessive contributions') has unfairly prejudiced the individual's creditors,

the court may make such order as it thinks fit for restoring the position to what it would have been had the excessive contributions not been made.

(3)   Subsection (4) applies where the court is satisfied that the value of the rights under the arrangement is, as a result of rights of the individual under the arrangement or any other pension arrangement having at any time become subject to a debit under section 29(1)(a) of the Welfare Reform and Pensions Act 1999 (debits giving effect to pension-sharing), less than it would otherwise have been.

(4)   Where this subsection applies—

(a)   any relevant contributions which were represented by the rights which became subject to the debit shall, for the purposes of subsection (2), be taken to be contributions of which the rights under the arrangement are the fruits, and

(b)   where the relevant contributions represented by the rights under the arrangement (including those so represented by virtue of paragraph (a)) are not all excessive contributions, relevant contributions which are represented by the rights under the arrangement otherwise than by virtue of paragraph (a) shall be treated as excessive contributions before any which are so represented by virtue of that paragraph.

(5)   In subsections (2) to (4) 'relevant contributions' means contributions to the arrangement or any other pension arrangement—

(a)   which the individual has at any time made on his own behalf, or

(b)   which have at any time been made on his behalf.

(6)   The court shall, in determining whether it is satisfied under subsection (2)(b), consider in particular—

(a)   whether any of the contributions were made for the purpose of putting assets beyond the reach of the individual's creditors or any of them, and

(b)   whether the total amount of any contributions—

(i)   made by or on behalf of the individual to pension arrangements, and

(ii)   represented (whether directly or indirectly) by rights under approved pension arrangements or excluded rights under unapproved pension arrangements,

is an amount which is excessive in view of the individual's circumstances when those contributions were made.

(7)   For the purposes of this section and sections 342B and 342C ('the recovery provisions'), rights of an individual under an unapproved pension arrangement are excluded rights if they are rights which are excluded from his estate by virtue of regulations under section 12 of the Welfare Reform and Pensions Act 1999.

(8)   In the recovery provisions—

'approved pension arrangement' has the same meaning as in section 11 of the Welfare Reform and Pensions Act 1999;

'unapproved pension arrangement' has the same meaning as in section 12 of that Act.

Part IV   Insolvency

342B.   Orders under section 342A

(1)   Without prejudice to the generality of section 342A(2), an order under section 342A may include provision—

    (a)   requiring the person responsible for the arrangement to pay an amount to the individual's trustee in bankruptcy,

    (b)   adjusting the liabilities of the arrangement in respect of the individual,

    (c)   adjusting any liabilities of the arrangement in respect of any other person that derive, directly or indirectly, from rights of the individual under the arrangement,

    (d)   for the recovery by the person responsible for the arrangement (whether by deduction from any amount which that person is ordered to pay or otherwise) of costs incurred by that person in complying in the bankrupt's case with any requirement under section 342C(1) or in giving effect to the order.

(2)   In subsection (1), references to adjusting the liabilities of the arrangement in respect of a person include (in particular) reducing the amount of any benefit or future benefit to which that person is entitled under the arrangement.

(3)   In subsection (1)(c), the reference to liabilities of the arrangement does not include liabilities in respect of a person which result from giving effect to an order or provision falling within section 28(1) of the Welfare Reform and Pensions Act 1999 (pension sharing orders and agreements).

(4)   The maximum amount which the person responsible for an arrangement may be required to pay by an order under section 342A is the lesser of—

    (a)   the amount of the excessive contributions, and

    (b)   the value of the individual's rights under the arrangement (if the arrangement is an approved pension arrangement) or of his excluded rights under the arrangement (if the arrangement is an unapproved pension arrangement).

(5)   An order under section 342A which requires the person responsible for an arrangement to pay an amount ('the restoration amount') to the individual's trustee in bankruptcy must provide for the liabilities of the arrangement to be correspondingly reduced.

(6)   For the purposes of subsection (5), liabilities are correspondingly reduced if the difference between—

    (a)   the amount of the liabilities immediately before the reduction, and

    (b)   the amount of the liabilities immediately after the reduction,

is equal to the restoration amount.

(7)   An order under section 342A in respect of an arrangement—

    (a)   shall be binding on the person responsible for the arrangement, and

    (b)   overrides provisions of the arrangement to the extent that they conflict with the provisions of the order.

342C.   Orders under section 342A: supplementary

(1)   The person responsible for—

    (a)   an approved pension arrangement under which a bankrupt has rights,

    (b)   an unapproved pension arrangement under which a bankrupt has excluded rights, or

    (c)   a pension arrangement under which a bankrupt has at any time had rights,

shall, on the bankrupt's trustee in bankruptcy making a written request, provide the trustee with such information about the arrangement and rights as the trustee may reasonably require for, or in connection with, the making of applications under section 342A.

(2)   Nothing in—

    (a)   any provision of section 159 of the Pension Schemes Act 1993 or section 91 of the Pensions Act 1995 (which prevent assignment and the making of orders that restrain a person from receiving anything which he is prevented from assigning),

    (b)   any provision of any enactment (whether passed or made before or after the passing of the Welfare Reform and Pensions Act 1999) corresponding to any of the provisions mentioned in paragraph (a), or

    (c)   any provision of the arrangement in question corresponding to any of those provisions,

applies to a court exercising its powers under section 342A.

(3)   Where any sum is required by an order under section 342A to be paid to the trustee in bankruptcy, that sum shall be comprised in the bankrupt's estate.

(4)   Regulations may, for the purposes of the recovery provisions, make provision about the calculation and verification of—

   (a)   any such value as is mentioned in section 342B(4)(b);
   (b)   any such amounts as are mentioned in section 342B(6)(a) and (b).

(5)   The power conferred by subsection (4) includes power to provide for calculation or verification—

   (a)   in such manner as may, in the particular case, be approved by a prescribed person; or
   (b)   in accordance with guidance—

      (i)   from time to time prepared by a prescribed person, and
      (ii)   approved by the Secretary of State.

(6)   References in the recovery provisions to the person responsible for a pension arrangement are to—

   (a)   the trustees, managers or provider of the arrangement, or
   (b)   the person having functions in relation to the arrangement corresponding to those of a trustee, manager or provider.

(7)   In this section and sections 342A and 342B—

   'prescribed' means prescribed by regulations;
   'the recovery provisions' means this section and sections 342A and 342B;
   'regulations' means regulations made by the Secretary of State.

(8)   Regulations under the recovery provisions may—

   (a)   make different provision for different cases;
   (b)   contain such incidental, supplemental and transitional provisions as appear to the Secretary of State necessary or expedient.

(9)   Regulations under the recovery provisions shall be made by statutory instrument subject to annulment in pursuance of a resolution of either House of Parliament.

342D.   Recovery of excessive contributions in pension-sharing cases

(1)   For the purposes of sections 339, 341 and 342, a pension-sharing transaction shall be taken—

   (a)   to be a transaction, entered into by the transferor with the transferee, by which the appropriate amount is transferred by the transferor to the transferee; and
   (b)   to be capable of being a transaction entered into at an undervalue only so far as it is a transfer of so much of the appropriate amount as is recoverable.

(2)   For the purposes of sections 340 to 342, a pension-sharing transaction shall be taken—

   (a)   to be something (namely a transfer of the appropriate amount to the transferee) done by the transferor; and
   (b)   to be capable of being a preference given to the transferee only so far as it is a transfer of so much of the appropriate amount as is recoverable.

(3)   If on an application under section 339 or 340 any question arises as to whether, or the extent to which, the appropriate amount in the case of a pension-sharing transaction is recoverable, the question shall be determined in accordance with subsections (4) to (8).

(4)   The court shall first determine the extent (if any) to which the transferor's rights under the shared arrangement at the time of the transaction appear to have been (whether directly or indirectly) the fruits of contributions ('personal contributions')—

   (a)   which the transferor has at any time made on his own behalf, or
   (b)   which have at any time been made on the transferor's behalf,

to the shared arrangement or any other pension arrangement.

(5)   Where it appears that those rights were to any extent the fruits of personal contributions, the court shall then determine the extent (if any) to which those rights appear to have been the fruits of personal contributions whose making has unfairly prejudiced the transferor's creditors ('the unfair contributions').

(6)   If it appears to the court that the extent to which those rights were the fruits of the unfair contributions is such that the transfer of the appropriate amount could have been made out of rights under the shared arrangement which were not the fruits of the unfair contributions, then the appropriate amount is not recoverable.

(7)   If it appears to the court that the transfer could not have been wholly so made, then the appropriate amount is recoverable to the extent to which it appears to the court that the transfer could not have been so made.

(8)   In making the determination mentioned in subsection (5) the court shall consider in particular—

(a)   whether any of the personal contributions were made for the purpose of putting assets beyond the reach of the transferor's creditors or any of them, and

(b)   whether the total amount of any personal contributions represented, at the time the pension-sharing transaction was made, by rights under pension arrangements is an amount which is excessive in view of the transferor's circumstances when those contributions were made.

(9)   In this section and sections 342E and 342F—

'appropriate amount', in relation to a pension-sharing transaction, means the appropriate amount in relation to that transaction for the purposes of section 29(1) of the Welfare Reform and Pensions Act 1999 (creation of pension credits and debits);

'pension-sharing transaction' means an order or provision falling within section 28(1) of the Welfare Reform and Pensions Act 1999 (orders and agreements which activate pension-sharing);

'shared arrangement', in relation to a pension-sharing transaction, means the pension arrangement to which the transaction relates;

'transferee', in relation to a pension-sharing transaction, means the person for whose benefit the transaction is made;

'transferor', in relation to a pension-sharing transaction, means the person to whose rights the transaction relates.

342E.   Orders under section 339 or 340 in respect of pension-sharing transactions

(1)   This section and section 342F apply if the court is making an order under section 339 or 340 in a case where—

(a)   the transaction or preference is, or is any part of, a pension-sharing transaction, and

(b)   the transferee has rights under a pension arrangement ('the destination arrangement', which may be the shared arrangement or any other pension arrangement) that are derived, directly or indirectly, from the pension-sharing transaction.

(2)   Without prejudice to the generality of section 339(2) or 340(2), or of section 342, the order may include provision—

(a)   requiring the person responsible for the destination arrangement to pay an amount to the transferor's trustee in bankruptcy,

(b)   adjusting the liabilities of the destination arrangement in respect of the transferee,

(c)   adjusting any liabilities of the destination arrangement in respect of any other person that derive, directly or indirectly, from rights of the transferee under the destination arrangement,

(d)   for the recovery by the person responsible for the destination arrangement (whether by deduction from any amount which that person is ordered to pay or otherwise) of costs incurred by that person in complying in the transferor's case with any requirement under section 342F(1) or in giving effect to the order,

(e)   for the recovery, from the transferor's trustee in bankruptcy, by the person responsible for a pension arrangement, of costs incurred by that person in complying in the transferor's case with any requirement under section 342F(2) or (3).

(3)   In subsection (2), references to adjusting the liabilities of the destination arrangement in respect of a person include (in particular) reducing the amount of any benefit or future benefit to which that person is entitled under the arrangement.

(4)   The maximum amount which the person responsible for the destination arrangement may be required to pay by the order is the smallest of—

(a) so much of the appropriate amount as, in accordance with section 342D, is recoverable,

(b) so much (if any) of the amount of the unfair contributions (within the meaning given by section 342D(5)) as is not recoverable by way of an order under section 342A containing provision such as is mentioned in section 342B(1)(a), and

(c) the value of the transferee's rights under the destination arrangement so far as they are derived, directly or indirectly, from the pension-sharing transaction.

(5) If the order requires the person responsible for the destination arrangement to pay an amount ('the restoration amount') to the transferor's trustee in bankruptcy it must provide for the liabilities of the arrangement to be correspondingly reduced.

(6) For the purposes of subsection (5), liabilities are correspondingly reduced if the difference between—

(a) the amount of the liabilities immediately before the reduction, and

(b) the amount of the liabilities immediately after the reduction,

is equal to the restoration amount.

(7) The order—

(a) shall be binding on the person responsible for the destination arrangement, and

(b) overrides provisions of the destination arrangement to the extent that they conflict with the provisions of the order.

342F. Orders under section 339 or 340 in pension-sharing cases: supplementary

(1) On the transferor's trustee in bankruptcy making a written request to the person responsible for the destination arrangement, that person shall provide the trustee with such information about—

(a) the arrangement,

(b) the transferee's rights under it, and

(c) where the destination arrangement is the shared arrangement, the transferor's rights under it,

as the trustee may reasonably require for, or in connection with, the making of applications under sections 339 and 340.

(2) Where the shared arrangement is not the destination arrangement, the person responsible for the shared arrangement shall, on the transferor's trustee in bankruptcy making a written request to that person, provide the trustee with such information about—

(a) the arrangement, and

(b) the transferor's rights under it,

as the trustee may reasonably require for, or in connection with, the making of applications under sections 339 and 340.

(3) On the transferor's trustee in bankruptcy making a written request to the person responsible for any intermediate arrangement, that person shall provide the trustee with such information about—

(a) the arrangement, and

(b) the transferee's rights under it,

as the trustee may reasonably require for, or in connection with, the making of applications under sections 339 and 340.

(4) In subsection (3) 'intermediate arrangement' means a pension arrangement, other than the shared arrangement or the destination arrangement, in relation to which the following conditions are fulfilled—

(a) there was a time when the transferee had rights under the arrangement that were derived (directly or indirectly) from the pension-sharing transaction, and

(b) the transferee's rights under the destination arrangement (so far as derived from the pension-sharing transaction) are to any extent derived (directly or indirectly) from the rights mentioned in paragraph (a).

(5) Nothing in—

(a) any provision of section 159 of the Pension Schemes Act 1993 or section 91 of the Pensions Act 1995 (which prevent assignment and the making of orders which restrain a person from receiving anything which he is prevented from assigning),

(b) any provision of any enactment (whether passed or made before or after the passing of the Welfare Reform and Pensions Act 1999) corresponding to any of the provisions mentioned in paragraph (a), or

(c) any provision of the destination arrangement corresponding to any of those provisions,

applies to a court exercising its powers under section 339 or 340.

(6) Regulations may, for the purposes of sections 339 to 342, sections 342D and 342E and this section, make provision about the calculation and verification of—

(a) any such value as is mentioned in section 342E(4)(c);

(b) any such amounts as are mentioned in section 342E(6)(a) and (b).

(7) The power conferred by subsection (6) includes power to provide for calculation or verification—

(a) in such manner as may, in the particular case, be approved by a prescribed person; or

(b) in accordance with guidance—

(i) from time to time prepared by a prescribed person, and

(ii) approved by the Secretary of State.

(8) In section 342E and this section, references to the person responsible for a pension arrangement are to—

(a) the trustees, managers or provider of the arrangement, or

(b) the person having functions in relation to the arrangement corresponding to those of a trustee, manager or provider.

(9) In this section—

'prescribed' means prescribed by regulations;

'regulations' means regulations made by the Secretary of State.

(10) Regulations under this section may—

(a) make different provision for different cases;

(b) contain such incidental, supplemental and transitional provisions as appear to the Secretary of State necessary or expedient.

(11) Regulations under this section shall be made by statutory instrument subject to annulment in pursuance of a resolution of either House of Parliament.

343. Extortionate credit transactions

(1) This section applies where a person is adjudged bankrupt who is or has been a party to a transaction for, or involving, the provision to him of credit.

(2) The court may, on the application of the trustee of the bankrupt's estate, make an order with respect to the transaction if the transaction is or was extortionate and was not entered into more than 3 years before the commencement of the bankruptcy.

(3) For the purposes of this section a transaction is extortionate if, having regard to the risk accepted by the person providing the credit—

(a) the terms of it are or were such as to require grossly exorbitant payments to be made (whether unconditionally or in certain contingencies) in respect of the provision of the credit, or

(b) it otherwise grossly contravened ordinary principles of fair dealing;

and it shall be presumed, unless the contrary is proved, that a transaction with respect to which an application is made under this section is or, as the case may be, was extortionate.

(4) An order under this section with respect to any transaction may contain such one or more of the following as the court thinks fit, that is to say—

(a) provision setting aside the whole or part of any obligation created by the transaction;

(b) provision otherwise varying the terms of the transaction or varying the terms on which any security for the purposes of the transaction is held;

(c) provision requiring any person who is or was party to the transaction to pay to the trustee any sums paid to that person, by virtue of the transaction, by the bankrupt;

(d) provision requiring any person to surrender to the trustee any property held by him as security for the purposes of the transaction;

(e)   provision directing accounts to be taken between any persons.

(5)   Any sums or property required to be paid or surrendered to the trustee in accordance with an order under this section shall be comprised in the bankrupt's estate.

(6)   Neither the trustee of a bankrupt's estate nor an undischarged bankrupt is entitled to make an application under section 139(1)(a) of the Consumer Credit Act 1974 (re-opening of extortionate credit agreements) for any agreement by which credit is or has been provided to the bankrupt to be re-opened.

But the powers conferred by this section are exercisable in relation to any transaction concurrently with any powers exercisable under this Act in relation to that transaction as a transaction at an undervalue.

360.   Obtaining credit; engaging in business

(1)   The bankrupt is guilty of an offence if—

(a)   either alone or jointly with any other person, he obtains credit to the extent of the prescribed amount or more without giving the person from whom he obtains it the relevant information about his status; or

(b)   he engages (whether directly or indirectly) in any business under a name other than that in which he was adjudged bankrupt without disclosing to all persons with whom he enters into any business transaction the name in which he was so adjudged.

(2)   The reference to the bankrupt obtaining credit includes the following cases—

(a)   where goods are bailed to him under a hire-purchase agreement, or agreed to be sold to him under a conditional sale agreement, and

(b)   where he is paid in advance (whether in money or otherwise) for the supply of goods or services.

(3)   A person whose estate has been sequestrated in Scotland, or who has been adjudged bankrupt in Northern Ireland, is guilty of an offence if, before his discharge, he does anything in England and Wales which would be an offence under subsection (1) if he were an undischarged bankrupt and the sequestration of his estate or the adjudication in Northern Ireland were an adjudication under this Part.

(4)   For the purposes of subsection (1)(a), the relevant information about the status of the person in question is the information that he is an undischarged bankrupt or, as the case may be, that his estate has been sequestrated in Scotland and that he has not been discharged.

(5)   This section applies to the bankrupt after discharge while a bankruptcy restrictions order is in force in respect of him.

(6)   For the purposes of subsection (1)(a) as it applies by virtue of subsection (5), the relevant information about the status of the person in question is the information that a bankruptcy restrictions order is in force in respect of him.

Note: Sub-sections in italics prosp ins Enterprise Act 2002, s 257(3), Sch 21, para 3.

PART XIII

INSOLVENCY PRACTITIONERS AND THEIR QUALIFICATION

389A.   Authorisation of nominees and supervisors

(1)   Section 389 does not apply to a person acting, in relation to a voluntary arrangement proposed or approved under Part I or Part VIII, as nominee or supervisor if he is authorised so to act.

(2)   For the purposes of subsection (1) and those Parts, an individual to whom subsection (3) does not apply is authorised to act as nominee or supervisor in relation to such an arrangement if—

(a)   he is a member of a body recognised for the purpose by the Secretary of State, and

(b)   there is in force security (in Scotland, caution) for the proper performance of his functions and that security or caution meets the prescribed requirements with respect to his so acting in relation to the arrangement.

(3)   This subsection applies to a person if—

(a)   he has been adjudged bankrupt or sequestration of his estate has been awarded and (in either case) he has not been discharged,

(b) he is subject to a disqualification order made or a disqualification undertaking accepted under the Company Directors Disqualification Act 1986 or to a disqualification order made under Part II of the Companies (Northern Ireland) Order 1989, or

(c) he is a patient within the meaning of Part VII of the Mental Health Act 1983 or section 125(1) of the Mental Health (Scotland) Act 1984.

(4) The Secretary of State may by order declare a body which appears to him to fall within subsection (5) to be a recognised body for the purposes of subsection (2)(a).

(5) A body may be recognised if it maintains and enforces rules for securing that its members—

(a) are fit and proper persons to act as nominees or supervisors, and

(b) meet acceptable requirements as to education and practical training and experience.

(6) For the purposes of this section, a person is a member of a body only if he is subject to its rules when acting as nominee or supervisor (whether or not he is in fact a member of the body).

(7) An order made under subsection (4) in relation to a body may be revoked by a further order if it appears to the Secretary of State that the body no longer falls within subsection (5).

(8) An order of the Secretary of State under this section has effect from such date as is specified in the order; and any such order revoking a previous order may make provision for members of the body in question to continue to be treated as members of a recognised body for a specified period after the revocation takes effect.

389B. *Official receiver as nominee or supervisor*

(1) The official receiver is authorised to act as nominee or supervisor in relation to a voluntary arrangement approved under Part VIII provided that the debtor is an undischarged bankrupt when the arrangement is proposed.

(2) The Secretary of State may by order repeal the proviso in subsection (1).

(3) An order under subsection (2)—

(a) must be made by statutory instrument, and

(b) shall be subject to annulment in pursuance of a resolution of either House of Parliament.

Note: Section in italics prosp ins (E&W) Enterprise Act 2002, s 264(1), Sch 22, para 3.

390. Persons not qualified to act as insolvency practitioners

(1) A person who is not an individual is not qualified to act as an insolvency practitioner.

(2) A person is not qualified to act as an insolvency practitioner at any time unless at that time—

(a) he is authorised so to act by virtue of membership of a professional body recognised under section 391 below, being permitted so to act by or under the rules of that body, or

(b) he holds an authorisation granted by a competent authority under section 393.

(3) A person is not qualified to act as an insolvency practitioner in relation to another person at any time unless—

(a) there is in force at that time security or, in Scotland, caution for the proper performance of his functions, and

(b) that security or caution meets the prescribed requirements with respect to his so acting in relation to that other person.

(4) A person is not qualified to act as an insolvency practitioner at any time if at that time—

(a) he has been adjudged bankrupt or sequestration of his estate has been awarded and (in either case) he has not been discharged,

(b) he is subject to a disqualification order made or a disqualification undertaking accepted under the Company Directors Disqualification Act 1986 or to a disqualification order made under Part II of the Companies (Northern Ireland) Order 1989, or

(c) he is a patient within the meaning of Part VII of the Mental Health Act 1983 or section 125(1) of the Mental Health (Scotland) Act 1984 or has had a guardian appointed to him under the Adults with Incapacity (Scotland) Act 2000 (asp 4).

(5) A person is not qualified to act as an insolvency practitioner while a bankruptcy restrictions order is in force in respect of him.

Note: Sub-section in italics prosp ins Enterprise Act 2002, s 257(3), Sch 21, para 4.

PART XVI

PROVISIONS AGAINST DEBT AVOIDANCE

423. Transactions defrauding creditors

(1)   This section relates to transactions entered into at an undervalue; and a person enters into such a transaction with another person if—

    (a)   he makes a gift to the other person or he otherwise enters into a transaction with the other on terms that provide for him to receive no consideration;

    (b)   he enters into a transaction with the other in consideration of marriage; or

    (c)   he enters into a transaction with the other for a consideration the value of which, in money or money's worth, is significantly less than the value, in money or money's worth, of the consideration provided by himself.

(2)   Where a person has entered into such a transaction, the court may, if satisfied under the next subsection, make such order as it thinks fit for—

    (a)   restoring the position to what it would have been if the transaction had not been entered into, and

    (b)   protecting the interests of persons who are victims of the transaction.

(3)   In the case of a person entering into such a transaction, an order shall only be made if the court is satisfied that it was entered into by him for the purpose—

    (a)   of putting assets beyond the reach of a person who is making, or may at some time make, a claim against him, or

    (b)   of otherwise prejudicing the interests of such a person in relation to the claim which he is making or may make.

(4)   In this section 'the court' means the High Court or—

    (a)   if the person entering into the transaction is an individual, any other court which would have jurisdiction in relation to a bankruptcy petition relating to him;

    (b)   if that person is a body capable of being wound up under Part IV or V of this Act, any other court having jurisdiction to wind it up.

(5)   In relation to a transaction at an undervalue, references here and below to a victim of the transaction are to a person who is, or is capable of being, prejudiced by it; and in the following two sections the person entering into the transaction is referred to as 'the debtor'.

435. Meaning of 'associate'

(1)   For the purposes of this Act any question whether a person is an associate of another person is to be determined in accordance with the following provisions of this section (any provision that a person is an associate of another person being taken to mean that they are associates of each other).

(2)   A person is an associate of an individual if that person is the individual's husband or wife, or is a relative, or the husband or wife of a relative, of the individual or of the individual's husband or wife.

(3)   A person is an associate of any person with whom he is in partnership, and of the husband or wife or a relative of any individual with whom he is in partnership; and a Scottish firm is an associate of any person who is a member of the firm.

(4)   A person is an associate of any person whom he employs or by whom he is employed.

(5)   A person in his capacity as trustee of a trust other than—

    (a)   a trust arising under any of the second Group of Parts or the Bankruptcy (Scotland) Act 1985, or

    (b)   a pension scheme or an employees' share scheme (within the meaning of the Companies Act),

is an associate of another person if the beneficiaries of the trust include, or the terms of the trust confer a power that may be exercised for the benefit of, that other person or an associate of that other person.

(6)   A company is an associate of another company—

(a)   if the same person has control of both, or a person has control of one and persons who are his associates, or he and persons who are his associates, have control of the other, or

(b)   if a group of two or more persons has control of each company, and the groups either consist of the same persons or could be regarded as consisting of the same persons by treating (in one or more cases) a member of either group as replaced by a person of whom he is an associate.

(7)   A company is an associate of another person if that person has control of it or if that person and persons who are his associates together have control of it.

(8)   For the purposes of this section a person is a relative of an individual if he is that individual's brother, sister, uncle, aunt, nephew, niece, lineal ancestor, lineal descendant, treating—

(a)   any relationship of the half blood as a relationship of the whole blood and the stepchild or adopted child of any person as his child, and

(b)   an illegitimate child as the legitimate child of his mother and reputed father;

and references in this section to a husband or wife include a former husband or wife and a reputed husband or wife.

(9)   For the purposes of this section any director or other officer of a company is to be treated as employed by that company.

(10)   For the purposes of this section a person is to be taken as having control of a company if—

(a)   the directors of the company or of another company which has control of it (or any of them) are accustomed to act in accordance with his directions or instructions, or

(b)   he is entitled to exercise, or control the exercise of, one third or more of the voting power at any general meeting of the company or of another company which has control of it;

and where two or more persons together satisfy either of the above conditions, they are to be taken as having control of the company.

(11)   In this section 'company' includes any body corporate (whether incorporated in Great Britain or elsewhere); and references to directors and other officers of a company and to voting power at any general meeting of a company have effect with any necessary modifications.

436. Expressions used generally

In this Act, except in so far as the context otherwise requires (and subject to Parts VII and XI)—

'the appointed day' means the day on which this Act comes into force under section 443;

'associate' has the meaning given by section 435;

'business' includes a trade or profession;

'the Companies Act' means the Companies Act 1985;

'conditional sale agreement' and 'hire-purchase agreement' have the same meanings as in the Consumer Credit Act 1974;

'the EC Regulation' means Council Regulation (EC) No 1346/2000;

'modifications' includes additions, alterations and omissions and cognate expressions shall be construed accordingly;

'property' includes money, goods, things in action, land and every description of property wherever situated and also obligations and every description of interest, whether present or future or vested or contingent, arising out of, or incidental to, property;

'records' includes computer records and other non-documentary records;

'subordinate legislation' has the same meaning as in the Interpretation Act 1978; and

'transaction' includes a gift, agreement or arrangement, and references to entering into a transaction shall be construed accordingly.

436A.   Proceedings under EC Regulation: modified definition of property

In the application of this Act to proceedings by virtue of Article 3 of the EC Regulation, a reference to property is a reference to property which may be dealt with in the proceedings.

SCHEDULE A1

MORATORIUM WHERE DIRECTORS PROPOSE VOLUNTARY ARRANGEMENT

PART I

INTRODUCTORY

5.   The Secretary of State may by regulations modify the qualifications for eligibility of a company for a moratorium.

PART VI

MISCELLANEOUS

Subordinate legislation

45.   (1) Regulations or an order made by the Secretary of State under this Schedule may make different provision for different cases.

(2)   Regulations so made may make such consequential, incidental, supplemental and transitional provision as may appear to the Secretary of State necessary or expedient.

(3)   Any power of the Secretary of State to make regulations under this Schedule may be exercised by amending or repealing any enactment contained in this Act (including one contained in this Schedule) or contained in the Company Directors Disqualification Act 1986.

(5)   Regulations under paragraph 5 of this Schedule are to be made by statutory instrument and shall only be made if a draft containing the regulations has been laid before and approved by resolution of each House of Parliament.

SCHEDULE B1

ADMINISTRATION

NATURE OF ADMINISTRATION

Administration

1.—(1) For the purposes of this Act 'administrator' of a company means a person appointed under this Schedule to manage the company's affairs, business and property.

(2)   For the purposes of this Act—

    (a)   a company is 'in administration' while the appointment of an administrator of the company has effect,

    (b)   a company 'enters administration' when the appointment of an administrator takes effect,

    (c)   a company ceases to be in administration when the appointment of an administrator of the company ceases to have effect in accordance with this Schedule, and

    (d)   a company does not cease to be in administration merely because an administrator vacates office (by reason of resignation, death or otherwise) or is removed from office.

2.   A person may be appointed as administrator of a company—

    (a)   by administration order of the court under paragraph 10,

    (b)   by the holder of a floating charge under paragraph 14, or

    (c)   by the company or its directors under paragraph 22.

Purpose of administration

3.—(1) The administrator of a company must perform his functions with the objective of—

    (a)   rescuing the company as a going concern, or

    (b)   achieving a better result for the company's creditors as a whole than would be likely if the company

were wound up (without first being in administration), or

(c) *realising property in order to make a distribution to one or more secured or preferential creditors.*

(2) *Subject to sub-paragraph (4), the administrator of a company must perform his functions in the interests of the company's creditors as a whole.*

(3) *The administrator must perform his functions with the objective specified in sub-paragraph (1)(a) unless he thinks either—*

(a) *that it is not reasonably practicable to achieve that objective, or*

(b) *that the objective specified in sub-paragraph (1)(b) would achieve a better result for the company's creditors as a whole.*

(4) *The administrator may perform his functions with the objective specified in sub-paragraph (1)(c) only if—*

(a) *he thinks that it is not reasonably practicable to achieve either of the objectives specified in sub-paragraph (1)(a) and (b), and*

(b) *he does not unnecessarily harm the interests of the creditors of the company as a whole.*

4. *The administrator of a company must perform his functions as quickly and efficiently as is reasonably practicable.*

Status of administrator

5. *An administrator is an officer of the court (whether or not he is appointed by the court).*

General restrictions

6. *A person may be appointed as administrator of a company only if he is qualified to act as an insolvency practitioner in relation to the company.*

APPOINTMENT OF ADMINISTRATOR BY COURT

Administration order

10. *An administration order is an order appointing a person as the administrator of a company.*

Conditions for making order

11. *The court may make an administration order in relation to a company only if satisfied—*

(a) *that the company is or is likely to become unable to pay its debts, and*

(b) *that the administration order is reasonably likely to achieve the purpose of administration.*

Administration application

12.—(1) *An application to the court for an administration order in respect of a company (an 'administration application') may be made only by—*

(a) *the company,*

(b) *the directors of the company,*

(c) *one or more creditors of the company,*

(d) *the justices' chief executive for a magistrates' court in the exercise of the power conferred by section 87A of the Magistrates' Courts Act 1980 (fine imposed on company), or*

(e) *a combination of persons listed in paragraphs (a) to (d).*

(2) *As soon as is reasonably practicable after the making of an administration application the applicant shall notify—*

(a) *any person who has appointed an administrative receiver of the company,*

(b) *any person who is or may be entitled to appoint an administrative receiver of the company,*

(c) *any person who is or may be entitled to appoint an administrator of the company under paragraph 14, and*

(d) such other persons as may be prescribed.

(3) An administration application may not be withdrawn without the permission of the court.

(4) In sub-paragraph (1) 'creditor' includes a contingent creditor and a prospective creditor.

Powers of court

13.—(1) On hearing an administration application the court may—

(a) make the administration order sought;

(b) dismiss the application;

(c) adjourn the hearing conditionally or unconditionally;

(d) make an interim order;

(e) treat the application as a winding-up petition and make any order which the court could make under section 125;

(f) make any other order which the court thinks appropriate.

(2) An appointment of an administrator by administration order takes effect—

(a) at a time appointed by the order, or

(b) where no time is appointed by the order, when the order is made.

(3) An interim order under sub-paragraph (1)(d) may, in particular—

(a) restrict the exercise of a power of the directors or the company;

(b) make provision conferring a discretion on the court or on a person qualified to act as an insolvency practitioner in relation to the company.

(4) This paragraph is subject to paragraph 39.

APPOINTMENT OF ADMINISTRATOR BY HOLDER OF FLOATING CHARGE

Power to appoint

14.—(1) The holder of a qualifying floating charge in respect of a company's property may appoint an administrator of the company.

(2) For the purposes of sub-paragraph (1) a floating charge qualifies if created by an instrument which—

(a) states that this paragraph applies to the floating charge,

(b) purports to empower the holder of the floating charge to appoint an administrator of the company,

(c) purports to empower the holder of the floating charge to make an appointment which would be the appointment of an administrative receiver within the meaning given by section 29(2), or

(d) purports to empower the holder of a floating charge in Scotland to appoint a receiver who on appointment would be an administrative receiver.

(3) For the purposes of sub-paragraph (1) a person is the holder of a qualifying floating charge in respect of a company's property if he holds one or more debentures of the company secured—

(a) by a qualifying floating charge which relates to the whole or substantially the whole of the company's property,

(b) by a number of qualifying floating charges which together relate to the whole or substantially the whole of the company's property, or

(c) by charges and other forms of security which together relate to the whole or substantially the whole of the company's property and at least one of which is a qualifying floating charge.

Restrictions on power to appoint

15.—(1) A person may not appoint an administrator under paragraph 14 unless—

(a) he has given at least two business days' written notice to the holder of any prior floating charge which satisfies paragraph 14(2), or

(b) the holder of any prior floating charge which satisfies paragraph 14(2) has consented in writing to the making of the appointment.

(2) One floating charge is prior to another for the purposes of this paragraph if—

(a) it was created first, or

(b) it is to be treated as having priority in accordance with an agreement to which the holder of each floating charge was party.

(3) Sub-paragraph (2) shall have effect in relation to Scotland as if the following were substituted for paragraph (a)—

'(a) it has priority of ranking in accordance with section 464(4)(b) of the Companies Act 1985,'.

16. An administrator may not be appointed under paragraph 14 while a floating charge on which the appointment relies is not enforceable.

17 An administrator of a company may not be appointed under paragraph 14 if—

(a) a provisional liquidator of the company has been appointed under section 135, or

(b) an administrative receiver of the company is in office.

Notice of appointment

18.—(1) A person who appoints an administrator of a company under paragraph 14 shall file with the court—

(a) a notice of appointment, and

(b) such other documents as may be prescribed.

(2) The notice of appointment must include a statutory declaration by or on behalf of the person who makes the appointment—

(a) that the person is the holder of a qualifying floating charge in respect of the company's property,

(b) that each floating charge relied on in making the appointment is (or was) enforceable on the date of the appointment, and

(c) that the appointment is in accordance with this Schedule.

(3) The notice of appointment must identify the administrator and must be accompanied by a statement by the administrator—

(a) that he consents to the appointment,

(b) that in his opinion the purpose of administration is reasonably likely to be achieved, and

(c) giving such other information and opinions as may be prescribed.

(4) For the purpose of a statement under sub-paragraph (3) an administrator may rely on information supplied by directors of the company (unless he has reason to doubt its accuracy).

(5) The notice of appointment and any document accompanying it must be in the prescribed form.

(6) A statutory declaration under sub-paragraph (2) must be made during the prescribed period.

(7) A person commits an offence if in a statutory declaration under sub-paragraph (2) he makes a statement—

(a) which is false, and

(b) which he does not reasonably believe to be true.

APPOINTMENT OF ADMINISTRATOR BY COMPANY OR DIRECTORS

Power to appoint

22. (1) A company may appoint an administrator.

(2) The directors of a company may appoint an administrator.

Restrictions on power to appoint

23.—(1) This paragraph applies where an administrator of a company is appointed—

(a) under paragraph 22, or

(b) on an administration application made by the company or its directors.

(2) *An administrator of the company may not be appointed under paragraph 22 during the period of 12 months beginning with the date on which the appointment referred to in sub-paragraph (1) ceases to have effect.*

24.—(1) If a moratorium for a company under Schedule A1 ends on a date when no voluntary arrangement is in force in respect of the company, this paragraph applies for the period of 12 months beginning with that date.

(2) *This paragraph also applies for the period of 12 months beginning with the date on which a voluntary arrangement in respect of a company ends if—*

    (a) *the arrangement was made during a moratorium for the company under Schedule A1, and*

    (b) *the arrangement ends prematurely (within the meaning of section 7B).*

(3) *While this paragraph applies, an administrator of the company may not be appointed under paragraph 22.*

25. *An administrator of a company may not be appointed under paragraph 22 if—*

    (a) *a petition for the winding up of the company has been presented and is not yet disposed of,*

    (b) *an administration application has been made and is not yet disposed of, or*

    (c) *an administrative receiver of the company is in office.*

Notice of intention to appoint

26.—(1) A person who proposes to make an appointment under paragraph 22 shall give at least five business days' written notice to—

    (a) *any person who is or may be entitled to appoint an administrative receiver of the company, and*

    (b) *any person who is or may be entitled to appoint an administrator of the company under paragraph 14.*

(2) *A person who proposes to make an appointment under paragraph 22 shall also give such notice as may be prescribed to such other persons as may be prescribed.*

(3) *A notice under this paragraph must—*

    (a) *identify the proposed administrator, and*

    (b) *be in the prescribed form.*

27.—(1) A person who gives notice of intention to appoint under paragraph 26 shall file with the court as soon as is reasonably practicable a copy of—

    (a) *the notice, and*

    (b) *any document accompanying it.*

(2) *The copy filed under sub-paragraph (1) must be accompanied by a statutory declaration made by or on behalf of the person who proposes to make the appointment—*

    (a) *that the company is or is likely to become unable to pay its debts,*

    (b) *that the company is not in liquidation, and*

    (c) *that, so far as the person making the statement is able to ascertain, the appointment is not prevented by paragraphs 23 to 25, and*

    (d) *to such additional effect, and giving such information, as may be prescribed.*

(3) *A statutory declaration under sub-paragraph (2) must—*

    (a) *be in the prescribed form, and*

    (b) *be made during the prescribed period.*

(4) *A person commits an offence if in a statutory declaration under sub-paragraph (2) he makes a statement—*

    (a) *which is false, and*

    (b) *which he does not reasonably believe to be true.*

28.—(1) An appointment may not be made under paragraph 22 unless the person who makes the appointment has complied with any requirement of paragraphs 26 and 27 and—

    (a) *the period of notice specified in paragraph 26(1) has expired, or*

    (b) *each person to whom notice has been given under paragraph 26(1) has consented in writing to the making of the appointment.*

(2) *An appointment may not be made under paragraph 22 after the period of ten business days beginning with*

the date on which the notice of intention to appoint is filed under paragraph 27(1).

Notice of appointment

29.—*(1) A person who appoints an administrator of a company under paragraph 22 shall file with the court—*

(a) *a notice of appointment, and*
(b) *such other documents as may be prescribed.*

(2) The notice of appointment must include a statutory declaration by or on behalf of the person who makes the appointment—

(a) *that the person is entitled to make an appointment under paragraph 22,*
(b) *that the appointment is in accordance with this Schedule, and*
(c) *that, so far as the person making the statement is able to ascertain, the statements made and information given in the statutory declaration filed with the notice of intention to appoint remain accurate.*

(3) The notice of appointment must identify the administrator and must be accompanied by a statement by the administrator—

(a) *that he consents to the appointment,*
(b) *that in his opinion the purpose of administration is reasonably likely to be achieved, and*
(c) *giving such other information and opinions as may be prescribed.*

(4) For the purpose of a statement under sub-paragraph (3) an administrator may rely on information supplied by directors of the company (unless he has reason to doubt its accuracy).

(5) The notice of appointment and any document accompanying it must be in the prescribed form.

(6) A statutory declaration under sub-paragraph (2) must be made during the prescribed period.

(7) A person commits an offence if in a statutory declaration under sub-paragraph (2) he makes a statement—

(a) *which is false, and*
(b) *which he does not reasonably believe to be true.*

30. *In a case in which no person is entitled to notice of intention to appoint under paragraph 26(1) (and paragraph 28 therefore does not apply)—*

(a) *the statutory declaration accompanying the notice of appointment must include the statements and information required under paragraph 27(2), and*
(b) *paragraph 29(2)(c) shall not apply.*

ADMINISTRATION APPLICATION: SPECIAL CASES

Application by holder of floating charge

35.—*(1) This paragraph applies where an administration application in respect of a company—*

(a) *is made by the holder of a qualifying floating charge in respect of the company's property, and*
(b) *includes a statement that the application is made in reliance on this paragraph.*

(2) The court may make an administration order—

(a) *whether or not satisfied that the company is or is likely to become unable to pay its debts, but*
(b) *only if satisfied that the applicant could appoint an administrator under paragraph 14.*

Intervention by holder of floating charge

36.—*(1) This paragraph applies where—*

(a) *an administration application in respect of a company is made by a person who is not the holder of a qualifying floating charge in respect of the company's property, and*
(b) *the holder of a qualifying floating charge in respect of the company's property applies to the court to have a specified person appointed as administrator (and not the person specified by the administration applicant).*

(2)   The court shall grant an application under sub-paragraph (1)(b) unless the court thinks it right to refuse the application because of the particular circumstances of the case.

Application where company in liquidation

37.—(1) This paragraph applies where the holder of a qualifying floating charge in respect of a company's property could appoint an administrator under paragraph 14 but for paragraph 8(1)(b).

(2)   The holder of the qualifying floating charge may make an administration application.

(3)   If the court makes an administration order on hearing an application made by virtue of sub-paragraph (2)—

    (a)   the court shall discharge the winding-up order,

    (b)   the court shall make provision for such matters as may be prescribed,

    (c)   the court may make other consequential provision,

    (d)   the court shall specify which of the powers under this Schedule are to be exercisable by the administrator, and

    (e)   this Schedule shall have effect with such modifications as the court may specify.

38.   (1) The liquidator of a company may make an administration application.

(2)   If the court makes an administration order on hearing an application made by virtue of sub-paragraph (1)—

    (a)   the court shall discharge any winding-up order in respect of the company,

    (b)   the court shall make provision for such matters as may be prescribed,

    (c)   the court may make other consequential provision,

    (d)   the court shall specify which of the powers under this Schedule are to be exercisable by the administrator, and

    (e)   this Schedule shall have effect with such modifications as the court may specify.

Effect of administrative receivership

39.   (1) Where there is an administrative receiver of a company the court must dismiss an administration application in respect of the company unless—

    (a)   the person by or on behalf of whom the receiver was appointed consents to the making of the administration order,

    (b)   the court thinks that the security by virtue of which the receiver was appointed would be liable to be released or discharged under sections 238 to 240 (transaction at undervalue and preference) if an administration order were made,

    (c)   the court thinks that the security by virtue of which the receiver was appointed would be avoided under section 245 (avoidance of floating charge) if an administration order were made, or

    (d)   the court thinks that the security by virtue of which the receiver was appointed would be challengeable under section 242 (gratuitous alienations) or 243 (unfair preferences) or under any rule of law in Scotland.

(2)   Sub-paragraph (1) applies whether the administrative receiver is appointed before or after the making of the administration application.

EFFECT OF ADMINISTRATION

Dismissal of pending winding-up petition

40.—(1) A petition for the winding up of a company—

    (a)   shall be dismissed on the making of an administration order in respect of the company, and

    (b)   shall be suspended while the company is in administration following an appointment under paragraph 14.

(2)   Sub-paragraph (1)(b) does not apply to a petition presented under—

    (a)   section 124A (public interest), or

    (b)   section 367 of the Financial Services and Markets Act 2000 (petition by Financial Services Authority).

(3)   Where an administrator becomes aware that a petition was presented under a provision referred to in sub-paragraph (2) before his appointment, he shall apply to the court for directions under paragraph 63.

Dismissal of administrative or other receiver

41.—(1)   When an administration order takes effect in respect of a company any administrative receiver of the company shall vacate office.

(2)   Where a company is in administration, any receiver of part of the company's property shall vacate office if the administrator requires him to.

(3)   Where an administrative receiver or receiver vacates office under sub-paragraph (1) or (2)—

    (a)   his remuneration shall be charged on and paid out of any property of the company which was in his custody or under his control immediately before he vacated office, and

    (b)   he need not take any further steps under section 40 or 59.

(4)   In the application of sub-paragraph (3)(a)—

    (a)   'remuneration' includes expenses properly incurred and any indemnity to which the administrative receiver or receiver is entitled out of the assets of the company,

    (b)   the charge imposed takes priority over security held by the person by whom or on whose behalf the administrative receiver or receiver was appointed, and

    (c)   the provision for payment is subject to paragraph 43.

Moratorium on insolvency proceedings

42.—(1)   This paragraph applies to a company in administration.

(2)   No resolution may be passed for the winding up of the company.

(3)   No order may be made for the winding up of the company.

(4)   Sub-paragraph (3) does not apply to an order made on a petition presented under—

    (a)   section 124A (public interest), or

    (b)   section 367 of the Financial Services and Markets Act 2000 (petition by Financial Services Authority).

(5)   If a petition presented under a provision referred to in sub-paragraph (4) comes to the attention of the administrator, he shall apply to the court for directions under paragraph 63.

Moratorium on other legal process

43.—(1)   This paragraph applies to a company in administration.

(2)   No step may be taken to enforce security over the company's property except—

    (a)   with the consent of the administrator, or
    (b)   with the permission of the court.

(3)   No step may be taken to repossess goods in the company's possession under a hire-purchase agreement except—

    (a)   with the consent of the administrator, or
    (b)   with the permission of the court.

(4)   A landlord may not exercise a right of forfeiture by peaceable re-entry in relation to premises let to the company except—

    (a)   with the consent of the administrator, or
    (b)   with the permission of the court.

(5)   In Scotland, a landlord may not exercise a right of irritancy in relation to premises let to the company except—

    (a)   with the consent of the administrator, or
    (b)   with the permission of the court.

(6)   No legal process (including legal proceedings, execution, distress and diligence) may be instituted or

continued against the company or property of the company except—

(a) with the consent of the administrator, or

(b) with the permission of the court.

(7) Where the court gives permission for a transaction under this paragraph it may impose a condition on or a requirement in connection with the transaction.

(8) In this paragraph 'landlord' includes a person to whom rent is payable.

Interim moratorium

44.—(1) This paragraph applies where an administration application in respect of a company has been made and—

(a) the application has not yet been granted or dismissed, or

(b) the application has been granted but the administration order has not yet taken effect.

(2) This paragraph also applies from the time when a copy of notice of intention to appoint an administrator under paragraph 14 is filed with the court until—

(a) the appointment of the administrator takes effect, or

(b) the period of five business days beginning with the date of filing expires without an administrator having been appointed.

(3) Sub-paragraph (2) has effect in relation to a notice of intention to appoint only if it is in the prescribed form.

(4) This paragraph also applies from the time when a copy of notice of intention to appoint an administrator is filed with the court under paragraph 27(1) until—

(a) the appointment of the administrator takes effect, or

(b) the period specified in paragraph 28(2) expires without an administrator having been appointed.

(5) The provisions of paragraphs 42 and 43 shall apply (ignoring any reference to the consent of the administrator).

(6) If there is an administrative receiver of the company when the administration application is made, the provisions of paragraphs 42 and 43 shall not begin to apply by virtue of this paragraph until the person by or on behalf of whom the receiver was appointed consents to the making of the administration order.

(7) This paragraph does not prevent or require the permission of the court for—

(a) the presentation of a petition for the winding up of the company under a provision mentioned in paragraph 42(4),

(b) the appointment of an administrator under paragraph 14,

(c) the appointment of an administrative receiver of the company, or

(d) the carrying out by an administrative receiver (whenever appointed) of his functions.

Publicity

45.—(1) While a company is in administration every business document issued by or on behalf of the company or the administrator must state—

(a) the name of the administrator, and

(b) that the affairs, business and property of the company are being managed by him.

(2) Any of the following commits an offence if without reasonable excuse he authorises or permits a contravention of sub-paragraph (1)—

(a) the administrator,

(b) an officer of the company, and

(c) the company.

(3) In sub-paragraph (1) 'business document' means—

(a) an invoice,

(b) an order for goods or services, and

(c) a business letter.

PROCESS OF ADMINISTRATION

Announcement of administrator's appointment

46.—(1) This paragraph applies where a person becomes the administrator of a company.

(2)   As soon as is reasonably practicable the administrator shall—

(a)   send a notice of his appointment to the company, and
(b)   publish a notice of his appointment in the prescribed manner.

(3)   As soon as is reasonably practicable the administrator shall—

(a)   obtain a list of the company's creditors, and
(b)   send a notice of his appointment to each creditor of whose claim and address he is aware.

(4)   The administrator shall send a notice of his appointment to the registrar of companies before the end of the period of 7 days beginning with the date specified in sub-paragraph (6).

(5)   The administrator shall send a notice of his appointment to such persons as may be prescribed before the end of the prescribed period beginning with the date specified in sub-paragraph (6).

(6)   The date for the purpose of sub-paragraphs (4) and (5) is—

(a)   in the case of an administrator appointed by administration order, the date of the order,
(b)   in the case of an administrator appointed under paragraph 14, the date on which he receives notice under paragraph 20, and
(c)   in the case of an administrator appointed under paragraph 22, the date on which he receives notice under paragraph 32.

(7)   The court may direct that sub-paragraph (3)(b) or (5)—

(a)   shall not apply, or
(b)   shall apply with the substitution of a different period.

(8)   A notice under this paragraph must—

(a)   contain the prescribed information, and
(b)   be in the prescribed form.

(9)   An administrator commits an offence if he fails without reasonable excuse to comply with a requirement of this paragraph.

Statement of company's affairs

47.—(1) As soon as is reasonably practicable after appointment the administrator of a company shall by notice in the prescribed form require one or more relevant persons to provide the administrator with a statement of the affairs of the company.

(2)   The statement must—

(a)   be verified by a statement of truth in accordance with Civil Procedure Rules,
(b)   be in the prescribed form,
(c)   give particulars of the company's property, debts and liabilities,
(d)   give the names and addresses of the company's creditors,
(e)   specify the security held by each creditor,
(f)   give the date on which each security was granted, and
(g)   contain such other information as may be prescribed.

(3)   In sub-paragraph (1) 'relevant person' means—

(a)   a person who is or has been an officer of the company,
(b)   a person who took part in the formation of the company during the period of one year ending with the date on which the company enters administration,
(c)   a person employed by the company during that period, and
(d)   a person who is or has been during that period an officer or employee of a company which is or has been during that year an officer of the company.

(4)   For the purpose of sub-paragraph (3) a reference to employment is a reference to employment through a contract of employment or a contract for services.

(5)   In Scotland, a statement of affairs under sub-paragraph (1) must be a statutory declaration made in accordance with the Statutory Declarations Act 1835 (and sub-paragraph (2)(a) shall not apply).

48.—(1) A person required to submit a statement of affairs must do so before the end of the period of 11 days beginning with the day on which he receives notice of the requirement.

(2)   The administrator may—

  (a)   revoke a requirement under paragraph 47(1), or
  (b)   extend the period specified in sub-paragraph (1) (whether before or after expiry).

(3)   If the administrator refuses a request to act under sub-paragraph (2)—

  (a)   the person whose request is refused may apply to the court, and
  (b)   the court may take action of a kind specified in sub-paragraph (2).

(4)   A person commits an offence if he fails without reasonable excuse to comply with a requirement under paragraph 47(1).

Administrator's proposals

49.—(1) The administrator of a company shall make a statement setting out proposals for achieving the purpose of administration.

(2)   A statement under sub-paragraph (1) must, in particular—

  (a)   deal with such matters as may be prescribed, and
  (b)   where applicable, explain why the administrator thinks that the objective mentioned in paragraph 3(1)(a) or (b) cannot be achieved.

(3)   Proposals under this paragraph may include—

  (a)   a proposal for a voluntary arrangement under Part I of this Act (although this paragraph is without prejudice to section 4(3));
  (b)   a proposal for a compromise or arrangement to be sanctioned under section 425 of the Companies Act (compromise with creditors or members).

(4)   The administrator shall send a copy of the statement of his proposals—

  (a)   to the registrar of companies,
  (b)   to every creditor of the company of whose claim and address he is aware, and
  (c)   to every member of the company of whose address he is aware.

(5)   The administrator shall comply with sub-paragraph (4)—

  (a)   as soon as is reasonably practicable after the company enters administration, and
  (b)   in any event, before the end of the period of eight weeks beginning with the day on which the company enters administration.

(6)   The administrator shall be taken to comply with sub-paragraph (4)(c) if he publishes in the prescribed manner a notice undertaking to provide a copy of the statement of proposals free of charge to any member of the company who applies in writing to a specified address.

(7)   An administrator commits an offence if he fails without reasonable excuse to comply with sub-paragraph (5).

(8)   A period specified in this paragraph may be varied in accordance with paragraph 107.

Creditors' meeting

50.—(1) In this Schedule 'creditors' meeting' means a meeting of creditors of a company summoned by the administrator—

  (a)   in the prescribed manner, and
  (b)   giving the prescribed period of notice to every creditor of the company of whose claim and address he is aware.

(2)   A period prescribed under sub-paragraph (1)(b) may be varied in accordance with paragraph 107.

(3)   A creditors' meeting shall be conducted in accordance with the rules.

Requirement for initial creditors' meeting

51.—(1) Each copy of an administrator's statement of proposals sent to a creditor under paragraph 49(4)(b) must be accompanied by an invitation to a creditors' meeting (an 'initial creditors' meeting').

(2)   The date set for an initial creditors' meeting must be—

(a)   *as soon as is reasonably practicable after the company enters administration, and*

(b)   *in any event, within the period of ten weeks beginning with the date on which the company enters administration.*

(3)   An administrator shall present a copy of his statement of proposals to an initial creditors' meeting.

(4)   A period specified in this paragraph may be varied in accordance with paragraph 107.

(5)   An administrator commits an offence if he fails without reasonable excuse to comply with a requirement of this paragraph.

52.—(1) Paragraph 51(1) shall not apply where the statement of proposals states that the administrator thinks—

(a)   *that the company has sufficient property to enable each creditor of the company to be paid in full,*

(b)   *that the company has insufficient property to enable a distribution to be made to unsecured creditors other than by virtue of section 176A(2)(a), or*

(c)   *that neither of the objectives specified in paragraph 3(1)(a) and (b) can be achieved.*

(2)   But the administrator shall summon an initial creditors' meeting if it is requested—

(a)   *by creditors of the company whose debts amount to at least 10% of the total debts of the company,*

(b)   *in the prescribed manner, and*

(c)   *in the prescribed period.*

(3)   A meeting requested under sub-paragraph (2) must be summoned for a date in the prescribed period.

(4)   The period prescribed under sub-paragraph (3) may be varied in accordance with paragraph 107.

Business and result of initial creditors' meeting

53.—(1) An initial creditors' meeting to which an administrator's proposals are presented shall consider them and may—

(a)   *approve them without modification, or*

(b)   *approve them with modification to which the administrator consents.*

(2)   After the conclusion of an initial creditors' meeting the administrator shall as soon as is reasonably practicable report any decision taken to—

(a)   *the court,*

(b)   *the registrar of companies, and*

(c)   *such other persons as may be prescribed.*

(3)   An administrator commits an offence if he fails without reasonable excuse to comply with sub-paragraph (2).

Revision of administrator's proposals

54.—(1) This paragraph applies where—

(a)   *an administrator's proposals have been approved (with or without modification) at an initial creditors' meeting,*

(b)   *the administrator proposes a revision to the proposals, and*

(c)   *the administrator thinks that the proposed revision is substantial.*

(2)   The administrator shall—

(a)   *summon a creditors' meeting,*

(b)   send a statement in the prescribed form of the proposed revision with the notice of the meeting sent to each creditor,

(c)   send a copy of the statement, within the prescribed period, to each member of the company of whose address he is aware, and

(d)   present a copy of the statement to the meeting.

(3)   The administrator shall be taken to have complied with sub-paragraph (2)(c) if he publishes a notice undertaking to provide a copy of the statement free of charge to any member of the company who applies in writing to a specified address.

(4)   A notice under sub-paragraph (3) must be published—

(a)   in the prescribed manner, and

(b)   within the prescribed period.

(5)   A creditors' meeting to which a proposed revision is presented shall consider it and may—

(a)   approve it without modification, or

(b)   approve it with modification to which the administrator consents.

(6)   After the conclusion of a creditors' meeting the administrator shall as soon as is reasonably practicable report any decision taken to—

(a)   the court,

(b)   the registrar of companies, and

(c)   such other persons as may be prescribed.

(7)   An administrator commits an offence if he fails without reasonable excuse to comply with sub-paragraph (6).

Failure to obtain approval of administrator's proposals

55.—(1) This paragraph applies where an administrator reports to the court that—

(a)   an initial creditors' meeting has failed to approve the administrator's proposals presented to it, or

(b)   a creditors' meeting has failed to approve a revision of the administrator's proposals presented to it.

(2)   The court may—

(a)   provide that the appointment of an administrator shall cease to have effect from a specified time;

(b)   adjourn the hearing conditionally or unconditionally;

(c)   make an interim order;

(d)   make an order on a petition for winding up suspended by virtue of paragraph 40(1)(b);

(e)   make any other order (including an order making consequential provision) that the court thinks appropriate.

Further creditors' meetings

56.—(1) The administrator of a company shall summon a creditors' meeting if—

(a)   it is requested in the prescribed manner by creditors of the company whose debts amount to at least 10% of the total debts of the company, or

(b)   he is directed by the court to summon a creditors' meeting.

(2)   An administrator commits an offence if he fails without reasonable excuse to summon a creditors' meeting as required by this paragraph.

Creditors' committee

57.—(1) A creditors' meeting may establish a creditors' committee.

(2)   A creditors' committee shall carry out functions conferred on it by or under this Act.

(3)   A creditors' committee may require the administrator—

(a)   to attend on the committee at any reasonable time of which he is given at least seven days' notice, and

(b)   to provide the committee with information about the exercise of his functions.

Correspondence instead of creditors' meeting

58.—(1) Anything which is required or permitted by or under this Schedule to be done at a creditors' meeting may be done by correspondence between the administrator and creditors—

    (a)   in accordance with the rules, and

    (b)   subject to any prescribed condition.

(2)   A reference in this Schedule to anything done at a creditors' meeting includes a reference to anything done in the course of correspondence in reliance on sub-paragraph (1).

(3)   A requirement to hold a creditors' meeting is satisfied by conducting correspondence in accordance with this paragraph.

FUNCTIONS OF ADMINISTRATOR

General powers

59.—(1) The administrator of a company may do anything necessary or expedient for the management of the affairs, business and property of the company.

(2)   A provision of this Schedule which expressly permits the administrator to do a specified thing is without prejudice to the generality of sub-paragraph (1).

(3)   A person who deals with the administrator of a company in good faith and for value need not inquire whether the administrator is acting within his powers.

60.   The administrator of a company has the powers specified in Schedule 1 to this Act.

61.   The administrator of a company—

    (a)   may remove a director of the company, and

    (b)   may appoint a director of the company (whether or not to fill a vacancy).

62.   The administrator of a company may call a meeting of members or creditors of the company.

63.   The administrator of a company may apply to the court for directions in connection with his functions.

64.—(1) A company in administration or an officer of a company in administration may not exercise a management power without the consent of the administrator.

(2)   For the purpose of sub-paragraph (1)—

    (a)   'management power' means a power which could be exercised so as to interfere with the exercise of the administrator's powers,

    (b)   it is immaterial whether the power is conferred by an enactment or an instrument, and

    (c)   consent may be general or specific.

Distribution

65.—(1) The administrator of a company may make a distribution to a creditor of the company.

(2)   Section 175 shall apply in relation to a distribution under this paragraph as it applies in relation to a winding up.

(3)   A payment may not be made by way of distribution under this paragraph to a creditor of the company who is neither secured nor preferential unless the court gives permission.

66.   The administrator of a company may make a payment otherwise than in accordance with paragraph 65 or paragraph 13 of Schedule 1 if he thinks it likely to assist achievement of the purpose of administration.

General duties

67.   The administrator of a company shall on his appointment take custody or control of all the property to which he thinks the company is entitled.

68.—(1) Subject to sub-paragraph (2), the administrator of a company shall manage its affairs, business and property in accordance with—

    (a)   any proposals approved under paragraph 53,

    (b)   any revision of those proposals which is made by him and which he does not consider substantial, and

    (c)   any revision of those proposals approved under paragraph 54.

(2)   If the court gives directions to the administrator of a company in connection with any aspect of his management of the company's affairs, business or property, the administrator shall comply with the directions.

(3)   The court may give directions under sub-paragraph (2) only if—

    (a)   no proposals have been approved under paragraph 53,

    (b)   the directions are consistent with any proposals or revision approved under paragraph 53 or 54,

    (c)   the court thinks the directions are required in order to reflect a change in circumstances since the approval of proposals or a revision under paragraph 53 or 54, or

    (d)   the court thinks the directions are desirable because of a misunderstanding about proposals or a revision approved under paragraph 53 or 54.

Administrator as agent of company

69.   In exercising his functions under this Schedule the administrator of a company acts as its agent.

Charged property: floating charge

70.—(1)   The administrator of a company may dispose of or take action relating to property which is subject to a floating charge as if it were not subject to the charge.

(2)   Where property is disposed of in reliance on sub-paragraph (1) the holder of the floating charge shall have the same priority in respect of acquired property as he had in respect of the property disposed of.

(3)   In sub-paragraph (2) 'acquired property' means property of the company which directly or indirectly represents the property disposed of.

Charged property: non-floating charge

71.—(1)   The court may by order enable the administrator of a company to dispose of property which is subject to a security (other than a floating charge) as if it were not subject to the security.

(2)   An order under sub-paragraph (1) may be made only—

    (a)   on the application of the administrator, and

    (b)   where the court thinks that disposal of the property would be likely to promote the purpose of administration in respect of the company.

(3)   An order under this paragraph is subject to the condition that there be applied towards discharging the sums secured by the security—

    (a)   the net proceeds of disposal of the property, and

    (b)   any additional money required to be added to the net proceeds so as to produce the amount determined by the court as the net amount which would be realised on a sale of the property at market value.

(4)   If an order under this paragraph relates to more than one security, application of money under sub-paragraph (3) shall be in the order of the priorities of the securities.

(5)   An administrator who makes a successful application for an order under this paragraph shall send a copy of the order to the registrar of companies before the end of the period of 14 days starting with the date of the order.

(6)   An administrator commits an offence if he fails to comply with sub-paragraph (5) without reasonable excuse.

Protection for secured or preferential creditor

73.   (1)   An administrator's statement of proposals under paragraph 49 may not include any action which—

    (a)   affects the right of a secured creditor of the company to enforce his security,

(b)　would result in a preferential debt of the company being paid otherwise than in priority to its non-preferential debts, or

(c)　would result in one preferential creditor of the company being paid a smaller proportion of his debt than another.

(2)　Sub-paragraph (1) does not apply to—

(a)　action to which the relevant creditor consents,

(b)　a proposal for a voluntary arrangement under Part I of this Act (although this sub-paragraph is without prejudice to section 4(3)), or

(c)　a proposal for a compromise or arrangement to be sanctioned under section 425 of the Companies Act (compromise with creditors or members).

(3)　The reference to a statement of proposals in sub-paragraph (1) includes a reference to a statement as revised or modified.

Challenge to administrator's conduct of company

74.—(1) A creditor or member of a company in administration may apply to the court claiming that—

(a)　the administrator is acting or has acted so as unfairly to harm the interests of the applicant (whether alone or in common with some or all other members or creditors), or

(b)　the administrator proposes to act in a way which would unfairly harm the interests of the applicant (whether alone or in common with some or all other members or creditors).

(2)　A creditor or member of a company in administration may apply to the court claiming that the administrator is not performing his functions as quickly or as efficiently as is reasonably practicable.

(3)　The court may—

(a)　grant relief;

(b)　dismiss the application;

(c)　adjourn the hearing conditionally or unconditionally;

(d)　make an interim order;

(e)　make any other order it thinks appropriate.

(4)　In particular, an order under this paragraph may—

(a)　regulate the administrator's exercise of his functions;

(b)　require the administrator to do or not do a specified thing;

(c)　require a creditors' meeting to be held for a specified purpose;

(d)　provide for the appointment of an administrator to cease to have effect;

(e)　make consequential provision.

(5)　An order may be made on a claim under sub-paragraph (1) whether or not the action complained of—

(a)　is within the administrator's powers under this Schedule;

(b)　was taken in reliance on an order under paragraph 71 or 72.

(6)　An order may not be made under this paragraph if it would impede or prevent the implementation of—

(a)　a voluntary arrangement approved under Part I,

(b)　a compromise or arrangement sanctioned under section 425 of the Companies Act (compromise with creditors and members), or

(c)　proposals or a revision approved under paragraph 53 or 54 more than 28 days before the day on which the application for the order under this paragraph is made.

Misfeasance

75.—(1) The court may examine the conduct of a person who—

(a)　is or purports to be the administrator of a company, or

(b)　has been or has purported to be the administrator of a company.

(2)　An examination under this paragraph may be held only on the application of—

(a)　the official receiver,

    (b)   *the administrator of the company,*

    (c)   *the liquidator of the company,*

    (d)   *a creditor of the company, or*

    (e)   *a contributory of the company.*

(3)   An application under sub-paragraph (2) must allege that the administrator—

    (a)   *has misapplied or retained money or other property of the company,*

    (b)   *has become accountable for money or other property of the company,*

    (c)   *has breached a fiduciary or other duty in relation to the company, or*

    (d)   *has been guilty of misfeasance.*

(4)   On an examination under this paragraph into a person's conduct the court may order him—

    (a)   *to repay, restore or account for money or property;*

    (b)   *to pay interest;*

    (c)   *to contribute a sum to the company's property by way of compensation for breach of duty or misfeasance.*

(5)   In sub-paragraph (3) 'administrator' includes a person who purports or has purported to be a company's administrator.

(6)   An application under sub-paragraph (2) may be made in respect of an administrator who has been discharged under paragraph 98 only with the permission of the court.

ENDING ADMINISTRATION

Automatic end of administration

76.—(1) The appointment of an administrator shall cease to have effect at the end of the period of one year beginning with the date on which it takes effect.

(2)   But—

    (a)   *on the application of an administrator the court may by order extend his term of office for a specified period, and*

    (b)   *an administrator's term of office may be extended for a specified period not exceeding six months by consent.*

77.—(1) An order of the court under paragraph 76—

    (a)   *may be made in respect of an administrator whose term of office has already been extended by order or by consent, but*

    (b)   *may not be made after the expiry of the administrator's term of office.*

(2)   Where an order is made under paragraph 76 the administrator shall as soon as is reasonably practicable notify the registrar of companies.

(3)   An administrator who fails without reasonable excuse to comply with sub-paragraph (2) commits an offence.

78.—(1) In paragraph 76(2)(b) 'consent' means consent of—

    (a)   *each secured creditor of the company, and*

    (b)   *if the company has unsecured debts, creditors whose debts amount to more than 50% of the company's unsecured debts, disregarding debts of any creditor who does not respond to an invitation to give or withhold consent.*

(2)   But where the administrator has made a statement under paragraph 52(1)(b) 'consent' means—

    (a)   *consent of each secured creditor of the company, or*

    (b)   *if the administrator thinks that a distribution may be made to preferential creditors, consent of—*

        (i)   *each secured creditor of the company, and*

        (ii)   *preferential creditors whose debts amount to more than 50% of the preferential debts of the company, disregarding debts of any creditor who does not respond to an invitation to give or withhold consent.*

(3)   Consent for the purposes of paragraph 76(2)(b) may be—

(a)   *written, or*

(b)   *signified at a creditors' meeting.*

(4)   *An administrator's term of office—*

(a)   *may be extended by consent only once,*

(b)   *may not be extended by consent after extension by order of the court, and*

(c)   *may not be extended by consent after expiry.*

(5)   *Where an administrator's term of office is extended by consent he shall as soon as is reasonably practicable—*

(a)   *file notice of the extension with the court, and*

(b)   *notify the registrar of companies.*

(6)   *An administrator who fails without reasonable excuse to comply with sub-paragraph (5) commits an offence.*

Court ending administration on application of administrator

79.—(1) *On the application of the administrator of a company the court may provide for the appointment of an administrator of the company to cease to have effect from a specified time.*

(2)   *The administrator of a company shall make an application under this paragraph if—*

(a)   *he thinks the purpose of administration cannot be achieved in relation to the company,*

(b)   *he thinks the company should not have entered administration, or*

(c)   *a creditors' meeting requires him to make an application under this paragraph.*

(3)   *The administrator of a company shall make an application under this paragraph if—*

(a)   *the administration is pursuant to an administration order, and*

(b)   *the administrator thinks that the purpose of administration has been sufficiently achieved in relation to the company.*

(4)   *On an application under this paragraph the court may—*

(a)   *adjourn the hearing conditionally or unconditionally;*

(b)   *dismiss the application;*

(c)   *make an interim order;*

(d)   *make any order it thinks appropriate (whether in addition to, in consequence of or instead of the order applied for).*

Termination of administration where objective achieved

80.—(1) *This paragraph applies where an administrator of a company is appointed under paragraph 14 or 22.*

(2)   *If the administrator thinks that the purpose of administration has been sufficiently achieved in relation to the company he may file a notice in the prescribed form—*

(a)   *with the court, and*

(b)   *with the registrar of companies.*

(3)   *The administrator's appointment shall cease to have effect when the requirements of sub-paragraph (2) are satisfied.*

(4)   *Where the administrator files a notice he shall within the prescribed period send a copy to every creditor of the company of whose claim and address he is aware.*

(5)   *The rules may provide that the administrator is taken to have complied with sub-paragraph (4) if before the end of the prescribed period he publishes in the prescribed manner a notice undertaking to provide a copy of the notice under sub-paragraph (2) to any creditor of the company who applies in writing to a specified address.*

(6)   *An administrator who fails without reasonable excuse to comply with sub-paragraph (4) commits an offence.*

Court ending administration on application of creditor

81.—(1) *On the application of a creditor of a company the court may provide for the appointment of an administrator of the company to cease to have effect at a specified time.*

(2)   *An application under this paragraph must allege an improper motive—*

  (a)   *in the case of an administrator appointed by administration order, on the part of the applicant for the order, or*

  (b)   *in any other case, on the part of the person who appointed the administrator.*

(3) *On an application under this paragraph the court may—*

  (a)   *adjourn the hearing conditionally or unconditionally;*

  (b)   *dismiss the application;*

  (c)   *make an interim order;*

  (d)   *make any order it thinks appropriate (whether in addition to, in consequence of or instead of the order applied for).*

Public interest winding-up

82.—*(1)   This paragraph applies where a winding-up order is made for the winding up of a company in administration on a petition presented under—*

  (a)   *section 124A (public interest), or*

  (b)   *section 367 of the Financial Services and Markets Act 2000 (petition by Financial Services Authority).*

(2)   *This paragraph also applies where a provisional liquidator of a company in administration is appointed following the presentation of a petition under any of the provisions listed in sub-paragraph (1).*

(3)   *The court shall order—*

  (a)   *that the appointment of the administrator shall cease to have effect, or*

  (b)   *that the appointment of the administrator shall continue to have effect.*

(4)   *If the court makes an order under sub-paragraph (3)(b) it may also—*

  (a)   *specify which of the powers under this Schedule are to be exercisable by the administrator, and*

  (b)   *order that this Schedule shall have effect in relation to the administrator with specified modifications.*

Moving from administration to creditors' voluntary liquidation

83.—*(1)   This paragraph applies in England and Wales where the administrator of a company thinks—*

  (a)   *that the total amount which each secured creditor of the company is likely to receive has been paid to him or set aside for him, and*

  (b)   *that a distribution will be made to unsecured creditors of the company (if there are any).*

(2)   *This paragraph applies in Scotland where the administrator of a company thinks—*

  (a)   *that each secured creditor of the company will receive payment in respect of his debt, and*

  (b)   *that a distribution will be made to unsecured creditors (if there are any).*

(3)   *The administrator may send to the registrar of companies a notice that this paragraph applies.*

(4)   *On receipt of a notice under sub-paragraph (3) the registrar shall register it.*

(5)   *If an administrator sends a notice under sub-paragraph (3) he shall as soon as is reasonably practicable—*

  (a)   *file a copy of the notice with the court, and*

  (b)   *send a copy of the notice to each creditor of whose claim and address he is aware.*

(6)   *On the registration of a notice under sub-paragraph (3)—*

  (a)   *the appointment of an administrator in respect of the company shall cease to have effect, and*

  (b)   *the company shall be wound up as if a resolution for voluntary winding up under section 84 were passed on the day on which the notice is registered.*

(7)   *The liquidator for the purposes of the winding up shall be—*

  (a)   *a person nominated by the creditors of the company in the prescribed manner and within the prescribed period, or*

  (b)   *if no person is nominated under paragraph (a), the administrator.*

(8)   In the application of Part IV to a winding up by virtue of this paragraph—

    (a)   section 85 shall not apply,

    (b)   section 86 shall apply as if the reference to the time of the passing of the resolution for voluntary winding up were a reference to the beginning of the date of registration of the notice under sub-paragraph (3),

    (c)   section 89 does not apply,

    (d)   sections 98, 99 and 100 shall not apply,

    (e)   section 129 shall apply as if the reference to the time of the passing of the resolution for voluntary winding up were a reference to the beginning of the date of registration of the notice under sub-paragraph (3), and

    (f)   any creditors' committee which is in existence immediately before the company ceases to be in administration shall continue in existence after that time as if appointed as a liquidation committee under section 101.

Moving from administration to dissolution

84.—(1)   If the administrator of a company thinks that the company has no property which might permit a distribution to its creditors, he shall send a notice to that effect to the registrar of companies.

(2)   The court may on the application of the administrator of a company disapply sub-paragraph (1) in respect of the company.

(3)   On receipt of a notice under sub-paragraph (1) the registrar shall register it.

(4)   On the registration of a notice in respect of a company under sub-paragraph (1) the appointment of an administrator of the company shall cease to have effect.

(5)   If an administrator sends a notice under sub-paragraph (1) he shall as soon as is reasonably practicable—

    (a)   file a copy of the notice with the court, and

    (b)   send a copy of the notice to each creditor of whose claim and address he is aware.

(6)   At the end of the period of three months beginning with the date of registration of a notice in respect of a company under sub-paragraph (1) the company is deemed to be dissolved.

(7)   On an application in respect of a company by the administrator or another interested person the court may—

    (a)   extend the period specified in sub-paragraph (6),

    (b)   suspend that period, or

    (c)   disapply sub-paragraph (6).

(8)   Where an order is made under sub-paragraph (7) in respect of a company the administrator shall as soon as is reasonably practicable notify the registrar of companies.

(9)   An administrator commits an offence if he fails without reasonable excuse to comply with sub-paragraph (5).

Discharge of administration order where administration ends

85—(1) This paragraph applies where—

    (a)   the court makes an order under this Schedule providing for the appointment of an administrator of a company to cease to have effect, and

    (b)   the administrator was appointed by administration order.

(2)   The court shall discharge the administration order.

Notice to Companies Registrar where administration ends

86.—(1) This paragraph applies where the court makes an order under this Schedule providing for the appointment of an administrator to cease to have effect.

(2)   The administrator shall send a copy of the order to the registrar of companies within the period of 14 days beginning with the date of the order.

(3)   An administrator who fails without reasonable excuse to comply with sub-paragraph (2) commits an offence.

REPLACING ADMINISTRATOR

Resignation of administrator

87.—(1) An administrator may resign only in prescribed circumstances.

(2)   Where an administrator may resign he may do so only—

(a)   *in the case of an administrator appointed by administration order, by notice in writing to the court,*

(b)   *in the case of an administrator appointed under paragraph 14, by notice in writing to the person who appointed him,*

(c)   *in the case of an administrator appointed under paragraph 22(1), by notice in writing to the company, or*

(d)   *in the case of an administrator appointed under paragraph 22(2), by notice in writing to the directors of the company.*

Removal of administrator from office

88.   The court may by order remove an administrator from office.

Vacation of office: discharge from liability

98.—(1) Where a person ceases to be the administrator of a company (whether because he vacates office by reason of resignation, death or otherwise, because he is removed from office or because his appointment ceases to have effect) he is discharged from liability in respect of any action of his as administrator.

(2)   The discharge provided by sub-paragraph (1) takes effect—

(a)   *in the case of an administrator who dies, on the filing with the court of notice of his death,*

(b)   *in the case of an administrator appointed under paragraph 14 or 22, at a time appointed by resolution of the creditors' committee or, if there is no committee, by resolution of the creditors, or*

(c)   *in any case, at a time specified by the court.*

(3)   For the purpose of the application of sub-paragraph (2)(b) in a case where the administrator has made a statement under paragraph 52(1)(b), a resolution shall be taken as passed if (and only if) passed with the approval of—

(a)   *each secured creditor of the company, or*

(b)   *if the administrator has made a distribution to preferential creditors or thinks that a distribution may be made to preferential creditors—*

(i)   *each secured creditor of the company, and*

(ii)   *preferential creditors whose debts amount to more than 50% of the preferential debts of the company, disregarding debts of any creditor who does not respond to an invitation to give or withhold approval.*

(4)   Discharge—

(a)   *applies to liability accrued before the discharge takes effect, and*

(b)   *does not prevent the exercise of the court's powers under paragraph 75.*

GENERAL

Presumption of validity

104.   An act of the administrator of a company is valid in spite of a defect in his appointment or qualification.

Majority decision of directors

105.   A reference in this Schedule to something done by the directors of a company includes a reference to the same thing done by a majority of the directors of a company.

Penalties

106.—(1) *A person who is guilty of an offence under this Schedule is liable to a fine (in accordance with section 430 and Schedule 10).*

(2)   *A person who is guilty of an offence under any of the following paragraphs of this Schedule is liable to a daily default fine (in accordance with section 430 and Schedule 10)—*

(a)   *paragraph 20,*

(b)   *paragraph 32,*

(c)   *paragraph 46,*

(d)   *paragraph 48,*

(e)   *paragraph 49,*

(f)   *paragraph 51,*

(g)   *paragraph 53,*

(h)   *paragraph 54,*

(i)   *paragraph 56,*

(j)   *paragraph 71,*

(k)   *paragraph 72,*

(l)   *paragraph 77,*

(m)   *paragraph 78,*

(n)   *paragraph 80,*

(o)   *paragraph 84,*

(p)   *paragraph 86, and*

(q)   *paragraph 89.*

Extension of time limit

107.—(1) *Where a provision of this Schedule provides that a period may be varied in accordance with this paragraph, the period may be varied in respect of a company—*

(a)   *by the court, and*

(b)   *on the application of the administrator.*

(2)   *A time period may be extended in respect of a company under this paragraph—*

(a)   *more than once, and*

(b)   *after expiry.*

108.—(1) *A period specified in paragraph 49(5), 50(1)(b) or 51(2) may be varied in respect of a company by the administrator with consent.*

(2)   *In sub-paragraph (1) 'consent' means consent of—*

(a)   *each secured creditor of the company, and*

(b)   *if the company has unsecured debts, creditors whose debts amount to more than 50% of the company's unsecured debts, disregarding debts of any creditor who does not respond to an invitation to give or withhold consent.*

(3)   *But where the administrator has made a statement under paragraph 52(1)(b) 'consent' means—*

(a)   *consent of each secured creditor of the company, or*

(b)   *if the administrator thinks that a distribution may be made to preferential creditors, consent of—*

(i)   *each secured creditor of the company, and*

(ii)   *preferential creditors whose debts amount to more than 50% of the total preferential debts of the company, disregarding debts of any creditor who does not respond to an invitation to give or withhold consent.*

(4)   *Consent for the purposes of sub-paragraph (1) may be—*

(a)   *written, or*

(b)   *signified at a creditors' meeting.*

(5)   *The power to extend under sub-paragraph (1)—*

(a)   *may be exercised in respect of a period only once,*

(b) *may not be used to extend a period by more than 28 days,*

(c) *may not be used to extend a period which has been extended by the court, and*

(d) *may not be used to extend a period after expiry.*

109. Where a period is extended under paragraph 107 or 108, a reference to the period shall be taken as a reference to the period as extended.

Amendment of provision about time

110.—(1) The Secretary of State may by order amend a provision of this Schedule which—

(a) *requires anything to be done within a specified period of time,*

(b) *prevents anything from being done after a specified time, or*

(c) *requires a specified minimum period of notice to be given.*

(2) An order under this paragraph—

(a) *must be made by statutory instrument, and*

(b) *shall be subject to annulment in pursuance of a resolution of either House of Parliament.*

Interpretation

111.—(1) In this Schedule—

> *'administrative receiver' has the meaning given by section 251,*
> *'administrator' has the meaning given by paragraph 1 and, where the context requires, includes a reference to a former administrator,*
> *'company' includes a company which may enter administration by virtue of Article 3 of the EC Regulation,*
> *'correspondence' includes correspondence by telephonic or other electronic means,*
> *'creditors' meeting' has the meaning given by paragraph 50,*
> *'enters administration' has the meaning given by paragraph 1,*
> *'floating charge' means a charge which is a floating charge on its creation,*
> *'in administration' has the meaning given by paragraph 1,*
> *'hire-purchase agreement' includes a conditional sale agreement, a chattel leasing agreement and a retention of title agreement,*
> *'holder of a qualifying floating charge' in respect of a company's property has the meaning given by paragraph 14,*
> *'market value' means the amount which would be realised on a sale of property in the open market by a willing vendor,*
> *'the purpose of administration' means an objective specified in paragraph 3, and*
> *'unable to pay its debts' has the meaning given by section 123.*

(2) A reference in this Schedule to a thing in writing includes a reference to a thing in electronic form.

(3) In this Schedule a reference to action includes a reference to inaction.

Scotland

112—116. (applies to Scotland only)

Note: Schedule in italics prosp ins Enterprise Act 2002, s 248, Sch 16.

SCHEDULE 1

POWERS OF ADMINISTRATOR OR ADMINISTRATIVE RECEIVER

1. Power to take possession of, collect and get in the property of the company and, for that purpose, to take such proceedings as may seem to him expedient.

2. Power to sell or otherwise dispose of the property of the company by public auction or private contract or, in Scotland, to sell, feu, hire out or otherwise dispose of the property of the company by public roup or private bargain.

3. Power to raise or borrow money and grant security therefor over the property of the company.

4.   Power to appoint a solicitor or accountant or other professionally qualified person to assist him in the performance of his functions.

5.   Power to bring or defend any action or other legal proceedings in the name and on behalf of the company.

6.   Power to refer to arbitration any question affecting the company.

7.   Power to effect and maintain insurances in respect of the business and property of the company.

8.   Power to use the company's seal.

9.   Power to do all acts and to execute in the name and on behalf of the company any deed, receipt or other document.

10.   Power to draw, accept, make and endorse any bill of exchange or promissory note in the name and on behalf of the company.

11.   Power to appoint any agent to do any business which he is unable to do himself or which can more conveniently be done by an agent and power to employ and dismiss employees.

12.   Power to do all such things (including the carrying out of works) as may be necessary for the realisation of the property of the company.

13.   Power to make any payment which is necessary or incidental to the performance of his functions.

14.   Power to carry on the business of the company.

15.   Power to establish subsidiaries of the company.

16.   Power to transfer to subsidiaries of the company the whole or any part of the business and property of the company.

17.   Power to grant or accept a surrender of lease or tenancy of any of the property of the company, and to take a lease or tenancy of any property required or convenient for the business of the company.

18.   Power to make any arrangement or compromise on behalf of the company.

19.   Power to call up any uncalled capital of the company.

20.   Power to rank and claim in the bankruptcy, insolvency, sequestration or liquidation of any person indebted to the company and to receive dividends, and to accede to trust deeds for the creditors of any such person.

21.   Power to present or defend a petition for the winding up of the company.

22.   Power to change the situation of the company's registered office.

23.   Power to do all other things incidental to the exercise of the foregoing powers.

SCHEDULE 4

POWERS OF LIQUIDATOR IN A WINDING UP

PART I

POWERS EXERCISABLE WITH SANCTION

1.   Power to pay any class of creditors in full.

2.   Power to make any compromise or arrangement with creditors or persons claiming to be creditors, or having or alleging themselves to have any claim (present or future, certain or contingent, ascertained or sounding only in damages) against the company, or whereby the company may be rendered liable.

3.   Power to compromise, on such terms as may be agreed—

(a)   all calls and liabilities to calls, all debts and liabilities capable of resulting in debts, and all claims (present or future, certain or contingent, ascertained or sounding only in damages) subsisting or supposed to subsist between the company and a contributory or alleged contributory or other debtor or person apprehending liability to the company, and

(b)   all questions in any way relating to or affecting the assets or the winding up of the company, and take any security for the discharge of any such call, debt, liability or claim and give a complete discharge in respect of it.

3A.   Power to bring legal proceedings under section 213, 214, 238, 239, 242, 243 or 423. [Ital para prosp ins]

PART II

POWERS EXERCISABLE WITHOUT SANCTION IN VOLUNTARY WINDING UP, WITH SANCTION IN WINDING UP BY THE COURT

4.   Power to bring or defend any action or other legal proceeding in the name and on behalf of the company.

5.   Power to carry on the business of the company so far as may be necessary for its beneficial winding up.

PART III

POWERS EXERCISABLE WITHOUT SANCTION IN ANY WINDING UP

6.   Power to sell any of the company's property by public auction or private contract with power to transfer the whole of it to any person or to sell the same in panels.

7.   Power to do all acts and execute, in the name and on behalf of the company, all deeds, receipts and other documents and for that purpose to use, when necessary, the company's seal.

8.   Power to prove, rank and claim in the bankruptcy, insolvency or sequestration of any contributory for any balance against his estate, and to receive dividends in the bankruptcy, insolvency or sequestration in respect of that balance, as a separate debt due from the bankrupt or insolvent, and rateably with the other separate creditors.

9.   Power to draw, accept, make and indorse any bill of exchange or promissory note in the name and on behalf of the company, with the same effect with respect to the company's liability as if the bill or note had been drawn, accepted, made or indorsed by or on behalf of the company in the course of its business.

10.   Power to raise on the security of the assets of the company any money requisite.

11.   Power to take out in his official name letters of administration to any deceased contributory, and to do in his official name any other act necessary for obtaining payment of any money due from a contributory or his estate which cannot conveniently be done in the name of the company.

In all such cases the money due is deemed, for the purpose of enabling the liquidator to take out the letters of administration or recover the money, to be due to the liquidator himself.

12.   Power to appoint an agent to do any business which the liquidator is unable to do himself.

13.   Power to do all such other things as may be necessary for winding up the company's affairs and distributing its assets.

SCHEDULE 4A

BANKRUPTCY RESTRICTIONS ORDER AND UNDERTAKING

Bankruptcy restrictions order

1.—(1) A bankruptcy restrictions order may be made by the court.

(2)   An order may be made only on the application of—

(a)   the Secretary of State, or
(b)   the official receiver acting on a direction of the Secretary of State.

Grounds for making order

2.—(1) The court shall grant an application for a bankruptcy restrictions order if it thinks it appropriate having regard to the conduct of the bankrupt (whether before or after the making of the bankruptcy order).

(2)   The court shall, in particular, take into account any of the following kinds of behaviour on the part of the bankrupt—

(a)   *failing to keep records which account for a loss of property by the bankrupt, or by a business carried on by him, where the loss occurred in the period beginning 2 years before petition and ending with the date of the application;*

(b)   *failing to produce records of that kind on demand by the official receiver or the trustee;*

(c)   *entering into a transaction at an undervalue;*

(d)   *giving a preference;*

(e)   *making an excessive pension contribution;*

(f)   *a failure to supply goods or services which were wholly or partly paid for which gave rise to a claim provable in the bankruptcy;*

(g)   *trading at a time before commencement of the bankruptcy when the bankrupt knew or ought to have known that he was himself to be unable to pay his debts;*

(h)   *incurring, before commencement of the bankruptcy, a debt which the bankrupt had no reasonable expectation of being able to pay;*

(i)   *failing to account satisfactorily to the court, the official receiver or the trustee for a loss of property or for an insufficiency of property to meet bankruptcy debts;*

(j)   *carrying on any gambling, rash and hazardous speculation or unreasonable extravagance which may have materially contributed to or increased the extent of the bankruptcy or which took place between presentation of the petition and commencement of the bankruptcy;*

(k)   *neglect of business affairs of a kind which may have materially contributed to or increased the extent of the bankruptcy;*

(l)   *fraud or fraudulent breach of trust;*

(m)   *failing to cooperate with the official receiver or the trustee.*

(3)   *The court shall also, in particular, consider whether the bankrupt was an undischarged bankrupt at some time during the period of six years ending with the date of the bankruptcy to which the application relates.*

(4)   *For the purpose of sub-paragraph (2)—*

   'before petition' shall be construed in accordance with section 351(c),
   'excessive pension contribution' shall be construed in accordance with section 342A,
   'preference' shall be construed in accordance with section 340, and
   'undervalue' shall be construed in accordance with section 339.

Timing of application for order

3.—(1) *An application for a bankruptcy restrictions order in respect of a bankrupt must be made—*

(a)   *before the end of the period of one year beginning with the date on which the bankruptcy commences, or*

(b)   *with the permission of the court.*

(2)   *The period specified in sub-paragraph (1)(a) shall cease to run in respect of a bankrupt while the period set for his discharge is suspended under section 279(3).*

Duration of order

4.—(1) *A bankruptcy restrictions order—*

(a)   *shall come into force when it is made, and*

(b)   *shall cease to have effect at the end of a date specified in the order.*

(2)   *The date specified in a bankruptcy restrictions order under sub-paragraph (1)(b) must not be—*

(a)   *before the end of the period of two years beginning with the date on which the order is made, or*

(b)   *after the end of the period of 15 years beginning with that date.*

Interim bankruptcy restrictions order

5.—(1) *This paragraph applies at any time between—*

(a)   *the institution of an application for a bankruptcy restrictions order, and*

(b)   *the determination of the application.*

(2)   *The court may make an interim bankruptcy restrictions order if the court thinks that—*

(a)   there are prima facie grounds to suggest that the application for the bankruptcy restrictions order will be successful, and

(b)   it is in the public interest to make an interim order.

(3)   An interim order may be made only on the application of—

(a)   the Secretary of State, or

(b)   the official receiver acting on a direction of the Secretary of State.

(4)   An interim order—

(a)   shall have the same effect as a bankruptcy restrictions order, and

(b)   shall come into force when it is made.

(5)   An interim order shall cease to have effect—

(a)   on the determination of the application for the bankruptcy restrictions order,

(b)   on the acceptance of a bankruptcy restrictions undertaking made by the bankrupt, or

(c)   if the court discharges the interim order on the application of the person who applied for it or of the bankrupt.

6.—(1) This paragraph applies to a case in which both an interim bankruptcy restrictions order and a bankruptcy restrictions order are made.

(2)   Paragraph 4(2) shall have effect in relation to the bankruptcy restrictions order as if a reference to the date of that order were a reference to the date of the interim order.

Bankruptcy restrictions undertaking

7.—(1) A bankrupt may offer a bankruptcy restrictions undertaking to the Secretary of State.

(2)   In determining whether to accept a bankruptcy restrictions undertaking the Secretary of State shall have regard to the matters specified in paragraph 2(2) and (3).

8.   A reference in an enactment to a person in respect of whom a bankruptcy restrictions order has effect (or who is 'the subject of' a bankruptcy restrictions order) includes a reference to a person in respect of whom a bankruptcy restrictions undertaking has effect.

9.—(1) A bankruptcy restrictions undertaking—

(a)   shall come into force on being accepted by the Secretary of State, and

(b)   shall cease to have effect at the end of a date specified in the undertaking.

(2)—The date specified under sub-paragraph (1)(b) must not be—

(a)   before the end of the period of two years beginning with the date on which the undertaking is accepted, or

(b)   after the end of the period of 15 years beginning with that date.

(3)   On an application by the bankrupt the court may—

(a)   annul a bankruptcy restrictions undertaking;

(b)   provide for a bankruptcy restrictions undertaking to cease to have effect before the date specified under sub-paragraph (1)(b).

Effect of annulment of bankruptcy order

10.   Where a bankruptcy order is annulled under section 282(1)(a) or (2)—

(a)   any bankruptcy restrictions order, interim order or undertaking which is in force in respect of the bankrupt shall be annulled,

(b)   no new bankruptcy restrictions order or interim order may be made in respect of the bankrupt, and

(c)   no new bankruptcy restrictions undertaking by the bankrupt may be accepted.

11.   Where a bankruptcy order is annulled under section 261, 263D or 282(1)(b)—

(a)   the annulment shall not affect any bankruptcy restrictions order, interim order or undertaking in respect of the bankrupt,

(b)   the court may make a bankruptcy restrictions order in relation to the bankrupt on an application instituted before the annulment,

(c)   the Secretary of State may accept a bankruptcy restrictions undertaking offered before the annulment, and

(d)   an application for a bankruptcy restrictions order or interim order in respect of the bankrupt may not be instituted after the annulment.

Registration

12.   *The Secretary of State shall maintain a register of—*

(a)   *bankruptcy restrictions orders,*

(b)   *interim bankruptcy restrictions orders, and*

(c)   *bankruptcy restrictions undertakings.*

Note: Schedule in italics prosp ins Enterprise Act 2002, s 257, Sch 20.

SCHEDULE 6

THE CATEGORIES OF PREFERENTIAL DEBTS

Category 1: Debts due to Inland Revenue

1.   *Sums due at the relevant date from the debtor on account of deductions of income tax from emoluments paid during the period of 12 months next before that date.*

The deductions here referred to are those which the debtor was liable to make under section 203 of the Income and Corporation Taxes Act 1988 (pay as you earn), less the amount of the repayments of income tax which the debtor was liable to make during that period. [ital para prosp rep]

2.   *Sums due at the relevant date from the debtor in respect of such deductions as are required to be made by the debtor for that period under section 559 of the Income and Corporation Taxes Act 1988 (sub-contractors in the construction industry).* [Ital para prosp rep]

Category 2: Debts due to Customs and Excise

3.   *Any value added tax which is referable to the period of 6 months next before the relevant date (which period is referred to below as 'the 6-month period').*

For the purposes of this paragraph—

(a)   *where the whole of the prescribed accounting period to which any value added tax is attributable falls within the 6-month period, the whole amount of that tax is referable to that period; and*

(b)   *in any other case the amount of any value added tax which is referable to the 6-month period is the proportion of the tax which is equal to such proportion (if any) of the accounting reference period in question as falls within the 6-month period;*

and in sub-paragraph (a) 'prescribed' means prescribed by regulations under the Value Added Tax Act 1984. [Ital para prosp rep]

3A.   *Any insurance premium tax which is referable to the period of 6 months next before the relevant date (which period is referred to below as 'the 6-month period').*

For the purposes of this paragraph—

(a)   *where the whole of the accounting period to which any insurance premium tax is attributable falls within the 6-month period, the whole amount of that tax is referable to that period; and*

(b)   *in any other case the amount of any insurance premium tax which is referable to the 6-month period is the proportion of the tax which is equal to such proportion (if any) of the accounting period in question as falls within the 6-month period;*

and references here to accounting periods shall be construed in accordance with Part III of the Finance Act 1994. [Ital para prosp rep]

3B.   *Any landfill tax which is referable to the period of 6 months next before the relevant date (which period is referred to below as 'the 6-month period').*

For the purposes of this paragraph—

(a) *where the whole of the accounting period to which any landfill tax is attributable falls within the 6-month period, the whole amount of that tax is referable to that period; and*

(b) *in any other case the amount of any landfill tax which is referable to the 6-month period is the proportion of the tax which is equal to such proportion (if any) of the accounting period in question as falls within the 6-month period;*

and references here to accounting periods shall be construed in accordance with Part III of the Finance Act 1996. [Ital para prosp rep]

3C. Any climate change levy which is referable to the period of 6 months next before the relevant date (which period is referred to below as 'the 6-month period').

For the purposes of this paragraph—

(a) *where the whole of the accounting period to which any climate change levy is attributable falls within the 6-month period, the whole amount of that levy is referable to that period; and*

(b) *in any other case the amount of any climate change levy which is referable to the 6-month period is the proportion of the levy which is equal to such proportion (if any) of the accounting period in question as falls within the 6-month period;*

and references here to accounting periods shall be construed in accordance with Schedule 6 to the Finance Act 2000. [Ital para prosp rep]

3D. Any aggregates levy which is referable to the period of 6 months next before the relevant date (which period is referred to below as 'the 6-month period').

For the purposes of this paragraph—

(a) *where the whole of the accounting period to which any aggregates levy is attributable falls within the 6-month period, the whole amount of that levy is referable to that period; and*

(b) *in any other case the amount of any aggregates levy which is referable to the 6-month period is the proportion of the levy which is equal to such proportion (if any) of the accounting period in question as falls within the 6-month period;*

and references here to accounting periods shall be construed in accordance with Part 2 of the Finance Act 2001. [Ital para prosp rep]

4. The amount of any car tax which is due at the relevant date from the debtor and which became due within a period of 12 months next before that date. [Ital para prosp rep]

5. Any amount which is due—

(a) *by way of general betting duty, bingo duty or gaming duty, or*

(b) *under section 12(1) of the Betting and Gaming Duties Act 1981 (general betting duty and pool betting duty recoverable from agent collecting stakes),*

from the debtor at the relevant date and which became due within the period of 12 months next before that date. [Ital para prosp rep]

5A. The amount of any excise duty on beer which is due at the relevant date from the debtor and which became due within a period of 6 months next before that date. [Ital para prosp rep]

5B. Any amount which is due by way of lottery duty from the debtor at the relevant date and which became due within the period of 12 months next before that date. [Ital para prosp rep]

5C. Any amount which is due by way of air passenger duty from the debtor at the relevant date and which became due within the period of six months next before that date. [Ital para prosp rep]

Category 3: Social security contributions

6. All sums which on the relevant date are due from the debtor on account of Class 1 or Class 2 contributions under the Social Security Contributions and Benefits Act 1992 or the Social Security (Northern Ireland) Act 1975 and which became due from the debtor in the 12 months next before the relevant date. [Ital para prosp rep]

7.   All sums which on the relevant date have been assessed on and are due from the debtor on account of Class 4 contributions under either of those Acts of 1975, being sums which—

    (a)   are due to the Commissioners of Inland Revenue (rather than to the Secretary of State or a Northern Ireland department), and

    (b)   are assessed on the debtor up to 5th April next before the relevant date,

but not exceeding, in the whole, any one year's assessment. [Ital para prosp rep]

Category 4: Contributions to occupational pension schemes, etc.

8.   Any sum which is owed by the debtor and is a sum to which Schedule 4 to the Pension Schemes Act 1993 applies (contributions to occupational pension schemes and state scheme premiums).

Category 5: Remuneration, etc, of employees

9.   So much of any amount which—

    (a)   is owed by the debtor to a person who is or has been an employee of the debtor, and

    (b)   is payable by way of remuneration in respect of the whole or any part of the period of 4 months next before the relevant date,

as does not exceed so much as may be prescribed by order made by the Secretary of State.

10.   An amount owed by way of accrued holiday remuneration, in respect of any period of employment before the relevant date, to a person whose employment by the debtor has been terminated, whether before, on or after that date.

11.   So much of any sum owed in respect of money advanced for the purpose as has been applied for the payment of a debt which, if it had not been paid, would have been a debt falling within paragraph 9 or 10.

12.   So much of any amount which—

    (a)   is ordered (whether before or after the relevant date) to be paid by the debtor under the Reserve Forces (Safeguard of Employment) Act 1985, and

    (b)   is so ordered in respect of a default made by the debtor before that date in the discharge of his obligations under that Act,

as does not exceed such amount as may be prescribed by order made by the Secretary of State.

Interpretation for Category 5

13.   (1) For the purposes of paragraphs 9 to 12, a sum is payable by the debtor to a person by way of remuneration in respect of any period if—

    (a)   it is paid as wages or salary (whether payable for time or for piece work or earned wholly or partly by way of commission) in respect of services rendered to the debtor in that period, or

    (b)   it is an amount falling within the following sub-paragraph and is payable by the debtor in respect of that period.

    (2) An amount falls within this sub-paragraph if it is—

    (a)   a guarantee payment under Part III of the Employment Rights Act 1996 (employee without work to do);

    (b)   any payment for time off under section 53 (time off to look for work or arrange training) or section 56 (time off for ante-natal care) of that Act or under section 169 of the Trade Union and Labour Relations (Consolidation) Act 1992 (time off for carrying out trade union duties etc.);

    (c)   remuneration on suspension on medical grounds, or on maternity grounds, under Part VII of the Employment Rights Act 1996; or

    (d)   remuneration under a protective award under section 189 of the Trade Union and Labour Relations (Consolidation) Act 1992 (redundancy dismissal with compensation).

14.   (1) This paragraph relates to a case in which a person's employment has been terminated by or in consequence of his employer going into liquidation or being adjudged bankrupt or (his employer being a company not in liquidation) by or in consequence of—

    (a)   a receiver being appointed as mentioned in section 40 of this Act (debenture-holders secured by floating charge), or

    (b)   the appointment of a receiver under section 53(6) or 54(5) of this Act (Scottish company with property subject to floating charge), or

    (c)   the taking of possession by debenture-holders (so secured), as mentioned in section 196 of the Companies Act.

(2) For the purposes of paragraphs 9 to 12, holiday remuneration is deemed to have accrued to that person in respect of any period of employment if, by virtue of his contract of employment or of any enactment that remuneration would have accrued in respect of that period if his employment had continued until he became entitled to be allowed the holiday.

(3) The reference in sub-paragraph (2) to any enactment includes an order or direction made under an enactment.

15.   Without prejudice to paragraphs 13 and 14—

    (a)   any remuneration payable by the debtor to a person in respect of a period of holiday or of absence from work through sickness or other good cause is deemed to be wages or (as the case may be) salary in respect of services rendered to the debtor in that period, and

    (b)   references here and in those paragraphs to remuneration in respect of a period of holiday include any sums which, if they had been paid, would have been treated for the purposes of the enactments relating to social security as earnings in respect of that period.

Category 6: Levies on coal and steel production

15A. Any sums due at the relevant date from the debtor in respect of—

    (a)   the levies on the production of coal and steel referred to in Articles 49 and 50 of the ECSC Treaty, or

    (b)   any surcharge for delay provided for in Article 50(3) of that Treaty and Article 6 of Decisions 3/52 of the High Authority of the Coal and Steel Community.

Orders

16.   An order under paragraph 9 or 12—

    (a)   may contain such transitional provisions as may appear to the Secretary of State necessary or expedient;

    (b)   shall be made by statutory instrument subject to annulment in pursuance of a resolution of either House of Parliament.

PART V

COMMERCIAL

Misrepresentation Act 1967

1.   Removal of certain bars to rescission for innocent misrepresentation

Where a person has entered into a contract after a misrepresentation has been made to him, and—

(a)   the misrepresentation has become a term of the contract; or

(b)   the contract has been performed;

or both, then, if otherwise he would be entitled to rescind the contract without alleging fraud, he shall be so entitled, subject to the provisions of this Act, notwithstanding the matters mentioned in paragraphs (a) and (b) of this section.

2.   Damages for misrepresentation

(1)   Where a person has entered into a contract after a misrepresentation has been made to him by another party thereto and as a result thereof he has suffered loss, then, if the person making the misrepresentation would be liable to damages in respect thereof had the misrepresentation been made fraudulently, that person shall be so liable notwithstanding that the misrepresentation was not made fraudulently, unless he proves that he had reasonable ground to believe and did believe up to the time the contract was made that the facts represented were true.

(2)   Where a person has entered into a contract after a misrepresentation has been made to him otherwise than fraudulently, and he would be entitled, by reason of the misrepresentation, to rescind the contract, then, if it is claimed, in any proceedings arising out of the contract, that the contract ought to be or has been rescinded, the court or arbitrator may declare the contract subsisting and award damages in lieu of rescission, if of opinion that it would be equitable to do so, having regard to the nature of the misrepresentation and the loss that would be caused by it if the contract were upheld, as well as to the loss that rescission would cause to the other party.

(3)   Damages may be awarded against a person under subsection (2) of this section whether or not he is liable to damages under subsection (1) thereof, but where he is so liable any award under the said subsection (2) shall be taken into account in assessing his liability under the said subsection (1).

3.   Avoidance of provision excluding liability for misrepresentation

If a contract contains a term which would exclude or restrict—

(a)   any liability to which a party to a contract may be subject by reason of any misrepresentation made by him before the contract was made; or

(b)   any remedy available to another party to the contract by reason of such a misrepresentation,

that term shall be of no effect except in so far as it satisfies the requirement of reasonableness as stated in section 11(1) of the Unfair Contract Terms Act 1977; and it is for those claiming that the term satisfies that requirement to show that it does.

Unfair Contract Terms Act 1977

PART I

AMENDMENT OF LAW FOR ENGLAND AND WALES AND NORTHERN IRELAND

1.   Scope of Part I

(1)   For the purposes of this Part of this Act, 'negligence' means the breach—

    (a)   of any obligation, arising from the express or implied terms of a contract, to take reasonable care or exercise reasonable skill in the performance of the contract;

    (b)   of any common law duty to take reasonable care or exercise reasonable skill (but not any stricter duty);

    (c)   of the common duty of care imposed by the Occupiers' Liability Act 1957 or the Occupiers' Liability Act (Northern Ireland) 1957.

(2)   This Part of this Act is subject to Part III; and in relation to contracts, the operation of sections 2 to 4 and 7 is subject to the exceptions made by Schedule 1.

(3)   In the case of both contract and tort, sections 2 to 7 apply (except where the contrary is stated in section 6(4)) only to business liability, that is liability for breach of obligations or duties arising—

    (a)   from things done or to be done by a person in the course of a business (whether his own business or another's); or

    (b)   from the occupation of premises used for business purposes of the occupier;

and references to liability are to be read accordingly but liability of an occupier of premises for breach of an obligation or duty towards a person obtaining access to the premises for recreational or educational purposes, being liability for loss or damage suffered by reason of the dangerous state of the premises, is not a business liability of the occupier unless granting that person such access for the purposes concerned falls within the business purposes of the occupier.

(4)   In relation to any breach of duty or obligation, it is immaterial for any purpose of this Part of this Act whether the breach was inadvertent or intentional, or whether liability for it arises directly or vicariously.

2.   Negligence liability

(1)   A person cannot by reference to any contract term or to a notice given to persons generally or to particular persons exclude or restrict his liability for death or personal injury resulting from negligence.

(2)   In the case of other loss or damage, a person cannot so exclude or restrict his liability for negligence except in so far as the term or notice satisfies the requirement of reasonableness.

(3)   Where a contract term or notice purports to exclude or restrict liability for negligence a person's agreement to or awareness of it is not of itself to be taken as indicating his voluntary acceptance of any risk.

3.   Liability arising in contract

(1)   This section applies as between contracting parties where one of them deals as consumer or on the other's written standard terms of business.

(2)   As against that party, the other cannot by reference to any contract term—

    (a)   when himself in breach of contract, exclude or restrict any liability of his in respect of the breach; or

    (b)   claim to be entitled—

        (i)   to render a contractual performance substantially different from that which was reasonably expected of him, or

        (ii)   in respect of the whole or any part of his contractual obligation, to render no performance at all,

except in so far as (in any of the cases mentioned above in this subsection) the contract term satisfies the requirement of reasonableness.

4.   Unreasonable indemnity clauses

(1)   A person dealing as consumer cannot by reference to any contract term be made to indemnify another person (whether a party to the contract or not) in respect of liability that may be incurred by the other for negligence or breach of contract, except in so far as the contract term satisfies the requirement of reasonableness.

(2)   This section applies whether the liability in question—

(a)   is directly that of the person to be indemnified or is incurred by him vicariously;

(b)   is to the person dealing as consumer or to someone else.

5.   'Guarantee' of consumer goods

(1)   In the case of goods of a type ordinarily supplied for private use or consumption, where loss or damage—

(a)   arises from the goods proving defective while in consumer use; and

(b)   results from the negligence of a person concerned in the manufacture or distribution of the goods,

liability for the loss or damage cannot be excluded or restricted by reference to any contract term or notice contained in or operating by reference to a guarantee of the goods.

(2)   For these purposes—

(a)   goods are to be regarded as 'in consumer use' when a person is using them, or has them in his possession for use, otherwise than exclusively for the purposes of a business; and

(b)   anything in writing is a guarantee if it contains or purports to contain some promise or assurance (however worded or presented) that defects will be made good by complete or partial replacement, or by repair, monetary compensation or otherwise.

(3)   This section does not apply as between the parties to a contract under or in pursuance of which possession or ownership of the goods passed.

6.   Sale and hire-purchase

(1)   Liability for breach of the obligations arising from—

(a)   section 12 of the Sale of Goods Act 1979 (seller's implied undertakings as to title, etc);

(b)   section 8 of the Supply of Goods (Implied Terms) Act 1973 (the corresponding thing in relation to hire-purchase)

cannot be excluded or restricted by reference to any contract term.

(2)   As against a person dealing as consumer, liability for breach of the obligations arising from—

(a)   section 13, 14 or 15 of the 1979 Act (seller's implied undertakings as to conformity of goods with description or sample, or as to their quality or fitness for a particular purpose);

(b)   section 9, 10 or 11 of the 1973 Act (the corresponding things in relation to hire-purchase),

cannot be excluded or restricted by reference to any contract term.

(3)   As against a person dealing otherwise than as consumer, the liability specified in subsection (2) above can be excluded or restricted by reference to a contract term, but only in so far as the term satisfies the requirement of reasonableness.

(4)   The liabilities referred to in this section are not only the business liabilities defined by section 1(3), but include those arising under any contract of sale of goods or hire-purchase agreement.

7.   Miscellaneous contracts under which goods pass

(1)   Where the possession or ownership of goods passes under or in pursuance of a contract not governed by the law of sale of goods or hire-purchase, subsections (2) to (4) below apply as regards the effect (if any) to be given to contract terms excluding or restricting liability for breach of obligation arising by implication of law from the nature of the contract.

(2)   As against a person dealing as consumer, liability in respect of the goods' correspondence with description or sample, or their quality or fitness for any particular purpose, cannot be excluded or restricted by reference to any such term.

(3)   As against a person dealing otherwise than as consumer, that liability can be excluded or restricted by reference to such a term, but only in so far as the term satisfies the requirement of reasonableness.

(3A) Liability for breach of the obligations arising under section 2 of the Supply of Goods and Services Act 1982 (implied terms about title etc in certain contracts for the transfer of the property in goods) cannot be excluded or restricted by references to any such term.

(4)   Liability in respect of—

  (a)   the right to transfer ownership of the goods, or give possession; or
  (b)   the assurance of quiet possession to a person taking goods in pursuance of the contract,

cannot (in a case to which subsection (3A) above does not apply) be excluded or restricted by reference to any such term except in so far as the term satisfies the requirement of reasonableness.

(5)   This section does not apply in the case of goods passing on a redemption of trading stamps within the Trading Stamps Act 1964 or the Trading Stamps Act (Northern Ireland) 1965.

9.   Effect of breach

(1)   Where for reliance upon it a contract term has to satisfy the requirement of reasonableness, it may be found to do so and be given effect accordingly notwithstanding that the contract has been terminated either by breach or by a party electing to treat it as repudiated.

(2)   Where on a breach the contract is nevertheless affirmed by a party entitled to treat it as repudiated, this does not of itself exclude the requirement of reasonableness in relation to any contract term.

10.   Evasion by means of secondary contract

A person is not bound by any contract term prejudicing or taking away rights of his which arise under, or in connection with the performance of, another contract, so far as those rights extend to the enforcement of another's liability which this Part of this Act prevents that other from excluding or restricting.

11.   The 'reasonableness' test

(1)   In relation to a contract term, the requirement of reasonableness for the purposes of this Part of this Act, section 3 of the Misrepresentation Act 1967 and section 3 of the Misrepresentation Act (Northern Ireland) 1967 is that the term shall have been a fair and reasonable one to be included having regard to the circumstances which were, or ought reasonably to have been, known to or in the contemplation of the parties when the contract was made.

(2)   In determining for the purposes of section 6 or 7 above whether a contract term satisfies the requirement of reasonableness, regard shall be had in particular to the matters specified in Schedule 2 to this Act; but this subsection does not prevent the court or arbitrator from holding, in accordance with any rule of law, that a term which purports to exclude or restrict any relevant liability is not a term of the contract.

(3)   In relation to a notice (not being a notice having contractual effect), the requirement of reasonableness under this Act is that it should be fair and reasonable to allow reliance on it, having regard to all the circumstances obtaining when the liability arose or (but for the notice) would have arisen.

(4)   Where by reference to a contract term or notice a person seeks to restrict liability to a specified sum of money, and the question arises (under this or any other Act) whether the term or notice satisfies the requirement of reasonableness, regard shall be had in particular (but without prejudice to subsection (2) above in the case of contract terms) to—

  (a)   the resources which he could expect to be available to him for the purpose of meeting the liability should it arise; and
  (b)   how far it was open to him to cover himself by insurance.

(5)   It is for those claiming that a contract term or notice satisfies the requirement of reasonableness to show that it does.

12.   'Dealing as consumer'

(1)   A party to a contract 'deals as consumer' in relation to another party if—

  (a)   he neither makes the contract in the course of a business nor holds himself out as doing so; and
  (b)   the other party does make the contract in the course of a business; and

(c)   in the case of a contract governed by the law of sale of goods or hire-purchase, or by section 7 of this Act, the goods passing under or in pursuance of the contract are of a type ordinarily supplied for private use or consumption.

(1A)   But if the first party mentioned in subsection (1) is an individual paragraph (c) of that subsection must be ignored.

(2)   But the buyer is not in any circumstances to be regarded as dealing as consumer—

(a)   if he is an individual and the goods are second-hand goods sold at public auction at which individuals have the opportunity of attending the sale in person;
(b)   if he is not an individual and the goods are sold by auction or by competitive tender.

(3)   Subject to this, it is for those claiming that a party does not deal as consumer to show that he does not.

13.   Varieties of exemption clause

(1)   To the extent that this Part of this Act prevents the exclusion or restriction of any liability it also prevents—

(a)   making the liability or its enforcement subject to restrictive or onerous conditions;
(b)   excluding or restricting any right or remedy in respect of the liability, or subjecting a person to any prejudice in consequence of his pursuing any such right or remedy;
(c)   excluding or restricting rules of evidence or procedure;

and (to that extent) sections 2 and 5 to 7 also prevent excluding or restricting liability by reference to terms and notices which exclude or restrict the relevant obligation or duty.

(2)   But an agreement in writing to submit present or future differences to arbitration is not to be treated under this Part of this Act as excluding or restricting any liability.

14.   Interpretation of Part I

In this Part of this Act—

'business' includes a profession and the activities of any government department or local or public authority;
'goods' has the same meaning as in the Sale of Goods Act 1979:
'hire-purchase agreement' has the same meaning as in the Consumer Credit Act 1974;
'negligence' has the meaning given by section 1(1);
'notice' includes an announcement, whether or not in writing, and any other communication or pretended communication; and
'personal injury' includes any disease and any impairment of physical or mental condition.

26.   International supply contracts

(1)   The limits imposed by this Act on the extent to which a person may exclude or restrict liability by reference to a contract term do not apply to liability arising under such a contract as is described in subsection (3) below).

(2)   The terms of such a contract are not subject to any requirement of reasonableness under section 3 or 4.

(3)   Subject to subsection (4), that description of contract is one whose characteristics are the following—

(a)   either it is a contract of sale of goods or it is one under or in pursuance of which the possession or ownership of goods passes; and
(b)   it is made by parties whose places of business (or, if they have none, habitual residences) are in the territories of different States (the Channel Islands and the Isle of Man being treated for this purpose as different States from the United Kingdom).

(4)   A contract falls within subsection (3) above only if either—

(a)   the goods in question are, at the time of the conclusion of the contract, in the course of carriage, or will be carried, from the territory of one State to the territory of another; or
(b)   the acts constituting the offer and acceptance have been done in the territories of different States; or
(c)   the contract provides for the goods to be delivered to the territory of a State other than that within whose territory those acts were done.

27. Choice of law clauses

(1)   Where the law applicable to a contract is the law of any part of the United Kingdom only by choice of the parties (and apart from that choice would be the law of some country outside the United Kingdom) sections 2 to 7 and 16 to 21 of this Act do not operate as part of the law applicable to the contract.

(2)   This Act has effect notwithstanding any contract term which applies or purports to apply the law of some country outside the United Kingdom, where (either or both)—

    (a)   the term appears to the court, or arbitrator or arbiter to have been imposed wholly or mainly for the purpose of enabling the party imposing it to evade the operation of this Act; or

    (b)   in the making of the contract one of the parties dealt as consumer, and he was then habitually resident in the United Kingdom, and the essential steps necessary for the making of the contract were taken there, whether by him or by others on his behalf.

(3)   [Applies to Scotland only.]

28. Temporary provision for sea carriage of passengers

(1)   This section applies to a contract for carriage by sea of a passenger or of a passenger and his luggage where the provisions of the Athens Convention (with or without modification) do not have, in relation to the contract, the force of law in the United Kingdom.

(2)   In a case where—

    (a)   the contract is not made in the United Kingdom, and

    (b)   neither the place of departure nor the place of destination under it is in the United Kingdom,

a person is not precluded by this Act from excluding or restricting liability for loss or damage, being loss or damage for which the provisions of the Convention would, if they had the force of law in relation to the contract, impose liability on him.

(3)   In any other case, a person is not precluded by this Act from excluding or restricting liability for that loss or damage—

    (a)   in so far as the exclusion or restriction would have been effective in that case had the provisions of the Convention had the force of law in relation to the contract; or

    (b)   in such circumstances and to such extent as may be prescribed, by reference to a prescribed term of the contract.

(4)   For the purposes of subsection (3)(a), the values which shall be taken to be the official values in the United Kingdom of the amounts (expressed in gold francs) by reference to which liability under the provisions of the Convention is limited shall be such amounts in sterling as the Secretary of State may from time to time by order made by statutory instrument specify.

(5)   In this section—

    (a)   the references to excluding or restricting liability include doing any of those things in relation to the liability which are mentioned in section 13 or section 25(3) and (5); and

    (b)   'the Athens Convention' means the Athens Convention relating to the Carriage of Passengers and their Luggage by Sea, 1974; and

    (c)   'prescribed' means prescribed by the Secretary of State by regulations made by statutory instrument;

and a statutory instrument containing the regulations shall be subject to annulment in pursuance of a resolution of either House of Parliament.

29. Saving for other relevant legislation

(1)   Nothing in this Act removes or restricts the effect of, or prevents reliance upon, any contractual provision which—

    (a)   is authorised or required by the express terms or necessary implication of an enactment; or

    (b)   being made with a view to compliance with an international agreement to which the United Kingdom is a party, does not operate more restrictively than is contemplated by the agreement.

(2)   A contract term is to be taken—

    (a)   for the purposes of Part I of this Act, as satisfying the requirement of reasonableness;

(b)   [Applies to Scotland only]

if it is incorporated or approved by, or incorporated pursuant to a decision or ruling of, a competent authority acting in the exercise of any statutory jurisdiction or function and is not a term in a contract to which the competent authority is itself a party.

(3)   In this section—

'competent authority' means any court, arbitrator or arbiter, government department or public authority;
'enactment' means any legislation (including subordinate legislation) of the United Kingdom or Northern Ireland and any instrument having effect by virtue of such legislation; and
'statutory' means conferred by an enactment.

SCHEDULE 1

Section 1(2)

SCOPE OF SECTIONS 2 TO 4 AND 7

1.   Sections 2 to 4 of this Act do not extend to—

(a)   any contract of insurance (including a contract to pay an annuity on human life);
(b)   any contract so far as it relates to the creation or transfer of an interest in land, or to the termination of such an interest, whether by extinction, merger, surrender, forfeiture or otherwise;
(c)   any contract so far as it relates to the creation or transfer of a right or interest in any patent, trade mark, copyright or design right, registered design, technical or commercial information or other intellectual property, or relates to the termination of any such right or interest;
(d)   any contract so far as it relates—

(i)   to the formation or dissolution of a company (which means any body corporate or unincorporated association and includes a partnership), or
(ii)   to its constitution or the rights or obligations of its corporators or members;

(e)   any contract so far as it relates to the creation or transfer of securities or of any right or interest in securities.

2.   Section 2(1) extends to—

(a)   any contract of marine salvage or towage;
(b)   any charterparty of a ship or hovercraft; and
(c)   any contract for the carriage of goods by ship or hovercraft;

but subject to this sections 2 to 4 and 7 do not extend to any such contract except in favour of a person dealing as consumer.

3.   Where goods are carried by ship or hovercraft in pursuance of a contract which either—

(a)   specifies that as the means of carriage over part of the journey to be covered, or
(b)   makes no provision as to the means of carriage and does not exclude that means,

then sections 2(2), 3 and 4 do not, except in favour of a person dealing as consumer, extend to the contract as it operates for and in relation to the carriage of the goods by that means.

4.   Section 2(1) and (2) do not extend to a contract of employment, except in favour of the employee.

5.   Section 2(1) does not affect the validity of any discharge and indemnity given by a person, on or in connection with an award to him of compensation for pneumonoconiosis attributable to employment in the coal industry, in respect of any further claim arising from his contracting that disease.

SCHEDULE 2

Sections 11(2), 24(2)

'GUIDELINES' FOR APPLICATION OF REASONABLENESS TEST

The matters to which regard is to be had in particular for the purposes of sections 6(3), 7(3) and (4), 20 and 21 are any of the following which appear to be relevant—

(a)   the strength of the bargaining positions of the parties relative to each other, taking into account (among other things) alternative means by which the customer's requirements could have been met;

(b)   whether the customer received an inducement to agree to the term, or in accepting it had an opportunity of entering into a similar contract with other persons, but without having to accept a similar term;

(c)   whether the customer knew or ought reasonably to have known of the existence and extent of the term (having regard, among other things, to any custom of the trade and any previous course of dealing between the parties);

(d)   where the term excludes or restricts any relevant liability if some condition is not complied with, whether it was reasonable at the time of the contract to expect that compliance with that condition would be practicable;

(e)   whether the goods were manufactured, processed or adapted to the special order of the customer.

Sale of Goods Act 1979

PART I

CONTRACTS TO WHICH ACT APPLIES

1. Contracts to which Act applies

(1)   This Act applies to contracts of sale of goods made on or after (but not to those made before) 1 January 1894.

(2)   In relation to contracts made on certain dates, this Act applies subject to the modification of certain of its sections as mentioned in Schedule 1 below.

(3)   Any such modification is indicated in the section concerned by a reference to Schedule 1 below.

(4)   Accordingly, where a section does not contain such a reference, this Act applies in relation to the contract concerned without such modification of the section.

PART II

FORMATION OF THE CONTRACT

2. Contract of sale

(1)   A contract of sale of goods is a contract by which the seller transfers or agrees to transfer the property in goods to the buyer for a money consideration, called the price.

(2)   There may be a contract of sale between one part owner and another.

(3)   A contract of sale may be absolute or conditional.

(4)   Where under a contract of sale the property in the goods is transferred from the seller to the buyer the contract is called a sale.

(5)   Where under a contract of sale the transfer of the property in the goods is to take place at a future time or subject to some condition later to be fulfilled the contract is called an agreement to sell.

(6)   An agreement to sell becomes a sale when the time elapses or the conditions are fulfilled subject to which the property in the goods is to be transferred.

3. Capacity to buy and sell

(1)   Capacity to buy and sell is regulated by the general law concerning capacity to contract and to transfer and acquire property.

(2)   Where necessaries are sold and delivered to a minor or to a person who by reason of mental incapacity or drunkenness is incompetent to contract, he must pay a reasonable price for them.

(3)   In subsection (2) above 'necessaries' means goods suitable to the condition in life of the minor or other person concerned and to his actual requirements at the time of the sale and delivery.

4. How contract of sale is made

(1)   Subject to this and any other Act, a contract of sale may be made in writing (either with or without seal), or by word of mouth, or partly in writing and partly by word of mouth, or may be implied from the conduct of the parties.

(2)   Nothing in this section affects the law relating to corporations.

5. Existing or future goods

(1)   The goods which form the subject of a contract of sale may be either existing goods, owned or possessed by the seller, or goods to be manufactured or acquired by him after the making of the contract of sale, in this Act called future goods.

(2)   There may be a contract for the sale of goods the acquisition of which by the seller depends on a contingency which may or may not happen.

(3)   Where by a contract of sale the seller purports to effect a present sale of future goods, the contract operates as an agreement to sell the goods.

6.   Goods which have perished

Where there is a contract for the sale of specific goods, and the goods without the knowledge of the seller have perished at the time when the contract is made, the contract is void.

7.   Goods perishing before sale but after agreement to sell

Where there is an agreement to sell specific goods and subsequently the goods, without any fault on the part of the seller or buyer, perish before the risk passes to the buyer, the agreement is avoided.

8.   Ascertainment of price

(1)   The price in a contract of sale may be fixed by the contract, or may be left to be fixed in a manner agreed by the contract, or may be determined by the course of dealing between the parties.

(2)   Where the price is not determined as mentioned in subsection (1) above the buyer must pay a reasonable price.

(3)   What is a reasonable price is a question of fact dependent on the circumstances of each particular case.

9.   Agreement to sell at valuation

(1)   Where there is an agreement to sell goods on the terms that the price is to be fixed by the valuation of a third party, and he cannot or does not make the valuation, the agreement is avoided; but if the goods or any part of them have been delivered to and appropriated by the buyer he must pay a reasonable price for them.

(2)   Where the third party is prevented from making the valuation by the fault of the seller or buyer, the party not at fault may maintain an action for damages against the party at fault.

10.   Stipulations about time

(1)   Unless a different intention appears from the terms of the contract, stipulations as to time of payment are not of the essence of a contract of sale.

(2)   Whether any other stipulation as to time is or is not of the essence of the contract depends on the terms of the contract.

(3)   In a contract of sale 'month' prima facie means calendar month.

11.   When condition to be treated as warranty

(1)   This section does not apply to Scotland.

(2)   Where a contract of sale is subject to a condition to be fulfilled by the seller, the buyer may waive the condition, or may elect to treat the breach of the condition as a breach of warranty and not as a ground for treating the contract as repudiated.

(3)   Whether a stipulation in a contract of sale is a condition, the breach of which may give rise to a right to treat the contract as repudiated, or a warranty, the breach of which may give rise to a claim for damages but not to a right to reject the goods and treat the contract as repudiated, depends on each case on the construction of the contract; and a stipulation may be a condition, though called a warranty in the contract.

(4)   Subject to section 35A below, where a contract of sale is not severable and the buyer has accepted the goods or part of them, the breach of a condition to be fulfilled by the seller can only be treated as a breach of warranty, and not as a ground for rejecting the goods and treating the contract as repudiated, unless there is an express or implied term of the contract to that effect.

(6)   Nothing in this section affects a condition or warranty whose fulfilment is excused by law by reason of impossibility or otherwise.

(7)   Paragraph 2 of Schedule 1 below applies in relation to a contract made before 22 April 1967 or (in the application of this Act to Northern Ireland) 28 July 1967.

12. Implied terms about title, etc

(1)   In a contract of sale, other than one to which subsection (3) below applies, there is an implied term on the part of the seller that in the case of a sale he has a right to sell the goods, and in the case of an agreement to sell he will have such a right at the time when the property is to pass.

(2)   In a contract of sale, other than one to which subsection (3) below applies, there is also an implied term that—

   (a)   the goods are free, and will remain free until the time when the property is to pass, from any charge or encumbrance not disclosed or known to the buyer before the contract is made, and

   (b)   the buyer will enjoy quiet possession of the goods except so far as it may be disturbed by the owner or other person entitled to the benefit of any charge or encumbrance so disclosed or known.

(3)   This subsection applies to a contract of sale in the case of which there appears from the contract or is to be inferred from its circumstances an intention that the seller should transfer only such title as he or a third person may have.

(4)   In a contract to which subsection (3) above applies there is an implied term that all charges or encumbrances known to the seller and not known to the buyer have been disclosed to the buyer before the contract is made.

(5)   In a contract to which subsection (3) above applies there is also an implied term that none of the following will disturb the buyer's quiet possession of the goods, namely—

   (a)   the seller;

   (b)   in a case where the parties to the contract intend that the seller should transfer only such title as a third person may have, that person;

   (c)   anyone claiming through or under the seller or that third person otherwise than under a charge or encumbrance disclosed or known to the buyer before the contract is made.

(5A)   As regards England and Wales and Northern Ireland, the term implied by subsection (1) above is a condition and the terms implied by subsections (2), (4) and (5) above are warranties.

(6)   Paragraph 3 of Schedule 1 below applies in relation to a contract made before 18 May 1973.

13. Sale by description

(1)   Where there is a contract for the sale of goods by description, there is an implied term that the goods will correspond with the description.

(1A)   As regards England and Wales and Northern Ireland, the term implied by subsection (1) above is a condition.

(2)   If the sale is by sample as well as by description it is not sufficient that the bulk of the goods corresponds with the sample if the goods do not also correspond with the description.

(3)   A sale of goods is not prevented from being a sale by description by reason only that, being exposed for sale or hire, they are selected by the buyer.

(4)   Paragraph 4 of Schedule 1 below applies in relation to a contract made before 18 May 1973.

14. Implied terms about quality or fitness

(1)   Except as provided by this section and section 15 below and subject to any other enactment, there is no implied term about the quality or fitness for any particular purpose of goods supplied under a contract of sale.

(2)   Where the seller sells goods in the course of a business, there is an implied term that the goods supplied under the contract are of satisfactory quality.

(2A)   For the purposes of this Act, goods are of satisfactory quality if they meet the standard that a reasonable person would regard as satisfactory, taking account of any description of the goods, the price (if relevant) and all the other relevant circumstances.

(2B)   For the purposes of this Act, the quality of goods includes their state and condition and the following (among others) are in appropriate cases aspects of the quality of goods—

   (a)   fitness for all the purposes for which goods of the kind in question are commonly supplied,

   (b)   appearance and finish,

   (c)   freedom from minor defects,

   (d)   safety, and

  (e) durability.

(2C) The term implied by subsection (2) above does not extend to any matter making the quality of goods unsatisfactory—

  (a) which is specifically drawn to the buyer's attention before the contract is made,

  (b) where the buyer examines the goods before the contract is made, which that examination ought to reveal, or

  (c) in the case of a contract for sale by sample, which would have been apparent on a reasonable examination of the sample.

(2D) If the buyer deals as consumer or, in Scotland, if a contract of sale is a consumer contract, the relevant circumstances mentioned in subsection (2A) above include any public statements on the specific characteristics of the goods made about them by the seller, the producer or his representative, particularly in advertising or on labelling.

(2E) A public statement is not by virtue of subsection (2D) above a relevant circumstance for the purposes of subsection (2A) above in the case of a contract of sale, if the seller shows that—

  (a) at the time the contract was made, he was not, and could not reasonably have been, aware of the statement,

  (b) before the contract was made, the statement had been withdrawn in public or, to the extent that it contained anything which was incorrect or misleading, it had been corrected in public, or

  (c) the decision to buy the goods could not have been influenced by the statement.

(2F) Subsections (2D) and (2E) above do not prevent any public statement from being a relevant circumstance for the purposes of subsection (2A) above (whether or not the buyer deals as consumer or, in Scotland, whether or not the contract of sale is a consumer contract) if the statement would have been such a circumstance apart from those subsections.

(3) Where the seller sells goods in the course of a business and the buyer, expressly or by implication, makes known—

  (a) to the seller, or

  (b) where the purchase price or part of it is payable by instalments and the goods were previously sold by a credit-broker to the seller, to that credit-broker,

any particular purpose for which the goods are being bought, there is an implied term that the goods supplied under the contract are reasonably fit for that purpose, whether or not that is a purpose for which such goods are commonly supplied, except where the circumstances show that the buyer does not rely, or that it is unreasonable for him to rely, on the skill or judgment of the seller or credit-broker.

(4) An implied term about quality or fitness for a particular purpose may be annexed to a contract of sale by usage.

(5) The preceding provisions of this section apply to a sale by a person who in the course of a business is acting as agent for another as they apply to a sale by a principal in the course of a business, except where that other is not selling in the course of a business and either the buyer knows that fact or reasonable steps are taken to bring it to the notice of the buyer before the contract is made.

(6) As regards England and Wales and Northern Ireland, the terms implied by subsections (2) and (3) above are conditions.

(7) Paragraph 5 of Schedule 1 below applies in relation to a contract made on or after 18 May 1973 and before the appointed day, and paragraph 6 in relation to one made before 18 May 1973.

(8) In subsection (7) above and paragraph 5 of Schedule 1 below references to the appointed day are to the day appointed for the purposes of those provisions by an order of the Secretary of State made by statutory instrument.

15. Sale by sample

(1) A contract of sale is a contract for sale by sample where there is an express or implied term to that effect in the contract.

(2) In the case of a contract for sale by sample there is an implied term—

  (a) that the bulk will correspond with the sample in quality;

(c) that the goods will be free from any defect, making their quality unsatisfactory, which would not be apparent on reasonable examination of the sample.

(3) As regards England and Wales and Northern Ireland, the term implied by subsection (2) above is a condition.

(4) Paragraph 7 of Schedule 1 below applies in relation to a contract made before 18 May 1973.

15A. Modification of remedies for breach of condition in non-consumer cases

(1) Where in the case of a contract of sale—

(a) the buyer would, apart from this subsection, have the right to reject goods by reason of a breach on the part of the seller of a term implied by section 13, 14 or 15 above, but

(b) the breach is so slight that it would be unreasonable for him to reject them,

then, if the buyer does not deal as consumer, the breach is not to be treated as a breach of condition but may be treated as a breach of warranty.

(2) This section applies unless a contrary intention appears in, or is to be implied from, the contract.

(3) It is for the seller to show that a breach fell within subsection (1)(b) above.

(4) This section does not apply to Scotland.

PART III

EFFECTS OF THE CONTRACT

16. Goods must be ascertained

Subject to section 20A below where there is a contract for the sale of unascertained goods no property in the goods is transferred to the buyer unless and until the goods are ascertained.

17. Property passes when intended to pass

(1) Where there is a contract for the sale of specific or ascertained goods the property in them is transferred to the buyer at such time as the parties to the contract intend it to be transferred.

(2) For the purpose of ascertaining the intention of the parties regard shall be had to the terms of the contract, the conduct of the parties and the circumstances of the case.

18. Rules for ascertaining intention

Unless a different intention appears, the following are rules for ascertaining the intention of the parties as to the time at which the property in the goods is to pass to the buyer.

Rule 1 – Where there is an unconditional contract for the sale of specific goods in a deliverable state the property in the goods passes to the buyer when the contract is made, and it is immaterial whether the time of payment or the time of delivery, or both, be postponed.

Rule 2 – Where there is a contract for the sale of goods and the seller is bound to do something to the goods for the purpose of putting them into a deliverable state, the property does not pass until the thing is done and the buyer has notice that it has been done.

Rule 3 – Where there is a contract for the sale of specific goods in a deliverable state but the seller is bound to weigh, measure, test, or do some other act or thing with reference to the goods for the purpose of ascertaining the price, the property does not pass until the act or thing is done and the buyer has notice that it has been done.

Rule 4 – When goods are delivered to the buyer on approval or on sale or return or other similar terms the property in the goods passes to the buyer—

(a) when he signifies his approval or acceptance to the seller or does any other act adopting the transaction;

(b) if he does not signify his approval or acceptance to the seller but retains the goods without giving notice of rejection, then, if a time has been fixed for the return of the goods, on the expiration of that time, and, if no time has been fixed, on the expiration of a reasonable time.

Rule 5 –

(1)   Where there is a contract for the sale of unascertained or future goods by description, and goods of that description and in a deliverable state are unconditionally appropriated to the contract, either by the seller with the assent of the buyer or by the buyer with the assent of the seller, the property in the goods then passes to the buyer; and the assent may be express or implied, and may be given either before or after the appropriation is made.

(2)   Where, in pursuance of the contract, the seller delivers the goods to the buyer or to a carrier or other bailee or custodier (whether named by the buyer or not) for the purpose of transmission to the buyer, and does not reserve the right of disposal, he is to be taken to have unconditionally appropriated the goods to the contract.

(3)   Where there is a contract for the sale of a specified quantity of unascertained goods in a deliverable state forming part of a bulk which is identified either in the contract or by subsequent agreement between the parties and the bulk is reduced to (or to less than) that quantity, then, if the buyer under that contract is the only buyer to whom goods are then due out of the bulk—

(a)   the remaining goods are to be taken as appropriated to that contract at the time when the bulk is so reduced; and

(b)   the property in those goods then passes to that buyer.

(4)   Paragraph (3) above applies also (with the necessary modifications) where a bulk is reduced to (or to less than) the aggregate of the quantities due to a single buyer under separate contracts relating to that bulk and he is the only buyer to whom goods are then due out of that bulk.

19.   Reservation of right of disposal

(1)   Where there is a contract for the sale of specific goods or where goods are subsequently appropriated to the contract, the seller may, by the terms of the contract or appropriation, reserve the right of disposal of the goods until certain conditions are fulfilled; and in such a case, notwithstanding the delivery of the goods to the buyer, or to a carrier or other bailee or custodier for the purpose of transmission to the buyer, the property in the goods does not pass to the buyer until the conditions imposed by the seller are fulfilled.

(2)   Where goods are shipped, and by the bill of lading the goods are deliverable to the order of the seller or his agent, the seller is prima facie to be taken to reserve the right of disposal.

(3)   Where the seller of goods draws on the buyer for the price, and transmits the bill of exchange and bill of lading to the buyer together to secure acceptance or payment of the bill of exchange, the buyer is bound to return the bill of lading if he does not honour the bill of exchange, and if he wrongfully retains the bill of lading the property in the goods does not pass to him.

20.   Passing of risk

(1)   Unless otherwise agreed, the goods remain at the seller's risk until the property in them is transferred to the buyer, but when the property in them is transferred to the buyer the goods are at the buyer's risk whether delivery has been made or not.

(2)   But where delivery has been delayed through the fault of either buyer or seller the goods are at the risk of the party at fault as regards any loss which might not have occurred but for such fault.

(3)   Nothing in this section affects the duties or liabilities of either seller or buyer as a bailee or custodier of the goods of the other party.

(4)   In a case where the buyer deals as consumer or, in Scotland, where there is a consumer contract in which the buyer is a consumer, subsections (1) to (3) above must be ignored and the goods remain at the seller's risk until they are delivered to the consumer.

20A.   Undivided shares in goods forming part of a bulk

(1)   This section applies to a contract for the sale of a specified quantity of unascertained goods if the following conditions are met—

(a)   the goods or some of them form part of a bulk which is identified either in the contract or by subsequent agreement between the parties; and

(b)   the buyer has paid the price for some or all of the goods which are the subject of the contract and which form part of the bulk.

(2)   Where this section applies, then (unless the parties agree otherwise), as soon as the conditions specified in paragraphs (a) and (b) of subsection (1) above are met or at such later time as the parties may agree—

    (a)   property in an undivided share in the bulk is transferred to the buyer, and

    (b)   the buyer becomes an owner in common of the bulk.

(3)   Subject to subsection (4) below, for the purposes of this section, the undivided share of a buyer in a bulk at any time shall be such share as the quantity of goods paid for and due to the buyer out of the bulk bears to the quantity of goods in the bulk at that time.

(4)   Where the aggregate of the undivided shares of buyers in a bulk determined under subsection (3) above would at any time exceed the whole of the bulk at that time, the undivided share in the bulk of each buyer shall be reduced proportionately so that the aggregate of the undivided shares is equal to the whole bulk.

(5)   Where a buyer has paid the price for only some of the goods due to him out of a bulk, any delivery to the buyer out of the bulk shall, for the purposes of this section, be ascribed in the first place to the goods in respect of which payment has been made.

(6)   For the purposes of this section payment of part of the price for any goods shall be treated as payment for a corresponding part of the goods.

20B.   Deemed consent by co-owner to dealings in bulk goods

(1)   A person who has become an owner in common of a bulk by virtue of section 20A above shall be deemed to have consented to—

    (a)   any delivery of goods out of the bulk to any other owner in common of the bulk, being goods which are due to him under his contract;

    (b)   any dealing with or removal, delivery or disposal of goods in the bulk by any other person who is an owner in common of the bulk in so far as the goods fall within that co-owner's undivided share in the bulk at the time of the dealing, removal, delivery or disposal.

(2)   No cause of action shall accrue to anyone against a person by reason of that person having acted in accordance with paragraph (a) or (b) of subsection (1) above in reliance on any consent deemed to have been given under that subsection.

(3)   Nothing in this section or section 20A above shall—

    (a)   impose an obligation on a buyer of goods out of a bulk to compensate any other buyer of goods out of that bulk for any shortfall in the goods received by that other buyer;

    (b)   affect any contractual arrangement between buyers of goods out of a bulk for adjustments between themselves; or

    (c)   affect the rights of any buyer under his contract.

21.   Sale by person not the owner

(1)   Subject to this Act, where goods are sold by a person who is not their owner, and who does not sell them under the authority or with the consent of the owner, the buyer acquires no better title to the goods than the seller had, unless the owner of the goods is by his conduct precluded from denying the seller's authority to sell.

(2)   Nothing in this Act affects—

    (a)   the provisions of the Factors Act or any enactment enabling the apparent owner of goods to dispose of them as if he were their true owner;

    (b)   the validity of any contract of sale under any special common law or statutory power of sale or under the order of a court of competent jurisdiction.

23.   Sale under voidable title

When the seller of goods has a voidable title to them, but his title has not been avoided at the time of the sale, the buyer acquires a good title to the goods, provided he buys them in good faith and without notice of the seller's defect of title.

Part V Commercial

24. Seller in possession after sale

Where a person having sold goods continues or is in possession of the goods, or of the documents of title to the goods, the delivery or transfer by that person, or by a mercantile agent acting for him, of the goods or documents of title under any sale, pledge, or other disposition thereof, to any person receiving the same in good faith and without notice of the previous sale, has the same effect as if the person making the delivery or transfer were expressly authorised by the owner of the goods to make the same.

25. Buyer in possession after sale

(1)   Where a person having bought or agreed to buy goods obtains, with the consent of the seller, possession of the goods or the documents of title to the goods, the delivery or transfer by that person, or by a mercantile agent acting for him, of the goods or documents of title, under any sale, pledge, or other disposition thereof, to any person receiving the same in good faith and without notice of any lien or other right of the original seller in respect of the goods, has the same effect as if the person making the delivery or transfer were a mercantile agent in possession of the goods or documents of title with the consent of the owner.

(2)   For the purposes of subsection (1) above—

   (a)   the buyer under a conditional sale agreement is to be taken not to be a person who has bought or agreed to buy goods, and

   (b)   'conditional sale agreement' means an agreement for the sale of goods which is a consumer credit agreement within the meaning of the Consumer Credit Act 1974 under which the purchase price or part of it is payable by instalments, and the property in the goods is to remain in the seller (notwithstanding that the buyer is to be in possession of the goods) until such conditions as to the payment of instalments or otherwise as may be specified in the agreement are fulfilled.

(3)   Paragraph 9 of Schedule 1 below applies in relation to a contract under which a person buys or agrees to buy goods and which is made before the appointed day.

(4)   In subsection (3) above and paragraph 9 of Schedule 1 below references to the appointed day are to the day appointed for the purposes of those provisions by an order of the Secretary of State made by statutory instrument.

26. Supplementary to sections 24 and 25

In sections 24 and 25 above 'mercantile agent' means a mercantile agent having in the customary course of his business as such agent authority either—

   (a)   to sell goods, or
   (b)   to consign goods for the purpose of sale, or
   (c)   to buy goods, or
   (d)   to raise money on the security of goods.

PART IV

PERFORMANCE OF THE CONTRACT

27. Duties of seller and buyer

It is the duty of the seller to deliver the goods, and of the buyer to accept and pay for them, in accordance with the terms of the contract of sale.

28. Payment and delivery are concurrent conditions

Unless otherwise agreed, delivery of the goods and payment of the price are concurrent conditions, that is to say, the seller must be ready and willing to give possession of the goods to the buyer in exchange for the price and the buyer must be ready and willing to pay the price in exchange for possession of the goods.

29. Rules about delivery

(1)   Whether it is for the buyer to take possession of the goods or for the seller to send them to the buyer is a question depending in each case on the contract, express or implied, between the parties.

(2)   Apart from any such contract, express or implied, the place of delivery is the seller's place of business if he has one, and if not, his residence; except that, if the contract is for the sale of specific goods, which to the knowledge of the parties when the contract is made are in some other place, then that place is the place of delivery.

(3)   Where under the contract of sale the seller is bound to send the goods to the buyer, but no time for sending them is fixed, the seller is bound to send them within a reasonable time.

(4)   Where the goods at the time of sale are in the possession of a third person, there is no delivery by seller to buyer unless and until the third person acknowledges to the buyer that he holds the goods on his behalf; but nothing in this section affects the operation of the issue or transfer of any document of title to goods.

(5)   Demand or tender of delivery may be treated as ineffectual unless made at a reasonable hour; and what is a reasonable hour is a question of fact.

(6)   Unless otherwise agreed, the expenses of and incidental to putting the goods into a deliverable state must be borne by the seller.

30.   Delivery of wrong quantity

(1)   Where the seller delivers to the buyer a quantity of goods less than he contracted to sell, the buyer may reject them, but if the buyer accepts the goods so delivered he must pay for them at the contract rate.

(2)   Where the seller delivers to the buyer a quantity of goods larger than he contracted to sell, the buyer may accept the goods included in the contract and reject the rest, or he may reject the whole.

(2A)   A buyer who does not deal as consumer may not—

(a)   where the seller delivers a quantity of goods less than he contracted to sell, reject the goods under subsection (1) above, or

(b)   where the seller delivers a quantity of goods larger than he contracted to sell, reject the whole under subsection (2) above,

if the shortfall or, as the case may be, excess is so slight that it would be unreasonable for him to do so.

(2B)   It is for the seller to show that a shortfall or excess fell within subsection (2A) above.

(2C)   Subsections (2A) and (2B) above do not apply to Scotland.

(2D)   [applies to Scotland only]

(2E)   [applies to Scotland only]

(3)   Where the seller delivers to the buyer a quantity of goods larger than he contracted to sell and the buyer accepts the whole of the goods so delivered he must pay for them at the contract rate.

(5)   This section is subject to any usage of trade, special agreement, or course of dealing between the parties.

31.   Instalment deliveries

(1)   Unless otherwise agreed, the buyer of goods is not bound to accept delivery of them by instalments.

(2)   Where there is a contract for the sale of goods to be delivered by stated instalments, which are to be separately paid for, and the seller makes defective deliveries in respect of one or more instalments, or the buyer neglects or refuses to take delivery of or pay for one or more instalments, it is a question in each case depending on the terms of the contract and the circumstances of the case whether the breach of contract is a repudiation of the whole contract or whether it is a severable breach giving rise to a claim for compensation but not to a right to treat the whole contract as repudiated.

32.   Delivery to carrier

(1)   Where, in pursuance of a contract of sale, the seller is authorised or required to send the goods to the buyer, delivery of the goods to a carrier (whether named by the buyer or not) for the purpose of transmission to the buyer is prima facie deemed to be a delivery of the goods to the buyer.

(2)   Unless otherwise authorised by the buyer, the seller must make such contract with the carrier on behalf of the buyer as may be reasonable having regard to the nature of the goods and the other circumstances of the case; and if the seller omits to do so, and the goods are lost or damaged in course of transit, the buyer may decline to treat the delivery to the carrier as a delivery to himself or may hold the seller responsible in damages.

Part V   Commercial

(3)   Unless otherwise agreed, where goods are sent by the seller to the buyer by a route involving sea transit, under circumstances in which it is usual to insure, the seller must give such notice to the buyer as may enable him to insure them during their sea transit; and if the seller fails to do so, the goods are at his risk during such sea transit.

(4) In a case where the buyer deals as consumer or, in Scotland, where there is a consumer contract in which the buyer is a consumer, subsections (1) to (3) above must be ignored, but if in pursuance of a contract of sale the seller is authorised or required to send the goods to the buyer, delivery of the goods to the carrier is not delivery of the goods to the buyer.

33.   Risk where goods are delivered at distant place

Where the seller of goods agrees to deliver them at his own risk at a place other than that where they are when sold, the buyer must nevertheless (unless otherwise agreed) take any risk of deterioration in the goods necessarily incident to the course of transit.

34.   Buyer's right of examining the goods

Unless otherwise agreed, when the seller tenders delivery of goods to the buyer, he is bound on request to afford the buyer a reasonable opportunity of examining the goods for the purpose of ascertaining whether they are in conformity with the contract and, in the case of a contract for sale by sample, of comparing the bulk with the sample.

35.   Acceptance

(1)   The buyer is deemed to have accepted the goods subject to subsection (2) below—

(a)   when he intimates to the seller that he has accepted them, or
(b)   when the goods have been delivered to him and he does any act in relation to them which is inconsistent with the ownership of the seller.

(2)   Where goods are delivered to the buyer, and he has not previously examined them, he is not deemed to have accepted them under subsection (1) above until he has had a reasonable opportunity of examining them for the purpose—

(a)   of ascertaining whether they are in conformity with the contract, and
(b)   in the case of a contract for sale by sample, of comparing the bulk with the sample.

(3)   Where the buyer deals as consumer or (in Scotland) the contract of sale is a consumer contract, the buyer cannot lose his right to rely on subsection (2) above by agreement, waiver or otherwise.

(4)   The buyer is also deemed to have accepted the goods when after the lapse of a reasonable time he retains the goods without intimating to the seller that he has rejected them.

(5)   The questions that are material in determining for the purposes of subsection (4) above whether a reasonable time has elapsed include whether the buyer has had a reasonable opportunity of examining the goods for the purpose mentioned in subsection (2) above.

(6)   The buyer is not by virtue of this section deemed to have accepted the goods merely because—

(a)   he asks for, or agrees to, their repair by or under an arrangement with the seller, or
(b)   the goods are delivered to another under a sub-sale or other disposition.

(7)   Where the contract is for the sale of goods making one or more commercial units, a buyer accepting any goods included in a unit is deemed to have accepted all the goods making the unit; and in this subsection 'commercial unit' means a unit division of which would materially impair the value of the goods or the character of the unit.

(8)   Paragraph 10 of Schedule 1 below applies in relation to a contract made before 22 April 1967 or (in the application of this Act of Northern Ireland) 28 July 1967.

35A.   Right of partial rejection

(1)   If the buyer—

(a)   has the right to reject the goods by reason of a breach on the part of the seller that affects some or all of them, but
(b)   accepts some of the goods, including, where there are any goods unaffected by the breach, all such goods

he does not by accepting them lose his right to reject the rest.

(2)   In the case of a buyer having the right to reject an instalment of goods, subsection (1) above applies as if references to the goods were references to the goods comprised in the instalment.

(3)   For the purposes of subsection (1) above, goods are affected by a breach if by reason of the breach they are not in conformity with the contract.

(4)   This section applies unless a contrary intention appears in, or is to be implied from, the contract.

36.   Buyer not bound to return rejected goods

Unless otherwise agreed, where goods are delivered to the buyer, and he refuses to accept them, having the right to do so, he is not bound to return them to the seller, but it is sufficient if he intimates to the seller that he refuses to accept them.

37.   Buyer's liability for not taking delivery of goods

(1)   When the seller is ready and willing to deliver the goods, and requests the buyer to take delivery, and the buyer does not within a reasonable time after such request take delivery of the goods, he is liable to the seller for any loss occasioned by his neglect or refusal to take delivery, and also for a reasonable charge for the care and custody of the goods.

(2)   Nothing in this section affects the rights of the seller where the neglect or refusal of the buyer to take delivery amounts to a repudiation of the contract.

PART V

RIGHTS OF UNPAID SELLER AGAINST THE GOODS

38.   Unpaid seller defined

(1)   The seller of goods is an unpaid seller within the meaning of this Act—

   (a)   when the whole of the price has not been paid or tendered;
   (b)   when a bill of exchange or other negotiable instrument has been received as conditional payment, and the condition on which it was received has not been fulfilled by reason of the dishonour of the instrument or otherwise.

(2)   In this Part of this Act 'seller' includes any person who is in the position of a seller, as, for instance, an agent of the seller to whom the bill of lading has been indorsed, or a consignor or agent who has himself paid (or is directly responsible for) the price.

39.   Unpaid seller's rights

(1)   Subject to this and any other Act, notwithstanding that the property in the goods may have passed to the buyer, the unpaid seller of goods, as such, has by implication of law—

   (a)   a lien on the goods or right to retain them for the price while he is in possession of them;
   (b)   in case of the insolvency of the buyer, a right of stopping the goods in transit after he has parted with the possession of them;
   (c)   a right of re-sale as limited by this Act.

(2)   Where the property in goods has not passed to the buyer, the unpaid seller has (in addition to his other remedies) a right of withholding delivery similar to and co-extensive with his rights of lien or retention and stoppage in transit where the property has passed to the buyer.

41.   Seller's lien

(1)   Subject to this Act, the unpaid seller of goods who is in possession of them is entitled to retain possession of them until payment or tender of the price in the following cases—

   (a)   where the goods have been sold without any stipulation as to credit;
   (b)   where the goods have been sold on credit but the term of credit has expired;
   (c)   where the buyer becomes insolvent.

Part V Commercial

(2)   The seller may exercise his lien or right of retention notwithstanding that he is in possession of the goods as agent or bailee or custodier for the buyer.

42.   Part delivery

Where an unpaid seller has made part delivery of the goods, he may exercise his lien or right of retention on the remainder, unless such part delivery has been made under such circumstances as to show an agreement to waive the lien or right of retention.

43.   Termination of lien

(1)   The unpaid seller of goods loses his lien or right of retention in respect of them—

      (a)   when he delivers the goods to a carrier or other bailee or custodier for the purpose of transmission to the buyer without reserving the right of disposal of the goods;

      (b)   when the buyer or his agent lawfully obtains possession of the goods;

      (c)   by waiver of the lien or right of retention.

(2)   An unpaid seller of goods who has a lien or right of retention in respect of them does not lose his lien or right of retention by reason only that he has obtained judgment or decree for the price of the goods.

44.   Right of stoppage in transit

Subject to this Act, when the buyer of goods becomes insolvent the unpaid seller who has parted with the possession of the goods has the right of stopping them in transit, that is to say, he may resume possession of the goods as long as they are in course of transit, and may retain them until payment or tender of the price.

45.   Duration of transit

(1)   Goods are deemed to be in course of transit from the time when they are delivered to a carrier or other bailee or custodier for the purpose of transmission to the buyer, until the buyer or his agent in that behalf takes delivery of them from the carrier or other bailee or custodier.

(2)   If the buyer or his agent in that behalf obtains delivery of the goods before their arrival at the appointed destination, the transit is at an end.

(3)   If, after the arrival of the goods at the appointed destination, the carrier or other bailee or custodier acknowledges to the buyer or his agent that he holds the goods on his behalf and continues in possession of them as bailee or custodier for the buyer or his agent, the transit is at an end, and it is immaterial that a further destination for the goods may have been indicated by the buyer.

(4)   If the goods are rejected by the buyer, and the carrier or other bailee or custodier continues in possession of them, the transit is not deemed to be at an end, even if the seller has refused to receive them back.

(5)   When goods are delivered to a ship chartered by the buyer it is a question depending on the circumstances of the particular case whether they are in the possession of the master as a carrier or as agent to the buyer.

(6)   Where the carrier or other bailee or custodier wrongfully refuses to deliver the goods to the buyer or his agent in that behalf, the transit is deemed to be at an end.

(7)   Where part delivery of the goods has been made to the buyer or his agent in that behalf, the remainder of the goods may be stopped in transit, unless such part delivery has been made under such circumstances as to show an agreement to give up possession of the whole of the goods.

46.   How stoppage in transit is effected

(1)   The unpaid seller may exercise his right of stoppage in transit either by taking actual possession of the goods or by giving notice of his claim to the carrier or other bailee or custodier in whose possession the goods are.

(2)   The notice may be given to the person in actual possession of the goods or to his principal.

(3)   If given to the principal, the notice is ineffective unless given at such time and under such circumstances that the principal, by the exercise of reasonable diligence, may communicate it to his servant or agent in time to prevent a delivery to the buyer.

(4) When notice of stoppage in transit is given by the seller to the carrier or other bailee or custodier in possession of the goods, he must re-deliver the goods to, or according to the directions of, the seller; and the expenses of the re-delivery must be borne by the seller.

47. Effect of sub-sale etc by buyer

(1) Subject to this Act, the unpaid seller's right of lien or retention or stoppage in transit is not affected by any sale or other disposition of the goods which the buyer may have made, unless the seller has assented to it.

(2) Where a document of title to goods has been lawfully transferred to any person as buyer or owner of the goods, and that person transfers the document to a person who takes it in good faith and for valuable consideration, then—

   (a) if the last-mentioned transfer was by way of sale the unpaid seller's right of lien or retention or stoppage in transit is defeated; and
   (b) if the last-mentioned transfer was made by way of pledge or other disposition for value, the unpaid seller's right of lien or retention or stoppage in transit can only be exercised subject to the rights of the transferee.

48. Rescission: and re-sale by seller

(1) Subject to this section, a contract of sale is not rescinded by the mere exercise by an unpaid seller of his right of lien or retention or stoppage in transit.

(2) Where an unpaid seller who has exercised his right of lien or retention or stoppage in transit re-sells the goods, the buyer acquires a good title to them as against the original buyer.

(3) Where the goods are of a perishable nature, or where the unpaid seller gives notice to the buyer of his intention to re-sell, and the buyer does not within a reasonable time pay or tender the price, the unpaid seller may re-sell the goods and recover from the original buyer damages for any loss occasioned by his breach of contract.

(4) Where the seller expressly reserves the right of re-sale in case the buyer should make default, and on the buyer making default re-sells the goods, the original contract of sale is rescinded but without prejudice to any claim the seller may have for damages.

PART 5A

ADDITIONAL RIGHTS OF BUYER IN CONSUMER CASES

48A. Introductory

(1) This section applies if—

   (a) the buyer deals as consumer or, in Scotland, there is a consumer contract in which the buyer is a consumer, and
   (b) the goods do not conform to the contract of sale at the time of delivery.

(2) If this section applies, the buyer has the right—

   (a) under and in accordance with section 48B below, to require the seller to repair or replace the goods, or
   (b) under and in accordance with section 48C below—

      (i) to require the seller to reduce the purchase price of the goods to the buyer by an appropriate amount, or
      (ii) to rescind the contract with regard to the goods in question.

(3) For the purposes of subsection (1)(b) above goods which do not conform to the contract of sale at any time within the period of six months starting with the date on which the goods were delivered to the buyer must be taken not to have so conformed at that date.

(4) Subsection (3) above does not apply if—

   (a) it is established that the goods did so conform at that date;
   (b) its application is incompatible with the nature of the goods or the nature of the lack of conformity.

48B. Repair or replacement of the goods

(1)   If section 48A above applies, the buyer may require the seller—

    (a)   to repair the goods, or

    (b)   to replace the goods.

(2)   If the buyer requires the seller to repair or replace the goods, the seller must—

    (a)   repair or, as the case may be, replace the goods within a reasonable time but without causing significant inconvenience to the buyer;

    (b)   bear any necessary costs incurred in doing so (including in particular the cost of any labour, materials or postage).

(3)   The buyer must not require the seller to repair or, as the case may be, replace the goods if that remedy is—

    (a)   impossible, or

    (b)   disproportionate in comparison to the other of those remedies, or

    (c)   disproportionate in comparison to an appropriate reduction in the purchase price under paragraph (a), or rescission under paragraph (b), of section 48C(1) below.

(4)   One remedy is disproportionate in comparison to the other if the one imposes costs on the seller which, in comparison to those imposed on him by the other, are unreasonable, taking into account—

    (a)   the value which the goods would have if they conformed to the contract of sale,

    (b)   the significance of the lack of conformity, and

    (c)   whether the other remedy could be effected without significant inconvenience to the buyer.

(5)   Any question as to what is a reasonable time or significant inconvenience is to be determined by reference to—

    (a)   the nature of the goods, and

    (b)   the purpose for which the goods were acquired.

48C. Reduction of purchase price or rescission of contract

(1)   If section 48A above applies, the buyer may—

    (a)   require the seller to reduce the purchase price of the goods in question to the buyer by an appropriate amount, or

    (b)   rescind the contract with regard to those goods,

if the condition in subsection (2) below is satisfied.

(2)   The condition is that—

    (a)   by virtue of section 48B(3) above the buyer may require neither repair nor replacement of the goods; or

    (b)   the buyer has required the seller to repair or replace the goods, but the seller is in breach of the requirement of section 48B(2)(a) above to do so within a reasonable time and without significant inconvenience to the buyer.

(3)   For the purposes of this Part, if the buyer rescinds the contract, any reimbursement to the buyer may be reduced to take account of the use he has had of the goods since they were delivered to him.

48D. Relation to other remedies etc

(1)   If the buyer requires the seller to repair or replace the goods the buyer must not act under subsection (2) until he has given the seller a reasonable time in which to repair or replace (as the case may be) the goods.

(2)   The buyer acts under this subsection if—

    (a)   in England and Wales or Northern Ireland he rejects the goods and terminates the contract for breach of condition;

    (b)   in Scotland he rejects any goods delivered under the contract and treats it as repudiated;

    (c)   he requires the goods to be replaced or repaired (as the case may be).

48E. Powers of the court

(1)   In any proceedings in which a remedy is sought by virtue of this Part the court, in addition to any other power it has, may act under this section.

(2)   On the application of the buyer the court may make an order requiring specific performance or, in Scotland, specific implement by the seller of any obligation imposed on him by virtue of section 48B above.

(3)   Subsection (4) applies if—

    (a)   the buyer requires the seller to give effect to a remedy under section 48B or 48C above or has claims to rescind under section 48C, but

    (b)   the court decides that another remedy under section 48B or 48C is appropriate.

(4)   The court may proceed—

    (a)   as if the buyer had required the seller to give effect to the other remedy, or if the other remedy is rescission under section 48C

    (b)   as if the buyer had claimed to rescind the contract under that section.

(5)   If the buyer has claimed to rescind the contract the court may order that any reimbursement to the buyer is reduced to take account of the use he has had of the goods since they were delivered to him.

(6)   The court may make an order under this section unconditionally or on such terms and conditions as to damages, payment of the price and otherwise as it thinks just.

48F. Conformity with the contract

For the purposes of this Part, goods do not conform to a contract of sale if there is, in relation to the goods, a breach of an express term of the contract or a term implied by section 13, 14 or 15 above.

PART VI

ACTIONS FOR BREACH OF CONTRACT

49.   Action for price

(1)   Where, under a contract of sale, the property in the goods has passed to the buyer and he wrongfully neglects or refuses to pay for the goods according to the terms of the contract, the seller may maintain an action against him for the price of the goods.

(2)   Where, under a contract of sale, the price is payable on a day certain irrespective of delivery and the buyer wrongfully neglects or refuses to pay such price, the seller may maintain an action for the price, although the property in the goods has not passed and the goods have not been appropriated to the contract.

50.   Damages for non-acceptance

(1)   Where the buyer wrongfully neglects or refuses to accept and pay for the goods, the seller may maintain an action against him for damages for non-acceptance.

(2)   The measure of damages is the estimated loss directly and naturally resulting, in the ordinary course of events, from the buyer's breach of contract.

(3)   Where there is an available market for the goods in question the measure of damages is prima facie to be ascertained by the difference between the contract price and the market or current price at the time or times when the goods ought to have been accepted or (if no time was fixed for acceptance) at the time of the refusal to accept.

51.   Damages for non-delivery

(1)   Where the seller wrongfully neglects or refuses to deliver the goods to the buyer, the buyer may maintain an action against the seller for damages for non-delivery.

(2)   The measure of damages is the estimated loss directly and naturally resulting, in the ordinary course of events, from the seller's breach of contract.

(3)　Where there is an available market for the goods in question the measure of damages is prima facie to be ascertained by the difference between the contract price and the market or current price of the goods at the time or times when they ought to have been delivered or (if no time was fixed) at the time of the refusal to deliver.

52.　Specific performance

(1)　In any action for breach of contract to deliver specific or ascertained goods the court may, if it thinks fit, on the plaintiff's application, by its judgment or decree direct that the contract shall be performed specifically, without giving the defendant the option of retaining the goods on payment of damages.

(2)　The plaintiff's application may be made at any time before judgment or decree.

(3)　The judgment or decree may be unconditional, or on such terms and conditions as to damages, payment of the price and otherwise as seem just to the court.

53.　Remedy for breach of warranty

(1)　Where there is a breach of warranty by the seller, or where the buyer elects (or is compelled) to treat any breach of a condition on the part of the seller as a breach of warranty, the buyer is not by reason only of such breach of warranty entitled to reject the goods; but he may—

(a)　set up against the seller the breach of warranty in diminution or extinction of the price, or
(b)　maintain an action against the seller for damages for the breach of warranty.

(2)　The measure of damages for breach of warranty is the estimated loss directly and naturally resulting, in the ordinary course of events, from the breach of warranty.

(3)　In the case of breach of warranty of quality such loss is prima facie the difference between the value of the goods at the time of delivery to the buyer and the value they would have had if they had fulfilled the warranty.

(4)　The fact that the buyer has set up the breach of warranty in diminution or extinction of the price does not prevent him from maintaining an action for the same breach of warranty if he has suffered further damage.

(5)　This section does not apply to Scotland.

54.　Interest

Nothing in this Act affects the right of the buyer or the seller to recover interest or special damages in any case where by law interest or special damages may be recoverable, or to recover money paid where the consideration for the payment of it has failed.

PART VII

SUPPLEMENTARY

55.　Exclusion of implied terms

(1)　Where a right, duty or liability would arise under a contract of sale of goods by implication of law, it may (subject to the Unfair Contract Terms Act 1977) be negatived or varied by express agreement, or by the course of dealing between the parties, or by such usage as binds both parties to the contract.

(2)　An express term does not negative a term implied by this Act unless inconsistent with it.

(3)　Paragraph 11 of Schedule 1 below applies in relation to a contract made on or after 18 May 1973 and before 1 February 1978, and paragraph 12 in relation to one made before 18 May 1973.

57.　Auction sales

(1)　Where goods are put up for sale by auction in lots, each lot is prima facie deemed to be the subject of a separate contract of sale.

(2)　A sale by auction is complete when the auctioneer announces its completion by the fall of the hammer, or in other customary manner; and until the announcement is made any bidder may retract his bid.

(3)　A sale by auction may be notified to be subject to a reserve or upset price, and a right to bid may also be reserved expressly by or on behalf of the seller.

(4)   Where a sale by auction is not notified to be subject to a right to bid by or on behalf of the seller, it is not lawful for the seller to bid himself or to employ any person to bid at the sale, or for the auctioneer knowingly to take any bid from the seller or any such person.

(5)   A sale contravening subsection (4) above may be treated as fraudulent by the buyer.

(6)   Where, in respect of a sale by auction, a right to bid is expressly reserved (but not otherwise) the seller or any one person on his behalf may bid at the auction.

59.   Reasonable time a question of fact

Where a reference is made in this Act to a reasonable time the question what is a reasonable time is a question of fact.

60.   Rights etc enforceable by action

Where a right, duty or liability is declared by this Act, it may (unless otherwise provided by this Act) be enforced by action.

61.   Interpretation

(1)   In this Act, unless the context or subject matter otherwise requires,—

'action' includes counterclaim and set-off, and in Scotland condescendence and claim and compensation;
'bulk' means a mass or collection of goods of the same kind which—

(a)   is contained in a defined space or area; and

(b)   is such that any goods in the bulk are interchangeable with any other goods therein of the same number or quantity;

'business' includes a profession and the activities of any government department (including a Northern Ireland department) or local or public authority;
'buyer' means a person who buys or agrees to buy goods;
'contract of sale' includes an agreement to sell as well as a sale;
'consumer contract' has the same meaning as in section 25(1) of the Unfair Contract Terms Act 1977; and for the purposes of this Act the onus of proving that a contract is not to be regarded as a consumer contract shall lie on the seller;
'credit-broker' means a person acting in the course of a business of credit brokerage carried on by him, that is a business of effecting introductions of individuals desiring to obtain credit—

(a)   to persons carrying on any business so far as it relates to the provision of credit, or

(b)   to other persons engaged in credit brokerage;

'delivery' means voluntary transfer of possession from one person to another except that in relation to sections 20A and 20B above it includes such appropriation of goods to the contract as results in property in the goods being transferred to the buyer;
'document of title to goods' has the same meaning as it has in the Factors Acts;
'Factors Acts' means the Factors Act 1889, the Factors (Scotland) Act 1890, and any enactment amending or substituted for the same;
'fault' means wrongful act or default;
'future goods' means goods to be manufactured or acquired by the seller after the making of the contract of sale;
'goods' includes all personal chattels other than things in action and money, and in Scotland all corporeal moveables except money; and in particular 'goods' includes emblements, industrial growing crops, and things attached to or forming part of the land which are agreed to be severed before sale or under the contract of sale and includes an undivided share in goods;
'plaintiff' includes pursuer, complainer, claimant in a multiplepoinding and defendant or defender counter-claiming;
'producer' means the manufacturer of goods, the importer of goods into the European Economic Area or any person purporting to be a producer by placing his name, trade mark or other distinctive sign on the goods;
'property' means the general property in goods, and not merely a special property;
'repair' means, in cases where there is a lack of conformity in goods for the purposes of section 48F of this Act, to bring the goods into conformity with the contract;
'sale' includes a bargain and sale as well as a sale and delivery;

Part V   Commercial

'seller' means a person who sells or agrees to sell goods;

'specific goods' means goods identified and agreed on at the time a contract of sale is made and includes an undivided share, specified as a fraction or percentage, of goods identified and agreed on as aforesaid;

'warranty' (as regards England and Wales and Northern Ireland) means an agreement with reference to goods which are the subject of a contract of sale, but collateral to the main purpose of such contract, the breach of which gives rise to a claim for damages, but not to a right to reject the goods and treat the contract as repudiated.

(3)   A thing is deemed to be done in good faith within the meaning of this Act when it is in fact done honestly, whether it is done negligently or not.

(4)   A person is deemed to be insolvent within the meaning of this Act if he has either ceased to pay his debts in the ordinary course of business or he cannot pay his debts as they become due.

(5)   Goods are in a deliverable state within the meaning of this Act when they are in such a state that the buyer would under the contract be bound to take delivery of them.

(5A) References in this Act to dealing as consumer are to be construed in accordance with Part I of the Unfair Contract Terms Act 1977; and, for the purposes of this Act, it is for a seller claiming that the buyer does not deal as consumer to show that he does not.

(6)   As regards the definition of 'business' in subsection (1) above, paragraph 14 of Schedule 1 below applies in relation to a contract made on or after 18 May 1973 and before 1 February 1978, and paragraph 15 in relation to one made before 18 May 1973.

62.   Savings: rules of law etc

(1)   The rules in bankruptcy relating to contracts of sale apply to those contracts, notwithstanding anything in this Act.

(2)   The rules of the common law, including the law merchant, except in so far as they are inconsistent with the provisions of this Act, and in particular the rules relating to the law of principal and agent and the effect of fraud, misrepresentation, duress or coercion, mistake, or other invalidating cause, apply to contracts for the sale of goods.

(3)   Nothing in this Act or the Sale of Goods Act 1893 affects the enactments relating to bills of sale, or any enactment relating to the sale of goods which is not expressly repealed or amended by this Act or that.

(4)   The provisions of this Act about contracts of sale do not apply to a transaction in the form of a contract of sale which is intended to operate by way of mortgage, pledge, charge, or other security.

Commercial Agents (Council Directive) Regulations 1993, SI 1993/3053

PART I

GENERAL

1.   Citation, commencement and applicable law

(1)   These Regulations may be cited as the Commercial Agents (Council Directive) Regulations 1993 and shall come into force on 1st January 1994.

(2)   These Regulations govern the relations between commercial agents and their principals and, subject to paragraph (3), apply in relation to the activities of commercial agents in Great Britain.

(3)   A court or tribunal shall:

(a)   apply the law of the other member State concerned in place of regulations 3 to 22 where the parties have agreed that the agency contract is to be governed by the law of that member State;

(b)   (whether or not it would otherwise be required to do so) apply these regulations where the law of another member State corresponding to these regulations enables the parties to agree that the agency contract is to be governed by the law of a different member State and the parties have agreed that it is to be governed by the law of England and Wales or Scotland.

2.   Interpretation, application and extent

(1)   In these Regulations—

'commercial agent' means a self-employed intermediary who has continuing authority to negotiate the sale or purchase of goods on behalf of another person (the 'principal'), or to negotiate and conclude the sale or purchase of goods on behalf of and in the name of that principal; but shall be understood as not including in particular:

(i)   a person who, in his capacity as an officer of a company or association, is empowered to enter into commitments binding on that company or association;

(ii)   a partner who is lawfully authorised to enter into commitments binding on his partners;

(iii)   a person who acts as an insolvency practitioner (as that expression is defined in section 388 of the Insolvency Act 1986) or the equivalent in any other jurisdiction;

'commission' means any part of the remuneration of a commercial agent which varies with the number or value of business transactions;

'EEA Agreement' means the Agreement on the European Economic Area signed at Oporto on 2nd May 1992 as adjusted by the Protocol signed at Brussels on 17th March 1993;

'member State' includes a State which is a contracting party to the EEA Agreement;

'restraint of trade clause' means an agreement restricting the business activities of a commercial agent following termination of the agency contract.

(2)   These Regulations do not apply to—

(a)   commercial agents whose activities are unpaid;

(b)   commercial agents when they operate on commodity exchanges or in the commodity market;

(c)   the Crown Agents for Overseas Governments and Administrations, as set up under the Crown Agents Act 1979, or its subsidiaries.

(3)   The provisions of the Schedule to these Regulations have effect for the purpose of determining the persons whose activities as commercial agents are to be considered secondary.

(4)   These Regulations shall not apply to the persons referred to in paragraph (3) above.

(5)   These Regulations do not extend to Northern Ireland.

Part V Commercial

PART II

RIGHTS AND OBLIGATIONS

3.   Duties of a commercial agent to his principal

(1)   In performing his activities a commercial agent must look after the interests of his principal and act dutifully and in good faith.

(2)   In particular, a commercial agent must—

(a)   make proper efforts to negotiate and, where appropriate, conclude the transactions he is instructed to take care of:

(b)   communicate to his principal all the necessary information available to him:

(c)   comply with reasonable instructions given by his principal.

4.   Duties of a principal to his commercial agent

(1)   In his relations with his commercial agent a principal must act dutifully and in good faith.

(2)   In particular, a principal must—

(a)   provide his commercial agent with the necessary documentation relating to the goods concerned:

(b)   obtain for his commercial agent the information necessary for the performance of the agency contract, and in particular notify his commercial agent within a reasonable period once he anticipates that the volume of commercial transactions will be significantly lower than that which the commercial agent could normally have expected.

(3)   A principal shall, in addition, inform his commercial agent within a reasonable period of his acceptance or refusal of, and of any non-execution by him of, a commercial transaction which the commercial agent has procured for him.

5.   Prohibition on derogation from regulations 3 and 4 and consequence of breach

(1)   The parties may not derogate from regulations 3 and 4 above.

(2)   The law applicable to the contract shall govern the consequence of breach of the rights and obligations under regulations 3 and 4 above.

PART III

REMUNERATION

6.   Form and amount of remuneration in absence of agreement

(1)   In the absence of any agreement as to remuneration between the parties, a commercial agent shall be entitled to the remuneration that commercial agents appointed for the goods forming the subject of his agency contract are customarily allowed in the place where he carries on his activities and, if there is no such customary practice, a commercial agent shall be entitled to reasonable remuneration taking into account all the aspects of the transaction.

(2)   This regulation is without prejudice to the application of any enactment or rule of law concerning the level of remuneration.

(3)   Where a commercial agent is not remunerated (wholly or in part) by commission, regulations 7 to 12 below shall not apply.

7.   Entitlement to commission on transactions concluded during agency contract

(1)   A commercial agent shall be entitled to commission on commercial transactions concluded during the period covered by the agency contract—

(a)   where the transaction has been concluded as a result of his action; or

(b)   where the transaction is concluded with a third party whom he has previously acquired as a customer for transaction of the same kind.

(2)   A commercial agent shall also be entitled to commission on transactions concluded during the period covered by the agency contract where he has an exclusive right to a specific geographical area or to a specific group of customers and where the transaction has been entered into with a customer belonging to that area or group.

8.   Entitlement to commission on transactions concluded after agency contract has terminated

Subject to regulation 9 below, a commercial agent shall be entitled to commission on commercial transactions concluded after the agency contract has terminated if—

(a)   the transaction is mainly attributable to his efforts during the period covered by the agency contract and if the transaction was entered into within a reasonable period after that contract terminated; or

(b)   in accordance with the conditions mentioned in regulation 7 above, the order of the third party reached the principal or the commercial agent before the agency contract terminated.

9.   Apportionment of commission between new and previous commercial agents

(1)   A commercial agent shall not be entitled to the commission referred to in regulation 7 above if that commission is payable, by virtue of regulation 8 above, to the previous commercial agent, unless it is equitable because of the circumstances for the commission to be shared between the commercial agents.

(2)   The principal shall be liable for any sum due under paragraph (1) above to the person entitled to it in accordance with that paragraph, and any sum which the other commercial agent receives to which he is not entitled shall be refunded to the principal.

10.   When commission due and date for payment

(1)   Commission shall become due as soon as, and to the extent that, one of the following circumstances occurs:

(a)   the principal has executed the transaction; or

(b)   the principal should, according to his agreement with the third party, have executed the transaction; or

(c)   the third party has executed the transaction.

(2)   Commission shall become due at the latest when the third party has executed his part of the transaction or should have done so if the principal had executed his part of the transaction, as he should have.

(3)   The commission shall be paid not later than on the last day of the month following the quarter in which it became due, and, for the purposes of these Regulations, unless otherwise agreed between the parties, the first quarter period shall run from the date the agency contract takes effect, and subsequent periods shall run from that date in the third month thereafter or the beginning of the fourth month, whichever is the sooner.

(4)   Any agreement to derogate from paragraphs (2) and (3) above to the detriment of the commercial agent shall be void.

11.   Extinction of right to commission

(1)   The right to commission can be extinguished only if and to the extent that—

(a)   it is established that the contract between the third party and the principal will not be executed; and

(b)   that fact is due to a reason for which the principal is not to blame.

(2)   Any commission which the commercial agent has already received shall be refunded if the right to it is extinguished.

(3)   Any agreement to derogate from paragraph (1) above to the detriment of the commercial agent shall be void.

12.   Periodic supply of information as to commission due and right of inspection of principal's books

(1)   The principal shall supply his commercial agent with a statement of the commission due, not later than the last day of the month following the quarter in which the commission has become due, and such statement shall set out the main components used in calculating the amount of the commission.

(2)   A commercial agent shall be entitled to demand that he be provided with all the information (and in particular an extract from the books) which is available to his principal and which he needs in order to check the amount of the commission due to him.

(3)   Any agreement to derogate from paragraphs (1) and (2) above shall be void.

Part V   Commercial

(4)   Nothing in this regulation shall remove or restrict the effect of, or prevent reliance upon, any enactment or rule of law which recognises the right of an agent to inspect the books of a principal.

PART IV

CONCLUSION AND TERMINATION OF THE AGENCY CONTRACT

13.   Right to signed written statement of terms of agency contract

(1)   The commercial agent and principal shall each be entitled to receive from the other, on request, a signed written document setting out the terms of the agency contract including any terms subsequently agreed.

(2)   Any purported waiver of the right referred to in paragraph (1) above shall be void.

14.   Conversion of agency contract after expiry of fixed period

Any agency contract for a fixed period which continues to be performed by both parties after that period has expired shall be deemed to be converted into an agency contract for an indefinite period.

15.   Minimum periods of notice for termination of agency contract

(1)   Where an agency contract is concluded for an indefinite period either party may terminate it by notice.

(2)   The period of notice shall be—

(a)   1 month for the first year of the contract;
(b)   2 months for the second year commenced;
(c)   3 months for the third year commenced and for the subsequent years;

and the parties may not agree on any shorter periods of notice.

(3)   If the parties agree on longer periods than those laid down in paragraph (2) above, the period of notice to be observed by the principal must not be shorter than that to be observed by the commercial agent.

(4)   Unless otherwise agreed by the parties, the end of the period of notice must coincide with the end of a calendar month.

(5)   The provisions of this regulation shall also apply to an agency contract for a fixed period where it is converted under regulation 14 above into an agency contract for an indefinite period subject to the proviso that the earlier fixed period must be taken into account in the calculation of the period of notice.

16.   Savings with regard to immediate termination

These Regulations shall not affect the application of any enactment or rule of law which provides for the immediate termination of the agency contract—

(a)   because of the failure of one party to carry out all or part of his obligations under that contract; or
(b)   where exceptional circumstances arise.

17.   Entitlement of commercial agent to indemnity or compensation on termination of agency contract

(1)   This regulation has effect for the purpose of ensuring that the commercial agent is, after termination of the agency contract, indemnified in accordance with paragraphs (3) to (5) below or compensated for damage in accordance with paragraphs (6) and (7) below.

(2)   Except where the agency contract otherwise provides, the commercial agent shall be entitled to be compensated rather than indemnified.

(3)   Subject to paragraph (9) and to regulation 18 below, the commercial agent shall be entitled to an indemnity if and to the extent that—

(a)   he has brought the principal new customers or has significantly increased the volume of business with existing customers and the principal continues to derive substantial benefits from the business with such customers; and
(b)   the payment of this indemnity is equitable having regard to all the circumstances and, in particular, the commission lost by the commercial agent on the business transacted with such customers.

(4)   The amount of the indemnity shall not exceed a figure equivalent to an indemnity for one year calculated from the commercial agent's average annual remuneration over the preceding five years and

if the contract goes back less than five years the indemnity shall be calculated on the average for the period in question.

(5) The grant of an indemnity as mentioned above shall not prevent the commercial agent from seeking damages.

(6) Subject to paragraph (9) and to regulation 18 below, the commercial agent shall be entitled to compensation for the damage he suffers as a result of the termination of his relations with his principal.

(7) For the purpose of these Regulations such damage shall be deemed to occur particularly when the termination takes place in either or both of the following circumstances, namely circumstances which—

    (a) deprive the commercial agent of the commission which proper performance of the agency contract would have procured for him whilst providing his principal with substantial benefits linked to the activities of the commercial agent; or

    (b) have not enabled the commercial agent to amortize the costs and expenses that he had incurred in the performance of the agency contract on the advice of his principal.

(8) Entitlement to the indemnity or compensation for damage as provided for under paragraphs (2) to (7) above shall also arise where the agency contract is terminated as a result of the death of the commercial agent.

(9) The commercial agent shall lose his entitlement to the indemnity or compensation for damage in the instances provided for in paragraphs (2) to (8) above if within one year following termination of his agency contract he has not notified his principal that he intends pursuing his entitlement.

18. Grounds for excluding payment of indemnity or compensation under regulation 17

The indemnity or compensation referred to in regulation 17 above shall not be payable to the commercial agent where—

    (a) the principal has terminated the agency contract because of default attributable to the commercial agent which would justify immediate termination of the agency contract pursuant to regulation 16 above; or

    (b) the commercial agent has himself terminated the agency contract, unless such termination is justified—

        (i) by circumstances attributable to the principal, or

        (ii) on grounds of the age, infirmity or illness of the commercial agent in consequence of which he cannot reasonably be required to continue his activities; or

    (c) the commercial agent, with the agreement of his principal, assigns his rights and duties under the agency contract to another person.

19. Prohibition on derogation from regulations 17 and 18

The parties may not derogate from regulations 17 and 18 to the detriment of the commercial agent before the agency contract expires.

20. Restraint of trade clauses

(1) A restraint of trade clause shall be valid only if and to the extent that—

    (a) it is concluded in writing; and

    (b) it relates to the geographical area or the group of customers and the geographical area entrusted to the commercial agent and to the kind of goods covered by his agency under the contract.

(2) A restraint of trade clause shall be valid for not more than two years after termination of the agency contract.

(3) Nothing in this regulation shall affect any enactment or rule of law which imposes other restrictions on the validity or enforceability of restraint of trade clauses or which enables a court to reduce the obligations on the parties resulting from such clauses.

Part V Commercial

PART V

MISCELLANEOUS AND SUPPLEMENTAL

21.   Disclosure of information

Nothing in these Regulations shall require information to be given where such disclosure would be contrary to public policy.

22.   Service of notice etc

(1)   Any notice, statement or other document to be given or supplied to a commercial agent or to be given or supplied to the principal under these Regulations may be so given or supplied:

(a)   by delivering it to him;

(b)   by leaving it at his proper address addressed to him by name;

(c)   by sending it by post to him addressed either to his registered address or to the address of his registered or principal office;

or by any other means provided for in the agency contract.

(2)   Any such notice, statement or document may—

(a)   in the case of a body corporate, be given or served on the secretary or clerk of that body;

(b)   in the case of a partnership, be given to or served on any partner or on any person having the control or management of the partnership business.

23.   Transitional provisions

(1)   Notwithstanding any provision in an agency contract made before 1st January 1994, these Regulations shall apply to that contract after that date and, accordingly any provision which is inconsistent with these Regulations shall have effect subject to them.

(2)   Nothing in these Regulations shall affect the rights and liabilities of a commercial agent or a principal which have accrued before 1st January 1994.

THE SCHEDULE

Regulation 2(3)

1.   The activities of a person as a commercial agent are to be considered secondary where it may reasonably be taken that the primary purpose of the arrangement with his principal is other than as set out in paragraph 2 below.

2.   An arrangement falls within this paragraph if—

(a)   the business of the principal is the sale, or as the case may be purchase, of goods of a particular kind; and

(b)   the goods concerned are such that—

(i)   transactions are normally individually negotiated and concluded on a commercial basis, and

(ii)   procuring a transaction on one occasion is likely to lead to further transactions in those goods with that customer on future occasions, or to transactions in those goods with other customers in the same geographical area or among the same group of customers, and

that accordingly it is in the commercial interests of the principal in developing the market in those goods to appoint a representative to such customers with a view to the representative devoting effort, skill and expenditure from his own resources to that end.

3.   The following are indications that an arrangement falls within paragraph 2 above, and the absence of any of them is an indication to the contrary—

(a)   the principal is the manufacturer, importer or distributor of the goods;

(b)   the goods are specifically identified with the principal in the market in question rather than, or to a greater extent than, with any other person;

(c)   the agent devotes substantially the whole of his time to representative activities (whether for one principal or for a number of principals whose interests are not conflicting);

(d)   the goods are not normally available in the market in question other than by means of the agent;

(e)   the arrangement is described as one of commercial agency.

4.   The following are indications that an arrangement does not fall within paragraph 2 above—

    (a)   promotional material is supplied direct to potential customers;

    (b)   persons are granted agencies without reference to existing agents in a particular area or in relation to a particular group;

    (c)   customers normally select the goods for themselves and merely place their orders through the agent.

5.   The activities of the following categories of persons are presumed, unless the contrary is established, not to fall within paragraph 2 above—

Mail order catalogue agents for consumer goods.
Consumer credit agents.

PART VI

EU

The EC Treaty (as amended by Treaty of Amsterdam)

PART ONE

PRINCIPLES

Article 2

The Community shall have as its task, by establishing a common market and an economic and monetary union and by implementing common policies or activities referred to in Articles 3 and 4, to promote throughout the Community a harmonious, balanced and sustained development of economic activities, a high level of employment and of social protection, equality between men and women, sustainable and non-inflationary growth, a high degree of competitiveness and convergence of economic performance, a high level of protection and improvement of the quality of the environment, the raising of the standard of living and quality of life, and economic and social cohesion and solidarity among Member States.

Article 3

(1)   For the purposes set out in Article 2, the activities of the Community shall include, as provided in this Treaty and in accordance with the timetable set out therein:

(a)   the prohibition, as between Member States, of customs duties and quantitative restrictions on the import and export of goods, and of all other measures having equivalent effect;

(b)   a common commercial policy;

(c)   an internal market characterised by the abolition, as between Member States, of obstacles to the free movement of goods, persons, services and capital;

(d)   measures concerning the entry and movement of persons as provided for in Title IV;

(e)   a common policy in the sphere of agriculture and fisheries;

(f)   a common policy in the sphere of transport;

(g)   a system ensuring that competition in the internal market is not distorted;

(h)   the approximation of the laws of Member States to the extent required for the functioning of the common market;

(i)   the promotion of co-ordination between employment policies of the Member States with a view to enhancing their effectiveness by developing a co-ordinated strategy for employment;

(j)   a policy in the social sphere comprising a European Social Fund;

(k)   the strengthening of economic and social cohesion;

(l)   a policy in the sphere of the environment;

(m)   the strengthening of the competitiveness of Community industry;

(n)   the promotion of research and technological development;

(o)   encouragement for the establishment and development of trans-European networks;

(p)   a contribution to the attainment of a high level of health protection;

(q)   a contribution to education and training of quality and to the flowering of the cultures of the Member States;

(r)   a policy in the sphere of development co-operation;

(s)   the association of the overseas countries and territories in order to increase trade and promote jointly economic and social development;

(t)   a contribution to the strengthening of consumer protection;

(u)   measures in the spheres of energy, civil protection and tourism.

(2)   In all the activities referred to in this Article, the Community shall aim to eliminate inequalities, and to promote equality, between men and women.

Article 12

Within the scope of application of this Treaty, and without prejudice to any special provisions contained therein, any discrimination on grounds of nationality shall be prohibited.

The Council, acting in accordance with the procedure referred to in Article 251, may adopt rules designed to prohibit such discrimination.

PART TWO

CITIZENSHIP OF THE UNION

Article 17

1.   Citizenship of the Union is hereby established. Every person holding the nationality of a Member State shall be a citizen of the Union. Citizenship of the union shall complement and not replace national citizenship.

2.   Citizens of the Union shall enjoy the rights conferred by this Treaty and shall be subject to the duties imposed thereby.

PART THREE

COMMUNITY POLICIES

TITLE I

FREE MOVEMENT OF GOODS

Article 23

1.   The Community shall be based upon a customs union which shall cover all trade in goods and which shall involve the prohibition between Member States of customs duties on imports and exports and of all charges having equivalent effect, and the adoption of a common customs tariff in their relations with third countries.

2.   The provisions of Article 25 and of Chapter 2 of this Title shall apply to products originating in Member States and to products coming from third countries which are in free circulation in Member States.

Article 25

Customs duties on imports and exports and charges having equivalent effect, shall be prohibited between Member States. This prohibition shall also apply to customs duties of a fiscal nature.

Article 28

Quantitative restrictions on imports and all measures having equivalent effect shall be prohibited between Member States.

Article 29

Quantitative restrictions on exports, and all measures having equivalent effect, shall be prohibited between Member States.

Article 30

The provisions of Articles 28 and 29 shall not preclude prohibitions or restrictions on imports, exports or goods in transit justified on grounds of public morality, public policy or public security; the protection of health and life of humans, animals or plants; the protection of national treasures possessing artistic, historic or archaeological value; or the protection of industrial and commercial property. Such prohibitions or restrictions shall not, however, constitute a means of arbitrary discrimination or a disguised restriction on trade between Member States.

TITLE III

FREE MOVEMENT OF PERSONS, SERVICES AND CAPITAL

Article 39

1.   Freedom of movement for workers shall be secured within the Community.

2.   Such freedom of movement shall entail the abolition of any discrimination based on nationality between workers of the Member States as regards employment, remuneration and other conditions of work and employment.

3.   It shall entail the right, subject to limitations justified on grounds of public policy, public security or public health:

(a)   to accept offers of employment actually made

(b)   to move freely within the territory of Member States for this purpose;

(c)   to stay in a Member State for the purpose of employment in accordance with the provisions governing the employment of nationals of that State laid down by law, regulation or administrative action;

(d)   to remain in the territory of a Member State after having been employed in that State, subject to conditions which shall be embodied in implementing regulations to be drawn up by the Commission.

4.   The provisions of this Article shall not apply to employment in the public service.

Article 43

Within the framework of the provisions set out below, restrictions on the freedom of establishment of nationals of a Member State in the territory of another Member State shall be prohibited. Such prohibition shall also apply to restrictions on the setting up of agencies, branches or subsidiaries by nationals of any Member State established in the territory of any Member State.

Freedom of establishment shall include the right to take up and pursue activities as self-employed persons and to set up and manage undertakings, in particular companies or firms within the meaning of the second paragraph of Article 48, under the conditions laid down for its own nationals by the law of the country where such establishment is effected, subject to the provisions of the Chapter relating to capital.

Article 44

1.   In order to attain freedom of establishment as regards as regards a particular activity, the Council, acting in accordance with the procedure referred to in Article 251 and after consulting the Economic and Social Committee, shall act by means of directives.

2.   The Council and the Commission shall carry out the duties devolving upon them under the preceding provisions, in particular:

(a)   by according, as a general rule, priority treatment to activities where freedom of establishment makes a particularly valuable contribution to the development of production and trade;

(b)   by ensuring close co-operation between the competent authorities in the Member States in order to ascertain the particular situation within the Community of the various activities concerned;

(c)   by abolishing those administrative procedures and practices, whether resulting from national legislation or from agreements previously concluded between Member States, the maintenance of which would form an obstacle to freedom of establishment;

(d)   by ensuring that workers of one Member State employed in the territory of another Member State may remain in that territory for the purpose of taking up activities therein as self-employed persons, where they satisfy the conditions which they would be required to satisfy if they were entering that State at the time when they intended to take up such activities;

(e)   by enabling a national of one Member State to acquire and use land and buildings situated in the territory of another Member State, insofar as this does not conflict with the principles laid down in Article 33(2);

(f)   by effecting the progressive abolition of restrictions on freedom of establishment in every branch of activity under consideration, both as regards the conditions for setting up agencies, branches or subsidiaries in the territory of a Member State and as regards the conditions governing the entry of personnel belonging to the main establishment into managerial or supervisory posts in such agencies, branches or subsidiaries;

(g)   by co-ordinating to the necessary extent the safeguards which, for the protection of the interests of members and others, are required by Member States of companies or firms within the meaning of the second paragraph of Article 48 with a view to making such safeguards equivalent throughout the Community;

(h)   by satisfying themselves that the conditions of establishment are not distorted by aids granted by Member States.

Article 45

The provisions of this Chapter shall not apply, so far as any given Member State is concerned, to activities which in that State are connected, even occasionally, with the exercise of official authority.

The Council may, acting by a qualified majority on a proposal from the Commission, rule that the provisions of this Chapter shall not apply to certain activities.

Article 46

1.   The provisions of this Chapter and measures taken in pursuance thereof shall not prejudice the applicability of provisions laid down by law, regulation or administrative action providing for special treatment for foreign nationals on grounds of public policy, public security or public health.

2.   The Council shall, acting in accordance with the procedure referred to in Article 251, issue directives for the co-ordination of the above mentioned provisions.

Article 47

1.   In order to make it easier for persons to take up and pursue activities as self-employed persons, the Council shall, acting in accordance with the procedure referred to in Article 251, issue directives for the mutual recognition of diplomas, certificates and other evidence of formal qualifications.

2.   For the same purpose, the Council shall, acting in accordance with the procedure referred to in Article 251, issue directives for the co-ordination of the provisions laid down by law, regulation or administrative action in Member States concerning the taking up and pursuit of activities as self-employed persons. The Council, acting unanimously throughout the procedure referred to in Article 251, shall decide on directives the implementation of which involves in at least one Member State amendment of the existing principles laid down by law governing the professions with respect to training and conditions of access for natural persons. In other cases the Council shall act by qualified majority.

3.   In the case of the medical and allied and pharmaceutical professions, the progressive abolition of restrictions shall be dependent upon co-ordination of the conditions for their exercise in the various Member States.

Article 48

Companies or firms formed in accordance with the law of a Member State and having their registered office, central administration or principal place of business within the Community shall, for the purposes of this Chapter, be treated in the same way as natural persons who are nationals of Member States.

'Companies or firms' means companies or firms constituted under civil or commercial law, including co-operative societies, and other legal persons governed by public or private law, save for those which are non-profit making.

Article 49

Within the framework of the provisions set out below, restrictions on freedom to provide services within the Community shall be prohibited in respect of nationals of Member States who are established in a State of the Community other than that of the person for whom the services are intended.

The Council may, acting by a qualified majority on a proposal from the Commission, extend the provisions of this Chapter to nationals of a third country who provide services and who are established within the Community.

Article 50

Services shall be considered to be 'services' within the meaning of this Treaty where they are normally provided for remuneration, insofar as they are not governed by the provisions relating to freedom of movement for goods, capital and persons.

'Services' shall in particular include:

    (a)   activities of an industrial character;
    (b)   activities of a commercial character;
    (c)   activities of craftsmen;
    (d)   activities of the professions.

Without prejudice to the provisions of the Chapter relating to the right of establishment, the person providing a service may, in order to do so, temporarily pursue his activity in the State where the service is provided, under the same conditions as are imposed by that State on its own nationals.

Article 55

The provisions of Articles 45 to 48 shall apply to the matters covered by this Chapter.

TITLE VI

COMMON RULES ON COMPETITION, TAXATION AND APPROXIMATION OF LAWS

Chapter 1

Rules on competition

Article 81

1. The following shall be prohibited as incompatible with the common market: all agreements between undertakings, decisions by associations of undertakings and concerted practices which may affect trade between Member States and which have as their object or effect the prevention, restriction or distortion of competition within the common market, and in particular those which:

    (a) directly or indirectly fix purchase or selling prices or any other trading conditions;

    (b) limit or control production, markets, technical development, or investment;

    (c) share markets or sources of supply;

    (d) apply dissimilar conditions to equivalent transactions with other trading parties, thereby placing them at a competitive disadvantage;

    (e) make the conclusion of contracts subject to acceptance by the other parties of supplementary obligations which, by their nature or according to commercial usage, have no connection with the subject of such contracts.

2. Any agreements or decisions prohibited pursuant to this Article shall be automatically void.

3. The provisions of paragraph 1 may, however, be declared inapplicable in the case of:

    — any agreement or category of agreements between undertakings;

    — any decision or category of decisions by associations of undertakings;

    — any concerted practice or category of concerted practices,

which contributes to improving the production or distribution of goods or to promoting technical or economic progress, while allowing consumers a fair share of the resulting benefit, and which does not:

    (a) impose on the undertakings concerned restrictions which are not indispensable to the attainment of these objectives;

    (b) afford such undertakings the possibility of eliminating competition in respect of a substantial part of the products in question.

Article 82

Any abuse by one or more undertakings of a dominant position within the common market or in a substantial part of it shall be prohibited as incompatible with the common market insofar as it may affect trade between Member States.

Such abuse may, in particular, consist in:

    (a) directly or indirectly imposing unfair purchase or selling prices or unfair trading conditions;

    (b) limiting production, markets or technical development to the prejudice of consumers;

    (c) applying dissimilar conditions to equivalent transactions with other trading parties, thereby placing them at a competitive disadvantage;

    (d) making the conclusion of contracts subject to acceptance by the other parties of supplementary obligations which, by their nature or according to commercial usage, have no connection with the subject of such contracts.

Chapter 2

Tax provisions

Article 90

No Member State shall impose, directly or indirectly, on the products of other Member States any internal taxation of any kind in excess of that imposed directly or indirectly on similar domestic products.

Furthermore, no Member State shall impose on the products of other Member States any internal taxation of such a nature as to afford indirect protection to other products.

Chapter 3

Approximation of laws

Article 94

The Council shall, acting unanimously on a proposal from the Commission and after consulting the European Parliament and the Economic and Social Committee, issue directives for the approximation of such laws, regulations or administrative provisions of the Member States as directly affect the establishment or functioning of the common market.

Article 95

1.   By way of derogation from Article 94 and save where otherwise provided in this Treaty, the following provisions shall apply for the achievement of the objectives set out in Article 14. The Council shall, acting in accordance with the procedure referred to in Article 251 and after consulting the Economic and Social Committee, adopt the measures for the approximation of the provisions laid down by law, regulation or administrative action in Member States which have as their object the establishment and functioning of the internal market.

2.   Paragraph 1 shall not apply to fiscal provisions, to those relating to the free movement of persons nor to those relating to the rights and interests of employed persons.

3.   The Commission, in its proposals envisaged in paragraph 1 concerning health, safety, environmental protection and consumer protection, will take as a base a high level of protection, taking account in particular of any new development based on scientific facts. within their respective powers, the European Parliament and the Council will also seek to achieve this objective.

4.   If, after the adoption by the Council of a harmonisation measure, a Member State deems it necessary to maintain national provisions on grounds of major needs referred to in Article 30, or relating to the protection of the environment or the working environment, it shall notify the Commission of these provisions as well as the grounds for maintaining them.

5.   Moreover, without prejudice to paragraph 4, if, after the adoption by the Council or by the Commission of a harmonisation measure, a Member State deems it necessary to introduce national provisions based on new scientific evidence relating to the protection of the environment or the working environment on grounds of a problem specific to that Member State arising after the adoption of the harmonisation measure, it shall notify the Commission of the envisaged provisions as well as the grounds for introducing them

6.   The Commission shall, within six months of the notifications as referred to in paragraphs 4 and 5, approve or reject the national provisions involved after having verified whether or not they are a means of arbitrary discrimination or a disguised restriction on trade between Member States and whether or not they shall constitute an obstacle to the functioning of the internal market.

In the absence of a decision by the Commission within this period the national provisions referred to in paragraphs 4 and 5 shall be deemed to have been approved.

When justified by the complexity of the matter and in the absence of danger for human health, the Commission may notify the Member State concerned that the period referred to in this paragraph may be extended for a further period of up to six months.

7.   When, pursuant to paragraph 6, a Member State is authorised to maintain or introduce national provisions derogating from a harmonisation measure, the Commission shall immediately examine whether to propose an adaptation to that measure.

8.   When a Member State raises a specific problem on public health in a field which has been the subject of prior harmonisation measures, it shall bring it to the attention of the Commission which shall immediately examine whether to propose appropriate measures to the Council.

9.   By way of derogation from the procedure laid down in Articles 226 and 227, the Commission and any Member State may bring the matter directly before the Court of Justice if it considers that another Member State is making improper use of the powers provided for in this Article.

10.   The harmonisation measure referred to above shall, in appropriate cases, include a safeguard clause authorising the Member States to take, for one or more of the non-economic reasons referred to in Article 30, provisional meaures subject to a Community control procedure.

TITLE XI

SOCIAL POLICY, EDUCATION, VOCATIONAL TRAINING AND YOUTH

Chapter 1

Social Provisions

Article 136

The Community and the Member States, having in mind fundamental social rights such as those set out in the European Social Charter signed at Turin on 18 October 1961 and in the 1989 Community Charter of the Fundamental Social Rights of Workers, shall have as their objectives the promotion of employment, improved living and working conditions, so as to make possible their harmonisation while the improvement is being maintained, proper social protection, dialogue between management and labour, the development of human resources with a view to lasting high employment and the combating of exclusion.

To this end the Community and the Member States shall implement measures which take account of the diverse forms of national practices, in particular in the field of contractual relations, and the need to maintain the competitiveness of the Community economy.

They believe that such a development will ensue not only from the functioning of the common market, which will favour the harmonisation of social systems, but also from the procedures provided for in this Treaty and from the approximation of provisions laid down by law, regulation or administrative action.

Article 137

1.   With a view to achieving the objectives of Article 136, the Community shall support and complement the activities of the Member States in the following fields:

—   improvement in particular of the working environment to protect workers' health and safety;

—   working conditions;

—   the information and consultation of workers;

—   the integration of persons excluded from the labour market, without prejudice to Article 150;

—   equality between men and women with regard to labour market opportunities and treatment at work.

2.   To this end, the Council may adopt, by means of directives, minimum requirements for gradual implementation, having regard to the conditions and technical rules obtaining in each of the Member States. Such directives shall avoid imposing administrative, financial and legal constraints in a way which would hold back the creation and development of small and medium-sized undertakings.

The Council shall act in accordance with the procedure referred to in Article 251 after consulting the Economic and Social Committee and the Committee of the Regions.

The Council, acting in accordance with the same procedure, may adopt measures designed to encourage co-operation between Member States through initiatives aimed at improving knowledge, developing exchanges of information and best practises, promoting innovative approaches and evaluating experiences in order to combat social exclusion.

3.   However, the Council shall act unanimously on a proposal from the Commission, after consulting the European Parliament, the Economic and Social Committee and the Committee of the Regions in the following areas:

- social security and social protection of workers;

- protection of workers where their employment contract is terminated;

- representation and collective defence of the interests of workers and employers, including co-determination, subject to paragraph 6;

- conditions of employment for third-country nationals legally residing in Community territory;

- financial contributions for promotion of employment and job-creation, without prejudice to the provisions relating to the Social Fund.

4.   A Member State may entrust management and labour, at their joint request, with the implementation of directives adopted pursuant to paragraphs 2 and 3.

In this case, it shall ensure that, no later than the date on which a directive must be transposed in accordance with Article 249, management and labour have introduced to take any necessary measure enabling it at any time to be in position to guarantee the results imposed by that directive.

5.   The provisions adopted pursuant to this Article shall not prevent any Member State from maintaining or introducing more stringent measures compatible with this Treaty.

6.   The provisions of this Article shall not apply to pay, the right of association, the right to strike or the right to impose lock-outs.

Article 141

1.   Each Member State shall ensure that the principle of equal pay for male and female workers for equal work or work of equal value is applied.

2.   For the purpose of this Article, 'pay' means the ordinary basic or minimum wage or salary and any other consideration, whether in cash or in kind, which the worker receives directly or indirectly, in respect of his employment, from his employer.

Equal pay without discrimination based on sex means:

(a)   that pay for the same work at piece rates shall be calculated on the basis of the same unit of measurement;

(b)   that pay for work at time rates shall be the same for the same job.

3.   The Council, acting in accordance with the procedure referred to in Article 251, and after consulting the Economic and Social Committee, shall adopt measures to ensure the application of the principle of equal opportunities and equal treatment of men and women in matters of employment and occupation, including the principle of equal pay for equal work or work of equal value.

4.   With a view to ensuring full equality in practice between men and women in working life, the principle of equal treatment shall not prevent any Member State from maintaining or adopting measures providing for specific advantages in order to make it easier for the under-represented sex to pursue a vocational activity or to prevent or compensate for disadvantages in professional careers.

PART FIVE

INSTITUTIONS OF THE COMMUNITY

TITLE I

PROVISIONS GOVERNING THE INSTITUTIONS

Chapter 1

The institutions

Section 4

The Court of Justice

Article 226

If the Commission considers that a Member State has failed to fulfil an obligation under this Treaty, it shall deliver a reasoned opinion on the matter after giving the State concerned the opportunity to submit its observations.

If the State concerned does not comply with the opinion within the period laid down by the Commission, the latter may bring the matter before the Court of Justice.

Article 230

The Court of Justice shall review the legality of acts adopted jointly by the European Parliament and the Council, of acts of the Council, of the Commission and of the ECB, other than recommendations and opinions, and of acts of the European Parliament intended to produce legal effects vis-à-vis third parties.

It shall for this purpose have jurisdiction in actions brought by a Member State, the Council or the Commission on grounds of lack of competence, infringement of an essential procedural requirement, infringement of this Treaty or of any rule of law relating to its application, or misuse of powers.

The Court of Justice shall have jurisdiction under the same conditions in actions brought by the European Parliament, by the Court of Auditors and by the ECB for the purpose of protecting their prerogatives.

Any natural or legal person may, under the same conditions, institute proceedings against a decision addressed to that person or against a decision which, although in the form of a regulation or a decision addressed to another person, is of direct and individual concern to the former.

The proceedings provided for in this Article shall be instituted within two months of the publication of the measure, or of its notification to the plaintiff, or, in the absence thereof, of the day on which it came to the knowledge of the latter, as the case may be.

Article 234

In Court of Justice shall have jurisdiction to give preliminary rulings concerning:

(a)   the interpretation of this Treaty;
(b)   the validity and interpretation of acts of the institutions of the Community and of the ECB;
(c)   the interpretation of the statues of bodies established by an act of the Council, where those statues so provide.

Where such a question is raised before any court or tribunal of a Member States, that court or tribunal may, if it considers that a decision on the question is necessary to enable it to give judgment, request the Court of Justice to give a ruling thereon.

Where any such question is raised in a case pending before a court or tribunal of a Member State against whose decisions there is no judicial remedy under national law, that court or tribunal shall bring the matter before the Court of Justice.

Chapter 2

Provisions common to several institutions

Article 249

In order to carry out their task and in accordance with the provisions of this Treaty, the European Parliament acting jointly with the Council, the Council and the Commission shall make regulations and issue directives, take decisions, make recommendations or deliver opinions.

A regulation shall have general application. It shall be binding in its entirety and directly applicable in all Member States.

A directive shall be binding, as to the result to be achieved, upon each Member State to which it is addressed, but shall leave to the national authorities the choice of form and methods.

A decision shall be binding in its entirety upon those to whom it is addressed.

Recommendations and opinions shall have no binding force.

Council Directive 64/221 on the co-ordination of special measures concerning the movement and residence of foreign nationals which are justified on grounds of public policy, public security or public health
(Preamble omitted)

Article 1

1.   The provisions of this Directive shall apply to any national of a Member State who resides in or travels to another Member State of the Community, either in order to pursue an activity as an employed or self-employed person, or as a recipient of services.

2.   These provisions shall apply also to the spouse and to members of the family who come within the provisions of the regulations and directives adopted in this field in pursuance of the Treaty.

Article 2

1.   This Directive relates to all measures concerning entry into their territory, issue or renewal of residence permits, or expulsion from their territory, taken by Member States on grounds of public policy, public security or public health.

2.   Such grounds shall not be invoked to service economic ends.

Article 3

1.   Measures taken on grounds of public policy or of public security shall be based exclusively on the personal conduct of the individual concerned.

2.   Previous criminal convictions shall not in themselves constitute grounds for the taking of such measures.

3.   Expiry of the identity card or passport used by the person concerned to enter the host country and to obtain a residence permit shall not justify expulsion from the territory.

4.   The State which issued the identity card or passport shall allow the holder of such document to re-enter its territory without any formality even if the document is no longer valid or the nationality of the holder is in dispute.

Article 4

1.   The only diseases or disabilities justifying refusal of entry into a territory or refusal to issue a first residence permit shall be those listed in the Annex to this Directive.

2.   Diseases or disabilities occurring after a first residence permit has been issued shall not justify refusal to renew the residence permit or expulsion from the territory.

3.   Member States shall not introduce new provisions or practices which are more restrictive than those in force at the date of notification of this Directive.

Article 5

1.   A decision to grant or to refuse a first residence permit shall be taken as soon as possible and in any event not later than six months from the date of application for the permit.

The person concerned shall be allowed to remain temporarily in the territory pending a decision either to grant or to refuse a residence permit.

2.   The host country may, in cases where this is considered essential, request the Member State of origin of the applicant, and if need be other Member States, to provide information concerning any previous police record. Such enquiries shall not be made as a matter of routine. The Member State consulted shall give its reply within two months.

Article 6

The person concerned shall be informed of the grounds of public policy, public security, or public health upon which the decision taken in his case is based, unless this is contrary to the interests of the security of the State involved.

Part VI   EU

Article 7

The person concerned shall be officially notified of any decision to refuse the issue or renewal of a residence permit or to expel him from the territory. The period allowed for leaving the territory shall be stated in this notification. Save in cases of urgency, this period shall be not less than fifteen days if the person concerned has not yet been granted a residence permit and not less than one month in all other cases.

Article 8

The person concerned shall have the same legal remedies in respect of any decision concerning entry, or refusing the issue or renewal of a residence permit, or ordering expulsion from the territory, as are available to nationals of the State concerned in respect of acts of the administration.

Article 9

1.   Where there is no right of appeal to a court of law, or where such appeal may be only in respect of the legal validity of the decision, or where the appeal cannot have suspensory effect, a decision refusing renewal of a residence permit or ordering the expulsion of the holder of a residence permit from the territory shall not be taken by the administrative authority, save in cases of urgency, until an opinion has been obtained from a competent authority of the host country before which the person concerned enjoys such rights of defence and of assistance or representation as the domestic law of that country provides for.

This authority shall not be the same as that empowered to take the decision refusing renewal of the residence permit or ordering expulsion.

2.   Any decision refusing the issue of a first residence permit or ordering expulsion of the person concerned before the issue of the permit shall, where that person so requests, be referred for consideration to the authority whose prior opinion is required under paragraph I. The person concerned shall then be entitled to submit his defence in person, except where this would be contrary to the interests of national security.

Article 10

1.   Member States shall within six months of notification of this Directive put into force the measures necessary to comply with its provisions and shall forthwith inform the Commission thereof.

2.   Member States shall ensure that the texts of the main provisions of national law which they adopt in the field governed by this Directive are communicated to the Commission.

Article 11

This Directive is addressed to the Member States.

Done at Brussels, 25 February 1964.

Annex

A.   Diseases which might endanger public health:

1.   Diseases subject to quarantine listed in International Health Regulation No 2 of the World Health Organisation of 25 May 1951;

2.   Tuberculosis of the respiratory system in an active state or showing a tendency to develop;

3.   Syphilis;

4.   Other infectious diseases or contagious parasitic diseases if they are the subject of provisions for the protection of nationals of the host country.

B.   Diseases and disabilities which might threaten public policy or public security:

1.   Drug addiction

2.   Profound mental disturbance; manifest conditions of psychotic disturbance with agitation, delirium, hallucinations or confusion.

Council Directive 68/360 on the abolition of restrictions on movement and residence within the Community for workers of Member States and their families
(Preamble omitted)

Article 1

Member States shall, acting as provided in this Directive, abolish restrictions on the movement and residence of nationals of the said States and of members of their families to whom Regulation (EEC) No 1612/68 applies.

Article 2

1. Member States shall grant the nationals referred to in Article 1 the right to leave their territory in order to take up activities as employed persons and to pursue such activities in the territory of another Member State. Such right shall be exercised simply on production of a valid identity card or passport. Members of the family shall enjoy the same right as the national on whom they are dependent.

2. Member States shall, acting in accordance with their laws, issue to such nationals, or renew, an identity card or passport, which shall state in particular the holder's nationality.

3. The passport must be valid at least for all Member States and for countries through which the holder must pass when travelling between Member States. Where a passport is the only document on which the holder may lawfully leave the country, its period of validity shall be not less than five years.

4. Member States may not demand from the nationals referred to in Article 1 any exit visa or any equivalent document.

Article 3

1. Member States shall allow the persons referred to in Article 1 to enter their territory simply on production of a valid identity card or passport.

2. No entry visa or equivalent document may be demanded save from members of the family who are not nationals of a Member State. Member States shall accord to such persons every facility for obtaining any necessary visas.

Article 4

1. Member States shall grant the right of residence in their territory to the persons referred to in Article 1 who are able to produce the documents listed in paragraph 3.

2. As proof of the right of residence, a document entitled 'Residence Permit for a National of a Member State of the EEC' shall be issued. This document must include a statement that it has been issued pursuant to Regulation (EEC) No 1612/68 and to the measures taken by the Member States for the implementation of the present Directive. The text of such statement is given in the Annex to this Directive.

3. For the issue of a Residence Permit for a National of a Member State of the EEC, Member States may require only the production of the following documents;

— by the worker:

(a) the document with which he entered their territory;
(b) a confirmation of engagement from the employer or a certificate of employment;

— by the members of the worker's family:

(c) the document with which they entered the territory;
(d) a document issued by the competent authority of the State of origin or the State whence they came, proving their relationship;
(e) in the cases referred to in Article 10(1) and (2) of Regulation (EEC) No 1612/68 a document issued by the competent authority of the State of origin or the State whence they came, testifying that they are dependent on the worker or that they live under his roof in such country.

4. A member of the family who is not a national of a Member State shall be issued with a residence document which shall have the same validity as that issued to the worker on whom he is dependent.

Article 5

Completion of the formalities for obtaining a residence permit shall not hinder the immediate beginning of employment under a contract concluded by the applicants.

Article 6

1.   The residence permit:

    (a)   must be valid throughout the territory of the Member State which issued it;

    (b)   must be valid for at least five years from the date of issue and be automatically renewable.

2.   Breaks in residence not exceeding six consecutive months and absence on military service shall not affect the validity of a residence permit.

3.   Where a worker is employed for a period exceeding three months but not exceeding a year in the service of an employer in the host State or in the employ of a person providing services, the host Member State shall issue him a temporary residence permit, the validity of which may be limited to the expected period of the employment. Subject to the provisions of Article 8(1)(c), a temporary residence permit shall be issued also to a seasonal worker employed for a period of more than three months. The period of employment must be shown in the documents referred to in paragraph 4(3)(b).

Article 7

1.   A valid residence permit may not be withdrawn from a worker solely on the grounds that he is no longer in employment, either because he is temporarily incapable of work as a result of illness or accident, or because he is involuntarily unemployed, this being duly confirmed by the competent employment office.

2.   When the residence permit is renewed for the first time, the period of residence may be restricted, but not to less than twelve months, where the worker has been involuntarily unemployed in the Member State for more than twelve consecutive months.

Article 8

1.   Member States shall, without issuing a residence permit, recognise the right of residence in their territory of:

    (a)   a worker pursuing an activity as an employed person, where the activity is not expected to last for more than three months. The document with which the person concerned entered the territory and a statement by the employer on the expected duration of the employment shall be sufficient to cover his stay; a statement by the employer shall not, however, be required in the case of workers coming within the provisions of the Council Directive of 25 February 1964 on the attainment of the freedom of establishment and freedom to provide services in respect of the activities of intermediaries in commerce, industry and small craft industries.

    (b)   a worker who, while having his residence in the territory of a Member State to which he returns as a rule, each day or at least once a week, is employed in the territory of another Member State. The competent authority of the State where he is employed may issue such worker with a special permit valid for five years and automatically renewable;

    (c)   a seasonal worker who holds a contract of employment stamped by the competent authority of the Member State on whose territory he has come to pursue his activity.

2.   In all cases referred to in paragraph 1, the competent authorities of the host Member State may require the worker to report his presence in the territory.

Article 9

1.   The residence documents granted to nationals of a Member State of the EEC referred to in this Directive shall be issued and renewed free of charge or on payment of an amount not exceeding the dues and taxes charged for the issue of identity cards to nationals.

2.   The visa referred to in Article 3(2) and the stamp referred to in Article 8(1)(c) shall be free of charge.

3.   Member States shall take the necessary steps to simplify as much as possible the formalities and procedure for obtaining the documents mentioned in paragraph 1.

Article 10

Member States shall not derogate from the provisions of this Directive save on grounds of public policy, public security or public health.

(All remaining provisions omitted.)

Council Regulation 1612/68 on freedom of movement for workers within the Community
(Preamble omitted)

TITLE I ELIGIBILITY FOR EMPLOYMENT

Article 1

1.   Any national of a Member State, shall, irrespective of his place of residence, have the right to take up an activity as an employed person, and to pursue such activity, within the territory of another Member State in accordance with the provisions laid down by law, regulation or administrative action governing the employment of nationals of that State.

2.   He shall, in particular, have the right to take up available employment in the territory of another Member State with the same priority as nationals of the State.

Article 2

Any national of a Member State and any employer pursuing an activity in the territory of a Member State may exchange their applications for and offers of employment, and may conclude and perform contracts of employment in accordance with the provisions in force laid down by law, regulation or administrative action, without any discrimination resulting therefrom.

Article 3

1.   Under this Regulation, provisions laid down by law, regulation or administrative action or administrative practices of a Member State shall not apply:

— where they limit application for and offers of employment, or the right of foreign nationals to take up and pursue employment or subject these to conditions not applicable in respect of their own nationals; or
— where, though applicable irrespective of nationality, their exclusive or principal aim or effect is to keep nationals of other Member States away from the employment offered.

This provision shall not apply to conditions relating to linguistic knowledge required by reason of the nature of the post to be filled.

2.   There shall be included in particular among the provisions of practices of a Member State referred to in the first subparagraph of paragraph 1 those which:

(a)   prescribe a special recruitment procedure for foreign nationals;
(b)   limit or restrict the advertising of vacancies in the press or through any other medium or subject it to conditions other than those applicable in respect of employers pursuing their activities in the territory of that Member State;
(c)   subject eligibility for employment to conditions of registration with employment offices or impede recruitment of individual workers, where persons who do not reside in the territory of that State are concerned.

Article 4

1.   Provisions laid down by law, regulation or administrative action of the Member States which restrict by number or percentage the employment of foreign nationals in any undertaking, branch of activity or region, or at a national level, shall not apply to nationals of the other Member States.

2.   When in a Member State the granting of any benefit to undertakings is subject to a minimum percentage of national workers being employed, nationals of the other Members States shall be counted as national workers, subject to the provisions of the Council Directive of 15 October 1963.

Article 5

A national of a Member State who seeks employment in the territory of another Member State shall receive the same assistance there as that afforded by the employment offices in that State to their own nationals seeking employment.

Article 6

1.   The engagement and recruitment of a national of one Member State for a post in another Member State shall not depend on medical, vocational or other criteria which are discriminatory on grounds of nationality by comparison with those applied to nationals of the other Member State who wish to pursue the same activity.

2.   Nevertheless, a national who holds an offer in his name from an employer in a Member State other than that of which he is a national may have to undergo a vocational test, if the employer expressly requests this when making his offer of employment.

TITLE II EMPLOYMENT AND EQUALITY OF TREATMENT

Article 7

1.   A worker who is a national of a Member State may not, in the territory of another Member State, be treated differently from national workers by reason of his nationality in respect of any conditions of employment and work, in particular as regards remuneration, dismissal, and should he become unemployed, reinstatement or re-employment.

2.   He shall enjoy the same social and tax advantages as national workers.

3.   He shall also, by virtue of the same right and under the same conditions as national workers, have access to training in vocational schools and retraining centres.

4.   Any clause of a collective or individual agreement or of any other collective regulation concerning eligibility for employment, employment, remuneration and other conditions of work or dismissal shall be null and void in so far as it lays down or authorises discriminatory conditions in respect of workers who are nationals of the other Member States.

Article 8

1.   A worker who is a national of a Member State and who is employed in the territory of another Member State shall enjoy equality of treatment as regards membership of trade unions and the exercise of rights attaching thereto, including the right to vote; he may be excluded from taking part in the management of bodies governed by public law and from holding an office governed by public law. Furthermore, he shall have the right of eligibility for workers' representative bodies in the undertaking. The provisions of this Article shall not affect laws or regulations in certain Member States which grant more extensive rights to workers coming from the other Member States.

2.   This Article shall be reviewed by the Council on the basis of a proposal from the Commission which shall be submitted within not more than two years.

Article 9

1.   A worker who is a national of a Member State and who is employed in the territory of another Member State shall enjoy all the rights and benefits accorded to national workers in matters of housing, including ownership of the housing he needs.

2.   Such worker may, with the same right as nationals, put his name down on the housing lists in the region in which he is employed, where such lists exist; he shall enjoy the resultant benefits and priorities. If his family has remained in the country whence he came, they shall be considered for this purpose as residing in the said region where national workers benefit from a similar presumption.

TITLE III WORKERS' FAMILIES

Article 10

1.   The following shall, irrespective of their nationality, have the right to install themselves with a worker who is a national of one Member State and who is employed in the territory of another Member State:

   (a)   his spouse and their descendants who are under the age of 21 years or are dependents;
   (b)   dependent relatives in the ascending line of the worker and his spouse.

2.   Member States shall facilitate the admission of any member of the family not coming within the provisions of paragraph 1 if dependent on the worker referred to above or living under his roof in the country whence he comes.

3.   For the purposes of paragraphs 1 and 2, the worker must have available for his family housing considered as normal for national workers in the region where he is employed; this provision, however must not give rise to discrimination between national workers from the other Member States.

Article 11

Where a national of a Member State is pursuing an activity as an employed or self-employed person in the territory of another Member State, his spouse and those of the children who are under the age of 21 years or dependent on him shall have the right to take up any activity as an employed person throughout the territory of that same State, even if they are not nationals of any Member State.

Article 12

The children of a national of a Member State who is or has been employed in the territory of another Member State shall be admitted to that State's general education, apprenticeship and vocational training courses under the same conditions as the nationals of that State, if such children are residing in its territory. Member States shall encourage all efforts to enable such children to attend these courses under the best possible conditions.

(All remaining provisions omitted).

Part VI EU

Commission Regulation (EC) No 2790/1999 of 22 December 1999 on the application of Article 81(3) of the Treaty to categories of vertical agreements and concerted practices

THE COMMISSION OF THE EUROPEAN COMMUNITIES,

Having regard to the Treaty establishing the European Community,

Having regard to Council Regulation No 19/65/EEC of 2 March 1965 on the application of Article 85(3) of the Treaty to certain categories of agreements and concerted practices (1), as last amended by Regulation (EC) No 1215/1999(2), and in particular Article 1 thereof,

Having published a draft of this Regulation (3),

Having consulted the Advisory Committee on Restrictive Practices and Dominant Positions,

Whereas:

(1) Regulation No 19/65/EEC empowers the Commission to apply Article 81(3) of the Treaty (formerly Article 85(3)) by regulation to certain categories of vertical agreements and corresponding concerted practices falling within Article 81(1).

(2) Experience acquired to date makes it possible to define a category of vertical agreements which can be regarded as normally satisfying the conditions laid down in Article 81(3).

(3) This category includes vertical agreements for the purchase or sale of goods or services where these agreements are concluded between non-competing undertakings, between certain competitors or by certain associations of retailers of goods; it also includes vertical agreements containing ancillary provisions on the assignment or use of intellectual property rights; for the purposes of this Regulation, the term 'vertical agreements' includes the corresponding concerted practices.

(4) For the application of Article 81(3) by regulation, it is not necessary to define those vertical agreements which are capable of falling within Article 81(1); in the individual assessment of agreements under Article 81(1), account has to be taken of several factors, and in particular the market structure on the supply and purchase side.

(5) The benefit of the block exemption should be limited to vertical agreements for which it can be assumed with sufficient certainty that they satisfy the conditions of Article 81(3).

(6) Vertical agreements of the category defined in this Regulation can improve economic efficiency within a chain of production or distribution by facilitating better coordination between the participating undertakings; in particular, they can lead to a reduction in the transaction and distribution costs of the parties and to an optimisation of their sales and investment levels.

(7) The likelihood that such efficiency-enhancing effects will outweigh any anti-competitive effects due to restrictions contained in vertical agreements depends on the degree of market power of the undertakings concerned and, therefore, on the extent to which those undertakings face competition from other suppliers of goods or services regarded by the buyer as interchangeable or substitutable for one another, by reason of the products' characteristics, their prices and their intended use.

(8) It can be presumed that, where the share of the relevant market accounted for by the supplier does not exceed 30%, vertical agreements which do not contain certain types of severely anti-competitive restraints generally lead to an improvement in production or distribution and allow consumers a fair share of the resulting benefits; in the case of vertical agreements containing exclusive supply obligations, it is the market share of the buyer which is relevant in determining the overall effects of such vertical agreements on the market.

(9) Above the market share threshold of 30%, there can be no presumption that vertical agreements falling within the scope of Article 81(1) will usually give rise to objective advantages of such a character and size as to compensate for the disadvantages which they create for competition.

(10) This Regulation should not exempt vertical agreements containing restrictions which are not indispensable to the attainment of the positive effects mentioned above; in particular, vertical agreements containing certain types of severely anti-competitive restraints such as minimum and fixed resale-prices, as well as certain types of territorial protection, should be excluded from the benefit of the block exemption established by this Regulation irrespective of the market share of the undertakings concerned.

(11) In order to ensure access to or to prevent collusion on the relevant market, certain conditions are to be attached to the block exemption; to this end, the exemption of non-compete obligations should be limited to obligations which do not exceed a definite duration; for the same reasons, any direct or indirect obligation causing the members of a selective distribution system not to sell the brands of particular competing suppliers should be excluded from the benefit of this Regulation.

(12) The market-share limitation, the non-exemption of certain vertical agreements and the conditions provided for in this Regulation normally ensure that the agreements to which the block exemption applies do not enable the participating undertakings to eliminate competition in respect of a substantial part of the products in question.

(13) In particular cases in which the agreements falling under this Regulation nevertheless have effects incompatible with Article 81(3), the Commission may withdraw the benefit of the block exemption; this may occur in particular where the buyer has significant market power in the relevant market in which it resells the goods or provides the services or where parallel networks of vertical agreements have similar effects which significantly restrict access to a relevant market or competition therein; such cumulative effects may for example arise in the case of selective distribution or non-compete obligations.

(14) Regulation No 19/65/EEC empowers the competent authorities of Member States to withdraw the benefit of the block exemption in respect of vertical agreements having effects incompatible with the conditions laid down in Article 81(3), where such effects are felt in their respective territory, or in a part thereof, and where such territory has the characteristics of a distinct geographic market; Member States should ensure that the exercise of this power of withdrawal does not prejudice the uniform application throughout the common market of the Community competition rules or the full effect of the measures adopted in implementation of those rules.

(15) In order to strengthen supervision of parallel networks of vertical agreements which have similar restrictive effects and which cover more than 50% of a given market, the Commission may declare this Regulation inapplicable to vertical agreements containing specific restraints relating to the market concerned, thereby restoring the full application of Article 81 to such agreements.

(16) This Regulation is without prejudice to the application of Article 82.

(17) In accordance with the principle of the primacy of Community law, no measure taken pursuant to national laws on competition should prejudice the uniform application throughout the common market of the Community competition rules or the full effect of any measures adopted in implementation of those rules, including this Regulation,

HAS ADOPTED THIS REGULATION:

Article 1

For the purposes of this Regulation:

(a) 'competing undertakings' means actual or potential suppliers in the same product market; the, product market includes goods or services which are regarded by the buyer as interchangeable with or substitutable for the contract goods or services, by reason of the products' characteristics, their prices and their intended use;

(b) 'non-compete obligation' means any direct or indirect obligation causing the buyer not to manufacture, purchase, sell or resell goods or services which compete with the contract goods or services, or any direct or indirect obligation on the buyer to purchase from the supplier or from another undertaking designated by the supplier more than 80% of the buyer's total purchases of the contract goods or services and their substitutes on the relevant market, calculated on the basis of the value of its purchases in the preceding calendar year;

(c) 'exclusive supply obligation' means any direct or indirect obligation causing the supplier to sell the goods or services specified in the agreement only to one buyer inside the Community for the purposes of a specific use or for resale;

(d) 'Selective distribution system' means a distribution system where the supplier undertakes to sell the contract goods or services, either directly or indirectly, only to distributors selected on the basis of specified criteria and where these distributors undertake not to sell such goods or services to unauthorised distributors;

(e) 'intellectual property rights' includes industrial property rights, copyright and neighbouring rights;

(f) 'know-how' means a package of non-patented practical information, resulting from experience and testing by the supplier, which is secret, substantial and identified: in this context, 'secret' means that the know-how, as a body or in the precise configuration and assembly of its components, is not generally known or easily accessible; 'substantial' means that the know-how includes information which is indispensable to the buyer for the use, sale or resale of the contract goods or services; 'identified' means that the know-how must be described in a sufficiently comprehensive manner so as to make it possible to verify that it fulfils the criteria of secrecy and substantiality;

(g)   'buyer' includes an undertaking which, under an agreement falling within Article 81(1) of the Treaty, sells goods or services on behalf of another undertaking.

Article 2

1.   Pursuant to Article 81(3) of the Treaty and subject to the provisions of this Regulation, it is hereby declared that Article 81(1) shall not apply to agreements or concerted practices entered into between two or more undertakings each of which operates, for the purposes of the agreement, at a different level of the production or distribution chain, and relating to the conditions under which the parties may purchase, sell or resell certain goods or services ('vertical agreements').

This exemption shall apply to the extent that such agreements contain restrictions of competition falling within the scope of Article 81(1) ('vertical restraints').

2.   The exemption provided for in paragraph 1 shall apply to vertical agreements entered into between an association of undertakings and its members, or between such an association and its suppliers, only if all its members are retailers of goods and if no individual member of the association, together with its connected undertakings, has a total annual turnover exceeding EUR 50 million; vertical agreements entered into by such associations shall be covered by this Regulation without prejudice to the application of Article 81 to horizontal agreements concluded between the members of the association or decisions adopted by the association.

3.   The exemption provided for in paragraph 1 shall apply to vertical agreements containing provisions which relate to the assignment to the buyer or use by the buyer of intellectual property rights, provided that those provisions do not constitute the primary object of such agreements and are directly related to the use, sale or resale of goods or services by the buyer or its customers. The exemption applies on condition that, in relation to the contract goods or services, those provisions do not contain restrictions of competition having the same object or effect as vertical restraints which are not exempted under this Regulation.

4.   The exemption provided for in paragraph 1 shall not apply to vertical agreements entered into between competing undertakings; however, it shall apply where competing undertakings enter into a non-reciprocal vertical agreement and:

(a)   the buyer has a total annual turnover not exceeding EUR 100 million, or
(b)   the supplier is a manufacturer and a distributor of goods, while the buyer is a distributor not manufacturing goods competing with the contract goods, or
(c)   the supplier is a provider of services at several levels of trade, while the buyer does not provide competing services at the level of trade where it purchases the contract services.

5.   This Regulation shall not apply to vertical agreements the subject matter of which falls within the scope of any other block exemption regulation.

Article 3

1.   Subject to paragraph 2 of this Article, the exemption provided for in Article 2 shall apply on condition that the market share held by the supplier does not exceed 30% of the relevant market on which it sells the contract goods or services.

2.   In the case of vertical agreements containing exclusive supply obligations, the exemption provided for in Article 2 shall apply on condition that the market share held by the buyer does not exceed 30% of the relevant market on which it purchases the contract goods or services.

Article 4

The exemption provided for in Article 2 shall not apply to vertical agreements which, directly or indirectly, in isolation or in combination with other factors under the control of the parties, have as their object:

(a)   the restriction of the buyer's ability to determine its sale price, without prejudice to the possibility of the supplier's imposing a maximum sale price or recommending a sale price, provided that they do not amount to a fixed or minimum sale price as a result of pressure from, or incentives offered by, any of the parties;
(b)   the restriction of the territory into which, or of the customers to whom, the buyer may sell the contract goods or services, except:

- the restriction of active sales into the exclusive territory or to an exclusive customer group reserved to the supplier or allocated by the supplier to another buyer, where such a restriction does not limit sales by the customers of the buyer,
- the restriction of sales to end users by a buyer operating at the wholesale level of trade,
- the restriction of sales to unauthorised distributors by the members of a selective distribution system, and
- the restriction of the buyer's ability to sell components, supplied for the purposes of incorporation, to customers who would use them to manufacture the same type of goods as those produced by the supplier;

(c)   the restriction of active or passive sales to end users by members of a selective distribution system operating at the retail level of trade, without prejudice to the possibility of prohibiting a member of the system from operating out of an unauthorised place of establishment;

(d)   the restriction of cross-supplies between distributors within a selective distribution system, including between distributors operating at different level of trade;

(e)   the restriction agreed between a supplier of components and a buyer who incorporates those components, which limits the supplier to selling the components as spare parts to end-users or to repairers or other service providers not entrusted by the buyer with the repair or servicing of its goods.

Article 5

The exemption provided for in Article 2 shall not apply to any of the following obligations contained in vertical agreements:

(a)   any direct or indirect non-compete obligation, the duration of which is indefinite or exceeds five years. A non-compete obligation which is tacitly renewable beyond a period of five years is to be deemed to have been concluded for an indefinite duration. However, the time limitation of five years shall not apply where the contract goods or services are sold by the buyer from premises and land owned by the supplier or leased by the supplier from third parties not connected with the buyer, provided that the duration of the non-compete obligation does not exceed the period of occupancy of the premises and land by the buyer;

(b)   any direct or indirect obligation causing the buyer, after termination of the agreement, not to manufacture, purchase, sell or resell goods or services, unless such obligation:

- relates to goods or services which compete with the contract goods or services, and
- is limited to the premises and land from which the buyer has operated during the contract period, and
- is indispensable to protect know-how transferred by the supplier to the buyer,

and provided that the duration of such non-compete obligation is limited to a period of one year after termination of the agreement; this obligation is without prejudice to the possibility of imposing a restriction which is unlimited in time on the use and disclosure of know-how which has not entered the public domain;

(c)   any direct or indirect obligation causing the members of a selective distribution system not to sell the brands of particular competing suppliers.

Article 6

The Commission may withdraw the benefit of this Regulation, pursuant to Article 7(1) of Regulation No 19/65/EEC, where it finds in any particular case that vertical agreements to which this Regulation applies nevertheless have effects which are incompatible with the conditions laid down in Article 81(3) of the Treaty, and in particular where access to the relevant market or competition therein is significantly restricted by the cumulative effect of parallel networks of similar vertical restraints implemented by competing suppliers or buyers.

Article 7

Where in any particular case vertical agreements to which the exemption provided for in Article 2 applies have effects incompatible with the conditions laid down in Article 81(3) of the Treaty in the territory of a Member State, or in a part thereof, which has all the characteristics of a distinct geographic market, the competent authority of that Member State may withdraw the benefit of application of this Regulation in respect of that territory, under the same conditions as provided in Article 6.

Article 8

1. Pursuant to Article 1 a of Regulation No 19/65/EEC, the Commission may by regulation declare that, where parallel networks of similar vertical restraints cover more than 50% of a relevant market, this Regulation shall not apply to vertical agreements containing specific restraints relating to that market.

2. A regulation pursuant to paragraph 1 shall not become applicable earlier than six months following its adoption.

Article 9

1. The market share of 30% provided for in Article 3(1) shall be calculated on the basis of the market sales value of the contract goods or services and other goods or services sold by the supplier, which are regarded as interchangeable or substitutable by the buyer, by reason of the products' characteristics, their prices and their intended use; if market sales value data are not available, estimates based on other reliable market information, including market sales volumes, may be used to establish the market share of the undertaking concerned. For the purposes of Article 3(2), it is either the market purchase value or estimates thereof which shall be used to calculate the market share.

2. For the purposes of applying the market share, threshold provided for in Article 3 the following rules shall apply:

   (a) the market share shall be calculated on the basis of data relating to the preceding calendar year;
   (b) the market share shall include any goods or services supplied to integrated distributors for the purposes of sale;
   (c) if the market share is initially not more than 30% but subsequently rises above that level without exceeding 35%, the exemption provided for in Article 2 shall continue to apply for a period of two consecutive calendar years following the year in which the 30% market share threshold was first exceeded;
   (d) if the market share is initially not more than 30% but subsequently rises above 35%, the exemption provided for in Article 2 shall continue to apply for one calendar year following the year in which the level of 35% was first exceeded;
   (e) the benefit of points (c) and (d) may not be combined so as to exceed a period of two calendar years.

Article 10

1. For the purpose of calculating total annual turnover within the meaning of Article 2(2) and (4), the turnover achieved during the previous financial year by the relevant party to the vertical agreement and the turnover achieved by its connected undertakings in respect of all goods and services, excluding all taxes and other duties, shall be added together. For this purpose, no account shall be taken of dealings between the party to the vertical agreement and its connected undertakings or between its connected undertakings.

2. The exemption provided for in Article 2 shall remain applicable where, for any period of two consecutive financial years, the total annual turnover threshold is exceeded by no more than 10%.

Article 11

1. For the purposes of this Regulation, the terms 'undertaking', 'supplier' and 'buyer' shall include their respective connected undertakings.

2. 'Connected undertakings' are:

   (a) undertakings in which a party to the agreement, directly or indirectly:

      – has the power to exercise more than half the voting rights, or
      – has the power to appoint more than half the members of the supervisory board, board of management or bodies legally representing the undertaking, or
      – has the right to manage the undertaking's affairs;

   (b) undertakings which directly or indirectly have, over a party to the agreement, the rights or powers listed in (a);
   (c) undertakings in which an undertaking referred to in (b) has, directly or indirectly, the rights or powers listed in (a);

(d) undertakings in which a party to the agreement together with one or more of the undertakings referred to in (a), (b) or (c), or in which two or more of the latter undertakings, jointly have the rights or powers listed in (a);

(e) undertakings in which the rights or the powers listed in (a) are jointly held by:

– parties to the agreement or their respective connected undertakings referred to in (a) to (d), or
– one or more of the parties to the agreement or one or more of their connected undertakings referred to in (a) to (d) and one or more third parties.

3. For the purposes of Article 3, the market share held by the undertakings referred to in paragraph 2(e) of this Article shall be apportioned equally to each undertaking having the rights or the powers listed in paragraph 2(a).

Article 12

1. The exemptions provided for in Commission Regulations (EEC) No 1983/83(4), (EEC) No 1984/83(5) and (EEC) No 4087/88(6) shall continue to apply until 31 May 2000.

2. The prohibition laid down in Article 81(1) of the EC Treaty shall not apply during the period from 1 June 2000 to 31 December 2001 in respect of agreements already in force on 31 May 2000 which do not satisfy the conditions for exemption provided for in this Regulation but which satisfy the conditions for exemption provided for in Regulations (EEC) No 1983/83, (EEC) No 1984/83 or (EEC) No 4087/88.

Article 13

This Regulation shall enter into force on 1 January 2000.

It shall apply from 1 June 2000, except for Article 12(1) which shall apply from 1 January 2000.

This Regulation shall expire on 31 May 2010.

This Regulation shall be binding in its entirety and directly applicable in all Member States.

Done at Brussels, 22 December 1999.

PART VII

COMPANY FORMS

10

**Please complete in typescript,
or in bold black capitals.**

CHWP000

Notes on completion appear on final page

First directors and secretary and intended situation of registered office

Company Name in full

Proposed Registered Office

(PO Box numbers only, are not acceptable)

Post town

County / Region   Postcode

If the memorandum is delivered by an agent for the subscriber(s) of the memorandum mark the box opposite and give the agent's name and address.

Agent's Name

Address

Post town

County / Region   Postcode

Number of continuation sheets attached

You do not have to give any contact information in the box opposite but if you do, it will help Companies House to contact you if there is a query on the form. The contact information that you give will be visible to searchers of the public record.

Tel

DX number   DX exchange

Companies House receipt date barcode
This form is been provided free of charge by Companies House

Form April 2002

When you have completed and signed the form please send it to the Registrar of Companies at:
Companies House, Crown Way, Cardiff, CF14 3UZ   DX 33050 Cardiff
for companies registered in England and Wales
or
Companies House, 37 Castle Terrace, Edinburgh, EH1 2EB
for companies registered in Scotland   **DX 235 Edinburgh**

Company Secretary (see notes 1-5)

Company name	

	NAME	*Style / Title		*Honours etc	

* Voluntary details

Forename(s)	
Surname	
Previous forename(s)	
Previous surname(s)	

†† Tick this box if the address shown is a service address for the beneficiary of a Confidentiality Order granted under section 723B of the Companies Act 1985 otherwise, give your usual residential address. In the case of a corporation or Scottish firm, give the registered or principle office address.

Address ††

Post town	
County / Region		Postcode	
Country	

I consent to act as secretary of the company named on page 1

Consent | | **Date** | |

Directors (see notes 1-5)

Please list directors in alphabetical order

	NAME	*Style / Title		*Honours etc	

Forename(s)	
Surname	
Previous forename(s)	
Previous surname(s)	

†† Tick this box if the address shown is a service address for the beneficiary of a Confidentiality Order granted under section 723B of the Companies Act 1985 otherwise, give your usual residential address. In the case of a corporation or Scottish firm, give the registered or principle office address.

Address ††

Post town	
County / Region		Postcode	
Country	

	Day	Month	Year		
Date of birth				Nationality	

Business occupation	
Other directorships	

I consent to act as director of the company named on page 1

Consent signature | | **Date** | |

Directors (see notes 1-5)

Please list directors in alphabetical order

| NAME | *Style / Title | | *Honours etc | |

Forename(s)

Surname

Previous forename(s)

Previous surname(s)

† Tick this box if the address shown is a service address for the beneficiary of a Confidentiality Order granted under section 723B of the Companies Act 1985 otherwise, give your usual residential address. In the case of a corporation or Scottish firm, give the registered or principle office address.

Address †

Post town

County / Region   Postcode

Country

Date of birth

Day   Month   Year

Nationality

Business occupation

Other directorships

I consent to act as director of the company named on page 1

Consent signature   Date

This section must be signed by
Either

an agent on behalf of all subscribers   Signed   Date

Or the subscribers   Signed   Date

(*i.e those who signed as members on the memorandum of association).*   Signed   Date

Signed   Date

Signed   Date

Signed   Date

Signed   Date

Notes

1. Show for an individual the full forename(s) NOT INITIALS and surname together with any previous forename(s) or surname(s).

   If the director or secretary is a corporation or Scottish firm - show the corporate or firm name on the surname line.

   Give previous forename(s) or surname(s) except that:

   - for a married woman, the name by which she was known before marriage need not be given,

   - names not used since the age of 18 or for at least 20 years need not be given.

   A peer, or an individual known by a title, may state the title instead of or in addition to the forename(s) and surname and need not give the name by which that person was known before he or she adopted the title or succeeded to it.

   Address:

   Give the usual residential address.

   In the case of a corporation or Scottish firm give the registered or principal office.

   Subscribers:

   The form must be signed personally either by the subscriber(s) or by a person or persons authorised to sign on behalf of the subscriber(s).

2. Directors known by another description:

   - A director includes any person who occupies that position even if called by a different name, for example, governor, member of council.

3. Directors details:

   - Show for each individual director the director's date of birth, business occupation and nationality. **The date of birth must be given for every individual director.**

4. Other directorships:

   - Give the name of every company of which the person concerned is a director or has been a director at any time in the past 5 years. You may exclude a company which either **is** or at **all times during the past 5 years,** when the person was a director, **was:**

   - dormant,

   - a parent company which wholly owned the company making the return,

   - a wholly owned subsidiary of the company making the return, or

   - another wholly owned subsidiary of the same parent company.

   If there is insufficient space on the form for other directorships you may use a separate sheet of paper, which should include the company's number and the full name of the director.

5. Use Form 10 continuation sheets or photocopies of page 2 to provide details of joint secretaries or additional directors.

Company Secretary (see notes 1-5)

Form 10 Continuation Sheet

CHWP000

Company Name

NAME   *Style / Title   *Honours etc

* Voluntary details

Forename(s)

Surname

Previous forename(s)

Previous surname(s)

† Tick this box if the address shown is a service address for the beneficiary of a Confidentiality Order granted under section 723B of the Companies Act 1985 otherwise, give your usual residential address. In the case of a corporation or Scottish firm, give the registered or principle office address

Address †

Post town

County / Region   Postcode

Country

I consent to act as secretary of the company named on page 1

Consent signature   Date

Directors (see notes 1-5)

Please list directors in alphabetical order

NAME   *Style / Title   *Honours etc

Forename(s)

Surname

Previous forename(s)

Previous surname(s)

† Tick this box if the address shown is a service address for the beneficiary of a Confidentiality Order granted under section 723B of the Companies Act 1985 otherwise, give your usual residential address. In the case of a corporation or Scottish firm, give the registered or principle office address

Address †

Post town

County / Region   Postcode

Country

Day   Month   Year

Date of birth   Nationality

Business occupation

Other directorships

I consent to act as director of the company named on page 1

Consent signature   Date

Company Secretary (see notes 1-5)

	NAME	*Style / Title		*Honours etc	

* Voluntary details

Forename(s)	

Surname	

Previous forename(s)	

Previous surname(s)	

† Tick this box if the address shown is a service address for the beneficiary of a Confidentiality Order granted under section 723B of the Companies Act 1985 otherwise, give your usual residential address. In the case of a corporation or Scottish firm, give the registered or principle office address

Address †	

Post town	

County / Region		Postcode	

Country	

I consent to act as secretary of the company named on page 1

Consent signature		**Date**	

Directors (see notes 1-5)

Please list directors in alphabetical order

	NAME	*Style / Title		*Honours etc	

Forename(s)	

Surname	

Previous forename(s)	

Previous surname(s)	

† Tick this box if the address shown is a service address for the beneficiary of a Confidentiality Order granted under section 723B of the Companies Act 1985 otherwise, give your usual residential address. In the case of a corporation or Scottish firm, give the registered or principle office address

Address †	

Post town	

County / Region		Postcode	

Country	

	Day	Month	Year		
Date of birth				**Nationality**	

Business occupation	

Other directorships	

I consent to act as director of the company named on page 1

Consent signature		**Date**	

Companies House
for the record

*Please complete in typescript,
or in bold black capitals.*

CHWP000

Declaration on application for registration

12

Company Name in full

I,

of

† Please delete as appropriate.

do solemnly and sincerely declare that I am a † [Solicitor engaged in the formation of the company][person named as director or secretary of the company in the statement delivered to the Registrar under section 10 of the Companies Act 1985] and that all the requirements of the Companies Act 1985 in respect of the registration of the above company and of matters precedent and incidental to it have been complied with.

And I make this solemn Declaration conscientiously believing the same to be true and by virtue of the Statutory Declarations Act 1835.

Declarant's signature

Declared at

	Day	Month	Year

On

❶ Please print name.

before me ❶

Signed   **Date**

† A Commissioner for Oaths or Notary Public or Justice of the Peace or Solicitor

Please give the name, address, telephone number and, if available, a DX number and Exchange of the person Companies House should contact if there is any query.

Tel
DX number   DX exchange

Companies House receipt date barcode

This form has been provided free of charge by Companies House.

Form revised June 1998

When you have completed and signed the form please send it to the Registrar of Companies at:

Companies House, Crown Way, Cardiff, CF14 3UZ   **DX 33050 Cardiff**
for companies registered in England and Wales
or
Companies House, 37 Castle Terrace, Edinburgh, EH1 2EB
for companies registered in Scotland   **DX 235 Edinburgh**

Companies House
—— *for the record* ——

Please complete in typescript,
or in bold black capitals
CHWP000

225

Change of accounting reference date

Company Number	

Company Name in Full	

NOTES

You may use this form to change the accounting date relating to either the current or the immediately previous accounting period.

a. You **may not** change a period for which the accounts are already overdue.

b. You **may not** extend a period beyond 18 months unless the company is subject to an administration order.

c. You **may not** extend periods more than once in five years unless:

   1. the company is subject to an administration order, or

   2. you have the specific approval of the Secretary of State, (please enclose a copy), or

   3. you are extending the company's accounting reference period to align with that of a parent or subsidiary undertaking established in the European Economic Area, or

   4. the form is being submitted by an oversea company.

The accounting reference period ending

	Day	Month	Year

is Shortened   † so as to end

	Day	Month	Year

Subsequent periods will end on the same day and month in future years.

If extending more than once in five years, please indicate in the box the number of the provision listed in note c. on which you are relying.

Signed [   ] **Date** [   ]

† *Please delete as appropriate*

† a director / secretary / administrator / administrative receiver / receiver and manager / receiver (Scotland) / person authorised on behalf of an oversea company

Please give the name, address, telephone number, and if available, a DX number and Exchange, for the person Companies House should contact if there is any query

Tel
DX number   DX exchange

Companies House receipt date barcode

This form has been provided free of charge by Companies House.

When you have completed and signed the form please send it to the Registrar of Companies at:

Companies House, Crown Way, Cardiff, CF14 3UZ   DX 33050 Cardiff
for companies registered in England and Wales
or
Companies House, 37 Castle Terrace, Edinburgh, EH1 2EB
for companies registered in Scotland   **DX 235 Edinburgh**

Form revised July 1998

Please complete in typescript, or in bold black capitals.
CHWP000

88(2)

Return of Allotment of Shares

Company Number

Company name in full

Shares allotted (including bonus shares):

	From			To		
Date or period during which shares were allotted *(If shares were allotted on one date enter that date in the "from" box)*	Day	Month	Year	Day	Month	Year

Class of shares *(ordinary or preference etc)*			
Number allotted			
Nominal value of each share			
Amount (if any) paid or due on each share *(including any share premium)*			

List the names and addresses of the allottees and the number of shares allotted to each overleaf

If the allotted shares are fully or partly paid up otherwise than in cash please state:

% that each share is to be treated as paid up			

Consideration for which the shares were allotted *(This information must be supported by the duly stamped contract or by the duly stamped particulars on Form 88(3) if the contract is not in writing)*	

Companies House receipt date barcode

This form has been provided free of charge by Companies House.

When you have completed and signed the form send it to the Registrar of Companies at:

Companies House, Crown Way, Cardiff CF14 3UZ   **DX 33050 Cardiff**
For companies registered in England and Wales

Companies House, 37 Castle Terrace, Edinburgh EH1 2EB   **DX 235**
For companies registered in Scotland   **Edinburgh**

Form Revised January 2000

Names and addresses of the allottees *(List joint share allotments consecutively)*

Shareholder details	Shares and share class allotted	
Name Address UK Postcode ⌞ ⌞ ⌞ ⌞ ⌞ ⌞ ⌞	Class of shares allotted	Number allotted
Name Address UK Postcode ⌞ ⌞ ⌞ ⌞ ⌞ ⌞ ⌞	Class of shares allotted	Number allotted
Name Address UK Postcode ⌞ ⌞ ⌞ ⌞ ⌞ ⌞ ⌞	Class of shares allotted	Number allotted
Name Address UK Postcode ⌞ ⌞ ⌞ ⌞ ⌞ ⌞ ⌞	Class of shares allotted	Number allotted
Name Address UK Postcode ⌞ ⌞ ⌞ ⌞ ⌞ ⌞ ⌞	Class of shares allotted	Number allotted

Please enter the number of continuation sheets (if any) attached to this form

Signed _____ **Date** _____

A director / secretary / administrator / administrative receiver / receiver manager / receiver   *Please delete as appropriate*

Please give the name, address, telephone number and, if available, a DX number and Exchange of the person Companies House should contact if there is any query.

Tel	
DX number	DX exchange

G

COMPANIES FORM No. 123

Notice of increase in nominal capital

123

CHWP000

Pursuant to section 123 of the Companies Act 1985

**Please complete
legibly, preferably
in black type, or
bold block lettering**

To the Registrar of Companies
(Address overleaf)

For official use

Company number

Name of company

* insert full name
of company

*

gives notice in accordance with section 123 of the above Act that by resolution of the company

dated _____ the nominal capital of the company has been

increased by £ _____ beyond the registered capital of £ _____ .

† the copy must be
printed or in some
other form approved
by the registrar

A copy of the resolution authorising the increase is attached. †

The conditions (eg. voting rights, dividend rights, winding-up rights etc.) subject to which the new

shares have been or are to be issued are as follows :

Please tick here if
continued overleaf

‡ Insert
Director,
Secretary,
Administrator,
Administrative
Receiver or
Receiver
(Scotland) as
appropriate

Signed

Designation ‡

Date

Presentor's name address and
reference (if any) :

For official Use
General Section

Post room

Notes

The address for companies registered in England and Wales or Wales is :-

The Registrar of Companies
Companies House
Crown Way
Cardiff
CF4 3UZ

or, for companies registered in Scotland :-

The Registrar of Companies
Companies House
37 Castle Terrace
Edinburgh
EH1 2EB

G

CHFP001

COMPANIES FORM No. 169

Return by a company purchasing its own shares

169

Pursuant to section 169 of the Companies Act 1985

Please do not write in this margin

Please complete legibly, preferably in black type, or bold block lettering

* insert full name of company

Note
This return must be delivered to the Registrar within a period of 28 days beginning with the first date on which shares to which it relates were delivered to the company

§ A private company is not required to give this information

‡ Insert Director, Secretary. Receiver, Administrator, Administrative Receiver or Receiver (Scotland) as appropriate

To the Registrar of Companies **(address overleaf)**

For official use

Company number

Please do not write in the space below. For Inland Revenue use only.

Name of company

*

Shares were purchased by the company under section 162 of the above Act as follows:

Class of shares			
Number of shares purchased			
Nominal value of each share			
Date(s) on which the shares were delivered to the company			
Maximum prices paid § for each share			
Minimum prices paid § for each share			

The aggregate amount paid by the company for the shares to which this return relates was:	£
Stamp duty payable on the aggregate amount at the rate of ½ % rounded up to the nearest multiple of £5.00	£

Signed   Designation‡   Date

Presentor's name address and reference (if any):

For official Use

General Section   Post room

CHAD 07/12/99

1. Before this form is delivered to Companies House it must be "stamped" by an Inland Revenue Stamp Office to confirm that the appropriate amount of Stamp Duty has been paid. Inland Revenue Stamp Offices are located at:

Birmingham Stamp Office	Bristol Stamp Office	Manchester Stamp Office
Ground Floor	The Pithay	Alexandra House
City House	All Saints Street	Parsonage
140-146 Edmund Street	Bristol	Manchester
Birmingham B3 2LG	BS1 2NY	M60 9BT
DX: 15001 Birmingham 1	DX: 7899 Bristol 1	DX: 14430 Manchester
Tel: 0121 200 3001	Tel: 0117 927 2022	Tel: 0161 833 0413

Newcastle Stamp Office
15th Floor, Cale Cross House
156 Pilgrim Street
Newcastle Upon Tyne
NE1 6TF

Edinburgh Stamp Office
Mulberry House
16 Picardy Place
Edinburgh
EH1 3NF

DX: 61021 Newcastle Upon Tyne 1
Tel: 0191 261 1199

DX: ED 303 Edinburgh 1
Tel: 0131 556 8998

London Stamp Office
(Personal callers only)
South West Wing
Bush House
Strand
London WC2B 4QN

Worthing Stamp Office
(Postal applications only)
Room 35
East Block
Barrington Road
Worthing BN12 4SE

DX: 3799 Worthing 1
Tel: 020 438 7252/7452   Tel: 01903 508962

Cheques for Stamp Duty must be made payable to "Inland Revenue - Stamp Duties" and crossed "Not Transferable".

NOTE: This form must be presented to an Inland Revenue Stamp Office for stamping together with the payment of duty within 30 days of the allotment of shares, otherwise Inland Revenue penalties may be incurred.

2. After this form has been "stamped" and returned to you by the Inland Revenue it must be sent to:

For companies registered in:

England or Wales:	Scotland:
The Registrar of Companies	The Registrar of Companies
Companies House	Companies House
Crown Way	37 Castle Terrace
Cardiff CF14 3UZ	Edinburgh EH1 2EB
DX: 33050 Cardiff	DX: 235 Edinburgh

G

CHFP001

COMPANIES FORM No. 173

Declaration in relation to the redemption or purchase of shares out of capital

173

Please do not write in this margin

Pursuant to section 173 of the Companies Act 1985

Please complete legibly, preferably in black type, or bold block lettering

To the Registrar of Companies
(Address overleaf - Note 4)

For official use

Company number

Name of company

* insert full name of company

*

Note
Please read the notes on page 2 before completing this form.

ø insert name(s) and address(es) of all the directors

I/We ø _____

_____

_____

_____

_____

_____

_____

_____

† delete as appropriate

[the sole director][all the directors]† of the above company do solemnly and sincerely declare that:

The business of the company is:

§ delete whichever is inappropriate

(a) that of a [recognised bank][licensed institution]† within the meaning of the Banking Act 1979§

(b) that of a person authorised under section 3 or 4 of the Insurance Companies Act 1982 to carry on insurance business in the United Kingdom§

(c) that of something other than the above§

The company is proposing to make a payment out of capital for the redemption or purchase of its own shares

The amount of the permissible capital payment for the shares in question is £ _____
(note 1)

Continued overleaf

Presentor's name address and reference (if any):

For official Use
General Section

Post room

JFL0104a / Rev 5.2 10/99

I/We have made full enquiry into the affairs and prospects of the company, and I/we have formed the opinion:

(a)   as regards its initial situation immediately following the date on which the payment out of capital is proposed to be made, that there will be no grounds on which the company could then be found unable to pay its debts (note 2), and

(b)   as regards its prospects for the year immediately following that date, that, having regard to my/our intentions with respect to the management of the company's business during that year and to the amount and character of the financial resources which will in my/our view be available during that year, the company will be able to continue to carry on business as a going concern (and will accordingly be able to pay its debts as they fall due) throughout that year. (note 2)

And I/we make this solemn declaration conscientiously believing the same to be true and by virtue of the provisions of the Statutory Declarations Act 1835.

Declared at _____   Declarant(s) to sign below

_____

_____

| | Day | Month | Year |

on

before me _____

A Commissioner for Oaths, or Notary Public, or Justice
of the Peace, or Solicitor having the powers conferred
on a Commissioner for Oaths.

Notes

1   'Permissible capital payment' means an amount which, taken together with
   (i) any available profits of the company; and
   (ii) the proceeds of any fresh issue of shares made for the purposes of the redemption or purchase;
   is equal to the price of redemption or purchase.
   'Available profits' means the company's profits which are available for distribution (within the meaning of section 172 and 263 of the Companies Act 1985).
   The question whether the company has any profits so available and the amount of any such profits is to be determined in accordance with section 172 of the Companies Act 1985.

2   Contingent and prospective liabilities of the company must be taken into account, see sections 173(4) & 517 of the Companies Act 1985.

3   A copy of this declaration together with a copy of the auditors report required by section 173 of the Companies Act 1985, must be delivered to the Registrar of Companies not later than the day on which the company publishes the notice required by section 175(1) of the Companies Act 1985, or first publishes or gives the notice required by section 175(2), whichever is the earlier.

4.   The address for companies registered in England and Wales or Wales is:-

   The Registrar of Companies
   Companies House
   Crown Way
   Cardiff
   CF14 3UZ

   or, for companies registered in Scotland:-

   The Registrar of Companies
   Companies House
   37 Castle Terrace
   Edinburgh
   EH1 2EB

Page 2

Companies House
for the record

*Please complete in typescript,
or in bold black capitals.*
CHWP000

287

Change in situation or address of Registered Office

Company Number

Company Name in full

New situation of registered office

NOTE:

The change in the
situation of the
registered office does
not take effect until the
Registrar has registered
this notice.

For 14 days beginning
with the date that a
change of registered
office is registered, a
person may validly serve
any document on the
company at its previous
registered office.

PO Box numbers only
are not acceptable.

Address

Post town

County / Region 　　　　　Postcode

Signed 　　　　　**Date**

† Please delete as appropriate.

Please give the name, address,
telephone number and, if available,
a DX number and Exchange of
the person Companies House should
contact if there is any query.

† a director / secretary / administrator / administrative receiver / liquidator / receiver manager / receiver

Tel

DX number　　　DX exchange

Companies House receipt date barcode

*This form has been provided free of charge
by Companies House.*

Form revised June 1998

When you have completed and signed the form please send it to the
Registrar of Companies at:
Companies House, Crown Way, Cardiff, CF14 3UZ　　**DX 33050 Cardiff**
for companies registered in England and Wales
or
Companies House, 37 Castle Terrace, Edinburgh, EH1 2EB
for companies registered in Scotland　　　　　**DX 235 Edinburgh**

Companies House
for the record

Please complete in typescript,
or in bold black capitals.

CHWP000

288a

APPOINTMENT of director or secretary
(NOT for resignation (use Form 288b) or change of particulars (use Form 288c))

Company Number [ ]

Company Name in full [ ]

Appointment form

Notes on completion appear on reverse.

†† Tick this box if the address shown is a service address for the beneficiary of a Confidentiality Order granted under the provisions of section 723B of the Companies Act 1985

* Voluntary details.
† Directors only.
**Delete as appropriate

	Day	Month	Year			Day	Month	Year
Date of appointment				**†Date of Birth**				

Appointment as director [ ] as secretary [ ] *Please mark the appropriate box. If appointment is as a director and secretary mark both boxes.*

NAME *Style / Title* [ ] *Honours etc* [ ]

Forename(s) [ ]

Surname [ ]

Previous Forename(s) [ ] Previous Surname(s) [ ]

†† **Usual residential address** [ ]

Post town [ ] Postcode [ ]

County / Region [ ] Country [ ]

†Nationality [ ] †Business occupation [ ]

†Other directorships (additional space overleaf) [ ]

I consent to act as ** director / secretary of the above named company

Consent signature [ ] **Date** [ ]

A director, secretary etc must sign the form below.

Signed [ ] **Date** [ ]

(**a director / secretary / administrator / administrative receiver / receiver manager / receiver)

You do not have to give any contact information in the box opposite but if you do, it will help Companies House to contact you if there is a query on the form. The contact information that you give will be visible to searchers of the public record..

Tel [ ]

DX number [ ] DX exchange [ ]

When you have completed and signed the form please send it to the Registrar of Companies at:

Companies House, Crown Way, Cardiff, CF14 3UZ   DX 33050 Cardiff
for companies registered in England and Wales   **or**
Companies House, 37 Castle Terrace, Edinburgh, EH1 2EB
for companies registered in Scotland   **DX 235 Edinburgh**

Companies House receipt date barcode
This form has been provided free of charge by Companies House

Form April 2002

Company Number

† Directors only.

†Other directorships

NOTES

Show the full forenames, NOT INITIALS. If the director or secretary is a corporation or Scottish firm, show the name on surname line and registered or principal office on the usual residential line.

Give previous forenames or surname(s) except:
- for a married woman, the name by which she was known before marriage need not be given.
- for names not used since the age of 18 or for at least 20 years

A peer or individual known by a title may state the title instead of or in addition to the forenames and surname and need not give the name by which that person was known before he or she adopted the title or succeeded to it.

Other directorships.

Give the name of every company incorporated in Great Britain of which the person concerned is a director or has been a director at any time in the past five years.

You may exclude a company which either is, or at all times during the past five years when the person concerned was a director, was
- dormant
- a parent company which wholly owned the company making the return, or
- another wholly owned subsidiary of the same parent company.

Companies House
for the record

**Please complete in typescript,
or in bold black capitals.**
CHWP000

288b

Terminating appointment as director or secretary
*(NOT for appointment (use Form 288a) or change
of particulars (use Form 288c))*

Company Number

Company Name in full

	Day	Month	Year

Date of termination of appointment

as director   **as secretary**

Please mark the appropriate box. If terminating appointment as a director and secretary mark both boxes.

NAME   ***Style / Title**   ***Honours etc**

Please insert
details as
previously
notified to
Companies House.

Forename(s)

Surname

	Day	Month	Year

†Date of Birth

A serving director, secretary etc must sign the form below.

Signed   **Date**

* Voluntary details.
† Directors only.
** Delete as appropriate

(** serving director / secretary / administrator / administrative receiver / receiver manager / receiver)

Please give the name, address,
telephone number and, if available,
a DX number and Exchange of
the person Companies House should
contact if there is any query.

Tel

DX number   DX exchange

Companies House receipt date barcode

*This form has been provided free of charge
by Companies House.*

Form revised 1999

When you have completed and signed the form please send it to the
Registrar of Companies at:
Companies House, Crown Way, Cardiff, CF14 3UZ   DX 33050 Cardiff
for companies registered in England and Wales   **or**
Companies House, 37 Castle Terrace, Edinburgh, EH1 2EB
for companies registered in Scotland   **DX 235 Edinburgh**

Please complete in typescript,
or in bold black capitals.

CHWP000

288c

CHANGE OF PARTICULARS for director or secretary *(NOT for appointment (use Form 288a) or resignation (use Form 288b))*

Company Number

Company Name in full

Changes of particulars form

Complete in all cases

Date of change of particulars

Day	Month	Year

Name

Style / Title

Honours etc

Forename(s)

Surname

Day	Month	Year

† Date of Birth

Change of name *(enter new name)* Forename(s)

Surname

Change of usual residential address ††

(enter new address)

†† Tick this box if the address shown is a service address for the beneficiary of a Confidentiality Order granted under the provisions of section 723B of the Companies Act 1985

Post town

County / Region   Postcode

Country

Other change
(please specify)

A serving director, secretary etc must sign the form below.

* Voluntary details.
† Directors only.
**Delete as appropriate.

Signed   **Date**

*(** director / secretary / administrator / administrative receiver / receiver manager / receiver)*

You do not have to give any contact information in the box opposite but if you do, it will help Companies House to contact you if there is a query on the form. The contact information that you give will be visible to searchers of the public record..

Tel

DX number   DX exchange

Companies House receipt date barcode

This form has been provided free of charge by Companies House

When you have completed and signed the form please send it to the Registrar of Companies at:
Companies House, Crown Way, Cardiff, CF14 3UZ   DX 33050 Cardiff
for companies registered in England and Wales   **or**
Companies House, 37 Castle Terrace, Edinburgh, EH1 2EB
for companies registered in Scotland   **DX 235 Edinburgh**

Form April 2002

COMPANIES FORM No. 395

Particulars of a mortgage or charge

395

CHWP000

A fee of £10 is payable to Companies House in respect of each register entry for a mortgage or charge.

Please do not
write in
this margin

Pursuant to section 395 of the Companies Act 1985

*Please complete
legibly, preferably
in black type, or
bold block lettering*

To the Registrar of Companies
(Address overleaf - Note 6)

For official use

Company number

* insert full name
of Company

Name of company

*

Date of creation of the charge

Description of the instrument (if any) creating or evidencing the charge (note 2)

Amount secured by the mortgage or charge

Names and addresses of the mortgagees or persons entitled to the charge

Postcode

Presentor's name address and
reference (if any) :

For official Use
Mortgage Section

Post room

Time critical reference

Page 1

Short particulars of all the property mortgaged or charged

Particulars as to commission allowance or discount (note 3)

Signed _____   Date _____

On behalf of [company][mortgagee/chargee]†

Notes

1   The original instrument (if any) creating or evidencing the charge, together with these prescribed particulars correctly completed must be delivered to the Registrar of Companies within 21 days after the date of creation of the charge (section 395). If the property is situated and the charge was created outside the United Kingdom delivery to the Registrar must be effected within 21 days after the date on which the instrument could in due course of post, and if dispatched with due diligence, have been received in the United Kingdom (section 398). A copy of the instrument creating the charge will be accepted where the property charged is situated and the charge was created outside the United Kingdom (section 398) and in such cases the copy must be verified to be a correct copy either by the company or by the person who has delivered or sent the copy to the registrar. The verification must be signed by or on behalf of the person giving the verification and where this is given by a body corporate it must be signed by an officer of that body. A verified copy will also be accepted where section 398(4) applies (property situate in Scotland or Northern Ireland) and Form No. 398 is submitted.

2   A description of the instrument, eg "Trust Deed", "Debenture", "Mortgage", or "Legal charge", etc, as the case may be, should be given.

3   In this section there should be inserted the amount or rate per cent. of the commission, allowance or discount (if any) paid or made either directly or indirectly by the company to any person in consideration of his:
      (a) subscribing or agreeing to subscribe, whether absolutely or conditionally, or
      (b) procuring or agreeing to procure subscriptions, whether absolute or conditional,
for any of the debentures included in this return. The rate of interest payable under the terms of the debentures should not be entered.

4   If any of the spaces in this form provide insufficient space the particulars must be entered on the prescribed continuation sheet.

5   Cheques and Postal Orders are to be made payable to **Companies House**.

6   The address of the Registrar of Companies is:-

Companies House, Crown Way, Cardiff CF14 3UZ

TRANSFER FORM

J30

(Above this line for Registrars only)

Certificate lodged with the Registrar

Consideration Money £ . . . .

(For completion by the Registrar/Stock Exchange)

Full name of Under-taking	
Full description of Security	
Number or amount of Shares, Stock or other security and, in figures column only, number and denomi-nation of units, if any.	Words Figures (units of)
Name(s) of regis-tered holder(s) should be given in full; the address should be given where there is only one holder. If the transfer is not made by the regis-tered holder(s) insert also the name(s) and capacity (e.g., Executor(s)) of the person(s) making the transfer.	In the name(s) of Account Designation (if any)

PLEASE SIGN HERE ⇨

I/We hereby transfer the above security out of the name(s) aforesaid to the person(s) named below *or to the several persons named in Parts 2 of Brokers Transfer Forms relating to the above security:*

Stamp of Selling Broker(s) or, for transactions which are not stock exchange transactions, of Agent(s), if any, acting for the Transferor(s).

Delete words in italics except for stock exchange transactions.
Signature(s) of

1. . . . .

2. . . . .

3. . . . .

4. . . . .

A body corporate should execute this transfer under its common seal or otherwise in accordance with applicable statutory requirements

Date . . . .

Full name(s) and full postal address(es) (in-cluding County or, if applicable, Postal Dis-trict number) of the person(s) to whom the security is transferred.

Please state title, if any, or whether Mr., Mrs. or Miss.

Please complete in typewriting or in Block Capitals.

Account Designation (if any)

I/We request that such entries be made in the register as are necessary to give effect to this transfer.

Stamp of Buying Broker(s) (if any)	Stamp or name and address of person lodging this form (if other than the Buying Broker(s))

Reference to the Registrar in this form means the registrar or registration agent of the undertaking, <u>not</u> the Registrar of Companies at Companies House

FORM of CERTIFICATE REQUIRED WHERE TRANSFER IS NOT LIABLE TO STAMP DUTY
Pursuant to the Stamp Duty (Exempt Instruments) Regulations 1987

(1) Delete as appropriate
(2) Insert "A", "B" or appropriate category

(1) I/We hereby certify that this instrument falls within category (2) _____ in the schedule to the Stamp Duty (Exempt Instruments) Regulations 1987, set out below.

*Signature(s)

*Description: "Transferor", "Solicitor", or state capacity of other person duly authorised to sign and giving the certificate from his known knowledge of the transaction.

_____

_____

_____

_____

_____

_____

Date _____

*NOTE - The above certificate should be signed by (i) the transferor(s) or (ii) a solicitor or other person (e.g. bank acting as trustee or executor) having a full knowledge of the facts. Such other person must state the capacity in which he signs, that he is authorised so to sign and gives the certificate from his own knowledge of the transactions.

SCHEDULE

A. The vesting of property subject to a trust in the trustees of the trust on the appointment of a new trustee, or in the continuing trustees on the retirement of a trustee.
B. The conveyance or transfer of property the subject of a specific devise or legacy to the beneficiary named in the will (or his nominee).
C. The conveyance or transfer of property which forms part of an intestate's estate to the person entitled on intestacy (or his nominee).
D. The appropriation of property within section 84(4) of the Finance Act 1985 (death: appropriation in satisfaction of a general legacy of money) or section 84(5) or (7) of that Act (death: appropriation in satisfaction of any interest of surviving spouse and in Scotland also of any interest of issue).
E. The conveyance or transfer of property which forms part of the residuary estate of a testator to a beneficiary (or his nominee) entitled solely by virtue of his entitlement under the will.
F. The conveyance or transfer of property out of a settlement in or towards satisfaction of a beneficiary's interest, not being an interest acquired for money or money's worth, being a conveyance or transfer constituting a distribution of property in accordance with the provisions of the settlement.
G. The conveyance or transfer of property on and in consideration only of marriage to a party to the marriage (or his nominee) or to trustees to be held on the terms of a settlement made in consideration only of the marriage.
H. The conveyance or transfer of property within section 83(1) of the Finance Act 1985 (transfers in connection with divorce etc.).
I. The conveyance or transfer by the liquidator of property which formed part of the assets of the company in liquidation to a shareholder of that company (or his nominee) in or towards satisfaction of the shareholder's rights on a winding-up.
J. The grant in fee simple of an easement in or over land for no consideration in money or money's worth.
K. The grant of a servitude for no consideration in money or money's worth.
L. The conveyance or transfer of property operating as a voluntary disposition *inter vivos* for no consideration in money or money's worth nor any consideration referred to in section 57 of the Stamp Act 1891 (conveyance in consideration of a debt etc.).
M. The conveyance or transfer of property by an instrument within section 84(1) of the Finance Act 1985 (death: varying disposition).

Instructional Notes
1. In order to obtain exemption from Stamp Duty on transactions described in the above schedule the Certificate must be completed and may then be lodged for registration or otherwise acted upon. Adjudication by the Stamp Office is not required
2. This form does not apply to transactions falling within categories (a) and (b) in the form of certificate required where the transfer is not liable to ad valorem stamp duty set out below. In these cases the form of certificate printed below should be used. Transactions within either of those categories require submission of the form to the Stamp Office and remain liable to £5 duty.

FORM OF CERTIFICATE REQUIRED WHERE TRANSFER IS NOT LIABLE TO
AD VALOREM STAMP DUTY

Instruments of transfer are liable to a fixed duty of £5 when the transaction falls within one of the following categories:-

a   Transfer by way of security for a loan or re-transfer to the original transferor on repayment of a loan.
b   Transfer, not on sale and not arising under any contract of sale and where no beneficial interest in the property passes: (i) to a person who is a mere nominee of, and is nominated only by, the transferor; (ii) from a mere nominee who has at all times, held the property on behalf of the transferee; (iii) from one nominee to another nominee of the same beneficial owner where the first nominee has at all times held the property on behalf of that beneficial owner.   (NOTE - this category does not include a transfer made in any of the following circumstances: (i) by a holder of stock, etc., following the grant of an option to purchase the stock, to the person entitled to the option or his nominee; (ii) to a nominee in contemplation of a contract for the sale of the stock, etc., then about to be entered into; (iii) from the nominee of a vendor, who has instructed the nominee orally or by some unstamped writing to hold stock, etc., in trust for a purchaser, to such a purchaser.)

(1) _____ hereby certify that the transaction in respect of which this transfer is made is one which falls within the category (2) _____ above
(3) _____

_____

_____

_____

(1) "I" or "We"

(2) Insert "(a)" or "(b)"

(3) Here set out concisely the facts explaining the transaction Adjudication may be required.

*Signature(s)

*Description ("Transferor", "Solicitor", etc.)

_____

_____

_____

_____

_____

_____

Date _____

*NOTE - The above certificate should be signed by (1) the transferor(s) or (2) a member of a stock exchange or a solicitor or an accredited representative of a bank acting for the transferor(s): in cases falling within (a) where the bank or its official nominee is a party to the transfer, a certificate, instead of setting out the facts, may be to the effect that "the transfer is excepted from Section 74 of the Finance (1909-10) Act 1910". A certificate in other cases should be signed by a solicitor or other person (e.g. a bank acting as trustee or executor) having a full knowledge of the facts

This certificate relates to an instrument made on _____ between:-

COMPANIES FORM No. 403a

Declaration of satisfaction in full or in part of mortgage or charge

403a

CHWP000

Please do not
write in
this margin

Pursuant to section 403(1) of the Companies Act 1985

*Please complete
legibly, preferably
in black type, or
bold block lettering*

To the Registrar of Companies
(Address overleaf)

For official use

Company number

Name of company

* insert full name
of company

*

I, _____

of _____

† delete as
appropriate

[a director][the secretary][the administrator][the administrative receiver]† of the above company, do
solemnly and sincerely declare that the debt for which the charge described below was given has been
paid or satisfied in **[full][part]**†

\# insert a description
of the instrument(s)
creating or
evidencing the
charge, eg
'Mortgage',
'Charge',
'Debenture' etc

Date and description of charge # _____

Date of registration ø _____

ø the date of
registration may be
confirmed from the
certificate

Name and address of [chargee][trustee for the debenture holders]† _____

_____

§ insert brief details
of property

Short particulars of property charged § _____

_____

And I make this solemn declaration conscientiously believing the same to be true and by virtue of the
provisions of the Statutory Declarations Act 1835.

Declared at _____

Declarant to sign below

_____

	Day	Month	Year
on			

before me _____

A Commissioner for Oaths or Notary Public or Justice of
the Peace or a Solicitor having the powers conferred on a
Commissioner for Oaths.

Presentor's name address and
reference (if any) :

For official Use (02/00)
Mortgage Section

Post room

Notes

The address of the Registrar of Companies is:-

The Registrar of Companies
Companies House
Crown Way
Cardiff
CF14 3UZ

Register of Members

Name

Address

Dividends to

Class of share

Denomination

Date of entry as member

Date of cessation of membership

Date of Allotment OR Entry of Transfer	References in Register		No. of Share Certificate	Amount paid or agreed to be considered as paid	Acquisitions	Disposals	Balance	Remarks
	Allotments	Transfers						

CK3.A4

Register of Directors

Surname _____
(or Corporate Name if appropriate)

Forename(s) _____

Any former Forenames or Surnames _____

Residential Address _____
(or Registered or Principal Office if appropriate)

_____

_____

Nationality _____

Date of Birth _____

Business Occupation _____

DATES OF:

Appointment _____   Resignation or Cessation _____

Minute _____   Minute _____

Filing Particulars _____   Filing Particulars _____

Other Directorships	Date of resignation

CK4.A4

Register of Directors' Interests

Name & address of person interested		Classes of share capital or debenture (a) _____ (b) _____							
Entry		Date of		Nature of Event	No of shares involved		No of shares in which interested after event	Price or consideration	Remarks
No	Date	Event	Notification		Acquisitions	Disposals			

CK6 A4

Register of Secretaries

Surname
(or Corporate Name if Appropriate)

Forename(s)

Any former Forenames or Surnames

Residential Address
(or Registered or Principal Office if appropriate)

DATES OF:

Appointment | Resignation or Cessation

Minute | Minute

Filing Particulars | Filing Particulars

Surname
(or Corporate Name if Appropriate)

Forename(s)

Any former Forenames or Surnames

Residential Address
(or Registered or Principal Office if appropriate)

DATES OF:

Appointment | Resignation or Cessation

Minute | Minute

Filing Particulars | Filing Particulars

Register of Mortgages and Charges

Entry No	Particulars of Charges			Rate of interest	Description of property charged	Name and address of persons entitled to Charge	Date of discharge of Charge	Remarks and date of filing
	Date	Description of Instrument creating Charge	Amount of Charge					

CK7 A4